BOOKS BY THOMAS MALLON

FICTION

Arts and Sciences
Aurora 7
Henry and Clara
Dewey Defeats Truman
Two Moons
Bandbox
Fellow Travelers
Watergate
Finale
Landfall
Up With the Sun

NONFICTION

Edmund Blunden
A Book of One's Own
Stolen Words
Rockets and Rodeos
In Fact
Mrs. Paine's Garage
Yours Ever
The Very Heart of It

The Very Heart of It

The Very Heart of It

NEW YORK DIARIES
1983–1994

THOMAS MALLON

Alfred A. Knopf

NEW YORK

2025

A BORZOI BOOK

FIRST HARDCOVER EDITION

PUBLISHED BY ALFRED A. KNOPF 2025

Published by Alfred A. Knopf, a division of Penguin Random
House LLC, 1745 Broadway, New York, NY 10019.

Knopf, Borzoi Books, and the colophon are registered trademarks
of Penguin Random House LLC.

Portions of this book originally appeared,
in different form, in *The New Yorker.*

Library of Congress Cataloging-in-Publication Data
Names: Mallon, Thomas, [date] author.
Title: The very heart of it : New York diaries, 1983–1994 /
Thomas Mallon.
Description: First edition. | New York : Alfred A. Knopf, 2025. |
Identifiers: LCCN 2024044324 |
ISBN 9780593801802 (hardcover) | ISBN 9780593801819 (ebook)
Subjects: LCSH: Mallon, Thomas, [date]—Diaries. |
Authors, American—20th century—Biography. |
Gay authors—United States—Biography. | LCGFT: Diaries.
Classification: LCC PS3563.A43157 Z46 2025 |
DDC 813/.54 [B]—dc23/eng/20250124
LC record available at https://lccn.loc.gov/2024044324

penguinrandomhouse.com | aaknopf.com
Printed in the United States of America
2 4 6 8 9 7 5 3 1

The authorized representative in the EU for product safety
and compliance is Penguin Random House Ireland,
Morrison Chambers, 32 Nassau Street, Dublin D02 YH68, Ireland,
https://eu-contact.penguin.ie.

This book is for Billy—

William Gene Bodenschatz

—with love and thanks for the past thirteen thousand days.

The Very Heart of It

PREFACE

Forty years and a few million words ago, while writing a book about other people's diaries, I briefly described what were then the mere thirty notebooks containing my own, wondering why the second-person signifier so often appeared in my practice of this ultimate first-person form: "Who is this 'you' that's made its way more and more often into these pages in the last few years, this odd pronoun I sometimes find myself talking to like a person at the other end of a letter? . . . I can say without a trace of coyness that I have no idea who 'you' is."

Now, with the publication of these journals, I at last know that the "you" in them—for example, on March 25, 1985: "to give you an idea of how bad things are"—is *you*, the person with this book in hand. Back in the 1980s I had no notion of publishing these diaries, but as a student of the genre I felt certain that all diarists were, even unconsciously, looking for some eventual audience, even if it consisted of a single person.

I continue keeping diaries to this day, in pretty much the way I mentioned in *A Book of One's Own*: "I'm always behind . . . I often don't get around to writing up a day until several more have gone by. But I manage to keep them all separate." Everything is hand-written. After selecting a fraction of their material for this book, the only transcriptive changes I have made are ones to rectify obvious slips of my hasty pen (writing, say, "for" when I meant "to") and to correct occasional misspellings and poor punctuation choices. I have even retained such irritating idiosyncrasies as using an ampersand for "and," a habit I seem finally to have broken later in the 1990s.

Why, with a half century of diaries to choose from, have I drawn this book from 1983–1994? A few years ago, when I was getting the diaries ready for an appraiser to look at, in advance of their acquisition by the Library of Congress, I began to read and type out portions of the notebooks from my early days in New York City. I was struck by a manic quality to their narrative. I might be generally rhapsodic about the city and delighted by the bit of traction I was starting to get as a writer, but the relentless spread of AIDS constantly thwarted the happy entries, blunting them with others that contained terrible medical news: some new scientific study with exponential forecasts of impending death, or a private word I'd received that yet another friend of mine was sick. I was frightened, continually, about the state of my own health, aware that I had been exposed to the virus but for years unwilling to take the test that would confirm whether or not I had it.

When this book opens, in the fall of 1983, I am about to turn thirty-two, getting ready for that book on diaries to come out. I am on the verge of becoming a tenured English professor at Vassar College but about to escape my faculty apartment in Poughkeepsie for a tiny walk-up near Grand Central Terminal. What I really want is to break free altogether from academic life and to make my living as a novelist and critic. I have just been through a brief, disappointing love affair with a postdoctoral fellow in classics at Johns Hopkins, Tom Curley, whose illness and death are about to plunge me into a whirlwind of grief and fear. And yet, in these early New York years, as I worry that my end may be near, I feel not so much that I am starting over as starting out—"living my twenties in my thirties," as I put it, on the "game board" of Manhattan's street grid during a gaudy but grim time for the city.

This is a chronicle of sex and death; of lovesickness and eventual joy; of friendship and gossip, of political fervor and ambivalence; of ambitions both frustrated and fulfilled; and of a now vanished literary life, some of it lived within the always drama-filled hallways of Condé Nast.

Any sizable diary becomes a kind of ramshackle autobiography. The reader of these pages will learn or figure out that I grew up Catholic and middle-class on Long Island before going off as an undergraduate to Brown, where I wrote a thesis on Mary McCarthy, eventually a mentor and friend. After five subsequent years earning a PhD at Harvard, I was off to an improbable one-year academic job in West Texas. Then, in 1979, it was on to Vassar.

In these pages the moment always counts for more than the larger arc and shape of things. My judgments, often unkind, are the products of immediate feeling rather than lengthy reflection. I have kept footnotes and bracketed identifications to a minimum. Sometimes people are identified by initials or a pseudonym, but more often, as in the original diaries, by name.

Compiling this book has left me grateful to all the friends and lovers and colleagues and antagonists who filled my life: to those who died during the years of these pages or in the decades after; and to those who—like Bill, first and foremost—are still sharing the present with me.

T.M.

1983

OCTOBER 7: Sometime around 6:00 this morning there was an earthquake. I slept through it. You were supposed to be able to feel it from Canada to (yes) Baltimore. Well, Tommy, my rumble [in Poughkeepsie] is your rumble; at [least] we're tremored together. But a phone call would be too much. Rachel* came into my office in the morning (while I was reading more of the Donaldson biography [of F. Scott Fitzgerald]). She tells me that another part of Tom's conversation last Sunday involved his horror of AIDS. I thought this might have abated by now, but it hasn't. So he will be hiding in his house. In an awful perverse way does this make me think: ok, at least he isn't with anyone else? Maybe he'll come back to me?

. . .

A nice breezy Friday night. Fall is here. It seemed criminal, walking around in the twilight, not to have someone to share it with. O mysterious reader, if 3 months from tonight I am not gone from this town, read no more. There would be no point to it. For nothing will happen between that page and the grave.

---

* Rachel Kitzinger, professor of classics at Vassar; taught Tom Curley at Amherst in the 1970s and introduced me to him when he was a job candidate at Vassar.

OCTOBER 9: The October 10 issue of *New York* magazine reports that the vacancy rate below 96th St. is less than 1% and that the whole housing situation is likely to get even worse. I will not let this deter me. I am getting out of this place over Christmas.

OCTOBER 11: I taught Heaney in the morning; they really don't know Northern Ireland from northern New Jersey, but they were attentive enough. (They all showed up, all 19, but since that effort is sufficiently heroic some of them reserved the right to shamble in 10 minutes late.)

OCTOBER 12: Drinks at Ann's* . . . My plans to move to New York came up—and Barbara† responded with stony silence. Suspected disloyalty to the old plantation?

OCTOBER 13: Matthew Bruccoli—the Fitzgerald biographical industry—lectured to a sparse crowd in Rocky 300 at 7:00 . . . He says the real tools of the biographer are jet planes and widows and Xerox machines. If it ain't published, it ain't scholarship, he said—responding to charges that he bursts into print too often.

OCTOBER 17: The October break—which lasts until Wednesday—has begun. The students go off to places like California & London; the faculty may get as far as Vermont. How lonely I feel this time. The sense of emptiness in this apartment is fairly splitting me in two—as if that's the only way to get somebody else into it. Me and me.

OCTOBER 17: There was an ad on Friday & Sat. in the *NYT* for a place on E. 43rd St. (151, #4A) for the absurdly *low* price of $508 a month. [Went to] the office on 2nd Ave., between 52nd & 53rd. The broker (a *very* cute boy named Jamie Niblock, whom I'm thinking of asking out for a drink) said I should get down

---

* Ann Imbrie, who joined the Vassar English department when I did in the fall of 1979.
† Barbara Page, a senior colleague in the English department.

there right away, since other brokers in the firm would be free to send people down too. "I strongly suggest you take a taxi," he said.

I raced to the street, found a cab, cursed the traffic and arrived at the place just as 2 girls from Barnard did. An agent brought all 3 of us in together. I took a very fast look. It's *small*, but it's livable—and only a block from Grand Central. (It's between Lexington & 3rd. You look right coming out of it & you see the station. You look left & you see the U.N.) I knew I had to get back to the broker before the girls did, so putting self-interest ahead of gallantry I raced to the street and got a cab back to 2nd & 53rd. I beat them by about a minute and a half.

And now it's mine . . . My heart raced. Will I be able to manage it? . . . My instincts keep telling me I will. I'll review books like crazy on the train to help pay the bills. In fact, one of the first things I did was call *Newsday* and sign on for two more.

OCTOBER 18: Number 151 is framed by two small yellow door lights—very inviting & O. Henryish. It's above a Xerox store & there's a super named Pat McCormack who lives on the premises. It occurs to me that my generation is desperately trying to pay large sums of money to live in the same apartments their parents fled for the suburbs . . .

OCTOBER 21: I've done one of the stupidest things I've ever done. My only consolation is that he's done one of the stupidest things *he's* ever done. That may be the only thing that saves me from reaping the whirlwind.

Barbara gave a great boozy bash to celebrate Dixie's[*] 40th birthday. Among the many present was [HPS[†]], who was looking handsome and more than relaxed. He was flying a bit. Well, he was drunk and I was drunk & when we sat on the couch he started pouring out his troubles to me. I made the mistake of listening, and before I knew it we were upstairs & sort of groping one another. It didn't get very far; I was too drunk to worry

---

* Dixie Sheridan, Vassar College administrator; later a photojournalist specializing in theater.
† Dean of the college.

about it, and I thought it was over. But it was still very much on his mind. He rode me home & I invited him in for a cup of tea because I could see he was still feeling nervous & agitated. He was talking a mile a minute—his position, his past loves, his lover, etc. It didn't make much sense, but neither did I. In any case, I wound up turning the water off before it boiled . . . It wasn't much more than a drunken fumble, but when he left he seemed to be alternating between overwhelming regret & apprehension—& the feeling that this might be the start of something big. How he has been interested in me for years, how he could do this a thousand times, etc. I was already deep into oh-my-God-what-have-I-done thoughts, & wondering if I was going to be sick.

OCTOBER 22: Ann tells me this will all blow over & that if there's any impropriety it's more his than mine. But I somehow keep thinking there's going to be trouble out of it. *At least in my head.*

OCTOBER 24: I'm infinitely relieved. I saw [HPS] at about 5:30 in his office. He was so nervous he appeared stricken by some sorcerer for a moment. But we quickly saw it was going to be fine. We tripped over ourselves to say that we'd both been drunk, that there was nothing to be ashamed of, that we weren't always like this, and that it would of course be wrong to go on with it. We both seemed to exhale at once. And then we wound up wanting to talk college business—to get away from it.

   Until he came back to it in a delicate way. He said—all these things almost as asides—that he had "enjoyed it" (not just that there was nothing to be embarrassed about); that I was sweet; that he found me easy to talk to (not that we were both just drunk). He said that there was a quality of innocence on both sides that he liked about it. He lamented how he had no one to talk to here because of his position, and how he wished he could see someone away from here: as it is, whenever he travels it's always on some sort of college business. (I'd mentioned the New York apartment to him.)

OCTOBER 25: [Paul Fussell] is a Californian, but you wouldn't know it. He looks a lot like Russell Baker and even sounds a little like him. His lecture (about a bogus WW2 diary) was clever & well delivered. (Beth* sat next to me & drove me creepy-crazy; she was all set to emote over the discovery of another Anne Frank before P.F. got to the kicker.)

. . . At last I settled down to write my letter to Tom. To make it friendly, almost detached, funny. I have no idea whether he'll respond to it. Enfeebled as he is, he doesn't need me. And I still need him. I told him that Byron said friendship was love without wings & that that wasn't such a bad idea.

But there are still better ones.

OCTOBER 27: I watched Reagan's speech on Grenada & Lebanon (he had more to talk about than he had time for). More and more the mission is beginning to look as if it was not such an outrageous idea after all. And then there was Jeane Kirkpatrick's[†] speech to watch—much tougher & more entertaining than *Hill Street Blues*.

OCTOBER 29: I've started to pack. Some of the picture frames have four years of dust on top. Specks accumulating through . . . the thousands of papers graded; the nearly two thousand risings and sleepings; all the words thought and written in this same place. I'm ready to go.

NOVEMBER 1: Tommy called. And we talked for an hour. Everything so different, so peculiar, in many ways so fine.

He is better. Several weeks ago things were so bad that he was telling his chairman he wasn't sure he could finish out the semester. Since then he's been given a pill—some sort of antidepressant he takes 3 times a day while seeing the shrink. The result: he is looking for jobs, writing his book, waking up in the morning amazed he's not feeling awful . . . All through the talk I had the strangest feeling that he wants me to be happy—not because he wants to share in my life, but also not because he wants me settled so he can forget about me and I won't bother him. No, because

---

* Beth Darlington, Victorian scholar and senior English department colleague.
† Neoconservative U.S. ambassador to the United Nations.

he feels tender towards me . . . But what comes now? Do I go on being in love with him?

NOVEMBER 2: [A department meeting about developing a more rigorous version of English 105] Bill Gifford sits there looking wounded—as Lynn Bartlett* says, he sees his whole life being undone. He wants to keep the touchie-feely version of the course he's taught for 20 years, the one in which the students talk about how literature relates to their deepest feelings. . . .

NOVEMBER 5: I'm gradually bringing a lot of stuff that I won't have room for in the apartment over [to my office]. And it makes me wonder if some of the "senior members," as we always call them, won't be thinking that he's making himself at home a bit prematurely.

NOVEMBER 7: . . . Lunch with Barbara and Bob[†] in the Retreat. Charlie Beye[‡] will, on the basis of a story Bob tells, forever be known as The Man Who Came to Dinner at the Maces'.[§] It seems he was there last night . . . The predictable unbearability of such a gathering was heightened by Dean's wispy moans about the decline of standards here and there, and a few choice anti-Semitic remarks just to spice things up. Charlie was so disgusted and disbelieving that when Dean at one point lamented how awful all the young people in the English department are, Charlie turned to him and said, "Well, with an old queen like you in the department they must be pretty miserable." Dean—who is more than a queen; he's more like Empress of India—responded in a little whisper: "You're very sophisticated."

NOVEMBER 8: The students continue to be crazy about Updike. I told one of them in office hours I was surprised they were so

---

* English department colleague, at the college since 1952.
† Robert Pounder, professor of classics.
‡ A visiting professor in the same department.
§ Dean Mace was a longtime senior member of the English department.

enthusiastic about [*Rabbit Redux*], and explained to me: "It's all the sex." . . . Today was Election Day. Nothing much on the ballot except the transportation bond issue, which, with the self-interest of a new commuter, I voted for.

NOVEMBER 9: The composition class went very well. We did the sonnet, & as I was mentally comparing Walker Gaffney to a summer's day, the students were catching on nicely.

NOVEMBER 11: I'm writing this sitting on my sleeping bag on the floor of #4A, 151 E. 43rd St. I got here late this afternoon and got the keys next door.

As soon as I put the suitcases on the floor I went out for a walk. The lights were coming on up and down Fifth Ave.

I live here now.

NOVEMBER 12: A boy in a fish store was pouring clams over ice in the window; near it was another fish store—hobby fish. After Poughkeepsie one's eyes suffer a sort of mercantile overload. One can't quite believe all of these stores are just outside one's door. All at once I feel very much at home and very much a rube.

NOVEMBER 13: [Moving my things from Poughkeepsie] What should have been an ordeal turned into an idyll. Oliver [my Irish brother-in-law] arrived with his two Salvadoran helpers (one of them escaped on the floor of a truck and has been here only a month) and we loaded up in about an hour . . . [Once in Manhattan] We double-parked the truck and made dozens of trips up the stairs—and finally got the couch up four flights . . . I don't think I'll ever forget the twilit moment when I waved good-bye to them. We were all laughing and our eyes kept darting from the Chrysler Building to Grand Central to "Naciones Unitas!"

And there we were—three different kinds of immigrants, each dreaming the different phases of the same dream. . . .

NOVEMBER 14: My review of the Fitzgerald biography is out in *NR* [*National Review*]—with my picture next to [John] Simon's &

Buckley's. Charlie Beye says it's a wonderful picture & that I don't look at all like it.

NOVEMBER 15: Barbara battered Beth's intellect so much over some faulty proposal of hers for a new College Course that Beth finally got weepy—& then Barbara got weepy over her failure to be recommended for promotion. Our feminists!

NOVEMBER 18: [A surprise 60th-birthday party for my widowed mother] Our ruse worked. Ollie (who had gone to pick her up at work) stalled Mom until about 7:35. She never suspected anything. In fact, she was so surprised—shocked—that she burst into tears as we were singing "Happy Birthday" and had trouble stopping. She actually had to go upstairs for a minute or two to compose herself. As [Aunt] Belle, who is quietly wise, said to me, "It's 'cause she's lonesome."

NOVEMBER 19: I love it here. I don't intend to leave. Right now the job just feels like a means toward living here, and if it falls through I just have to look for something else. Geography seems far more important than tenure all of a sudden . . .

Dallas is 20 years ago Tuesday, and we're going through a national orgy of commemoration. JFK is on virtually every magazine cover & all over the television—his face is far more present these days than Ronald Reagan's. It's all quite eerie. It's as if we've decided to be governed by an apparition for a month or so.

NOVEMBER 20: The whole country was expected to watch *The Day After* (Kansas gets nuked), but I declined.

NOVEMBER 22: Everyone has been telling his where-I-was-twenty-years-ago-today tale. Rachel was at the Madeira School having lunch with Blair Brown when the news came. Twenty years later to the night I was at Ann's watching Blair Brown, the actress, portraying Jacqueline Kennedy with a blood-spattered face in the last minutes of the TV mini-series that ended tonight.

NOVEMBER 27: I walked along the park up through the 70s before turning back. A little boy's helium balloon escaped his hand, and I made a run and a leap for it & *almost* got it. But I didn't. And even though I heard him call me a "nice man" to his mother, I felt blue and ineffectual for hundreds of yards afterwards.

DECEMBER 1: [Vacating my Vassar apartment] I'll probably remember it as the place where I really discovered lovemaking. If you put on the wall lamp in the bedroom while you made love on the sofa bed in the living room, the light was perfect.

DECEMBER 6: I was at Alumnae House by 6:30 for dinner with Andrew Motion,* who [seems] less gay and about as pretty as I remember him from June . . . Beth was nauseatingly Anglo, in that way that makes you cringe for the guest & for the reputation of the college. But Andrew Motion is a bit of a wet (not politically—there were the usual Labor pieties about England's becoming "a car park for Cruise miss*isles*"—but a wet blanket) . . . We were pretty drunk by 8:30 & I had to articulate my consonants pretty carefully when we got to the introduction in the Old Faculty Parlor.

DECEMBER 7: A long faculty meeting in the Aula. Computers and foreign languages—and pieties, pieties, pieties. I sat next to Demo† and paid more attention to the expanse of skin between the sock & pants on his crossed leg than I did to the meeting.

DECEMBER 13: . . . A letter from Tommy inside a blue-and-white envelope from the Johns Hopkins classics department. A long page of élite type—probably more words than he sent me all the time I was in England . . . Full of good news. The "Limbitrol" is working miracles, which he's wise enough to realize only buy him time. Nonetheless, he's not anxiety-ridden; he's finished revising the dissertation (the book will be out in the fall); he's had another

* British author and editor; eventually, from 1999 to 2009, British poet laureate.
† Robert DeMaria Jr., distinguished eighteenth-century scholar; later chairman of the Vassar English department.

article accepted; and he's eager to get to the convention in Cincinnati and find a job. It's a staggering difference.

He wants to get together in NY just before he goes off to Ohio. He suggests the de Kooning exhibition at the Whitney. (All those breasts. Maybe he's turning straight to boot?)

DECEMBER 15: ... A busy day full of little things that kept jerking my mood around. (*We're* not manic-depressive; *life* is manic-depressive.)

DECEMBER 16: Charlie [Pierce]* gave a huge cocktail party for Betty [Daniels], in honor of her retirement as chairman. So Ann and I drove out to the house he and Barbara have in Salt Point. The backyard is the size of a small New England state. Inside one feels inclined to ask what wing, or time zone, one should put one's coat in. John Christie† has risen, looking very hale. I got into a bit of a chat with him & with Dean [Mace]. Both of them pleasant, and I was pleased that I wasn't going to any special lengths to be the good boy in front of the powers that shouldn't be.

DECEMBER 19: I've never been so saturated with Christmas, or what's supposed to be Christmas, as I am living here. The relentless decoration and the energy passing for cheer ... It's mostly, I've already begun thinking, for the "out-of-towners."

... Dropped into the little modern art museum Philip Morris runs on 42nd St. An exhibit of Hollywood publicity photos, including one of a body-hairless Ronald Reagan sunning himself with Jane Wyman in 1947. Not an abundance of muscle tone there. Who would have thought he'd age so slowly.

DECEMBER 20: ... Typed up my annual report for the dean. Well, he knows what I was doing on Oct. 21.

... Every time I go out on the streets and look at it all, and hear it all, I think: I never want to leave. Never. Why not just

---

* The new chairman of the Vassar English department; later director of the Morgan Library in New York.
† At Vassar since 1946.

chuck the Vassar job right now and stay here & write & find something else to do to make money? One minute it seems like the easiest thing imaginable, and the next minute I slow myself down. . . .

Watched Reagan's press conference. Mostly about Lebanon. Nothing bothers him, and people like that. If he's defeated in '84 it'll be a surprise.

Strange doings downstairs. I think in fact that the man in the apartment below died. The dog was howling last night, but I assumed he was just out. But tonight there were 2 cops there talking to a relative & there was discussion about what to do with the "beautiful dog."

DECEMBER 22: A still very optimistic Tommy called just after 10:00 tonight . . . He has interviews at San Diego State, Michigan, U. of Wash., Berkeley, Columbia, & American College in Paris . . . We talked for almost an hour, and I had to stop myself from thinking "What if he's at Columbia?" or "What if he's in Paris?"—for how much is it likely to mean either way ever again? We actually spent a lot of time talking about my future: whether I'll get it [tenure], whether I'll want it. And somehow we went through role reversal. He seemed like the secure young professional and I seemed like the one who could be sliding into the void. And I didn't like it.

DECEMBER 23: The man downstairs, by the way, is dead. I got the story from Pat McCormack this morning. He was shot in the head on 76th St.—probably by someone he owed money. Pat says he was "a bad one"—gambling, loan sharking. He'd run games—even a roulette wheel—right in #3A. The cops had their eyes on him & they were here the other night to search the place . . . Well, it's a lot more interesting than living across the hall from [Vassar sociology professor] Jean Pin.

DECEMBER 24: A cruelly cold day (the homeless seem to have vanished from the streets—to shelters?) . . . E. 43rd St. had a Dodge City feel. (Wrong allusion: I'm looking for a ghost town, not a shoot-'em-up place; I just can't think of the name. Does that mean I have Alzheimer's Disease? It's *the* disease this year, the way it was

Tourette Syndrome a couple of years back, and anorexia a little before then.)

DECEMBER 28: [A drink with Ann at] the MLA convention . . . A wonderful place to overhear conversations that make you want to kill yourself when you realize you're connected to it (actually, I've stopped paying my dues).

DECEMBER 29: Mostly it's Tom that's on my mind. I can't walk down a street without wondering if he walked down it at 9, or 17.
   . . . [On 6th Ave.] Man shouting in that ceaseless schizophrenic way that's a constant feature of the streets here. The only 2 words I could make out were "straight razors."

DECEMBER 30: The battlefields in France: "That'd give you a reason to come stay with me." That's what Tommy said when I mentioned these dilemmas [what book to write next] at lunch. (He's solidly in favor of my staying at Vassar if I get tenure, and of my doing the Sassoon book.) He said I could stay with him because we're both sure he's going to be teaching at the American College in Paris . . . We talked about all the different schools and interviews in a French restaurant on 2nd Avenue. We'd met at the Citicorp Building. Every time I see him he's seemed to age 2 more years instead of a few months, but he is still more beautiful than any man I've seen . . . We walked all the way to his mother's apartment at 1st and 22nd. I passed his grammar school (the Epiphany School). He would point out one thing or another and irrevocably, to my mind, stamp it as his, shower it with an aura . . . I am still hopelessly in love with him; everything in the city only means something if it pertains to him.

1984

JANUARY 4: Ran into Rachel in the Retreat. I neglected to mention that yesterday she told me she is worried about Tom. She talked to a few people at the convention who said he was *not* interviewing well, and that the word from Hopkins (*pace* Diskin Clay[*]) is that his troubles are all too apparent.

JANUARY 6: One drawback about working here in the day. The flower man who stands outside Sam Goody hawks his wares with Italian leather lungs for hours at a time. . . .

I took a walk down to E. 17th St. tonight and looked at #222, where he grew up. A pretty house. It can't have changed much since Henry James was in NY. I can see Tom's mother wheeling him in the park & then coming back upstairs from Rutherford Place to fight with the father.

JANUARY 7: I finally reached Bob [Pounder] this evening. He'd just gotten back from the hospital. Don [Rawlinson] is dying; he's not expected to live more than a few days. He has a virulent kind of pneumonia, the usual sort of "opportunistic" infection AIDS patients die from. Bob brought him to the hospital a few days

---

* Professor of Greek and chair of Classics (1976–1983) at Johns Hopkins.

ago—he'd found him looking like "a living corpse," alone in his apartment, not eating, afraid to go to the hospital because he knew what they'd do to him & knew he'd never leave. (He's on a respirator now, unconscious.). Bob said that he was hallucinating and seeing snakes and old ladies . . . I still won't think about it. Prefer to keep my mind on newspaper reports of how the number of new reported cases is beginning to drop. Prefer to think that only Tommy's [psychiatric] medicine was making him look so old & tired last week.

JANUARY 10: [Don Rawlinson] spent his whole life wanting someone to love him, someone to thrill him. He looked like a cuddly child, was a gifted doctor, went to leather bars, was a mess, a good and sweet-natured person who didn't deserve this horror, who was dealt so many bad deals by life, who's gone. Bob was good to him at the end.

JANUARY 12: An eerie message on the answering machine. Just a roar of traffic with a voice too faint to be made out. Anxiety-producing.

JANUARY 13: I am desperately horny, and tomorrow I'm going to a memorial service for someone who died of AIDS.

JANUARY 14: [A gathering in Don Rawlinson's apartment near Lincoln Center] It began with Don's lovely birdlike cousin Betty, his executor and heir, saying she was glad to welcome us "to Don's home." Somehow this moved me as much as anything else—it had a grace and an intimacy; it was as if that bare, white, modernist apartment, which seemed so much a mirror of his unhappiness, had at last been humanized . . . A number of people recalled how difficult Don could be, and no one more movingly than the doctor who hired him at St. Luke's, and who said that at first he tried to keep him there because Don was a brilliant doctor & in spite of his outbursts; and then, in some ways, because of his outbursts. He said he'd never met anyone so willing to appear vulnerable and to let people see into his unhappiness. He was put off by this at first, but then he realized that there was something crazily courageous about it, and that he was somehow privileged to be its witness. What this tall, serious and hugely intelligent—and completely straight—man was saying was that gay, neurotic, hysterical Don had made him a better person. He was realizing this only now, and with a kind of unfolding awe. It was the most profound part of the night.

AIDS was never mentioned. It was left literally unspeakable.

JANUARY 17: Tuesdays will be the hardest day [of my once-or-twice-a-week commute]. It's the one day of the week I'll be going both up [to Vassar] & back. But at least it's now begun & I'm coping. It's peculiar, going through Ardsley at 7 a.m. and reading an interview with Howard Nemerov in a book you've got to review, but I'm convinced this is going to pay off eventually.

JANUARY 20: [With David Kelley, Vassar's libertarian philosophy professor] We talked about the election; the inauguration is a year from today. Since my boy Glenn is doing so badly we're counting him out. I admitted I couldn't vote for Mondale at this point. David gave me a list of reasons to vote for Reagan but I shook my head and just smiled; there are limits to what one can do for one's anti-Communism and country.

JANUARY 21: Rachel still seems indifferent to her own career, somehow more interested in other people's happiness than her own—not in the standard pre-feminism way (with all its concealed bitternesses), but in some odd, and maybe beautiful, fundamental way.

JANUARY 22: [My mother visits my new apartment.] She really liked the place & brought it some pillows and flowers. I was expecting lots of frettings and warnings about locks, fire escapes, smoke detectors—anything that could possibly go wrong. But she was all enthusiasm. Since Dad died she's developed better instincts for what people need to make them happy, what moves they need to make. She knows this is right & so she responds happily. (If only she would leave messages instead of narratives on the answering machine.) The changes are amazing: she tells me about a party [my sister] Loree's giving and wants me to go to; I express no real interest; she responds: "Why don't you go? There'll be a gay couple there."

JANUARY 26: . . . A long faculty meeting over the language requirement (still) & a clause for the catalogue saying that Vassar doesn't discriminate on the basis of "sexual orientation." Ken [Weedin] butches up his voice & speaks well on its behalf. A few timid demurrings, the subtext of which is: won't this mean a lot more queer kids coming here?

JANUARY 27: I was not alone in the apartment. A mouse skittered across the kitchen floor at about 8:30. "Jesus!" I shouted & went upstairs to confer with little Mitchell. He'd seen one too the other night. Pat McCormack [the super] gave me two traps & at about 12:30 I heard one of them slam down on a couple of inches of gray fur.

JANUARY 28: [On the movie line to get into Woody Allen's *Broadway Danny Rose*] I listened to paired New Yorkers talking. One of them was reading the *Daily News* out loud, an article about a microsurgeon who's suing someone over an accident that has hurt his hand and leaves him "unable to handle certain instruments." "Yeah," replied the woman listening, "like a five iron."

JANUARY 29: Ronald Reagan just announced he's running again. The old boy milked dry what little suspense there was, referring to a "difficult decision" at the beginning of the 5-minute broadcast . . . Went off to Lamb's Theatre on W. 44th at 3 to see *Painting Churches* . . . It couldn't settle into any real attitude. At first it tries to show that senility is cute, and then in the 2nd-act climax it tries to convince you it's a piss-stained nightmare.

JANUARY 30: It will be a year tomorrow night that I met Tommy . . . And he's going to be a long time leaving my mind. I finally mailed him a card tonight, just before getting the taxi to the bus. I fear things have not gone well. Why wouldn't he call if there were good news?

JANUARY 31: The poetry class went well, even though (probably because) they—most of them—don't like Carolyn Forché's poems. ("OK, so she saw a lot of severed ears.")

FEBRUARY 3: I thought of going into the gay bar a few blocks from here, but I think I'll put that off for a while and see if something arises more "naturally." Why that should still seem so unnatural, I don't know.

FEBRUARY 4: Read more of Cyril Connolly. Odd to review a book that talks so much about reviewing. He says if you spend more than two years at it you become a hack. That means I'm close to completing a full year of hackdom, I suppose. But if you burn out after two years of that how long does it take to burn out as a grader of student essays? I think I lost any interest in it around 1975, months after I started it . . .

FEBRUARY 5: [A visit to Long Island with my almost-three-year-old nephew] Seán comes out with the oddest things. The other day when the squirrels were going through their garbage he said, "Maybe the squirrels will move uptown." (Origin: he'd heard Billy Joel singing "Uptown Girl" on the radio in the kitchen.)

FEBRUARY 6: A mixed day on Grub St. Nina King calls and asks me to add [the] David Pryce-Jones book on Cyril Connolly to my piece on the essays & to take another hundred dollars. She also says I can do the new Françoise Sagan book.

FEBRUARY 8: I deposited a check from *Newsday* today that brought my bank balance to over $10,000. If things here don't work out [with tenure], I've got a six-months' lifeline. If they do work out, I intend to spend a lot of money foolishly this summer.

FEBRUARY 10: I want a private life utterly divorced from Vassar whether I stay there or not.

FEBRUARY 11: Wanting to make a complete new romantic start— but feeling paralyzed all day. Don't know how I'm going to meet people down here; absurdly, that never really occurred to me while I was moving . . . The tenure uncertainty has been getting to me more than I've been admitting to this book or letting on to others.

FEBRUARY 12: Passing the Roosevelt and hearing a hundred squealing Puerto Rican teenage girls orgasming in unison as one of Menudo (the rock band of Puerto Rican teenage boys) raced into his limo. Walking past the Pierre and seeing Frank Perdue, the chicken king, strolling with a blonde on his arm.

FEBRUARY 13: [On the bus to Vassar] Finished *Nowhere Man* [a 1967 novel by Tom Curley's father]. By the end of it I hated [all the characters]. As Rachel once said: "If Tom is twelve, his father is two." Determined to intellectualize everything to death, to make every experience hollow & ghastly, to admit what they do and to wish, secretly, for applause for doing it. A terrifying book: talented, pretentious, ugly.

FEBRUARY 15: I'm trying to show as much grace under pressure in the halls as possible. It's clear to me that next week is my week to be discussed [for tenure] by the fulls & associates. Eamon [Grennan, the poet] makes a grumbling joke about how much I've written & says he has to spend this weekend reading it. Demo walks by with the whole stack of it under his arm. Susan Morgan tells me that she's just finished my article on Sassoon and that the last paragraph almost made her cry. So Monday is probably the day—a good morning to stay in New York.
. . . Went to bed reading a biography of Dorothy Kilgallen, a bizarre Valentine from Beverly. Just your average Catholic girl sleeping with a gay crooner and talking to the President's murderer's murderer.

FEBRUARY 15: [Our faculty performance of] *The Tempest* went off all right. The wine bottle I had to gulp from had some real wine in it, & I was pretty far gone by the end of things. Lynn [Bartlett], in a Queen Victoria sweatshirt, made a roaring Caliban—not such a bad sensation to have a full professor kiss one's feet a few days before one gets discussed for tenure. The students loved it. Doug

Anderson looked terrific in black tights. The Grennan kiddies played little sprites . . .

FEBRUARY 18: [With Charles Edwards, a graduate student at the Institute of Fine Arts] . . . We strolled around St. Mark's Place. Charles impulsively bought me a book of Eudora Welty's because we'd talked about her over drinks. And that was the last clue I needed to tell me that it was going to happen. We went into a gay bar next to the bookstore—a weird place done up like a 1950s family rec room. I had the fascinated creeps, but by this time I was drunk & proceeded to make out in a bar for the 1st time in my life.

We didn't want to wait any longer so we got in a cab & came back here . . . I always get cold feet *afterwards*.

FEBRUARY 19: Maybe I should be waiting until something realer comes along.

But what's real? . . . My mind, incidentally, keeps running towards the Ultimate Horror, Killer AIDS. People used to die for love; now you can die for sex, too. Although there would seem to be little chance of that here. Charles has been a good boy for a good while now & has been out of the country for the better part of the last four years. Still, I think about it.

FEBRUARY 20: I watched the Iowa caucuses . . . Glenn was wiped out. Hart finished second—even though he's 30 pts. behind he's a winner because he did "better than expected." But Mondale looks very strong. It's an idiotic system. You've got people saying it's all over—and it may be—because a bunch of Democratic cornhuskers in a small Republican state have held a bunch of town meetings at which you don't even get to cast a secret ballot.

FEBRUARY 21: Peter Elkoff failed to make it [to class] again today, because he overslept. He'd been out until 2:00 at a party given by Melia Tataki, Vassar's Greek shipping heiress. She'd decided to rent out Poughkeepsie's only night club and throw a Monday night party for about 200 close friends.

FEBRUARY 23: Erotic high point of the day: a conference, on the run between the library and Avery, with Walker Gaffney . . . Actually, it wasn't erotic. As I think I've already said here once, Walker is so absurdly beautiful that he's almost anaphrodisiacal—more of an aesthetic experience.

FEBRUARY 25: In the course of grading the character sketches from the Composition class I discovered that about half of them had elected to write on me. (Does my "rail-thin" face really have an "academic pallor" year-round? . . .)

[Sex with Charles] He has the gusto and virtuosity of Tom. I'm completely relaxed with him, enough to enjoy it thoroughly, as I never could with Tom. But there's that missing element—love is the only thing you can call it—that can make you stand outside yourself as you do it, contemplate it, and feel a glory that passes understanding.

FEBRUARY 29: A department meeting . . . Dan Peck & Frank Bergon fighting for their American literature turf in that awful Vassar way—the mediocre reach their 40s, realize they aren't at Yale or Harvard, and . . . take to college politics as a substitute for accomplishment (the way at Harvard they took to it as a substitute for sex).

MARCH 3: Met Doug [MacKay, a former student] at 8:15 in front of the theatre on 58th St. The movie was *A Woman in Flames*, a German neo-Fassbinder film about a dominatrix. Much more funny than scary—amazing, the solemnity of some of the reviews. The woman in it looked a little like a skinny Ingrid Bergman on a bad day.

Afterwards we went to Tony Roma's, the huge ribs place on 57th St. over near 1st Ave. A bad piano player mauled Cole Porter. It's a fun place—chunky waitresses in mini-skirts. It can't tell whether it wants to be NY or some big Friday-night Formica-tabled suburban place.

MARCH 7: The [tenure] letter was in my box this morning. I got it . . . I stood against the bookshelf a few minutes ago & looked out the window of Avery. This office: am I finally supposed to put up curtains, put down a rug[?] I looked at the pictures of Mary McCarthy & Edmund Blunden & wondered if they'd be hanging there 32 years from tonight.

MARCH 9: I was with Charlie [Pierce, the department chairman] for an hour and a half . . . He said my teaching was considered very good at all levels of the curriculum; they liked my energy, good humor, etc. (What he was talking about, without using the usual word, was my "collegiality.") He said the range and quantity of my scholarship were admired as well as the fact that I actually completed things I started. (This would be a small thing in most places, but not at Vassar.)

MARCH 10: Why is [Tommy] on my mind? Because of what I was feeling during sex last night? The lack of frenzy?

MARCH 13: I've gone from being the rebellious outsider of the Vassar English department to being a member of its establishment—in five days. Charlie Pierce called this morning to ask me if I'd agree to succeed Barbara as chairman of advisors. What [it] means practically: a few more nights in Poughkeepsie at the beginning of each term—but a course off. A 2–2 load for the next 3 years! . . . God: am I going to become one of *them*? Climbing the academic ladder, wanting to be a chairman, caring who's on committees, etc.? I don't think so. I know I'm saying yes to this so I can have more time for myself.

MARCH 14: When I went outside this morning there were cops and sawhorses blocking off E. 43rd Street, and a crowd of people looking up at the Chrysler Building. A jumper, I thought. No: it was ice falling off the building in chunks. Whenever I wanted to go in and out I had to tell the cops I lived at 151 . . . Trashed out in front of *Dynasty*—I fixate on the actor who plays Adam. He looks like Tom; he sounds like Tom; his pattern of chest hair is the same as Tom's.

MARCH 15: Talked to Katrina [Kenison, my editor] on the phone. Once again the publication date has been pushed back—this time to Nov. 7. The theory (advanced at a Houghton Mifflin meeting on Tuesday) is that September is the time for blockbuster novels; my book will get more review attention if it's delayed until November. (Do people read book reviews during the weeks of presidential elections?)

MARCH 17: I watched part of the parade . . . I was out on the streets to pick up a review copy of a biography of King George V—not a really appropriate errand for this day. I watched as much as I could, but unless you're drunk you get bored pretty fast: how many fire companies from Orange County can one watch go down the green line painted up 5th Ave.?

MARCH 18: Charley [Edwards] has not called, & I think some of our conversation Friday night may have to do with it—the little investigations one makes into people's pasts in the middle of an epidemic.

MARCH 19: Each day I'm more anxious about Tommy, and yet I don't dare call him.

MARCH 20: Opened an IRA for $2,000 this morning at Marine Midland . . . Inevitable Yuppieism.

MARCH 22: I met Ed Herrmann for lunch at the Oyster Bar at 1:30. He was wearing an old Washington Senators baseball cap. He's gotten back from California, where he shot more Xerox commercials. (The audio versions have just started coming over the radio.). He's finished the new Woody Allen movie in a studio up on 127th St. and is off to Toronto to film *Mrs. Soffel* with Diane Keaton. (Terrible title: if the reviewers don't like it they'll keep calling it *Mrs. Awful.*)

MARCH 23: . . . Met Charley outside the Guggenheim. We went through the Picasso exhibit (the last things, 1963 to 1973) on the ramp of that ridiculous seashell where your weight is always on your right foot. Some of the paintings seemed moving and joyous to me; the theatre aquatints weren't much—they looked like Hirschfelds; you kept wanting to count "Nina"s.

MARCH 25: It's 10:30 p.m. and I've just gotten off the phone with Rachel. She says she's tried to call Tom several times in the past week, but she's been unable to reach him . . . It's raining, and I haven't been out of the house for a whole hour at a time. And every time I flush the toilet it sends a spectacular spray of water out from the tank; as if you've hit a jackpot.

And I'm back in that state—I don't know how long it'll last—when the more I think about Tommy the more I think about Tommy.

MARCH 29: [While fighting a cold] We pulled into New York at 8:30 and my head already felt less congested. I took some codeine, put on the television, got into bed & waited for Charley, who came over and made love to me. It was different this time. More affectionate, more full of caresses and nips and whispers; less of Tom peering through the kitchen window at me. Maybe this represents evolution to something more. Or maybe it's just making up after last week's fight. Or maybe it was just the codeine.

MARCH 30: . . . Walked over to Simon & Schuster to get the review copy of Joan Didion's new novel [*Democracy*] with the requisite anorectic jacket photo. Things are picking up on the reviewing front: I've been offered a voting membership in the National Book Critics Circle . . .

APRIL 1: [As the New York presidential primary approached] At this point I have no idea what I'll do in November. But I do know that my domestic "liberalism," if that's what it is, can't extend itself to the foreign policy the Democrats talk about. When Hart says "The enemy in Central America is poverty, not Communism," I can't imagine greater naivete. It's both, of course . . .

APRIL 2: Read some of Didion's new novel & believe it's going to turn into the only bad book she's ever written. How could she allow herself to fall into this awful self-parody?

APRIL 3: Had a letter from [my college friend] John Graham—he's gay, he says; he lives with an ex-student of his. Surprise! Actually, it is: it still has that shock of revelation somehow, even when it comes from somebody you "always suspected."

APRIL 4: Loree reports the following review session on numbers between Oliver and [three-year-old] Seán:

> OLIVER: What comes after 1?
> SEÁN: 2.
> OLIVER: What comes after 2?
> SEÁN: 3.
> OLIVER: What comes after 3?
> SEÁN: Blind mice.

APRIL 5: [Robert Kiely, my Harvard dissertation advisor, came to give a lecture at Vassar.] We went down to the pub for tea and talked about Vassar, and my tenure, and Harvard. He told me funny Herschel Baker stories, and gradually I eased things around to the [business of Walter Jackson Bate and his protégé James Engell]. He was only slightly guarded; mostly he talked to me as a colleague, even a friend, instead of a student. Admits there was a "love affair" aspect to the whole thing, and that Bate went "off the deep end." When it came time to vote on Engell's tenure there would be midnight phone calls, "Are you gonna vote for Jim?" Kiely loves Bate and says the whole thing was a terrible embarrassment, a sort of temporary-insanity episode that hurt Engell but that Bate has now come out of. The eighteenth century has been passed on, and Bate feels content.

APRIL 6: I had a sudden feeling that I was going to get it all: tenure, books written, magazines, Manhattan, a string of boyfriends, a great love. I had a rush of emotion, an ecstasy, a disbelief that

I had all I now have . . . I was in the kitchen, looking at the sky-scrapers of 45th St. and I sent a hymn of thanks up to God.

APRIL 10: Copies of the 3 "outside evaluators" letters came in the unstamped today. (The rules now have the candidate and department chairman getting copies.) Letterheads and signatures are blocked out, but I know one is from Phyllis [Rose]* (almost embarrassing in its praise; I'll treasure it), one is from [Benjamin] DeMott (also a rave), and the last is from [Bernard] Bergonzi in England. He's got some serious reservations (in a very British way) about me, but on the whole he's praising, and I must say I agree with him about my own weak spots. I *am* thin where he says I am. In fact, he understands what I've realized about myself: I write better than I think. But since the Vassar English department is full of people who can do neither, I probably do deserve a few laurels.

APRIL 12: Reached the limits of my patience in English 226. Nicholas Katz failed to show up for the 10th time out of 22, so I sent a note to [the dean of studies] informing him that he may not take the exam. He was here later—& stunned. But I would not relent. Then came the usual tale of "problems," counseling . . . I listened, nodded, said I understood. We talked about life for half an hour or so. He left saying "For someone who's just thrown me out of his course, you've been very sympathetic." . . . Everyone is bitching about [the students]: Ann has blown up once again; Beth walked out of her seminar. You see, they don't do their work because they have "problems"—emotions of one kind or another: that's all "problems" means. And the underlying assumption is a hyper-romantic one that the emotions make work impossible, that it is an inevitable & necessary thing for work to give way before them. That work can sometimes be an escape from emotion never occurs to them, because it never occurs to them that emotions sometimes should be escaped. That would be "artificial" and "insincere."

APRIL 13: Charley came over at 9:30 and we made love. With almost astounding vigor . . . Both of us lay beached in front

---

* Biographer and essayist; a friend since the late 1970s.

of the TV with that hit-by-a-truck feeling afterwards. It was affectionate—I'm fond of him, I missed him all week—but there's still a point above which my affections cannot rise.

APRIL 16: Sights of the city: yesterday in Grand Central—a little white kid, maybe 10 years old, break dancing with crutches. His right leg was amputated at the hip.

APRIL 17: . . . Up to Rachel's office. She told me that she spoke to Tommy last night. He did get the Paris job—a month ago. But he is more depressed . . . he didn't seem to want to talk to her at all. He was pushing her away. It may be that he's got going one of his usual schemes for starting an entirely new life and that it means cutting off everything pre-Paris. He'll be gone by August. Rachel says I shouldn't expect him to get in touch with me—& that there's no point in feeling this is unreasonable after how friendly we were at Christmas. It's just Tom's illness . . . The job will be good for him; it will let him, at 30, run away from home. It won't be too demanding (they don't even make you come up for tenure). He'll hide there. He'll have a series of romances, none that will last. (It's odd how little jealousy I feel amidst all this despair; I know he'll never give to anyone what he wouldn't give to me.). He'll survive there somewhat better than he would in most places . . . As Rachel said, truthfully, matter-of-factly, when we imagined him in Paris: "He'll grow old there." . . . [But] I'll *never* stop thinking of him if I can't ever see him. I want to see him so I can forget him.

APRIL 22: When I got home on Friday there was a message on the machine from James [Raimes, my former editor at Ticknor & Fields] about how "my [Doubleday] colleague Jackie Onassis" had suggested that he use her name in talking to the Frick director if there was any difficulty about their cooperation [with a book idea I'd been contemplating].

APRIL 23: No dice. Everett Fahy [the Frick's director] . . . wants to write his own book, & is waiting for Henry Clay Frick's 98-year-old daughter Helen to die so that he can have all the papers he needs . . . says the real difficulty isn't his book (sure); it's that the Frick abhors publicity. He couldn't cooperate, couldn't speak to me, or allow others to . . . We got nowhere & clearly loathed one another by the end of the conversation. It's hopeless. I can't write it if they're hostile to it. So the thing to do is cut my losses right now. I put the books back on the bookshelves & threw the file away. I brooded and muttered and took a walk, but I was over it in an hour. I may not know how to abandon romantic ships, but I'm learning how to jump from professional ones.

APRIL 27: Read and dozed on the train home. It was five before I got here, & ran to the Fold 'n' Fondle [what I used to call my laundry on E. 49th St.] before it closed—the proprietor's helper was in full drag (if a leotard held by a woman's belt, make-up, curls, and wedgies qualify).

APRIL 30: Talked to James this morning—the 1st chance I've had to get him since talking to Fahy. He doesn't think the Frick thing is much of a debacle. He's used to getting a dozen ideas & discarding them within an hour. We'll-think-of-something is his attitude right now.

. . . Managed to reach Bruce Chatwin by phone. He can't come as writer-in-residence [at Vassar] next year, but he'd love to come in '85–'86. He sounds much older than he is, but we had a terrible connection. He seemed charming & approachable; I had a little bit of a crush on him (good sign) after a 5-minute conversation.

. . . I want to stay here forever. Everything seemed fine today— even lunch in the coffee shop on 44th with the waitress who called me "Cookie" . . .

MAY 3: . . . Went up this morning to Ticknor & Fields, and tacked to Katrina's bulletin board was the mock-up of my book cover. A beautiful marbled-endpaper Victorian sort of thing with a gold strip holding Beardsley/Gorey lettering. It's exquisite . . . I would guess that I've looked at it several hundred times.

. . . Chester Kerr [the publisher of Ticknor & Fields] sat next to me at the awards ceremony [for Mary McCarthy at the New York Public Library]. He gave me a nice sell, too: "I think it's terrible the way James Raimes is hunting you." And proceeded to tell me that I should stay at Ticknor & Fields for my own good. He introduced me to Stephen Spender by saying, "This is Tom Mallon. He's my claim to fame." I ate it all up like a college kid. He also says he and Katrina have been brainstorming about a [next] book for me.

Brooke Astor gave Mary her medal. Mary's anti-Reagan speech was charming. Mrs. Astor, her speech slurred by (she said) bronchitis, commended Mary for her exploration of the moral consequences of our "auctions."

MAY 4: [Katrina Kenison] told me what she and Chester Kerr have cooked up for me. It seems that a few years ago Chester asked Michael Wood to write a book about plagiarism for T&F. A contract was signed, and the advance was paid. But he [never delivered] and the contract was cancelled.

Picture this: a lively book of famous "cases"; right up through [John] Gardner & [D. M.] Thomas & [Penelope] Gilliatt. A sort of ethical and psychological inquiry à la Sissela Bok or Susan Jacoby. This could be my "crime book" in a way. It would force me to write narrative, & it would hoist me up on my ethical high horse. It would also be sufficiently scholarly (about literature) to get me promoted a few years from now if I stay at Vassar. It would be a logical "By the author of *A Book of One's Own*" follow-up. There's actually a lot to be said for it. I'm going to think about it. When she first said "plagiarism" I thought—pretty dull. But I see possibilities now. And look at what somebody like Frances FitzGerald (who was at the party last night) can do with an inquiry into American history textbooks.

MAY 5: Fifth Avenue was blocked off for a parade on behalf of Soviet Jews. Thousands of marchers. I stopped around 45th St. and watched for a while, long enough to see the politicians come by: Moynihan in the same Irish hat I used to see outside Harvard Yard; nerdy, owlish D'Amato; and, of course, Ed Koch, in a blue shirt, strutting, thumbs high in the air, doing a star turn to the crowd's applause. He might have been a Macy's balloon . . . It was nice to have Manhattan turned into an anti-Communist paradise for a few hours.

MAY 10: If I die in the next few years, mark this as the day I found out it might happen . . .

[Charley told me] he can't stand this halfway relationship we've got, that it's been tearing him up. I didn't know what to say, but I felt as if he were reading my lines. I'm always supposed to be the one too much in love . . .

Tom has been Charley's great problem . . . He says I never fail to bring him up . . . He said I ought to just keep pursuing Tom if I'm in love with him. He would. "I live completely on a fantasy level these days," he said. His face was contorted. I felt so awful looking at him, but the rotten truth is that from the moment Tom's name came into the conversation I was thinking more about him than Charley.

So when Charley left—angry, in tears—and I felt awful in such an uncustomary way, I decided to do just what Charley suggested: call Tom. Maybe to find out if I *could* be feeling less for him . . .

. . .

And then I learned what's really been going on.

I teased him about not calling me, and in a rush he started telling me why he hadn't. He's afraid he may have AIDS. He's had a case of thrush, and tests reveal he has a bad "T-cell ratio." So he's spent the last couple of months trying to be excited about Paris, but also wondering if he's going to die.

There are all sorts of ways to explain the thrush and T-cell stuff (the anti-depression medicine, the depression itself, childhood immunizations for summer trips to Spain, hypochondria, etc.)—but it's ominous. Very ominous . . .

He didn't tell me because he didn't want to worry me. Or so he says. After all, he says, the chances that he could have passed it on to me are so remote. Who says? And what business is it of his to decide this? It's *my* life we're talking about. His not telling me was pure selfishness. He wanted to spare himself the embarrassment. Instead, he told Rachel. She's never let on to me, but that was what he told her a few weeks ago on the phone. That's the position he put her in . . . I called Rachel, frantically. I think she was relieved I finally knew. But she doesn't think there's much to worry about, really. (Then why does she think I should have a check-up?)

No one knows anything about this disease, even if they've found the virus that supposedly causes it. Does it always transmit itself? They used to say you could have it for 2 years before you got sick and died. Now they say 5. They say every blood test is ultimately inconclusive. The only thing they know for sure is that if you do have it, you die.

MAY 11: I called Charley in the morning and said I had to see him. I took the subway up to the Institute and we crossed 5th Avenue into the sunny park. We had hot dogs for lunch, and I got mustard all over me as we sat on the bench and I told him what's happening. He took it very well—no real shock or blame or visible upset. He says he's more worried about my state of mind than anything else, since I'm one step further up the line of fire . . . We made bad jokes about dying. He walked me to the subway, but I decided to walk home. Everything was extremely beautiful, clarified, outlined—and I kept wondering if I had those odd-shaped cells in my body. And whether I would live to write another book.

I kept my date with Doug MacKay. We saw *The Bounty*, a very good, morally complicated movie. All day I'd been making bargains with God: just let me live and I'll be content with work and writing and friendship—I'll retire from sex forever. Then I saw Mel Gibson on the screen and thought: this isn't going to be easy.

MAY 12: I took a walk down 1st Avenue this afternoon (smoking cigarettes on my "since I'm probably going to die" principle). I went past all the hospitals, Bellevue included, and wondered whether I'd die in any of them. I wondered, too, when and where Tommy would die. I walked past Peter Cooper Village, just north of Stuyvesant Town, where his mother lives, and then I went just a little southwest to E. 17th St. I stood in front of number 222, where he grew up, and then I crossed Rutherford Place and sat down in Stuyvesant Square Park. I sat on the bench and watched the gold hands on the clock on the Episcopal church tower move toward 3.

I thought about him being wheeled in a pram through this park in the 50s; about what collection of decisions and circumstances eventually brought us to the same dinner table and same

bed . . . And I wondered if, when he made love to me, he was literally killing me.

I wonder, too, whether he cares if I live or die. If he didn't
bother to tell me because it was just too much trouble . . .

And I read the obituaries in the *Times*. A 56-year-old director
of musical comedies, who leaves his mother as his principal survivor, has died of pneumonia. Guess what he really died of.

MAY 13: (He had had the tests before he saw me at Christmas; he
was waiting for the results. I would never have embarked on an
affair with Charley if I'd known. Forget about me: what right does
he have to allow me to put a third person at risk?)

Rachel called to see how I was. We talked a long time and
I was calm throughout. She says his not telling me was "outrageous." Typically, she doesn't complain about the nasty position
he forced *her* into. It's Rachel's way to take care of whoever's most
troubled. . . .

She says the odds that anything is wrong with me are extremely
small. But the fact remains that because of the nature of this thing
(the long incubation period, etc.), I'm going to have to live in a
"gray area" for a while. (I remember Ann once telling me: "You
have a low tolerance of ambiguity.")

MAY 15: [Dr. Liu] doesn't seem panicked . . . and he says there
could be other reasons for all Tom's symptoms, but he also says he
can't give me any absolute "reassurances." If Tom has it, then I've
been exposed to it; but that doesn't mean it transmitted itself. He's
going to give me a complete physical next week, including the
"T-cell" test—which goes out to a lab—but if it says I'm healthy,
all it means is I'm healthy now. It doesn't say anything about 6
months from now. Nor, if my T cells are off, does it mean I have
a problem. So what is the point? But I'll do it anyway. He's sympathetic even though it's clear he thinks gays are from another
galaxy.

MAY 16: I really enjoyed the [English department honors] meeting, except for Ken, who was pouting and flouncing his petticoats

because his candidate hadn't won. It was the old creepy Ken. He may be out of the closet, but he's not out of the woodwork.

MAY 17: Tommy called tonight while Charley was here. He's still in Baltimore. He decided not to come this weekend because he's been sick. The flu. Why this didn't alarm me (it alarms him) I'm not sure. Maybe because he actually sounded better on the phone tonight than he did a week ago, when he was coughing and his chest sounded congested.

. . . When I mentioned my only health problem of the moment—an aching back—he launched happily into chiropractor talk and his theory that it's probably caused by the fact that "[my] shoulders are always shrugged." He says I walk around in a sort of hunched, frightened way. Well, maybe I do around him. (My bad back is from sleeping on a sofa bed.)

MAY 18: It was getting dark, and the jackhammers were starting up on E. 43rd. (The Kent Building is converting to gas and they're looking for the right spots and connections.). They've been going on and off for a couple of weeks now. "Goo ti bed with a bottle of Scotch," Pat [the Irish super] advised as the only way to get to sleep.

MAY 19: [Graduation weekend at Vassar] At seven Ann and I went off to the President's House for dinner with the Lehrer family[*] and Virginia.[†] Jamie had invited Ann and me since we've both taught her. Her mother is a gorgeous Texas belle, and her little sisters chatter like birds and obviously adore her. Grandma Staples has that tough, stringy look one still associates with older Texans. Jim Lehrer himself is charming and youthful-looking, until you get up close. Then you see the lines and strains from the recent heart attack. He turned 50 today.

. . .

[*] Newsman Jim Lehrer and his wife, Kate, a novelist; I had taught their daughter Jamie.
[†] Virginia B. Smith (1923–2010) was the president of Vassar College from 1977–1986.

Then to the bonfire . . . A great roaring suburban Nazi affair. [The students] throw books, notes, old furniture, and TV sets onto it. (It's sunk into them that it's less than humane to throw clothes on.) And yet there's a curious element of sobriety and control to it, too. The fire truck stands by, and there's almost no alcohol to be found. Some of the kids are very subdued, sad and worried about graduating.

MAY 21: I've got to live—even if it's only living "in the meantime."

MAY 24: They took 4 test-tubefuls of blood out of my left arm and are going to be looking for hepatitis, lymphocyte count, etc. and Dr. Liu says that unless there's a problem indicated, he's not going to bother with the T-cell test. He says it would cost me $100 and probably only panic me if (for one of the many possible reasons) something was "imbalanced." If this test they're developing for the AIDS virus itself (due in the fall) is sufficiently "specific," we'll think about that.

. . .

Got back here at about 10:30. Tommy's ghostly voice was on my Sanyo, giving his mother's number as the one I could reach him at. He's here.

MAY 25: We are such a doomed pair. Even on the phone this morning (he was sectioning a grapefruit as I reached him) there was crackling and static and we could barely hear one another. But we made a date to meet outside MOMA at 12:30.

We went to lunch a few doors down. I looked carefully at him. Physically, he appears *healthier* than in December—less reddish and dried out. (He kept licking the inside of his mouth throughout lunch; it's constantly dry from the limbotril [sic].) But he looked careworn . . .

. . .

What do we really have to talk about? A little about my tenure, a little about moving to Paris (I sense he's worried about whether he'll be able to manage giving four courses). Some family stories. Tommy is still looking for a pot of sanity at the farthest back end of the Freudian rainbow. He tells me some of the things he goes over in analysis: how he took 10 mos. to get out of the womb; how his mother went back to work 2 weeks after he was born (this was in 1953) . . . Tom thinks all these things somehow explain him.

. . .

The line outside MOMA was too long, so when we left the restaurant we decided to go to the Knoedler Gallery and see the show of recent Diebenkorn paintings. So we walked up to E. 70th. It was while we were walking that Tommy said, "Tom, you're going to have to slow down." It was then I realized the extent of the lack of vitality in him . . .

The Diebenkorn paintings are cool, serene, controlled. They have a certain beauty, but it's a life-denying beauty. That's why he'd like them on his walls . . .

MAY 31: I called the Poughkeepsie Medical Center this afternoon and was told that the results of all the tests were "fine." I'm supposed to talk to Dr. Liu tomorrow about details . . .

I don't feel I'm living in a "grey" area. I'm happy. Happy that the rain has stopped. Happy that when I go to buy typing paper now I go to buy it in the Graybar Building, with its impossibly shiny floor, rather than at the Vassar Coop. Happy to go out for a newspaper tonight and realize how paltry the stars are compared to the Chrysler Building.

JUNE 1: I spent a couple of hours with Katrina this afternoon, and we mapped out my future with Ticknor & Fields. If they can make sure Michael Wood still isn't writing a plagiarism book, I'll do it . . . And she says that [they] will give a serious look to a revised *Arts & Sciences* [my first novel] . . . Corlies Smith[*] said, "We'll see a lot of you." . . .

JUNE 6: Read the long excerpt from Vidal's *Lincoln* in last month's *Atlantic*. The writing is pretty silly—how come the elegant lizard of the essays turns into James Michener when he writes fiction?—but all the right details are there. . . .

[*] Corlies "Cork" Smith (1929–2004), legendary book editor at Lippincott, Viking, and Ticknor & Fields.

JUNE 7: Pat McCormack, dripping sweat, God bless him, put my air conditioner in the window late this afternoon. "She's goin' nowhere" he contentedly proclaimed after he'd secured it with a base of boards on the ledge and brackets on the window. It's amazing more of them don't go somewhere, though—right down into the street. You walk along 2nd Avenue and see them dangling at crazy angles from the old buildings.

I'm reading Johnson's *Life of Savage*, and I've got 3 books to review, but I didn't want to spend the evening reading, cool as the apartment might be. So I took the subway to Astor Place (all the white males there look like either Jack Wrangler or Leon Trotsky) and went up to Charley's. We drank wine and looked at *Hill Street Blues* and walked around St. Mark's Place. But he was curiously unresponsive. You figure him out. Figure *anyone* out.

JUNE 8: I worked at the [Mid-Manhattan Library] both morning and afternoon. I'm quickly getting deep into the plagiarism book. I like working there instead of in Lockwood up at Vassar. I don't know anyone, so I'm not interrupted for shop talk every ten minutes. I only know faces and habits: there's the bag lady who reads Xenophon, for instance.

JUNE 9: [Seeing Hitchcock's *Rope*] . . . The gay boys with the body in the chest were such evil queens that you could only laugh at them. About once a month I thank God I was born in 1951 instead of 1931.

JUNE 12: . . . A call from Nina King [at *Newsday*] about the last couple of sentences of my Taki review, which is about to go into the paper. We had to iron out some ambiguity. God, how I hate writing over the phone.

Back at the library in the afternoon. I wrote letters to George O'Brien & Rachel, finished Spark and read about Coleridge. I ogle a cute Chinese boy. An Indian man ogles me. Yesterday I was panhandled by somebody sitting at the next table.

JUNE 13: [Charley] then proceeded to tell me, after I asked what was wrong, that "Everything!" was wrong. "Look at my life!"

he said. It's true: it's a mess. No money, vagabonding from one apartment-sitting job to another, an incomplete dissertation, these temporary jobs he'll have at Manhattanville and Vassar but which won't be enough to keep him going for long. And other troubles he said he didn't even want to talk about.

JUNE 14: I picked up pounds and pounds of proof this morning, and Katrina and I settled on the jacket photo. I set to work on the index when I got back here.

JUNE 15: Several blocks north of here a woman was lying motionless on the ground and a man was shaking and bleeding. A truck had plowed up over the curb and run them down. A cop was rushing to them. And the crowd standing around them had those nervous (or is it there-but-for-the-grace-of-God-satisfied) smiles that one sees in Weegee photographs.

JUNE 19: I did more indexing today. At first it was fun ("love (see marriage, courtship and homosexuality)"), but I'm already tired of the sight of the proofs and simply want the book out in the stores.

. . .

. . . A bus up 3rd Ave. to Charley's latest apartment. We had a few laughs, and then we made love with such hollow gusto that I felt depressed, even ashamed.

JUNE 20: [*Glengarry Glen Ross* is] really less about money than it is about swearing—how quickly "fuck" exhausts itself into all-purpose meaninglessness, but how fresh something like "He couldn't find his dick with two hands and a map" can sound.

JUNE 21: More indexing and awful fact-checking in the library. An hour to run down something that inevitably turns out to be what I thought it was in the first place. I don't know where meticulousness ends and neurosis begins.

JUNE 23: Talked to Loree over the phone. We wound up arguing over the Church—she's quite the ultramontane these days, appalled that I don't think the Church's position on abortion should necessarily be U.S. law. But when the discussion turned to how the Church is refusing to obey Koch's anti-discrimination order about hiring homosexuals (for work contracted by the city), she immediately softened and said that here, of course, the Church was wrong. I realized that Loree must long ago have drawn her own conclusions about me. . . .

JUNE 26: Sirens are just what Midtown has instead of birds.

JULY 1: Lillian Hellman has gone to that great fabrication factory in the sky. Whether this will end the libel suit [against Mary McCarthy] still isn't wholly clear; but I'll bet there's joy in Castine. (I still remember how two summers ago, when informed of bad weather on Martha's Vineyard, Mary smiled and said contentedly, "I'm glad.")

JULY 3: I should be taking some stretch of time off (weeks, in fact), but there's something phobic in me. If I don't spend at least some part of *every* day working, I fear I'm doing something wrong. And I suppose something bad will happen.

JULY 4: The fireworks were further down the river, and I never even crossed 1st Ave., but it was still spectacular enough . . . As for the U.N.: that great green slab of corruption never looked so good as it did in all the colored outbursts.

JULY 5: I fear that tiny 151 E. 43rd can't last forever. A new skyscraper is going up on the corner, and I'm sure we will be demolished to make way for another one before much time goes by.

JULY 7: Tommy called this morning. He sounded drugged up to the eyeballs. He is at his mother's. He says he's been sick, and that it was "scary" moving with no energy. His father and brother went to Baltimore to help. This information I more or less had to piece together. For stretches he mumbled and made little sense. He wanted to see me, but I told him I couldn't today. When I said I'd come tomorrow & we decided on 1:00, he wrote this information down, and couldn't get straight what day it was. I don't know if he's on a new drug or whether he's just scared out of his wits over AIDS. But I'm frightened.

JULY 8: I think Tommy may be dying. And losing his mind.

I got to Peter Cooper Village at 1:30. Mrs. Curley, who is slight and friendly and whom I immediately liked, opened the door. Tom remained seated. He extended his hand, which trembled. His dry mouth has a blister. He coughs up great quantities of phlegm every so often. I saw a piece of his handwriting in a folder about Plato's signatures (a topic he's been working on). It was almost recognizable—the way it shouldn't be until he's 90. He offered me a drink, but he asked me to get it myself. He did manage to rise later, but he hobbles & holds on to things. His feet hurt.

He can't follow conversation. He mumbles, then says a few sentences that are regular, and then he loses the thread . . . He went to the bathroom while the 3 of us were making lunch. As soon as he was out of earshot, Mrs. Curley said to me that she thought she'd go crazy if this went on much longer. And that's how we plunged into two frantic, whispered conversations. (The other was when, later, I went into her bedroom to say goodbye.). She has been home from work for a week because she's afraid to leave him alone. But she's got to go back tomorrow. She doesn't know whether this is real or not, and she doesn't know what to do. She gave me her # at work & I said I'd call her . . . Did he summon me there today to show me he was dying? Was he crying for help? Is that why he spent so long in the bathroom—did he want his mother and me to talk?

JULY 11: [Seeing *Design for Living*] I thought Jill Clayburgh was fine—not at all the snorting, braying thing John Simon forced one to imagine.

JULY 12: Louise Curley called early this morning. Tom is being taken (he was, this afternoon, by his brother Mark) to Columbia-Presbyterian. She'll call me tomorrow to tell me about visiting hours and so forth. The doctors have also discovered that he has anemia, and she wonders if this explains the lethargy and vagueness. I don't think it does, and I don't think this sudden discovery of anemia makes sense in any case: with all the complicated blood tests he's had done, they're just discovering this now?

. . .

Mondale has picked Geraldine Ferraro for Vice-President. He's in desperate need of the appearance of excitement, so it's probably a good idea. But they still look as if they're going to be murdered by Reagan. And when the Democrats lose they usually deserve to.

JULY 14: Tommy has a spot on his lung that is probably pneumonia. They are doing tests for AIDS. The results so far are not definitive, but they're discouraging. One of the doctors has told [Louise] not to be optimistic.

Tommy is so frightened that on Thursday afternoon he ripped out his IV tubes and tried to flee the hospital . . . I went up to see him at about 5:00. The hospital was ringed with pickets—there's a strike going on. He's on the 8th Floor of the Harkness Pavilion. You can only see him if you're wearing a gown, a mask, gloves.

He is less disoriented than he was on Sunday, but his mind still wanders. He won't talk about tests, procedures, prognoses. He's not willing to deal with it yet. But he's facing it in some ways, making oblique acknowledgments. He told me that he cared about me a lot, that it was good of me to come. Tom, who had such trouble with terms of endearment last year, was forcing them out of himself now. I told him he could count on me—whatever happens.

How bad does he look? It's hard to say. He's not pallid—but Daddy never was either, if only because of fever. He's not emaciated. His robe was open to his waist, and his chest and stomach looked as beautiful as they did when he lay naked next to me in Baltimore and in Poughkeepsie.

But he is hooked to the tubes and is coughing great quantities of sputum into cups. The hall is filled with AIDS patients.

He gave me his new article on Plato. I said I would get it typed. But I read a page of it on the subway & fear it's too illegible and incoherent . . . As I left, I touched him on the knee and told him I loved him.

And for the first time he told me he loved me.

JULY 15: For a few hours today I thought I might lose my mind or die of fright. For one thing, I'm sick with a summer cold. But no cold will ever be just a cold for the next few years . . . I don't think I'd mind dying so much as being known as a person who'd died of *that* . . . I tried to watch the pre-convention news on the television, but keeping my mind on anything is too hard. One minute I think: if he dies, I want to die with him. The next I think: I want at least ten years to write more books.

If I get two more years, the odds are that I'll get 40.

JULY 16: He barked at me in frustration once and spilled his yogurt all over my jeans and the floor. I bought him a Walkman so he could listen to music without bothering anyone if he couldn't sleep. He liked this, but I wonder if it's wise to give him one more opportunity to tune out from reality. He even had the phones on his head while I was talking to him at one point. And he'd go on talking as he listened to the music. Sometimes he'd make sense and sometimes he wouldn't.

And yet I'm convinced there's something selective about the degree of lucidity he shows. When Paul Sachner & Charles Gandee, his old *Architectural Record* friends, came up at about 6:00, he seemed much more normally conversational. (And succeeded in making me absurdly jealous.)

JULY 17: I listened to Jesse Jackson's speech. Everyone at this convention is a star except Mondale.

JULY 18: He looks better, his fever is down, and he's much more lucid. The 3-way-ness of the conversation also seemed to help him mentally. At one point we were all laughing hard as Rachel and I got into a comical debate over English cooking. Then Tommy suddenly closed his eyes. I asked him if he was tired & we should leave. He said, "No, I'm just feeling very sad all of a sudden."

. . . Rachel & I went down to Peter Cooper Village. His mother told us what the week before he went into the hospital was really like. Tommy threw everything from the medicine cabinet into the toilet; he stopped it up another time with toilet paper; he lay on the bed saying "I forgive Mark" (his happy brother);

he went through some old family pictures with Mark, and every time he came to one of himself smiling he would say "Here's one of you"—he would only accept sad-expressioned photographs as ones of himself; he lay on his bed and named all the objects on the dresser across the room—he looked at an owl bank and said "There's the owl. Hoot. Hoot." And he lay on the couch once, whispering, "All the AIDS symptoms are gone. The thrush. The swollen lymph glands. Gone." . . . When we finally got up to go, Mrs. Curley threw her arms around me.

JULY 19: [Rachel and I] drove on into Massachusetts & up to Leverett. Tommy crept back into the conversation. Rachel said that the first time she met him—after he'd gotten out of Austen Riggs—they read Ovid together for an hour—& tears never stopped streaming down his face.

JULY 20: We drove to Shelburne Falls and went swimming in these spectacular rock pools. Rachel did deep dives on dares from the twelve-year-old boys around. They obviously thought she was a goddess & they were right.

As I swam from one ridge or rock to another, and felt the sun on my face and chest and back, and made my arms and muscles go, I had one thought: I don't want to die.

I threw a 1984 penny into the water and made a wish.

JULY 21: Tommy has cancer. His mother called tonight and said that the small brown spot on his nose—which he'd told me was a blood blister—is, in fact, Kaposi's sarcoma, the skin cancer that many AIDS victims get. I don't know why I never thought of this when I saw that spot—maybe there were just so many other enormities to concentrate on.

Dr. Weissman has also told her that he's psychotic, and that he'll never work again. Told her in those terms of breezy cruelty that [our family doctor] Harold Draffen used to specialize in.

JULY 23: I went up to the hospital late this afternoon. On the way I bought Tommy chocolate bars and some hand-grippers he can exercise with. I think they frustrated him more than anything else.

He soon lost interest in them. But when his father came in & tried them successfully Tommy felt obliged to pick them up again.

. . .

Tommy was cranky and withdrawn. He came up with one-word answers or nothing at all. But then he motioned for me to come sit beside him on the bed. When I did, he made a satisfied smile as if now everything were cozy & ok. He asked me not to go.

. . .

I talked to his father, who had tears in his eyes, in front of the elevators. The doctor has now told Tommy that his "immunological system is impaired"—his father couldn't say "AIDS"; maybe even the doctor couldn't—but that he can probably go home at the end of the week. (How Mrs. Curley will cope with this I don't know.). . . .

JULY 25: I bought Tommy—our *Greystoke*[*] joke—more bananas at a Spanish stand near the hospital. He is so frail & childlike. He was in a sweet mood today, a little boy who wanted to be teased, verbally cuddled. At one point he grabbed my wrist and wouldn't let go, daring me to try to tickle him again. I read to him from *Vanity Fair*—Becky's disgust over being at Miss Pinkerton's.

But he was as vague as he was sweet. He is not in touch with reality. At one point he uttered the word AIDS for the first time since he's been in the hospital. But what he said was: "It's amazing. It's been two years since the AIDS scare began, and I still don't have any of the crucial symptoms." Jesus. I nearly jumped out the 8th-floor window.

JULY 26: The doctor who a week ago said Tommy was psychotic now says he can go home and that [Louise] shouldn't pamper him too much. He now explains Tommy's lack of touch with reality by saying "Hospitals are disorienting places."

JULY 27: When Mrs. Curley and I were at the hospital we spotted Weissman in the elevator. Now he says yes, Tommy does have AIDS. And he warns her that things will not be easy when Tommy

* The Tarzan movie with Christopher Lambert.

is home . . . Tommy has lost memory & he's incapable of doing things like adding up the value of four coins. These functions don't get lost, the neurologist says, unless there's physiological damage. (Or unless you don't *want* to tell the neurologist how much the damned coins add up to . . . Why should Tommy be *expected* to be in touch with reality when the reality is that he's dying of AIDS?)

. . .

I told [Louise] the whole story of our affair last year. She says she always wanted him to have a relationship. "A good homosexual relationship is still a relationship. I've known lots of lousy heterosexual relationships."

. . .

Louise says that when he came home from Vassar after meeting me he was "ecstatic." And she said: "Did you see how he lit up when you came into the room this afternoon?" It's true, and these things keep me going.

She says when he was four & suspected of cutting up the Rubbermaid dishpan, he was told to tell the truth. It was important to tell the truth & he wouldn't be punished: "What if all truth were lies & all lies truth?" he responded.

. . .

I'm writing all these things down in no particular order. It's just that when he's dead I want to remember everything I can about him.

JULY 29: I talked to Tommy for a couple of minutes from Loree's. He asked what time I'd be coming tomorrow: "that way I'll have something to look forward to." Hearing that made me feel happy; the heart is easily pleased in the short run.

JULY 30: I got back to the city around 11 & talked with the landlord and the super about the mouse . . . Pat [the super] says the problem is the building they've torn down at the corner of 43rd & Lex. The mice are leaving a sinking edifice. The rectory cat next door is said to be stuffed . . .

Tommy is the worst I've ever seen him. Maybe it's the antipsychotic drugs, but he's plunging further & further into a state we won't be able to drag him back from. He stares ahead with big glassy eyes. He wanted to hold hands but not say anything— except for a few spooky things . . . he looked at my arm & [saw] 2 moles I've always had & a spaghetti sauce fleck from lunch and said: "If that were my arm they'd say I had skin cancer." There's no point in telling him he *does* have cancer. That realization just comes + goes in him.

JULY 31: I've been so agitated that Mom was wondering if there wasn't more than I was saying. And the strain of not letting on was getting to be more than I could stand. So I sat her down at the kitchen table late this morning—the same kitchen table where I told her about Tom and me a year and a half ago—and I told her . . . I laid it out straight & brutally. She has taken in the fact that I'm at risk & she's accepted it. The only assurance she wanted was that I wasn't lying to her when I said I'm ok as of now. Other than that her focus was on Tom. All her instincts and values are dead right and pure. She knows that this is a slaughter of innocents going on. And she said: "I don't know him, but I love him."

AUGUST 1: I got to the hospital at 3:00 and found Tommy sprawled on the floor. He'd collapsed on his way back from the bathroom. I lifted him into bed. "You're strong," he said, with a kind of matter-of-fact surprise. Once I had him in (and had noticed all the sprinkled lesions on his legs) he was too weak to adjust his position by as much as an inch. I put him under the blankets, petted him, told him I loved him, said he had to hang on—that his mother & I would figure out just what was going on.

After he drifted off to sleep I went out & told the nurse how I'd found him. She asked how long ago this had happened. "About a half hour ago," I said. "You should have told us sooner. What's your name? I have to fill out an incident report."

They're still talking, the nurse says, about bringing him home. "Have you seen him?" I asked her.

AUGUST 2: . . . Keep checking my arm for freckles that aren't freckles.

AUGUST 3: Watched a broad-shouldered American girl [Mary Lou Retton] beat the leotards off a couple of little Romanians on the balance beam. . . .

Tommy and I made love a year ago tonight. It was the last time. . . .

AUGUST 4: . . . Uptown to Tommy. (The most depressing part of the trip may be the walk across to the "A" train. Today I saw a girl with a blank face & bleeding mouth walking next to the boyfriend, or maybe pimp, who'd just socked her.)

. . . He's off Haldol, thank God . . . But the stuff is still in his system & his hands shake. Actually, they more than shake; they practically flap, and every so often they levitate off the bed, as if in devotion. He's got blisters on his feet and is now in booties. He's afraid of losing feeling in his legs & knocks himself out trying to move them every few minutes. To stop the hands from shaking he grabbed onto mine.

. . . He said he's bothered by terrible "pictures." He remembered the picture I took of him in Woodstock a year ago ("I had on a blue shirt, right?"), and then says "Pictures! Enough already! Go away!" and makes a dismissing movement. I said, "Do you want me to go away?" "No," he said, hurt that I'd mistaken his meaning & patting my hand. He wants the pictures to go away.

What is he seeing?

AUGUST 6: [Louise] saw a psychiatrist herself last week. She asked her, "Do you mind if I smoke?" The psychiatrist said, "Yes, I do." Louise won't make another appointment . . .

On the way out of the hospital, she asked, "Do you think you make him feel guilty?" It's true he didn't light up as he did when I came in on the two of them the other week. But I can't tell if it's bedsores or his psyche. But I felt hurt that she even suggested it. I don't want to start thinking that he'd be better off without me.

. . . Mary [McCarthy] had brain surgery for her balance problem a few weeks ago. The thing that seemed to bother her most was having to have half her head shaved.

AUGUST 9: I got to the hospital in the afternoon and found Katy paying her first visit—mask, gown, gloves. Very emotional when she came out into the hall . . . her father, an immunologist, says that anyone with AIDS who's alive 6 months from now may have a chance. That's how fast work on it is going. But I don't believe any good news on this subject. I keep thinking of Blunden and WWI: "surely we we[re] born for this, naught else."

. . .

Katrina said she called Mary [in Maine] and heard the story of the brain surgery. But Mary said, "I'm going back upstairs into bed right now, and I'm going to read Tom's book. I'll call you with the quotation as soon as I'm finished."

AUGUST 10: There was a letter from François in Paris advising [Tommy] to have "courage." Tom had Louise read it to him. "This is going to be awful," he said.

Beat when I got back here. Bob [Pounder] & Charley came by at 9:00 (after I talked to Rachel), and we went out to this dreary gay bar on 2nd Ave. called The Last Call. Complete with dirty videos. All I wanted to do was leave. But here's Bob smiling up at this dirty movie when tomorrow he has to scatter Don's ashes over Fire Island.

AUGUST 11: . . . The ghastly power of love. A year ago I was being battered and ground by unrequited—or briefly requited and brutally snatched—love. Now I'm facing someone's death and my own possible fatal illness. And the truth of the matter is that the second set of circumstances is, moment by moment, easier to live with. The constant self-hatred, the feeling of exile from paradise: these things aren't there.

AUGUST 12: That curious, exhilarating sense I have these days of how all my perceptions are poignantly sharpened, all my feelings strong, excessive even, but somehow beyond sentimentality. I feel fully, complicatedly, dangerously alive.

AUGUST 14: [Flying home from a visit to friends in South Bend, Indiana] The weird sort of ecstasy I've been feeling and writing about here . . . when the Chrysler Building, in all its silver-jagged defiance, swam past the window on the turn into LaGuardia, I very nearly sobbed.

AUGUST 16: Weisman called [Louise], or she him, and he says she mustn't give up hope. Tommy will have one more spinal tap, but then they can bring him home (towards the end of next week). Weisman says that the more they learn about AIDS the more shades of gray they're starting to see. People live with it (yes, but for how long?). When Tommy gets home he is to get dressed, sit up, and generally be forced back into the land of the living. And Louise needn't wash his things separately or keep him in isolation. All of this made her feel good.

AUGUST 17: NBC News . . . says that 64% of all gay men in San Francisco have had sexual contact with someone who's got AIDS. That means there are tens of thousands of people in that one city in my position. There are two ways of looking at this. You can say, "Well, that's comforting; surely they can't *all* die." But after that you can say, "What's to *say* they won't die?"

AUGUST 18: The human capacity for relativism can be a wonderful thing. I was happy coming home on the A train because Tommy was having a good day. A good day for this beautiful, brilliant 30-year-old man now means being able to smile when you come in the room, to make a little bit of conversation before he drifts off to sleep holding your hand, to sit up a little while you spoonfeed him vanilla ice cream.

AUGUST 20: [Tommy's] father read several Shakespeare sonnets from the book on the table. Difficult to listen to how the fairest should procreate, how at forty their brows will be creased.

AUGUST 21: A letter from Mary praising the book and telling me about her shunt operation . . . She sounds full of beans.
      . . . New York stories: the cab driver . . . who told me about the cop who gave him 2 tickets back in '79. Then the cabbie, a

Greek, put a curse on him. "And then, New Year's Eve, he got his throat slashed. I read it in the *Post*."

AUGUST 22: Tommy continues to be more alert mentally. And he's eating ravenously—yogurt, jello, ice cream, a frappe, all in quick succession. The best evidence that he's more in touch with reality may have come when he winced at one point, as he just lay there, and said, "Sometimes I just want to cry."

. . .

One lovely moment today: the Goodyear blimp sailing splendiferously above 2nd Avenue. An Italian girl turned to me and said, "Is so beautiful. Is like the cinema."

AUGUST 23: . . . We may revert to a kind of gay celibacy. The epidemic will make people like me start to fall in love with beautiful, unattainable straight men. There may be a couple of Christopher Fields* ahead of me yet. This may be the way we survive. If we survive.

. . . Ann despises Kirkpatrick, & is appalled that I may vote for Reagan. . . .

AUGUST 24: Did bureaucracy with Irene [Grabowski, the English department secretary] and at one point couldn't keep my mind on what we had in front of us because I was sure one of my glands felt swollen.

AUGUST 25: . . . Tommy's brain seems to be coming back remarkably. He is conversational now—no more one-word answers. He even plays on words. He doesn't drift off to sleep during visits. He is altogether more with it. [One attendant's] replacement, a dislikeable guy, mutters something about how Tommy won't be able to go home until his sore is healed, and Tommy, annoyed at the pessimism and at how we were being interrupted, told him to shut

* Christopher Field, a close friend, and the object of a long, serious crush during my years as a Harvard graduate student. Later an accomplished translator of Japanese and a broadcaster.

up . . . I even think his libido is coming back: he made a salacious grin when I told him I had running shorts instead of underwear on underneath my other shorts (I was telling him that the [laundry] had been closed this morning). And when I mentioned one of these AIDS patients who'll be discussed in a TV documentary next week, someone's who's had the disease for a long time and living more or less normally with it, Tommy asked: "Does he have sex?"

AUGUST 26: I got a call this afternoon from Tom Stevenson, a former student of Katherine's.[*] He's in NY looking for a job; he's left graduate school. He's 25, 6'4", blond, adorable, boyish, Iowan. And gay. Sweet as can be.

He came over tonight and had a couple of drinks and we took a walk. He looked at the U.N. and Tudor City and all sorts of things with gosh-oh-golly genuineness. And told me how much he liked Truman Capote [who had died the day before] . . .

AUGUST 27: Mary is in the paper getting her MacDowell Medal & wearing a cloth hat to cover what she told the reporter was surgery on her "scalp."

AUGUST 28: He's coming home tomorrow. I was in the room with him when he got the news over the telephone from his mother. She'd just talked to Weisman.

He is both happy and afraid, I think. Reaches out over the bed and clutches my ankle. Wants to be touched, reassured . . .

AUGUST 29: I had a letter from the *L.A. Times* saying they may at some point have some work for me. And I had what I thought was a flirtatious postcard from Bruce Chatwin.

      . . .

New York was glorious today. I'm in love with it. Every part of it. Even the deranged man who makes imaginary machine-gunner movements in front of St. Agnes'.

---

* Mary Katherine Tillman (1940–2022), a scholar of John Henry Newman and a longtime professor at Notre Dame; a close friend when we were both on sabbatical at St. Edmund's House, University of Cambridge, from 1982 to 1983.

SEPTEMBER 1: [For his birthday] Bought Tommy an Alexander Julian shirt at Saks . . . Talked to [him] and Louise on the phone. Tommy already hates his nurse ("home attendant") but otherwise seems to be managing.

SEPTEMBER 2: . . . Tommy looks pretty dreadful: his hair is wispy; the sarcoma on his face is larger; he's very thin . . . Paul Sachner was also [at Louise's]. (Was I jealous? At first, yes. I'm not the only claimant. But I liked Paul a lot. And he's stuck by Tommy. Most of his NY friends gave up on him long before AIDS—they just couldn't take the other "problems," the incessant despairs.) Louise cooked a roast. A very good dinner. Tommy tunes in and out . . . We kept going until 10:00. The talk turned to New York stories. Tommy sat on the sidelines. We wound up treating him as one treats the very old.

Mark and Big Tom* did the dishes. Louise changed Tommy's dressing. We all said good-night to him in his bedroom (taking care to use the other bathroom) one by one. The family left to go uptown. Louise, nervous, not wanting everyone to go at once, got Paul & me to stay. The three of us chatted, hopefully, as Tommy's coughs came out of the bedroom.

Paul & I walked 23rd St. before I got into a cab. He says a year or so ago he slept with someone who's now dead.

SEPTEMBER 3: Talked to Doug MacKay [now a GMHC volunteer] about a new "buddy" for Tommy and then relayed the information to Louise. Big Tom picked up the phone down there. She was in the bedroom, probably changing Tommy's dressing. I had the impression they'd be[en] squabbling. I wonder if it all feels eerily like taking care of the baby back in 1953.

SEPTEMBER 4: [Katrina] says that *Saturday Review*, which I thought was out of business, has said it will review my book. And we talked about a minuscule error I've discovered in Ch. 7 of *ABOOO*. She says not to worry—the only book she's ever seen go out perfect into the world is Louis Simpson's poems. But it still wounds me . . .

* Tom Curley's father, the novelist Thomas Curley (1925–2005).

I hate the idea of any error in print . . . It's eternity—the idea that it's there forever, the very thing that attracted one to writing in the first place—that gnaws at one.

SEPTEMBER 5: Bob, the home attendant, is fussy but very diligent. It took him a long time to leave, and he puts 2-page-long reports to Louise on the frig door.

SEPTEMBER 7: [Paul Sachner and I] met downtown, right outside the door to Tommy's building, a little after 4:00. The visit was not a success. Tommy seems to have plunged in the past 48 hours. He's back to one-word answers, hobbling, and a distracted look. We dressed him up in his duck jacket with a sweater under-neath. What little hair he has left stood up in wild wisps. The old ladies of Peter Cooper Village thought Paul and I, who had Tommy by one arm apiece, were escorting a drunk or a lunatic. He'd be less conspicuous in a wheelchair. We made it less than halfway around the playground before we had to sit down.

But I don't think that's the worst of it. The worst of it is Bob . . . his old queen of an attendant. He can't give Tommy a pill or a glass of juice without pawing him. He has obviously con-ceived a crush on Tommy; it's just as obvious that he intended to do that with whatever patient he was assigned. Louise has told him to back off; his supervisor says this is part of the "bonding" process the program encourages.

SEPTEMBER 9: He looks awful. He'd just had a bath, and it had taken a lot out of him. His hair is somehow more depressing than anything else. He and Louise both seem resigned to keeping Bob . . . particularly since the Saturday substitute didn't show up and the substitute's substitute arrived at 11:00 with a hangover . . . I'm more instead of less preoccupied with it. Somehow more fear-ful for myself, & more aware of the enormity of what's happening to him. Paul Sachner, whom I talked to on the phone, says it's the same way with him. He spaces out. Last night at a dinner party his hostess said, "Paul, you're not yourself."

SEPTEMBER 10: . . . I still feel my real boy—my real might-have-been, my had-but-lost—is dying twenty blocks away from me.

SEPTEMBER 12: [Louise] says it's been a bad week. Tommy seems to be up more in the middle of the night than in the daytime. She's having trouble sleeping herself. The other night he got up, wandered around the apartment, and fell down.

SEPTEMBER 13: Found Pat McCormack sweeping as I got back to 151. "Good *evenin'*, sor!" And it was a lovely evening, the last commuters making it at 7:00 towards Grand Central, the last light of day shining on the Chrysler Building. In the mailbox a letter from Mary inviting me to Maine, and the first review of *A Book of One's Own*—from *Booklist*. Descriptive, not judgmental.

. . . [Sex with Charley] With our usual vigor. And with increasing tenderness. Lovely. Made love even though last night I'd had a dream that made me come in my sleep—I can't remember when that last happened. I don't usually put this sort of thing in here. Maybe it's reading all the Boswell.

SEPTEMBER 14: I sat and talked with Louise, who is frantic & discouraged. She says I "buoy her up." But we know it's hopeless, & for the first time I could sense we were syllables away from saying we wish he'd die soon.

I went in to say good-bye to him. I kissed his blue-striped robe and told him I loved him & would see him soon. He opened his eyes & said "I love you, too" and then went back to sleep.

. . . Still in love with the night. Maybe in love with this tragedy? On some level I'm awed by what fate is doing to me.

SEPTEMBER 15: . . . Ran into the San Gennaro Festival before getting to the Performing Garage on Wooster St. There I met Charley, Michael and Alison West [Mary McCarthy's stepdaughter, eventually a close friend]. We went to see Jeff Weiss's *And That's How the Rent Gets Paid, Part IV*, a four-hour series of blackout sketches about Conrad Gerhardt, actor, legend, fag, alter ego of a Finnish gymnast; wanted for murder by Detective Persky, various lesbian ex-wives and Adonis sons.

SEPTEMBER 16: I walked up to the Book Fair on 5th, between 48th and 57th. Jimmy Breslin, the star of the Ticknor & Fields booth, wasn't supposed to arrive until 1:00. But across the street, hawking *Gender Gap*, was Bella Abzug herself, under a smart grey hat. She and a man were arguing about Ferraro and abortion. "Now I'm not a Catholic," she explained. Stop press.

. . .

[Tommy] was racked with chills and had a bandage over his eyebrow. I thought it might be a new lesion, but it was a cut—he fell again & cut himself on a humidor . . . [He] stayed awake as long as he could, and then I held onto his arm as he hobbled back to bed. Paul & I stayed to talk to Louise.

Weissman (it's got 2 S's) tells Paul that celibacy is not necessary. He ought to know, says Paul. It turns out he's gay himself.

SEPTEMBER 17: A biography of Eleonora Duse has arrived from the *LA Times* for me to review. All I know about Eleonora Duse is the Fats Waller line "They're makin' Duses of all the chanteuses," but I'll do it anyway.

SEPTEMBER 18: [A visiting faculty member in the Vassar art department] told us the story of how years ago he spent a day acting in a porno film called *Rough House*—complete with details of how they use a bottle of Ivory Liquid when the lead is sated by too many takes.

SEPTEMBER 20: This should have been a good day for me. I taught well and came back down here to find a *Kirkus Reviews* notice Katrina sent me: I'm unpedantic, perky, vivid and informative.

And completely bewildered.

SEPTEMBER 21: Tommy is a little better than Sunday. We managed to look at a book of Bonnard's paintings together. He took a real interest in it, & we kept making comparisons, whether it was to Van Gogh or Monet, that clearly encouraged him to keep thinking. A wheelchair is supposed to arrive next week. Once again there are fantastic plans that we'll actually make it to some-

place like the Morgan Library . . . Still, he is in touch with reality
enough to say, "This is a strange existence."

. . .

I was resolved to spend the evening alone and feel self-
sufficient . . . Then the phone rang. A very merry Tom Stevenson
called and suggested we go out to a gay bar. Well, okay. We did.
To one in this neighborhood. Then we got a cab downtown and
sat outside until 1:00 at a café drinking wine. And after that we
went dancing (yes, *I* went dancing with a man) . . . We ended the
night by sitting on the steps of a beautiful old house on W. 9th
St. . . . He was very affectionate, romantic, silly—saying we ought
to fly to Brazil in the morning, saying we had to go into a particular bar when we heard "Embraceable You" coming out of it.

SEPTEMBER 22: . . . One thing I'm realizing about my life down
here is that I have few *friends*, pure and simple. Everyone I see has
some sort of sexual relevance . . . every encounter has an erotic
dimension. No wonder I don't relax. No wonder I feel wonderful
and horrible ten times a day.

SEPTEMBER 23: Went down to Tommy's at about 8:00 . . . Mark
and Missy[*] and Louise there. I realize, partly from the quality of
the circle of people, that I'm coming to love Tommy in a whole
new way—as family, as my invalid brother . . . He was in a sweater,
wrapped up in blankets. An hour later his temperature was 103°.
He tuned in and out of conversation . . . We talked about the election and politics . . . Muhammad Ali is in Columbia-Presbyterian
for Parkinson's syndrome, and we talked about that. . . .
    . . . As I left I thought: all right, this is awful & tragic, but
there was love in that room tonight; sweetness; solicitude; common cause against enormity. Why can't it continue like this? I can
accept this. Why does he have to *die*?

SEPTEMBER 24: Ronald Reagan today became the third American President I've laid eyes on . . . He's in NY to make nice with

* Mary Ellen Curley, wife of Mark Curley and sister-in-law of Tom.

Andrei Gromyko, whose legendary madcap charm was on display at the U.N. today. His limo looks more like a battleship than a car, but you get enough of a glimpse of him to realize his hair is dyed a lighter brown than you thought . . . I didn't hear a single boo on the streets. . . .

SEPTEMBER 25: . . . Thinking about Paul Sachner. He called here tonight. He's been feeling awful all week—exhausted, dizzy, slightly nauseated. And he's terrified.

The train has sped up to a hundred miles an hour. No one's going to make it out of the way.

SEPTEMBER 27: [Paul Sachner] feels much better after seeing Weissman . . . convinced he's had some ordinary bug that panic has made him believe is AIDS. Weissman tells him he should go ahead with the 2-week trip to Italy that he's making for the magazine. Weissman's added prescription was, "Go and get laid."

SEPTEMBER 28: Tommy is scheduled to have a blood transfusion on Wednesday. He is very weak (albeit without fever) and everyone is going through one of those periods of wondering, without speaking, if this is the beginning of the end.

. . . The book jacket is out and looks awfully good—I'm all happy teeth—but everything else at T&F is vexed. There was no meeting of the HM [Houghton Mifflin] board this week (everyone's at the book fair in Frankfurt), but there are murmurs that they don't want to take a chance on the plagiarism book until they see some good reviews of *ABOOO*. I'm beginning to feel jerked around, and Katrina admits I have a right to.

SEPTEMBER 29: [Went with Tom Stevenson] to a piano bar, Arthur's, on Grove St. . . . After a few more drinks I just blurted that not the least of my difficulties in this situation is my developing a first-rate crush on him.

Well, his response was to squeeze my knee in a sweet, protective way that made my heart sink.

SEPTEMBER 30: I spoke to Louise. I told her I had a depressing weekend and that I wasn't sure I could make it down tomorrow. She told me I was charming, a great person, not to berate myself. (I'd told her that I feel I can't relate to anyone these days & I know she immediately knew I was talking about the shadow of AIDS. What surprised me was her obvious & instant sympathy, for what am I suffering compared to Tommy?)

OCTOBER 2: I've been scared. I have a sore throat. I've been feeling light-headed and tired. I wish it would develop into a full-blown cold; otherwise I keep wondering if I've got thrush or my blood is turning completely scarlet.

OCTOBER 3: I had a postcard (forwarded from *Newsday*) from Jessica Mitford praising the Toynbee review. Rather nice of her since I'd, in the middle of praise, called her slippery & vulgar.

OCTOBER 4: I left Kendrick [House at Vassar] about 8:30 and crossed Raymond Ave. After I got through the Main Gate I saw Rachel coming toward me, and I thought that was odd. I also thought it was odd that she looked so unhappy, almost heavy with age. But I never made any connections until she told me that Tommy had died yesterday in the hospital.

Louise went up with him in the ambulette. He was very bad—unable to walk even with the cane and walker. One of his lungs was filled with fluid. As soon as they saw him at C-P they decided he would have to be admitted. They prepared a room . . . Big Tom was called from Xavier. And Missy was called. Mark was playing handball in Central Park; Missy called the ranger, who got him off the court. They all saw him. He knew who they were, but could only mumble a few words. He never had the transfusion . . . an attendant came in and told them that he'd just died on his way to the X-Ray room.

. . .

I was back in the city by six. I went down to Peter Cooper because Louise asked me to. I had dinner with her, Big Tom, Missy and Mark: Big Tom's face puffed up with pain; Louise looking like a bird whose spine was about to crack; Missy strong and helpful; Mark running into the bathroom at one point to weep for the brother who was so utterly different from himself.

. . . He's being buried with the Friers [Louise's family] in Milton, Mass. on Monday.

Terry McKiernan, who went to Fordham Prep with Tommy and Mark, and who is a sweet old-fashioned fellow, came by for a while. He cheerfully argued politics with Louise, who did her affectionate Gerry Ferraro imitation: "Lemme tell ya . . ."

I only cried once while I was there—when at the dinner table Big Tom and Louise asked me if I'd be a pallbearer.

OCTOBER 5: Rachel came to the apartment at 7:00 and we took a taxi to the funeral parlor at 2nd and 21st. The casket was closed. The place looked a little like where you'd have an Italian wedding reception. "How he'd have hated this room," Rachel said. (When Louise had to pick out the casket yesterday, she decided to do the sensible & tasteful thing and buy the cheapest. But when the salesman pointed out the rayon lining to her, she decided she had to get the next one up the line: Tommy's *GQ* soul would not have peace wrapped in rayon.)

OCTOBER 6: We were assembled at the funeral parlor at 9:00. We said prayers around the coffin, directed by a mafioso-type who did everything by the book.

I thought my heart would break as we picked up the casket—me, Mark, Terry, Brad and two professionals—and carried it to the hearse . . . Carrying it up the steps was worse. I saw Big Tom and Louise holding on to one another. How do parents bury a child?

The curious thing about pallbearing is that it's more than ceremonial; it's hard work. Even bodies that perish at 105 pounds are heavy when they're put inside a wooden box. I remembered picking him up off the hospital floor.

. . . When the priest (who taught Tommy at Fordham Prep one year) prayed that our sacrifice of bread be acceptable to Him, I thought: "What more does that Great Bastard want?" Tommy's corpse wasn't ten feet from the chalice.

OCTOBER 9: I did all right until about 7:15 p.m. Then NBC news had a story about how AIDS is now thought to be carried in saliva, and they showed a clip of a man with Kaposi's sarcoma, and I became absolutely convinced that the bruise on my chest . . . was a lesion . . .

It is inhuman. I cannot live like this. But I know that my real fears are likely to be starting only now. There's no more Tommy to worry about and do things for . . . The only thing that exceeds my fear is my ludicrous self-pity. A couple of times today I caught myself thinking that Tommy was lucky to be out of it.

And yet I know I don't want to be out of it. Not when I'm having such a good time teaching Keats that I look up and find it's 2:45 when I was expecting it to be about 2:20; not when everyone who comes into my office oohs and aahs over the new book on my desk.

OCTOBER 11: Just before I left for home I ran into Brett [Singer] . . . To give you an idea of how out of touch we've been, she said: "Do you still see your friend Tom?"

OCTOBER 12: Paul called early in the evening. I was surprised he was back from Italy already, and yet I for some reason then assumed that since he was he'd already been into the office and talked to Charles Gandee. But he hadn't. So I had to tell him that Tommy was dead . . . He told me Weissman said Tom had the most aggressive case of AIDS he'd ever seen . . . An hour later I was in a coffee shop . . . A radio report about some kind of mouth disease connected to AIDS came on in the background. I just threw my silverware down onto the table and pushed my food aside.

OCTOBER 13: I was down at Louise's just past 6:30 . . . It was the same group as the birthday party—except for Tommy himself . . . Louise was surprised (and maybe pleased, maybe she felt a little less odd) to learn from Paul that his own life was just as fast as Tommy's, that many people's lives were . . . [she] says her only consolation now is that Tommy's life was always so miserable that he may be better off. We recalled how you'd call him up & ask how he was & he'd say "Surviving." When he was little, Louise says, he was so afraid of going to sleep that he'd hold his eyelids up with his fingers.

OCTOBER 15: [The movie *Garbo Talks*] was charming. And then came the credits—they showed that the faggy director [character] who pushed Hermione Gingold around was played by Court Miller. Court Miller has AIDS . . . He came to visit Tommy at Peter Cooper a few weeks ago, to give him a pep talk. He told him to get rid of all the doctors and he left him books on magic.

OCTOBER 16: Maybe 2000 dead isn't all that many—because maybe we're all gay. Sometimes that's the way it seems. Remember Mitchell, the little blond choirboy who lived upstairs? He moved out a couple of months ago. Tonight there was a letter for him, waiting to be forwarded, lying on the radiator near the mailboxes. The return address was the Boy Bar on St. Mark's Place.

OCTOBER 17: Dinner at the Brauhaus [in Poughkeepsie] with the DeMarias and Beverly. From there to Eamon & Rachel's. They were supposed to be having coffee. It turned out that the coffee was champagne and the icing on the dessert said "A Cake of One's Own."

OCTOBER 18: . . . Over to Lincoln Center for Mary [McCarthy's] reading (at the Bruno Walter Auditorium). One of the early chapters of her "intellectual autobiography." I almost felt nostalgic when Uncle Myers & Aunt Margaret reappeared. God, isn't autobiography the perfect form for Mary? She gets to combine her critical faculties & her touches of egotism and it comes out splendid—diction & syntax clear as gin . . . About ten of us went over to The Ginger Man after that. I sat between Mary & Niccolò Tucci. Lizzie [Hardwick] and Dotson Rader (a drunken idiot) talked about the supposedly missing (and perhaps never written) manuscript of the rest of *Answered Prayers*. Kevin McCarthy, who remains spectacularly handsome, made a brief, fortuitous appearance. One of Mary's old students from Bard was there too . . . When Mary greeted me after the reading she said "A fellow author!"

OCTOBER 19: Houghton Mifflin bought the [plagiarism book proposal] at yesterday's meeting.

OCTOBER 23: I'm back to scraping my tongue and wondering if any tiny fleck of white may be a harbinger of death. Otherwise it's been an easy day.

OCTOBER 25: It's certainly my moment. And it's coming faster and easier than I'd ever have expected. When I got home at 7:00 there was a message on the tape from Anatole Broyard at the *Times*. He wants me to call him about doing a review for them. He says he's gotten my name from Phyllis [Rose] (O my Lady Gregory!) and that he's gotten hold of *ABOOO* and finds it "interesting" . . . I can't screw this up. I thought it would happen, but not until *ABOOO* had gotten some good reviews & I'd sent a portfolio and so forth . . . Opened a beer and watched *Cheers* & *Hill Street Blues* and kept thinking omigosh-I've-done-it thoughts.

OCTOBER 26: I met Damo [Damian Leader]* for lunch. We talked about Tommy. He was very sympathetic, but I kept feeling he was looking at me like a possibly doomed creature, and I'm too busy feeling like a star . . . Broyard is very friendly. (I expected a jerk from some of his essays and TV appearances—he struck me as someone who was comfortable with David Susskind.) He assures me that if this piece—on the Vita [Sackville-West] to Virginia [Woolf] letters—works out there will be more. Likes my book, & altogether encouraging. I went back through Times Square on air.

. . . [Tom S. and I] decided to have a nightcap in midtown. . . . Tom suggested we go into Rounds, which turns out to be a hustlers' bar. All these fat old men being paid thoroughly friendly attention by the gorgeous young boy hookers. (One of them next to me couldn't have been 19 yet.) Quite a spectacle, and it gets ugly around 1:00. I heard one paunchy guy who was just looking being told "you can't afford me" in tremendously indignant

* Historian and foreign-service officer; a friend made during my sabbatical at St. Edmund's House in Cambridge.

terms by a not-very-good-looking hustler. God knows whether they thought we were buying or selling.

OCTOBER 27: . . . Drinks at [Paul Sachner's] place. Hamburgers at a Columbia spot (he lives on W. 103) called The Abbey. Friendly, slightly stiff conversation—at just such a pitch that made it hard to tell if this was the nervousness of courtship or just a lack of much to say. From there to a gruesome, nearly deserted bar called the Knight Deposit. Talk turned sexy, playful; so obviously did we want to forget Tommy, forget disease (I still hate writing the acronym).

And then back to the apartment, where one thing led to another & finally nothing. Amorousness on the couch and then naked to bed. Where shortly before we finished we stopped. Tommy might as well have been rattling the bedsprings (it's the same apartment where they had their affair; Paul's been there 7 years).

OCTOBER 28: I came home from dinner at the Curleys' with a huge bagful of Tommy's beautiful clothes: jackets, trousers, shirts . . . Louise was disappointed that I didn't take even more.

OCTOBER 29: I don't know how much more of this I can bear. At 3:15 I met Big Tom on the corner of 3rd & 29th and we went to have coffee. A few nervous pleasantries before he got to the main business: asking me if I thought Tommy felt reconciled to him before he died . . . I kept trying to figure out what the human thing to do was; and I also kept imagining Tommy listening in from beyond, amazed at the question, amazed by its being asked to me.

I stumbled; said things about how there's always unfinished business between people; talked about me and Daddy; said that the fact that their relationship was troubled showed it was something of consequence, not indifference. I have no idea if I made him feel any better. And I'm not sure he wanted to.

But there we were, talking again about the hospital, Baltimore, my chances for coming down with AIDS, how Tommy was a nervous child . . .

We stayed together for about an hour. Then we walked up

3rd Avenue. It was already dark, and starting to rain, at 4:30. Weird to see the skyscraper lights on so early. I tried to get him to talk about the coming grandchild.

It was dark back upstairs in the apartment—only the lights from the Kent Building across the street coming through the window. And I sat in the dark and I looked at Tommy's picture and I cried all over again.

. . .

I didn't mention this: Paul said that Tommy described our relationship as "stormy," ascribing no particular blame to either one of us. The only thing that surprises me is that Tommy mentioned it at all.

OCTOBER 30: Angelica Garnett spoke in Taylor Hall tonight about her [Bloomsbury] parents [Vanessa Bell and Duncan Grant]. A different lecture from what she gave here a few years ago, and meant to accompany the exhibition in the Art Gallery. Her disposition seems sunnier, and this time her dress looked like a white graduation robe instead of a black graduation robe. The main thing I caught from her lecture was that for the last 43 years of her life Vanessa was in a state of intense sexual ("seksyooal," as her daughter would say) deprivation.

. . . [Bob Pounder] showed me a copy of Tommy's dossier from when he was a job candidate here. The letter of recommendation from one Princeton professor describes Tommy as a "very stable personality."

OCTOBER 31: Mrs. Gandhi's baleful streaked head is gone. "Sikh or treat?" is today's joke.[*]

NOVEMBER 1: And so now I want this. What I had tonight. Coming up to Apartment 4A, my little warren amid the twinkling towers, and finding Tom [S.] working on dinner. I want this: to call out, "Hi, sweetie, I'm home!" We made spaghetti, salad, opened up wine, ate our fill, lay back on the couch and argued politics and cuddled. . . .

---

[*] Indira Gandhi, the prime minister of India, was assassinated by two Sikh bodyguards.

Jesse Jackson was at Vassar this morning. He talked in the chapel and the Main Gate was crowded with police cars. Rachel asked me afterwards if I'd gone to hear him. I told her I had too much to do before I caught the train back to "Hymietown."

NOVEMBER 2: Nancy cuts my hair & asks whom I'm voting for. I tell her I'm leaning toward Reagan. She says "Little people should vote for Mondale." . . . Tom [S.] and I were not connecting. We wandered around and he wanted to go into the Boy Bar. I didn't . . . I don't want to be some old Virgil offering him sage advice (of which I have none) as he explores his own sexual worries and perambulates around the "scene."

NOVEMBER 3: I got my Vita piece written in the morning and it's not bad. A hash of cross-outs at the moment, but there are some good lines in it. I think it'll do.

A beautiful fall day—the season is here at last. I walked all the way up to the Museum & met Louise outside it at 3:15. We saw the Van Gogh exhibit, a beautiful, intelligently arranged thing, but packed to the point of outrageousness. I was four rows of people (with headphones) from some of the paintings & sketches. I had a better view of Ronald Reagan a few weeks ago. . . .

We went to a fancy coffee place on Madison afterwards . . . She started talking about Tommy, about the prize she wants to set up at Amherst or Princeton. I gave her the pictures. We felt suddenly awkward with one another, newly distant after all we'd been through.

NOVEMBER 5: I taped an interview at National Public Radio this morning in the weird soundlessness of a control booth hooked up by satellite to Washington. It's to be dovetailed with an interview with Susan Cheever. The first question they asked me was whether she'd have had a harder time writing her book about her father without his journals. I think I said something like "I guess so" . . .

Brought my review over to the *Times*. The *Book Review* office is as grubby as a police precinct. Broyard doesn't even have his own office—just one desk in a sea of them. He called back in the afternoon, said the piece reads well, and we fiddled with a few sentences. . . .

I'm in the stores now. I went into all of them on Fifth Avenue, & it's there. On shelves, alas, and not tables, but in Scribner's Philip Larkin's essays are spine-outwards and I'm front-cover-forwards on the same shelf.

NOVEMBER 6: [Reagan won] a staggering majority. But I'm not part of it. I got into the booth on E. 45th St. and just couldn't pull the lever for either one of them. I just voted for the rest (Goodman, Stein). Yes, I've leaned toward Reagan for months, so conservative have my foreign politics become in the last several years. But there were all the other things: the Supreme Court, the religious crazies, the rest of it. I just couldn't do it.

NOVEMBER 10: I met Phyllis [Rose] at 1095 Park Avenue a little after 7:00 . . . We went to Nirvana on Central Park South for an Indian dinner . . . It's perhaps the most beautiful restaurant I've ever been in, but how it gets by the fire code with the cloth-covered ceilings & walls & everything else, I'll never know.

NOVEMBER 12: I went up to Scribner's to get a copy of *As You Like It* for Thursday night's departmental reading. I just hope it goes fast, because Jaques intends to be on the 10:26 home to New York that evening.

NOVEMBER 14: A quiet evening. Graded papers, prepared Emily [Dickinson], and went over to Patty's to watch Joan Collins get sprung from the Denver Detention Center before her hairdo deteriorated any further. They were very into designer food tonight. Even the prison meals seemed color-coordinated.

NOVEMBER 17: At about ten this morning I was sitting here with a hangover, in my underwear, listening to the radio and reading yesterday's *New York Post* . . . Then Bob called to tell me congratulations. John Gross had reviewed my book, favorably, in the morning's *Times*. I went out to the terminal and got 3 copies.

It's a good review—four columns across. One or two jabs at

what may be occasionally excessive perkiness and breathlessness, but lots of praise. A happy idea; a wise decision; "commendable zest . . . lively curiosity"; an ending (Barbellion) that's "an eloquent close to an enjoyable book." I've read the article about 315 times by now & have decided that it's indeed good. In fact, I'm digesting it more proportionately than I do student evaluations, even though several million people are looking at it. People have called to congratulate me, and on the street I've had a slight urge to be recognized.

. . .

Tom [S.] and I went at 7:30 to a mass sponsored by Dignity, the organization of gay Catholics. A good idea, I thought when he suggested it. But where should it be held? Unbelievably enough, at St. Francis Xavier. But I went anyway. And liked it. Lots of shapes and ages: not a gay bar with pews. About 200 people. Low key, dignified. (With a few camp moments: the gospel was the parable of the talents—that least paradoxical and satisfying of all Biblical stories. After the poor servant was left waiting and gnashing and the priest closed with the formula "And this is the good news of Jesus Christ," a faggy voice behind me said, "This is the *good* news? What's the bad news?") . . . Afterwards there was a "social" in the basement. Members of the gay synagogue from the neighborhood put on a gay, Jewish version of *Dynasty* (Anorexis instead of Alexis, etc.). I laughed and laughed and wondered about John [Cardinal] O'Connor walking in. The whole thing is oddly sanctioned & disapproved of. A bit like early Christians meeting risk-free in the catacombs.

NOVEMBER 18: I kept inside & to myself most of the day . . . imagined people all over Manhattan emptying their vacuum bags onto my picture, as I am literally yesterday's news.

[Louise and I] had a spaghetti dinner and I told her about the strange Xavier experience last night. She has been hurting herself by reading Tommy's awful Amherst diaries.

NOVEMBER 20: Bad news in the evening while I prepare the war poets & read Mary Chesnut for the *LA Times*. Patty calls to say that Lisa Schiller, who used to be an English major (an advisee of mine) and then switched to Spanish, has been killed in a car crash. She was driving to Green Haven; she did tutoring in the prison. She'd been happy doing this for a long time. I'd see her on the path & she'd say, "Mr. Mallon, I'm going to see the boys this afternoon." She had a sunny disposition, a little ditzy and no doubt good-hearted. And so she's the one to placate the actuarial gods this year.

NOVEMBER 21: . . . Made dinner with an extraordinarily affection-ate hello-kiss-on-the-mouth from Tom [S.] . . . I went with him to a gay bar. Because he wanted a kind of chaperone . . . And the duenna got picked up.

I brought somebody home from a bar. At 33. In the middle of an epidemic. As soon as Tom left for God-knows-where, so much for my forceful example, I saw this good-looking blond named Carl, who's from Munich, and who sells jewelry and got mentioned in Eugenia Sheppard's column, but maybe, for all I know, is an international jewel thief. He leaves for Munich on Monday, comes back several weeks later, wants to live here permanently, and when he's here lives with an ex-boyfriend on E. 60th St.

I went home with him after a half an hour of conversation. He made love to me twice, with an authority & power I've not known since—Tom. We did it safely. If there is such a way. He stayed until 5:00, hugging and kissing me and telling me I was "silly little boy." He's 31 . . .

This was sheer, idiotic, wonderful & dangerous fantasy. I even saw spots on his leg. He's says they're from blood poisoning 5 years ago. He got it when he cut his leg on a rock on Mykonos. And I don't know whether I believe him & don't know why I'm not more panic-stricken . . . Perhaps I'm finally determined to have what others always thought was a good time now that we're in the last days of Pompeii. In his thick German accent telling me "I make you feel good" and "Inside you are naïve little boy, professore . . . You dream of me." And then he left—taking my telephone number and giving me his.

NOVEMBER 22: He called . . . I'm supposed to talk to him Friday. After I get home from Thanksgiving—during which he told me to eat seven slices of turkey ("You need to gain much weight") and think of him when I ate the seventh . . . I was in a sleepless daze through a miserable Thanksgiving. Loree was unforgivably awful to everyone. Going to Ireland has begun to seem like doom to her. . . .

NOVEMBER 24: I called his number twice & got his Greek roommate. He's not at home. Doesn't know when he'll be back. "But what can *I* do for you, Tom?" the Greek asks.

. . .

Nice Terry McKiernan was in town and we went to lunch down at Suspenders. We talked about Tommy . . . The famous story of the moon-landing weekend: "that," Tommy told me, "was the weekend I first discovered my father had a girlfriend & he first discovered I had a boyfriend."

NOVEMBER 25: I am out of control. At 6:00 I was crying at the sink because he hadn't called. At 9:30 I was prancing up and down the apartment because I finally reached him: he met old friends (do I believe this?) at that party Friday night—"centuries old"—and went away for the weekend. ("You are funny boy. You do not like secrets, but you write book about secrets.")

NOVEMBER 26: [In order to see Carl I'm] not going to a party Weds. night that Mary McCarthy's invited me to—a note came today . . . I'd rather see my Aryan ne'er-do-well. (Wednesday night it was cold in here. He said, "Do you have fireplace? We put books you write in it to get warm." I replied: "Oh, imposing your national customs on me already.")

. . .

Well, the day wasn't such a loss . . . I'm 95% sure I saw Greta Garbo. I picked up shirts at the Chinese laundry in the afternoon. It was so beautiful I decided to keep walking. Eventually I got as far as Beekman, then Sutton. Saw her there. Brown coat, straight hair, ramrod posture. Saw someone else doing a double take.

NOVEMBER 28: . . . It's 8:35 p.m.; and he of course hasn't shown up.

NOVEMBER 30: A phone call from Broyard. The bad news is my Vita piece won't run until Dec. 16. The good news is that everybody at the *Book Review* is "taken with it," so I'm a regular. (Alas, regulars aren't very regular. No one can write more than once every 3 mos. . . .)

DECEMBER 1: Tom [S.] and I went to the Dignity mass & the social afterwards. I met a very cute boy named John Champagne (really) and we exchanged phone numbers. . . .

The day's lovely moment: seeing in the B. Dalton on 8th St. that *A Book of One's Own* is alphabetically shelved in "Literary Criticism" next to *The Writing on the Wall* by Mary McCarthy.

DECEMBER 2: Are you ready for this? A few hours ago one Carl Furstenburg called from a little town outside Munich—where he says he grew up with a lot of cute, frustrated farm boys. The man who stood me up twice spends an hour on the transatlantic phone calling me his little koala bear, telling me he'll teach me to enjoy life, talking about going to the Caribbean with me in January.

DECEMBER 5: I was back in Avery after dinner. A couple of hours with senior papers, and I made progress. My only interruption from poor sonless Lynn [Bartlett], who pops in and out a half dozen times a day. He tells me a funny story about how in his first year at Vassar Caroline Mercer discreetly prevented him from flunking out the Weyerhauser fortune.

DECEMBER 7: Went down to Louise's for dinner . . . Mostly we talked about our own days in graduate school. Her stories are more interesting than mine. She was one of three women studying for an Economics Ph.D. at M.I.T. in the 40s. (She went to Simmons instead of Radcliffe as an undergraduate because tuition at the former was $300; at the latter it was $400.) . . . It was a nice evening. And yet when I walked across the paths and around the flagpole at Peter Cooper, I wished he could have been sitting—lying—inside on the couch—however sick, however feverish, just so he was alive & able to say hello in his hollow voice.

We are inside a tornado. Doug MacKay stopped by here a little after 9:00 for a drink. He was coming from Bellevue, where he was visiting an AIDS patient. (Doug was substituting for somebody else in the Gay Men's Health Crisis; his own patient, in Brooklyn, is out of money & down to a couple of cans of soup—he had to run some money out to him before going to Bellevue.)

The one in Brooklyn threatened suicide the other night. The one in Bellevue was attached to an oxygen mask as he watched Lena Horne on the TV. This is how we live in 1984. And yet Doug & I managed to go out and sit in a diner & laugh while I told him about Carl.

DECEMBER 9: I have a new appreciation for Brooke Shields . . . Nancy Kessler, the charming, competent and chunky *Time* photographer, took 144 pictures of me—4 rolls of 36. Some at the desk, some on the couch, some outside the door, some outside the church, and probably the best of all on the third-floor landing with the fire escape visible behind me: a 1940s struggling-young-writer look. The camera generally likes me, but I'm not relaxed around it, and I was in need of a nap after I came back up the stairs.

DECEMBER 11: Freshman conferences in the afternoon. Also a meeting with the one Paul Russell calls "Eraserhead" and thinks may be part of the first wave of "acid babies" from hippie parents.

DECEMBER 13: [Tom S.] gave me a warning. He's met one or two Carl types . . . He says: "they get off on being loved." There may be a wisdom in this remark that I didn't really think Tom capable of.

DECEMBER 15: Just as I was turning down the bed, at 12:40 a.m., the phone rang. I knew it would be Carl. "Good morning, honey." Well, it was morning for him—& I'm sure he hadn't been to bed. I wonder where he gets the money; actually it may be best not to know. He says Daddy is rich, but whether Daddy is sugar daddy or biological daddy I don't know. I mention money because he stayed on the phone for an hour and twenty minutes. And he says he'll

call again before he gets back here on December 29. He wants us
to go to Puerto Rico. He got up to get a guidebook to the Caribbean. When I said it sounded like an awful long distance he'd just
walked, he said, "Is six rooms, honey. Not little bullshit apartment like yours." He tells me: "I *love* your letter. You are so funny,
honey." And: "Why you *think* I call you?"—if, that is, I don't care
about you.

Well, I was in a state of erotic seizure. And when I told him I
was so horny I felt like going out & jumping a sidewalk Santa, he
said: "First sensible thing you ever say."

DECEMBER 19: Getting off the train at Christmastime with my
students: one of the few times I'm in love with the idea of being
a teacher.

DECEMBER 20: I picked up my advance check for *Stolen Words* (I
wish I wanted to write the book) in the morning. At 12:30 I went
to Scudder, Stevens & Clark at 345 Park to pick up Louise. We
went to Eamonn Doran on 2nd Ave. for lunch . . . I think the only
time Tommy came up was when she mentioned his father. She
said "Big Tom" & then stopped for a second before saying, "I
guess I don't have to call him that anymore." . . .

I did a tour of bookstores on 5th & was alarmed to find
ABOOO missing from a number of them that have been stocking
it. Pleased, of course, that they've been sold—but of all the weekends not to have it on shelves!

DECEMBER 21: Off to Macy's in the afternoon. Did not enjoy
Christmas shopping. Got Seán Tinker Toy because I couldn't find
the right kind of blocks. (Part of the problem seems to be that
there are two of everything in Macy's: a toy department on the
7th floor and another on the 5th.) A little top for Kissy[*]—I passed
up the designer dresses for 3-year-olds—$40 or so—which sent
visions of starving Ethiopians dancing in my head. . . .

. . . Walked east to the Rutledge. Tom [S.] was getting up from

---

[*] Family nickname for my two-year-old niece, Christina.

his nap. The floor was littered with little presents from his students. (Should he accept the $20 check from Joseph Blandino's mom?) One girl gave him a kiss and told him, "Mr. Stevenson, you've gotta get some muscles over Christmas!" I loved being in that hotel room with him, the traffic below, the gifts on the floor, the school papers strewn everywhere, Tom gazing at me and saying, happily and slowly and à propos of nothing: "I like you."

It was more fun than our little Christmas later in the evening, actually . . . I had a garland up over the kitchen, & a candle lit, & pâté & herring & cookies & Louise's fruitcake & wine, & he brought champagne: but Tom has little boy tastes in food and didn't really want the pâté & herring. He wanted to be infantile, as he often does around me—to revert to making nonsense statements & just nonsense noises. And I found it irritating. The truth is the poor boy is just completely worn out. He fell asleep on the couch for two hours. I did the dishes . . . And then it seemed tranquil; it even seemed Christmas. And I loved him & my absurd life & I loved New York, the Chrysler Building twinkling across the street like the world's ultimate Christmas tree.

DECEMBER 22: I spent a lot of the day reading *Dancer from the Dance*, a gay novel by Andrew Holleran. It's from about 6 years back, about the fast world of the 70s. I kept feeling I was getting little glimpses of Tommy (they even sit in the park near 17th St.). The atmosphere is all damned and doomed—but for reasons other than the novelist knows. It's a pre-AIDS book. And it's difficult to think of the suicides, baths fires and drug overdoses as particularly tragic. The real holocaust was just beginning to grow in the intestines of probably a dozen people in lower Manhattan. But nobody knew it yet.

DECEMBER 23: Rachel and I met at Louise's at 4:30. Big Tom came down too, and we had tea and cake. Mark's operation is an apparent success and the four of us talked happily enough. Rachel is so beautiful and endlessly intelligent that all eyes focus on her; it's like a worship service as much as a tea party. There was a little talk about the prize in memory of Tommy. It's being set up at Princeton & will not really be a prize at all—rather, more of an emergency fund for graduate students. It makes sense; Tommy's whole life was an emergency. Big Tom tells me he's read my book (I feel awkward about my so-called success in front of him); and I see Louise even has *Edmund Blunden* out on a table (Tommy's copy, plucked from one of the Baltimore boxes).

1985

JANUARY 1: I lay on the couch under a blanket a lot of the time, catching sleep and making resolutions. Chief among them is that this sort of instant business from bar to bedroom must not happen again. Hysteria is called for.

JANUARY 2: . . . I continued to call Germany every couple of hours and hear nothing but beeps.

JANUARY 3: I called Nicos' this evening, and he was there. And has been since Tuesday night. He came home via Miami—"business." So why hasn't he called? And why does he now not think Puerto Rico is a good idea? Because, haaahney, he was bothered by my second letter—thinks I'm getting too involved, etc. The usual malarkey. (And true too.)

JANUARY 4: Talked to Nina [King] on the phone about assignments. I've got this Lady Gregory book to do, but I'm sick of literary biographies and after that one I've asked for a book on the Yorkshire Ripper as a change of pace.

 . . .

 . . . When I was walking home at about 5:30, in the silvery Manhattan dark of Friday night rush hour . . . I passed a stationery store at 51st & Madison & saw a sign about Christmas cards being 70% off. I went in and bought a box of hideous ones. I've put them in my closet. Next December I intend to be healthy, to pull them out of their bag, and to send them—rejoicing that I'm alive & that I've passed through the shadow on the other side.

JANUARY 5: I went to Dignity . . . At Mass they invited people to call out the names of loved ones who died in 1984, and it went on and on and on, and you know what they all died of. We might as well have been reading the wall at Verdun.

On the way home I walked past 55 W. 14th St., home of Bernhard Goetz* . . . Inside, hung over the lobby, a computer-graphics "Welcome Home, Bernie" sign. Anticipating his release on bail.

JANUARY 6: So he came here at 8:00 and I gave him a hesitant kiss on the cheek and he—cock of the walk, a little surprised and still pleased with himself—said "That's all?" We had a drink and then walked and took a cab downtown. We had a snack in the Figaro on Bleecker St. ("You need to eat more, haaahney," he said, looking at a plate of fruit and nuts I picked at), and then went off to a bar on Christopher St. The whole time we were sparring, doing shtick, exaggerating my naivete, his worldliness . . . As we sat in the bar a handsome man passed the window. He saw Carl from behind, stopped, walked back a few steps and hailed him through the glass. Carl went out to the street. Hugs. Conversation. Five minutes later he returns. "Old friend. Amadeus. I was in love with him. Years ago. But we never fuck." He must be the only one.

We went to a dance place, but it was one of those awful infernos, and I didn't want to stay, so we stood in the bar upstairs while the piano player played Sondheim songs and a lot of gay men sang along pretending to be happy. Carl stood with vodka tonic after vodka tonic admiring himself for being admired. I kept drinking, wondering why I was sticking out the evening when I knew I had to be on the train by 8:50 [in the morning]. He was alternately protective and exasperated with me, going so far at one point as to

---

* In December 1984, Goetz, the "subway vigilante," shot four teenagers he said were trying to rob him.

give my face a little slap followed by a caress. And I loved it. That's why I kept drinking.

Every so often we talked. And the whole story of Tommy ("the pretty boy in silver picture frame") came out. The reaction of the philosopher was predictable. Is sad, but *so what*. You live and you die and you take your chances.

"Go home, haaaney. Take some money and get in cab." He put a bunch of bills in my pocket, but I gave them back. But I did get in the cab.

"I call you for sure," he said.

And as the cab went uptown and I got into bed in the silvery lamplight of Manhattan at 2:30 a.m., I felt hopeless and peaceful.

JANUARY 9: There were so many messages that the tape had run out and shut the machine off. The best news among them was that there's been a British sale of *ABOOO* (£2500; I get 80% of it)—to Picador, Mehta's jazzy house. Everyone's pleased.

Talked to Carl ("Get off the phone, haaaney. *Dynasty* is starting"), and we'll talk again over the weekend. To Loree, too—she & the kids were in Manhattan straightening out passports. Kissy went up to a screaming crazy in Penn Station and sweetly informed him: "You're givin' me a headache."

JANUARY 12: Tomorrow night he has a dinner party, but he'll call me ("I 100 per cent promise") and we'll set something up for sometime soon. I think he's curious to know whether I could go on sleeping with him, occasionally, without becoming involved. I'm curious to know the same thing actually. ("But haaaney," he tells me, "you can't even say 'fuck' without turning purple.")

JANUARY 13: On the phone much of the day. Once with Carl, who was dressing for his dinner party ("I look *great*," he interrupts himself to say).

JANUARY 14: I stood perplexed this morning, on the 5th floor of Macy's, before about 75 television sets playing color reruns of *Bewitched*. I came home with a Sharp (reduced from $429 to

$269)—my present to myself instead of the trip to Puerto Rico. I also called to get hooked up to the cable. Tired of the ghosts from the Chrysler Building's shadows.

. . .

Doug and I ate Mexican on 1st Ave. (Mañana). His AIDS patient in Bellevue is dead, and he was emotional, affectionate. . . .

Walked home unambivalently in love with the city, desperate to stay alive right *here*. (Joke: What does GAY mean? Answer: "Got AIDS yet?")

JANUARY 15: Alice Truax called from *The New Yorker* this afternoon and asked if I'd like an advance copy of next week's issue. I walked over to 25 W. 43rd to get it. I've got the lead review and it's an undiluted rave. Naomi Bliven says [*A Book of One's Own* is] "charming, diverting and exceptionally intelligent." She was originally scheduled to do a brief on it, but she asked if she could do the lead instead and they said yes. I went out of that building walking on air. Even though I've always loathed that magazine, theirs is the stamp of approval that counts more than any other . . .

I did a radio interview with a morning talk show in St. Paul. I just sat here in the apartment in my bathrobe and talked and my voice went into cars driving around Minneapolis and crossing the Mississippi . . . The announcer was a typical radio jock with a lounge singer's oily patter. "Hey, how about diaries?" he asked the audience as my lead-in. I followed a George Carlin tape, and when he cut to the weather he asked the meteorologist, "Hey, Karen, do *you* keep a diary?" He kept referring to the book as *A Book of One's Own People*.

. . .

Talked to Carlo. I may or may not see him tomorrow night. I told him that I was a star, and that *The New Yorker* says I know a lot about life, and he howled with laughter.

JANUARY 17: I called Herr Furstenberg to bawl him out. A lot of good that did. He says he never called back because I'm boring and childish. *He* was angry at *me*. "But now that is over. How are you, *haaaney*?"

JANUARY 19: I don't want to do anything halfway any more, which is one of the reasons I did not go to the party Alison West gave for Charley tonight . . . The truth is that the next time I sleep with someone I'd like to be in love with him. Or at least close to it.

JANUARY 20: Watched Ronnie take the oath inside the White House. He looks no older than he did 4 years ago. The Democrats are now calling him "America's Host."

JANUARY 21: I can't recall a day so cold. (The Inaugural parade was cancelled.). I went out twice—the briefest forays, for a sandwich & to take the typewriter to a repair shop in the subway arcade of the Chanin Building.

JANUARY 23: Spent most of the morning in Howie's dental chair. My teeth are in good shape, but my gums are in trouble. I bled streams as the assistant cleaned and scraped and plucked. Since I could never master or sustain flossing, I'm supposed to "stimudent," which involves poking and pressing with a blunted orange toothpick. If things are not better in a couple of weeks, more drastic measures may be needed. I asked Howie what was the matter, and he used the word "infection." For a minute I went liquid in the chair. . . .

JANUARY 24: [Carl and I] sat in a bar on Christopher St. and he told me how when he was 16 his first lover would keep him locked up when he went out. He said he couldn't sleep with me again because if we tried we would laugh & talk during it & that would ruin it. It's the usual gay pathology, of course, but somehow in his case it doesn't seem pathological. He is the least unhappy person I've ever met. We went dancing. Afterwards, a lecture: "You dance good. A little old-fashioned, but good. But, haaaney, what's dis?" He imitates my hunched shoulders. He says, "Dis mean, 'Please don' touch me, I am afraid.' Haaaney, you are ten times better than these people—me, I am twenty—and yet you are scared of them" . . . He gave me a bone-crushing hug & a gorgeous kiss.

I went home at 4 a.m. He, of course, didn't.

JANUARY 25: I had to be up at 9:30 to get to Ticknor & Fields, but I wasn't the least tired. The reason is simple. Carl Furstenberg does not depress me.

I went over permissions matters with Katrina and Laurie for the British and paperback editions. Then I talked with Katrina about *Arts & Sciences*. She's worried that it's a little dated, that Artie remains too twitty at the end, and that Angela's reasons for being with him aren't made clear soon enough. But she is clearly interested. She says Cork is reading it right now. "Give us a little time," she says. I'm surprised; I didn't expect it to get even this far with them. God, how I'd love it to come out of cold storage, to come to life.

. . .

A quick diner dinner on 17th St. with Tom [S.]. Last night Carl was yelling at me as if I were a schoolboy. Tonight I was having to say "Tom, don't play with your food". . . .

JANUARY 26: I finished reading *Lady Gregory*, and I went down to Dignity at 7:00. It really seems a lost cause. I lasted about five minutes at the social. There was absolutely no one I wanted to talk to. The ironic thing about going to church is that it's teaching me to be a Pharisee.

JANUARY 27: Maybe I'm kidding myself by thinking I've got my haaaney problem under control. When he told me tonight that in April he's thinking of going to Mykonos for several months, and when he said good-bye "my dear friend" with a big kiss into the receiver, I felt a little too much the way one feels when one's in love and those things happen.

. . .

Tom [S.] and I walked up to the Frick just before 5:00 and listened to Jeffrey Kahane play Mozart, Bach & Schumann. (Why does he have to make so many faces when he plays? I don't make faces when I write.)

JANUARY 28: Why am I watching this shlocky Bobby Kennedy [miniseries]? They of course make LBJ look like an evil buffoon when the fact is he was a greater man than all the Kennedys put together.

. . .

To Cable News [CNN] in Penn Plaza this afternoon to do *Media Watch*. Chris Chase is a bubbly, blond, non-bazoomed ex-starlet. Very charming. It's easy as pie to do these things. We retape the questions to get nod shots to avoid jump cuts. When you see Mike Wallace nodding skeptically to a *60 Minutes* grillee, the grillee has probably already gotten a cab home.

JANUARY 31: I'm rich and famous. Katrina called this morning to tell me that the [Quality Paperback Book] Club has decided to make me a main selection. This increases the price they pay from $5,000 to $25,500 and my take is $12,500 . . . It's not sunk in yet, but I'm beginning to think buying an apartment down here may not always be beyond me.

. . . Sat with Katrina and Gwen* as the NBCC Awards were presented. At the cocktail party beforehand people came up to me on the strength of my name tag: yes, *I'm* Tom Mallon. God, it's fun.

Katrina said she had a call from Michael Korda about *ABOOO*. It seems Graham Greene saw himself mentioned in the *Time* review & called Korda to complain that he'd not given permission for his books to be quoted. Katrina explained the citations were clearly fair use & he was satisfied. (In fact, I wrote Viking for permission & they never responded.) It's rather hilarious that Michael Korda concerns himself with such things, but I suppose it's the old family-Hollywood connection to Greene.

Katrina, Gwen & I went to Damon's on Columbus Ave. to celebrate the QPB news. At last Ticknor & Fields has bought me a bottle of champagne. . . .

A dusting of snow was on the ground, and the streets and the park were beautiful as we came out, & I still can't get accustomed to the new glamor in my life. (And I'm already worried: will they take *Arts & Sciences*? How can the next book possibly live up to all this?) Went back to midtown in a cab with Gwen & Paul. Then,

* Gwen North Reiss, Ticknor & Fields publicist, and later a poet.

back up here, I called Carlo. "Haaaney, think of all the things you can buy me!"

FEBRUARY 1: Gwen shepherded me to 245 Park Ave. this morning for an interview with Canadian radio. The interviewer was a charming woman named Freda [Garmaise] . . . eccentric and British, in her fifties. She remembered keeping a diary as a girl during the Second World War. "I seemed to be terribly preoccupied with food. There I was with the Blitz whizzing all around me and writing things like plum duff today!"

FEBRUARY 3: . . . To W. 27th St. to see Stockard Channing & Jim Dale in the revival of *Joe Egg*. Bloody marvelous, as Tony Wohl (whom Jim Dale sounds like) might say . . . She ends the first act with a "where there's life, there's hope" soliloquy (literally), and as my throat caught in seat N5 of the high-school-auditorium-looking theatre (part of F.I.T.) I heard little pools of water click in the throats of N3 & N7, too.

After that down to the Village to drink and dance with Carlo until 3 in the morning. He makes me happy. And I make him happy, too, I think . . . He's not liking or getting on in NY as he should (this is a city for people who work), and he knows he'll wind up going to work in a bar near his house on Mykonos. He'll go soon, too, I bet . . . Yes, I know you can find lapses right in this book, but on the whole I'm handling this in a way I never could have even a year ago. He laughs; he grabs and kisses me unexpectedly; he drags me out to dance a second time, again. And then I go home. And he stays. And I don't even feel lonely in the cab. I feel happy, whizzing home at three in the morning.

FEBRUARY 4: [Dinner at the Bartletts' in Poughkeepsie] I rather enjoyed Maggie . . . for all her starched, prim faculty-wifeliness. At one point we were talking about the election and she spoke of her admiration for Ferraro. She said, referring to her own pretty white hair, "You know, I'd always rather liked the Bushes—perhaps because she's one of the few women my age that I know of who doesn't dye her hair—but, you know, after what they said about Ferraro, well, I just think they're both absolute shits."

FEBRUARY 7: . . . My first really nasty review. From *The Washing-ton Post*, by some academic clone from Leon Edel's biographical factory in Hawaii. It was reviewed with 2 other (very academic) books. After saying that my book was actually the most success-ful of the three—"delightful," in fact—he goes on to warn the reader about my "relentlessly jolly schoolboy style." The impulse to send a fuck-you telegram is so strong. (The offending sentence he quotes—"Along with a great job, he's got a swell wife"—would be recognized by a freshman for what it is: not me, but a kind of indirect free style for what Pepys would sound like if he were writ-ing now.)

FEBRUARY 8: Ticknor & Fields has turned down *Arts & Sciences*. This was not, despite Katrina's noises a couple of weeks ago, a surprise. (She doesn't make decisions; Cork does.). And in and of itself it doesn't bother me much. But their reasons do. They seem to have less to do with the book than with their view of what I ought to be doing. They are afraid if I spend more time revis-ing this that I'll cut into the time I should be spending on *Stolen Words* . . . Very low in the evening. Even a funny call from Carlo couldn't really pick me up. I tried to do that by going out to two bars. The result was that I stood around looking at 3 people who didn't want to look at me; being looked at by 3 people I didn't want to be looked at by; and watching one of the people I looked at who didn't want to look at me pair off with one of the people who looked at me but whom I didn't want to be looked at by.

FEBRUARY 13: The seminar went all right. Fifteen years ago, when I started college, we thought of [D. H.] Lawrence as a radical, a liberator; we were all so eager to be liberated into any kind of sex. Then of course the feminist critique came; and as late as five years ago he'd provoke fierce debate in class. Now he more or less bores or amuses the students; they merely think he's preposterous, a mastodon, something of purely historical interest.

FEBRUARY 14: And then Carlo called! He did get my Valentine and he was in a mood to go out with his Barney (derived from early confusion between "Miller" and "Mallon"). So he came here, late (after commiserating with some Greek ladies; Nicos' aunt just died), and [we] went out. Our usual two stops. And we sparred and argued and kissed, and I listened to him say things like "You better do" and "You better don't" . . . happy, even when the point came for his admonitions to make their inevitable change from "Stay awake, honey" to "Is time for you to go, honey." I left him standing near the stairway with a black guy named Ashley and a Frenchman who had just come to New York "to study." As for me: a Puerto Rican boy came up to me singing "Take Me Home." But I didn't.

FEBRUARY 15: [Uncle] Tom left ½ of everything to Belle & Joe; ¼ to Mom; ¼ to Loree. Carol & I are to split a bankbook worth about $8400. He was anxious that [my cousin] Carol & I not feel slighted by the will & told Joe that he reasoned I was successful now, and Carol very settled. Whereas he seemed to have doubts about Loree, perhaps about the prospects for her marriage. If that was his reasoning it was both wise and generous. He didn't owe me anything in any case. He lent me $500 the first awful year I was at Harvard. I needed it badly and I'll always be grateful to him for it. Loree was a much better niece than I was a nephew; she never neglected him. She visited, wrote, did things with him.

. . .

Went to the library and then down to 21st St. to see Mary Evans, one of the agents Katrina recommended . . . And became angrier than I was before at Katrina who, according to Mary, called her a few days ago: "She's very worried about your career." It sounds as if she's recommended an agent for me & then gone and given reasons to the agent why I shouldn't be handled—as if Mary would be hurting a friend (Katrina) if she took me on and pushed *Arts & Sciences*.

. . . Down to see *Tom & Viv* at the Public at 8. A silly, stilted play, but well acted. I don't think Ed Herrmann is quite right for T. S. Eliot . . . Ed & I went to the Riviera café afterwards. This was the first he'd heard of the book club news, and he was wonderfully enthusiastic . . . We rode back to 43rd St. on the 3rd Avenue bus and talked about reviews. I got no worse in *The Washington Post* than he got from John Simon in *New York*.

FEBRUARY 16: We buried Uncle Tom this morning in Flushing Cemetery with his father & Grandma . . . We went back to the house . . . Despite all the little changes and painting Tom did, someone struck blind in 1940 could still find his way around in it. Everything was there: the pedal-push trash can I'd step on every time I was there; the clock in the dining room; the candy dishes, the plates on the wall. I almost swooned with memories: the Easters and Christmases, the coal pile in the basement, the vase I was always afraid of breaking.

FEBRUARY 17: [After I'd gone home with someone the night before] I worried a lot about myself today. And with good reason, too. I walked around nervous, guilty, scared. I only felt better talking to Carlo later. He's not the right father confessor for this, since his assigned penance is "go out and do again"—but, actually, he has enough imagination to know that I'm not he and to know that I'm upset. So he listened to me and calmed me down. I talked to him after the first installment of Jackie Collins' *Hollywood Wives* was aired. "They are ruining a great novel," he told me.

FEBRUARY 20: In the morning I was on the phone with Mary Evans & Katrina. Mary thinks the novel is good—publishable after some work. But she doesn't think she can sell *me* to a publisher without my being able to offer them my next non-fiction book, too. "You're an attractive writer, but at the moment you're not a very attractive package."

FEBRUARY 22: Tired back at home. I stayed in to try to give the coup de grâce to my cold. Read John O'Hara—coarse, vulgar, terrific.

FEBRUARY 23: At six I went down to 186 Sullivan St. for a party given by Phyllis (who leaves for Paris Friday) and her glamorous friend Wendy Gimbel . . . A real *literary* party: Jean Strouse just loves the book; Ed Mendelson (who gives his card to people he meets) introduces himself as Tom Mallon's former teacher; I exchange nice words with Katha Pollitt; Lois Gould blunders into the bathroom while I'm peeing; Annie Dillard says she ought to push me down the stairs[*] (and 51% of her means it; but her husband was sweet) . . . I had a good time and stayed late. It certainly was more fun than being at Vassar, which Nancy Milford describes as "a terrible place; the women are all sots."

How great all these women in their 40s look. And how fast their husbands deteriorate—all fat and ear hairs. The gay men look terrific, of course, if they're not dead yet.

FEBRUARY 25: T&F are going to try to give me $1000 and a letter saying it's understood I'll be working on the ms. of *A&S* & that if the revisions are to their liking they'll publish it . . .

In any case, Mary Evans is now officially my agent.

. . .

Had lunch with Doug at Madigan's on 60th St. After I left I decided to call Carlo—after all, it was a beautiful day and I was only a block away. The phone rang four times. Someone picked it up and then put it down again without speaking. 2:00 p.m.: too early to get up.

MARCH 1: I called 355-3189 at 3:30 this afternoon and asked for Carl. Nicos said he had just left—for Germany. He may be back in a month, if the apartment they're thinking of buying comes through, or he may not be back until September. He was called away suddenly, by the jewelry man he works for. Or so it seems. Nicos seemed very cautious about answering questions. "Sometimes there's work to do," he explained, less than particularly.

He said his plane was leaving in two hours. I called Lufthansa and found out there was a flight to Munich at 5:30. Figuring that must be it, I left the apartment and got a bus to Kennedy.

All the way through the tunnels and over the pocked parkways I realized I wasn't the least bit angry with him . . . I am far surer of his fondness for me than I am of the fondness of people who are correctly nice to me all the time. What I realized instead was what I was losing, how much those silly nights dancing and laughing meant to me. I hadn't laughed in a long while when I met him; he

---

[*] She was less than pleased with what I wrote about her book *Holy the Firm* in *A Book of One's Own.*

put some fizz back into life. He wound up making me feel warm and happy and curiously safe . . .

I realized, in fact, that I was racing to the airport to thank him . . . I didn't make it. There was maddening traffic & stop after stop before we got to Lufthansa.

MARCH 2: . . . We went to another place & Tom [S.] wanted to borrow money . . . I wanted, of course, to be with Carlo instead, to hear him, instead of borrowing, asking for change of a fifty: "Have you got any little money, haaaney?"

MARCH 5: *People* called this morning. They're going to interview me on Saturday . . . It will be curious to try to figure out which of my colleagues will have seen the interview but won't admit it.

MARCH 7: Dinner [in Poughkeepsie] at Milanese. I sit next to [William] Trevor [during his writer's residency at Vassar], who says I remind him a little of a salesman—always rushing about with my suitcase. He says he thinks *ABOOO* will do well in England, and we talk about John O'Hara's being a better writer than John Cheever.

MARCH 9: [The *People* interviewer] knew the book very well (a peculiar feeling to see your own book underlined and annotated) and she asked good questions. But it went on too long: six hours. We broke for lunch at the U.N. Plaza Hotel, but even during the meal the machine was running. (I was recorded over a tape of Chevy Chase.)

MARCH 10: Overheard while walking home along E. 33rd St.—a mother to her little boy, approximately three years old: "Well, Mickey, when you're older you'll understand *why* I hate your goddamned father."

MARCH 11: Bad news from Germany . . . He's not coming back next month. He's had it with New York ("It didn't like me, haaaney"—something he finds inexplicable) . . . I told him "I miss you." The ordinary human response to this, of course, is "I miss you, too." Carl's is "I understand."

 . . .

 Chernenko is dead—it's like musical funerals over there. The new leader is young (54) with a chic wife & a big birthmark on his forehead. Margaret Thatcher claims to like him. . . .

MARCH 12: I've gotten most of the lecture [for Vassar's spring Convocation] written . . . I take a break down at the bar late in the evening. I know this sounds like a lot of gay-bar-hopping, but nothing's really happening & I've learned just to go in, have a drink, & enjoy the [music] videos. Still, though, I guess one always is looking for something to happen, and a little disappointed & relieved each time it doesn't.

MARCH 13: I had Louise coming over for drinks. She got here at 5:30, the first time she's been here. I told her how Tommy, the one time he was here, pronounced it all right. That's about how much we talk of him now: one or two remarks per meeting, almost ritualistic. And that's it.

MARCH 15: [A trip to Texas] I was back on the Lubbock moon-scape, being made much of and happy to be here. Of course, if I'd never left here my life would have been a disaster. I'd be no writer, a 4th-rate scholar in a hopeless backwater without water— "centrally isolated," as Lynn [Hatfield] puts it. I'd have remained everyone's puppy, childish & virginal, a freak. I would have died for lack of an embrace, fallen in love with cowboy after cowboy in my classes. Would have died from the shock of my own failure when I woke up some morning in a cold sweat, years from now.

 But I wouldn't be facing the fright & the fear I am now. I don't want to go home. I'm afraid I'm going to go under.

MARCH 16: I may have come upon a great plagiarism case. Jim Brink & a couple of other guys in the history department told me about a real lulu they had here . . . Everyone wants to talk about it. We sat around the kitchen table at 1:00 a.m. & I got a preview of it. It's got everything—a real "human interest" narrative could be fashioned from it. To my delight I found myself getting excited about *Stolen Words*, almost for the first time.

Took a walk before the party. Around the grid of streets named for cities near [Mary and Lynn Hatfield's] house. Huge, darkening sky. I'm the only pedestrian. Almost no trees. The space-station houses. A few barking dogs. I felt exotic, displaced. And all the time my mind keeps coming back to disease. Mary says even people from Harrison, Arkansas, have died of AIDS.

MARCH 17: Back to the Hatfields' in the afternoon. It all seems so normal and happy. Chris and Ginny fly in and out with their friends, turn on the TV, bang on the computer, raid the refrigerator, pet the cat. Mary and Lynn are alternately oblivious and amused. We sit down to dinner and the kids are giggly, good-humored, smart, participating. They know their parents are fun & that they're lucky. I have one of those rare (and, finally, false) moments when I think this is how it should have turned out for me, too. Better just to think that there's an odd piece of that world with which I have a friendly diplomatic connection. But it's not my world.

MARCH 18: My lecture was . . . a big hit. Lots of laughter, and serious appreciation at the end. Very polite audience of about 150. About a third of them people I knew here. I sold about 30 or 40 books at the autograph party afterwards. I was very good at the small talk, not at all stiff. I really do love a little stardom.

MARCH 20: Before Mary took me out past the feed lots and grain elevators to the airport, we stopped downtown at the new statue of Buddy Holly and took each other's pictures . . . A lot of Texans on the plane of course. When we came down over Queens, over all its middle-class apartment houses, somebody said: "It's a brick farm."

MARCH 21: I had my worst AIDS scare in months. I saw a reddish patch on my leg that may be a bruise or dry skin (I think it *is* one of those now), but I was convinced when I saw it that it was a sarcoma and I began to cry. I walked around outside afterwards trying to calm myself down and resign myself to death. This is the way we live now. I'll be checking my leg every half hour now for the next week, and if it's not gone after a week has passed, I'll be feeling suicidal.

MARCH 22: [Seeing old graduate-school friends in Maine] I got the plane to Portland from Newark, and then a bus ride to Lewiston . . . Sanford meets me with a strong hug at the bus station. He's a little balder, a little heavier, and minus his steel-rimmed glasses (in exchange for contacts, which don't become him). He is just as kindly, a real mensch, not a pseudo-one like Jerry Badanes.* He took me back to his and Carole's enormous old house, which overlooks poor and weatherbeaten Lewiston. It's a beautiful old barn of a place, and once more (as I did in the Lubbock ranch houses or in Katherine's house in South Bend) I wondered why I was living in about 300 sq. feet. Of course I do know, as a few hours in Lewiston, Maine make clear—it's a tired place, as garishly old as Lubbock is garishly new.

MARCH 23: [I'd come to Bates College as an outside examiner for some honors theses.] The oral exams went well. The charming [Wilfred] Owen girl got high honors; the Woolf girl mere honors. There's a Ken Weedin clone at Bates named Werner Somebody, who fusses about typos and pushes his favorites. He's very effeminate and twisted and troubled; Sanford says that years ago someone actually threw stones at him.

MARCH 24: At Carole and Sanford's breakfast table this morning I wound up telling them about Tommy. I suppose I'd been wanting to, but it just tumbled out before I realized I was actually doing it. They are knowledgeable as well as sympathetic. (Carole is the advisor to something called the Gay-Straight Alliance on campus.) Sanford nearly began to cry. I realized what he was seeing was little Tom, myself at 24, vulnerable, threatened. He wanted to protect me, and I was touched.

---

* An instructor in the English department.

MARCH 25: I felt overwhelmed today: tired from the travel, anxious about my erotic scrapes, doubtful about my romantic future. Above all, overworked. I couldn't summon up the will to do anything but reread *Turn of the Screw* and pick up the laundry. At four o'clock I was sitting, barely alive, unable to clean the kitchen. Tom [S.] came by, and to give you an idea of how bad things are, *he* took charge of *me*. We put *My Fair Lady* on the record player & he mopped the bathroom and kitchen floors. I managed to clean the refrigerator, where several cans of Coke had exploded over the weekend.

MARCH 26: The *NYTBR* piece is at last out. [Katrina] says the review is "fine"—& then, when I ask what's not so good in it, she reads me the ¶ about my "unfortunate metaphors." The reviewer quotes some of the same lines others have singled out as being stylish & fun & calls them "crassly fatuous" and "risibly portentous."

It makes no difference that he liked a lot of the book; it makes no difference that he's Brad Leithauser, whose novel was recently ripped apart for its pomposity in *The New Yorker*; it makes no difference that I've said cruel things in reviews; it makes no difference that the sales rep at T&F is delighted and thinks it's a selling review. I feel disembowelled, eviscerated, mortally wounded . . . All because of one paragraph by someone named Brad, a name that's always attached to an asshole . . . If Carl were here he'd say one sharp "Basta!" to me as I kept fretting, and it would help.

MARCH 29: I went to Ticknor & Fields and Gwen told me funny stories about how Gloria Naylor deals with nasty reviews. (Jimmy Breslin, whose essay collection is being returned by the hundreds, called while I was there.) We talked about how this isn't such a bad review, anyway, and how I have such a stack of good ones.

. . .

The highlight of my day was the long-delayed arrival of the cable-TV man. I am already an MTV junkie.

MARCH 30: There was a nude talk show on [public access] Channel J. A white couple, the woman in chains, was being interviewed by a black host, who, in casual Merv-and-Johnny style, asked questions like "Just how big is your cock?"

APRIL 2: All day long [at Vassar] people have come up to me . . . and said, "Nice review in the *Times*." Maybe they can't read. Or maybe they're humoring me. Or maybe it isn't so bad after all. Rachel says the last is the truth. "*You* can't read," she tells me.

APRIL 6: James Lord,[*] who must have been a knockout 25 years ago, took David Schorr[†] and me to lunch this afternoon at the Four Seasons. The bill came to over $200; he paid cash. We got drunk & happy. (The restaurant actually is ugly; sort of the executives' cafeteria.) James loves *ABOOO*. He was supposed to review it for *The New Criterion* but declined because he can't think of anything to say (he says) about diaries beyond what I already have. It's unclear whether they'll assign it to someone else. He says he met with the editors this week & they don't think it needs a further boost after "that nice review in the *Times*."

APRIL 8: . . . I feel blessed to be on Lexington Ave. picking out muffins at 11 p.m. One of those moments—I still have them—when I realize that moving down here was the real stroke of genius in my life. I don't know why I should be awash in well-being tonight, after feeling so desperate last week, but don't question miracles.

APRIL 9: . . . 3 hours getting to Poughkeepsie. We lost power in the tunnel. The conductor said we had trouble getting up the hill and were going back "to take another run at it." But we had the little engine that couldn't, and the train was "annulled." We were put on the 8:20 local.
   . . . An 87-year-old man from Michigan who's been keeping a diary for 60 years writes me.

---

[*] Artists' biographer and memoirist; longtime resident of Paris.
[†] Artist and professor at Wesleyan University; colleague and close friend of Phyllis Rose.

APRIL 10: [A dinner with Rachel Kitzinger's parents] The distinguished Ernst Kitzinger is very merry and sweet. Susan, his wife, is a solid old English Quaker—steady, reliable, kind, and capable of sudden twinkles and deep, satisfied laughs. I really enjoyed them both. The conversation was mostly about the worst and most hilariously hopeless students we've known . . . At one point during dinner, when the other four people were in a conversation of their own, Susan turned to me and said, "Rachel tells me you were a friend of Tom Curley's." He was "such a nice man," she said.

Yes, he was, in many ways. There was a sweetness trying to get out from under all the fear and snobbery.

APRIL 11: . . . Virginia Smith called. She's resigning from Vassar at the end of the year and she wanted to let some friends know before she makes the announcement in the Villard Room at 8:15 tomorrow morning . . . We're not going to find somebody as good as VBS. Her enemies didn't like her because she was a fat lesbian who was impatient with social niceties. They didn't understand she's a shy person who likes a good time (ping-pong and cards and booze) and who has never asked a stupid question in her life.

APRIL 12: . . . I do not have a death wish. The truth is that I am trying to meet someone—someone I can, yes, have a "relationship" with. And there are no methods of courtship in the gay world. And I am so desperate to have a real relationship again that I'm willing to take what may be absurd risks to get one started.

His name is Thom McClean, and he's a dancer with the Joffrey. About 25. He is beautiful. And smart. And this will probably never work . . . I met him because he kept smiling at me. When I introduced myself he asked me if I was the one who was sending him drinks all night. I wasn't. And ten minutes after I started talking to him another drink came over on a tray. We never found out who sent them. [The sender] eventually lost interest and left, I guess. I was hoping for something romantic, like a punch in the nose.

APRIL 13: . . . To Dignity, where the priest who has Ed Herrmann's voice explained the laying on of hands and the anointing.

It seems that extreme unction is no longer just for the nearly dead. And the "healing" it seeks to effect does not have to be just physical. I approached the altar with everyone else—the sermon had been partly about doubting Thomas—& I had the oil put on my forehead and palms. I take these things more seriously than I used to, although I'm not sure what's involved here: new maturity, new credulity, or new desperation.

APRIL 14: I met Bob Massa [a drama critic for *The Village Voice*] down at the Public Theater and we saw *Salonika* . . . Jessica Tandy & Elizabeth Wilson very good, but not so dazzling as the nude Maxwell Caulfield—the front as nice as the back. We were in the second row . . . Massa is astonishingly like Jonathan [Kahn].* The same body, only a bit shorter; the same sweet face, handsome when it smiles, but scarred from a bad adolescence. The same shyness. The whole thing together is eerie . . . Now this boy is not a dreamboat, but I could grow very fond of him. He's smart and steady. So why fall into the beauty trap? Why pursue Thom McClean (for that's what I'll wind up doing?) when it would never last?

Why is everything suddenly opening up?

APRIL 15: . . . Tonight on the news they say that between 500,000 to 1,000,000 Americans have the AIDS virus. They may not catch the disease in a wholesale way, but they may remain susceptible to "a variety of diseases throughout their lifetimes." So I may not "get it," but I may die of cancer at, say, 42.

APRIL 19: *People*'s idea of a natural shot is to put me out on the fire escape writing the diary. So there I am, shaking, wondering if this rusty thing will hold. Then she says she's getting glare from my glasses, so I have to hand them to her through the window. More shakes. But midtown was roaring with life below me—delivery trucks, lunchtime shouts, screamers. It was hot as summer, and I was seeing the Chrysler Building gargoyles and the St. Agnes flag and cross as I'd never seen them before. I was totally, zanily alive.

* A student of veterinary medicine, Jonathan was a friend of mine at St. Edmund's House in Cambridge (U.K.) during my 1982–83 sabbatical from Vassar.

. . . There's an article about T&F (which is very hot right now) in this week's *Publishers Weekly*. It mentions that *Stolen Words* is "as yet unscheduled." Try unwritten, unresearched and unthought of in weeks!

APRIL 20: I couldn't get hold of Robert Massa, but I did read his two pieces in this week's *Voice*. His main subject? AIDS plays. He writes well.

APRIL 21: On 5th Avenue I ran into a Salute to Israel Parade (signs vs. Reagan's visit to Bitburg). Later, down Third Ave.: I stopped into a drug store to buy a pack of condoms. When I came out I saw John Simon, who's in boiling water over making AIDS jokes. . . .

And then Thom got here at 7:30, looking pretty & delicate. We drank and then we ate Mexican at Lillie Langtry. And then we bought beer and went back to his tiny apartment in the old McAlpin Hotel.

There are literally scores of Eva Perón pictures on the walls. His happiest experience in the theatre was doing that show in Vienna. Tomorrow he auditions for a summer touring company.

He gave me his 8" x 10" glossy and signed it "To my favorite descamisado." We talked about the theatre. (Where does he get the bravery? It doesn't seem he's accomplished much, but he keeps on and on. And he's not 24-ish; he's 29, soon to be 30, he admitted sheepishly. I admired him hugely tonight, through all the campy, draggy silliness. He's more courageous than I am, God knows.)

APRIL 24: [My Vassar Convocation speech] Ann and I picked Mom up at the train and she looked very nervous. Her hand tremor was noticeable; she was walking on eggs, hunched; her face was blotched. But as the day went on she relaxed, got prettier, younger—became, in fact, the belle of the ball. She says it was the proudest day of her life. . . .

The chapel was more crowded than usual, I think. I must have looked very small and foolish in one of the great baronial chairs, Virginia in the other.

I'll never forget the introduction—she compared my charm

and wit to Mary McCarthy's. Now if that's not the kind of validation the boy in those diaries wanted, I don't know what could be.

I was very nervous at first, preoccupied with the microphones.
But after a few laughs, I hit my stride and performed. I read it well,
knew I had them, thought I lost them for a minute, but no, I had
them. Really had them. . . .

On the steps outside, after the recessional, I was kissed,
squeezed, given flowers, petted and praised and told that it was
the best Convocation speech ever. (Mind you, there have been
some easy acts to follow.) . . .

Dinner at Virginia's—the head table . . . Mom succeeded in
charming both Barbara & Charlie [Pierce]—everyone, for that
matter. It turned into a real party . . . At about 10:30 Rachel and
Eamon (who said, by mistake, "Pleased to meet you, Mrs. Curley") took Mom back to Alumnae House. Virginia went to bed
(after I put in a few good words for Beverly's tenure case) & the
rump party got going. . . .

APRIL 25: Only a few hours sleep. (How could I have AIDS and
have this much energy?) . . .

APRIL 26: The lack of sleep caught up with me tonight, and I nodded off during Dr. Ruth's latest televised sermon on ewections.

APRIL 28: [My mother was moving from the house I'd grown up
in to a smaller place] It was raining when we moved into the house
on July 31, 1958. And it was raining when I left it for the last time
today. I went out to Stewart Manor in the afternoon & had dinner with Mom . . . I went to the basement, touched all the walls,
remembered Johnny Rodabaugh next door—dead more than 20
years now. Remembered Daddy coming in the door, the oxygen
tank coming up the stairs. It felt as if we were getting ready to
give away our lives . . . I walked around the yard. Loree chalked
"1963" on one of the garage walls & it's still there; the license
plates Harry Koch hung in 1931 are there too.

I walked out of my room for the last time, and I was crying.
Then Mom approached, talking, from the master bedroom. She

passed Loree's room, which was open and completely bare, and suddenly her voice bounced through a series of echoes. All at once I could hear us there, the four of us, as if it were Christmas morning & we were getting ready to go downstairs.

I couldn't stand to stay more than another few minutes. I remembered, going out, that the first thing Loree & I did when we walked into that house was bang the chimes [which rang with the doorbell]. So that was the last thing I did before leaving—for both of us.

APRIL 30: . . . In a springtime rite of moral self-congratulation, the students have "taken" Main Gate to protest apartheid. I'm writing this at my desk in Kendrick after midnight—every so often their campsite bursts into applause or shouts.

MAY 3: Had a letter from James Lord in Paris. A long description of a party he was at with Phyllis & Mary [McCarthy] & Jim. It's also something of a love letter: I've "become the destination of quite a few of [his] thoughts and impressions, all better left unrecorded (as the greatest diary reader in history well knows!)."

MAY 4: I went over to Lincoln Center to see American Ballet Theatre this afternoon. I've got a subscription for the next few weeks. It's not the way it was ten years ago, when I got caught up in the dance boom along with everybody else. Here were Cynthia Gregory and Fernando Bujones doing some of *Raymonda* at a matinee, and there were lots of empty seats in the house. People just aren't as mad for it as they once were.

MAY 9: A lot of kids have been coming by the office asking me to sign *ABOOO*—sometimes for their mothers (who usually have different names; at Vassar everyone has divorced parents).

MAY 10: I went over to Time-Life this afternoon and picked up six copies of next week's *People* . . . The picture is 5" x 8," the size of the book, and I am as lovely as any Scavullo woman. (Also as unreal; this isn't really me, of course. Oh, hell, as Martha Mitchell said, "It is *too* me; that's how I always look.") Everyone is supposedly entitled to one great photograph of himself—didn't someone say this—& this is mine.

MAY 11: . . . Blazing summer afternoon—I met Paul Sachner for a drink at the Ginger Man & then a hamburger at O'Neal's. Depressing. It turned into an AIDS conversation—all his dead friends, not just Tommy. (Tommy isn't even the only dead "C" in his address book.) Paul says he "behaves" when he's in NY, but not when he travels. He knows that this makes no sense, but he does it anyway & then talks about it with his psychiatrist . . .

. . .

And then what should happen? I met someone at the "social" [after the Dignity Mass]. [W.], late 30s . . . He's a lawyer, used to teach French at Queens College. And he approached me.

MAY 13: He's Frank O'Connor's legal aide & he's at work on a decision in the Jean Harris appeal. He can't really talk about it, & I can tell this is a guy who plays by the rules. Sweet, awkward; he even stutters a little.

MAY 14: . . . Went to the party for retiring faculty at Alumnae House. One of the retirees was Pamela Askew (art); I met her for the first time and stood next to her while Susan Kuretsky gave the only witty speech of the afternoon. Evert Sprinchorn came up to her and asked if she plans to spend her retirement writing books. "Evert," she responded, "how unfrivolous you are."

MAY 17: At 8:30 I took a subway and taxi to [W.'s] pretty apartment—built in the 30s, it overlooks the courtyard & garden—across the street from the Chelsea Hotel. We had drinks & then went downtown and had dinner in the garden of Emilio's.

He's so shy, I kept thinking. In some ways closeted; not the least camp. An athlete, a swimmer—and, to my astonishment, I was told he's 42. He looks ten years younger, but it's a natural, boyish, athletic youth—not the creams-and-facial-exercises youth of most gays in their 40s. Quiet, conservative: his female lawyer friends are still trying to marry him off or marry him themselves.

. . .

We were back on the street at 1 a.m., more or less ready to go our separate ways. And then he stopped and said in a way that was so direct and so befuddled at the same time that I'll always remember it: "Now would you like to come home and sleep with me?"

Yes, I would. And I did. After we had a brief, embarrassed health discussion. We decided to be cautious, to assume we had both been "exposed." . . . He's been in New York for the last 15 years. He says he's only been to the baths twice, that Tennessee Williams once held his hand in a taxicab after a party, and that he was once in the Chelsea Hotel "under seamy circumstances."

. . . He is a wonderful lover; lean, ardent, emotional. Purrs of contentment. Hand-holding and nuzzling afterwards. I felt wonderful—and I was only with him. Usually, at the last moment, I'm with somebody else in my mind. . . .

MAY 18: I could hear the birds in the garden this morning, and the light that came up from it dappled us awake. We stayed in bed until after ten and kissed and caressed and murmured. Then he made coffee and we sat and drank it until past noon & we talked about the law. This is a controlled person, somebody who cares about limits, their just establishment. I suspect he's a better lawyer than he was a literary critic . . . The paper of course had a particularly frightening article about AIDS. Sometimes I think I'm walking into the future on nerve alone, sure at some small spot inside that God & destiny will protect me from the bullets.

MAY 20: [In Washington, D.C., for a Vassar Club event] I met Daniel Boorstin for lunch at 12:30. For someone who writes fan letters he turned out to be rather squirrelly and stodgy. We raced through lunch (brought in by a waiter to a private dining room in the Madison Building—and Lord what a view of the city). His idea of conversation is to ask you a rapid series of questions . . . Went to Ford's Theatre in the afternoon to get my imagination working on Booth.* The theatre itself was closed for emergency

---

* An idea for a biography of John Wilkes Booth that eventually turned into my novel *Henry and Clara*.

repairs, but the museum downstairs was open. I saw the gun; it's about the size of a hash pipe.

MAY 24: Why am I not crying "Eureka!"? Is it because [W.] is so shy that I'm afraid he'll never be able to connect with me at that ultimate depth where I think It, perfection, must be? Am I afraid I'll scare him away? . . . He is so beautiful, so slim and youthful, and so vulnerable during it—he murmurs all the time. When he said "Time for bed," it was as if we'd been doing this for years. It's nice; in fact, it's heavenly.

MAY 26: Mario Cuomo is probably the best political speaker in the U.S. today, but he was a little flat at this morning's commencement. Mostly bromides, and a jockstrap joke that would have gone over better at St. John's than at Vassar. It was broiling hot. I sat in front of Karen [Stolley],* back from her own Commencement at Yale . . . Josh [Lerman]'s mother, VC '54, recalled how Adlai Stevenson spoke to her graduation & said he'd never had the pleasure of addressing so many Republicans before. Things have changed.

MAY 28: Dinner with David Schorr. I went to his apartment on 86th St. off CPW. Beautiful photos, some of Phyllis [Rose], on the walls. (Also the full frontal Nureyev nudes done by Richard Avedon and never published; well, forget those rumors that it was a sock in the costume.) . . .

. . . Went home in a taxi in the rain . . . I talked to [W.] before getting into bed. He talks in his sweet, hesitating Jimmy Stewart way. He has a longstanding dinner plan for Friday night. He says he could come over late, "but, uh, ah, maybe, uh, you don't like that idea." I told him I like the idea.

---

* Vassar friends to whom I remained close ever after included Karen Stolley and Pat Kenworthy (professors of Hispanic Studies); David Littlefield (Karen's husband); and Jim Montoya, Vassar's admissions director and later an executive with the College Board.

MAY 29: . . . I'm moving through Dotson Rader's pathetic book on Tennessee Williams. He doesn't just drop names—he drops them, after aiming, into shit.

MAY 31: . . . He looked impossibly fresh and adorable, his white shirt like a moving star against the night . . . It's sweet to hear him talking like a lawyer. He always says "individuals" instead of people . . . I don't think I've ever known sex more tender. We take a long time, and occasionally just stop and gaze into one another's eyes—"I love your eyes," he says—and caress each other's faces and exchange a score of little kisses.

JUNE 1: The telephone ringing about 3 seconds before orgasm and the two of us laughing. "Oh, Jesus! Don't answer it."

        . . .

Went to the travel agent to see about my ticket to Ireland [to visit my sister and her family] before walking over to the ballet—*Coppélia*, pretty and heartless . . . I walked home in the sun thinking how, for all its fears and disappointments, my life has been so lucky. I've had love, passion, rejection, books, a taste of fame. I've had New York. I've been exhilarated. I want it to go on and on. But in the plague one must always think of losing it. But it's easier to face losing something than losing nothing . . .

Passed all the hotel strikers shouting on 59th St. Half expected to see Leona Helmsley strafing them with machine gun fire from the Park Lane.

JUNE 2: Louise came over at three & we walked over to the Rousseau exhibit at the Modern. A happy exhibit; you can see it making people feel good. In some ways it looks like an exhibition of children's wallpaper. (His paintings of children themselves are ghastly.)

JUNE 3: Greenwood Village itself is quite all right. The house is sturdy & more spacious than I'd expected. Mom already has everything out & in place. The houses make trim rows & there's a lot of building going on. New, skinny trees being put in place. It reminded me of East Meadow in the 50s. And surely there must be a number of people who have a sense of coming full circle—from G. I. Bill homes on L.I. that looked like this 35 years ago.

JUNE 7: Went by myself tonight to see *Perfect* down on 34th St. It features John Travolta doing aerobic exercises with half an erection.

JUNE 8: Instead of getting books about plagiarism I'm reading books—or looking for books—about Catholic orphans in New York City in the 1860s (part of my Booth idea).

Went to Dignity at 7:30 . . . The social was held in the gym instead of the cafeteria, & that's where I caught up with [W.], who looked as fresh as could be. Tom [S.] laughed when he saw him from the balcony above: "He's just like you," he said, pointing to the protective body language . . .

JUNE 9: . . . For the first time in my life I actually have a man keeping a toothbrush at my apartment . . .

JUNE 10: At 3:30 I was at 321 E. 45th St. looking at studios. One (on the ground floor, which makes me a little squeamish) is for $90,000. Two others are for $98,000. I could do them, so long as I thought of the apartment as my bank account. I liked the building & the street—even the agent, who was like an Italian Susan Anton. I may be rushing, but I'm ready to do it. I'm tired of E. 43rd St., the noise, the construction, the mini-Bowery we've got across from the terminal.

JUNE 11: [W.] & I also had our first "fight." We were making plans for Friday night & dealing with the fact that we both have to be up early on Saturday. I suggested that we could be "good boys" on Friday—get to bed early & not make love until 4:30 a.m. And he cringed at the "good boys" phrase—as if it were campy self-loathing . . . I hadn't meant it that way—I meant it to refer to our having to be childlike (getting to bed early). This got us into a long discussion of language and gayness . . . And, oh, I had breakfast at Howard Johnson's on 42nd St. & saw John F. Kennedy, Jr. eating at the counter. "Boy, is he cute"—that's how I described him to [W.] & wondered if that was a mistake, too.

JUNE 13: I went down to Walter & Samuels on Park Ave. So. this morning and put in a bid of $88,000 on the apartment. I was told I got it. I probably, in fact, could have gotten it for less, but I didn't want to lose this poker game to anyone else, and I'm feeling pretty lucky just as is. I brought the bewilderingly large [co-op] prospectus home and read it at lunchtime. Now the financing dance starts.

. . .

Claus von Bülow has just testified before the highest court in the land: Barbara Walters, on 20/20. He has the swagger that must come with being certified innocent. And if the jury had seen this a few days ago they probably would have convicted him.

JUNE 14: I went to see [W.] at about 8:00. He'd just come back from swimming and looked wonderful. And what conversations we have: they went from the Claudel play he was reading, to Jean Harris, to whether or not *cliché* (shopworn phrase) and *cliché* (post-card picture) are *faux amis*. We walked around the Village and ate pizza and went home to bed.

JUNE 16: I want us to break out of the pattern of weekend "dates"— to give the relationship some of the texture of dailiness.

JUNE 17: Anatole Broyard called this afternoon to ask if I felt like working. Mortgage payments in mind—& glad that he's called again after all these months—I said yes. I'm not crazy about the books he's offered (a biography of Radclyffe Hall & the diary of her steady—the *NYTBR* seems to think I specialize in lesbians), but I'll do them.

. . .

. . . "Day 4" of the hijacking.* It's all sickeningly reminiscent of '79-'80 . . . the "moderate" with whom we can "talk," but who

---

* TWA flight 847, en route from Athens to Rome, was hijacked by terrorists on June 14, 1985.

in fact probably can't deliver anything (Berri = Bani Sadr & a year from now he'll be in exile or dead); the yellow ribbons. If Reagan doesn't hit back at these people he deserves to see his presidency fall into the same ruins that Carter's did.

JUNE 18: I wrote and got the biggest checks of my life today. I saw Reba Miller and put down $8800 on the apartment less than an hour after my Houghton Mifflin royalties for $17,541 came.

. . .

Jesse Jackson has jumped into the hostage crisis . . . He's off to make a "moral appeal" to the terrorists, to "break the cycle of pain." This particular moral appeal is being offered to people who broke every rib of the young navy diver they killed; who smashed his face before shooting him & throwing him out on the tarmac.

. . . [Pride Month] I had never seen the gay bar so packed . . . People were celebrating, forgetting about AIDS for a night— dancing vs. death & some of them probably going home to exchange more death. I remember the news of the Stonewall riot; the week I was graduated from high school. I remember being interested in it; thinking—knowing fearfully—that it had some-thing to do with me. But I was afraid even to have a reaction to it. Afraid to feel even secret sympathy.

I still think it: even with AIDS around, I have to feel we're lucky. If I'd been born 20 years earlier my life might have been a miserable lie. Other people have fought my battles.

JUNE 19: Just when I was settled down to my reading this evening, [W.] called. He had two passes into Area, the new disco down on Hudson St. that's been written up everywhere. They were for a party to celebrate the opening of a play an old friend is in—some camp thing called *Vampire Lesbians of Sodom* (and I'm not supposed to say "boy"!). Never mind: I had a wonderful time. I hopped into the shower and rattled down there in a cab.

Area changes its décor every month or so. Torture seemed to be the current theme. Lots of leather masks and severed heads. Still somehow, the effect was rather like that of a high school prom in a gymnasium—maybe because the crowd was so young. A little less than half heterosexual, I'd say . . . When some old Michael

Jackson record came on everyone squealed to life and started dancing.

Including [W.]! Who dances roughly as well as Jonathan, which is to say like a sweet little stick, but I was surprised he would at all. We stood near one of the speakers and the bass hammered the solar plexus—the pounding was enough to clear bronchial passages and pulverize kidney stones.

JUNE 20: 1) In the supermarket this afternoon a man barked at an old lady on the checkout line (they were disputing conveyor belt space): "You ought to learn that the world doesn't revolve around old ladies." 2) Ann and I saw a drugged crazy shouting abuse at cops and finally kicking their patrol car door. They came out & waved nightsticks at him but didn't arrest him. He disappeared into the 8th St. subway station. 3) I passed a 3rd Ave. bar called "Life of Reilly" on my walk home. Some men and women—one of the women had blood streaming down her forehead—were explaining things to cops.

JUNE 23: [W. and I] went—walking quickly—up to 8th Ave. & 47th St. to see a 10:00 showing of *Charade*. An odd neighborhood for it. The theatre must have been a converted (& recently) porno palace. But there it was playing host to a Yuppie crowd and showing Audrey on screen.

. . .

At the moment of orgasm I was simply looking at his face. It was so beautiful, so perfect & so serene. I was stunned by it. And I climaxed. Simply by looking at the beauty of his face.

JUNE 24: I stopped into the Whitney Annex on the way home & looked at an exhibit of surreal cityscapes: weirding the lily. . . .

And then, at 7:00, Tom [S.] came by for our farewell night . . . We went through the Terminal—& for the 1st time Tom noticed the stars on the ceiling . . . [He] told me how much I meant to him & how when he'd gone into the bathroom at David's he'd started to cry.

There was so much I wanted to tell him & couldn't. Not in that silly place. How I don't think I could have gotten through last September if I didn't have his freshness to come back to, from school, from Tommy's death-couch. How I loved coming back to him on Thursday nights, going up to his room on the 8th Fl. in the snail's-pace elevator of that lousy hotel. As the months went on he made me impatient—he always seemed so needy & weak & undisciplined—but I still loved his freshness of heart. And I did, finally, love being depended on, loved being unquestionably the one in New York that he needed and truly knew.

He brought me a single, perfect rose.

JUNE 25: The city felt quiet, underpopulated, underwater, as I ran my errands this afternoon. I was feeling his absence . . . Now I'll miss his phone calls—not a day would go by without them— wheedling me to go out with him. I'd hit the message machine & know it was his voice coming up from the traffic roar coming through the pay phone.

Well, back to work. I'm having trouble with Olwyn Hughes, who's going to charge a huge fee [in the British edition of *ABOOO*] for quotations from Sylvia Plath (her sister-in-law). She wants £240; a thief. And she wonders if the last quotation (Plath's, not mine) might not be in questionable taste . . . To Theatre 80 to see *Queen Christina*. That shot of Garbo on the prow at the end: is there anything remotely like it? She's so beautiful she's almost repellent.

JUNE 26: I took the subway up to the reservoir this morning— I was there in minutes—& ran . . . Effortlessly. The cool breeze, devoid of humidity, pumped air into the lungs like some mechanical supplement. I had more than enough to spare. The buildings south and east, distant, stood like a city without people, a thing of neutron-bombed perfection, as if God had finally had enough of us and our imperfections, clearing us out and leaving the real pride of his creation to stand.

JUNE 27: Lots of delays at Kennedy. The charter business is confusing with vouchers, double lines, etc. A lot of loud American-Irish, aggressive about the beauties of the old country, were lined up in their fisherman's sweaters. The most sentimental race imaginable.

JUNE 28: Loree and Ollie picked me up at Shannon and drove me to Ballinasloe. On the way we stopped—although I was punchy with fatigue—in Gort, to see Thoor Ballylee. It's rather a strange relic; they've not restored it. Nothing has been put inside (except a bed) to give you a sense of what it was like when WBY [Yeats] was there. Only a few uninteresting display cases and large incongruous heaters keeping nothing warm. One room was covered with mouse droppings, and we saw a rat jump onto the river bank.

. . . Heading home to "Avondale," which its owners named for one of Parnell's houses. Everything is vast and green. The hay is newly mown & the sheep are recently shorn . . . A country dinner of blood pudding & potatoes. We relaxed when the children were in bed. Life is centered in the kitchen. I felt transported to another planet. (Seán thinks Ireland is just that—that the plane flies to another globe—and I'm more inclined toward his point of view now.)

JUNE 29: Loree and I went for a walk after supper—it stays light until after ten. We passed the handsome fortyish farmer who's just taken a wife and built the grandest house in Newtown. Loree says that at first she was put off by small town life, but now she inevitably takes an interest in the gossip. She says she had a great time recently at the big local dinner for the Irish Wheelchair Association.

JUNE 30: [Loree] tells me to watch what I say in the hotel as the grand sport is eavesdropping. A look around the dining room, full of craned heads, confirms this.

JULY 1: Well, more about Clonmacnoise elsewhere. [I was visiting the ancient Irish monastery on assignment from the *New York Times* Travel section.] . . . Things not good in the evening. The children were fussing & Loree was beset with hay fever (so am I). And she began one of her rages, shouting at the kids, at Oliver, running around crazy . . . I was in my room, feeling imprisoned, & wondering how Mom is supposed to put up with this for three weeks.

JULY 2: I worked on my Clonmacnoise piece as [Loree] did her errands. At twelve we met for lunch at Rourke's, a tea shop. I was sullen, clearly still angry over last night. This further infuriated Loree, who thinks of this as "carrying a grudge" . . . Back home we were no more calm. We sat in the kitchen, and Loree—who is as preoccupied with Freudian explanations and childhood grudges as Tommy was—talked about growing up in my successful shadow even though I was the younger child. Of not being allowed to do this and that. The implication was that her life is hard & mine has always been easy. And I couldn't stand this & decided to fight back. I just shouted: "Oh, use your imagination! Do you think this friend of mine who died last year was just a friend?" And I left the kitchen for my room, conscious on the way that I had "done it."

She turned out to be wonderful . . . After dinner the two of us bicycled for miles through Roscommon. My head was a poisoned balloon from the hay fever, but I barely minded. It was the nicest hour or two I can remember spending with Loree. I felt as if I had come alive before her, as if I were no longer the emotional cipher, Uncle Tom's replacement . . . We went in and played Scrabble with Ollie and Paraic. I came in dead last. Ollie and Paraic may not make the oddest words, but they have an Irish eye for "Double Word Score" squares—almost as if they've spotted a good tract of land.

JULY 3: Dublin itself is even a little shabbier than I remember it—sort of like Jackson Heights during a recession. The country is mortgaged to the eyebrows: everyone owes a foreigner $2200.

But it was pretty enough on St. Stephen's Green, where I walked before getting the #11 bus out to [Joe Dunne's] new house in Clonskeagh, which is much nicer than Dundrum. He seems to be moving up in the world materially, but otherwise he frets about being stalled. He and Laura have broken up, and he's unhappy to be unmarried at 37. (How is this possible? He's the only handsome man in Ireland. What woman would say no?) And I wasn't surprised to hear that he still hasn't finished the dissertation.

JULY 4: From there to the Wax Museum—which is recently recovered from an attack. (Somebody cleavered Margaret Thatcher.)

The only one who looks like himself is Boy George, as if he's the only one used to wearing make-up.

JULY 5: A long ride to the airport . . . I don't think I ever hugged Loree so hard. In fact, something in me usually flinches when she hugs me. But today I flung myself into it. I wanted to be hugged, as I now believed I was actually palpable to her.

JULY 6: Read the paper and looked at *The Way We Were* on television. When I first saw it a dozen years ago, I couldn't "relate" to scenes like the one where she tries to get him back late at night in the kitchen. I had no experience. And now I saw myself in that scene—her brains, her struggle to control, to let strategy take over, to hold her tongue, to rise from defeat.

JULY 10: Joyce Thomas came by for a drink & we went out for dinner in the Citicorp Building. First time I've seen her in ten years . . . when I was at Brown I used to feel so jealous knowing that she and Tom [Lewis] were going back from wherever we were to make love in his dorm room. Now they're divorced & she's a lesbian, & we've got more in common than they did.

JULY 13: We walked around Chelsea for awhile, all the way over to the seminary near 10th Avenue, before going back to his place. We put on Nimet (not Mimette, it turns out) & listened to her program of French songs for Bastille Day as we made love. [W.] was a million miles away . . . He knows he's distant, says he knows he's not giving me signs of affection & reassurance. Says it's because he's preoccupied. More or less holding my breath. I ask whether it's another person. He says no (convincingly). It's mostly his career, & his sense that he's not where he should be . . . He's starting to see a therapist, and he's even going to go to two est* sessions. I would have been really alarmed if he'd not had enough irony to smile as he said this. But he's still going to do it, & he says

* Erhard Seminars Training, a cultish self-help program of the 1970s and early 1980s; later softened into The Forum, which was what W. attended.

he feels "threatened" by me—I'm doing just what I like, am very successful at it . . . He said he went to see an exhibition of Géricault drawings at the Morgan this afternoon so that he could tell me about it & I would approve intellectually. I laughed at this & told him it's just the sort of thing I'm doing over *him*, afraid he's going to find me glib, silly, superficial. All of this came as a great surprise to us both. (Especially to me, certain as I am that I never cross the mind of anyone the moment I leave the room.)

JULY 16: An utterly astonishing storm in the afternoon. Sheets of water and hail poured down into 43rd St. In the Kent Building each window had an amazed office worker pressed against it looking out. A weirdly secure community feeling. I felt peaceful & happy, though what was beyond the glass couldn't have been more violent.

JULY 17: A letter from Dick Ellmann, who's read *ABOOO* & likes it a lot. Don't know whether he discovered it on his own or if Picador sent him a copy for a quotation. The second letter was from Jono, a sweet one, but also containing a sentence about how he's become "very anti-American." Some real bitterness follows. Well, how does one respond to that?

Took the train to Mom's . . . Bea & Edie[*] were out to see her last Saturday & for a housewarming present Bea gave her a set of crystal that belonged to Mom's mother. It was a wedding present to her from her last employer, a New York lady named Mrs. Sinclair. I remember it in Bea's house 30 years ago—the little knife holder that looks like a dog's bone. It seems to me Mom could have been given some of it a few decades before now. After all, it was her mother, not Bea's. But Mom is still Cinderella against the 2 wicked stepsisters. In fact, tonight she admitted to me that after all these years she's still afraid of Bea.

JULY 23: In the evening to see *Prizzi's Honor* (a nasty little movie, actually; and awfully overrated). I met Robert Massa (I still can't

---

[*] My mother's half sisters.

figure him out) outside the Sutton on 57th. He was carrying the afternoon *Post* with its screaming headline about Rock Hudson & AIDS.

JULY 24: At 6:00 we all met at the Ginger Man. I was late, but I hurried as fast as I could on foot (past the ventriloquist in Columbus Circle, whose dummy looked at my white linen jacket and sunglasses and said: "Hey, Miami Vice!" and made the crowd of about a hundred laugh).

JULY 25: We went to Orso on Restaurant Row, and I had the most delicate pizza I've ever eaten—almost a pizza crêpe. A couple of tables away some Broadway types were talking about the merits of a particular lyricist: "He's even done a number about supply-side economics."

JULY 28: A bit panicky. I spent last night riding fever and chills in alternating swoops. And my glands are swollen just where they say it means danger. Now of course your glands do swell when you're fighting off a bug, and it's been months and months since I've had any bug at all; but I still feel scared.

Matters were not helped by having a date with Louise this afternoon. Not that I didn't want to see her. But there we were walking up 3rd Avenue and talking about Rock Hudson; and sitting in the balcony watching *Kiss of the Spider Woman*, in which William Hurt plays a "flamboyant" homosexual; and making occasional remarks about Tom—while I was all the time thinking of my swollen glands. It was a small nightmare. It'll be comical to read this if things turn out all right; if they don't, this will be one of those pages where the organ chords begin.

JULY 29: Hmmmn. [W.] called tonight, tired, a little less buoyant about the whole Forum thing, I thought, than last week. But it turns out that the final session is really tomorrow night, for 3 hours, to which the recently graduated bring their friends—so that they can see what their loved ones have been through, and, frankly, so that they can be subjected to a hard sell.

Now there's no way on earth I'd sign up for this thing—& I
don't feel any real pressure from [W.]. And yet he wants me to go,
that's clear. . . .

. . .

. . . And Anatole Broyard drove me crazy this afternoon. At
first he called me to say that he loves the Radclyffe Hall piece but
that the Una [Troubridge] book has to be dropped: they like it so
much they want to run it soon (as at *Newsday*, the cupboard gets
bare in the summertime). So will I chop off Una & write a new
ending? (Una must be dropped because the pub. date isn't until
late September.) And yet when I sat down at my desk, looking
at this stuff I've been away from for a month, I got angrier and
angrier. I ended up throwing the galleys across the room . . . So
I called back + took this line: Anatole, I can't possibly do this by
Thursday . . . And he said: "Let me motivate you." It turns out
"they" (Levitas?) like the piece so much they want to use it on the
front page (a split page with one other piece). In other words, they
want to make me into a star & I shouldn't argue with them . . .
Then I got to work. And then the phone rang. Anatole: "Tom,
good news. Don't do a thing. There's a problem with the other
review & we've had to dissolve that whole front page. We'll run
your review as is in September."

JULY 30: [W.] came by here at about 6:00 and we went off to "The
Forum," which is held in the old East Side Airlines Terminal . . .
It's a little like a salesman's convention, I think. Anything is possible; you take charge. ([W.] looks on all this as a revelation—as if
he's now in charge of his world; in fact, he still won't take Communion because he's sure God's angry at him.) They use the same
sports metaphors again & again—& after 2 hours it still meant
nothing to me. It's too superficial to be sinister. (It's a derivation
of est—they let you go to the bathroom & don't scream at you
anymore.)

JULY 31: Went to the *Times* at lunchtime to drop off my Clonmacnoise piece with Nora Kerr. About a dozen people over there have
dropped (and been cured) from Legionnaire's Disease. I won-

dered if I should wear a mask going in—but then I also thought: God, Legionnaire's Disease, what a *little* disease to worry about. It doesn't even always kill its victims.

In the evening to Louise's. The final proofs of Tommy's book have arrived and they've got to be gone over quickly. (Rachel is still out of the country.). So we started working on them at the dining room table after dinner.

Tommy wrote well—with authority, *confidence*—that's what most distinguishes it, I think. He had so little of that in most of life's areas; a lot of it in a few. He was very present tonight—he was closer to me than at any time since his death, I think. I could hear him, feel him on the typescript we were checking things against. (Someone from Hopkins sent Louise some pictures today—taken in the fall of '82—with Tom, lying on a couch with a drink at a party, looking handsome and relaxed. She burst into tears when she saw them, and we kept them out on the table as we worked.) . . . It felt peculiar walking out of Peter Cooper [Village], as if I'd just visited *him.* . . .

AUGUST 2: At home [W.] was quiet, unresponsive. Goddamned Nimet played Aaron Copland, too, & this put him into what I thought was a rather theatrical closed-eyed revery. And nothing happened in bed. I felt as if I was being brushed off in half a dozen ways, and I asked if I should leave. "No," was all he could say . . . even though he says my tendency to analyze everything some-times "drives him wild" . . . He says he feels "committed" to me and fondles me and kisses me, and I'm confused, completely.

AUGUST 3: Just before the alarm went off [W.] said, "I'm sure glad you didn't leave" and pulled me close to him . . . I felt very con-fused and scared and angry when he disappeared through the gate to track 14 [at Grand Central]. I even muttered "Fuck you" as I walked back here. Suddenly I'm frightened, unsure if this will go anywhere.

   . . .

I did go to Dignity & gave thanks for a curious anniversary. It's been 2 years since Tommy & I last made love. I know they say it can incubate for 5 years now, but they used to say 2, and when the scare for me really began—in May of '84—I vowed I would feel good if I got to this day & was healthy. And so I'm grateful. The closing hymn was "Amazing Grace" (not only gay priests but Protestant hymns, too!): grace brought me this far & it'll see me home.

AUGUST 5: I "closed" this morning in a cubicle in the law offices of Leslie Plump, Esq., on E. 40th St. I signed a lot of checks . . . I also signed an affidavit stating that I was none of the Thomas Mallons against whom there are records of outstanding judgments. There's a substantial list of deadbeat namesakes that I have.

Went back to Walter & Samuels on Park Ave. So. to get the keys from Farrah-haired Elaine, and then the place was mine. I walked over to it and met the Lurch-like doorman and just stood in the emptiness, amazed at the size and cleanliness of it.; the gracefulness of the beams; the friendliness of the bushes outside the window.

AUGUST 7: These big, nice guys from Astoria showed up at 12:15 and in under two hours moved everything I own from E. 43rd to E. 45th . . . I happen to know it takes two people to carry that air conditioner, but this guy put it on his shoulder so he would have one arm free for another box . . . At one point in the evening I went back to the old place . . . How many ghosts a room can fill up with in only 21 months; how many memories: the tenure days, Tom's dying, the book's excitement. New Tom, Carlo, [W.], Louise—all of it. Again I have the impulse to write down how nobody reading this book should ever think I didn't feel alive. Here I was joyful, sorrowful, excited, amazed & always fully *alive*. As I'd never been elsewhere. If anything happens to me, remember that.

AUGUST 12: A water main near 42nd St. broke today, and we had nothing from the taps until evening. Well, maybe it will help the drought crisis. As Ed Koch says: "You don't have to flush the toilet each toime you merely eeuuuurinate."

AUGUST 13: At 4 p.m. I turned on CNN & saw they were covering the big anti-apartheid demonstration about to move toward the U.N. I could simply have looked out the window.

AUGUST 17: I went down to church at 7:30. [W.] came late and sat in another pew—as I expected he would. He's shy about what he calls "the marriage of the unmarriageables"—he's half a dozen years behind me. It was the usual cheerful Dignity service: lots of called-out intentions for people just dead or diagnosed with AIDS; a boy in the pew in front of me with KS on his nose, in exactly the spot where Tommy had it; a singer who did the Communion hymn—beautifully, too—who, I later learned, is a PWA (Person With AIDS).

[W.] could stand to be with me when it came time for the social. And at 9:30 we walked out into the downtown evening without any plans. He'd already vetoed both a restaurant & a movie. We wound up walking home to my place—thirty blocks of eggshells.

AUGUST 18: . . . He's experiencing the old dichotomy, the same one in Tommy. The better he knows me, the harder it is to have sex. He's felt this before in his relationships, & it's what you always find in gay men who lived through the 70s. That much he's honest about . . . I ask him—as I hold my breath—if he wants to call it a day. He says yes & no. No, because I'm "sensitive" & he likes being with me; yes, because he'd have "one less commitment." Part of him would be disappointed if I walked away, but he emphasizes that part of him would be relieved—that would solve all the ambiguities for him . . . He told me he had had "great hopes for this." But he was just infatuated. Yes, he knows this always happens— that infatuation wears off & you wake up with a person instead of an idea—but he doesn't seem to feel that at 42 there's any point in fighting a pattern that's left him alone up to now.

. . .

I went down to Louise's. She gave me dinner & I cried it out on her shoulder. She was glad. Because she wanted to mourn Tommy tonight. So we drank too much & did both because it all seemed part of the same wretched whole. Why, she wanted to know, has she so carefully arranged all his Latin and Greek books? "He's not coming back," she admits. She gives me yet another picture of him. She tells me of her own disasters with Big Tom—even reads me some of a memoir she wrote when they were breaking up.

Why did I even try to fall in love again? Why not just be Tommy's ludicrous widow, the survivor of our brief deathbed marriage, even as I may be dying myself?

AUGUST 20: It's only 3:20 p.m. & I'm in the [Mid-Manhattan Library] on 40th St. . . . Across from me . . . on the other side of the table, is an extremely handsome Latin-looking man, about my age, doing calculus. I minded his books while he went for a cigarette & he smiles at me every so often. I want him to talk to me.

AUGUST 22: More [Vassar] bureaucracy with Charlie & Irene. Ken [Weedin] has begun his annual job of driving me crazy with his prancing temperamental queenliness. He's being difficult about registration and so forth. His apparel gets more aggressively gay: today he was wearing a little tee-shirt that strategically ended an inch or so above the waist, thereby allowing—indeed, making inevitable—an undesired view of his starved belly.

AUGUST 23: Paul Sachner called in the afternoon . . . We talked about [W.]—and his Jim. And it was darkly funny. Because things between him & Jim are almost exactly where things between me & [W.] are. And Paul is playing my part. We laughed at the ugly correspondences but we know the familiarity isn't funny. "It's as if you're barely breathing," Paul says of breakups. Two weeks ago Jim forgot his birthday—no small, cute sitcom incident in a relationship either. And Paul told him the plain truth: "I'm 35, and I'm too old to be spending my birthday alone."

AUGUST 24: [Another Saturday night with W.] After Mass . . . we wound up talking and sitting outside the White Horse Tavern drinking beer in the cool air. We talked about things like what sort of city Houston is. Stiff. Terrified of each other. There were certain silences so long that I was a second away from getting up and saying goodbye & putting an end to it for good. But I couldn't bring myself to; and I remembered that my rush to fill any silence with talk is one of the things I do that infuriates him . . .

AUGUST 25: I got a cab [home from W.'s] to Grand Central, forgetting I no longer live next door. Carmen McRae was singing "Like a Lover" on the cab's radio, & with that & the rain & Sunday I was just aware how peaceful and unbattered I felt compared to last Sunday. But I fear it's a false peace, just a little Armistice; the real defeat is yet to come.

AUGUST 26: Spent the morning on the telephone. Broyard would like me to write an essay for the *Book Review* for $1,000—but I can't think of anything just now. (One of those dully feminist copyeditors got her hands on my Radclyffe piece & was trying to make all sorts of little changes in the direction of blandness & liberal orthodoxy . . . Her most hilarious annotation—next to where I write that Una understood love more fully than R.H. or "for that matter, most people," she's queried: "How does he know?" Anatole says he will try to rescue me from her.)

AUGUST 27: I did my 3.2 miles up at the reservoir . . . How odd and lovely to ride the subway with a Cleo Laine tape playing into my ears. As of so many things, I revise my opinion: I used to think Walkmen were anti-social. Now I think they're lovely.

AUGUST 30: [Preparing to go through the Mary McCarthy papers in order to write remarks for a celebration of their acquisition by Vassar] Looking at some of the boxes I wondered again if I might not be making a mistake by not doing MMcC's biography—but no. I'd wind up being known as a faggy flame-keeper & identified with Vassar more than I already am.

AUGUST 30: Hours of paperwork and buttonhole advising in the afternoon before registration in the gym . . . One girl points to a course description reading "Chaucer, Spenser, Shakespeare, Donne & Milton" & inquires if they'll be reading a lot of poetry.

AUGUST 31: Went down to church in a cab. Sparse crowd—whoever isn't dead from AIDS is out at Fire Island for the last weekend of summer. Ran into Gerry Johnson at the social. Hadn't seen his easy Irish face in months. He tells me he's got "a new little companion." I thought it might be a 17-year-old Puerto Rican boy, but it turns out to be a wire-haired terrier.

SEPTEMBER 2: I ran my 3.2 up at the Park and spotted another lazy reservoir rat crossing the path as I made my way to the railings in order to do my pre-run stretches. It was a tricky day; it didn't seem hot, but once you started running you realized how thick the air was. Walked home down 5th after deciding to spend the dollar in my Nike on a soda instead of the subway. Had the headphones on and didn't want to be anywhere but New York.

SEPTEMBER 4: The bureaucracy has calmed somewhat, and I'm doing my best to insulate myself from the looniest tunes & their loopy demands. I had one girl come in yesterday to get a form signed and within two minutes she was telling me about her problems with anorexia & lithium.

SEPTEMBER 5: [G.] came to my office & asked me to reassign him as an advisee from Bob DeMaria to Ken Weedin—his boyfriend . . . I refused, since I only make reassignments "in cases of severe personality conflict between advisor and advisee." [G.], to his credit, admitted there was none. I told him he could continue to get Mr. Weedin's advice informally (indeed), but that he should keep Mr. DeMaria's perspective as well.

The trouble is that Ken himself left me a note requesting the change—though he knows full well he would have huffed & puffed & flounced his skirts if anyone had asked him to do such a thing when he was Chairman of Advisors. But that was before he discovered love. And since he's twenty years behind on kisses and orgasms he needs to go through a phase of consummating rituals: I suppose having [G.] made his advisee would be a sort of nuptials, some latter-day compensation for Ken's never having given his pin to anyone in high school. But, God, Ken, if you're coming out this late, could you just sort of skip over this phase of development—kind of like Communist China going from being an agrarian country to an industrial one with nothing in between?

. . . To the GM Building at 5th and 59th for a publishing party Ticknor & Fields was giving for Guy Vanderhaeghe, a Canadian novelist just my age. The co-sponsor of the party was the Canadian government & a little diplomat . . . made a little nationally self-effacing speech about how this shows Americans will buy the Canadian "product" if it's good enough.

SEPTEMBER 8: Another awful conversation with [W.] this morning—in some respects worse than 3 weeks ago. (But in some respects better: less cold, more angry, more honest.) . . . We end drained, each telling the other he cares about him, each not sure he means it.

He says he and I know more about one another than he and the person he once lived with—for 4½ years—knew about one another. That must have been some romance.

SEPTEMBER 10: Charles ran fevers in July & saw a doctor who said he's fine.

If Charles gets it, will I be blamed? Should I be? No. He knew about Tommy & his own life before he met me was ten times faster than mine. We've all been exposed, we're all living under the sword, & I'm no more lethal than anyone else. We're either going to get it or not. Period. I hate doing this algebra in my head, but maybe it helps keep one from going completely crazy.

SEPTEMBER 12: Mary [McCarthy] and Jim [West] were late getting to Pratt House after about 9 hours in the car from Castine. Jim appeared a bit doddering and tired, but Mary looks really well, thinner too. I was relieved that she seemed happy to see me, eager to hear all news, full of compliments on the Radclyffe Hall piece, calling me "dear Tom" . . . We went to Dixie's for dinner. Barbara also there, and Jean or Jane Someone from CBS News (they're doing an interview tomorrow). A great food fest and Mary enjoyed talking about each little piece of lamb or cheese. Barbara so ill at ease around Mary that her IQ drops 30 points—but some of it was regained by dessert. A taxi I called never came, so I stayed later than I expected and resigned myself to spending another night in Kendrick.

Marvelous Mary still hasn't lost the little jab. On the way home I apologized for being such a lousy guide, not being able to find the right street or the parking lot. I couldn't even manage to get a cab to come out there, after all. I told Mary my sense of direction suffered from always being a pedestrian. "That doesn't account for the cab," she smiled.

SEPTEMBER 13: [At the ballet in NY with W.] things were still so tense and formal between us. The program was dull and literally colorless—nothing but whites and blacks and diluted pastels going around the stage—watery Antony Tudor and a few other things that didn't provide much of a change of pace. But it wasn't *that* bad, and I thought there was something neurotic and niggardly in the way [W.] withheld applause at lots of moments. After all, it's much harder not to clap than otherwise.

SEPTEMBER 14: Got dressed and ready and walked up to Frances FitzGerald's apartment on E. 72nd—the last building before the river. Lizzie Hardwick was already there, out on the street in the limo, and she called out to me. On the way up [to Poughkeepsie] FitzGerald . . . did some homework—rereading something in *On the Contrary*. Lizzie and I talked about NY apartment prices & *The New York Times*. She agrees the copyeditors are awful. "If you say 'Picasso,'" she said in her Kentucky squawk, "they make you put 'the Spanish painter' after it. And talkin' to Nona Balakian is like talkin' to a dog." Alas, about five miles out of Poughkeepsie she asked me what I was working on now, and I told her. When Jacob Epstein's name came up she turned a bit frosty. "You cain't," she said, thinking of her good friend Barbara's boy. "You just cain't. It ruined his life." (Jacob has just been nominated for an Emmy for *Hill Street Blues*. It strikes me as a view typical of *The New York Review of Books* to think that this constitutes a ruined life.) She told me about how unfairly he was treated, and I told her that maybe that was the story I would have to tell. We were suddenly at Virginia's door, and it was left nowhere.

At lunch I told Mary that it looked as if the wagons were being drawn in a circle. She responded zestily & told me about one of Jason [Epstein]'s own thefts from the 40s, something she'd heard about. She said I could get the story from John Gross and from Terry Kilmartin (*The Observer*). So it seems like father like son.

. . . The ceremony itself, in brilliant sun under the sycamore, went very well. It was elegant but casual. Friendly, intimate. Mary had a lovely time. My speech went down well & she and I blew kisses to one another after it was over. Jovanovich, who just jetted in and out in his million-dollar suit, was the most off the cuff. Mary read the piece from her new autobiography about coming to Vassar and losing her virginity for the third time.

. . . I napped at Kendrick and was then back at VBS' for the dinner. Reuel* was on my left; Frankie FitzGerald on my right. Mary and Virginia nearby. Conversation not especially crackling, but Virginia was clearly having a good time, and I was glad.

I got whisked away in the limo [back to Manhattan]. I dozed in the front. Barbara Epstein, Lizzie & Frankie were in the back making themselves unattractive by cutting up Virginia and scrutinizing Renata Adler's love life.

SEPTEMBER 17: [Vassar advising] The most interesting meeting of the day: with Susan Watson, a black woman with children who's earned two years of transfer credit at Dutchess [Community College] over the last ten years as she's worked the night shift in a psychiatric hospital. She's still doing that as she takes a full program at Vassar. She says she's not had any trouble with race here, only class. It's the fact that she works, and at what, that the students can't relate to. She says she wants to complete her degree so that she doesn't have to spend the rest of her life tending to

---

* Reuel K. Wilson, b. 1938; longtime professor of European literature and a memoirist; the son of Edmund Wilson and Mary McCarthy.

"90-year-old schizophrenics who'd rather drink out of the toilet than a glass."

SEPTEMBER 18: I think Charlie has had two main goals as chairman: get a Xerox machine for Avery Hall and get rid of Jerry [Badanes]—who, as Susan Morgan says, is a hustler, and who's gotten an unbelievable break for 6 years. But Eamon & Bill Gifford make a sentimental pitch for him. The rules are now written so that Charlie can do what he wants and I don't think Jerry will last long.

I was once more in the office after dinner, working on grant applications. Demo came in for something he forgot. He was wearing a tee-shirt & I thought I'd pass out from the sight of such Michelangelan perfection.

SEPTEMBER 21: At 5:30 I called [W.], realizing he'd never get around to calling me if I didn't. And so—on my nickel—I was given my walking papers. Officially. Plus a tale of how he still feels "committed to me as a friend." (Esthole.) I also got an apology for the way he's treated me over the last six weeks.

I've known it was over—& known how deeply screwed up he is—for more than a month, but hearing the words is different. I could feel them moving through the silence a second before they were uttered, & it was like that moment between knowing you're going to hit the car in front of you & actually hitting it.

SEPTEMBER 22: I was aggressively sensible all day. I cleaned the house, read the paper, graded papers, got ready for Louise—& threw away his toothbrush.

. . . [Louise and I] laughed & told war stories from work & got sloshed & of course came back to AIDS. She says she's glad Tommy didn't live to see this summer's barrage of news on the subject—he couldn't have stood it without breaking down . . . She also says she's glad I own my apartment given the current hysteria. (What does she mean? The talk of quarantine? The possibility I'll get sick?)

SEPTEMBER 23: I felt better during lunch with Doug . . . I think he's become the nicest, most mature man I know. (I always fall for the truly cold—like [W.]—because I decide their reserve and awkwardness is really bottled-up warmth that they're waiting for me to release—an act for which they'll repay me with extravagant love.)

SEPTEMBER 24: At one point, after an appointment with a student, I had to catch my breath in the bathroom—that feeling I was going to pass out from sheer despair, that I'd die if I had to make one more minute of small or professional talk.

SEPTEMBER 25: Ended the day at a [Vassar] *Dynasty* premiere party (the sort of thing going on in every gay bar in New York) . . . The guest of honor was [the Spanish novelist Carmen Martín Gaite]. We explained to her this plot line about a typical American family . . . She laughed a lot and gave me her book. She is extremely affectionate toward me & I wonder if it's because Patty has told her about Tommy. Given the fact that this spring her own daughter died of AIDS. (Needles.)

SEPTEMBER 27: Hurricane Gloria turned out to be a big bust, at least as far as Manhattan went. I went out about 11:00 to buy provisions for what I thought would be a long siege. And things were pretty wild: rainwater racing across 2nd Ave. in lariat snaps; the banner above Dustin's flapping crazily and getting ready to tear. I got back here and found the 3 networks giving non-stop assassination-like coverage to it. "Fifteen minutes," they kept repeating, saying it would reach New York with the force of an atomic bomb.

    Well, before that happened I fell asleep. When I woke up at 1:30 it was sort of drizzling.

SEPTEMBER 28: . . . At 12:30 I was in a cab, hurtling across the park. At 1:00 I was in Uncle Charlie's very drunk, talking to a young doctor, very drunk. And very nice. And very plain. And at 3:00 we were back here. Fumbling around. Safely. He's the doctor. I was in bed with somebody very funny, very wry, very smart—&

I couldn't conceive the slightest romantic feeling for him because he wasn't pretty enough.

SEPTEMBER 30: After 9 days of making me suffer, he called. There was a message on the machine at 5:00. He identified himself [with his first and last names] (surely not the [W.] whose cock used to be against mine? some other [W.] perhaps?) & gave his number (just in case I'd forgotten it), including the area code (just in case I thought he lived in Bensonhurst). I think he's loony.

. . . Lunch with Aram & Gailyn Saroyan in Ridgefield, CT, where I'd not been in 20 years (a visit to the McLindens). I took the train to Katonah & Aram picked me up. I liked him & Gailyn very much. It's a little like being with the family in *Family Ties*: ex-quasi-hippies with a good long marriage & 3 kids, one of them already a sophomore in high school . . . We had a summery lunch & I heard that Gloria Vanderbilt, Carol Marcus [Aram's mother], & Oona Chaplin are really "three of the great bitches in the world". . . .

OCTOBER 2: Carmen very lively—in contrast to last night, when I ran into her in the Retreat & she was weepy over her daughter. We talked—last night—about depression (talk about expertise: this was the equivalent of Einstein & Fermi talking about the atom), how work, not diversion, is the only cure. The first builds up your self-respect, the second doesn't.

. . . Took the train home . . . First thing I saw outside the terminal was the *Post* announcing Rock Hudson's death. Poor bastard. One day before Tommy's anniversary. Poor all of us. The cover story in *New York* is about "the last word on avoiding AIDS." One doctor makes me feel safe; another makes me certain I've got better than a 1 in 3 chance of getting AIDS or ARC. And Diane McGrath, the Republican candidate for mayor, wants to close not only the baths, but the bars as well.

OCTOBER 3: Is it more unimaginable that he's been gone for a year or that he ever was? How can someone I knew so little have left such a mark on me? (He may yet, literally, be the death of me.)

OCTOBER 10: Who should be on the message tape but Carlo? He's coming back to NY in a few weeks & he'll call again. Did I ever think he'd resurface? In fact, yes. But not so soon. Come back, haaaaney, & make me happy. Take me dancing & make me smile.

OCTOBER 13: [A more-or-less annual reunion with graduate-school dorm-mates] It was a quiet, low-key, easy affair, the whole weekend. Things are changing as we age. At dinner last night we were drinking chablis & listening to Handel. Ten years ago it would have been beer and the Tubes. And most of our talk has been about mortgages and property . . . The jokes are stale to the point of timelessness, though, and in most ways it might as well be 1975.

. . .

[Michael Dowling dropped me off in Baltimore; I had about an hour before my train would leave.] I walked once more past Tommy's, and kept spotting things I'd remember—a store we stopped into that Friday afternoon, & his gay bar, The Hippo. I walked through the alleyway, sweating from the sun by now. I looked up at the back windows of 10 E. Madison & wondered if I'd caught my death there.

. . .

[Back in NY that night I learned from Phyllis Rose that she was] in love with the son of the man who wrote the Babar books. She thinks he's going to divorce his wife & marry her. She can't believe David [Schorr] has kept his mouth shut this long.

OCTOBER 15: The Carnegie Foundation has released a study that shows 38% of all college teachers wanting to leave the profession within the next five years.

OCTOBER 17: This afternoon I saw Jacqueline Onassis twice within one hour. I was headed from the 86th St. station to the reservoir & saw her coming toward me. She is bone-slim, looks masked and has hair that's unaccountably in place without look-ing lacquered. She's very tanned and looks older than her photo-graphs. "So, honey," I felt like saying, "how come you're not at

Doubleday? Playin' hooky?" Maybe she'd just come home for a quick late-lunch tuna melt & to feed the cat. Anyway, I ranked it just beneath my Garbo sighting. Well, after I did my 3.2 [miles], and was heading back to the subway, whom should I see once more, walking west this time instead of east? Herself. We passed one another crossing Park Ave. I saw her stifling a yawn as she waited for the light to change.

OCTOBER 18: [A speaking engagement in Iowa] To Lake Okoboji, the resort where the Iowa Writing Project was having its conference. I spotted Tom [S.] before we even got into the hotel parking lot. He is, of course, as he was: gangling, loving, prickly, lost. We took a walk down to the lake . . . then we went back to our room in the "lodge"—really just a big motel. Everyone at the conference registration tables, right near the check-in desk, saw me ask for an extra key. God knows what they thought of us. I felt as if I had G-A-Y written on me in big, Eastern, neon letters all day. But who cares? and what was there for them to worry about anyway? Tom and I were as innocent as two ten-year-olds. We napped in the same bed and hugged and kissed, and he smelled good, and that was it. We watched sitcom reruns on the TV and fell asleep until dinnertime. It was warm and intimate and, as I say, innocent, and it did nothing to diminish my loneliness by so much as a jot.

OCTOBER 19: I took a walk up and down the golf course behind our room. That I wanted to walk alone struck [Tom] as odd, but I didn't see it that way. I'm feeling lonely and gelded, built for friendship and not for love, and I almost want to deny myself—at least in spurts—to my friends, as a kind of revenge on all the lovers (some of them became the friends) who have forsaken me. . . . I was the only paying passenger on the plane from Spencer to Minneapolis. A pilot & co-pilot & two other airline workers rounded out the group. Under the circumstances the usual long "Welcome Aboard" set of instructions were foolish, and the captain wisely settled for "Sit up, shut up & buckle up" . . . I shortly thereafter became probably the first person ever to read *Zuleika Dobson* while flying between northwest Iowa & Minneapolis.

OCTOBER 21: Another date, another death-inviting disaster . . . We are in the middle of the Black Death and I still fuck first and ask questions later. Actually, not fuck. Safely, safely. Though he had no interest in safety; in fact, found my interest in it rather touchingly boyish. Made stupid remarks about fatalism.

OCTOBER 23: Tonight I walked up to the Whitney—the entire East Side blocked by limos and cops—to a reception for Cambridge alumni (I'm sort of one). I signed up for this instead of throwing the invitation in the wastebasket, because I figure I ought to be "meeting people." Well, there were only 2 recognizable gay men there (both, of course, from Peterhouse). But I did see Barbara Kirschten & Gwen Kinkead from Harvard; I hadn't seen either one in 8 or ten years. Barbara tells me that Jim Engell has married and fathered a child—much to Bate's bereavement. He's now all alone in his woodland cabin on the weekends.

OCTOBER 24: A bit of a pick-me-up. A letter from James Lord (complete with page of *Giacometti* manuscript) assures me I'm a half-dozen dazzling adjectives . . . And James Raimes takes me to lunch at Darjeeling on 49th St. for hot food under the greenhouse roof in the back. We talked about everything from *Booth* (how dare I underline it yet?) to Dick Ellmann, who, James says, is a shark and a double-dealer when it comes to business. Oxford U.P. has finally given up on the much-delayed *Oscar*, and it's gone to Knopf for $250,000.

. . . A double suicide on the news. Two men leapt from the 35th floor of a 3rd Ave. apt. house. One of them, 42, is thought to have had AIDS. He and his lover roped themselves together at the waist and jumped after toasting themselves with wine. The police found the apartment "immaculate." There were fresh cut flowers.

OCTOBER 26: Paul [Sachner] and I wandered around looking for a place to eat & wound up all the way up at Joe Burns'. We ate fish and talked about (what else?) AIDS. He says he went to a seminar (good word for it) on "safe sex" last weekend. It was sponsored by the GMHC in the Village. He says everyone left it more confused than they were upon arrival. They'd bring out one doctor who'd say that actual fucking is the only thing that's been *proved* to be dangerous; and then they bring out another who'd tell you you can die from tapping somebody on the shoulder.

OCTOBER 27: Went down to the Lucille Lortel this afternoon to see Ed Herrmann's play [*Not About Heroes*]. Didn't much like it: all I could see was Ed, not Sassoon. And the Owen guy was too normal—just a little callow & shook up by the war, whereas I think there was something fundamentally squirrelly about the real W.O. Sat with Ed in his dressing room afterwards. He's got pictures of S.S. and Blunden in it, and I joked to him that all this paraphernalia looked suspiciously liked Method Acting . . . The play (which I heard on the radio when I was at St. Ed's) is really very hokey. The best thing about it was the way Ed aged Sassoon 15 years—just by lowering his eyelids a millimeter—when a flash-forward scene called for it. Owen was played by Dylan Baker, who, alas, is only a little cuter than the real W.O. was.

OCTOBER 28: . . . I went back to the office to mark more papers. I realize that in the last few days I've written as many words of marginal annotation and comments as it would take to fill a chapter of my unwritten book.

OCTOBER 29: An hour ago on the news they reported that some doctors in Paris have succeeded in completely refiring the immune systems of 2 AIDS patients in a matter of 5 days with the use of some drug. This will probably turn out to be nothing. "It will be years before . . ." the news stories will go. But tonight there are thousands of men in New York desperate to get to France.

OCTOBER 30: [My students] sat like unbreathing mounds of protoplasm all through our two hours on Yeats. When I commented on how "Easter, 1916" is relatively free of end stops, compared to what we'd read a moment before, one of them looked at me as if it were weird for anyone to take an interest in such things. And this kid is a senior English major.

OCTOBER 31: [Editing my piece on Clonmacnoise for the Travel section of *The New York Times*] As with the *Book Review*, everything has got to be rubbed into its most banal, literal and unconfusing form—clouds must not merely "roll across"; they must "roll across the sky."

. . .

Just before I was ready to wind up office hours and get on the train, cute, full-of-himself [C.A.] walks in—fuming. He's resentful that almost all my comments on his recent paper deal with mechanics instead of his "ideas." I gently suggest that his paper . . . was so full of sentence fragments & every other kind of "mechanical" mistake that it was difficult to find the "ideas." He fumes and sputters and then begins to cry. He then starts saying "It's not the paper, it's not the paper." I ask him what it is then, but he just gets up to go. I ask him to sit, please, and tell me what's bothering him and [ask] if there's anything I can do. But he says no, he's "not going to do this"—as if I'm forcing him into some sort of display—& walks out.

I am sick of these emotional spectacles of the overprivileged. I am sick of being their captive audience. Two years ago I would have called the dorm and talked to the House Fellow, put a note in the unstamped [campus mail]. Today I just say the hell with it. I get on the train. Let him grow up on his own time.

NOVEMBER 2: [At a 34th birthday dinner for me at Doug MacKay & Bruce Shostak's, with Bob Pounder] Bob drove me occasionally crazy with the way he dotes on Bruce, every one of whose comments is a pearl beyond price. He can't stop giving him little pats either. Just as he can't stop—well, let's say he occasionally finds himself—making cute little intimate references to our days together. References that make my flesh crawl.

NOVEMBER 3: The only living part of the day: my [return] call to Carlo in L.A. To be called Barney and Bugsy & be teased for being much more innocent than I am.

. . .

There was a message to be answered—"if you're in before 12:30 or 1:00"—from Virginia . . . We wound up talking for an hour (on my nickel—the curse of these message machines). About everything from the equation of sexy & sexist to [HPS's] delusions to the First Amendment. Coherent night thoughts. Hers, anyway. I'll miss her when she goes. One hell of a smart lady. One hell of a good patron.

NOVEMBER 4: [At a Viking Penguin publishing party] for William Burroughs, which means that all the high-risk AIDS groups, except for Haitians, were represented. I met Jim Carroll, carrot-headed & unmistakeable, who said he liked what I wrote about him in *ABOOO*. But he seemed so strung out on something that he found [himself] unable to look me (or anybody) in the eye. They're making a movie of *Basketball Diaries* & the little redheaded boy who's playing him (and who's part of the new *Saturday Night Live* cast) was there.[*] Allen Ginsberg was in a black leather jacket taking flash pictures of everybody . . . The new fiction editor of *Esquire*, who's the son of the Castelli Gallery, was there, looking about 12. Peter Manso was there, and I avoided him because of the bad review I gave *Mailer* in *USA Today*. Burroughs himself looked like a bewildered old street person—so skinny the back of his ribcage was almost coming through his suit. I kept looking at him and thinking: this man killed his wife.

NOVEMBER 5: I got up even earlier than usual this morning to go across the street and vote for Koch, who won by the predicted astronomical margin . . . I voted for Carol Greitzer, the City Councilwoman, but I had a pang I didn't expect. David Rothenberg, the gay activist she beat in the Democratic primary, was still on the ballot, as a Liberal. And for a second I thought I should vote for him. Here, I thought, is my gay brother (cornball, yes), and here we are now in the middle of this holocaust—I should vote for him. All the conflicts in my life—mainstream person vs. gay person—came welling up for a second.

   In the end, though, I didn't do it. I thought, I've never been a kind of single-issue politician and I'm not going to start now.

---

[*] The film wouldn't be made for another decade, and it would star Leonardo DiCaprio, not Anthony Michael Hall.

NOVEMBER 7: The news: the city has shut down the Mineshaft, the torture bar down on Washington Street, as a health hazard. I know of 2 people who have been there. They're both dead. Tommy and Don Rawlinson. How can one have regrets about their shutting it down: a hellhole of piss and whips and microbes? And yet you wonder: what's going to be next? And where are these people going to move to? The "regular" bars?

NOVEMBER 8: I hit a low point tonight. I called [W.], because I couldn't figure out what had happened since the Ed Herrmann date fell through. He was eager to hear me, I could tell, and as soon as I was on the phone I was sorry I was calling . . . Then there's a buzzing sound in the background. He says it's a drill in the next apartment. It happens again, ten seconds later. And then he admits it's the doorbell. A new boyfriend . . . I walked up First Avenue & felt sorry for myself. I had the Streisand Broadway album playing in my Walkman. I felt sad, sentimental, victimized. Coming back along 47th St.—the park between 1st & 2nd—I tried to give $10 to a bag lady, but she wouldn't take it & shouted at me instead . . . When I got home from my walk, I took out a story I wrote 9 years ago called "Amours de Voyage." Parts of it are respectably bad. And it's the same old me of love inside it.

NOVEMBER 10: [W.] came over tonight at about 8:30. He kissed me on the mouth when he came in the door—smelling fresh-shaven and beautiful. He was relaxed. I wasn't. But we sat and drank. For hours. For two hours we talked about everything but "us"—that obsolete pronoun. And then, gradually, we got to it . . . He says he analyzed it: "If Tom is x, y, and z—all these things you want and find attractive—and you can't make it work with him, maybe you don't want a relationship at all."

NOVEMBER 11: [Book-club appearance in tony Millbrook, near Poughkeepsie] What a bunch. I knew Millbrook was rich, but not *this* rich . . . I don't really know why they *have* a book club. They don't seem particularly interested in literature, though most of them had dutifully read *ABOOO*. (There was one woman there who'd typed the Lindberghs' diaries.) I think they would rather have been talking about the real hot news in Millbrook: somebody has absconded with a bunch of Episcopalian silver from the local church.

NOVEMBER 12: [Ann Imbrie] is, I think obsessed with the lives of her cute young male students, both homo and hetero . . . (On Saturday she threw herself a birthday party—most of the guests were students, who drank up her liquor.) I guess she'd explain it by saying she's nervous about her [tenure] review, & that she's lonely on the weekends with Beverly & me in NY. But I don't know, there's something extravagant & self-destructive about it. I ran into Beverly on the train yesterday morning & she said that for all Ann's love of self-analysis & psychological categories she's got absolutely no insight into herself.

NOVEMBER 13: I taught a bang-up class on Hopkins, as I do every year. After that to the shortest faculty meeting I can recall. I sat all the way over on the right side of the Aula next to Karen. (I've discovered it has the wonderful advantage of making almost everything said from the floor inaudible.) . . . Once back here [in Manhattan] I put on PBS to watch a documentary [about] Harvey Milk . . . To think there was a time when Anita Bryant was all we had to worry about.

Well, I felt pretty morose after that film & I went out to the bar. I ran into [J.S.], the doctor from that drunken night in September. And with a minimum of embarrassment we talked with one another. And I realized that he isn't merely sweet and furry. He says he's had to take 2 weeks leave from the hospital. I thought, well, stress of NY, of medical residency, etc. Then he shyly said, "Actually, I've had a nervous breakdown." And then he left.

NOVEMBER 15: I went downtown at about 10:00 to a publishing party for John Ash, a British poet . . . A lot of theatre people were there; the apartment, a loft on W. 29th, belongs to some director. (There are really two New Yorks; one city sublets from the other.) I spent a lot of time talking to a woman named Renfrew . . . She's a displaced 60s person who's been through a marriage or two and lots of years of drifting. She had glitter above her eyes and she told me about the surgeon who did Viva's facelift. She once wrote a book about The Living Theatre and recalled how one time she was in a hotel room with Julian Beck while he was lighting up a joint. "I think it's important to break the law at least once a day," he said. She told me about the recent funeral of Jackie Curtis, one of Warhol's transvestite superstars. He died (surprisingly enough) not from AIDS. Just a plain old overdose. Renfrew didn't go to the wake for a day or two, she says, because: "You never went to Jackie's openings. They were always a disaster. Usually by closing night he had it together."

NOVEMBER 16: I went down to church in the pouring rain & spent Mass watching him look like an angel in the choir. They sang "Swing Low, Sweet Chariot" at the Offertory (what's with all these Protestant hymns?), and he pressed his hand to his flat stomach as he opened his mouth. He looked like a Christmas card. I kept trying to find fault with him & couldn't . . . I went home alone. Except for the *Times*. My Clonmacnoise piece is out—with so many changes, and all so pointless, that I half wish they'd have taken my by-line off it. I crawled into bed at my worst—a night of fear, brought on, of course, by depression. I keep thinking: these microbes are in my body. They're going to kill me eventually.

NOVEMBER 18: There was an article in the paper yesterday about a South African woman held in jail for dissidence. It mentioned how she'd learned to do "fast time"—a prisoner's term for training your body to sleep the days away. That's what I wanted to do today. I couldn't get out of bed. All I wanted to do was sleep, and let all the nothingness be drowned in greater nothingness.

NOVEMBER 22: Nancy cut my hair in the morning & urged a special dye on me. I said no—I feel if I keep it gray then I won't grow bald: the gods will be propitiated. She tells me the problems her son is having with his Italian professor, "who's very effeminate." We waltz around that one for a while.

In the afternoon to Arthur Greene on the 43rd floor at 101 Park Avenue. He's the accountant Ed Herrmann recommended. I know I can't afford him (he handles Mike Nichols, for Christ's sake), but I've gone ahead anyway. He handles a lot of writers & maybe he can save me heaps of money. His basic premise is that writers are working all the time—soaking up empirical effluvia, the impressions that will inform their work. So his considered message is that my whole life is deductible, which sounds nice. I liked him. He's hugely fat & quiet & obviously *likes* writers. He sits in a fancy office in a cardigan sweater & he adds the figures on his green ledger sheet with his head instead of a calculator. Behind him is a picture of his son, so gorgeous you can't believe he proceeds from the loins of this unassuming roly-poly gnome. The Empire State Building, braving the rain outside the office window, seems close enough to touch, even to break in two like a piece of chalk.

NOVEMBER 24: Autumn in NY: in the space of a few days the other week, Doug witnessed: a Carey bus with a fender bloodied from hitting a pedestrian (who was covered with a sheet); and a (non-fatal) stabbing. There was something else, too: a purse-snatching or someone defecating in the street, but I've already forgotten.

NOVEMBER 25: Turned down an offer from Princeton Univ. Press to evaluate a huge edition of Robert Graves's letters (for $25!).

NOVEMBER 26: I decided to treat myself and call Carlo in L.A. "Make it quick, Barney, I am missing *Bloopers*." He says he cannot wait to see my palazzo. Oh, God, come home and make me laugh.

NOVEMBER 27: [Bob DeMaria and I] had coffee together this morning. What a gorgeous, gentle, brilliant soul. Every time he sees me these days he gives me this intimate, protective hug. I think it's because he knows about Tommy. Does he wonder if I might be dying?

NOVEMBER 28: [Thanksgiving dinner on Long Island] I sat near Kathleen, who is something of a maidenly pain in the ass to [my aunt] Belle, calling her every day; but I got on with her well enough. She told me about her days (1945–72) as assistant chief operator at the St. Moritz: Walter Winchell's temper; Joan Kennedy's bad complexion.

NOVEMBER 29: I was so thoroughly fed up that at 10:00 I went out for a drink. And came home with someone named Stephen Smith, who's 32, from New Orleans (moved to NY 3 months ago), works for American Express. He stayed all night . . . I'll tell you what scares me. Not what we did: we were so careful that nobody could possibly have gotten hurt. What scares me is that this man is good-looking, kind, interested in someone permanent, & clearly smitten with me. And I don't want to see him again . . . I can't help but feel that I'm better off being lonely than feeling hollow after every orgasm. I should just calm down, stop this hysterical searching, spend the next 6 mos. celibate and calm and not looking. . . .

DECEMBER 3: Charlie called me into the office & told me that he is going to lower the boom on Jerry Badanes next week. Not only will there be nothing for him in the English dep't. any more; there won't be anything anywhere else either. Charlie has it in writing from Sullivan, and American Culture & Religion (Jerry's sidelines) are also on board. Charlie has been calling all the tenured members in and softening up potential Jerry-defenders like Eamon + Bill. Jerry will be told just after classes have ended & the last [*Miscellany News*, Vassar's student newspaper] is out. Charlie has gotten every trap door under Jerry ready to spring.

This is going to be very ugly. Jerry, fake mensch (I know: I didn't think so once), will make all sorts of phony moral appeals, will shout at Charlie, imply anti-Semitism & talk about himself as a special genius & conscience. But he will lose . . . I went back to Avery [after dinner]. Lynn was still there after 9:00 and dropped in. He and I got to talking about Jerry. He says Jerry has already (anticipating) been trying to get people to lobby for him. "Nancy [Willard] Lindbloom was in to see me the other day, but before she could even plant her elfin feet on the floor I told her it was no sell."

DECEMBER 5: As soon as I got back in the door of #1E tonight the phone was ringing. It was Mom. She has at last been to the neurologist for her hand tremor and the verdict has come in with instant finality. Parkinson's Disease. She is taking this as "good news." The doctor tells her she doesn't have a brain tumor (which, of course, we never considered; we were thinking along the lines of a pinched nerve). She has to take 3 pills a day.

DECEMBER 6: . . . In the lobby of the News Building an all-black choir of school kids was singing carols, & they were so good, & their white teacher so serious & energetic, that I was almost lifted into the "spirit of the season"—I've been feeling coerced ever since Thanksgiving, resistant, but today I caught some of it . . . Went running just before it got dark. I crunched snow on the northern pieces of the reservoir track, but I never slipped. Made my 3.2 miles in 25 minutes, feeling glorious in the white and gold and blue. I will live in no other place on earth. This *is* the absolute door prize of the universe. . . .

DECEMBER 7: This afternoon, as I was walking back from Sloan's [supermarket], a nicely dressed woman about my age approached me. I thought she was going to ask directions. Instead she screamed: "*Omni* magazine says men can get pregnant! It's against nature!"

DECEMBER 8: Talked to Mom. She's in a very good mood. The pills have already restored her handwriting. She spent the afternoon filling out Christmas cards.

I read the paper. (Robert Graves is dead & I'm one of the "Notable Books of 1985.")

DECEMBER 9: Yes, Steve [Smith] did come here, and he spent the night . . . But I can't feel it's right. I just don't feel IT, and he does. He adores me, says it, repeats it—and then says he'll have me any way I'm willing, he'll take me on my terms and so forth, and then I see this sweet, decent, attractive man acting the way I always act. And I look at him with pity & guilt & feel that he's being sadly ridiculous. If this keeps up, he'll have to go through a big BREAK-

UP, and he doesn't deserve that. I shouldn't see him again. But I will. (Did he leave his watch here intentionally?)

DECEMBER 10: After I got off the train & dropped my things in Kendrick, I went to the library. On my way out, getting near the doors, I was buttonholed by a student. I stopped and talked. Then Jerry Badanes came by. I said hello. Well, as the saying goes, he had "murder in his eyes." He said nothing, barrelled past me, and nearly took one of the library doors off its hinges. When I got to Avery I found a note from Charlie to all tenured members saying that Jerry had gotten his pink slip.

DECEMBER 11: The last faculty meeting of the term in the Aula. Barbara had to defend a Women's Studies proposal against several attackers. She did it with a bored professionalism, picking off these mental Lilliputians trying to scale her with ropes and hooks and dropping them like so many dead mice into the fireplace. It was fun to watch.

DECEMBER 12: [My student] Chris Bull came into my office at about 3:30 for his final conference for English 207 . . . Well, the floodgates opened. He told me how recently he'd come to terms with being gay; how he's not had any romance; how scared he is of AIDS; how he's not sure whether he's attractive to gay males (the most sweetly hilarious point of the conversation—he's probably the prettiest boy in the senior class); how so many gays—but not me—seem sad to him; how he feels dishonest about not telling *everyone*, including his parents. A dozen things.

And, boy, was I good. Friendly, comforting, and still professional. I talked of my own experience . . . I was an absolutely perfect goddamn role model, and I gave no hint of the fact that I would have been delighted to lean across the desk and kiss his adorable little face. I felt useful as a teacher, for about the first time this term.

DECEMBER 14: I graded papers & made a quick trip to the Toulouse-Lautrec exhibit at MOMA. Beautiful stuff, but the crowds were impossible. One felt, well, dwarfish, trying to stand on one's toes to see over the rows of people between oneself and the paintings.

. . .

Robert Massa, back from Germany, calls. He spent a lot of time in the East. He says it's not so bad except you realize that any friend you make will never come visit you. And if you mention fear of flying, no one knows what you're talking about. He said he realized he was back in New York when the other day he saw a well-dressed man and a well-dressed woman, both carrying shopping bags full of Christmas presents, having a fist fight over a taxicab.

DECEMBER 16: The *capo di tutti capi* got rubbed out tonight [at Sparks Steak House] a few blocks from here (3rd & 46th). The police say no one will admit to being an eyewitness. Can't imagine why.

DECEMBER 18: . . . A sleepless night (a young woman braying to a young man, outside my window about how "sensitive" she is) . . .

DECEMBER 23: I just hope it doesn't turn out that I can't love [Steve Smith] because he loves me. If that turns out to be the beast in my jungle, the real repeating condition in my psychology—well, then I really would be better off dead.

DECEMBER 28: [At the movies, alone, to see *A Chorus Line*, when I see [W.] come in with a date] I didn't get a good look at the boyfriend, but enough of one to convince me he's handsome. Wearing a black shirt. I'm sure [W.] saw me—they came part way up the aisle, facing me—but I pretended I was looking elsewhere. I panicked, thought I should leave as soon as the lights went down. Felt I had LONELY FRUMP written on me in neon letters. But my self respect & cheapness battled back: damn it, I'm an American citizen who's paid $6 to see this movie & I'm going to see it.

So I stayed. And managed to keep my mind on the film for maybe 75% of the time. When the kid sang "I Can Do That," I thought, "I can get past this." And when Cassie sang "What I Did for Love"—I wondered if he might just be thinking of me thinking of him.

DECEMBER 31: [New Year's Eve with Doug and Bruce] We went over to Chez Napoleon way over on the West Side near Daddy's birth block. Ate a good dinner until about 10:30 and then actually dared to go to Times Sq. Rain, mounted police, sawhorses, surging crowds, roaring, a feeling of being trapped, violence and stampeding possible at any second—and still somehow insanely happy. We loved it in spite of ourselves and even though we didn't stay. We left at about 11:00, having had enough of a taste of pandemonium. We walked back to the East Side through the forties, joking, jostling, Bruce & I blaring horns in Doug's ears & in response to hornblowings from the hotels in the canyons. We blew salutes to Leona in the Helmsley Walk, blared greeting to the trains below the gratings on 46th St. I was in love with New York and everything all over again.

The actual ringing in was a little bizarre. We decided to find a gay bar. We didn't have much time [until midnight] & I said I thought there was one called Sapphire on 1st Ave. We found it—& it turned out to be full of old white men slavering over little Asian geisha boys.

1986

JANUARY 1: Mom called from Georgiana's, where she spent last night. She had a New Year's announcement. She says she wants me to have the money from Uncle Tom, which will be coming through in a month or two. What am I to do about this? How does one say yes? How does one say no? She says she doesn't need any more: her house is paid for and she's got $60,000 in the bank. I can give her some of the interest. I can put it into the apartment. I can feel less chained to Vassar . . . I just mumbled an ungracious sort of "please, no," & said we'd talk about it another time. My God. Think about it.

JANUARY 2: I recently became entranced with an old *Life* cover showing Rene Carpenter watching her husband go up into space in 1962 . . . So I went to locate it in used magazine stores—God, they smell wonderful—on W. 43rd and W. 26th. Got it at the latter. Got a frame for it up near 57th & 3rd. I did a very good job of framing it all by myself. It's on the wall above my desk now . . . I don't know what I think of it. It's romantic, patriotic, sad (they got divorced), exhilarating & dangerous ("55 Minutes That Lasted Forever"). It speaks to me. It interests me. I can tell you, though, what it is not. It is not Pop Art and it is not "ironic."

JANUARY 3: [Katrina Kenison and I] began to rip apart *Arts & Sciences* with serious relish . . . came to an agreement that its flaws are more ones of plot than style or character. And then we talked about remedies: maybe giving Artie Angela at the end; perhaps having him win big academically (which is what Mary McCarthy always thought best). By the end of the meeting I was all fired up to get back to it & fairly sure that after all the vicissitudes it still has a shot over at T&F and I should go ahead.

JANUARY 5: [In a gay bar] heard a conversation between 2 men. The one who was doing the flirting was telling his object how hard it is for anyone to get AIDS. He knows because he used to work at Pfizer pharmaceuticals.

. . . I've been at my desk tonight, chipping away at *Stolen Words* & *Arts & Sciences*. (The choice of phrase is revealing: "chipping away." I don't view any writing as the creation of something; it's really just a task to be completed, something that results in neurotic relief.)

Read more of Spender's journals—a few bits about Isherwood. Between those bits I heard on the TV that Isherwood has died in California.

JANUARY 6: Dinner with Big Tom. I went up to his place on East End Avenue . . . It's a depressing apartment: old manuscripts that won't be published; dog-eared journals; a bachelor mess with some beautiful Tommy pictures redeeming it. But he doesn't really live there, I suppose. It's more of a studio. He spends most of his time at Gloria's. Still, it looks like the Nowhere Man's place.

We went out to dinner at Monte Carmela on 1st Ave. & it wasn't awkward at all. He's much stronger than he was a year ago. We did talk about Tommy, but he wasn't searching for posthumous solutions and absolutions. We also talked about AIDS. He said he hoped I was being "careful." . . . He says that when it came to sex Tommy was an addict. He tried to warn him against excesses years ago, but there was no point to it.

JANUARY 8: Tried to take care of my cold. Read Spender: as drowsy-making as the cold medicine. Wrote out my application for a Rockefeller Fellowship & watched Bill the super try one more time to fix my radiator.

JANUARY 10: [London] Checked into a hotel in Tottenham Court Road and went out wandering. Found [the British edition of] *ABOOO* in a couple of bookstores and felt pleased, though, God, is the cover ever ugly. Amazed by how *little* London seems. It's so *airy*. I used to be struck by its massiveness. I was scared of it: I was a poacher of its literature, intimidated by the supposedly smarter Brits. Everything gave off a feeling of immensity. Now New York is thoroughly inside me & I look at London & think what Horace Walpole is supposed to have said about Versailles: "What a huge heap of littleness."[*]

JANUARY 11: Began the day in terror in a teashop. I was writing postcards (all with the wrong date) and reading the *Herald Tribune*, which carried a story about how it's now thought vastly more people exposed to the AIDS virus will actually get it than was previously reckoned. Weeks have gone by without my worrying. I think: "Thank God, it's now 3 years." But people are still getting sick 6 years after being exposed. Maybe I've been kidding myself. Maybe this diary is just a long good-bye note.

JANUARY 12: [Returning to St. Edmund's House in Cambridge, where I'd been a visiting scholar in 1982–83] I was too tired and terrified to get much sleep. Got up and went down into the chapel at 6 a.m. to pray. . . .

I felt better when I got up from my [knees]. I went back upstairs and sat down, struggling with the gas fire, to read Spender's poems. I wrote my review of them and the journals tonight, & I think it's the best short piece I've done in a while.

. . . Took a walk into town after [breakfast]. Cold & windy & bright. The streets nearly empty; term hasn't started yet. I could

---

[*] Walpole actually referred to a judgment by Thomas Gray.

hear each of my footfalls make a satisfying click as I walked past King's. Came back here with the papers. The *Observer* says *ABOOO* has been "justly applauded." Julian Symons in the *TLS* says it's "engaging" and "sophisticated." So I'm pleased . . .

Carried the water and wine to the altar at offertory. So many familiar faces in the chapel: the Elsmores, Mrs. Archdeacon (who's retired as proprietress of the Cow & Calf: she used to have a panic button under the bar—it would flip off whatever IRA song was playing on the jukebox when she saw a British patron taking offense).

. . . The place does get a little smarter, and a little less Catholic, each time I come to it.

JANUARY 13: I was sitting in the Combination Room with the papers just before breakfast when Sylvia walked through and gave me a hug: "'Allo, luv, you don't look a die aoulder." We had a nice chat. She told me all about the attempts to tart up the place, which she doesn't like, and about [Father Coventry's] last days, when he was pretty much manic-depressively off his head. The medication only made things worse for a while. "It was 'is tablets." He's in London now and doing fine. "'E was a cantankerous old sausage," Sylvia says, and she clearly misses him.

His portrait is in the refectory now—looking right down on the place he used to sit.

. . . [With my friend Jonathan Kahn in Grantchester, about which I was doing a travel article for *The New York Times*] Weirdly enough, Jono's father is buried right near the church. He worked in Cambridge in the 70s & had an apartment in the new Vicarage. He got on well with the new vicar, who fixed things so that Mr. Kahn, an unbelieving Jew, could be buried in the churchyard in 1978 . . . We tramped around for about an hour and a half looking for local color—which today was mostly gray.

JANUARY 14: [Visiting Claire Blunden, widow of my dissertation subject, WWI poet Edmund Blunden] Walked down to Mawson Road at lunchtime . . . Dear Claire very much as always. She'd just come back from her yoga class. She told me all about the ceremony in the Abbey, which was something of a scandal of thought-lessness. There are 17 on the stone. Excerpts were read from 15 of the poets, and Blunden was one of the two left out. What a stupid, callous thing to do. But Claire still described it all merrily. They all had to file past the stone, which was flanked by two lighted tapers—one of which her grandson proceeded to blow out.

. . .

Dinner in. Sat near David Wallace who told me briefly about sharing a place in Stanford last year with a man whose lover had died of AIDS. "He hadn't kissed anyone in five years." And David says he began to get a little worried about himself. (Perhaps he was afraid he'd catch it from a doorknob.) There was nothing unkind in this—he couldn't know what torment he was putting me in, that I really wanted to scream as I was sitting there nodding gravely.

JANUARY 15: . . . Off in a taxi to make the 8:52 to Liverpool Street. The tube was in a snarl, but I managed to get out to Bush House, between Aldwych and the Strand, to do a quick [BBC] interview with kind and twinkling Edward Blishen, whose book on school-mastering I'd been enjoying in the train. The tape we made goes out to about 60 countries, so somebody will be eating his morning toast to my words about six weeks from now in Botswana. Even so, it's not a very high-tech operation, and the microphone I spoke into looked as if it could have been used for the abdication speech by the Duke of Windsor.

JANUARY 18: [Dinner in NY with Greg Ullman] He grew up in Florida and was an undergraduate at UF. He's very preppy-looking, & admits to having been his fraternity president. (While he was sleeping with one of his fraternity brothers.) At Columbia Law he was president of the gay students' association. . . .

JANUARY 20: It's the 1st Martin Luther King Day. And George Wallace, still governor of Alabama, gave a speech in his honor.

JANUARY 22: . . . Karen & David & Jim & I sat around watching *Dark Victory* on the VCR and eating popcorn . . . On my way back to Kendrick I saw the *USA Today* box: through the glass, fifty years later, Reagan [who played in the movie] was saying he won't raise taxes.

JANUARY 25: [An evening in New York with Elmer and Sophie Blistein, my favorite Brown professor and his wife] . . . They seem ageless to me: Sophie never changes her hairstyle, and Elmer still has a mum in his lapel. They made much of *A Book of One's Own* & everything else . . . We were doing our Homer & Artie act. (I've never yet told him anything about *Arts & Sciences*, but he'll be pleased to have a walk on.) We talked about the old days— Cambodia & Kent State & Vietnam—and we might have been talking about the 100 Years' War.

JANUARY 28: The space shuttle blew up this morning 72 seconds after it left the ground. All 7 crew members, including the charming high-school teacher from New Hampshire, died. The tape is played over and over on TV, like Kennedy's exploding head. But the odd thing about this explosion is that it is easily as beautiful— great billows of orange, white and blue—as it is terrifying. People are, it seems, deeply affected by it . . . The odd thing is that it will probably rekindle interest in the space program—by returning to it some of the original danger that made it so attractive.

JANUARY 29: . . . A long meeting of tenured members of the department to discuss salaries for the "lower ranks." I love Lynn Bartlett. He finds something nice to say about everyone, as if he were one of the Cheeryble brothers telling the comptroller to dig in deeper for a better raise for the person being discussed. Charlie would recommend an "average" raise for someone, and then Lynn would come back with "Now, Charles," and mention how he always hears whomever's being talked about conferring with students after 5:00 . . .

FEBRUARY 1: Steve left me this morning to go to work with lots of kisses and whispers. Why can't I contrive some way to let this be It? But of course I can't. Still, I didn't feel regretful . . . I felt comfortable, realistic, physically relieved.

. . .

[Seeing the musical version of *The Mystery of Edwin Drood* with Louise]: Cleo Laine was wonderful, smoky & raunchy. Betty Buckley's voice is thin but affecting. The only thing I object to was the fact that they're all miked within an inch of their lives. You can hear their body mikes scraping their buttons when they dance. Ethel Merman must be scowling in her grave.

We ended the evening in "Harry's Bar" in Leona's Harley Hotel (just renamed for Helmsley, actually; a last little tribute from her before the old coot dies, I suppose).

FEBRUARY 4: Congratulated Demo—OUP has taken his book for a British version; he's quietly, luxuriously, anticipating the moment he'll tell Charlie—he's sucking on it like a candy. And he looks better than ever. I asked Ann if she'd heard the news about the book & she said, "Yeah, I got a hug out of it." (So did I.)

. . . Sat down at the microfilm reader & looked at old clips about Scott & Rene Carpenter, who fascinate me. The Loud family of space. By '68 she was dressing like a go-go girl and talking like a "kook" (her word). She was travelling around as Ethel Kennedy's "sidekick" in the '68 primary campaign. After '68 she disappears from the papers. Scott Carpenter only shows up every so often in the 70s with some crazy business venture (wasp-raising; methanol fuel). I'd like to write about them. I'd like to write about everything. But I have no time.

FEBRUARY 6: Nice mail at home: a letter from Mary in Paris; a knitted tie from Loree; a letter from Wlady [Pleszczynski] at *The American Spectator* saying he wishes I could be in every issue. And Mike Leahy called from the *Times* to say he loves the Grantchester piece. A good writerly day.

FEBRUARY 7: [An evening with Steve]: The proof that sex is mostly in the imagination is that "safe sex" can be just as frenzied as what's now "dangerous." We are perfectly comfortable and friendly with one another—& know almost nothing about one another.

FEBRUARY 8: [At the movies with Greg] The juggler entertaining across the street from the long ticket line wound around 59th St. ought to have been arrested as a public menace; he dropped his flaming, flying sticks twice.

FEBRUARY 12: Ended the evening red-penning *Arts & Sciences*. God, is there a lot of jiggling fat that's coming off. I'm always explaining my jokes in extra clauses.

FEBRUARY 13: Dinner in the pub with Nancy & Eric Lindbloom. This was planned long ago. Ann & I once made a list of all the happy people in Poughkeepsie & they were the only people on it. . . .

Back to Avery—Lynn Bartlett's office—for my first nighttime personnel meeting . . . Charlie did do a weird invocation of the departed spirit of John Christie—quoting something he once said about the need for open-mindedness. This was rather like beginning a meeting of the League of Women Voters with a saying from Ferdinand Marcos.

FEBRUARY 15: On Saturday mornings Steve will put his arm around my waist while we lie in bed, and if I'm sexually greedy I'll respond and we'll do it again. And if I'm not, I'll find myself unable to respond with even simple physical affection. What can he get out of this?

FEBRUARY 16: Talked with Mom about all the complicated business of investing this $80,000. We're so nervous and worried and would-rather-not-think-about-it that you'd think we were talking about a debt instead of a windfall.

FEBRUARY 17: It's midnight and I'm feeling awful. We had our first meeting about Ann tonight, & things are looking much closer than I'd expected . . . Ken, who hasn't written a syllable in 20 years, claims to be disturbed by Ann's approach to Spenser in an article she's published.

I do think she's got the votes to come through, but the result is likely to be weak—something like 8 to 5 . . . Demo & I are in there fighting hard.

FEBRUARY 20: Susan Sontag is coming next week to do a panel discussion on genre (something after Michael Murray's[*] hermeneutical heart) and I'm supposed to do the introduction (the king of cute glibness).

FEBRUARY 21: [Another meeting about Ann's tenure] [W. & P.] are unbelievable: they always make these speeches of high-minded pap about how we should *listen* to one another (like Charlie invoking John Christie!), about how we should "exchange views" and not adopt "strenuous" positions that are "adversarial." The real meaning of these speeches is the implication that anyone who's spoken strongly has acted in bad faith. It's amazing how they get away with this. It passes for "statesmanship" with a lot of the dimmer bulbs, too. But it's fake. The only open parts of [P.'s] mind are the empty ones—a considerable terrain.

FEBRUARY 23: [A Lambda cocktail party in NYC] Lambda is all so respectable. Congressman Weiss was there; a *Saturday Night Live* star; Larry Kramer; the gay City Council candidate (Rothenberg) . . . [Someone] talked to me about his work for the New Alliance party, and how great they'll be for gays. I asked him if these weren't the same New Alliance people I saw demonstrating on behalf of Farrakhan on 3rd Avenue the other day. Well, yes, he admitted. But he really thinks Farrakhan is trying to have a "dialogue" with Jews and gays, & that it's important for all left-of-center people to come together. Of course Farrakhan wants the Jews and gays to speak their side of the dialogue while they're marching off to the gas chamber. But I didn't say this. I just said "no sale" & excused myself over to the *hors d'oeuvres*.

FEBRUARY 27: . . . The panel on genre with Susan Sontag, who I thought was a thumping bore. She never thanked me for my

---

[*] Michael Murray, Vassar professor of philosophy from 1970 to 2013.

introduction; she condescended to the students; and she went crazy when I inadvertently waved the red flag of Norman Mailer. I raised his name innocently enough—in connection with the New Journalism and the blending of genres. Well, she (who personalizes everything) started growling about how she's no fan of Mailer's; how *The Armies of the Night* isn't a good book; how the New Journalism is just a base coinage of "the lowest minds" in journalism itself; how they (the New Journalists) were all too illiterate to know they weren't doing anything different from what Defoe did. Blah, blah, blah. And it was all because of Mailer, who reduced her to tears at the PEN conference last month.

And Barbara sat there reverentially through the whole thing. Even when SS trotted out the hoariest lines ("Perhaps I pick a violent metaphor because I live in a violent country").

MARCH 1: Talked to Mom on the phone: she advises me to join a health club to meet boys. My mom—Woman of the 80s!

. . . [With Doug and Bruce] saw a movie called *My Beautiful Laundrette*. It's British, about London Pakistanis who are making it (while losing their souls, of course). The great twist is that the entrepreneurial kid has an affair with a sexy MALE punker who's become sold on Thatcherism—or at least work. One still gasps seeing two men make love on screen in anything but a porno movie. (A few straight women could be seen exchanging have-we-got-the-wrong-film? glances on the ticket line.) . . . The punker, who licks the other boy's choice little brown neck, was played by C. Day Lewis's son—a better actor than his father was a poet.

MARCH 2: I'm fully recovered from the flu—without antibiotics, either. And I ran 6.4 miles today. (My immune system has to be working. I *can't* have it.)

MARCH 4: Worked in the office & listened to Tom Beller complain about his advisor, Beverly Haviland. (Her real trouble is that she refuses to find him adorable.)

MARCH 6: [The NBCC awards down at NYU] I sat in front of Joni Evans, the brash Simon & Schuster executive profiled in *New York* this week . . . She and her brassy friends cluck about how badly reviewers are paid—not out of sympathy with the reviewers, but with a superior feeling about what dumb schmucks reviewers are. Almost nobody shows up to pick up his award. Anne Tyler, Leon Edel, William Gass—all absent. And it's not like the Oscars where sometimes another star fills in. Here all you get is an agent or an editor. Louise Glück, who won the poetry award and who was there to accept it, gave a beautiful little speech that ended with her saying how "encouraged" she was. . . . .

MARCH 7: Down to [Uncle] Charlie's. And whom do I meet? A pretty, smiling young man of 28; a lawyer; funny, grew up in Red Cloud, Nebraska (Willa Cather's town); affectionate; looking for someone special. God, I thought. Look what I'm meeting. *Here*, of all places . . .

And then I learn the other important fact: his law firm is sending him to Singapore for a year. He leaves in 2 weeks.

And I went home with him anyway.

MARCH 9: It occurs to me that most of my dates are with handsome lawyers who own studio co-ops.

MARCH 10: [Dinner at Parnell's with my Vassar colleague Iva Deutchman] She writes letters to William Safire fulminating about sexist language, and tonight at dinner she tells me she likes a man who holds doors for her. Her politics are Vladivostok and her outfits are Vegas. Arafat is her idea of a political good guy & Sidney Sheldon her idea of a good read.

MARCH 11: Jay & I, in 96 hours, have run through a whole affair. We're already in let's-be-friends "aftermath" . . . We started having a what-do-you-want-out-of-life conversation . . . Only gay men use the phrase "love of my life"—usually about some semi-straight college roommate who got away. Only gay men talk about their "ideal body type," assuming any affair to be properly doomed if the partner is off by a millimeter or an eye color . . .

MARCH 14: Tinkered with the reviews in the afternoon & at 5:30 started out to meet Louise . . . at La Boîte au Bois on W. 68th St. . . . [After dinner] we walked to Avery Fisher Hall. Boulez is back at the Philharmonic. And people are once more walking out. The program was Stravinsky, Debussy & Boulez. His own stuff was 3 Mallarmé poems set, atonally and excruciatingly, to music. They were shrieked, syllable by syllable, in a frightening way by a soprano who looked like Kate Smith before Kate Smith shrank to the size of Rose Kennedy.

MARCH 15: I got my hair cut by Nancy, who of course had her own slant on the Donald Manes death [the Queens borough president had stabbed himself]: "He didn't do it; the *wife* did it." Then up to the Plaza to meet James Lord in the Oyster Bar . . . The two of us had 2 bowls of stew, a few glasses of wine, a plate of oysters (his), a bowl of strawberries (mine). Well, that came to $105. Out of his money clip . . . He told me that Giacometti's widow is circulating a petition vs. the book—saying it's all lies—in Paris. Simone de Beauvoir is one of the signers, though he's sure she's never read the book. He tells me about the day he went to interview Sartre for it. When he arrived outside the apartment door he heard de Beauvoir reading to him—"in a fast voice, without any tone or rhythm, like a machine." Well, lunch was grand, and we walked out into the sun—the sun! after so much wretched rain—James toward Tiffany's and I, slightly drunk, toward home.

MARCH 18: [In Portland with my college friend Jay Geary] People tell me my memory is good. But I don't remember him coming down to Well St. And I don't remember him coming to the Galbraiths'. And I don't remember seeing the Henry Miller documentary at the Orson Welles together. But he brings up details of all these occasions. Maybe I was so in love with him once that I forever dissociate him from any bits of real life in my memories.

MARCH 19: . . . I did one of those *Good Morning, Portland* type shows before a "live studio audience" of schoolkids mostly, who clap happily on command.

MARCH 20: All day long I seemed a step ahead or behind Ronald Reagan's daughter. At 9:30 I was in Rob & Jane's kitchen [in Seattle] eating cereal and watching her on *Good Company* . . . She was pushing her book about Daddy and Mommy. A half hour later I was on the same set taping a segment with the same glib, pancaked host. From there Susan Ruddy—pretty as Sue Ellen Ewing and, I discover, interesting, too—drove me to a radio station where I did several minutes. The interviewer had Patti Davis's book on his console. "Oh, has she been here?" I asked. "No, she's coming later."

. . .

I hate that queer, dear neutered feeling that comes over me when I'm with my friends' children—and it's heightened by a new feeling of being a potential AIDS bogeyman from the city of sin—but I was quite content in their living room. [Rob and Jane Doggett] couldn't be more loving, & I wonder what the hell it is that makes me seem so special to them. We did wind up talking about Tommy's death & disease—they started it. I didn't want to get into it, but I admired them—loved them, even—for bringing it up.

MARCH 21: Read the *Times* on the plane [back to New York]. The gay rights bill has passed the City Council & the rate of increase in AIDS cases in the city has levelled off. Dear God, somehow get me through this. Stop the killing & don't let me be in the last set of casualty figures.

MARCH 24: I didn't get the Guggenheim. I didn't expect it & they granted less than a tenth of the applications. I can make it through my six payless months next year by drawing on the interest the Scudder fund will make. So this is not any disaster. Still, it makes one blue. It's as if your book has gotten a bad review before it's written.

MARCH 25: Iva, as usual, is politically mad, says Qaddafi is saner than Reagan . . . Frankly I don't care if RR bombs the whole goddamned country, so long as none of them demonstrate on E. 45th St.

MARCH 28: Here it is Good Friday & I'm like one of the moneychangers in the temple. I spent most of the morning with roly-poly Arthur Greene & his executive phone doing my tax return. I talked Keogh Plans, IRAs and deductibles. . . .

MARCH 30: I went down to Louise's late in the afternoon. She asked me if I wanted my letters to Tommy. I was shocked that he'd saved them. But it turns out they were all there . . . She found a letter from a monastery in MN from May 1981. The head monk was responding to an inquiry of Tommy's. Unfortunately Tommy's letter had gotten chewed up in the mail sorter, & the monk was having to respond as best he could: "Regarding your remarks (questions?) about celibacy: this portion of the letter is particularly mangled." Louise read this and laughed so hard she nearly cried. She says she's never seen a clearer intervention of God's hand . . .

How desperate he was. O my dear desperate darling.

I walked home in the beautiful Easter sunshine thinking that what I want is to feel what I felt when I met him. No more of these cheap, sordid half-way budget romances. But the real scarifying thing again. I reread those little cards and letters [I sent Tommy] from England. How often I'm addressing his pain, or saying how happy I am over his telling me he's had a good week. And that awful letter from August. Which is the only really honest one. The rest are all so sadly clever: desperate to please, straining to be adorable, fake spontaneity that's gone through a rough draft or two.

MARCH 31: . . . To an exhibition of Halsman photographs in the Paine Webber Building: Magnani's meaty eyelids; Clement Greenberg's big pores; what must be a misdated JFK; a crazed-looking Father D'Arcy; and one of the "jump" pictures of Nixon, who still looks, mid-air, as if he's giving a speech.

APRIL 5: At the MML xeroxing junk for my crazy Carpenter notion & not writing my real book [about plagiarism].

APRIL 8: Lunch by myself & then a very good class on Auden. An hour on "Spain" and an hour on the Yeats elegy. Rachel peeked in during the break between the halves. I went out into the hall & she whispered to me that she's pregnant.

APRIL 11: I walked up to the Regent East for a nightcap. The only time I've been in there alone. I stood frozen. Nobody talked to me or vice versa. I just had this Dantesque vision of myself standing there ten years from tonight sweating and singing "What I Did for Love" with the rest of them around the piano.

APRIL 12: Tonight Robert Massa and I went to see Meredith Monk at La MaMa. It was just awful. We left halfway through. He wasn't writing about it, just seeing it to help him make up his mind about Obie Awards voting. Half of it was enough for that. I suppose it had something to do with the "blocked creative process"—I think she may have been trying to illustrate that—but it was a lot of schizy, chanting, repetitive sounds with a lot of schizy, jerky movements. If you saw a homeless person doing it outside Grand Central you wouldn't look twice . . . It is impossible to have an aesthetic reaction to anything that gives an impression of randomness.

APRIL 14: [Before tax filing] Went from bank to bank sheltering money: IRA at Marine Midland, Keogh at Chase. (All these secretaries on line with IRA contributions—it really is the ordinary person's little gold mine, everybody getting a little nugget of the Reagan strike.)

APRIL 16: [Nancy Graves was the President's Distinguished Visitor at Vassar] I can see how she gets the sculptures to stand up, but I can't imagine how she gets the hairdo to . . . A weird moment when she presented a sculpture to the college. She set it on a pedestal near the lectern. We all applauded this object that none of us could really see.

APRIL 17: I taught, had conferences, and late in the afternoon went over to the art gallery to see an exhibit of Nancy Graves's work . . .

Some of them are beautiful things: witty, delicate. And the colors are wonderful, everything enamelled in little light-catching swirls. The paintings did nothing for me, but I had an acquisitive response to the sculptures . . .

[Over dinner at the nearby Culinary Institute of America] Nancy Graves *very* serious, even severe. No one seems to know much about her except that along with being a good artist she's a good businesswoman.

. . . I didn't get out of Poughkeepsie until 10:26, and it was 12:30 when I was back in New York. I was still a little drunk from dinner, and coming down from three busy days, so what do I do? I go down to Charlie's. And have another drink . . . When I go down to that bar I know what I'm doing. I'm putting myself in a situation where I can't lose. In the back of my mind, I want to go home with someone. And if I do, I've "scored." And if I don't I've "resisted temptation," skirted danger and come through. Either way I get a little jolt.

APRIL 18: Yesterday Becky Goodheart (that wonderful Dickensian name) came into my office. She's an adorable little Brit, sort of a female Jonathan, and we had a long discussion. Her father is a Conservative MP (he came in in 1959 in the Macmillan-Gaitskell election). She is not keen on [Reagan's] Libya raid, but for an interesting, moderate reason: she says it will give the Laborites an argument for getting rid of the American Air Force bases (since Mrs. T. gave permission for the planes to take off from them), and she doesn't want to see that happen. Most of the Europeans loathe us just now, & I think that's fine.

APRIL 20: . . . I stayed up to watch my favorite program on television, with the exception of *Moonlighting*: *Naked City*. I think I would have liked living in New York when it was in black & white.

APRIL 25: I got it [a Rockefeller Fellowship run through the Poetry Center of the 92nd St. Y]. I reached Shelley Mason this morning & she told me. She says they found my proposal "very idiosyncratic" but interesting. They were a little hesitant to give me the award because they like the winners to live up at the Y. But she says I can use the room as an office & stay over when I want. I can also use the gym and the pool and the library. All I've got to do for the $20,000 is give a sort of one-night-a-week mini-course on the diary in the fall or spring . . . This is a financial, professional and personal bonanza. Even sweeter since I'd given up on it.

APRIL 26: [Greg Ullman and I] discussed the awful Buckley tattoo piece in the *Times* (there's to be a demonstration in front of *NR* on Wednesday). He thinks I should pull whatever copy I have at *NR*. I asked him if he thinks I should stop writing for the *Times*; they ran the [Buckley] piece.

APRIL 28: Forgot to mention that on Saturday I talked with Louise, back from seeing Halley's Comet in Peru. She said there was an 88-year-old woman there who said it didn't compare with 1910.

MAY 2: . . . A party the Trustees were giving in Connecticut for Virginia [Smith] . . . took place in a huge old barn in Greenwich, on some rich man's estate, that's been converted into a kind of whirling funhouse. Slot machines, test-your-strength machines, player pianos—on and on and all clicking and whizzing at once. A little as one imagines Michael Jackson's bedroom to be.
    . . . Going home I talked a little with Mrs. Mason Smith. She's the daughter of Olive Higgins Prouty, Sylvia Plath's patroness. She asks me if I'd like sometime to take a look at a lot of the correspondence she still has relating to Plath's hospitalization at McLean. She says OHP was outraged by how the McLean doctors used to let SP just sit and veg. Get her to type something, OHP suggested. The McLean people replied that they had nothing for her to type. Then let her type out the poems of Keats, OHP wrote back.

MAY 6: Everyone is telling Chernobyl jokes now instead of *Challenger* ones. ("Did you hear about the next generation of Swedes? Blue hair and blond eyes.")

MAY 8: Tom [S.], back in Iowa, called. He says his mother has found out he's gay. She emptied the pockets of a jacket & discovered a map of Amsterdam with some strategic locations marked on it.

MAY 9: [With Doug MacKay at lunch] He was a little glum: the co-op hassles; having to fire his secretary; being account executive during an unbelievably boorish and butch campaign by Schmidt's beer ("It's not for interior decorators; it's not for . . .")

MAY 10: My wing chair was finally delivered this morning. It's as if some big Edwardian spaceship has landed in the apartment. The wings are wide enough to fall asleep against. The whole thing is big enough to make love in. It is so vulgar, butch and beautiful.

MAY 11: Shelley Mason called about 7:00 and said that her introducer for Alice Walker tomorrow night has dropped out. Could I possibly do it? I said yes, though I shouldn't have. I've read about half an essay by Alice Walker . . . The lecture hall is bound to be packed and I'll be doing a "But I did see the movie!" introduction. I went down to the Book Worm on 3rd Avenue before it closed & came home with a couple of her books.

MAY 12: Well, Alice Walker isn't *terribly* warm, but she's a lot nicer than Susan Sontag.

. . .

Brought my review over to the *Times*. Anatole took it; he's spacier than ever. Says he read about my Rockefeller in the paper, which I don't think is possible. His hair is so light & he's so thin. He seems to be evaporating.

MAY 15: Ticknor & Fields was having a big publication party for Jimmy Breslin in the saloon of the Oyster Bar. "This is costing us the equivalent of four weddings," Katrina said; but they hope the new novel, *Table Money*, will be a huge seller. Breslin, who gave me a how-ah-ya handshake, is even the host of *Saturday Night Live* this week.

MAY 17: [A gallery opening for an exhibit of David Schorr's illustrations for Phyllis Rose's *Parallel Lives*] They were selling for

$900 each, and for a moment I deeply desired the one of Charles Dickens, which is surely the best of the lot. It's funny: in the text of *Parallel Lives* the women always come off better than the men; in the drawings it's the men who almost always look better. I suppose that's what happens when you get a feminist & a gay man collaborating.

MAY 18: . . . At Lincoln Center at 9:00 for the AIDS Walk . . . A rally in front of the band shell in Damrosch Park before the march. Ed Koch says, "You *know* this must be an important event if *The Village Voice* is sponsoring it and I'm here." Then, after an uneasy murmur, he says, "It's just a *joke*." Lots of gay politicians . . . Peter Allen is the only glitz. He comes out and sings a new song about how "what we don't have is time."

MAY 25: Went way down 3rd Avenue for a drink . . . Someone from Queens came up to me and started a conversation. I believe his fourth line was "Do you enjoy being blown?" I should have said "What's not to like?" but I just gave him a no-thanks smile.

MAY 28: I am already fretting about having to go back to Vassar a year from now, about having to face the fact that I can only be a writer one year in every four.

   . . .

[At the 92nd St. Y, E. L. Doctorow read a story] about a German boy around 1910 who catches his mother having sex with his tutor. Doctorow says he read [it] at a German university not long ago. After he finished, a German boy asked him why Jewish-American writers are so sex-obsessed. Doctorow replied: "Because we're trying to assimilate."

MAY 29: Got a late start. I'm still dazed by the fact of being on leave. I'm wandering around like the Count of Monte Cristo or something. I've clawed my way out of a dungeon, and now I'm stumbling around in the light, looking for the highway. I'm too confused and excited to settle down.

MAY 30: We ate outside at the café near the tram & 59th St. bridge, traffic pleasantly roaring all around us. Louise in good form, I thought. Grimmest subject matter: the death of Perry Ellis—from encephalitis, the papers say. It's AIDS, of course, but I suppose if you're the surviving directors of a rich sportswear company, you don't want Mrs. Shopper in Dubuque to have that on her mind.

. . .

I like [Robert Massa], but I never know what will register with him & what won't. He's tremendously bright but sometimes he's like the Moneymatic when it's not up to speed. You wait an extra ten seconds for the cash. It comes, but it comes slowly. It's like that with Robert—he lets every penny go through an extra set of chutes and gates before he finally lets you see it drop.

MAY 31: [At the NYPL] I noticed that the painting of the blind Milton being read to by his daughters has been taken down from the landing of the north staircase. Is it just being cleaned? Stored? Since 1968 I've never been in the library without seeing it. This feels ominous, as if a sea-change in my life is about to happen.

JUNE 2: [*National Review*'s Chilton Williamson tells me my review of John O'Hara's short stories] has never run because he thinks it's "a little thin." He may still run it, but it might have to go as a brief. I'm insulted, and I tell him I think it's one of the best pieces I wrote for him . . . I honestly think that the trouble at *NR* is ideological (aside from Chilton's sloth & carelessness—losing copy, etc.). I think in '81 and '82 they were pretty hot for me—people even wrote in & said they liked me; I got nice notes from them and so forth. Then I praised Vidal & panned Muggeridge & I think they got suspicious. I think the word went out that I was a good writer but ideologically unreliable . . . I'm not comfortable there now anyway—not with Buckley proposing tattoos for AIDS victims. It ain't easy being a gay neoconservative. Well, *NR* gave me my start as a commercial writer 5 years ago, and for that I'm grateful & always will be. But this is it. I'm not going to write briefs for them while the front of the magazine gets ever more dubious.

JUNE 7: Dear Doug is really a model citizen—this morning he was taking on a new patient for GMHC (a 51-year-old street vendor now in St. Luke's with pneumocystis; he's been married twice, but he hints he used to fool around with boys, though he doesn't want to talk about it).

JUNE 8: The Voyager probe—our planet's greeting card to other civilizations out there. And whose voice offers those greetings? Kurt Waldheim's. Sailing millions of miles into the universe are the tones of a Nazi—elected president of Austria today—saying y'all come.

JUNE 11: [With Karen Stolley and David Littlefield at a matinee of *House of Blue Leaves*] . . . The idea that this is a great American play deserving of this splashy Lincoln Center revival: oh, please. It's high-level sitcom (& sometimes pilot-reject sitcom: the nuns braying for imported beer), with improbable lyricism thrown in: Bananas, the wacked-out wife, every so often speaks a purplish bit of Tennessee Williams . . . Suddenly you're supposed to weep for her. But I couldn't even feel sorry for her when she got strangled—it was like seeing a cartoon balloon get deflated. Lots of anachronisms, too: John Lindsay was not mayor of NY in 1965, and the 1st heart transplant didn't occur until 1967.

. . .

Saw Karen, wholesomely beautiful in a pink shirtwaist dress, holding hands with cute David & felt empty. Blessed in so many ways—me, that is—but not like that.

JUNE 12: Went to Saks and bought 2 pairs of Calvin Klein slacks . . . What I realize is that Tommy has already been dead so long that the clothes of his I have are already wearing out. I apprehend this with sadness & relief. But why relief? Do I really think I'm going to get away free? The lead story on NBC News tonight was that they expect there to be 200,000 AIDS cases by 1991. What's to say I still won't fall apart?

JUNE 16: Went down to Forbes at noon for a lunch to celebrate *Extraordinary Lives* [a book of essays on the craft of biography that

I reviewed]. Lunch was in Malcolm Forbes' office, which comfortably seated forty. MF was not there, but his nerdy son presided. That poor, awkward boy! Trying to be witty when nothing could possibly dispel the image of this skinny, geeky kid still cowering beneath plutocrat dad. I guess money makes up for a lot. It has to . . .

JUNE 17: Got into Dublin—dreary, undersized place—early. Booked a room at Wynn's Hotel on Lower Abbey St. Sign of age: usually I'm bounding right out of the room, soon as I've put my suitcase down, but not today. I just kept the torn lace curtains shut and went to sleep for five hours.

   . . .

Had dinner in a wine bar on O'Connell Street & read the paper, which is full of the debate on the divorce referendum, which takes place on the 26th. "Put compassion in the constitution," the posters on the street say. "Vote Yes on Divorce" says one right near the statue of Parnell. It seems the Irish are facing up to adultery a century after it brought him low. They should get around to acknowledging homosexuality in about a thousand years . . .

JUNE 18: Shopped on O'Connell Street. (I do love the statue of Jim Larkin with his hands in the air.). Went into Clery's for presents for the kids. Everything seems tacky, sad, derivative. On the street one notices that none of the clocks agree. Even the one for Jameson's jewelers is off by 15 minutes.

Took the afternoon train to Ballinasloe. Loree was at the station with [my niece and nephew] . . . Chrissie speaks in beautifully clear little sentences. Her voice is all Irish in accent & diction— she says "as well" instead of "too." Seán still has some of his Yank "gob." Chrissie likes Madonna & Boy George & can imitate Ian Paisley ("No surrender!").

JUNE 19: Walked Seán to the two-room schoolhouse down the road. Christina insists on coming along. "Mind the cow dung, Uncle Tommy," she says. This will give you an idea. They're on a first-name basis with donkeys and sheep along the way. The schoolhouse is a plain, ancient little affair. The country children are very shy when a stranger approaches—their heads go down and they offer timid, respectful smiles.

JUNE 22: Loree . . . is trapped in the web of pseudo-Freudian pseudo-insight . . . Mommy never loved her; she just bossed her. I was allowed to do whatever I wanted. (Whenever I am around both Loree & Mom together, I cease, in Loree's eyes, to be her brother; I become her mother's son instead and whatever amity there is between us disintegrates.)

JUNE 23: [At the Municipal Gallery to do a piece for the *Times* Travel section] . . . Ethna Waldron, the curator . . . took me into the Lane room (locked to visitors during the renovations) and I saw all the great pictures stacked against the walls.
    . . .
    [An evening in Dublin with my old St. Ed's friend Joe Dunne] He clearly wanted to talk about my little hopes & dreams & kept pushing the conversation in that direction. So eventually I was out with it & was talking about "men." I was aware of something almost humorously mechanical in it—one more revelation of It to an old friend. I must have good instincts for picking friends, because it never seems to make a difference, eliciting only sympathy, concern, naturalness. So now Joe too knows what he knew anyway.

JUNE 26: [Back in Manhattan] The people on the streets compared to those in Dublin! No more of that drab, pale homogeneity.

JUNE 28: I am the boy who cried wolf, and then went looking, again and again, for one more wolf.

JUNE 29: You always remember a few things. This time it'll be the way he tasted of Scotch; the way he grumbled indifferently when I said goodbye; the way his roommate came home at 5 in the morning and got into a bed across the room . . . Mom called from Ballinasloe at about 10 & I faked pep. She sounds all right. Doug called to find out if I'd changed my mind about going to the parade. I hadn't. I wasn't feeling particularly proud.

JULY 3: Liberty Weekend, beautiful and corny, has begun. I watched the relighting [of the Statue of Liberty] on TV tonight. Ronnie looked calm and happy; Mitterrand somewhat frightened and small.

JULY 4: Shopped for food and laid on dinner for Doug, Bruce & Josh, who got here about 5:00 from the beach. By 7:30 we were making our way to the PATH train and Jersey City, where a work friend of Bruce's, a black guy named Quinton, had invited us for a rooftop view of the fireworks.

Jersey City is a tired, rough-looking place, the sort of town that, if it advertised on late-night TV, would say it was "approved for veterans."

The statue was gorgeous, surrounded by a mad flotilla of tall ships, pleasure boats, luxury liners, aircraft carriers. I'll never forget the sight of it shivering in Doug's binoculars . . . Yes, God Bless America and keep my queer shoulder to the wheel. This is our country, where we'll eventually have our freedom as much as everyone else. Even with the microbiological slaughter going on, would I be anywhere else? At any other time? . . . Home on the PATH train. Talk about huddled masses yearning to breathe free. We were pushed together to the panic point, without air-conditioning. But everyone was in a good mood.

JULY 5: [At a Mets game with Vassar friends] I decided that Phil Garner, an Astro, was the best-looking player on either side, and was thinking how nice it would be to be his boyfriend. And then he hit a home run.

JULY 6: . . . Down to Louise's for supper. Walked down 1st Ave. and at one point looked left towards the Drive, and saw a tall ship, fully under sail, coming up the East River. As improbable as a strolling mammoth . . . We talked of course about the Statue of Liberty festivities & that led to talk of immigrants and ancestors.

She showed me pictures of her two grandmothers on the top shelf of a bookcase in what was Tommy + Mark's room. A picture of Tommy is near the grandmothers. "I hate having him up here with everybody who's dead," Louise said.

JULY 9: Suzanne . . . called from *Newsday* . . . She's running both my royals pieces on Sunday. She's deleted the word "old" from my description of the Duchess of Windsor at the end of her life. "It's such a mean, awful word," she says. I respond, "It's a mean, awful word because people are afraid to use it."

JULY 14: [At the Philharmonic concert outdoors in Central Park] I think I see Ed Koch more often than I do my mother. He came through the crowd tonight—blue-shirted, big-bellied, thumbs up—to start the concert. I'd say 4 people were clapping to every one who was booing: not a bad ratio for someone surrounded by scandal.

JULY 15: *National Review* has paid me almost double the usual for the O'Hara review. And a "nice going" from WFB. I'd love to figure all of this out.

JULY 16: [Running with Front Runners, the gay running club, in Central Park] A mixed, weedy lot, a little like Dignity, though they're in better shape . . . Dinner [with the group] at a big diner on Broadway & 75th after that. I wound up sitting next to a hairdresser, which brought out all my latent class prejudice & homophobia. (Really, no gay should allow himself to become a hairdresser for the next twenty years or so. It's too much like a black being a minstrel.)

JULY 18: Paul [Sachner] tells me about his new love, a 28-year-old named Tim, who's an accountant . . . He & Tim met at a movie— a dirty movie. Paul says he now goes twice a week to "Sexual Compulsives Anonymous" at the Gay Community Center downtown. In fact, he came to the movie right from a meeting. He says he only has safe sex these days but that he goes after it just as compulsively as ever—& with emotional results just as miserable.

JULY 21: [A Harvard friend, Michael Mazzaferro, and I came out to each other] His parents don't know (trans., he hasn't told them), but they would have a lot to rationalize—including half a house in Provincetown that he's bought. We agree that Jenks[*] will be the last one out of the closet. Maybe it's the Ken Weedin Inverts' Inverse rule—the more obvious you are, the longer you stay in.

JULY 22: I've been making progress on *Arts & Sciences*, but I'm at the point where I'm a little afraid of it—where I've got to be tweezering in new scenes & tweezering out old ones. It requires more finesse than what I had to do with the earlier chapters.

JULY 23: I got up early enough to catch the balcony kiss between Fergie & Andy. It was fun watching her—she was having a helluva good time. (I don't see why they keep complaining about her weight. He's the one with the royal love handles now.) They are more fun to watch than Chuck & Di because they so obviously turn one another on. With the other two, you had to wonder what it was—particularly in her case. An ear fetish?

. . . Another hot night. And the Hitachi sign near Columbus Circle lies. It never says worse than "warm"—I suppose because they don't want you associating Hitachi and discomfort.

JULY 24: [Running into W. on 34th St.] He was vague—not giving an emotional dime away, as usual. He just stood there looking stiff & neurotic & beautiful. When the conversation was in safe waters he navigated happily, eager for all my news and opinions on this & that. I represent his ideal friend. . . .

JULY 27: [A visit to the *Intrepid* aircraft carrier] The space museum isn't very good—they even have the date for Aurora 7 wrong on the photo montage, and most of the equipment displayed (a LEM & a Gemini capsule, etc.) comes from Paramount Studios—left over from the filming of James Michener's *Space*. But I got a kick out of the whole thing & it got me thinking of Aurora 7 again.

* James Janke (1954–1993), a Harvard friend who would die of AIDS.

JULY 30: I've at last bought a new sofa bed. A red Chesterfield one, a match for my chair, appeared in the Macy's sale catalogue & this morning I went down to 34th St. to order one from a gay man named Liam . . . I long to get rid of the old one, which is falling apart . . . It's uncomfortable as hell, but I think the other reason I want to get rid of it is that my whole sexual career has been carried out on it & I somehow feel that a new and truly serious relationship deserves a new bed if it's to have a chance at lasting.

. . . Up to Riverside Park for tonight's Front Runners run. (Struck by the # of homeless actually trying to live in the park—little shanties & cookers.). Someone else, not Richard Walker, led the pack tonight. He explained that there were so few people there because a lot of people were attending somebody's memorial service.

AUGUST 1: Chris Bull [now graduated] came by at 6:00 on the dot . . . He looks more beautiful than ever, even though 10 days ago he had his appendix out in Austria. He asked if I wanted to see the scar. And how!

AUGUST 3: It's been three years since I slept with Tommy. Will I make it to five? Will I stop worrying after that? Will I ever stop worrying? Part of me would love to gamble & take the test & rejoice if it turned out negative. But I can't risk what would happen to my mind if it came back positive. I can't do it. And a lot of doctors say one shouldn't for that very reason: don't risk the devastation.

AUGUST 4: A huge package of legal documents arrives from LA— sent by CBS' lawyers in the *Falcon Crest* case. Accompanying it is a note saying I shouldn't write about this case at all. I think they think I'm in agreement with Mrs. Kornfeld [the plaintiff, a novelist suing for plagiarism] when of course I'm not.

AUGUST 5: Roy Cohn's funeral was private. I picture him at the gate of Heaven, St. Peter asking: "Are you now, or have you ever been, a homosexual?" And Roy takes the 5th.

AUGUST 8: The truth is, I think I can finally say I wouldn't want [W.] if I could have him. He's beautiful, and bright and has moments of real charm, but there is such furious self-protection in him, such emotional miserliness, and such a capacity to convince me I'm in the wrong (my own projection, of course), that I would inevitably end up miserable. If anything, he seems more overregulated than before . . . Went home tired, relieved, sad—realizing that all my might-have-beens were really, always, couldn't-have-beens.

AUGUST 12: Tom Beller came by on his bicycle this afternoon for a beer—Ferris Bueller's day off. He's been working in a gallery and writing features for a paper called *The West Side Spirit* . . . He means well, but he is a Vassar student x 2. Thinks his teachers' private lives are his property; believes it's more important to grade a student's effort than anything else; wants fast success & financial reward as a writer. He talks a mile a minute and is very smart, though not as smart as he thinks he is.

AUGUST 15: Wait until Mrs. Mandela takes power. There'll be more blood on her hands than there was on Imelda's. She said something complimentary about "necklacing" the other week. . . .

AUGUST 16: About 3½ miles into my Front Runners run (in the usual awful Saturday morning humidity) I staggered over to a water fountain. A woman behind me said, "I should drink more water. Actually I should drink less wine." I turned around to her and said, "You've put your finger on it."

AUGUST 17: Louise and I went to see *The Perfect Party* (A. R. Gurney) down near Astor Place this afternoon. Sort of a sitcom-Updike affair, WASPs in bewildered decline, funny enough once you let yourself roll with it . . . On the way to the theatre—we walked—we went past 222 E. 17th St., where [the Curleys] lived until 1961 . . . The peculiar Hotel Seventeen across the street used to be home—though not in their day there; way back—to a lot of Tammany figures. We walked on to Union Square, where she & Big Tom used to take Mark & Tommy to play on Sunday afternoons while the loonies were holding forth Hyde Park–style . . .

On our walks to the theatre and back Louise kept remarking on all the places that had been pleasant in the 50s and squalid in the 60s & were now reviving—like Union Sq.

AUGUST 18: [After a dinner with Susan McCloskey and David Kelley] I walked them to their car in a garage on 46th St. & said good night. And all at once I felt lonely and freakish. And I went down to Charlie's & I met someone named Larry . . . and I really don't want to talk about it. Another safe mistake, though an intense, all-night one. Yes, I'm ashamed of myself; think, in fact, that I'm mad. (I'm writing about this with much more control than I feel.) But what am I supposed to do until Mr. Right, who's never coming, it seems, comes along? How many months at a time with no physical contact at all am I supposed to go? What sort of living death is life supposed to be?

. . .

I know that my great hunger is emotional, not sexual.

I know that I must not go into a bar alone, and I know I should not have more than one drink a day.

I know I've said these things before.

. . .

Would there be any point in telling you anything about him?

AUGUST 19: Do I secretly like the aftermaths of these disasters? The chance to feel small & tidy—my own man well at ease [quoting Mary McCarthy quoting Chaucer]—climbing out of the pit, cleansing myself? was today really such a bad day? didn't I almost enjoy my own reformist company, and feel good, like an A.A. member, about my cozy night alone at home?

AUGUST 22: [Although my leave was beginning, I went up to Poughkeepsie for a cocktail party welcoming Vassar's new president, Frances Fergusson.] There was fear on campus all day that Fergie might take office the way John Lindsay did in 1966: the secretaries' union came close to calling for a strike on Monday, but a settlement was reached late in the afternoon (much to the relief of Irene, who despises the union). It all gave faculty a chance to buzz and posture at lunch in the Retreat . . . At a meeting later in the afternoon Tom McHugh waxed pompously ethical about how he was from an old union family and wouldn't cross a picket line. (Actually, before you can cross the picket line you've got to get past the anti-apartheid shacks.)

AUGUST 26: The apartment smells a little like a tannery. The beautiful leather couch arrived. But. The sofabed, while strong, is a good deal narrower than I expected & I'm hoping this is not a portent of my future erotic life. This is "a passion bed," according to Doug, who came over to look at it this afternoon & allay my doubts. One would definitely have to be crazy about whoever was sharing it. . . .

AUGUST 29: Aching all over. The moving of Doug & Bruce turned into a twelve-hour epic. (We'd figured maybe 4.). We could have used an extra person: as it was, it was just Doug, Bruce, me & Quinton (from Viking Penguin)—& Quinton was ornery for part of the morning. He pulled a 20-minute sitdown strike in front of the television . . . It was 2:00 before the truck was loaded & we made the trip to 702 West End. The apartment is quite nice, if small. (I kept telling Doug how big it was.) We ate pizza on the stoop; it's a good-looking building from 1891. Then we began carrying everything five flights up. No elevator . . . By the time we were finished I was in a rubbery delirium . . . Doug and I went to bring the truck back to Ryder. And discovered that the battery was dead. (We'd had the hazard lights on for hours.). We went to two gas stations in search of a jump start & finally procured one from an Exxon place across from the cute Emily Dickinson School (P.S. 75 on W. 96th). At the Mobil station down the street Doug & I stood blocking the entrance to the manager's office while we inquired. A Yuppie woman pushed past us, saying "In or out, boys." We were livid (& speechless). God, now I know how women called girls feel.

AUGUST 31: Jim Connolly [from Front Runners] called and came over in the evening. We talked and drank beer & made out— stopping ourselves before things got out of hand. Which is probably a good thing. I know I would never be romantically inclined toward him. So why start one more sour little failure? He, I think, would like to get involved, but not until he's "sure," and after some sort of courtship. Which is nice, even admirable. He's very old-fashioned in all sorts of ways. He may be gay, but he's still a Woodside male: go out to a diner with him & he's likely to order pie & coffee.

SEPTEMBER 1: Labor Day, & no parade in New York. The unions decided there wasn't enough interest and not much to celebrate, so they let everyone go to the beach instead. Ronnie has gotten everything he ever wanted!

SEPTEMBER 2: [Frank Conroy's *Stop-Time*] It's a very beautiful book. I envy his lack of sentimentality. My own writing is so full of cheap warmth.

SEPTEMBER 3: Doug came over for a drink. He's distressed because he and Bruce are fighting worse than ever. Bruce has already thrown a blanket in his face, proclaimed his hatred for "this fucking apartment," and gone to sleep on the new rug from Bloomingdale's.

. . . I realized it was Tommy's birthday, so I called Louise. She'd just come back from Mark & Missy's. Big Tom was there too. They composed a two-sentence description of Tommy for a bio-line in the journal publishing one of his Boethius pieces.

He's been dead longer than I knew him alive.

SEPTEMBER 4: [Moving into my office at the 92nd St. Y] I've only brought a suitcase's worth of stuff. The fact is I don't want the place to have all the comforts, and distractions, of home. It's on the girls' floor (just my luck), but there do seem to be a lot of attractive Jewish men walking around this place. I'll have to figure out where they're going and hope they're not involved with classical music.

SEPTEMBER 5: Over to the West Side to meet Doug & Bruce for a movie. We saw *She's Gotta Have It*, a gentle (except for one scene) comedy . . . We were in a theatre near Lincoln Center and the audience was about 20% white. A strange, and probably salutary, feeling to be in such a minority. One felt a little like a voyeur, or a diplomat in a foreign capital. We didn't get some of the slang . . .

SEPTEMBER 6: I've been getting some peculiar phone calls lately—no one on the other end—& last night there was one at 4:15 a.m. Just some whispered "Hello." Unnerving. One suspects everyone if one starts thinking about it for more than a minute. And one thinks of all the jerks one's given one's number to—at parties, in bars—over the last few years.

SEPTEMBER 8: Nora Kerr called from the *Times* Travel section. She's sat on the Irish piece so long that now the 1st ¶, with references to the divorce debate & [the boxer] McGuigan, must be cut. It's no longer current. She thinks the piece is nicely written but that the museum subject matter is a little peculiar. She thought, in fact, that Mike Leahy might have commissioned it for Arts and Leisure. I hate *The New York Times*.

SEPTEMBER 9: Talked with cute Ken in the office and saw the Poetry Center's just-printed brochure for the coming year. The description of my mini-course on diaries says that reading will range from "Keats to Anne Frank." (I gave the description to Karl or Shelley over the phone, and whoever it was heard "Keats" for "Pepys.")

. . .

[After seeing a movie with Robert Massa]: We talk a little bit about "What Ever Happened to Gay People?"—a favorite question of Robert's. I think he still views the 70s as a good be-yourself time. It's odd when I get into such discussions. I'll be several years older than the person I'm talking with, but in effect several years younger: I don't know what I was missing. I wasn't in New York, I wasn't even "sexually active," as the phrase goes . . .

A nice jokey, light stroll after that through Times Square. We saw a puffy, glaucomatous David Susskind coming out of *Me and My Girl* and getting into a cab with two blondes (one of them that quasi-famous model from the 50s; Carmen?) and another man. If Robert and I had told him we were bona fide gay people he would probably have booked us for his show so he could ask us why we haven't taken the Aesthetic Realism course to reorient ourselves.

SEPTEMBER 10: The long Aurora 7 mission report did arrive via interlibrary loan, and I xeroxed the whole thing up at the Y. Some amazing stuff in [the transcript of Carpenter's radio communications]. "Oh, I hope not" & "Attitudes are of no concern to me whatsoever. I know I'm drifting freely. The moon crossed the window not too long ago."

SEPTEMBER 11: I finished *Arts & Sciences* today. I know I said this four years ago in England, but this time I've brought it, I think, to its true conclusion. Meaning: this is it. I can do no more with it. I wrote the final Angela-Artie dialogue very quickly, after a walk around the Y's neighborhood to collect my thoughts, and I think it reads well. If you add up all the changes I've made since '82, you'll find they're vast. First, the texture changes after Mary's [McCarthy] 1983 letter. Then, this year, dozens of pages of new text, dozens of pages of deleted text, and enormous parings and adjustments to what was left. The novel is very different in tone and plot. To some extent in characterization. The ms. has been so pummeled that only I can type it.

. . . As I was about to settle down with television I got a call. It was [Ken] from the Poetry Center. He wanted to have a drink. He came down here & we went off to Hobeau's. We were out past two, which is nothing when you're 21. And I listened to all his vocational anxieties & desires to be a writer & tales of drug therapy for panic attacks. Oh, Lord, here I am being Advisor to Cute Troubled Youth again. I do not want this role.

SEPTEMBER 12: Watched news about [Nicholas] Daniloff's "release" to the U.S. Embassy in Moscow (the Russians won hands down on this one) and an Evans & Novak interview with Walter Mondale, who has lost some of the tremendous excitement he conveyed in 1984.

SEPTEMBER 14: Doug and Bruce came by late in the morning and we went off to the 5th Ave. Book Fair . . . The closest thing we saw to a real writer there was Tama Janowitz, who's really a writer aspiring to be a talk-show guest.

SEPTEMBER 18: Should I kiss & make up with *National Review?* A few weeks ago they ran a cover story called "A Conservative States the Case for Gay Rights" and in the last issue there was an interesting, non-Neanderthal debate on the subject in the letters column.

SEPTEMBER 19: There was news today about AZT, a drug that's having some success with AIDS patients. No cure, but it's buying time. And they say it may be especially useful to those who have been exposed but are not yet sick. There is so little good news, ever, that one feels almost giddy about this. God knows it's made my day. I just hope it doesn't have to try saving my life.

Talked with Wlady in the morning. I'm to do Julie Nixon's book about Pat for *The American Spectator* (a galley came personally to them from Michael Korda, a rarity: the Big Dick himself may have arranged it, Wlady thinks). I'll also do the Tom Wolfe novel a few months from now.

SEPTEMBER 20: [Greg Ullman and Ben Petrone and I] ended up at The Works . . . I ran into Tom Wessel from Dignity and told him I had stopped going. So has he, he told me: "This is my Saturday night Mass."

SEPTEMBER 21: Between sections of the paper I walked down to the Morgan Library to see the Housman exhibit (what a "mo," as Doug would say). But I much more enjoyed the exhibition of Mrs. Delany's flowers, paper-cut collages of impossible intricacy made by an old lady in the 18th century. Yuppie mother to 8-year-old daughter: "Do you know this lady lived *200* years ago?" Daughter's reply: "So?"

SEPTEMBER 22: [Ted Hughes' reading at the 92nd St. Y] Something about him—the voice, the boxer's head ducked—reminded me of a Yorkshire Norman Mailer, but that makes him ridiculous & he's not. He's gorgeous & mean & no wonder two of his wives killed themselves. What a reading—not so much oral annotations of the poems (in advance) as great shaggy-dog narratives. Some wonderful WWI stuff about his father, and a beautiful heroic poem about a salmon at the end. I can't remember ever being as wiped out by a reading.

Then to the party for him at Shelley's on W. 70th St. And who should be there but his big ugly sister Olwyn, with whom I had that tetchy correspondence over the Plath journals. At about 11:00 the party was beginning to thin & I feared I'd get into a position where I'd have to introduce myself. I decided it was time to leave, but she was between me & the door. So I told Shelley my name was Fred, & she said gotcha, & she showed me out, saying, "So glad you could come, Fred!" and I made my escape into the Manhattan night.

SEPTEMBER 26: Typed at the office and read more of the Pat Nixon galley. Just as I was at the part where the first nasty thing got said about Haldeman, Doug called and said that Josh's roommate wants to fix me up with Peter Haldeman, H.R.'s 29-year-old son, who writes for *Esquire* & knows my work.

SEPTEMBER 27: [To the Met with Louise Curley] It's been so long since I've seen Gauguins—how little paint there is on the canvas. From far away the colors are so deep that one expects there must be gobs, but actually the surface is barely covered . . . Louise is off to Rome tomorrow for a couple of weeks (she says she wants to find a quiet chapel on the 3rd [the anniversary of Tom's death]) . . .

. . . Jim [Connolly] came over mid-evening & we never got to a movie (our plans were vague) because we sat here (& lay here) making out. And we came "as close as we could without going over the actual retail price." I was the one who stopped things fairly close to the last minute. I sensed some hesitation on his part & suddenly even more on my own.

SEPTEMBER 29: [At the 92nd St. Y] J. M. Coetzee read. A very *serious* demeanour, though not an unappealing one—a bit like his prose in fact—so lean there's not a modifier failing to pull its weight in a whole book. He looks twenty years older as soon as he stops reading. Some predictable questions afterwards. When he made an anti-government statement about South Africa people covered themselves with their own wild self-congratulatory applause.

I enjoyed the party at Shelley's this time, without evil Olwyn there. Met Irving Howe (who introduced Coetzee) and his very warm, attractive (and much younger) Israeli wife, Alana.

SEPTEMBER 30: Came home to a phone message from Greg. Dinner tomorrow night may fall through because Joe Norton, one of the guys we saw *The Color Purple* with, has died of AIDS. He was 24. I can't even remember his face—only Louis, the lover's. Oh, God help us all.

OCTOBER 1: Greg and I left phone messages with one another throughout the day & talked tonight. He went to the hospital. It turns out Joe won't be dead until tomorrow. (Now there's a hell of a sentence.). They won't get the 3rd flat electroencephalogram until then; and only then can they unplug him. So his parents & Louis have begun to grieve while the machine is still beeping. And Greg tells me that the volunteer group he works for (doing wills for AIDS victims) wants him to go to the Bronx; that's where they're dying fastest now—all these mad Hispanic queens who've done IV drugs and been fucked up the ass for years—and the Yuppie lawyers don't want to go up there.

. . .

A letter [to Shelley Mason at the Poetry Center] from Ted Hughes. He thanks her for cancelling the Q-&-A session after his reading: says he feared a question "about Sylvia" coming like "an arrow in the dark"—though he admits it would have been less likely than a few years ago, when it would have been a certainty.

. . . Had a disjointed letter from Mary [McCarthy] at Bard. Watched the dedication of Carter's library at lunchtime on TV. He's a mean little man.

OCTOBER 2: Nervous packing tonight [for a plagiarism-research trip to California]—the fact is I hate to travel; I'm taking a 6-day business trip & I feel like kissing every corner of Manhattan good-bye.

OCTOBER 3: I walked around the [Berkeley] campus in the hot sunlight feeling disembodied & vulnerable, the way I usually do travelling. I always have work to do, phone calls to make, but even now . . . I feel somehow that what I'm doing is harebrained. As I did wandering around London in '76 looking for Edward Shelley.* No faith in myself . . . I wondered where Louise was all day today—if she'd really found that little Italian chapel.

OCTOBER 4: [interview with Anita Clay Kornfeld in San Rafael] She is intelligent, humorous. She has character and charm. I am completely convinced she brought that suit in good faith & on principle. (She had tears in her eyes twice during the interview.) I'm also convinced most aspects of her case were weak & poorly handled. How do I write a chapter that shows her as admirable even while it shows a verdict that was correct? That's my task, I think. . . .

. . . Thought about all these things as I rode the Larkspur ferry back past Alcatraz and into San Francisco. Met Tom [Stevenson] near Pier 23 & we ate dinner . . . From there to Alta Plaza, a tasteful gay bar that some call the Ultra Plastic. I was tired by 10:00 & made my way back to Berkeley alone. Got the BART train near the Civic Center. Passed City Hall in a taxi and thought about Dan White climbing in the window to shoot Harvey Milk & Moscone.

On the platform, as I waited for the subway, a well-muscled Mexican smiled at me & sidled up to me and said: "I like what I see." I gave him a smiling thanks-but-no-thanks but got such a sexual thrill out of the proposition that for a moment I felt the whole sleazy, furtive gay world of hourlong encounters had more to recommend it than the highest forms of lifetime heterosexual devotion.

---

* Edward Shelley (1874–1951), a witness against Oscar Wilde in 1895; the subject of my first published article, "A Boy of No Importance," in 1978.

OCTOBER 6: [Interviewing Richard Lanham and Edward Condren, UCLA colleagues and competing expert witnesses in the *Falcon Crest* case] Lanham looks like a younger Rehnquist, is obviously brilliant, and speaks with complete detachment about the legal consulting he does. Condren is completely different—a handsome, tall ex-naval aviator, with an Irishman's passion and blarney. He sees Anita Kornfeld as a damsel in distress & a terrific writer, too. I'm shocked by what I've got him saying, on tape, about *Vintage*.

OCTOBER 7: I was at Rosenfeld, Meyer & Susman in Beverly Hills by 10:00 & discovered [lawyer William Billick to be] handsome & sexy as can be in a manner (blond, bald, lean) I imagine the brightest CIA operatives to have . . . He let me examine the transcripts for a couple of hours & xerox whatever I wanted . . . There were 85 cartons against the wall across the hall from where I worked.

A quick walk around Beverly Hills (Rodeo Drive is less attractive than Miracle Mile in Manhasset) before getting a $30 cab ride to downtown LA, a generally depressed area that hasn't changed much, it would seem, in 30 years. It's little more impressive than downtown Lubbock. They were shooting a movie with 40s costumes (*The Woo Woo Kid*[*]) on the steps of the City Hall one recognizes from cop shows.

[During my interview with Judge Richard Gadbois] . . . Beginning to realize about this case: a lot of bright, admirable people caught up in a brutal, elephantine fight over nothing. And yet it's also clear why none of the parties could see it as trivial, why it claimed passions.

OCTOBER 8: [Getting ready to take the redeye home] The weather's lovely & I've done everything I set out to. Yeah, I get lonely on trips like this, but I'm also a spunky, resourceful little guy. So let's hear it for Tom tonight! Now let's go to the airport, buy *People* magazine, buckle the seatbelt, run the headphones up high, order a drink & fly, fly, fly.

---

[*] Released the following year as *In the Mood*.

OCTOBER 9: Slept until noon and then got up to the Poetry Center, where poor Ken told me he'd been chewed out (for lateness or something) by austere Karl. Slept on my futon for another hour or so after typing my quota of pages from *Arts & Sciences*. Then threw together some things about Pepys for my first class. The Y holds all of them at an elementary school named for Bobby Kennedy on 88th between Park & Lex.

OCTOBER 10: Got a copy of Sunday's *Book Review* at B. Dalton on Fifth Avenue. There at last is my essay [on letters from readers to authors], sharing the front page with Alfred Kazin & Philip Roth. I'm happy about the front page, but am convinced they owe me more money—wasn't it supposed to be a thousand dollars, and not five hundred, if it made the front?

OCTOBER 11: [Out to dinner with Doug MacKay's parents and their friends from the Cookeville, TN theatre club] "Get ready for smalltown society," Doug told me before, & that's what it was. I sat between Doug's mother and Dr. Derryberry's wife, a bubbly former schoolteacher. Doug's sister Molly was across from me until she went off for a late date with some guy she says is connected.

OCTOBER 13: Listened to Reagan's speech about Iceland. Despite what the media say, I think Reykjavik may have been his finest hour. If Star Wars is such a will-o'-the-wisp, as the TV boys keep saying, why are the Russians so dead set vs. our having it?

OCTOBER 14: . . . Saw the headline about Elie Wiesel's Nobel Peace Prize when I got out of the subway at 86th St. And then, when I got to the Y, I found him giving a press conference, in English and French, in the auditorium.

OCTOBER 15: I feel back to all-work-&-no-lay . . . All the depressive symptoms are here: escape naps, etc. I read a *Falcon Crest* script & typed some *A&S* as the Lex. Ave. subway rumbled beneath the Y. The only really exciting event of the day: the Mets/

Astros game, which went to 16 innings & gave the Mets the pennant. Rich the doorman had half a dozen heart attacks listening to his transistor.

OCTOBER 17: I worked all afternoon at the Y and then took the subway all the way down to Louise's to meet Tommy's old friend François (with whom he was once in love; but Rachel said François knew Tommy would be trouble & never turned the friendship into anything else) . . . He works for Bristol-Myers in France. He is tanned and handsome, nearing that cusp where the appealing pretty boy begins to turn into the boyishly overaged queen. But what charm—I can see why he was always Tommy's idol of manners and class. Louise told him [she'd] give a cocktail party for any friends he had in New York, so that's what I found . . . complete with a cracked Bavarian-princess-by-marriage; an adorable Columbia art student named Alan Smith, who met François this summer in Paris & calls him Frank . . . and a beautiful girl named [L.A.], who thinks she's dating Alan . . . There was also a yuppie female lawyer there. When the conversation turned to drug addicts and pushers in the parks, she said, eighteen inches from Louise, "I can't wait for all the drug addicts to die of AIDS." Then, presumably, the parks will be nice.

[Later that night] I went down to Charlie's and wound up flirting with someone named Chuck and wound up going home with him and sleeping with him in such a way as to put me (probably) in no physical danger, just more psychological peril. Is this the way I'm going to live the next twenty years, assuming I get to live them? There are still thousands of living gay men who do. Just hoping that something wonderful will come along, but then, after another month or two has gone by and something wonderful hasn't come along, going out and finding something brief, and exciting, just plain releasing. Is this the only alternative to celibacy? The only thing between complete celibacy and something wonderful? I seemed to need nothing in between all through my twenties. But I wasn't here in NY then, & I wasn't psychologically out of my teens then. So here I am living my twenties in my thirties—in the middle of this plague. I am starting to cry as I write this—out of self-pity, out of anger at the world. I just don't know what I'm sup-posed to do. Send me a miracle. Send me a miracle.

OCTOBER 18: Going home in my dark glasses by late-morning light & sleeping it off. Sleeping off sleeping together. Frightened by how unmomentous this has become . . . Do you know what this morning's conversation [with Chuck] was mostly about? My lost sock.

And in a few days my body will start feeling hungry & I'll wonder if I shouldn't call him.

OCTOBER 19: Still trying to feel chastened, tidy, penitent, self-sufficient. Would I feel different if these weren't dangerous times? Or is there something about the loathing that has nothing to do with panic? Am I just, now and forever, a nice Catholic boy?

OCTOBER 22: Greg came by about 7:00 . . . The whole evening gave me a lift, made me feel this is a real friendship, that it's had enough of a push down the runway to get it up and flying steadily.

OCTOBER 25: Came back here [from the Y] in the early evening. Passed John DeLorean and what appeared to be his snorting buddies on Second Ave. They were probably on their way to a Mets-watching party. What a game this 6th one turned out to be. Sloppy baseball, full of errors, but what dramatics. All these dizzying reversals of fortune in the 9th + 10th innings. The Mets were one strike away from losing the Series & they came back to win the game. I'll never forget Ray Knight's run from 3rd base to home once he saw they'd done it. He seemed to propel himself more with his arms than his legs, like some joyful bird. And then the roar I could hear coming from Billy Munk across the street.

OCTOBER 27: Got to the lecture hall in the basement of the Don-nell Library and took my seat for Mary [McCarthy]'s reading. She offered (after the lazy, inevitable introduction by Lizzie Hardwick) another chapter of *How I Grew*, the one just about to appear in *The Paris Review*. It's still too-name-stuffed even for my reality-based taste. . . .

I talked to her for a few moments afterwards. She looked very pretty—her feathery new hairdo is becoming . . . Jim was sick with strep throat and was up at the Viscusis'. Mary herself had to go back to Bard this evening—she's got a class tomorrow. (Why on earth does she do it? If it's to recapture her youth, there must be less tiring ways?) Lizzie seemed to scoot away right after the reading, which is just as well, since I imagined she'd be looking at me as the tormenter of poor Jacob Epstein.

OCTOBER 28: Alan [Smith] was here by 7:05. And it was like that 3-hour phone call come to life. We made dinner and listened to Aretha Franklin & Cleo Laine & sat on the couch and laughed, and laughed, and laughed. We gazed into one another's eyes and kissed and held one another & agreed that we shouldn't do anything more on what we really think should be a first date. Let's give this a chance. Which is exactly what we ought to do. But in my sexually impetuous way I found it almost impossible. His face is so beautiful & so kind.

Will we really be able to have good sex together? Isn't there too much humor between us? And despite all those classic movie comedies, isn't a sense of humor fatal to sex? . . . I waved to him through the window. And then he was really gone. And I cleared plates and pushed back the dining room table and turned out the bed in a dreamy way. . . .

OCTOBER 29: Tell me I'm not falling: I almost missed my subway stop this afternoon because I was daydreaming of him.

OCTOBER 30: Fought my way through about 500 words of the *Falcon Crest* chapter. I can see that writing narrative is going to be hard. This diary encourages lazy habits in that regard. I don't have to worry what "you" (whoever you are) know, because in my present understanding "you" know everything I know. But in the chapter I've got to keep stopping myself in order to ask: will the reader be able to follow this? . . .

I took a walk around Yorkville, beautiful & crepuscular (a favorite word). . . .

NOVEMBER 1: [In Richmond with friends] We went to the Museum of the Confederacy, not far from the old Confederate White House. The captions to some of the exhibits still haven't quite surrendered: one mentions how the Abolitionists tended to concentrate on the bad aspects of slavery.

NOVEMBER 2: [My 35th birthday] Well, I'm halfway home. Will I still be around on Nov. 2, 2021? How about Nov. 2, 1991?

NOVEMBER 3: Fernando Arrabal read tonight [at the Y]. *Quel* clown . . . He told charming, smutty pseudo-anecdotes about his days as a young man around the elder Surrealists.

NOVEMBER 4: Came back here to watch the election. Reagan has lost control of the Senate, which on the whole I think is not a good thing. I think we'd be more likely to get a really good arms control agreement if he had his own party there. It's the only real reason I voted for D'Amato, whom I otherwise can't stand. I also voted for Mario & all the moderately liberal Manhattan good guys like [Roy] Goodman & [Bill] Green.

NOVEMBER 9: [My niece and nephew] wore me out—constant jumpy, shrieky jabber—but I had a good time. Loree was, as usually, snappish and gay by turns. (Christina once took Loree's face in her hands and said: "Is it the nerves, Mommy?") . . . Christina is the peacemaker who loves a good gab. She sits on your lap and says: "I'll tell ya somethin'." When she finishes that story she says: "I'll tell ya another."

NOVEMBER 10: I went to the party at Shelley's [for P. D. James and Nicolas Freeling] and stayed until about eleven. Then I went home to leave [a] message [for Alan Smith]. And after that, appalled and depressed, I went down the avenue to Charlie's and wound up talking to a handsome rancher from southern Texas who was up in NYC selling natural gas to the NY public schools. He told me about the 125 Mexicans on this ranch & how his own 13-year-old son had called today to say he'd shot his first buck. He then asked me if I'd like to leave with him; he was staying at the Gramercy

Park Hotel. For the record, I did not go with him, which was as much good sense as I was capable of today.

NOVEMBER 12: [A fix-up date courtesy of Phyllis Rose with Robert Levithan, beginning at his apartment near Washington Square] He works for a foundation for the blind now, having stopped producing for a while. We're both 35. He talked about writing with me; we laughed about Phyllis & David. It was a very *polite* conversation, friendly and considerate. We didn't have dinner because for one month he's on one of these crazy diets—not to lose weight (he's handsome and perfect, like a Jewish Rex Smith), but to be pure or something. He says it's also supposed to help one's immune system. . . .

NOVEMBER 14: What I really want to hear from [Alan] for is confirmation of my reality principle. That's what's burnt as much as my feelings. I wonder if that night even took place. But I know it did. It's in this book and what I wrote is true. All that looking in one another's eyes. No one ever means anything by it. It's all performance. Rehearsal for a show that never opens.

Doug grows impatient with me. We meet outside the News Building (damn the Christmas lights that are going up) and proceed down to Barrow St. and Le Bistroquet. "OK," he scolds. "You've been blown off. You've blown people off too. Get over it." True. But helpful only for a moment.

NOVEMBER 15: I got up to the Y by the afternoon & found [Ken] in my room (I gave him a key a long time ago & he sometimes works in there late at night). He was getting over an argument with his roommate & being stoned last night. I was still hungover & we both wound up chastely napping on the futon until he got up at 4:00 to go to his psychiatrist.

. . . [Greg] was at a wills-writing seminar at GMHC today. Someone says insurance companies are beginning to ask particular questions about neighborhood, etc., in order to keep certain bachelors from getting policies. Someone joked that anyone who answered "Yes" to the question "Have you ever used the word 'taupe'?" would be denied. A couple of weeks ago Fran [Walker] told me she'd seen a TV program about personal finances advising investors in insurance companies to switch their money into hospitals to take advantage of the coming boom in AIDS deaths.

NOVEMBER 16: I ache for this person I've seen twice. And all the time I know that the ache has really nothing to do with him. It's just that there's a part of me ready to flay myself bloody again. It happens according to some chemical schedule.

NOVEMBER 17: [At Mary Evans' office in Chelsea] I give her *Arts & Sciences* and tell her what I did with it. She tells me the problems my option clause with T+F may create if they don't want it & she has to sell it elsewhere. (Places may like *A&S* but not buy it because they can't buy me—I'm not a free man non-fictionwise.) She tells me she's resold my Municipal Gallery piece to the *International Herald Tribune*.

. . . [That Monday's reading at the Y] Two playwrights. August Wilson was good. He read well from *Fences*, an old-fashioned play soon to open . . . The other guy was a hustler, Reinaldo Povod. He wrote the play De Niro was in, *Cuba and His Teddy Bear*. He came out (after an introduction by Joe Papp) and read poems about his deprived childhood, accompanied by a friend with a conga drum. It was let's-wallow-in-white-guilt time out there in the audience. I bagged the party afterwards. . . .

NOVEMBER 18: At the old Terrace Pub in Tudor City . . . found that the sweet old place filled with old ladies and the occasional mouse has been redone as a glitzy yuppie Mexican spot. (I realize I've now been in NY long enough to begin complaining about the way things used to be.)

NOVEMBER 19: Mary Evans called and told me Sonny Mehta had just been in her office & that he is interested in both *Arts & Sciences* and *Stolen Words*. (I give the former to Katrina in NY on Dec. 4.) She says he told her *ABOOO* is doing well in England + is still getting reviews. He tells her the story of how he bought it. He was with someone from T&F who told him, when he picked it up, that it wasn't for him. The person's phone rang & while he was waiting out the conversation he opened the book and read a page & was convinced he had to buy it.

. . . Reagan's press conference went very badly. He's really stumbled over Iran, and the press are gleeful with pseudo-outrage. RR did not help himself tonight—could barely get a coherent sentence out.

NOVEMBER 22: Went to the Y. I found Shelley in my room. Like Ken she has a key. She spent the night there after working late. She wrote a poem to the man who dumped her & I talked her out of mailing it to him.

NOVEMBER 24: I was already dealing with a piece of the mail— a bill or something—before I bothered to read the postcard sticking out from the rest of the pile. The handwriting was unfamiliar, and it took a minute or two for me to figure out what it was:

> "Tom, I'm sorry I have been so callous and I appreciate your phone calls. It is a very difficult time for me and when I feel additional pressure I'm afraid I react badly. Anyway, I do like you and would like to be friends—when things are saner I will call or [if] you'd like please do the same. AS"

And that ended three gruesome weeks. I walked around in a sort of happy disbelief with the Walkman on. I wasn't fantasizing about him. I merely felt free to be a person again, as if some kind of excommunication had been lifted . . .

        . . .

[Robertson Davies read at the Y]: He milked it with long pauses & gestures—anyone who wears a beard like that is used to milking whatever he does, I'm sure—but the words themselves were awfully crisp and funny . . . the house was packed—and so the reception was at somebody's pretty apartment on E. 71st St. instead of at Shelley's. Anne Carson looked fabulous in a tight black dress.

NOVEMBER 26: Walked to the ICP to see exhibits of Eisenstaedt and "Chim." Stood disbelievingly before the picture of the armless blind boy learning to read Braille with his lips.

The Winston Link photos are still for sale. They're all $500 except for the one I really want: the drive-in. That one's $1000. Why don't I just buy it & tell myself it's an investment?

NOVEMBER 27: [At my mother's house for Thanksgiving] I discover that Mom shares the national mania for *Wheel of Fortune*. Knows all about Vanna White & what consonants to pick. She also says it's probably based on "Hang the Butcher," a word game we used to play on paper with Daddy & which I've not thought of since I don't know when. We also watched a 20/20 feature on a reunion of British war brides & I could tell how much she was missing Daddy [who served as a medic in England] & trying not to say anything maudlin. Instead she joked about the British girlfriend he's supposed to have had (Rosina, I think . . . an Italian girl in the U.K.). Grandma was terrified from his letters that he'd marry her. God, I could have had a Brit for a mother. Awful thought.

NOVEMBER 29: . . . Bob [Pounder] came by (on his way back to Pok from Thanksgiving in Princeton) to pick up keys—he'll be staying here for a couple of nights while I'm in Texas. I walked him to Grand Central and we ran into Mary McCarthy + Jim West getting out of a taxi. Time for a quick hello. Mary kisses me and says "dear Tom" and never relaxes her smile & crinkled eyes.

NOVEMBER 30: Watched bits of the Sunday morning political talk shows. Everyone telling Reagan what he should do to get out of this. The media may have bloodlust, but the Democrats are still scared of RR's popularity. Most of them talk in almost protective tones about how he must save himself from the bad guys around him (very different from the way things went for Nixon).

. . . Bob called this morning . . . told me about his trip back to Poughkeepsie with Mary + Jim. Mary asks how I am and whether I'm writing about the Epstein case yet. Bob says not yet. Mary says she's a little worried about it, that it's going to make me enemies, that Lizzie Hardwick is "concerned." Well, too bad. . . .

DECEMBER 1: Sat next to Tom Victor in Kaufmann Concert Hall tonight. James Merrill & William Alfred were the program . . . Alfred was wonderful. He read from something unfinished called *Nothing Doing*, full of speakeasies and bag ladies and alcoholic show people in 1931. Funny Brooklynese overlaid with beautiful lyricism. I loved every line he bumbled through—he kept taking off his glasses and being unable to get them quite back on.

I talked to him for a couple of seconds afterwards. Reminded him that he was my medieval examiner on my orals 10 years ago at Harvard. And boy was he sweet. Lobbed me lots of slow balls. At one point I pointlessly plugged in Julian of Norwich to one of my answers. Instead of upbraiding me for irrelevance, he said, "Isn't she wonderful!" and we gave little testimonials of pleasure that helped run out the clock & mask my lack of knowledge. And when the 1st hour was up & I was sent to pace the hall on a "break"— a peculiar bit of Harvard torture—he invented a bit of business with the secretary in Warren House & on his way to her pat-ted my arm & said, "It's going wonderfully." As Oscar Wilde said in another context: "Men have gone to heaven for smaller things than that."

DECEMBER 5: [In Lubbock for several days to do interviews for a chapter of *Stolen Words*] Lots of talk of bad times in Texas. Oil is a disaster; jobs are down; people are moving away; all a far cry from the "Freeze a Yankee" bumper stickers you used to see the year I lived here. It depresses me, even though I hated their pride back then. Even the weather seemed poor and unreal: a grey, wet day— cold, too—more like a NY December. . . .

DECEMBER 6: . . . We went to a party at that Norwegian col-league's of Lynn [Hatfield] . . . Got into conversation with a right-wing professor of electrical engineering and his wife. They'd just come back from South Africa & they'd just loved it. (What was he doing? Electrifying fences?)

DECEMBER 7: Worked in the [Brinks'] garage apt. in the afternoon before running . . . saw about 20 jackrabbits in a circle in that field between Indiana and Memphis. They looked as if they were holding a council.

A delicious dinner of thick soup and Pam's homemade bread. Pam tells stories of growing up in Kansas, being surrounded by grandparents & great-grandparents who were fun. She says she once broke a date with a boy so she could go to one of her grandparents' parties. . . .

DECEMBER 10: A fantastic coming-in low over Manhattan. The city looked like a game board, or like that twinkling map they used to have at the World's Fair. I could look one way and see Turtle Bay, look another and think "There's Greg," or "There's [W.]."

A mad, cursing cab driver & I was home. And then, at 1:45 a.m., I went to Charlie's. And met Chuck. And went back to his apartment. A stupid thing, but I think I knew I would do it the moment I stepped on the plane in Lubbock. I wanted to be free of my pre-sexual mascot self—however much I love Mary & Lynn & Pam & Jim & everyone down there. Wanted to rush back to the New Old World, with all its terrors: the world I almost missed living in.

So that's why I was sitting in a bar at 2 a.m. and at 3 a.m. having safe and empty sex with someone I'd [at least] met before.

DECEMBER 14: In the evening Doug & I went down to the GMHC Christmas party at the Saint. Very festive, even though most of the food ran out while we were still in line. A # of straight people there. Older women, especially. Mothers of dead sons. A few brave souls walking around with heaped plates and obvious KS on their faces. And bits of the old days, "the scene," too: arrogant, beautiful bartenders, etc.

Doug left at around 10:00. He had a 7:00 a.m. meeting to look forward to. I stayed on for a while. A very cute, 34-year-old ex-policeman from Houston—he'd even been shot once—flirted with me & asked what chance there was we would leave together.

DECEMBER 15: Shortly after midnight the phone rang. It was Ken, wondering why I wasn't at the reception, wondering if I can come out for a drink. I'm too tired, I say; I'm already undressed. Can he come here then? Just for a nightcap? OK, I say, not thinking much of it, remembering the last time.

He got here. We had a glass of wine. He tells me he missed me while I was in Texas. Tells me how much he likes me; asks if he can have a copy of one of my *People* pictures. Talks and talks about school and writing. I get up to go to the bathroom. When I come back he's lying in the bed—from which I'd just gotten up & to which he clearly wants me to return.

So I did . . .

Now *what* am I supposed to have done? I am not a saint. This adorable blond boy literally climbs into my bed. It took him 4 months to do this, but he's wanted to. (Even though he says he still thinks he mostly likes girls—another heterosexual homosexual, just like Alan: it must be the trend among Today's Young People.)

DECEMBER 16: Ken left his cigarettes and lighter here. When I got to the office this afternoon, he was sitting there smiling & working along with puritanical Karl. When Karl stepped away to the Xerox machine I tossed Ken the cigarettes & lighter & smiled.

. . . Talked to Mom . . . who told me she was watching a documentary on Ch. 13 about the "pre-Stonewall" era of gays. She was completely sympathetic & curious. I'd seen that program & we talked about it. I take the miracle of her understanding for granted. I shouldn't, and I should tell her I don't; I should stop every so often and say thank you. What keeps me from doing that?

DECEMBER 17: It was getting late—I had to meet Greg—and so I dashed to 2nd Ave. for a cab, and it was one of those winter coming-home-from-work hours, when New York is swimming in light and movement and relief, and I felt glorious; wouldn't exchange any life for mine. I felt ready for Christmas. No one should be entitled to live in Manhattan before the age of 30. One can't appreciate or deserve it until then.

. . . We couldn't get a cab, so [Greg and I] wound up walking to the new Equitable Building on 7th + 52nd. The party we went to was run by GLAAD, a network of gay & lesbian professional organizations . . . ran into Jenks! That's right: Jim Janke. Not many months ago Michael Maz & I were saying he'd be the last one out of the closet. He was embarrassed to see me, relieved and grateful that I just treated his being there as the most natural thing in the world. An awfully ugly friend of his interrupted us and said: "I just ran into my doctor and she told me the results of my test! I'm negative! Actually, I knew I would be." With all due allowance for his relief and joy, I thought this was an incredibly vulgar thing to say before someone you don't know—especially since no one knows what anyone else's story & terrors might be.

DECEMBER 21: Talked to Greg. He spent a lot of last night trying to help Jean-Luc—who's in jail. The man J-L was living with had sworn out a burglary complaint against him (over a couple of sweaters & an unpaid phone bill). The truth is that the guy is a vindictive drug-user angry with J-L's refusal to continue having sex. J-L spotted him—or he spotted J-L—when J-L entered The Works last night. He chased him out into the street & flagged down a cop & had J-L arrested. Amazing to think that they can "take you downtown" on nothing more than that. He's still there— he won't be arraigned until tonight. Greg is acting as his lawyer. The real problem is that J-L will have an arrest record while his immigration status is shaky.

DECEMBER 26: Robert Massa came by at about 9:00 and we had a quick drink before going off to see *Crimes of the Heart* on 34th St. . . . The last scene has the three sisters happily gobbling birthday cake in their crumbling old Mississippi house. When the lights went up, Robert turned to me and said: "But will they ever get to Moscow?"

DECEMBER 29: [Seeing Katy Aisenberg, Tom Curley's friend from Baltimore, when she was in town for the MLA convention] She says she could never understand why I was so bent out of shape by Tommy—"You seemed so together, & he so obviously wasn't. I couldn't understand why you let him make you so upset." Then she said: "I guess you were in love."

DECEMBER 30: [Dinner with someone] nice-looking, accomplished, stable. (Or so it seems; at least his circumstances are. Most people turn out to be emotionally less stable than you think they are at first.) He doesn't seem like trouble (Tommy, W.). And he doesn't seem to have that unbelievable charm (Alan Smith) that instantly thrills and victimizes. I still don't know exactly how old he is (45?). 45 isn't too old, but maybe *he* is too old in some ways—the college-age kids, etc. He's so *sensible*, Mr. Good Gay Citizen, causes, healthy relationships with his children, Front Runners, etc. I do feel more than 10 years younger than he is. But isn't that what I want? Stability? (Doug MacKay: "Let's give dull a try.")

1987

JANUARY 4: We made a date to see *The Common Pursuit* on Friday. I didn't detect much enthusiasm in his voice at first & that immediately made me more desirous.

JANUARY 5: [Introducing Veronica Geng and Ian Frazier at the Y] I must say, some of her stuff sails right over my head, but I laughed a lot at her piece about George Bernard Shaw at the LBJ ranch.

. . . Ken was flirtatious all day and he stuck close to me at the reception. Afterwards he insisted—I mean it—that I come up to his little apartment on E. 91st St. (his roommate is still in Iowa). So of course we went to bed . . . we've been *so* safe that we might as well be phoning it in, or doing it by radio waves. But I still felt bad afterwards—he's very sweet & very young & this seems pointless. I have *got* to settle down.

JANUARY 8: [Dinner with my college friend Arlene Redmond] at the Hors d'Oeuverie, part of Windows on the World. We spent $50 for a couple of rounds of drinks & nibbles, but it was worth it—the night was gorgeously clear and all of NY was below us (107th fl.). Such is my geography that I only later realized what I thought was an exceptionally rural or blacked out section of Queens was probably Jamaica Bay.

JANUARY 11: [Flew to Denver to do Vassar Club and Seven Sisters events]: Dinner was at the home of the Smith graduate who's head of College for a Day, or involved in it, anyway. As usual at these things, I am made much more of than I should be . . . During these affairs I generally retreat into the bathroom at least twice to calm my nerves.

JANUARY 12: I got a bus to Boulder, about an hour's ride across flat dishes between snowcapped mountains . . . I was in search of Scott Carpenter, or his spirit, and I walked a couple of miles until I found the corner of Aurora & 7th. I looked at the house . . . Looked up at the flatiron mountain practically in the backyard and tried to imagine him on it, on his horse.

JANUARY 15: Came back from the Y this afternoon to a message from Katrina: "Hi, Tom, I'm calling to talk to you about *Arts & Sciences*, which I've read with *great* pleasure. I think you've done a wonderful job revising it. I'll be talking to Mary [Evans], so I'll want to talk to you too." I've played back the message enough times to have it memorized. It was too late to call her or Mary; the offices were closed. So what does this *mean*? Are they going to buy it?

JANUARY 16: Talked to both Katrina & Mary this morning. Here's the story: it's not home free, but it's looking good. Katrina is very enthusiastic now. She's writing the memo that will go to the Trade Management Board. I ask: "But don't I always have trouble with the TMB?" And she says that T&F always wins their fights with them in the end and that I am now a person with a reputation as a valued (i.e., money-making) author . . . Katrina says she thinks the title should be changed to something like *The Education of Artie Dunne*; I've told her no. I think that eponymity stuff is clichéd with comic novels &, also, *A&S* suggests that the book is about something at least a *little* bigger than Artie.

. . . [That night Kenny] asked if he could come here. So I said ok, knowing what would happen. And it did. But in a safe, friendly, illusionless way. (Which may be why it was so incredibly satisfying physically.). I kept having to restrain him. "Can't we do X? Can't we do Y?" "No, no, no, not a good idea. Not safe." But even though I held us within the strictest limits it was very exciting.

JANUARY 17: I was at Joel's—from the Y, after working on Amis & Sokolow*—by 6. It turns out he'd already made plans for us to go to dinner with some of his friends. So I spent the evening at the apartment of 2 gay psychiatrists on Central Park West. They barely speak to one another, and then only to criticize. One of them spent a lot of the evening in another room. There was another couple there—& one of them was a psychiatrist too. I was the youngest there by at least 10 years.

Some couples stay together for the sake of the children. I got the feeling our hosts stay together for the sake of the apartment— a huge thing into which entirely too much thought and work has gone. Just as too much thought and work goes into the food, the cats, the music. By eleven o'clock the opera singer had come off the turntable in favor of Barbara Cook, and then the telephone rang and one of the psychiatrists got a call with the news that one of his closest friends had just died of AIDS out in Los Angeles.

I felt I was getting one-two punches: the worst of the Old Homosexuality and the worst of the New . . .

JANUARY 19: Anthony Hecht read at the Y tonight. Very academic stuff and appearance; worth hearing. He's best when he throws his voice into someone else's dramatic monologue . . . [Nick,] a very cute young Brit who's working on some Auden project with Ed Mendelson, was also there.

JANUARY 22: We're in the middle of a blizzard. I trudged out of the Y at about 5:30 & learned that there were no trains running south of 86th St. on the Lexington line. So I caught a bus at 84th & 2nd—one of the few running. It was packed, and we moved no faster than a block a minute. I kept looking at an ad that said 1 in every 100 people is schizophrenic. And naturally the 1 on

---

* The scandal involving historian Jayme A. Sokolow took up a long chapter of my book on plagiarism.

this bus carrying about 100 souls was standing and shouting right next to me.

JANUARY 23: [Greg and Ben and I] went to Private Eyes . . . 21st St., I think, just off 5th . . . It's a comfortable place, not hellishly dark. White walls, like a bathroom or high-tech rumpus room. And the usual couple of dozen TV screens. We drank too much. Greg gets very serious as he contemplates pretty faces on the dance floor.

JANUARY 26: Mary Evans called this morning & told me that Katrina has offered $6000 for the novel. That's low, but we're going to take it. In fact, I'm delighted . . . I could think about all sorts of things—like, why shouldn't I wait for Sonny Mehta to steal me over to Knopf? All I know is that I'm happy that at long last this silly but by now nicely written novel will be published.

. . . The reading [by poets Daryl Hine and Alfred Corn] went nicely, despite the cold and confusion. Backstage, after Tom Victor finished taking pictures, Daryl Hine mused: "Imagine all the boys who've put on greasepaint here." It wasn't a really butch evening. Daryl Hine was wearing a huge fur coat, the sort of thing a girl from Queens picks up at Antonovich. Alfred Corn is not a snob, but he reads like one. Both he & Hine (and McClatchy, who was eager to pump all the Poetry Center gossip out of Ken) professed to like [my] intro. Shelley was nice enough to announce the acceptance of *Arts & Sciences* from the stage before I came out.

JANUARY 27: . . . Ronnie's State of the Union address. He seemed to have considerable energy & there's obviously plenty of affection left for him on at least one side of the aisle. Finished McInerney— didn't like the last 1/3 of it at all. (Christ, at least I don't suddenly ask readers to feel *sorry* for characters who've been giving them a good time for 150 pages.)

JANUARY 28: [Worked on *Stolen Words*] after doing 5 miles in the park. The track around the reservoir had a hard pack of snow on it, but it was amazingly unslippery. My wind was good and I ran well. And at last this cough that's been hanging on seems to be going. I've been thinking more than usually about AIDS. Another part of the cycle everyone goes through, I suppose. On Monday, after I got the news from Katrina, I thought: will I live to see it come out?

Now Liberace. And of course the usual denials. It's pernicious anemia brought on by a watermelon diet; it's emphysema; it's heart disease. I saw him on a talk show over Christmas at Mom's. The second I saw the emaciated face on the screen, I thought: he's got it.

AIDS humor. From Doug, who was over here for a drink before a GMHC meeting. Their big slogan, of course, is "On Me, Not In Me"—it's everywhere: pamphlets, bars, etc. Except in the bathroom at GMHC headquarters. Above the toilet? A sign that says: "In Me, Not On Me."

JANUARY 29: The NBCC Awards. I went to the Publicists' lunch in the old 5th Ave. Hotel (Robert Levithan's building, or next to it). It's the lunch they give for the reviewers each year. They are a raucous lot, really. Pushing Barbara Pym or *Thin Thighs in Thirty Days*—it's pretty much all the same to them. I sat between Ben and a friend of his named Michelle, who works for Franklin Watts & who's loud and funny. She talked about that enormous woman who was finally arrested for pretending to be Aristotle Onassis' sister, but only after she was able to pass a mint's worth of phony checks. "I've gotta take a urine test to do business in my own bank," Michelle says, "and this one's buying out a whole Radio Shack with a rubber check and no I.D."

JANUARY 30: [After seeing *Platoon*] we went back to Doug & Bruce's for drinks. On the way we talked about Vietnam, and I felt like everyone's grandfather. This was, in fact, a war even *I* was almost too young for, the draft ending the week I was graduated from college. But Bruce is *so* young that he didn't even know there *were* draft deferments for undergraduates.

JANUARY 31: Went shopping during the day. The second volume of Arthur Cash's biography of Sterne costs an absurd $49. But then again, between *Arts & Sciences* & the giddy stock market, I'm so rich these days that I'm actually looking for things to spend money on. Which is completely unlike me. I went into Caswell-Massey this afternoon to buy ear plugs & came out with a $45 hairbrush. And I don't even brush my hair.

FEBRUARY 2: [Christopher Ricks hosted the first of three evenings at the Y featuring writers and celebrities reading from authors' letters; I was writing a piece about the event for *The New York Times'* Arts and Leisure section.] John Simon is avoided by most in the green room, but he was pleasant to me . . . John Gross was very friendly and Pickwickian, though he told me Blake Morrison, now literary editor of *The Observer*, is also writing a book about plagiarism. My heart—actually, my stomach—sank at this news, but I quickly cheered myself out of it. Reasoning: this was bound to happen; I'll probably beat him to the punch; we won't cover a lot of the same ground; the traffic can bear two books on this subject in any case. Still, he probably does have the inside track on Amis' story . . . John Lindsay, beautiful but dumb, read from Burke . . . Alexander Cockburn, handsome, but with that British appearance of having dressed in the dark, read from Horace Walpole . . .

Ricks himself was brilliant—the perfect snippets delivered before each speaker. At the party at Shelley's, afterwards, he was just the way I remember him at Vassar: all cranked up, a little bantam holding court against the wall, rapid-firing his wit—&, God, he is witty—in a generous way.

And, I think, looking for a girl for the night. I also think he found one.

He teased me mightily & asked: "Tell me, how did my husband-in-law [the awful Geoffrey Kirk] go down at Vassar?"

FEBRUARY 3: Liberace is dying & the Disease Control Center in Atlanta is talking about having everyone admitted to a hospital be required to take the AIDS test.

FEBRUARY 4: I called Joel and we made plans for Saturday . . . He seems to think the conservative elements of my character and outlook are things I'll grow out of, blind spots I'll overcome. They aren't & I won't. Most of them are components of the overall ambivalence that is, for lack of a better term, my world-view, full of supposed inconsistencies (supposed, that is, by knee-jerk liberals and knee-jerk conservatives), and difficultly lived. Sometimes with honesty and sometimes with less than that.

FEBRUARY 9: [After a dull dinner and sex with Joel] I didn't stay the night. I kissed [Joel] goodbye & caught a taxi & felt more free than failed riding home through the park.

FEBRUARY 8: I read the paper—my Y piece is pretty nicely laid out. It has one of those felicitous typos—"documents" became "moments," and it reads better that way.

FEBRUARY 9: [At a reception at the Y, after the second evening of letters-reading] met Judith Thurman, just back in NY from California. On the plane she met a rich Texan who wanted her to give him the names of some singles bars, and who then told her that the per capita incidence of AIDS in his town in Texas was greater than it is in NY . . . Went home by myself (though Kenny was hinting he'd like to come too) and watched the tape of Part 2 of *[The Two] Mrs. Grenvilles* that the VCR had so obligingly made & kept waiting—like a warm dinner in the oven. . . .

FEBRUARY 12: That's how I think these days. Just give me time enough to finish *Stolen Words*. Draft *Aurora* 7. Then I can get sick. Just as a year ago I was making a bargain with God: just let me finish revising *Arts & Sciences*. Maybe, if I'm lucky, I can keep this up for 40 years.

FEBRUARY 13: Went to Howie the dentist this morning. A thorough cleaning and no problems. But my AIDS fears travel everywhere with me. Why, I think, is he asking how my "general health" has been? And when he tells me that the remaining 2 wisdom teeth (those he didn't take out 6 years ago, in a procedure that shed more blood than the Tate-LaBianca murders) will eventually have to come out, I think: what if I have it done overnight in a hospital? And what if by then they're giving the AIDS test to everyone? Will I wake up to hear a nurse tell me that my wisdom teeth are out & that, by the way, I'm antibody-positive?

FEBRUARY 14: Item: at least one doctor is now saying that everyone infected with the virus will eventually get sick. Item: at least one other doctor is saying that a negative result from the AIDS test proves nothing—the virus has already mutated into scores of forms the test doesn't recognize.

FEBRUARY 15: I do have to think—in fact, I can't stop thinking—about what will happen if I get sick. I don't want to be in the middle of too many things. I want to have the chance to finish some of them.

I have to think like that. And at the same time I have to think: I'm not *going* to get sick. I have to think both things at once and then live & work & be happy in such an existential tug of war.

FEBRUARY 16: We talked a lot about the last couple of weeks & the assault of AIDS news. Bless Louise: she says I'm supposed to call her up any time I'm feeling scared.

FEBRUARY 18: [Seventh anniversary of my father's death] I think about you for no more than a few minutes each day of my life—a life I think you'd be mostly proud of. But then night comes, and I dream of you about three times a week. Dreams in which things are quite pleasant, in which you're always good company, reasonable, eager to be informed—much as you were in life. You're often only a supporting character in these dreams, and are entirely content to be such—to offer advice, to be a sounding board. I am invariably glad you're there. The psychiatrists would say my dreaming of you so often no doubt indicates a failure to "work something out" while you were alive. But I think it's more that I'm just craving your quiet companionship. Yes, we had things left to "work out." But does it matter that we didn't? I wasn't ready to . . . And part of me still has the perfectly childlike faith that we'll catch up on everything in heaven.

FEBRUARY 20: [Six hours with Nick] Talking about Auden (he may be over here for the next 2 years, working on an edition of the prose); about his eccentric father who's convinced that someone comes into the greenhouse to sabotage his prize cacti; about being the grandson of an Oxford don and the privileges that entailed when he lived with his grandparents—being able to smash into undergraduates with his tricycle and watch them have to be polite. . . .

FEBRUARY 22: What irony: all that worry over being homosexual. And then, not much after it began to seem okay to be so, we must learn to practice every self-restraint we can think of not to be so.

Stayed in until mid-afternoon. Declined Doug's invitation to go down to a fundraiser for GMHC. They're raising money to build a building. They're going to be here forever.

MONDAY, FEBRUARY 23: In the afternoon I called Joyce Thomas to make an appointment to have my will done (March 25). Melo-dramatic? Maybe the timing, though I've meant to do this any-way, since I do now have money, property, copyrights to think about. And consider this: she's thinking of getting out of the wills business—too many of her clients have ARC, get AIDS, die, leave lovers who fight with parents. It's become too depressing.

. . . I'm more aware of just how closed the doors to the Epstein case will prove. I had a nice letter from Mary in Paris, but she told me she'd rather I didn't use her anecdote on the subject.

The last evening of letters at the Y—the 20th century. It went on forever, mostly because Bill Alfred got things off to a hilariously garrulous start with Yeats. Amy Clampitt gibbers and claps like a monkey; Grace Schulman, who is a kind of saint, looks like an academic Olive Oyl. She's all bones, and none of them are mean.

FEBRUARY 24: I see mandatory AIDS testing coming. They won't exactly drag one off the streets to do it, but they'll make it a requirement for so many things—visas, hospital stays, insurance, licenses of all kinds—that it will become impossible to go much further through life without it. And millions will get psychological death sentences.

FEBRUARY 27: [An evening with (W.), who] came in the door at 8 with a bouquet of flowers & a big kiss. We never got to dinner. We just sat and nibbled and drank and laughed for 5 hours. I drank to keep up with him; I think he drank to get somewhere. To that place he rarely gets, where he can have a good time. This beautiful, weirdly boyish 43-year-old with a cruelly self-protective streak.

"I'm having such a good time!" he shouted out at one point, laughing—as if he'd suddenly found himself in a plane over the Andes. And by 1:00 we were fooling around with the VCR and he put his hand on my hair, stroking it, asking me if I'd come up to Orange Co. this summer.

And then, like two old friends, we went to bed.

FEBRUARY 28: This was different. I suspect it will never even happen again. I'm not even sure I want it to. This was simple, healing. I'm not obsessing about it.

MARCH 2: . . . I ran. At 5:00 there was that gaudy color-photograph effect on the eastern edge of the reservoir. The sky was inky dark blue, and the buildings were as white as Marilyn Monroe's teeth. A trick that God, the great showoff, kept up for a couple of minutes. It was spectacular. A strong wind, too—the track was sprinkled with feathers.

MARCH 3: While [my accountant, Arthur Greene] figures I sit silent, looking out the window at the extraordinary sight of everything in Manhattan below 40th St. from the 43rd floor. Stuyvesant Town + Peter Cooper Village look like a big adobe village, unexpectedly squat compared to all that surrounds them. I sit and gaze calmly, proud of all the work I did with my receipts. The perpetual student, I want Arthur to praise my hard work, to give me an A in tax-preparation preparation.

MARCH 4: Went into the [Poetry Center] office today & found Karl there alone . . . We talk about jury duty, which he did last fall & which I start tomorrow morning. I ask him if he at least got a poem out of the experience. He says only a bad one. He says the situation was "too new and strange"—conditions that don't seem to me like bad ones for producing a poem . . . Ran 5 miles in the park and 3x passed Jackie O, huffing like the rest of us, but wrapped in ski hat and smoky goggles. But it was she all right—complete with bird-dogging photographer down by the southern station-house of the reservoir.

MARCH 5: [Jury-duty voir dire] I was empanelled through most of the afternoon on *Carlos Espinoza vs. Soohoo* (I think; not Soho) *Cab Corp*. Not a judicial landmark-to-be, I daresay. A fender bender with supposed back injuries. Between 2 cabbies. Liability has already been conceded. The next part of the trial is just to determine damages . . . The lawyers are a study in contrasts. DeVries (for the plaintiff) is verbose and whippety and paces up and down. Tries to get close and friendly with each juror; comes out bad and condescending. Has a bad suit. An ambulance chaser? The other guy—Brisson—is gorgeous, a Gregory Harrison lookalike. Flirts with his smile. I count 2 other gay men in the little room, 201B. We're all in love with him, I'm sure . . . One middle-aged black woman is asked if she has any gripes vs. the "system" that might make it hard for her to serve on this case. She says, well, her husband "pulled two to three"—for burglary; a sentence running now—and she didn't think that was fair. But she thinks she can serve on this. She's gently disqualified.

MARCH 6: [After being picked as an alternate] We were out early enough for me to get up to the Y and run 5 miles. Back here to greet Doug & Bruce & Brad (a Viking Penguin guy) for drinks. We went down to Brasero for dinner. Brad is a nice straight guy whose 60-year-old father now has a 31-year-old boyfriend.

MARCH 9: [Arthur Miller reads at the Y.] Pompous, old, overrated bore. He read from his memoirs (I counted 3 grammatical errors) & had the dumb audience eating out of his hand. Even after he called it quits rather abruptly & left the stage at 9:00. At the party upstairs in the nursery school he never even took off his coat. Oh, Marilyn, how you must have missed Joe D.

MARCH 11: Hell revealed: it's sitting in a jury box for 3 hours listening to lawyers argue w/ doctors. DeVries had a good day, I'd say. His Pakistani guy was dignified, sincere, & knew his stuff. Brisson's high-priced Park Ave. guy came across as a know-it-all, & the real ambulance-chaser in the case. He's testified in court 54x since '81, and 53x he was for the defense . . . The judge was less cranky today & even seemed amused by it at points. But then he'd tell everyone to shut up & get on with it. The lawyers look so foolish that the jurors gain confidence watching them.

MARCH 12: We had lunch in the jury room . . . No one talks about the case; everyone takes the obligation seriously. We talk about what we'd do if we win the lottery instead. The black lady next to me shows me her ticket for the numbers game, which she plays every day—middle-class white boy that I am, I'd never even seen one before.

MARCH 13: The news: Gotti walks. So much for my faith in the jury system! But Mr. Espinoza did okay—he got $60,000 . . .

MARCH 14: Don't know how much longer I can take being Advisor to Gay Youth. Career counseling with Chris Bull. Theological discussion with Tom Stevenson. Reading Kenny's stories. And now Nick. On whom I have developed a terrific crush . . . [We] drank and talked, for seven hours this time. We ate in an Afghan restaurant on St. Mark's, right under Adrian Kitzinger's old apartment. Nick set his napkin on fire, and the handsome waiter put it out with his hand.

MARCH 18: Oh—how could I forget? Walking on 2nd Ave. in the 60s this morning I saw a blonde woman walking in the other direction. I thought: "Gee, she's pretty." The mind tends toward understatement sometimes. I got a few steps closer and realized it was Catherine Deneuve.

MARCH 20: [A drink with] Anne Carson (her arms are like pipe cleaners and all she ever seems to consume is decaffeinated coffee) at the Victory Cafe before going back downtown.

MARCH 22: [After seeing *Swimming to Cambodia* with Nick]: we went to a coffee shop across from Lincoln Center and sat and talked about everything for hours. He had a fingernail paring caught between his teeth and repeated efforts to dislodge it with a toothpick succeeded only in bloodying his gums. That I found all this adorable instead of disgusting will tell you where I am.

MARCH 23: Up to the Y to work a bit on the Epstein chapter and to hear Salman Rushdie read . . . He's the new Didion: she became a Central American expert in 2 wks. He took 3.

[At the party afterwards]: Mona Simpson & three girls from *Paris Review* were there . . . chattering amongst themselves—and only themselves—like quadruplets who'd been raised in the forest.

MARCH 26: [In San Juan with Greg Ullman] Greg flirts with a little barfly named José and makes an older man named Richard furious . . . Greg has the Vidalian fuck-&-move-on-&-count-on-your-friends-for-everything-else view. Which I accept as his, just as he understands my looking-for-the-Mr.-Right-One drive.

MARCH 27: Mostly our conversations run to such serious matters as the relative merits of Sun Block 10 and Sun Block 6, and whether the ice in this round of piñas isn't more finely chopped than it was in the last one.

MARCH 28: This was the day our vacation turned into a gay version of *Love Boat*. Tom & Greg meet Ramon & Waldy & find true, temporary romance . . . two new doctors, in their late 20s, who are sweet as can be and who instantly develop crushes on us (Ramon on me, Waldy on Gregito).

MARCH 29: Ramon & Waldy showed up again today and asked if we'd like to go out with them on the ferry from Old San Juan to Cataño. Which we did, smiling & chattering, & looking up at the Big Dipper . . . it really did turn out to be a kind of shipboard romance. These doctors without airs, still living at home, youthful, romantic, fresh, a little silly. . . .

MARCH 30: [Back home that night] I opened a pile of mail as I watched the Oscars. (Dianne Wiest shaking with lovely, genuine excitement; Oliver Stone telling us that his movie ended Vietnam for us—the sort of crap Hollywood loves to hear; Bette Davis mentally decomposing in front of a billion people.) And I called back a woman from the *Washington Post* Style section. She's doing a piece on diary writing. We did a quick interview and she agreed to find out for me if Rene Carpenter is still around Washington.

APRIL 1: I got to the Y and after a long nap on the futon my head seemed to be almost back to normal. (Colds do leave me quickly; yes, I am healthy . . . oh, yes, knock wood on this day, the first one on which Ronald Reagan publicly uttered the word AIDS.) Wrote my Ozick review. It's ok, nothing more. It feels funny writing for a new editor. I know what Nina or Bob or Wlady or Anatole like. But who's this David Brooks?
    . . . A long letter from Loree. One indication of Ireland's terrible economic state. The prize the other night on a TV game show was "a job."

APRIL 2: Worked here in the morning and got to the Y by lunchtime. Poor Kenny has conjunctivitis & is wearing shades and looks like a pubescent cocaine dealer.

APRIL 3: Typing [a chapter of the plagiarism book] before going for my haircut. A breakthrough during the latter: Nancy has decided she likes my gray hair and will no longer insist that I dye it so that I can look like Frankie Avalon.

APRIL 6: Doug calls & asks if I'd like to be on a segment of *Good Morning America* being produced by Eric Marcus. It's about love

in the 80s, & I'm supposed to function as representative successful, reasonably attractive youngish gay man—filmed running in
the Park, etc. Well, no, thanks. But I'm flattered.

APRIL 10: I reached Rene Carpenter on the telephone this afternoon. Very friendly—but it was so strange. I can't put the voice I
heard into that [Ralph Morse] picture on the wall . . . the person
in my imagination for the last year . . . She seems eager to help in
a motherly way. "Now, let's see, Scotty was born in '49 and Jay in
'52. And when were you born?" . . . by the end of the conversation
calls me "dear."

APRIL 12: Anne Carson & Kenny came here at 6. (Shelley has
taken off for California.). Hors d'oeuvres were hard [to prepare];
Anne (anorexic?) eats no sugar and claims she's allergic to it; and
Ken can have no cheese because of the head medicine he takes.
Ken very bubbly, though no hint that anything ever happened
between us. Anne very salty & New England schoolmarmish—
controlled, useful, fatally wounded. Dinner at Joe Burns & then
back here for pie and coffee.

APRIL 13: Mary's autobiography reviewed, not too nicely, in
today's *Times*. The reviewer was Lehmann-Haupt. As she once
said of him in Maine: "He's dumb." But it's true she's written better books.

APRIL 14: The Y is shut up pretty tight [for Passover]. But Karl
was in the office & I chatted with him while I typed letters of
recommendation for Kenny. (The Poetry Center's invitations are
really killers when they go to Italy—Calvino dropped dead shortly
after getting his a couple of years ago; and now poor Primo Levi
has thrown himself down the stairs.)
. . .
    Minor pleasure: seeing Art Garfunkel on my way to the Mid-
Manhattan P. L. this morning.
    Major pleasure: seeing Cleo Laine walking briskly around the
reservoir this afternoon in the park.

APRIL 17: [I had been tormenting myself over an infinitesimal mistake I'd made in describing the plot of John Gregory Dunne's most recent novel, in a review for *USA Today*.] Talked with Katrina this morning. Confessed to feeling incompetent, in a slump. We wound up having a fairly long talk—she was sitting at home editing three novels, *Arts & Sciences* among them. We have never had the editor-as-psychiatrist kind of relationship some writers enjoy; but today we were a little more personal than usual. She confessed to her own lousy week & fantasies of escape, & she tried to cheer me up. Tells me that someone at HM is editing a book with an essay of J. G. Dunne's in it, in which he confuses E. M. Forster with Nabokov. So I don't feel quite so dumb.

APRIL 19: I spent a couple of hours on *Aurora* 7 tonight. I had a wonderful time meshing [my character] Gregory's timetable with Scott's. It's all I want to do and I wish the horrible plagiarism book would burn up or just get lost.

APRIL 20: [Louise is] very blue just now. Tommy's book has come out & it's brought back all the old disbelief that this ever could have happened. We talked about the latest AIDS horror stories in the press & I walked her home as far as 34th St., down 1st, past the bums getting ready for the night in their cardboard boxes in Ralph Bunche Park.

APRIL 23: Spent the evening writing an odd memo Katrina wants—I'm supposed to list all the *A&S* characters & then say how they've deliberately been pointed away from any real-life bases. This sounds like an invitation to trouble . . . but Katrina says it's confidential & privileged. Cork recommends it—it's what they've done with Madison Bell, who's got an old girlfriend in one of his books.

APRIL 24: Ironic mail: Frank Bergon's editor would like me to give a publicity quote for his novel; & Jeane Geehr writes from Florida asking for advice about how to get her detective novel published.

APRIL 25: [An opening party for Laurent de Brunhoff's Babar pictures, at the Mary Ryan Gallery] (Did the sight of Celeste the elephant in her dresses put me off heterosexuality for good when I first confronted it as a child?)

David [Schorr] was there with his long hair unbanded. He'll be out of town on Tuesday but wants me & Giovanni [Forti] to go ahead with our blind date anyway, unchaperoned. Wendy [Gimbel] was there; she's now writing reviews for *The Nation* & tells me I ought to rig up a deal with Vassar like the one Phyllis has with Wesleyan: "she teaches about 15 minutes a year." . . . David Leavitt and Gary Glickman, too, of course. There are no bones in Leavitt's hand: it's like shaking a chicken patty. I asked Gary if he was teaching and he said he was waiting until after his novel is out because he'll be worth more . . . Jean Strouse, who is very nice, and Nancy Milford, who's not, were talking to one another. I wind up talking Epstein with everyone—probably not wise.

APRIL 26: [Conversation with Nick over dinner in the Village] There was an article in the *Times* today about young literary sets in NY: the stars, aside from McInerney & Janowitz, were, of course, Leavitt & Glickman—the Gertrude & Alice of our day. Oh, the pretensions of their remarks! Nick works himself into a froth over it; it's because he knows he's smarter than they but will have to learn all the logrolling rules of literary life here. (Such as writing meaningless positive gobbledegook reviews—like Marilynne Robinson's of John Updike in today's *Times*—instead of the actual, real criticism you still can sometimes find in the British papers.)

APRIL 27: Headline in the *Weekly World News*: "AIDS Fears Slash Vampire Attacks."

APRIL 28: I opened the door at 7:30 to Giovanni Forti, who, just as David said, is just this side of handsome, but with a beautiful compact build and Florentine blue eyes. He has a son who's 9. He and his ex-wife are both journalists & have been here for a year. He is charming, very smart, and very impetuous.

Yes. Satisfied? I'm no brighter than I ever was. But don't tell me I wasn't pushed. By 10:00 we'd killed a bottle of wine and he suggested we order in instead of going out for a meal. Well, that didn't leave much doubt.

If you want the truth without the details: we didn't do anything dangerous, but it was very exciting and romantic. Like with Carlo: I become very American, cute Tom Sawyer, with these Europeans, and they instantly know what little-boy buttons to push. And I was drunk & enjoying myself almost thoroughly, except I could hear the disquieting voice in the back of my head: why couldn't you wait? why couldn't he?

Why? Because it's unnatural to live without sex, even in the midst of this pandemic. Why do Haitians have children when they can't feed them? Because without them they feel dead.

But this is what really bothered me. He was playing *my* role—instantly smitten, on the verge of declaring love to someone he'd just met. And I could see the little laser point of truth somewhere behind my eyes. I'm not going to be able to feel it back; I know it.

. . . He didn't spend the night. He was going home because he had movers coming in the morning & had to take his son to school.

He kissed me goodbye. My body felt wonderful: I had come lovely safe rivers onto his side. And I could feel the headache & the regrets coming.

APRIL 30: [Long phone conversation with Giovanni] . . . He suggested I come over right away & we make love. Which I said was a bad idea, though I was incredibly excited. This led to a long discussion of what was a good idea and what wasn't. I kept saying slow down. He kept saying I was right. But I felt like a liar, because I knew I would never feel what he wanted me to . . . After all, one always knows immediately. Not necessarily if it's love, but if there's the possibility. Love, or at least the recognition of its chance, is *always* at first sight.

. . . James Lord was in town & he took me to lunch at Moby Dick on Madison Ave. . . . He was quiet today. I did most of the talking. Perhaps he's down because of Madame Giacometti's never-ending campaign against him. He told one funny story: last week a gypsy fortune-teller approached him & his friends in a restaurant, and James said: "Oh, go away, we're *already* rich."

MAY 1: A report on ABC News tonight says AIDS may kill 50 million people in Africa. I went into one of my panics—not, of course, for the 50 million Africans, but for myself.

MAY 2: I was at the Y this morning & I ran. Talked to Doug and read the paper: they think there are nearly 100,000 cases of ARC in the city. Probably nobody should be dating anyone at all, ever again.

MAY 3: [At the 92nd St. Y] down to the art gallery at 11:00 to give my talk. Anne Carson and I were both supposed to speak about our work-in-progress—a bit of singing for our supper before Rockefeller Foundation representatives. But none of them showed. So we just talked to about a dozen Poetry Center members and others who'd decided to spend their Sunday morning this way.

And who should be in the 3rd row, along with my ex-student Liza Wright, and one of her Vassar friends who works at the Museum of Broadcasting, but another person employed by the Museum of B.—yes, Alexandra Isles . . .

MAY 4: Got myself up to the Y for a reading by Keri Hulme. She has a lot of personality—big, beery, working-woman's confidence— which you can't say for everyone who gets up in Kaufman Hall. The Maori stuff didn't do much for me, but I liked her. Kenny played his saxophone up at the reception in the nursery school afterwards . . . I talked to the New Zealand consul and his wife, who's Austrian, and who's also soft on Waldheim.

MAY 5: [I cooked dinner at the apartment for Nick.] There were even moments tonight when I wasn't quite sure I liked him. He seemed a little bit too much the operator, the ambitious one, in a way that wasn't completely appealing, that made me a little suspicious. (Everyone I get a crush on always starts out seeming sweet and ends up seeming real.)

MAY 6: I had a cup of coffee with genial John Gross in the NY *Times* cafeteria this afternoon. He told me a number of interesting anecdotes about the Epsteins, father & son, and about how Jacob might better have handled his crisis back in 1980. When I asked if I might quote him on the latter subject, though, he recoiled in apologetic astonishment. "Oh, no, no, you mustn't. I *know* all these people . . ."

. . . I talked with Greg, who tomorrow night raises the subject of homosexuality with his church board. He's the perfect one to do it; with his butch little voice & preppy ways, he'll surprise some of them. They're supposed to be meeting to talk about what they can do in the AIDS crisis. But he's going to say they can't usefully talk about AIDS without talking about homosexuality itself. Their music director, incidentally, is dying of AIDS, and they all know it.

MAY 7: [At the ballet with Louise Curley] Is it my imagination, or does the audience seem less gay than it did back in the late 70s? Are that many of us dead already?

MAY 8: Ran 5 miles. Over the Walkman I heard how Speaker Wright says the Conn. Congressman's AIDS death shows we must act against the disease (i.e.—transfusion acquisition = innocence). Tonight, natch, his wife reveals that Rep. McKinney did do it with the boys. So will Wright now call for less money?

MAY 9: My day began at 2 a.m. The buzzer rang and my heart screamed. I leapt out of bed, unnerved in a way one can only be in the middle of the night in NYC.

It was Kenny. He was coming home from a party downtown and just happened to think maybe he'd stop by. Maybe we could watch a video. He is so young and bouncy that that would almost be plausible . . . Yes, I should have sent him home. But what am I supposed to be? A saint? (I've said this before here.) So, yes, we made love. Super safely—though I had to keep stopping him from doing more. He kept saying—can't we do this, can't we do that, I want that more than anything in the world—and I kept saying no, no, no.

It is ridiculous. It isn't worth it. Sex will never be fun again. If it doesn't kill you, it gives you a nervous breakdown. This should have been a lovely, blond surprise, but it wasn't.

What is going to happen to this 21-year-old boy a year from now? When he meets someone who won't worry much about letting him take risks?

MAY 11: Ran 5 miles up at the Y. Typed and Xeroxed. Saw Kenny just before Yevtushenko read. A reading I did not go to. I decided to give the Rod McKuen of Occupied Kabul a miss. I saw him about 15 years ago at the Felt Forum, when I was a starry-eyed détentist.

MAY 12: [A trip to Boston to see various people at Houghton Mifflin] I spent some time with Larry Cooper, who is meticulously editing *A&S* and putting little green postems all over the ms. . . . It was fun, and deeply satisfying, to think of this going on: the Harvard novel I never really expected to publish being readied and pruned by the Common.

MAY 15: [Lunch with a straight couple] [He] beautiful, yes, but so careworn—his face has a nervous tic to it, and he makes these troubled, automatic grunts now and then. There is always something odd about the two of them together . . . there's always a plate of glass between me & them. And they behave toward each other with a kind of glamorous but brittle affection—they're like film stars in a romantic comedy. I cannot for the life of me picture them alone together.

MAY 16: [Seeing *Gardens of Stone* with Giovanni Forti,] a blandly well-intentioned movie in which almost everybody is ludicrously nice. It makes it seem as if Vietnam were a kind of natural disaster which made people understandably nervous and brought on a kind of family quarrel; we may have lost our tempers, but surely we all meant well.

 . . . At the corner of 57th & 5th, on my way over to the West Side, I was stopped by one of a group of fresh-faced sailors. He said, genuinely polite and full of mischief, "Excuse me, sir, if you were looking for a good time and trying to meet some women, would you go that way [pointing west] or that way [pointing south]?"

MAY 17: [Up to Vassar on an evening train] Went to Ann's. Naturally, she was entertaining students . . . Ann lives totally through these boys and girls; they graduate and she grows older. She wants them to confide in her & she wants to exhibit herself to them. I think even the colossal messes in her apartment (she is compulsively sloppy, the way other people are compulsively neat) have to do with this. It's a form of exhibitionism: the professor leaves her bills and bras out in the open and thereby says to the students: "See, I'm flesh and blood, too. Doesn't that intrigue you?"

MAY 18: Demo [the new English department chairman] is already picking up the soothing euphemisms of administration, which came so naturally to Charlie. When I mentioned that we could "sucker" students into Romantic Poetry if we manipulated a few of the pre-requisites for senior seminars, Demo corrected me, laughingly: "*Channel* them, Tom; *channel* them."

MAY 19: [Katrina Kenison says] it's OK if the Sokolow chapter becomes disproportionately large. But she's violently opposed to its being published separately and early in *The Atlantic*—she says that kind of thing doesn't stimulate sales; it cuts into them.

MAY 20: Far from being "a little shit"—the characterization of him in 3 separate epigraphs to an *Esquire* profile of him—Martin Amis is, I think, perfectly sweet. At least he was to me. I cajoled a brief telephone interview out of him this afternoon. He didn't say anything startling, but he gave me a few things that are useful and quotable. I'm glad to have done with the business. I *hate* [calling] people for interviews; it's awful. My stomach does turns every time I get an answer, or the phone just rings, or there's a busy signal.

MAY 21: Up to the Y to meet Anne Carson for lunch. After shooting the breeze with Kenny, David and Karl (*can* one shoot the breeze with Karl?) Anne and I went over to a little place on Madison. She told me the story of her older brother, who jumped bail while he was up on drug charges 7 years ago. He left Canada for Copenhagen. He sends her about 3 postcards a year & calls her about once . . . He will never come home again, and his parents will never again feel happy.

MAY 22: Picked up the copyedited ms. of *A&S* on Vanderbilt Ave. Katrina & Larry have done a really meticulous job. Amazing how one *thinks* one knows how to spell & set up a story with clarity & continuity. Here and there I quibble, but on the whole I'm delighted to have people asking questions like: where did Shane's toothbrush suddenly come from?

. . . Dick Ellmann has been dead for about a week & I didn't know it until this morning when I picked up the *Times* and saw the OUP's "In Memoriam" ad. A great scholar and a lovely, genial man. Bless you, Dick, for giving me a push in the ancient days of Edward Shelley.* & for kindnesses like letters of recommendation to Vassar, to the Rockefeller Foundation, other things I can't remember. And for a lovely tour of the Bodleian—showing me P. Shelley's gold watch, I remember, & telling me it looked awfully bourgeois for an atheist revolutionary.

MAY 23: Don't know how much more I can take of undeclared anything with Nick. I had such a good day—until I had to stoke and stifle my crushing crush . . . [We] talked for 6 hours. A couple at his apartment; a couple over dinner at a little dump in the East Village; and a last couple at the Riviera Cafe. How beautiful, ambitious, brilliant he is. That thick, dark hair; the powder-blue eyes; the white flesh at the open collar. I feel stupid around him . . . Hardest part of the evening: hearing him run down Dick Ellmann. Imitating him: "Jice" for "Joyce." Thought Dick was comical, conceited, venal, stupid, literally drooling. Says his big conclusion about Wilde was that Wilde was a nice man. Recalled interviewing him as an undergraduate. . . .

---

* A figure in the Oscar Wilde trials and the subject of my first long article, "A Boy of No Importance," in 1978.

MAY 26: I've got another cold. The last one came only 2 months ago. So I start thinking the unthinkable for a minute or two. And then, because the unthinkable is by definition something one can't think about, at least not beyond a minute or two, I blow my nose, take two aspirin and think about something else.

MAY 28: To Reade St. for dinner at Les Bon Temps Rouler, with Doug's father + Bruce. Mr. MacKay had specifically asked that I come along—I think because I appear to be a model middle-aged, middle-class homosexual to worried parents. A reassuring possibility of their children's future. It's a false role in lots of ways, but I'm willing enough to play it, and Mr. MacKay is quite agreeable in any case. Doug compares him to Johnny Carson, & it's a good choice. He's clever, sharp, very American, a conservative but no stand-patter, someone who can tune into any conversation, make good banter with the waitress . . . and size you up.

MAY 30: Greg's on a date. Someone he met last week called Damian. He said . . . that one sign of having been around the block too many times was being able to compare someone named Damian with *another* Damian one once went out with.

MAY 31: My wonderful Italian mother: she tells me that if I meet someone I really like & we're being intimate, we should each wear *two* rubbers because she's heard on the news that rubbers sometimes break. It might as well be 1958: "Wear your rubbers when it rains."

JUNE 2: We sat on the couch for a long while after clearing the plates; jazz on the stereo; the rest of the wine on the table. I drink far less than he does. (I'm sort of on the wagon these days & doing pretty well at it.) He remarks on this & says it's for some reason I'm not telling him. (Partly: I don't want to make a sloppy pass and be rejected.) Does he *want* me to be drunk enough to make a pass? So he can accept it? Reject it? Does he think I'm just trying to get *him* drunk? . . . I don't think I have the strength to "force the moment to its crisis"—ever, perhaps.

And maybe I never should. Because sex is finished for us. The

AIDS conference in Washington assures that we get an hourly flood of apocalyptic predictions, panaceas, off-the-cuff jeremiads. Cuomo wants to put in jail people who pass the virus on to others; Koch wants to test all tourists coming into the city.

JUNE 4: Another portent, or at least signal, that I should write *Aurora 7*. I was at the Life Gallery this morning. Deborah Cohen was showing me the Carl Mydans pictures, which are wonderful . . . We talked about how I'd been in before. I said, yes, to buy some Ralph Morse pictures—of Scott & Rene Carpenter. Then she told me Scott had been in a few weeks ago to buy some Ralph Morse pictures—to use in promotional literature for his lecturing.

. . . At 6:00 I walked in the rain up to the Union Club for *The American Spectator*'s 20th anniversary party. I did a lot of log-rolling business: David Brooks of *The Wall St. Journal* would like me to do another review; Tim Ferguson would like me to do an essay. As would Wlady—who is soft, gentle & giggly—pretty much as I expected. Tyrrell[*] is exceptionally handsome and more nervous than suave. I am made much of. Wlady introduces me as "one of our finest writers"; Tyrrell says he's a "great admirer" of my work. Fine. But I am only half at home here: the half that's not at home at Vassar. It *is* nice to be in a room where *everyone* loathes Jimmy Carter. But I want to be in a world where one can hate Ortega & not be a fag-basher; rather like Star Wars *and* civil rights. I am extinct—just when I found my real, natural political point there was almost no one to share it with . . . I believe in God and believe He wants me to make love to men. Why should that be so hard?

. . . High point of the night: meeting Tom Wolfe in his white suit. Very easy to talk to. I tell him I'll be his introducer at the Y, and I tell him about *Aurora 7*. Another Carpenter portent: TW says: "I was talking to Scott this morning on the telephone." Heaven is telling me every other day to write this book.

JUNE 6: [At Vassar to speak at Reunion weekend] Cocktails and dinner with the ladies of '27 . . . These women are delightful and

[*] R. Emmett Tyrrell, Jr., editor in chief of *The American Spectator*.

sharp. One of them tells me about how she heard of Lindbergh's landing during a luncheon party at Prexy's the month they were graduated. But they don't live in the past: there was plenty of talk of Ollie North & Gary Hart, and of CD players their sons gave them for their 80th birthdays. They are more optimistic than my generation, & they talk about how glad they are to have seen certain changes. They are more articulate, more grammatical—& if their speech carries girlish "isn't it darling"s & other such phrases amidst what are more sophisticated utterances, how nice that the dead weight of one's talk should be stuff like that instead of the shits, pisses, fucks & grunts that punctuate the half-sentences of our contemporary lovelies at the college.

JUNE 8: Louise called tonight. She says the summers are always hard now; she relives the one in '84.

JUNE 10: A lovely morning—much as I'm going to imagine May 24, 1962. I got on the train for my next bit of research—a trip back to Stewart Manor School, which seemed as cheerful as I remember it 25 years ago . . . The principal, a peppy woman in her 40s, was proud of the [school's] reading scores and her art teacher. She told me Joe Cadigan [the principal in my days] still drops in, that Marilyn Spillane and Clara Taylor have "passed away." She gave me the run of the place . . . Believe it or not, Mr. Georgi is still teaching 6th grade—though in Room #1, not #2. When he was rung up (the little black telephones are now beige) and told there was an old student down the hall, he came out to greet me. "Just give me the initials," he said. "T.M.," I complied. "Tommy Mallon," he responded. He blew off the rest of the morning to talk to me, and I enjoyed it. It's hard to find out these great icons of one's youth are more like Mr. Deasy than anyone else, but it was a wonderful feeling just to walk in the building unannounced & find that someone who was chalking the blackboard the morning Aurora 7 flew was still there chalking it. In fact, the chalked word of the day appeared to be "Glasnost." "The best modern way"—it was ever thus at the Stewart Manor School.

Georgi is still the martinet. While we chatted near his desk, the children's murmur grew louder & less fearful. I found my own stomach tightening: I knew that any moment they'd be barked at.

You know, I needn't have gone back. My memories were vivid, specific, accurate. I suppose they wouldn't be with any other place; after a while you're too old for it to strike you indelibly . . . This was more confirming than evocative—more proof, as if I needed it, that *Aurora 7* is the next book for me to write.

JUNE 12: Bad news. I finally reached Rene Carpenter in Annapolis & I'm getting the feeling she's [now] not too keen to have anything to do with *Aurora 7* . . . I got her in the midst of remodeling commotion—I could hear saws + electric sanders. I said I might be coming down soon. She said ok, pick a weekend . . . But the scrapbooks that she mentioned last time will be packed up. Do I want to wait until fall? . . . if we don't hit it off there's going to be a pall cast over the writing of the whole book. I don't need her help, really; or Scott Carpenter's for that matter. It may even be better if I don't see them: they're *supposed* to be remote, mythic, glamorous, in the book. Maybe I should keep them that way in my head. . . .

JUNE 16: [The Bernhard Goetz verdict was being discussed on *Nightline*.] Absolutely guffawed over Earl Caldwell talking about the four "young people" as if they were valedictorians going off to the Peace Corps. When asked what *he* would have done if they'd approached him as they did B.G., asking for $5, he said, "I would have said no, & that would have been it." It sure would have . . .

JUNE 17: Katrina called this afternoon to say that Houghton Mifflin had just had a "launch" meeting about *Arts & Sciences*. The good news: the sales people all like it. "This book is a gas!" one of them said. And they seem eager to push it. But they and Katrina still favor a change of title . . . She says they won't impose one on me. But something zippier & clearer? I rack my brain, to coin a phrase: *Great Explications*, *Master of the Arts* (good, but sounds like a Bruce Lee movie), *Heroic Couplets* (cutesy). *Reading Angela*? Only half the story. I search in vain for some phrase from Keats I might adapt.

. . . Around 7:00 Anne Carson & I made our way downtown to the Top of the Village Gate, where we met Kenny. We took him to see *Beehive* & then out to an al fresco dinner at Cin Cin to celebrate his graduation from NYU . . . We all took a cab up to the Y, racing pleasantly through the Park Ave. tunnel . . .

A letter from Tom Wolfe in his wild calligraphy.

JUNE 18: [Late at night] the phone rings. It's Kenny. Wanting to come over.

I thought all this was over. But no. I said no. He wheedled & cajoled. And of course I gave in. And of course, etc., etc. And of course afterwards I made a little speech about how this is not a good idea . . .

JUNE 19: Spent the day feeling crummy & tired & half sated (which is the only way one can feel in this age of super-cautious coitus: Actually, "coitus" is not even right).

[At the disco Private Eyes, Fifth Ave. and 21st St., with Greg and friends] Spent a couple of hours amidst the inane thumping music. One feels as if one is swimming through an ocean of Clinique between buffettings by phony pecs and shoulders, all of them swollen not by honest work but by pissed-away hours in the gym. And Greg loves this sort of place. We left around 2:00. (I think I know why one goes at all: it feels so good when you stop; that blessed feeling of relief when you step out into the smokeless quiet of the street in the middle of the night.)

JUNE 21: [The new age of the VHS] Got up late & saw the rest of *The Right Stuff.* ("Finishing a movie" is something one does now in the morning, the way one used to finish the novel or magazine article one put on the night table before clicking out the light.)

JUNE 22: [I accompanied Louise Curley to an AMFAR benefit at Alice Tully Hall.] Dr. Krim—married to the Orion Krim—spoke very briefly. [Yves] Montand came out to make a gentle speech about how important it is to give to this . . . You can be an anti-Communist—albeit a late one—in France, without having to be a social-agenda nut. Vive Yves! . . . He also spoke in tribute to Fred Astaire, who died today.

Finger food and milling about after the remarks. Princess Radziwill rented official bipartisan Safe Date Jerry Zipkin for the evening. Demi-stars lunged for the *Entertainment Tonight* cameras. (Most of the really big ones were 20 blocks south at the 100th birthday party for George Abbott.)

JUNE 24: . . . Lonely and edgy, went out for dinner, late. Met a handsome guy named Jim [McK.] & he gave me his number. Gave it to me back at his place.

I am not in control. I am miserable about Nick, edgy about my work. I am losing confidence that I can straighten it out . . . I am lonely, confused, frantic. . . .

JUNE 25: [To Shea Stadium with Nick] It was a glorious day and the Mets creamed the Cubs, 8–2. Dedrugged Doc Gooden did nicely. It was a breeze. Alas, no Lenny [Dykstra] . . . The guys behind us shouted "Faggot!" when Darryl Strawberry grounded out.

JUNE 27: [After a brief trip to Washington I stayed with Michael and Barbara Dowling in Annapolis.] I reached Rene Carpenter this morning & while I'll be going home without talking to her, I feel better than I have in the past couple of weeks. She was very friendly—is back to calling me "dear." I realize she is in a period of genuine chaos. She is about to move; her whole family is descending on her—today—by car; she really doesn't seem to know whether she's coming or going . . . I am convinced that she is not hostile to my project . . . I don't feel blown off. I feel more as if this is one of those tough interviews writers talk about—the ones you eventually get after a lot of stroking and cultivation and phone calls & follow-ups. I should just grow up & realize that this is going to be one of those.

JUNE 30: Greg's 29th birthday . . . We had drinks—Ben was a little out of sorts—& then went up to Wylie's for ribs, racing through them, mouths like typewriter carriages, before plonking them into the stainless steel bucket the cute waiter had put in the middle of the table.

JULY 1: [Meeting Carl Mydans, one of whose pictures I'd just bought, at an opening reception for Nina Leen's work at the Life Gallery] He told me about his trip to Freer, TX to shoot that story for *Life* 50 years ago. He says the photos were exhibited not long ago in Fort Worth & a middle-aged man named Ben Franklin came up & identified himself as the little boy Mydans photographed leaning on the iron bedstead. Said his father kept the magazine around for years; used to pull it out & tell him that it was up to him to do well, so that he'd be able to look back on the conditions Mydans photographed as just a memory.

JULY 4: I'd like to tell you how much I wanted to kiss his dozing face, but if I could find the words for that I surely would have found the gumption to do it.

JULY 6: [With Doug and Bruce and their friend Kenton] Went over to the park for the Philharmonic . . . The fireworks all delicate and silvery toward the end, though the solar-plexus-bashing booms seemed louder than ever. Ed Koch walking through the crowd & screaming "Hi!" as if he (or anybody else) had never heard of Bess Myerson. I saw one black male out of about 10,000 people, & he was gay: this was a Dukakis-for-President crowd showing off its good taste & civic pride—civic pride really being a matter of pride in having enough money to live here.

JULY 7: [Watching the Oliver North hearings] He is often speaking in a heartfelt way; at moments, though, you can see him drawing on what he learned in the Philmont High School Drama Club: deliberately hammy catches in the voice; throwing down his pencil in a gee-whiz-goddammit kid's way—like scuffing the dirt near first base after a bad call . . . Interesting as today was, these hearings—the whole scandal—is missing something. What's really needed is someone like Martha Mitchell. A lot of laws may have been broken here, but there's too much *dignity* to the scan-

dal: ideological zealotry can't compete with venality, power madness, hysteria & sheer stupidity—all of which made Watergate so
exciting. . . .

JULY 8: David Littlefield stayed at the apartment tonight. I went
up to the Y where I smashed my foot on one of the metal doors
near 91st St. A great bloody mess, like a special effect in the movies, though I don't think I broke the bone.

JULY 9: Went down to Louise's in a cab tonight. We had drinks in
front of the air conditioner—it's sickeningly hot—& talked about
Ollie and Iran. She gave me an offprint of Tommy's Boethius article (the one I wrote the editor about, from the hospital): "What
we do know, what Boethius allows us to know is that, confronted
with death, he chose to practice philosophy and poetry." Oh, God.
Tommy.

JULY 10: [Lunch with Jean Strouse] We talked about Ollie, of
course . . . On Monday people were wondering if he'd go to jail;
now they're wondering what office he'll run for. Headline in *USA
Today*: "Olliemania Sweeps USA."

Jean asks me for the lowdown on Charlie Pierce [appointed
the new director of the Morgan Library] & says she hopes he's
more interested in her Morgan book than Ryskamp was. . . .

Back here in the afternoon I finished the Epstein chapter—
that is, I put the last word to a very sloppy, inchoate, jumbled-up
draft. But at least I have a whole pot of stuff to begin stirring.

Late in the evening I went up to the Y. Anne Carson & I are
a hobbling pair. She messed up her ankle while running the other
day. And she's very depressed over failing her driving test & at
coping with her feelings about leaving Princeton . . . We made
ourselves cheerful with Ken outside the Victory Cafe for an hour
or so around midnight.

JULY 11: Went down to Nick's at about 8:00 . . . We had our usual
6 hours of nonstop chatter about everything from tapeworms to
the *TLS*, which has asked him to do an essay. We ate at The Pink

Tea Cup (soul food) and then drank for hours at Chumley's, an old speakeasy that you still have to enter through an unsigned courtyard.

JULY 14: [Arriving in London too early to check into my hotel on Cromwell Road] Everyone talks about what a "civilized" city this is—what kind of city is it that has virtually no place in which you can sit down over a cup of coffee, or a small meal, before noon?

. . .

[Seeing *Breaking the Code*, about Alan Turing] A remarkable audience—a strange blend of sophistication & barbarity. When the catastrophe occurs (he's been arrested) & he must fess up to his mother, her horrified reaction prompts the audience to laugh—as if she were some Mrs. Grundy or Lady Bracknell whose prudishness is being scorned. But the scene was never meant to be comedy; it was meant to show some of the horror that people 30 years ago had to endure. That an audience today feels accepting enough of homosexuality to laugh at supposedly ancient prejudice is something of a miracle, one Alan Turing could never have imagined; that that same audience is too dumb to realize, or feel, however remotely, what those of their class actually inflicted on those of Turing's kind, is unforgivable.

JULY 15: [At the London Library] It sits snugly in one corner of the square. The direct hit it took from a German bomber in WWII was probably meant for Ike's headquarters, which were diagonally opposite . . .

The [Charles] Reade notebooks—a huge, crumbling and filthy lot—are kept in two wooden cupboards (locked by a skeleton key) not far from the circulation desk. Douglas Matthews, the librarian, & a large assistant, Miss Dodgson, were very helpful & I quickly got about my work in the reading room upstairs. I found the two smoking guns concerning [his plagiarism of] Mme. Reybaud soon enough. . . .

JULY 16: [At the Stuart Hotel] The stupid traffic—rumbling past the *Daily Express* ad picturing two corgis and promising royal gossip—stirred into my jet lag and kept me pitiably awake, made me turn to magazines and my Walkman in the middle of the night.

Got down to breakfast & found that the milk had gone off. It insulted my tongue horribly when I brought it up from the cereal bowl in a spoon, and it made a mephitic unstoppable whirlpool when poured into the tea. I could not make the non-English-speaking waitress understand. "Sour," I said. "You want salt?' she replied. I settled for a roll & read about [Admiral] Poindexter's [Iran-Contra] testimony—he does not finger Ron, so the worst of it is already over for the Prez. Whether you believe either one of them or not.

JULY 17: When the skies cleared I went walking and walking—into Islington & parts of East London I'd never been before. Thought of Isaac Rosenberg and passed the spot where Wesley is supposed to have felt his heart strangely warmed. Something that happened on May 24. Something perhaps to use in *Aurora* 7.

. . . Jeffrey Archer's wife refutes the testimony of the prostitute who says she was with him. The missus says he has lovely smooth skin—no spots, as the prostitute testifies. This occupies the front pages of the papers of a nation that keeps lecturing the United States about its political immaturity.

JULY 18: [A visit to an expanded and upgraded St. Edmund's House in Cambridge] The apotheosis of St. Ed's—now a college—occurred on June 12 when the Duke of Edinburgh came for lunch, unveiling a plaque (where a crucifix used to be, I think) near the dining hall—a plaque so self-referential that it commemorates nothing but itself.

[Old friends David Wallace and Jonathan Kahn] & I walked along the river after dinner at the Spade & Becket. We wound up at the Cow & Calf, now under new management . . . Poor Mrs. Archdeacon. When the place was sold she told Terry, "I know these new people are gonna make changes. They're gonna put heat in." There was an advert in the local papers, too, announcing that the Cow & Calf is now an *English* pub.

(Why is Jono so anti-American? It hurts me. It must be all the loud Yanks who come [to St. Edmund's] and upset the quivering English. When I proposed that he come to the States he almost shuddered. No, he'd much rather have me come visit him when he's settled here . . . This paralytic shyness that masks such strong antipathies. I suspect Michael Hambrey is the same way. As David Wallace says, "Put him in America and he'd feel he was being raped.")

JULY 20: It's amazing how well I always work here. I hacked away at Epstein this morning and between tea and dinner worked on the balloon scene of *Aurora* 7. This novel will be the labor of love of my life, I know that . . . One thing that will have to be solved: the question of tense. I think it's going to have to be present tense, even though I loathe that staple of our "contemporary American novelists." Actually, though, what I really think I hate is the way narrative neutrality and emotional deadness accompany it. If I can keep these last two elements out of it, I should be all right.

. . . Down to Mawson Road for lunch with Claire Blunden at one of her two locals. A very frail Alec Hardie [another Blunden scholar] was staying with her, so the three of us went out to eat ploughman's lunches & ham-&-tomäto sandwiches. Hardie is just back from China. China! He hardly looks as if he could make it to London. But he's just finished a fourth year of teaching there. How much nicer he is to me now than in '79—quite sweet, really, and all because, in the end, he liked [my Blunden] book.

JULY 21: I caught my cab to the bus station and the bus to Heathrow. The bus actually turned back, fifteen minutes after it left the bay, to pick up a passenger that had missed it. The radio told the driver to return. So a whole busload of people was put a half hour behind because of one person—Mrs. T. still has a lot left to do with these people.

JULY 22: I went out with Nick tonight and, though I know I've said this before, I think this thing has gone too far.
. . . It was very hot and yet, as I passed Washington Square

and headed to Cornelia St., I felt fresh with excitement. I climbed the stairs to the fifth floor, after buzzing the code that assures him it's not the crazy landlady, and got a big hug and kiss. I gave him the book of AIDS stories (Adam Mars-Jones and Edmund White) he wanted from England, along with a tie from Bodger's. We sat in the hot apartment for a while before going out to The Corner Bistro and going through the usual business of talking for hours and hours.

JULY 29: I spent the morning down at NYU with *Aurora* 7 and Mme. Reybaud. A beautiful day, cool and sunny. So at lunchtime I rang up Nick from a pay booth off Wash. Sq. Pk. Would he like to have lunch? He sounded agitated about something, but he quickly accepted. In a few minutes we were at the Riviera . . . A rat jumped off the awning above us and landed in the street with a loud but apparently undamaging splat. It recovered itself and ran across the street and into the salad restaurant opposite us. We waited for the patrons to begin jumping and screaming, as in a Blake Edwards movie, but it never happened.

. . . I went up to the Y, and ran 5 miles in the twilight (1st time since I hurt my toe), and then came back & composed a 3-page letter to [Nick] saying the fact was that I'd fallen in love with him, that I hoped we could get past this & be friends . . .

JULY 30: I woke up in the middle of the night and wondered: am I doing the right thing? By morning I had no more doubts. By 7:30 I was on the subway; before 8 I had the envelope taped to his mailbox. I wasn't going to put this into the U.S. mails and have to endure phone calls and a planned movie date before he got it.

. . . Talked to Greg, who listened to the whole story patiently, which was awfully good of him since the person he was supposed to date last night—a date he was really looking forward to—cancelled. Greg says I did the right thing. OK, says I, what do I do when he tells me he's flattered, and thinks the world of me, and wants so much to be friends, and wishes he could return my feelings but can't? "Tell him to cram it up his ass," Greg answers. Which is the only line that's given me a genuine guffaw in 48 hrs.

JULY 31: Now I really do have doubts I did the right thing. Why not have let it go on as before? Was it so bad? . . . After a day with Epstein and Mme. Reybaud I met him at the Plaza on 58th St. and we saw *La Bamba*, a lousy little biopic about Ritchie Valens . . . And then we came back here for pizza and beer. And I talked about everything but until he said "should we talk about it?" I said OK, but proceeded to make it all as easy as possible, to make *him* comfortable, to dispose of it with a little pact: if the situation becomes too painful for me, I'll tell him; if it becomes too embarrassing for him, he'll tell me. And pretty soon, after a little more talk about *his* love troubles . . . we were on to other things, so that I might as well never have done anything at all. We were back to the way we were before Wednesday with the crucial difference that there was no longer any equality between us. And suddenly it wasn't frustration I was fighting but a kind of agonized embarrassment.

AUGUST 3: Talked to Gwen Reiss in the morning. Ticknor & Fields will spring for a photo session with Tom Victor ($500)—so I guess I've, however temporarily, arrived.

AUGUST 5: The proofs of *Arts & Sciences* came at 8 this morning from Federal Express, and I uttered a prayer of thanks as I ripped open the package. 210 pages—it looks quite lovely and almost error-free.

   . . . Up to the Y . . . Took David Low out for a farewell lunch at the Victory Café. Then back to [room] #967 to work. Ken comes by and wants, with comic transparency, for us to make love. But with will power &—I think—good sense, I just, as our First Lady says, say no.

AUGUST 10: [After the dramatic departure of the Poetry Center's director, and her replacement by Karl Kirchwey] Saw Karl in the P.C. office this afternoon. He's back from his vacation & looks as if he's about to decompose. He was on the verge of tears throughout the conversation . . . I really do feel sorry for Karl, which is hard to do since he's such a dry stick . . . He's literally sick to [his stomach] from being wound so tight. He wonders if he shouldn't resign . . . (All the locks on the P.C. were changed over the weekend.) He also apologized to me and to absent Anne for all the turmoil we got caught up in: "This wasn't supposed to be part of the Rockefeller Scholar-in-Residence program."

AUGUST 11: Mary E. called today and said her movie person at William Morris didn't much like *Arts & Sciences*. But Cheryl Peterson, an independent who used to be with CAA, "loves it" and a copy of the ms. is on its way to Michael J. Fox's "people," with whom she has close ties. Mary quite properly began this conversation by saying, "Now the first thing to keep in mind about what I'm going to tell you is that it's never going to happen."

AUGUST 14: I learned from Katrina this morning that Viking Penguin has passed on the *Arts & Sciences* paperback: Dawn thought it was a little too much a Harvard in-joke, and they didn't want to pay what T&F were asking (I still don't know the figure).
. . . And by the way: Charles Merrill Mount, an art historian who has written me a couple of times in the last several months to say that he's a victim of plagiarists, has been arrested in Boston for trying to sell letters (of Lincoln & Whistler) that he stole from the Library of Congress.
And: on an NBC Newsbreak tonight, Maria Shriver announced the suicide of Joan Rivers' husband. Why I love this country: where else would a portion of a 1-minute newscast be devoted to the Valium overdose of a comedienne's spouse, the newscaster being the niece of a former U. S. President and the wife of a former Mr. Olympia?

AUGUST 17: At 7:00 I met Doug at the News Building & we took a taxi down to GMHC so he could drop off an "intake" package with a volunteer who reminded me a lot of Steve Smith. It's a humming, busy, non-spooky place; you might mistake it for a small commercial arts firm. You wouldn't guess they deal in helping people to die.

AUGUST 19: [On a visit to Mom's] I read *Newsday*, which she has delivered. Nina now has Christopher Hitchens doing reviews. He's much admired by Nick, and he is very good.

AUGUST 20: [At my mother's with my favorite aunt and uncle] Joe and Belle arrived at lunchtime & we all had a lot of laughs. Joe grows a bit vague and sentimental at times, but at others he snaps back into being very funny. Bless gentle Belle—the only Gemein-schaft Mallon or Moruzzi who knows What I Am and to whom it matters not at all. We watched the Mets beat the Giants on the TV. Belle and Joe are completely knowledgeable fans—Belle even will wear a Mookie Wilson button. Adorable Lenny [Dykstra] had a mixed day. He got thrown out trying to steal second—but at least he got a chance to slide. And unless he gets the opportunity to do that once a game he feels like a puppy that's been kept indoors.

AUGUST 21: Went down to Tom Victor's apartment/studio near 5th and 20th at 3:00. A huge loft; a movie producer's idea of how the successful photographer lives. His handsome black assistant (lover) Ben also there. Tom is very flirtatious & feel-copping: the desired effect is to relax the subject—in my case it has something of the opposite effect at first. But basically he's a nice guy & I did begin to enjoy myself. Felt a little like Tammy Faye Bakker when he applied eye liner, blusher, and lipstick to me, but this is s.o.p. Then came hundreds of snappings: on the couch, by the wall, by the bookshelves, out on the street against brick walls, against the iron railings near Teddy Roosevelt's house. It's a strange feeling of simultaneous self-esteem and depersonalization that it gives you: on the one hand you feel as if no one in any situation could ever again pay you this much attention; but on the other, you know that shampoo bottles must be photographed with just as much loving care for ad pages. Tom says the hardest subjects are straight men past 60 who have been successes with women: now that their looks are just beginning to go, they're anxious about them—& eager to look their best. You can't get them to be natural. Whereas women & gay men have always had to be concerned with their looks. So there's less novelty & desperation to a photo session for them: you can soothe them into relaxing.

Tom clicks and says: "Oh yes!"—click—"Yes!"—click—"Beautiful!"—click—"You're great!"—click—"Tom Mallon, dis-tinguished author and cutie pie!"—click—"Fabulous!"

Everyone should have an afternoon like this.

AUGUST 22: From the library to Macy's . . . In the little sports department where I got [running shoes] they had a videotape of the '61 Yankees running. I caught sight of a man standing beneath the TV wiping a tear from his eye.

AUGUST 23: Late in the afternoon I went up to the Y and out to the park & achieved a new personal best: 7 miles or just a hair under that. It was so blue and golden and cool that I never wanted to stop. I could feel myself, rounding the northern corner, counterclockwise, and catching sight of the skyline to the south, drinking in the city, storing it up against the Poughkeepsie to come.

AUGUST 28: [Packing up my little office at the 92nd St. Y] Spacy Grace Schulman had also wandered in out of the rain. (She really is a dear. Hadn't seen her in some time. We made a point to have lunch, which of course we never will. She entered my name in her address book near Bernard Malamud's [d. 1986], which gave me the creeps.)

Back down here I found a letter from Mary [McCarthy] in Maine. Will see her on the 21st—at the Y, in fact. She says no one asked her to write anything on the Iran-Contra hearings, which she hopes says something about the hearings instead of herself. *Corriere della Sera* asked her to cover the Barbie trial,[*] but she's glad she didn't.

Greg, just back from vacation in Miami, called. Of course I told him about Michael [a lawyer whom I had begun to date] . . . The only thing that bothers him, he says, is my Hamlet complex about romance. I want it & don't want it & immediately upon starting something find reasons to discontinue it. When Greg lectures he can be a little stricter than I'd like—but he's right.

AUGUST 30: Without my uptown pied-à-terre I'm back to my old routine of running with a subway token and $20 bill in my right Nike.

---

[*] Klaus Barbie (1913–1991), SS officer called "the Butcher of Lyon," was convicted of crimes against humanity on July 4, 1987.

AUGUST 31: [Lunch with my old editor James Raimes] James (beardless) looks very fit, though older. (He ought to; I've been seeing him for eight years.) He's had a rough ride lately: he was out of work for 8 mos. after Arbor House was taken over by Morrow. But he thinks he'll enjoy Columbia [University Press], and stability; away from the trade wars at last . . . I miss the days when I worked with James. I owe no one more. He made me a writer. He told me I could be one. And he was sufficiently bullying and believable to get me going.

SEPTEMBER 2: [Vassar Convocation] Frances Fergusson has a boundless capacity for institutional self-congratulation. She made all the predictable liberal orthodox noises against Bloom's *Closing of the American Mind* and told us why Vassar is a shining example of everything that's right with America.

SEPTEMBER 6: Nick told me that he's made the decision to abandon his thesis on Auden. He can't see spending 2 or 3 years at something he's not interested in just so he can gain entry to a profession he has no liking for. Instead, he's going to hit the ground running: do some long essays this fall & look for a job on a magazine after Christmas.

If I'd had more guts, and more gifts (say as many as he's got), I might have done the same thing 10 years ago.

SEPTEMBER 8: I've just graded my first student paper in 16 months. Like diving into a dirty swimming pool.

What's more: one of the students accidentally walked off with my edition of *The Rambler*. I don't know how I'm going to teach class Thursday. I've got no annotations.

SEPTEMBER 9: Faculty meeting . . . Fran Fergusson rubs me the wrong way. Her deep voice gives her an authority her imagination doesn't entitle her to.

After that an hour in my study drafting the Brooke review, before drinks and dinner (at Dick Smith's restaurant) with Bob & Evert Sprinchorn, who tells stories of Seabury Quinn [Jr.], an out-of-control drinker in the drama department in the 50s. He's the one who defined a Vassar girl as someone who says, "Oh, shit! I stepped in doo-doo."

SEPTEMBER 11: Tom [S.] called from Berkeley this afternoon. His test results are, thank God, negative. The swollen glands? Perhaps hypochondria, perhaps anxiety (getting sick with worry over the possibility of being sick), perhaps nothing. I am relieved, thankful, thrilled.

And of course it makes me wonder: maybe I should take the test. It's been over 4 years since Tommy. What if I found I was negative? Wouldn't it change my whole outlook on myself & existence? Wouldn't it lift a huge burden? Relax me?

The answer is yes and no. The truth is it's impossible to think about dying for much more than a half hour or so a day. I would continue to behave as I now behave; in fact, I might only be a little lazier. As for safe sex: one would have to continue having it that way in any case. Consider all these things against the possibility of a + result & you decide you can't do it.

. . .

And now the news I have been keeping from you, the "you'll never guess" tidbit, the *pièce de résistance*. At 7:00 tonight, on 3rd Ave near 66th, I saw a handsome gray-haired man walking with his arm draped, a bit youthfully, over a woman's shoulder as he strolled in his youthful bluejeans. No, I thought; it can't be. Then, yes, I realized—partly from a few words I caught of the voice—it is: Scott Carpenter.

I'm pretty sure he saw my jaw drop but fortunately I stopped myself from blundering out some introduction.

SEPTEMBER 12: Jay [Geary] called in the afternoon. He and Mary & Patrick are settled in Florida; he seems weary. God, I hope he takes the Shane business all right. [I had based a character in my soon-to-be-published novel on him.]

SEPTEMBER 13: . . . The death of John Christie. I will say this for John—maybe I've already said it here, when he retired: he was a son of a bitch, but with such force of personality that, far from ever thinking you needed to defer to or indulge him in his handicap, for a nickel you'd have ripped the other arm out of the socket. This has to be counted as a triumph for him.

SEPTEMBER 14: Met Nick for lunch at the Pot Belly. He's looking a little peaked from boozy nights on the town with Christopher Hitchens and a *TLS* friend.

SEPTEMBER 15: The Bork hearings have begun. He looks as if he should be playing Juliet's father, or running for Doge instead of Assoc. Justice.

SEPTEMBER 17: I got a call from a woman at *Nightline* today: would I help with a program they're putting together on Plagiarizing Joe Biden? They wanted political anecdotes, but thought the one I gave them about Disraeli was a little too esoteric.

SEPTEMBER 19: At 11:30 Greg, Michael, Steve & I got in a cab on Columbus Ave. to go out to Williamsburg for Jean-Luc's party. The cab driver greeted our announced destination with stony silence, but we got there, going over the crumbling bridge out of the Lower East Side, for 17 bucks. A decimated P.R. neighborhood— drug dealers & boosters all over. But the building Jean-Luc was in isn't so bad. And the party was a kind of wild Blake Edwards mix: Jean-Luc & his black lesbian green-card wife; some people just off a plane from Paris; an effeminate history graduate student, very sweet, named David; an angel-boy, a young Swiss drummer . . . a gay couple wearing identical children's pajamas passed out on a mattress in one of the bedrooms; a couple of artists, I think; little twinkies and punky beer drinkers; the sweet super of the building, from Ecuador.

SEPTEMBER 20: I went up to Michael's to watch the interminable Emmys, where every sitcom is an *Iliad* and every acceptance speech a tearfully grandiloquent account of climbing Everest. Michael and I, like a bored couple in Levittown, lay side by side on the couch and kept watching.

SEPTEMBER 21: [Introducing Mary McCarthy at the 92nd St. Y] Tom Victor was shooting Mary in the Green Room. She greeted me with the news that Jim had just finished the galley of *Arts & Sciences* & "thinks it's great." She emphasized this and later in the evening he came up to me and told me he loved it: "That Angela is some babe!" Mary says she wants to read it and give it a puff, but that she's swamped at Bard rereading things like *The Princess Casamassima*.

Her reading (part of "My Confession" & a piece of the next volume of memoirs, which Jim suggests calling *And Grew*[*]) went well. "She's so beautiful!" I heard a woman behind me whisper . . .

Reception up in the 6th floor nursery school afterwards . . . The horrible Vivian Siegal, dowager-queen of the Poetry Center committee who treats everyone like a servant, was also there and told me: "you did very well," as if she were complimenting me on the nice job I did waxing her Mercedes.

SEPTEMBER 23: A meeting about freshman English chaired by the murmuring Bill Gifford. I suggest, somewhat indirectly, that we consider abolishing freshman English—just let them dive into real literature courses, the way I was allowed to take "Age of Johnson" at Brown . . . My observation, my suggestion, was considered hugely unserious and speculative, like a journal article by Robert Bork.

SEPTEMBER 26: . . . Watched a contortionist perform on a corner. The Village was jumping with authentic & touristy life tonight. One fancy car got scraped by a taxi. Big argument between drivers. Cops come. Utterly stoned backseat occupant of fancy car weaves through intersection upon getting out, presumably to avoid cops . . .

SEPTEMBER 27: I'm despairing. I talked to [W.] tonight; he'd left a message on my machine a week or so ago. He spent 4 days in the hospital with a kidney infection at the beginning of the month, &

---

[*] The volume already published, earlier that year, was called *How I Grew*.

when he was feeling weak, with tubes in his arms, he agreed to his doctor's request that he take the AIDS test. He's now waiting for the results & regretting he took it.

This is awful. Worse than waiting out Tom S.'s results in Berkeley. I'm not worried for myself. There's no way it could have passed between him and me, in either direction, unless everything they say is completely wrong. We were by-the-book safe . . . But I'm scared. I don't care if I ever have arms around me again. All I want is to live. To finish these 2 books. That's all. How could I have complained about loneliness Friday night? (As if I won't be complaining about it next Friday.)*

. . .

I read the paper, finished Wolfe and met Michael for a brunch outside in the garden behind the original Jackson Hole on 64th St. We did about 10 blocks of the 3rd Ave. Street Fair after that—the usual crush of people looking at nothing at all, ASPCA booths and bad art, and eating shish kebab. The city at its most suburban.

OCTOBER 2: Mary Evans called this afternoon. Michael J. Fox's "people" have passed on *A&S* because Michael is seeking more "heroic" roles.

. . .

[At the movies in Manhattan, seeing *Maurice*,] a reasonably authentic filming of a phony book (a book Forster himself admitted was more utopian tract than novel). These Merchant-Ivory films (rapturously overpraised by the Channel 13 crowd) are not about anything other than their props . . . the clean, pretty boys; the clouds scudding past Cantabrigian battlements; the polished antique cars. The overheated theatre was full of people who chortled loudly over jokes about "the Greeks" & other such matters, to show that they'd taken Western Civ. 101 at some point . . .

OCTOBER 8: Worked down at NYU for some of the afternoon. Realized there's something in the Calisher piece [a review of Hortense Calisher's novel *Age* for the *NYTBR*] that may or may not be construable as an error. And realized that unless I get hold

---

* Three days later W.'s results came back negative.

of myself on the subject of perfectionism I'm going to torment myself out of the writing business. . . .

Both Nick & Greg were over here for dinner. That's right: both of them. A first meeting. And they got on very well, to my relief . . .

Nick left before 10—for a late date, with a girl. Gregory's verdict: nice, even cute, wouldn't mind at all the 3 of us going out together. But: immature; screwed up; someone who will investigate his feelings out of existence.

OCTOBER 12: *I do not want to grade these fucking papers for another 30 years.*

OCTOBER 15: I went out for a drink at South Dakota and began talking with an adorable, bright, exceptionally sweet fellow named Mike. Thirty-three years old and charming as can be. And with a name like that, what else could he be? A priest. A Franciscan (at least it's my favorite order) . . . He had a lover for 2 years, left, came back. Now? He's working it out, making his own rules—waiting for JPII and O'Connor to pass on, encouraging homosexuals in the confessional to take the sacraments & consider their ability to love a gift from God . . . He's aware of the contradiction that's riven his life & he's just determined to live with it.

And yes, he came back here.

OCTOBER 16: All day long I kept thinking, if he were a lawyer I'd be ecstatic. When he was getting ready to leave, after a wonderful, tender night (I felt as if I'd found my twin), I asked him what kind of look he got from people who realized he was just returning from the night before. "Oh, they don't mind," he said, "as long as you don't flaunt that freshly fucked look." He looked more like an altar boy than someone of Crucifixion age.

I know this is ridiculous . . . [Greg] thinks it's politically appalling ("They're the enemy") but appreciates its porno value: the thought of being with a cute little naked priest.

OCTOBER 17: Ran 5 miles up at the park and didn't feel much appalled by myself. I feel excited, young, illicit, happily stupid.

OCTOBER 19: Mike called this evening & we were on the phone for two hours. As if we'd known each other for a dozen years . . . It's all too strange. Or is it? It's the 1980s. I've read David Lodge.[*] I watch the news. Priests are *supposed* to be doing these things. No? No.

OCTOBER 20: The stock market crashed today. (A good-news, bad-news joke of a day for conservatives: we bombed Iran but the market crashed!) I saw a shrieking headline on a pile of *Post*s on 14th St. after I left Bobst [Library], where I'd written on Reade. But I figured it was just the *Post* . . . What does one do? What happens tomorrow? (What do you call a yuppie? "Waiter!")

OCTOBER 21: [Dinner with Louise at L'Incontro, down the block] She says to stay in [the market], that things will get better. At the moment, she says, no one really knows what's going on . . . (I saw twisted, frantic faces beneath the Merrill Lynch ticker in Grand Central today; someone on 5th Ave. was wearing a big button saying "DON'T PANIC!")

Talked to Greg later in the evening; I got another anti-clerical lecture from him. And then Mike called.

OCTOBER 22: . . . Ron's press conference tonight. God knows he doesn't set a very high standard with these things, but he was less than a disaster, I thought.

Mike called and came over and we laughed through sitcoms and then made love. I hinted that this was all getting thoughtlessly out of control (3 times in a week—so much for taking things slowly), but in his serene, smiling altar boy way Mike said he didn't think so—this was just the initial fucking frenzy; it would pass . . .

OCTOBER 23: From Bard . . . Mary sends down an odd puff for the jacket:

"A charming, sad book that moves one by an unusual alternation of extreme high spirits and low spirits. It's also very nicely written." I suppose there is enough sadness in it, though that's

---

* David Lodge (1935–2025), British comic novelist and critic; his fiction often involves the snares of university teaching and Roman Catholic doctrine.

certainly not how we're selling it. Anyway, it's lovely of her to do it at all—a second time, too.

OCTOBER 24: Four of us . . . went up to 8th Ave. and 40th to La Escuelita, this huge underground discothèque . . . Greg and John have a taste for such adventures and I went along. We were frisked at the door. Down below hundreds of Puerto Ricans—lots of lesbian couples amidst raging little queens and their boyfriends. A few white gawkers—more as the evening went on. (Puerto Ricans not at all hostile, just completely indifferent, to outsiders.) Hot pink lights, whoops & parrot trills from the dancers. I stayed long enough for Greg to think I was a good sport. I left at 1:20 & he waited for a cab with me out on 8th Ave.

OCTOBER 27: I meet so many people who talk about how relieved they are to have gotten out of the market in August that I wonder how it managed to avoid crashing then, if there were so many sellers.

OCTOBER 28: Karen & David & I watched the *Firing Line* debate among the 6 Republican "hopefuls" between 9 & 11. Bush did well: he's less inane & tinny in give-and-take than when he makes a speech. Dole looked embalmed, but loosened up later. Kemp's discharges are all canned, but his delivery isn't bad & he surprises people by being bright. Haig & du Pont more hapless. Haig seemed old, affable, & half in the bag . . . And then there was Robertson, with the same affectless, shit-eating grin on for every sentence. The 5 others are making just the mistake with him that the Democrats did with Jackson in '84—fawning over him, praising him for bringing new registered voters to the party . . . This will only hurt the party in the long run—the fawning, that is; it makes independent moderates sick.

OCTOBER 29: Got home at about 8—the train late for the second week in a row. Mike called and came over to watch TV. We talked about things & we realize it's hopeless. We're going to stop now before it becomes hurtful. Turn it into a friendship. We haven't actually said this yet, but it's clearly what we're going to do.

OCTOBER 30: Worked at NYU in the afternoon and about 6:15 met Greg in front of the Bar Association on W. 44th . . . We went inside to the Lambda benefit. We wind up talking to each other at these things, which is I suppose the wrong thing, since in some vague way we're supposed to be finding husbands. But at least we always feel good-looking. The pulchritude quotient for gay lawyers in NY—at least the ones who join this outfit—is not high. I looked at the paintings of Cyrus Vance & other Protestants on the walls & wondered about what they'd be thinking of this gaggle of homos.

. . . From there to *Into the Woods*, the new Sondheim musical at the Martin Beck. God knows he's brilliant . . . but he can't stop rhyming to please himself . . . The singing was uniformly beautiful & the microphoning was for once measured and sensible. Not much variety (or length) to the melodies: you realize what they mean when they say you leave his shows humming the chord changes. Greg and I kept making up our own lyrics to the endlessly replayed snatches. ("They sent out a lot of ads and promos; / That's why the balcony's full of homos.")

NOVEMBER 3: Got up even earlier than usual to go across the street and, pointlessly, vote—for things like unanimously endorsed Civil Court candidates. Got up to [Vassar] at 10:00 to find that Sandy . . . had scheduled 5 appts. for hours when I'm not even here. Chose to bite lip instead of blow stack. Went down hall to count to ten . . . I am [always] so overscheduled from Tuesday to Thursday that anything less than clockwork frustrates me to tears.

NOVEMBER 5: I cleared out on the 3:53 so I could get to the Houghton Mifflin party at Scribner's for *The Best American Short Stories 1987* and *The Best American Essays*. Ann Beattie—looking still buck-toothed but more glamorous—did the first, and Gay Talese the second . . . People wandered about the bookshelves with wine and hors d'oeuvres in hand, and the sight was a little bizarre: shopping with refreshments, it looked like. Phyllis [Rose], whose essay on torture is included in the Talese volume, gave me a huge hello. She's in great spirits: Laurent is in Paris getting his divorce; and she's just turned over the ms. of Josephine Baker to Georges Borchardt, who was also there.

NOVEMBER 6: [At a gay dance at Columbia, which I'd gone to with Greg Ullman, I ran into James Alan Smith] . . . I apologized. He apologized. We kissed each other. Told the last year to each other. He's at Union Theological Seminary now—another homo for Jesus, he admits. He likes it fine except he doesn't believe in God. He finally stopped tormenting pretty [L.A.] and broke things off by telling her "I suck cock."

We had a funny, happy conversation & I felt myself charmed without being instantly resmitten . . . Somehow seeing and hearing him again demystified him, brought him back from the dark side of the moon, made him less desirable by making him, literally, less inaccessible.

The taxi that brought me home must have done 70 mph down 5th Ave. at 2:30 a.m. I felt wonderful.

NOVEMBER 7: Spent the evening at Robert Massa's 30th birthday party on W. 13th St. (in Erika Munk's apartment, just below his) . . . Mixed in with all Robert's artistic friends and colleagues on the *Voice* and gay activists like David Rothenberg was his family from New Jersey. His short Italian parents seemed good-willed and a little bewildered, I'll-take-it proud of this son whose last piece in the *Voice* was about being arrested at the Supreme Court (a couple of days after the gay rights march) during the civil-disobedience demo. ("Your shoes don't match your gloves!" the protestors shouted to the D.C. policemen wearing plastic gloves to protect them from AIDS.) Robert's brother James, a priest, with whom he argues all the time, was also there. A quiet lookalike. We talked for a time. I told him that those of us who would like to be reconciled with the church are more mainstream in other ways than he may think . . . [We] talked at friendly cross-purposes.

. . .

Robert was all dressed up—he looked as if he were making his First Communion. He said, "It's worth turning thirty just to have your mother & Judith Malina in the same room." Yep, there she was looking like a shrunken grandma with dyed hair & a party dress doing nothing more outrageous than a quiet little frug.

Robert also said: "Just turning 30 these days seems like an accomplishment." AIDS, of course. It's never more than 10 minutes away from one's conscious mind. On my way to the party I ignored a panhandler in my usual slightly guilt-ridden way. He shouted after me: "I hope something *real* bad happens to you."

[Robert died in 1994.]

NOVEMBER 10: The real story—the only one anyone talks about—as much as they talked about the baby in the well a few weeks ago . . . is the story of the little girl battered to death by her monster drugged-up father & perhaps her mother, who was beaten for years by the father. Insane, bloody beatings on W. 10th St. "Parents" who went out of their way to adopt a child. The mother once wrote children's books.

NOVEMBER 17: Chris [Bull] & I should not talk politics. I see him for the 1st time in 6 mos. [he was back at Vassar for a visit] and we spend dinner barking about Nicaragua and separatism (the gay kind) & Paul Simon. And I did most of the barking, because I was tired and ornery and sick of Vassar liberal-orthodox bullshit . . . I felt embattled in the way I used to as a freshman at Brown. In fact, I feel this more and more often now . . .

NOVEMBER 18: Ran into Chris in the Retreat this morning. He said that last night when he told his ex-boyfriend that he'd seen Mr. Mallon for dinner, the ex-boyfriend replied: "Oh, yeah, Mr. Mallon. I've seen him in The Works."

A pub dinner with David, Karen & Patty. (Joke of the day: what do Jessica Hahn and Judge Douglas Ginsburg have in common? They both blew a little dope.)*

* Jessica Hahn was a church secretary who had sex with televangelist Jim Bakker. Douglas Ginsburg's intended nomination to the Supreme Court collapsed over his having smoked marijuana years earlier.

NOVEMBER 21: Was at the microfilm reader at the Mid-Manhattan [Library] this morning. Poor soul, smelling to high heaven, mad as can be, pretending to work at the next one, scratching random (though not to him) letters on a piece of paper. His arms covered with inscrutable ballpoint jottings. Where is he sleeping tonight? And from the library I went to Saks to buy a sweater I didn't need.

A party tonight at John Cahillane's on LaGuardia Place. A party to celebrate his friend Nicholas's green card. Maybe 40 people, almost all gay men. At one point I found myself talking to a 6'5" blond neurosurgeon, Harvard '77, a rower, a dream come true, who, in a sudden grab-assy movement—so endlessly taken by my charm was he—managed to spill half a glass of red wine, mine, on that new sweater I didn't need. I was flushed with wine, wine stain, and pride. Alas, by the time an hour more had passed, he had goosed nearly everyone in the room with the same degree of interest and gusto. They didn't get stained with wine, though.

NOVEMBER 22: Darling Chris [Bull] called. He says the *Gay Community News* had a weekend staff meeting in some house in Concord—a sort of retreat that turned into a fanatical self-criticism session. He & the moderates were excoriated for not admitting the transparent justice of giving women *more* coverage than men. Stuff like that. He says he was calling in part to say he could feel the point of what I was saying Tuesday night, a little more anyway. He is a darling boy. I told him if he can handle right-wing faggots like me, he can handle Commie homos too. I love him.

NOVEMBER 23: Nick came over around 7 & we headed up to the Y on foot & in taxi. My intro. went pretty well. Wolfe himself very gracious. With that style—of dress and writing—you expect him to be a bundle of affectations. But he isn't. And his wife is awfully nice, too. The reading went well & he was very at ease answering questions . . . He looked like a million bucks—or, one should probably say, a million & a half: that's how much the paperback rights to *Bonfire* just went for.

. . .

About Tom Victor [who took pictures in the Green Room]: he looks awful. He's dropped a lot of weight since I saw him last. His voice is hoarse & he does certain things sitting that you know he would do standing if he were feeling better.[*] He says he's been on a macrobiotic diet to lose weight. But one knows that macrobiotic diets are what scared people are going on to fire up their immune systems.

Oh, God, I hope not. He's a nice man.

NOVEMBER 25: Got a ride [from Vassar] to NY with Dan Kempton, thereby avoiding the Dr. Zhivago pre-Thanksgiving special train. Bless him. We stopped to pick up a goose at a store in Pleasant Valley; he was bringing it down to Beverly Haviland's for Thanksgiving. The rumor is they're dating (Dan & Beverly, not Dan & the goose). We had a nice chat all the way down the Taconic in the gathering dark. I felt depressed after a while: why did they fire this nice, competent, bright, even elegant man, who says, "Sorry, Tom. I drive *feelingly*," after he curses another motorist?

NOVEMBER 27: [Greg Ullman's parents, Charley and Louise, were visiting him for Thanksgiving weekend. With our friend Ben Petrone] we went to Wylie's for ribs and then in a cab (5 of us, illegally; Mrs. Ullman charmed the Latin driver into submission) up to Dangerfield's. Just like Stand Up NY. We were convulsed with laughter & today I can't remember a single joke . . . And— the grand surprise. Rodney himself! He came on about 11:00. In the bag, filthy, hostile, depressed, very funny and very nerve-wracking. It was on the verge of the ugly or maudlin for 20 minutes. But it never went over & he remained screamingly beloved by the crowd even as it wondered what might happen next. He said he dropped into his own club to check out his Italian partner & see how much he's being robbed of.

NOVEMBER 30: The Haitians were wailing all day on 42nd St., desperate after yesterday's violence, pleading for anyone to help,

---

* See picture in insert. The eyeglass frames, just visible on the vanity table, tell a tale. Tom Victor asked me to remove my glasses because they were causing glare, even though he knew, from our shoot three months before, that I hated being photographed without my eyeglasses. I think he may have asked me to get rid of them on this evening because he felt too weak to stand and adjust the lights.

making not a ripple in Turtle Bay, where one handsome town-house I passed today is up for sale with the sign: "SINGLE FAMILY OR CONSULATE."

DECEMBER 2: One measure of how agitated I am just now, how close my feelings are to the surface: at the end of the last seminar of the term, my standard-issue run through the war poets, I was reading them out a bit of Stanley Weintraub's book on the Armistice (an awful passage about an American kid shot five minutes before 11:00 a.m., 11/11/18) and I started to snuffle and break down & could barely get through it. Nothing to be embarrassed about (in fact, the students like that kind of thing), but not the sort of thing I usually do; I couldn't stop it from coming.

DECEMBER 4: No regrets about sleeping curled up against Mike's elfin body. He left at about 9:30, and I said I'd call before I went back to school. There's no reason to pretend that this will last long . . .

DECEMBER 5: [At the ballet with Nick; tickets to *The Nutcracker* courtesy of Lincoln Kirstein] At the intermission one realizes that the audience is, for once, overwhelmingly heterosexual. The yuppies force all their little girls into velvet and bows, a conspicuous consumption of Victoriana. The little girl playing Clara is having the high point of her life, all too early, this month—a few years from now she'll be just another bulimic from Brearley.

DECEMBER 8: [The U.S.-Soviet summit] Mike & Raisa are here, and I swear the skin on his forehead is not only growing but sprouting little islands. An archipelago, one might say. Jeane Kirkpatrick was sitting right next to him tonight when he returned Ronnie's toast, and she had an expression that seemed to say: why don't you cut this radioactive reindeer crap, you evil old fuck of a jailer?

DECEMBER 13: [Went over] the Ellmann piece, which I typed tonight. I had a lot of words to cut, and I wound up taking out every incidental criticism. I feel a little guilty about this, but Christ—better this extreme than another. Claude Rawson reviewed the late Donald Howard's Chaucer biography in the *Times* today—& was, I thought, hyper-professional. Made it seem as if Howard's dying before he could make all the necessary revisions was some sort of malingering.

DECEMBER 20: Last night, when we were fumbling our way onto the couch, I mumbled my usual stuff about how maybe this wasn't a good idea and [D.] said, "Why not? I've been thinking about this for six months."

Well, why not? He's cute, he's smart, he's stable. The only troubles: too young (27), and too young-looking (about 15!) The real trouble? I'd wind up being the dominant partner emotionally—or at least that's what I'd be expected to be—when I, in fact, am all raging Need, wanting to be protected, cuddled, adored—& then let alone. I'm always moaning about my lack of a relationship in this book. The moan is a half-truth. 23 hours of the day I don't need or want anybody. I want no one else's sound, smell & habits hovering around me.

DECEMBER 21: [Interview with a Vassar job candidate] We talk about how he teaches autobiography in his freshman course—he says he sees these books as "hauntings." A writer's past selves come back to him, haunt him, and are then exorcised in the writing of the book. This is a nice notion with which to bamboozle eager freshmen; of course it has no bearing on literary actuality.

DECEMBER 22: [More job candidates] It's ok for [Diana] Fuss to say, as she said to me, that she didn't read literature during the whole 3 years she was working on her dissertation; but [John] Unsworth gets crucified for demonstrating insufficient awareness of minority writers over lunch. This is the new Philistinism, & virtually everyone in the department is hot for it.

DECEMBER 24: [Christmas Eve with my mother in Manorville] So, the two of us, an imploded, almost posthumous family, ended the evening as we have many other times—watching the Alastair Sim version of *A Christmas Carol* and trying to be cheerful—"in keeping with the situation."

Christmas Day: Read Malcolm Bradbury's *Cuts* on the train back. It's terrible! Dumb, obvious humor. *Arts & Sciences* is *Lucky Jim* by comparison. I'm delighted.

Mike came over, straight from some ecumenical thing at St. Thomas's, where he was all excited by meeting & chatting with Jackie O. The cable is out, so we watched a video of *How to Marry a Millionaire*, which even Mrs. O's rival, Marilyn, couldn't save.

DECEMBER 29: Ken came over at about 8:30 & we went over to the awful Marriott Marquis hotel in Times Square. The philologists are having their convention here, and Anne Carson was in town to give a paper . . . We went down the street to Barrymore's and had a quiet table, manned by a peppy out-of-work actor waiter, before the theatre crowds got out. Anne is still laughing her weary laugh, disliking Emory as much as she disliked Karl, telling us how she wrecked her car while claiming it from a wrecker's— where the city of Atlanta had impounded it after finding it parked in the wrong place.

The three of us went back to the hotel in the flesh-ripping cold and rode the elevators a few times to the 45th floor and back. They're the kind that fly up and down through an atrium—like globules through arteries, little bubbles along tracks.

DECEMBER 30: Walked to the Life Gallery . . . Eisenstaedt himself, tiny and spry, comes in to chat with and tease Marthe Smith while I'm there . . . too shy to introduce myself. . . .

DECEMBER 31: [At a New Year's Eve party in Poughkeepsie] Iva made a list of our political predictions for '88. I said Dole & Kirkpatrick would beat Cuomo and Gore.

1988

JANUARY 1: [The newspapers still printed stock quotations.] Looked at the Mutual Funds lists and saw a huge drop in the Scudder Growth & Income share price. I figured I'd managed to lose $7,000 in a quiet day on the market & was a little frantic until I got home and called David [Littlefield], who told me it means they declared capital gains: I've made money. Well, easy go, easy come.

JANUARY 2: [Nick] told me about a New Year's party he went to with this British friend—he saw Joseph Brodsky breaking up with his girlfriend on the steps. The Nobel prizewinner appeared to be giving the girl notice, not vice versa.

. . . Went to Greg's in the middle of the evening. We exchanged Christmas presents & all of a sudden, for the first time ever, kisses. Strange: think of all the meaningless safe fucks in life; almost none of them was as thrilling as this kiss. Not because it was arousing. Because it *meant* something. My friendship with him has become the most important single relationship in my life just now. And every time he mentions [moving to] Miami I cringe.

JANUARY 7: [On the phone with David Brooks] he says he'll finally run the Calvin piece next week & asks my opinions about "feminist revisions of the literary canon"—he's contemplating doing an article on this . . .

At about 5:45 p.m. Pia Lindstrom was on *Live at Five* giving a review of the musical *The Chosen*. Ten minutes later there were about 50 screaming Palestinians right outside my window & beyond some hastily placed police sawhorses, screaming, "Stop the deportations! End the occupation!" O, New York, my city, feast of irony.

JANUARY 8: A long, laughing phone conversation with Nick, still in despair over Mrs. T.'s having surpassed Asquith's time in office to become the century's longest-serving P.M.

JANUARY 9: [After dinner with Greg and Ben] They went to Charlie's from there, but I went home with the paper. I may be reeling between inappropriate "relationships," but bars, I'm determined, are a thing of the past. I haven't been in one in weeks and weeks, not even with Greg. In fact, the other Charlie's—Uncle Charlie's South—where I first laid eyes on Carl Furstenberg—has shut. The "Zanzibar & Grill" has opened up there. The word is that the real Uncle Charlie (who's known as the Ray Kroc of the gay world) sold it off to help raise bail money; I think he's accused of killing his boyfriend.

JANUARY 15: Went to the Physics Building Library this morning to get a book on the constellations. The cozy, wooden place reminded me of the sets for old college movies, and Henry Albers, the kindly astronomy prof who helped me out, could have played in any one of them.

JANUARY 16: Worked down at NYU in the afternoon. My discovery: on May 24, 1962, Lee Harvey Oswald was in the American embassy in Moscow obtaining his visa to return to America. So here is a perfect ¶ for *Aurora* 7: the idyll threatened.

JANUARY 17: Ran 5 miles up at the park around 11:00. The track was muddy & everyone was splashing and steeplechasing and having a wonderful time.

JANUARY 25: A 10:00 [English department] meeting of surpassing ugliness . . . Morgan, Brisman and Wallace assume that any procedural stitch Demo may drop in this endlessly complicated hiring business is really evidence of some sort of fix; he's putting something over on them. They, along with Beth, just hate him, and they torment him as they might a substitute teacher in high school. Morgan is the worst—cruder by the month. She dismissed one candidate today as a "gung-ho boy" and I let her have it—told her to consider why it was OK to use that term for the now universally despised white male, and what would happen if someone in the room used its female equivalent. The whole thing got worse by the minute.

. . .

Ronnie gave his last State of the Union, a platitudinous affair marked by some comedy with props: big stacks of budget pork. He received a lot of affection, I thought, but didn't get any steam rising under the contras & SDI.

JANUARY 26: I get congratulations for what I said to Susan Morgan—from several people—but Demo reports that Barbara is displeased over some overcrossed "t" in what I said, and—as is her sometimes condescending way—needs to speak to me . . . I am tired of her being the official Woman on campus, and I think she's politically off her rocker these days: she had a letter in the Sunday *Times* magazine expressing disgust over Allan Bloom's being traumatized by the black militants with guns at Cornell 20 years ago. She thinks he lacked understanding of the *reasons* they brought guns into the building.

JANUARY 27: The awful English department. Susan Morgan bursts into tears in front of me today, saying Demo's told her everyone hates her & she assumes that includes me. I say it doesn't, but I feel a surprising lack of sympathy toward her: she fuck-yous her way through month after month and then when she discovers she's hurt people, the feminist turns on the tears.

A meeting to determine salaries in the junior ranks. Barbara once again affects the higher reasonableness. Pat Wallace wants to be Barbara and Barbara wants to be God.

JANUARY 29: Nick . . . had an extra ticket for the ballet and I leapt at it. We had a drink at the Ginger Man and then went over to see *Stravinsky Violin Concerto, Liebeslieder Walzer* (torture, I thought) and *Brahms/Handel* (witty and fun). Nick is full of stories from Lincoln Kirstein . . . Robert La Fosse is Jerome Robbins' boyfriend; Maria Calegari has been missing for 3 days; Darci Kistler . . . never travels without a Bible & recently sold her NY apartment so that her survivalist brothers in Calif. can build a bomb shelter.

FEBRUARY 8: I was supposed to have an Iowa caucuses party—the results start coming in in about an hour and a half—but Nick's got the flu and Greg is going to an ACT UP meeting.

FEBRUARY 12: Nice feeling in [my agent's Chelsea] office: [Ginger Barber's] Irish housekeeper & the cat moving about, books and mailers everywhere, a tidy little operation making money . . . [Mary E.] gives me a big official-publication-day hug two days early. I walked all the way home (the rain was lighter); Friday night rush-hour twinkling. I looked up at the Metropolitan Life clock—5:40—and felt dazzled by my luck. How could I have guessed, ten years ago, that I'd have come even this far, that I'd be here, making it?

FEBRUARY 13: Came home with the *Times* tonight. A front-page article on how the virus isn't spreading to many gay men anymore (so safe sex apparently is safe)—but how a great harvest of souls is imminent. They actually say that a large portion of the gay male population in S. Fran. & NY will be "wiped out" over the next several years. Everyone who got the virus in the early 80s—did I get it 5 years ago next week?—will be dying. Or nearly everyone. And you know what this means: since the virus has stopped spreading and heterosexuals are safe, the search for a cure will slow. The dying will be allowed to die—nature's adjustment of the surplus, perverted population. Gays won't be extinct; they'll just be reduced & contained. In their secret hearts many people will think the shriving a good thing.

And will I be gathered in with the quarter of a million still to die? I tell myself I want only to finish these 2 books—let me see them done & out & then I'll go quietly. That's what I tell myself, anyway.

FEBRUARY 15: Graded papers & reread *Vile Bodies* back here. It doesn't seem as inventive and amusing as it used to. (One can reread the life out of a book if one goes back to it often enough.)

FEBRUARY 16: The main waiting room at Grand Central filled with freshly lit cigarettes—scores of people getting off the Metro North trains had just lit up, smoking on the trains having been banned since yesterday.

FEBRUARY 25: Paul [Sachner] & I talked tonight about high school (Bristol, CT being even more Italian than Elmont) and, over dinner, inevitably, about AIDS. Paul wonders how he can possibly *not* get it. Especially after reading the now-famous *Times* article of a couple of weeks ago. We talked about how gay bars are disappearing all over Manhattan—"is it that we're dying?"[*] Or is it, at least partly, that NY is no longer a mecca for gays? They can now be gay, comfortably, in cities where 20 years ago that would have been impossible.

MARCH 7: Gwen showed me the [*Times*] review [of *Arts and Sciences*] (it comes out Sunday) and it literally took my breath away. All day long I've swung between tears, panic, rage, revenge fantasies (there's no point in writing a letter; one always winces for authors who do, and they never get the last word); and, of course, phone calls . . . Ben & Greg even sent me a bouquet of flowers in

***

[*] A slight misquotation of Wilfred Owen's "Exposure."

the afternoon; this sounds funny, but it was meant to be sweet . . . I was eager to ride the tailspin. So at 1:00 I went out and started drinking at Chaps and then South Dakota . . .

MARCH 8: On Sunday morning they will all see it . . . and I'll want to be under lead blankets.

MARCH 9: An hour ago I was in the Grand Central waiting room, under Pegasus, taking a decision. I am going to bet the farm, and I am going to bet it on myself. I am going to leave Vassar in June. I am going to give everything I have to writing. For six months after leaving I am going to do nothing but write. I will finish the plagiarism book & have *Aurora 7* outlined down to the last scene. If I make no big money—have no windfall from paperback or movie rights in that time—I'll look for a job, here in NY, after New Year's. And it won't be a teaching job either.

I spent another rotten day and tonight I was out on Third Avenue, the tears beginning to break out again. And then I saw the Chrysler Building, its silver chevrons pointing upward, upward . . . I'm going to do this in the face of AIDS, financial worry, bourgeois pride in my professorial status, complete unacquaintance with a life outside schools. I've had a bad, confidence-sapping week, & I'm going to respond to it by an act of faith in myself. If I fail, I fail. If I don't, look back on this night and read this page and say: this was a time he showed some character.

MARCH 16: Geoff Stewart* here in the early evening. We had a drink & then went up to Parnell's for dinner. (By drink, I should add, I mean seltzer.) Today was Geoff's big day: the Iran-Contra indictments came down. We talk about it a little at dinner, though there's much he can't say or hear. (Like Lawrence Walsh himself he's never been allowed to see Ollie's testimony before the committee last summer—lest he be tainted by it.) Two things of real

---

* A good friend for more than fifty years. We were undergraduate classmates at Brown and then both went on to Harvard, he to the law school and I to the English department.

interest that he did tell me: the Sandinistas are as up to their asses in drug-dealing as the Contras; and Fawn Hall has surprisingly fat legs.

MARCH 22: [First day back at Vassar after the review's appearance] As soon as I got off the train I imagined that everyone was looking at me, pitying me, and this feeling persisted all day . . . A number of people did come to console me, but that only made it worse. I got through the Expos class and even made a joke about it (few of them had seen it & they think it's amazing that you've gotten your name in the paper at all), but I still felt pretty awful.

The chief consolation: on Feb. 14 *The LA Times* gave the book a rave. This only turned up today because of a mishap with the clipping service. The woman who reviewed it (5 full columns) found all sorts of parallels between Artie and Keats that were never intended, but her piece was clever & fun. The awful thing is that no one around here (and, face it, it's your enemies, not your friends, you care about) will see it. . . .

Told Demo what I'd decided in the afternoon, and by 8:00 p.m. my letter of resignation was in the Unstamped [campus mail].

MARCH 24: Well, the *Chicago Tribune* gave the lead fiction review to *Arts & Sciences* on Sunday and said it was a *Catch-22* of the 70s. But that's not the real news. The real news is that Katrina (who is happy with the news of my resignation) remembers now who [the *Times* reviewer] is: someone whose novel she turned down several months ago. She couldn't remember her sooner because the novel was so dreadful she only read half a chapter of it.

MARCH 25: Met Ben & Greg & his Florida cousin Scott at Grampa's (it's run by Grampa Munster, the actor Al Lewis), on Bleecker St., right near Nick's corner (where there was a gangland rubout early in the week). From there to Charlie's, where we found Peter, who really had a buzz on. A nice balmy night. They were making a movie in Sheridan Square. The sky was flooded with man-made light & Kevin Kline was coming out of a building near the Monster.

APRIL 7: [A reading at the Cambridge, Massachusetts, Public Library]: Afterwards I signed books. Two nice nearing-retirement ladies from Wellesley who use *A Book of One's Own* in their freshman English sections came up to me. And then I was greeted by a distinguished 50ish gentleman. I said, "You look awfully familiar." And he replied: "I'm John Fox, Dean of the [Harvard] Graduate School." I burst out laughing & said I hoped they were taking this all right. He said they were & that they were even thinking of giving the book "a little push." He says graduate students are still miserable in all the same ways and perhaps the book can be a cheerful antidote for them.

Darling Chris [Bull] & Katrina & I walked back to the Square through the Yard . . . Katrina & I had a long dinner at Harvest, and I spilled the beans about *Aurora 7* to her. To my great relief, she was immensely enthused—says they'd consider buying it on the basis of just a chapter and a detailed description. This is wonderful news, and I was gleeful. We discussed my Vassar-less future, & how she'd like the plagiarism book out by August '89, & I was vastly energized.

APRIL 17: Read more of the Shaw letters—I'm going to be at them [for a review] for weeks . . . Phyllis called from Middletown. She'd heard about my leaving Vassar and called to offer encouragement. She says Judith Thurman makes $2000 a month by writing one anonymous column for *Self*.

APRIL 18: Well, tomorrow is the primary, and if I weren't a disaffected (unregistered) Democrat, I'd be voting for Al Gore (that Tipper is one lucky girl). He's the only one who sensibly backed what RR did in the Gulf today. Dukakis is just a mush-mouthed McGovern. The rehabilitated Richard Nixon more or less said so in his interview on CNN tonight.

APRIL 19: Gore has done awfully (it's 9:55 p.m.) and will probably quit the race tomorrow. Dukakis will be the Democratic nominee. And the voters and reporters are blaming Koch for telling some truths about Jackson . . . After dinner [in Poughkeepsie], Patty,

Karen & David & I crossed Raymond Ave. & saw a large, light-colored Cadillac travelling past us toward Main St. Inside it, in the front passenger seat was the Rev. Al Sharpton—the burly, bouffant Rev. Al (ordained by his mother) who has taken charge of Tawana Brawley's lies. He was coming from campus, where he was no doubt talking about IRA or cult links to the case or comparing the State Attorney General to Hitler. Rev. Al is quite a man & I gave him a clenched fist salute that I hope he caught while primping in the rear-view mirror.

APRIL 20: A lively seminar on Foster—the pusillanimous line about betraying one's country rather than one's friend always gets a good discussion going. They're always shocked to find that their teacher doesn't think it's a beautiful sentiment.

APRIL 21: Ann tells me that both Demo & I have made the "10 Sexiest Men on Campus" list in the women's bathroom of the library. Alas, I had an annotation: "Not really a hunk, but the conversation would be wonderful." Demo made it on raw sex.

. . .

[Nick] asks me if Mary McC is likely to sue over a passage in a book of recollections of Auden being put out by Alan Ansen & punched up by Nick. Auden said that during the early days of her marriage to [Bowden] Broadwater, Mary joined the "anti-Homintern" by speaking of bisexuality as an affliction. I told Nick she certainly wouldn't sue over such a thing. For one thing, she's not in a position to sue any writer after her stand against Hellman the Censor; and for another, and to her credit, if she still believes that I'm sure she'd make the same remark to my face—without either of us losing any respect for the other.

APRIL 22: Well, thank heavens for neocons. Lionel Abel was *The Wall Street Journal*'s reviewer, and he liked it. He reads it as a tale of sexual role reversal & questions Artie's "maleness" (a word choice that dates him, since today one would say "sexuality")—and I didn't have that stuff much on my mind—but more importantly he says it's a "light, vivacious and very winning" novel that "hums literately." So—one more fuck-you to [the *Times* reviewer].

APRIL 23: . . . Dinner afterwards at Au Natural at 55th St. We admired the cute manager & waiter. The burglar alarm then went off and they couldn't figure out how to turn it off. It whooped (OOO-LAY-OOO-LAY-OOO-LAY) for fifteen minutes. While they were poking at it in vain I realized that this was really a job for a heterosexual and that there wasn't one in the whole place.

APRIL 24: A cocktail party at Doug & Bruce's up on West End . . . a lot of people from Doug's agency, a lot of them talking about his awful boss . . . the one with the husband who irons her dresses and adores Barbra Streisand.

APRIL 25: Tonight they had the 4th annual International Center of Photography awards at the Hilton; Marthe Smith asked me to join the Life Gallery table, which was awfully nice of her. So after an hour of cocktails in a dim, low-ceilinged room (the Hilton is a horror), I got to see Eisenstaedt get the Lifetime Achievement Award . . . The strangest component of the evening: Cheryl Tiegs as co-host. She made cutesy, boop-boop-a-doop remarks & stood in front of projections of assorted avant-garde & Third-World-suffering photos, just as she had to stand mutely behind one guy who attacked the absence of female honorees. Someone who took lots of pictures of Mao on the Long March also got an award. Through this all she glistened in her green dress . . .

APRIL 30: Nick had 2 of Kirstein's $42 house seats for the NYCB's American Musical Festival. OK. We go in. We sit down in the 2 best seats in the theatre. (Robert Gottlieb is not far from us.) And then, ok, who comes to fill the seats directly to my left? No, you've got to guess. Come on. Yes, male. Yes, famous. Yes, beautiful. All right. I'll tell.

BARYSHNIKOV. And his date.

He sits next to ME.

OK, Nick & I exchange amazed let's-get-hold-of-ourselves glances. We decide to be Cool. For two hours . . . I had to keep resisting the impulse to MAKE CONVERSATION. ("Hey, I guess tomorrow's May Day. D'ya ever miss it?") He didn't like the first new piece, *Into the Hopper*. It was too cutesy for him. When the real-life dancers started darting in and out of a projected movie, he muttered, disgustedly, "unbel*eee*fable."

MAY 1: [On the phone with Jay Geary] I tell him about leaving Vassar . . . His response—I might have written it for Shane—to the announcement that I'm going to try to make my living writing: "God, you've got balls . . . it's surprising your voice isn't deeper."

MAY 2: A congressional aide who'd been the subject of an exposé in *The Washington Post* jumped out a 24th-floor window of the Helmsley Palace last night. The cop wouldn't say if the paper he left was a suicide note. "One got the sense that he wasn't too optimistic."

MAY 3: Taught my last class of non-senior non-English majors . . . They ascribe their glazed, beaten-up look to the fact that the VAX [the college's computer system] has been down for days & they've been staying up nights hoping for it, like Jesus or Tinker Bell, to revive. They compose papers at rows of terminals as if they were working in the Triangle Shirtwaist Factory. It's absurd.

MAY 7: Lots of pictures in the sun outside. Loree's old [high-school] friend Evie was there with her daughter. The children were mesmerized by a little bird embryo—you could see the teeny beak—that had fallen onto the steps. It looked like a right-to-life sermon in the making.

MAY 8: After I was home Greg came over for a beer & we got into a hell of an argument. He watched the *Aurora* 7 tape & I told him that the gay character in my novel (Tony DiPretorio) is a future AIDS victim. Greg says this is "trite" & that I should instead show strong gays surviving the 80s. So we get into a whole argument over affirmative-action literature and my hidden self-hatred & Lord knows what blah, and I thought: if I wanted to be talked down to like this I could find some Vassar undergraduate to do it.
                . . .
News item: it turns out Bess Myerson was arrested for shoplifting in Harrods in 1970, while she was Lindsay's Consumer

Affairs commissioner. I guess it was meant to be the ultimate tip to the thrifty buyer—if you want to save money on something, just walk out of the store with it.

MAY 10: To Vassar and back with the Shaw letters each way on the train. WHY WON'T HE DIE? I'm past page 700 and he just goes on and on.

MAY 11: I walked over to Lincoln Center for an ABT matinee. Me and a thousand powdered, curled, bespectacled matrons sucking hard candies and crackling the cellophane . . . But I enjoyed standing on the outdoor balcony during the intermissions, watching the posters; the azaleas in Damrosch Park; the rain coming down; the absurd little Statue of Liberty on the rooftop across the way. Yes, at the moment New York is my only boyfriend.

MAY 12: . . . While eating at the Washington Square Diner spotted Rob Lowe, Brat Packer, in the back, eating and smoking and wearing very dark sunglasses and sort of hoping he'd be recognized.

MAY 13: Went up to the West Side at about 7:00 for a welcome-back cocktail party for Jay Y. given by his former girlfriend. Yep, girlfriend. Shari Patrick, an awfully nice woman from Nebraska, who's a lawyer now in NY. They've remained close since she got the real story. She had a poster-board full of old snaps up, going back to a fraternity formal in 1978. They were adorable together. If this had happened 25 years ago instead of 10, they'd be married & miserable now.

MAY 17: Bad news in the morning. Katrina called to say there were no takers for the *A&S* paperback rights during a telephone auction. Late in April. The market is soft, etc. . . . The truth is also that my ego isn't very hurt. Plenty of first novels don't get paper backed. What really bothers me is the money—that's several more thousand dollars I'll have to scrape up in other ways.

MAY 18: It keeps raining & the stock market keeps falling. I had lunch with Nick in Washington Square. (On the way down I hear a loud gum-snapper sitting next to me: I turn, expecting to find a little Queens secretary; instead, I see a chic Ultrasuede woman reading a copy of *On Liberty*, by John Stuart Mill.)

MAY 19: Watched a program of great-ladies-of-musicals from the White House. Mary Martin forgot some of the words to "My Heart Belongs to Daddy," and Ronald Reagan wasn't able to notice.

MAY 21: . . . Up to Poughkeepsie for Barbara's 50th birthday party . . . a more select crowd than I expected; not *tout* Vassar at all. Good food and music and lots of liquor. Barbara's mother came & everyone danced a lot. (Elizabeth Schalk's huge grey bouffant hairdo fell down after midnight—there were hairpins all over the floor. No one had ever seen her without it up.)

MAY 24: Tonight I did a reading at the Vassar Club in NY . . . There was a modest crowd, and I started reading the 1st chapter [of *Arts and Sciences*]. I could tell it was not going over. (You can't just drone from a text to such a small group, about 20 or so—it's a formal act in informal circumstances & it won't work.) Anyway, it went on & I got through. Polite applause. Then questions. All of them friendly except one—no, two—from a battleaxe from the Class of '24 in a red fright wig. "How can you expect anyone to care about these characters? I was an editor & I can't imagine anyone caring about them." . . . She persisted, telling me how I had to know these things and that presumably that's why I'd come here in the first place . . . I smiled & said no, I just came to read and that it was a little late for feedback. "The novel's already out and I'm not displeased with the reviews or sales. I'm sorry, but I can't make you like the characters."

Most people were embarrassed by her, and I kept my tone polite even as I refused to play dead. Afterwards somebody told me that this is her usual way at these events, which she always shows up for. (Linda Fairstein '69, the woman who prosecuted Robert Chambers, spoke a couple of weeks ago and this same woman lit into her too.)

An absurd incident—comical, of course. But I can tell you that it ruined my day & I had a couple of drinks by myself before I went home . . . Have I really done the right thing, picking a line of work that requires an elephant's hide?

MAY 27: I'm back [at Brown] for my 15th reunion. Before leaving the apartment this morning I primed myself with a James Taylor album . . . Providence is certainly not the shabby place I walked into 19 years ago. The train station has been redone & there are cranes visible everywhere. The whole place is very spruce, especially the campus. (Exception: the West Quad. I went strolling through Archibald House, past my old room & Jay's—the place doesn't look as if it's been painted since we left.) . . . The campus dance was crowded, and very pretty under Japanese lanterns on a clear night . . . wandered up to the very top of Sayles Hall [with my friend Deborah Mayhew], where we stood at a window in a dark room & looked down on the dance. We realized how lucky we'd been to get this fancy start in life . . . The truth is you don't really come back to meet other people; the person you keep running into, the one you came back to see, is yourself. And you find him, around every corner, through every doorway.

MAY 28: A gorgeously sunny day. Late in the morning I walked to Elmer & Sophie's on Alumni Ave. near Moses Brown. (Thayer Street is pretty unrecognizable. The little shops have given way to franchises. Even Thayer Market is now a CVS.) . . . We drank coffee and talked about the search for Howard Swearer's successor at Brown. One rumor is that Gregorian (of the NYPL) is on the short list. In fact, Sophie & Elmer were off to a talk by him in the afternoon. Elmer reflects on the failed presidencies of Heffner & Hornig. Says Heffner's wife used to weep when student radicals confronted her husband; Lilli Hornig, by complete contrast, would have made a better president than Donald.

MAY 30: Greg came home from London last night. I went up to the West Side tonight & we sat outside the JG Melon at Amsterdam & 76th and drank beer. He told me about his adventures &

how he suddenly found himself attracted to "European men" (there was some Frenchman in London) & may be breaking out of his south-of-the-border pattern.

MAY 31: Greg wants me to go with him to some Broadway AIDS benefit Sunday night—one of the partners at Chadbourne and his wife are sponsors. Greg figures if he brings a male they'll figure out he's gay. In a way he wants them to. And he thinks I'd be an appropriate date. And that's why I don't want to do it . . . If I'm going to be his date, then we ought to be dating.

JUNE 1: Louise is just back from France, and she's off to Russia in August. She reports that François's marriage has—what a surprise!—already broken up. When she arrived the wife was already gone & he had 2 young men . . . staying with him. The wife apparently only wanted the marriage so she could get the French equivalent of the green card. And she's taking him to the cleaners, too.

JUNE 2: At the NYPL this afternoon, and at home tonight, I went on a great writing jag and finished the draft of the [last] chapter—which is to say the book [*Stolen Words*] . . . I feel I've got a manuscript now & can be immensely relieved. Everything from here on seems mechanical. A couple of hours a day typing and revising & doing all the production things, off & on over the next year. But no more having to secrete new prose. And I can turn to *Aurora* 7 without guilt.

JUNE 3: Dinner with Greg and Ben at The Yellow Rose of Texas up on Amsterdam Ave. . . . On the way home I saw what *People* magazine calls "America's Strangest Couple": aging chanteuse Margaret Whiting & gay porn star Jack Wrangler.

JUNE 4: A very encouraging letter from Mary [McCarthy] in Maine. She says she's sure I'm doing the right thing leaving Vassar; feels certain I can make a living writing. "In fact I rejoice for you."

JUNE 7: . . . Down to the corner of Broadway & Prince for my first PEN meeting . . . The awful Susan Sontag presided. It is a measure of her courtesy and warmth that the meeting started one hour late & she never once apologized or even alluded to that fact. She managed in the next hour and a half to insult Thomas Fleming and to give us a little lecture on the absence of human rights in Korea (South, of course).

JUNE 8: . . . Up to Olympic Tower to watch [Christopher Field] broadcast to Japan. At 5:30 p.m. our time it's 6:30 a.m. there & he and [Shirley] MacLaine's daughter start making happy talk in Japanese. Chris holds up the front page of *The NY Times* and talks about Dukakis' having clinched the nomination. They do CNN-like features on things like suntanning, cut away to tapes of Chris in front of the UN with a microphone & then Shevardnadze inside at the podium. It moves very fast . . . a St. Patrick's spire is their backdrop. The control room is a little frantic but they are smooth as silk when they chatter. (They really do say "Ah so.")

JUNE 11: . . . Finished Carol Gelderman's [biography of Mary McCarthy]. She doesn't make a whole of Mary, but she is good on one distinguishing feature: Mary's complete lack of cynicism. Whatever worldliness, bitchiness, and occasional pessimism she has, she is completely without that.

JUNE 14: Park City, Utah: On the plane out here I met Fran Kiernan, who was at *The New Yorker* for 20 years & is now at Houghton Mifflin . . . Cumulus clouds so small and regularly spaced over the Midwest that they looked like little peaks of whipped cream shot from a frosting gun.

JUNE 15: Lunch with the [*Writers at Work* conference] organizers on the patio. Lots of congratulations about the reading [last night]. This & the excessive respect of the wannabe writers here for the published ones is good for my ego—which has had its ups & downs since *A&S* came out . . . Ron Carlson & Sandra McPherson were tonight's readers. He did a charming story about 12-year-old boys. She was another story, reading poems about her schizophrenic daughter into a hand mike like a lounge singer. Fran & I, sitting near Nan [Chalat],[*] cringed a little.

JUNE 16: Had coffee with Richard Ford this morning. We were putting our heads together about our 11:00 panel on reviews . . . He's a thin, handsome Southern tough-guy, now a Westerner . . . we got on fine & did a very good show together . . . Richard won't write bad reviews & thinks nobody ought to write a review who hasn't written a book. I offered less of a Platonic ideal & more bits of information about how the business really works. RF said negative reviews "by an Edmund Wilson or a Tom Mallon" might be useful to a writer, which was sweet of him . . . Pretty Charles Baxter read a funny story tonight, & he was followed by helmet-haired May Swenson, whose poetry is mostly correct & a little dull, but which takes some nice playful turns. . . .

JUNE 17: The 2nd-to-last-night party back in the Summit Room of the Yarrow. The round tables around the dance floor remind me of a prom. Fran & I dance and merge with Charlie Baxter & ambitious little Rachel Simon. Ford sits near Fran; someone presses a request to send her a ms. The music gets eclectic & ends with Harry Belafonte & I go to bed happy. . . .

JUNE 18: My last panel came after lunch. Things get very touchy-feely topic-wise on the last day. Ron Carlson, Janet Burroway & I had to discuss "I'm OK, My Writing's OK." I took the classical view. Your writing is not such an extension of yourself as you probably think. You can be ok & your writing can be lousy. It's still more important to be a nice person than a good writer, and, above all, get your self-respect from something other than writing or love. Carlson was fun . . . [Burroway] has published a lot of books & is by any wannabee's definition a successful writer. But she is torn up by all the first-book adulation paid the Mona Simpsons of the world.

Nan took Fran & me up the chair lift (scary) & down the

[*] A college classmate and friend ever since. Longtime editor of *The Park Record* newspaper in Park City, Utah.

alpine luge (fun). I worked the brake too much; if we'd gone a second time I'd've been a little more hell-bent. A gorgeous view swung into place about halfway down: a great mountain dotted with human beings' houses. (I realize that landscape, no matter how spectacular, doesn't interest me much without some touch of man in it.)

. . .

The last reading was at the Kimball Arts Center. Poor Janet B. had to precede the star, Richard Ford. He read a good lean story, but before he did he pumped himself up into a real emotional tizzy by reading an exceptionally beautiful poem by Richard Hugo. As a result the reading was a little like watching a live Judy Garland performance. His voice quavered throughout & you wondered if he'd get through it. The deliberateness of this was a little obvious & offputting to me. He's very much a James Dean figure: the unbearably sensitive tough guy.

JUNE 19: High drama this morning. The police arrive at the Yarrow looking for 2 teenage boys who've been reported missing. I saw them last night in the hospitality suite; they were with a guy who runs a little paper in Salt Lake. He'd been sort of flirty with me at the pool & tried to give me a really strong drink, which I didn't want, in the hospitality suite. Other people have already connected the boys to him, but Nan urges me to call in what I know before I leave. I don't like giving my address & phone # to police in Utah an hour before I catch a plane, and I don't enjoy feeling like the faggot informer, but Nan says I'll feel bad if the boys are found in Hefty bags and I did nothing. So I tell them what I know over the phone. It will probably turn out that these kids just get a hiding from their parents for going off in search of more drinks with a harmless queen. . . .

. . .

Nothing too startling in the mail [at home in New York] or on the phone tape. Greg stops over for a drink after a late Sunday night in the office. I tell him the police story & he asks if I've considered that the 2 kids may have been hustlers & that the chubby publisher may be the one in a Hefty bag? Once he said that I thought, of course. In fact, if this had happened in NY it would have been the 1st thing I thought. I guess a week near Mormons dulled my gay sensibilities.

JUNE 21: Nan called this morning. The two Utah boys are safe and sound, but they *were* taken to the chubby guy's house and not found until 1 p.m. the next day. Nan couldn't find out if anything actually went on, or if any charges will be filed, but the kids were only 15. Jesus. She did say that about 30 people all together connected that guy to the 2 boys. So my call hardly mattered by itself.

. . .

An awful evening . . . I argued on behalf of the INF treaty, which [S.] said she'd sort of heard of but wasn't really familiar with, but she couldn't believe how *anybody* could *ever* have been against the nuclear freeze. I pointed out that if the freeze people had gotten what they want[ed] in '82, there would still be intermediate-range nuclear weapons in Europe—the ones that are now being dismantled.

JUNE 25: At about 1:00 Ben & I met at John C. & Magno's down at LaGuardia Place & began the preparations for Greg's [birthday] party. I had already picked up the huge cake (a great bargain) at Veniero's on E. 11th St. We got 6 cases of Rolling Rock from a distributor on E. 2nd St. after stopping for hot dogs at Katz's enormous deli-restaurant on Houston St. The place looks just as it must have 45 years ago, complete with signs saying "Send a Salami to Your Boy in the Army."

JUNE 26: I scoffed at Greg's description of Jimmy Carter as an intellectual, and he said, with a sneer, "well, maybe not a Harvard liberal arts intellectual" . . . [Chris Bull and I] walked all the way to the pier to see the remnants of the [Gay Pride] parade and dance—Chris eager as a colt. I was glad it was over when we got there. Still, a small crowd milled about. (Lots of female cops—less of an incitement to gays.) Everyone there pretending to be festive, while knowing it was on that stretch of Christopher St. that a lot of people caught their death. (A gaunt man with KS on his face passed us moments before we passed an apartment window hung with gaudy streamers.)

JUNE 27: . . . Uptown to The Gibbon, a little Japanese restaurant on 80th St. between 5th & Madison, to meet Fran Kiernan & her husband for dinner . . . Talked about tormented little David Updike (Fran says that John U. really rewrites the stories that David's grandma publishes in *The New Yorker*). . . .

JUNE 28: I'm very happy. This morning I called up Wlady at *The Spectator* and asked if I could cover the re-launching of the shuttle & write about the future of the [space] program. I had a careful list of reasons why I could do this, but he agreed after about 30 seconds. I'll get at least $1500, which means I'll clear about $1000. I'm delighted. Of course, I'll probably be the only person in the state of Florida who doesn't drive a car, but I'll work that out.

JUNE 29: Talked to Greg. We agree that we've been spatting too much. He thinks I was "grudging" about giving the party. I tell him I was only annoyed that, after Ben & I agreed to give it, he kept interfering and telling us what we were doing wrong . . . Tomorrow night—his actual birthday—he & John & Magno & Ben are going out to dinner. He says if I don't want to come, "it's okay"—i.e., I have his permission—since I've already helped give the party. I wonder if he knows what a little martinet he sometimes sounds like.

JULY 1: The appetizer was strips of seaweed—it looked as if we were spies eating microfilm.

JULY 2: Louise came up here at 11:00 this morning & we took [the] bus up to the Metropolitan Museum, walking over from 3rd Ave. to 5th. A beautiful, cool, breezy day—the streets deserted for the holiday weekend. We saw the Mantegna *Descent of Christ into Limbo*. (Eve is the calmest one in the picture, seemingly on her best behavior, thinking if she & Adam just shut up & act properly they may get out of here.)

JULY 7: I delivered *Stolen Words* to Katrina this afternoon. The third book I've handed over to Ticknor & Fields. Laurie Parsons & Fran Kiernan were also around & I got big congratulations.

Is it a good book? Yes, I think: with a good deal of pruning & polishing it will be. Katrina listens very carefully to my list of things to consider while reading it. She knows this book has been a struggle & she wonders if she will ever suggest a topic to an author again.

JULY 10: Wonderful city. The lasers—great green shoots—go every night now. And the new curved building on the NW corner of 57th and Lexington is a marvel.

JULY 14: *One* subway ride: I get panhandled twice while on line for a token; ahead of me on line a customer gets in a shouting match with the clerk; once on the #6 I see a drunk come in the car, weaving & dancing & banging on the doors.

JULY 15: [A weekend at the Kiernans' in Sag Harbor] We're already here: me; Fran; Elisabeth Biondi, a German picture editor at *Vanity Fair*; Vance, who works for *Life* and whose last name I still haven't gotten; and Gabe, who also works for *Life* . . . Fran is adorable—serene, pretty, a lot like Blythe Danner.

The house is enormous, room after room, a garden, a beautifully tended pool. We made late-night pasta in the big kitchen & got merry. Lots of conversation on the Expressway coming out about the magazine world: Tina Brown's flunked her driving test; Anna Wintour is terrorizing *Vogue.* . . .

JULY 16: A fine day in this country house full of people. Sat by the pool reading Sassoon this morning and getting a bad farmer's sunburn on my arms. Actually, when I take off my shirt I look like someone naked except for long red evening gloves . . . Took a midnight drive to the beach with Vance & Gabe. Except for one or two campfires going, a blackness as pitch as anything in Maine. Hard even to find the waterline.

JULY 17: We drove back very late, hoping—successfully—to beat the Sunday night traffic back from the Hamptons. We listened to a Patsy Cline tape in the car. The only traffic we hit was in the Queens-Midtown Tunnel, which only had one lane open. The other was being washed, and the ceiling was flecked with soap bubbles. It gave the place an ominous, leaky feeling.

JULY 18: Was at the library in the afternoon. Wrote the little loggerhead turtles scene for *A*7. Everyone in the reading room was looking up at two men perched in electrically-raised cherry pickers who were changing every single bulb in two of the chandeliers. One man mutters, "So that's how they do it."

The heat may never break. One can't wait for it to—& I absolutely refuse to worry about the Greenhouse Effect—so I just went running up in the Park while the thermometer still said 91°.

. . . Settled down in front of the [Democratic] convention. Ann Richards, the beehived keynoter from Texas, gave a spirited, shallow speech that got people laughing ("Poor George [Bush]—he was born with a silver foot in his mouth"). She was followed by awful, rheumy-eyed Jimmy Carter—as dreadful as ever.

JULY 19: JFK Jr. introduced Teddy. Jesse was the great climax & he delivered a rousing speech, but everyone was so *expecting* to be roused that something was missing. Still, it was hard not to go damp-eyed when seeing things like Rosa Parks singing "America the Beautiful" at the end.

JULY 24: The Winogrand show [at MoMA] was not as messy as his last years of work are said to be . . . Funny how even the geekiest subjects—one step above the Arbusian pit—seem to have unnatural amounts of *volition* in pictures. Since their positions are fixed you assume they must have chosen them. Yes, the photographer manipulated them, but they're manipulating you. They've somehow *decided* to look like this, and forever.

JULY 25: Well, business is good again. (Question: did any of us begin as many simple statements with "Well" before RR was President?) The *Chicago Tribune*'s Dianne Donovan called today; she'd just gotten my clips & immediately offered me the new Joseph Heller novel.

JULY 28: Nick and I were working side-by-side on different micro-film readers in the reading room—he was checking Auden things and I [researching my novel] was looking at old stories about Thalidomide.

JULY 29: God, the Heller thing is bad. All this cutesiness about historical parallelism—so many things I'm taking as guides of just what not to do in *Aurora 7*.

JULY 30: Met Ben & Greg at Macy's. Bought a new kettle—& a phone, thereby becoming the last person in NYC to get rid of a leased rotary one.

JULY 31: [Mom's] as thin as I've ever seen her . . . It's a combination of being worn out by the [grand]kids; conscious dieting; and widowhood: just no real interest in cooking for herself. But she looks good & the Parkinson's tremor seems no worse. I try to keep her off the subject of Loree.

AUGUST 1: I went up to happy hour at Bogart's, which is considerably less depressing than late-night hours in any gay bar. But no one there was as unbelievably handsome and sweet as the man who flirted with me in the Food Emporium at about 7:00. We talked on the check-out line—the only time I've ever wished it would move more slowly. He told me he lived in the Beaux Arts on 44th St. I think I'll modify my route to the library & the subway for the rest of my life.

AUGUST 2: One of the best walks around here: on First Avenue—from anywhere in the low 50s—back to my place. It's slightly downhill and you get a breeze coming off the river. And since, of course, the East River isn't a river, it's really an ocean breeze you're getting, and you can smell the salt.

AUGUST 3: I met Loree & Seán in front of Penn Station at 10:30 this morning & we went up to the top of the Empire State Building. Seán was terrified that one of us might lift him up so he could get a better look. As it was, you couldn't even see Central Park: a filthy layer of ozone was covering everything.

The difference between Seán and Chrissie: Seán brought Raggy, his rag doll, with him—it was in Loree's bag—& at one point on the observation deck he held it up, very tentatively, so Raggy "could see the city." Loree tells me that last night Chrissie asked her to bring [her] doll & throw it off the building & then tell her what it looked like. She's 5 years old & she watches *All My Children*. What's she going to be into at 15? Snuff movies?

AUGUST 4: Robert Massa called this afternoon & told me he's had a boyfriend for 4 mos. & that they're moving in together next week . . . I feel like a freak. In the last year it seems as if the whole gay world has coupled itself up.

AUGUST 5: From there we went to Michael's Pub (where we were joined by Jose, Jay's designer date) to hear Joan Rivers. A big cover and outrageous drinks prices. A warmup singer so blowsy . . . we weren't sure it wasn't meant as a postmodern goof. Then Joan. Loud, crazy, dirty, febrile, workaholic. (She'd just come from doing *Broadway Bound*.) Crazy stutterings between bursts of prepared material. (She did one cluster of jokes twice in twenty minutes. People lowered their heads and wondered and muttered about Alzheimer's.) She was plenty funny in places, and thank God, there were no direct references to Edgar's suicide. The audience was a mix of gay men, Vegas goers, and girls on a night out from Bklyn: Farrah hairdos, lots of cigarettes and fake nails.

AUGUST 8: Greg is apartment hunting. He's going to look at a place near Tompkins Square Park, right where they had the big riot the other night. It's in Christodora House—an old settlement house that the Black Panthers took over 20 years ago. It's now a fancy yuppie building & the object of punkie, commie wrath downtown.

AUGUST 10: Wrote my Heller piece in the [NYPL] reading room. [The book] is so bad that I couldn't keep pummeling it for more than about 625 words, and so I called Dianne Donovan in Chicago and asked if I could come up short.

AUGUST 11: I did the truly stupid thing of running 5 miles at 4 p.m. when it was 92°. I came off the track beet red, facial veins throbbing, earning stares from a couple at the edge of the reservoir. When I got back down into the subway the skin on my arm seemed weirdly puckered. And they say there will be no change in the weather—not even movement of the air—for 2 weeks.

AUGUST 12: . . . After a while a 30-year-old tax consultant named [G.C.], with movie-star good looks and blond hair, a swimmer, started talking to me & asking me if I'd like to go to the bar on the corner to play the bowling game. So there I was—was it 2 in the morning[?]—playing some sort of shuffleboard/pinball/bowling, dancing, having another drink bought for me, not believing the looks of this man or my good fortune—& knowing, of course, that I'd hate myself in the morning.

AUGUST 13: When we got up the sofa bed was full of quarters. He even had one stuck to his beautiful brown back as he walked to the bathroom. He was, he explained, planning to do laundry today. This as we fumbled through good-byes & thanks & I-guess-I-was-a-little-drunks, and exchanged telephone numbers more out of courtesy than expectation.

AUGUST 14: I ran 5 miles in the morning, while it's "cool" (the new standard for that is under 90°—it was only about 89 when I got off the track) . . . The whole city is indoors and enervated and feeling sorry for itself.

AUGUST 16: Bush has picked cute Dan Quayle from Indiana to run for V-P. He's rock solid on defense and—of course—full of New Right stuff on social issues. But I'm happy to take the defense stuff & wish there were more neocons like Jeane K., who addressed the convention tonight—and who probably couldn't have pleased the Far Right if Bush had taken her. (They wouldn't even have approved of Goldwater: he's pro-choice on abortion.)

AUGUST 19: Read some of *1 Henry VI* tonight, just because I was appalled to realize how long it's been since I've read or seen any Shakespeare.

Turned down an assignment from *The Washington Times*. Moonie money would bother me.

AUGUST 22: Lunch with Demo & Joanne on Vassar Lake Drive. Once more we talk about what I'm likely to do beyond next year. He thinks I should let him rig up a Nancy [Willard] deal for me—after all, if I'm going to teach the odd course now & then (and probably pretty regularly) I ought to have some existence on paper. This will protect me from the caprices of chairmen and the worst exploitations of part-timer salaries . . . no meetings, & one day of class a week. I'd always have half an office & access to letterhead, supplies, Xerox, etc. . . . I've already learned this summer that I can make 2/3 of a living writing—so why not take this & be done with it & realize I'll have pretty much everything I've ever wanted in the way of a career?

AUGUST 23: Dinner tonight at Elisabeth Biondi's. She's the *Vanity Fair* photography editor—a very sweet & lively German—I met at Fran & Howard's in Sag Harbor. The two of them, & Vance Muse, and a painter named Cora & an Irishman named Billy were also there. The apartment is way down [on] Jay St. & has, I think, the biggest bathroom in NYC. Conversation turned to politics, and I of course cheerfully get called a fascist (I really am *rara avis* in my own circles). Also lots about movies & magazines & Fran & Howard's appearance this afternoon, before a Co-op board. (One of the members, noting that she worked as an editor, said they wouldn't need to factor in her income.) Gossip courtesy of *Vanity Fair*: the awful girl in McInerney's new novel is Mort Janklow's daughter.

AUGUST 25: Very good news from Katrina this morning. She's at last read *Stolen Words* & seems to like it very much. The only chapter with any real problems is the Epstein one; it's overdone, she thinks, & mean-spirited. But even there it's mostly a matter of just chopping & toning down. (I got her to admit that in part she's fearful of the Es getting their minions to gang up on the book; but the changes probably make good sense in any case.)

AUGUST 26: Going through Grand Central after lunch: crazy black derelict screaming how God wants all the homos killed. At the top of his lungs. I thought of telling one of the cops across the station to do something about it, but I didn't. Then, back here later, watching *Live at Five*, I hear Sue Simmons interviewing the boxer who got in a street fight with Mike Tyson a few nights ago. He keeps calling Tyson a "homo." She keeps giggling and making nice & giving the guy a big thank-you for coming. So I called up WNBC to complain—I asked if she would have continued so cutesy & gracious if he'd been making racial slurs. The operator (who I think was black) thanked me for my observation & said he'd pass it on.

AUGUST 28: I came down 2nd Ave. and at the corner of 53rd St. heard one of the payphones ringing. Some lonely old man hoping one of the hooker boys will pick it up.

AUGUST 30: Talked to Ben tonight. He's just come back from Washington. He spent 3 days taking Patty Hearst around talk shows & publicity stops; she's pitching the paperback version of her book, a tie-in to the movie that's coming out. They closed the bar in the Mayflower Hotel the other night—she is now a sensible preppy matron from CT. . . .

AUGUST 31: . . . Vance Muse and I had a drink tonight at Joe Allen's . . . We came out and peeked into the Guardian Angels headquarters on Restaurant Row: they've been there all summer, supposedly fighting drug pushers.

SEPTEMBER 1: Thomas Mallon: *Stranger In Two Worlds*. Jean Harris took what could have been my title. Last week, at Elisabeth Biondi's, I was the crazy neocon. Tonight, at David Brooks's up on W. 90th St. I was the most liberal person at the table . . . David's wife is pretty and preppy—in fact, politically, the closest thing to me: she voted for Gore in the April [primary]. Also there: a colleague of David's from the *Journal* named Melanie; and pretty Donna Rifkind from *The New Criterion*. And then there was enormously fat Terry Teachout . . . He's always making nervous disparagement of gays in his articles, and I knew the topic would come up tonight. He said that homosexual literature was of much higher quality before gay liberation. I said this was rubbish. He said being "openly gay" hurt writers. I said the un-openly gay writers he admired (the pre-libs) must have been a little bit open or else he wouldn't even know they were gay. He said the "gay world" was too specific to make universal literature out of. As opposed to unparochial places like Yoknapatawpha County? He said gay literature suffered from being *political*, that its *agenda* hurt him. I asked him then how he could admire Flannery O'Connor, every one of whose stories was, by her own admission, a tract.

SEPTEMBER 5: Passed the listless Labor Day parade this afternoon (a group of flight attendants were carrying a Don't Fly TWA blimp) on my way to Saks. No, I am simply too short to wear a Perry Ellis camel-hair overcoat. Which is a good thing, since it cost $765.

SEPTEMBER 6: SOVIET SPACE DRAMA, as a Brit headline might have it. Faulty retrofire over South Atlantic nearly strands Ivan & Afghan partner in space . . . They were safely down by the time *Nightline* was on, and listening to the scientists' comments made one realize that this was really more a *glasnost* story than a space one. The Soviets let their own people know the guys were in trouble while they were still up there.

SEPTEMBER 8: Saw Nick at the library, where I wrote the Elizabeth Wheatley scene for *Aurora 7*. It's Mary, of course; but could she really object to it? I don't think it's any less affectionate than the Homer Blomberg piece of *Arts & Sciences*.

SEPTEMBER 9: . . . Went down to Gramercy Park South for a cocktail party at Shirley Johnson's. (Nice, scattered Shirley predictably ran out of gas on the Taconic on her way to her own party.) William Phillips (*Partisan Review*) was there, on a cane, looking frail,

making sour comments . . . one felt, in spite of himself; his infir-
mities were getting the better of his better nature.

A very unpleasant evening afterwards. Up to Greg's for a drink
(& then dinner at Alameda) with him & John Cahillane. John asks
us for advice: he has 2 subletting offers on his apartment in London. The better one is from the South African embassy, which
would like it for a diplomat. John's question: is it morally all right
to rent it to them? I say yes, since international relations, even
with murderous regimes, are generally something the world needs
to sustain. One might even argue that the cause of freedom for
blacks in S. Africa will be advanced by continued diplomatic contacts with the regime instead of its isolation. (I mean, Lord: look
what I live near in Turtle Bay—Libyans, Iranians, Soviets, you
name it.)

Anyway, the discussion turned more general and Greg, who
would not let me finish a sentence, barked: "You may be intelligent, but when it comes to politics, your head is up your ass!"

SEPTEMBER 10: Greg called early this afternoon & we had the
worst argument we ever had. A watershed argument, probably . . .
Well, I am tired of being pushed around by his moral high horse,
barked at and taken for granted.

SEPTEMBER 11: Loud rock concert outside. It was over at the
U.N., the postscript to a charity bicycle race (world hunger). But
it was deafening. Life here was unlivable for a couple of hours, &
they had already been practicing last night. So I called the police
(& I wasn't the only one to do so). Five years in NY & the only
time I call the police is to protest a charity event to fight world
hunger.

But as Louise said tonight when I told her this: what about
world deafness?

SEPTEMBER 13: . . . A call from David Schorr, who's back from 15
mos. in Italy, inviting me to a party Saturday night. "There'll be
some interesting men there," he says. David is as warm and silly
as ever. (I remember what a shock he was to Anne Carson, who
used to refer to him as "the man who kisses everyone.") And while

totally unbrutal, he's unbelievably direct—he comes right out and asks how my health is, a question gay men do not generally ask each other on their first phone conversation after 15 mos.

SEPTEMBER 14: I realize how the situation I've got now is perfect. Vassar has become a day in the country.

SEPTEMBER 15: Garth [C.] called tonight. Wow! "I said I'd be swamped until the 15th, but, well, it's the 15th!" I can't quite believe this gorgeous creature is really interested in dating me, but my ego has gone up 50 points.

Went to the Life Gallery this morning & Deborah showed me some Dmitri Kessel pictures . . . Eisenstaedt—"Eisie"—came in to talk to Deborah at one point. He was very befuddled, couldn't find something, muttered that the best thing that could happen to sales of his pictures is his own death.

SEPTEMBER 16: . . . Paul Konigsberg has had to have the woman who lives in the room above his arrested. She has for months, 2 or 3 times a week, pounded on her floor with some kind of battering ram. So forcefully that not only has Paul's ceiling fallen in, but also the plaster in the apartment *below* his is falling. He had to go to court about 8x before he got an order. She told the police she has to do it because "Mr. Paul have a ray gun he keep pointing up at me."

SEPTEMBER 17: At 9:00 to a late dinner party at David Schorr's up on W. 86th St. in that apartment that looks like an atelier over a Venetian canal—all the drawings of opera characters, the busts and dolls, the bottles and glasses . . . I'd never really heard [David] tell stories to a whole table, never really heard him hold forth, & he turns out to be terrific at it. Stories of the cocktail party held for Candy Darling at the home of 2 old aristocratic, New Englandy professors at Wesleyan; about seeing Holly Woodlawn on a talk show & hearing her answer the earnest host, who wanted her to counsel all the poor folks dealing with their compulsions, with this advice: "Always look your best." And a lot of other tales, all spun out to exactly the right length. Including one of how he told an Italian ex-love how Phyllis was advising David to give up conquests & settle down. The Italian listened attentively, lengthily, consideringly, and then said: "Feelis ees wrong."

SEPTEMBER 21: [A Vassar colleague's] expressions have gotten very odd. They don't always coordinate with what she's been saying & she looks like a film that's been badly dubbed.

SEPTEMBER 22: Saw Mme. Onassis on 86th St. after I ran. Her face like a fine beige suede, nicely worn. A loose scarf over her head.

SEPTEMBER 23: Lunch at the Princeton Club with nice Carol Houck Smith of Norton . . . She tells me how 25 years ago she was the freelance editor (for Ivan Obolensky) on Joan Didion's first novel. "Joan always wore a mantilla and dark glasses and she was so nervous she'd play with her jewelry and not look you in the eye. You never knew if she'd show up or not. She was always out all night at some place & living a really *weird* life. She made me feel awfully prim and proper."

. . . Nervously shopped and started cooking. Garth came over at about 8. At first I thought it was going to be torture, that we were running out of things to say. But things eased up over the food (and wine) & we started laughing a little & confiding the usual things about pasts and do-your-parents-know and so forth. And after that we watched some of the Olympics (bless them for showing male gymnastics tonight: a great aphrodisiac) and entwined on the couch and went to bed.

SEPTEMBER 24: Garth reverted to his strong-silent-military type this morning in a way that I found more endearing than worrying. He was out of here pretty quickly, neat as a pin . . .

Loree called. Christina cuts off the connection when it's time for *Pee-wee's Playhouse*.

SEPTEMBER 25: . . . The debate. Dukakis clearly won on pts. But I found myself *loathing* him, & I'll bet that was a common reaction across the country. As Joe Klein says, he is "limitlessly smug."

My literary ideal and mentoring friend: with Mary McCarthy, 1982.

Creaking stairs, a rickety fire escape, mice . . . and a paradisical escape from Vassar: my first New York apartment, on East 43rd Street, next door to St. Agnes Roman Catholic Church.

Tom Curley at breakfast in Baltimore, 1983.

Rachel Kitzinger, a mainstay during Tom Curley's illness and death.

Wear your rubbers when it rains: my mother was unfailingly supportive; Bill eventually made me a better, more patient son.

1985: what a time Tom Stevenson picked to arrive in New York!

"You better don't": the spirit-lifting Carl Furstenberg, 1985, making fun of my tiny television and my writing.

In Scribner's Fifth Avenue window . . . and not quite believing it; 1985.

Up in Yorkville, I'm pretty sure, with Anne Carson, my fellow Rockefeller Fellow, for 1986-87, at the 92nd Street Y's Poetry Center. I think we were both spending more time on projects other than the ones that had been funded.

With Greg Ullman, and not even arguing, on vacation in Puerto Rico, 1987.

Click. "Yes!" Click. "Beautiful!": my first professional jacket photo, by Tom Victor; see August 21, 1987.

The glasses (on the vanity table) tell a tale: Tom Victor's photo of me with Tom and Sheila Wolfe, as well as Karl Kirchwey, at the Poetry Center; see November 23, 1987.

1987: my niece and nephew, Christina and Seán, who were back and forth between New York and Ireland in the 80s.

Impossible, and often brave: my sister, Loree, 1988.

Doug MacKay, left (1988), and Chris Bull (1986); Vassar students who became my lifelong friends.

The incomparable Miriam Golombeck (1920–1990), Bill's friend and then mine, 1989.

Home at last: with Bill at Symphony House in New York.

Bill (right) on the Hudson with our Vassar mates for the past four decades. From left: David Littlefield, Jim Montoya, Karen Stolley, and Pat Kenworthy, 1990.

My many return visits to Lubbock always took me back to Mary Hatfield's kitchen.

Bill with Gene Moore of Tiffany's, for whom he created a series of elegant and whimsical window displays.

In Sag Harbor with Fran
Kiernan, briefly my editor
and thereafter a friend, 1989.

With Elisabeth Biondi, photo wizard of
Vanity Fair and *The New Yorker*; on the
beach near Sag Harbor, 1990.

Quiet but steely, Robert
Massa (1957–1994) was a
theatre critic at *The Village
Voice* and eventually its
AIDS editor.

E. Howard Hunt in 1990:
my *GQ* author, fellow Brunonian,
and eventual fictional character.

"A most lovely gentlemanlike man":
Elmer Blistein, my Shakespeare professor
at Brown, 1990, with his midsummer
night's dream of a spouse, Sophie.

Irene Grabowski, the discreet
secretary who was alert to
every folly in the Vassar
English department.

From 1989 on, April usually meant going with Bill to hear Dixie Carter at the Café Carlyle.

Not your usual astronaut: the wondering, complicated Scott Carpenter, 1992.

Delivery-truck days: *GQ*'s cover story on the Clinton-Gore ticket, 1992. Gore Vidal, its author, was always keenly interested in newsstand sales figures.

Opening with the bang-bang: Gore Vidal, during the time I edited him at *GQ*.

With my close undergraduate buddies—left to right, Jay Geary, Rob Doggett, and Geoff Stewart—back at Brown for our twentieth reunion in 1993.

I can't imagine why Dan Quayle is paying more attention to Bob Woodward than to me. We're interviewing him aboard *Air Force Two*, flying back from Indiana to Washington on July 4, 1991.

The sparkling Sallie Motsch, in 1994. She checked and nailed thousands of facts for me—and died far too young.

Most fun job ever: in my *GQ* office at Condé Nast, 1992.

With Lucy Kaylin, *GQ*'s witty ingenue writer, later a powerhouse magazine editor and executive.

Conferring with Art Cooper at—what else?—a party; this one was at the Lion's Head in New York City, 1993. Football star Frank Gifford is behind us, and *GQ*'s managing editor, Marty Beiser, is seated behind the plates.

With Louise Curley and Bill, more than twenty years after the harrowing summer of 1984.

SEPTEMBER 27: [Merritt Island, FL] It's 8:30 p.m. and I'm in Room 160 of the Holiday Inn . . . The badging station, where I picked up my credentials this afternoon, is on the edge of the [Kennedy Space Center], just outside the gate—& near an old Redstone rocket & Mercury capsule that look small enough to be a ride in a children's playground.

SEPTEMBER 28: It's actually 2:05 a.m. on the morning of the 29th, & the huge digital countdown clock in front of me says -5:32:49. And across, in the distance, at the foot of a huge totem of floodlight, is the shuttle . . . Everything went perfectly today. I got a ride out here with another press guy—a cameraman—in the motel. I met him over a beer in the lounge late last night . . . All day long there was a sheep-and-goats system. If you've got a green card, like an immigrant, you're lucky. But if you're writing for a monthly you don't get one. And you can only watch the shuttle go up from the Causeway . . . I managed to get a lady who wanted to go home for the day to jump me from the wait list to the privileged one. It makes all the difference in the world. The only people who will be between the people in these bleachers & the astronauts themselves are the fire-&-rescue team, somewhere in a bunker . . . It's now 2:30 [a.m.] and the place is filling up. So are the fuel tanks. The LOX and liquid hydrogen are in the fast-fill mode now . . . And if I hadn't given up tenure I'd be teaching freshman English tomorrow.

SEPTEMBER 29: There was real doubt for a while that it would go, but when it did there was beauty and joy. The sound takes a while to reach you, but when it does the whole bleachers and your body are vibrating. It disappeared too quickly for everyone's tastes, into the clouds. In fact, it was behind the clouds when the 73-second mark (the point at which *Challenger* exploded) was reached . . . I have a good story to write—complete with my 4 a.m. interview of the men in the firehouse lounge.

OCTOBER 1: Got an airport limo to Orlando, where Jay met me . . . [We] went running around a nearby lake—3 miles in the hot sun. He sometimes does up to 7. It's obviously the way he works off the tension & asserts control over himself. He is wound even more tightly than he was in '86, though. He'll be joking & reminiscing & seemingly fine & then you'll look down & see his hand is balled into a tight fist.

OCTOBER 3: Arrived back to a message from *The New York Times Book Review*. They want me to do 800-1000 words on Isabel Colegate's new novel. This is the first thing they've asked for since Hortense Calisher last year, and the first, of course, since they gored *Arts & Sciences*. Needless to say we didn't discuss that. It's such a boring, badly written rag. But you just don't say no.

OCTOBER 6: Jackie Deval, the pretty BOMC publicist who's gone to head the department at Doubleday, took me to lunch at Bice on E. 54th St. We had a very good time watching a waiter spill a whole bottle of sparkling water & someone else use a cellular phone at his table.

OCTOBER 7: Garth came down here at 8:30 . . . [The movie we went to] was sentimental & I could tell that at the end soldier Garth had a tear in his eye. Which I liked. Just as later, after we'd finished making love, and I was getting ready to leave [the] too-small bed & sleep on the foam couch, I liked him for saying, "No, stay here for a while. It'll be nice."

OCTOBER 8: Garth left early, but with a hug & kiss that were different, much more real, than the morning-after ones before. This was the first day I walked around a little dreamily, thinking of him . . .

. . . Talked to Mom, who was upset by an article about Parkinson's Disease in *Newsday* and now feels sure she will get worse. I calmed her down, realizing how lucky we've been so far, and how really strong she's been the last few years. I told her to do what I do with AIDS articles in the paper: skip them. By now there's nothing more I need to know.

OCTOBER 9: . . . The day was clear & beautiful & I walked up to the Whitney, as I'd been meaning to for weeks, to see the Robert Mapplethorpe show.

He was a Floral Park* boy, and now he's dying of AIDS. The pictures are very beautiful, whether they're of calla lilies or black musclemen or people in leather. It's a little like Cecil Beaton Goes to the Mineshaft. There's one that I thought was some still life of something made of metal and wood: get closer and you see it's a penis in a torture device like a mousetrap. Oh. . . . The show doesn't *épater les bourgeois*; that's hardly possible these days. It's more like a slavish offering—see, I can go down into the depths & bring these things back to you. I can make them pretty & expensive. I've even given my life in order to do it for you.

OCTOBER 13: Anatole Broyard called today, while I was running, and asked if I would do a "charming" essay for the Christmas number of *The NYTBR*. Something about Christmas in diaries, memoirs & letters. I said yes—glad for the exposure, glad for the money, but wondering if I'm a dispenser of nicely written Lit Lite. . . .

. . .

The *Newsday* paper boy outside Grand Central this morning: "Read about the sorry-ass Mets!"

OCTOBER 15: What I'd like is the courage to live decently alone, for work and friends and whatever awareness I might gain before I die. But I remain starved for romance—& mostly because I think I'm *supposed* to want it, am afraid my status in the world will drop if I'm perceived as a freakish spinster.

OCTOBER 16: Went to Mass at St. Agnes'. A little like Russia. Sparse population in the pews; most of those in them are old. I suppose that it's mostly a commuters' church, that the people who stream in and out at noontime go to their own parishes on the weekends; but it's still striking. And the priests are mostly old.

---

* The Long Island town next to the one where I grew up.

OCTOBER 17: Katrina called at about 5:30 to tell me she's leaving Houghton Mifflin on Dec. 9 . . . We never became personally close, but we respected each other. She knew when to praise and when to say something wouldn't do. My life is utterly different than it would have been without Ticknor & Fields . . . I honestly can't imagine life without trips to the 6th floor of 52 Vanderbilt Ave.

OCTOBER 18: Cleaned the house before Doug came by for a drink. Sweet Doug, he brought flowers to make up for having to cancel lunch. He's going to his prep school reunion back in Tennessee this weekend—with another gay graduate who works here in the city. He shows me the printout of the hotel reservations: 1 Room, 2 Queens.

OCTOBER 19: . . . To Geneva, on W. 55th, to meet Garth for dinner. He looked handsome in a different way: his glasses were on & his hair was tousled. We had a nice long dinner. No real trouble talking, but still more like a first date than a fourth or fifth. No real sense of history accruing. I also do not think he's in the mood for any long relationship; he speaks too happily of not very long ago adventures.

OCTOBER 20: Read more of Isabel Colegate & of Aram [Saroyan]'s book before Louise came by at 6. We had a couple of drinks and then went off to *Ain't Misbehavin'* & had a ball. It's miked to the point of eardrum-damage, of course, and Nell Carter isn't happy unless she can twist vowels beyond recognition, but the whole thing is still a blast . . . There were a lot of deaf people in the audience—some sort of special night—& it was actually signed (amusingly, too) by 2 people in a spotlight in a corner downstage.

OCTOBER 22: We went to Julius' later & had a really nice, easy, laughing conversation. Greg can be human there; it's not like Charlie's, which makes him crazily avid.

OCTOBER 26: Lunch with Nancy Dye, the new Dean, today . . . She's delighted to make a permanent 1/3 slot for me; she's even willing to let me keep my title of Associate Professor. I have absolutely no care either way about that—"Lecturer" would be fine. . . .

OCTOBER 27: Martin Beiser and his assistant at *GQ* took me to lunch at the Ambassador Grill this afternoon . . . they have black bear on the menu, but [I] ordered something else . . . I sold him on the little diaries piece & a 90th birthday profile of Alfred Eisenstaedt. They pay a dollar a word . . . Last March I expected a struggle, that I'd be counting every penny . . . [Demo] says Dan Peck has told him that if everyone were allowed to do what Tom Mallon is doing we'd end up with a department of part-time "satellites." Yeah, except that if he tried to do it, he'd fall to earth like a stone.

OCTOBER 29: Finished the draft of my Christmas essay. I think Anatole will find it a bit of a downer—I've got homelessness, AIDS and war in it . . .

. . .

At 8:00 I went to Garth's. (Tomorrow night's dinner isn't coming off, so he said he'd make dinner for me tonight instead.) The apartment is nice, a prewar version of mine, though a bit stark & in need of books & pictures. He has a cat with an off-center moustache named Groucho. He made a very good dinner and we were intermittently talkative and happy. And then we got ready for Marcia's party. He was gamer than I, although I allowed him to spray my hair with green & glitter. He went with black-&-white stripes on his face & looked like a gorgeous zebra . . . [Back home] we scrubbed and went to bed. Outside the bridge was twinkling & the tram was weaving.

OCTOBER 30: Today I was the one who turned quiet and eager-to-go in the morning. He wanted to cook me breakfast, but I just wanted orange juice and to be on my way.

OCTOBER 31: Autumn in New York. The Halloween parade goes on downtown. Imelda Marcos surrenders to authorities and is fingerprinted while wearing a Filipino butterfly dress. I pass Brooks

Brothers a minute after a Japanese tourist has had his pocket ripped, his wallet stolen, his wrist twisted raw—in the middle of the afternoon.

Read some of the Civil War letters I'm reviewing for *The Philadelphia Inquirer*; they're wonderful so far. Wrote the Tommy Shanahan scene at the NYPL; drafted Vidal tonight; and typed my *Times* essay. At this rate I will end up outproducing Joyce Carol Oates & Balzac put together.

NOVEMBER 4: Beautiful twilight coming home, east on 45th. My favorite time of the year in the city. I love it because everyone seems so busy, moving so fast. I'm like Balanchine: faster, faster, I want to tell everyone in the streets.

Dinner at Fran Kiernan's—she & Howard are now at 1185 Park Ave. . . . [Elisabeth Biondi] had just come from a birthday party for Robert Mapplethorpe, who has taken a turn for the better, is looking less cadaverous & working feverishly. (Bad pun not intended.)

NOVEMBER 7: Lots of telephone post mortems on the [birthday] party [Greg threw for me]. Greg, on seeing Garth for the first time without Halloween make-up: "Tom, I have to tell you this. If you weren't going out with him, I'd be trying to sleep with him." (This is a high compliment indeed, given the fact that Garth isn't at all his type.)

NOVEMBER 8: Bush in a walk. The Duke dully noble in defeat. The media begrudges Bush a "mandate"; the campaign was too "dirty" . . . (Joke: What does Dukakis mean in English? Answer: Mondale.)

NOVEMBER 10: At 5:30 I walked over to the Time-Life [Building] for Eisenstaedt's 90th-birthday show. A crowd was packed into the gallery and the space between the elevators on the 28th floor. Debra re-introduced me to "Eisie" & we confirmed the details of our appointment on Monday. They had Korbel, and a cake with 90 candles. I chatted with Dick Stolley & Marthe Smith . . . Came home in the drizzle carrying some of Eisie's books, lent to me by

Debra—and my Kessel photograph, which I'd just paid her for. That may be my last purchase: I'm out of walls.

NOVEMBER 11: Thrown for a loop this morning by Marty Beiser of *GQ*. He says he wasn't able to sell the Eisenstaedt [idea] . . . something is fishy. As late as yesterday afternoon he left a message on my machine saying he hoped to see me at the opening. (He never showed.). I think somebody told him at the last minute that Condé Nast wasn't in the business of celebrating Time-Life heroes . . . I *want* to write this piece. So I called Ridgely Ochs and sold it to *Newsday*'s Sunday magazine.

NOVEMBER 13: After I finished my Civil War piece for *The Phila. Inq.*, Garth & I had dinner at the Metropolitan Café. Followed by ice cream at his place—sitting up in bed & watching Tracey Ullman & the end of *Back to the Future*. Before making love. I have never been more comfortable with him. Much laughter; no awkward silences; a bit of history between us now. Still, I get no hopes up. Someone called around 11 & it wasn't business, I'm sure . . . I wanted to spend the night & he wanted me to as well. But I hadn't prepped for Eisie, so I left at midnight & back at home spread the photography books out on the floor & stayed up until a quarter to two making up interview questions.

NOVEMBER 14: It wasn't easy. I'm not a practiced interviewer; I remain conscious throughout that the person is doing me a favor, so I'm afraid to press. (And one can hardly press a 90-year-old man in any case. Sometimes he would answer my questions & sometimes he would just tell me whatever anecdotes he wanted to.)

NOVEMBER 19: Dinner with the Ullmans [Greg's parents] . . . the two of them are nice as pie & cute as buttons—just as Greg would be if you shaved off the dogmatic edge.

NOVEMBER 20: A fairly hilarious cocktail hour with [Karen Stolley's parents]. Maggie's brother is soon to be married for the 1st time. He's 54. The bride is 34—and still thinks her groom is 41.

Yes, that's what he's told her. Lots of jokes about what will happen when the Social Security checks arrive 13 years early, or he lets childhood recollections of FDR slip out.

NOVEMBER 22: Had a 10:30 meeting at *House & Garden* (lots of anorectic Condé Nast women running around) with Dana Cowin. We talked generally about changes in the magazine since Anna "Nuclear" Wintour's departure for *Vogue* & what I might do for them. . . .

Lunch with Dougie Thornburg . . . It was a brilliant day & we went up to the Met with our Georgia O'Keeffe tickets . . . It still seems like dorm-wall art. It actually looks better in magazines—much of it aspires to be textureless, and the brushstrokes just get in the way.

NOVEMBER 25: Went to Bloomingdale's, to the lamp sale. Bought a blue-&-white Chinese ceramic lamp. $149. It's very pretty, but best of all it can take a 3-way 150 watt bulb; it will help stave off blindness as I read more badly Xeroxed galleys. Tonight when I told Chris Bull about my purchase he said, "Wow, buying fancy lamps at Bloomingdale's. One more sign you've made it as a writer." He had a teasing smile on. I told him. "Actually, Chris, buying fancy lamps at Bloomingdale's is one more sign that you've made it as a homosexual."

NOVEMBER 26: Met Greg & his parents just before 8:00 outside the Music Box on W. 45th. We saw *Spoils of War*, Michael Weller's new play. Kate Nelligan has some powerhouse moments in her $2000 red wig, but it's an overrated play—a sort of neo-50s realist family drama, overwritten & self-consciously "searing." It's the sort of thing Mary would have given the kiss of death in *Partisan Review*.

NOVEMBER 29: Went down to South Dakota and played Space Station pinball before bed: 1,266,000 points.

Doug's mother was arrested for speeding while on her way to a garden club meeting.

DECEMBER 2: Unbelievably enough, the testimony of Hedda Nussbaum is being carried live on all three channels, and millions are watching her ruined, broken face as she testifies about Joel Steinberg and the night he battered a 6-year-old to death. People are gruesomely gripped by it—this is not how middle-class kids are supposed to die. If this had happened to a 6-year-old in Bedford-Stuyvesant there'd be no press at all after a day or two.

Will people stay gripped by it? Become bored? Revulsed? Joyce Johnson is pushing a book outline on the case, & Houghton Mifflin's got it now. Fran K. wonders if they should publish it. She & Vance & I discuss this over lunch at Costello's (corned-beef sandwiches across from the Thurber drawings done on the wall) . . .

DECEMBER 6: Talked to Garth, who got home Sunday night—completely exhausted, he said—from Key West. I didn't ask.

DECEMBER 7: I opened the blinds at 6:15 and saw the street already filling with black security cars . . . If ever there was a day not to be in Turtle Bay ("GORBY GRIDLOCK"), this was it, and I was glad to be on the 7:50 to Pok.

DECEMBER 8: Gorby has left early because of a massive earthquake in Armenia, so the neighborhood is completely normal . . .

Anatole called in the afternoon & we did the very last editing on the Christmas essay. At the end of our conversation he told me I was "the cleanest writer in the world." I wish *The New York Times* would spare me its unpublished praise.

. . .

Dear little Kenny came by for a beer tonight. First time I've seen him in many months. He told me of his adventures in the Columbia Writing Program . . . & how in the last six months he's decided he's completely gay. No more girlfriends. Now he's a member of Columbia GLA; goes to the dances; has lots of dates; has told his parents. All this is for the best. The only complaint he has is that he hasn't met the right person yet and can't understand why at 23 he isn't settled down with somebody.

DECEMBER 9: Aram Saroyan was in town having an autograph party up at Hudson News on 2nd at 66th. I went up briefly to see him & Gailyn . . . Richard Avedon, looking incredibly youthful, came in & we were introduced & I remembered what unkind line I'd just written about him in the Eisenstaedt article . . . I walked home in the twinkle of early evening, in love with New York, the bridge, what I do. Looked up at Garth's dark window & tried to spot Groucho on the kitchen sill.

DECEMBER 10: Garth came by around 9:00 & we went down to Jay Y's Christmas party . . . I think Garth was happy to be with me. He likes the elfin TM, and that's what I was, I guess, in my Christmas red suspenders.

DECEMBER 11: It's turned very cold all of a sudden. I was shivering as I walked down 1st Ave. to Louise's tonight. (There's a regular Hooverville of cardboard boxes in Ralph Bunche Park now.) . . . Katy Aisenberg has a poem about Tommy in the current *Partisan Review*. Louise showed it to me while we were having drinks & I really did shiver at the first italicized passage—just the way Tommy sometimes was, hopelessly resolute. The mood would vanish as quickly as he assumed it.

DECEMBER 12: Up to the Y at 7:30 to introduce Peter Carey, who looks like a taller, slightly more buck-toothed version of yours truly. Elizabeth Jolley also on the program. She's adorably spinsterish, padding to the platform in cardigan and low shoes after being introduced by the weird polar bear that is Tom Disch. And Thomas Keneally introduced Rodney Hall, who had the courage to read from his new novel even though Lehmann-Haupt had savaged it in this morning's *Times*. (Lehmann-Haupt was right.) . . . Nancy Crampton is now the house photographer for the Poetry Center. Tom Victor is too sick to work. He's gone home to a sister in the Midwest.

DECEMBER 14: Held office hours—talked more about excuses and deadlines [for the students' papers] than poetry—before running with David [Littlefield] along the cross-country trails behind the golf course. We did about 3 miles and felt wonderful afterwards. He and Karen are still waiting [for the birth of their first child]. When I saw her all I could think to say was, "Karen. *Push*."

DECEMBER 15: Worked on the "Postscript" of *Stolen Words* before going down to Lower Broadway and up to PEN Headquarters for the Christmas party in honor of members who'd published books this year.

Arts and Sciences was on display and I felt pleased. Susan Sontag wasn't there, so I felt even more pleased. And then a very nice-looking man about my age came up to me and said, "Tom?" It was Bob Polito, who started Harvard with me and whom I've not seen since '78 . . . He taught for years at Wellesley, did not get tenure, and is now trying to make it down here, teaching and writing at the New School. He read *Arts & Sciences* and recognized everyone in it . . . We talked about Bate & Engell & how awful it all was. Wellesley sounds even worse. He says someone who didn't vote for him came up and told him, "You know, all the work I had to do for the department is what broke up my first marriage and stalled my writing. We don't see you as someone willing to let that happen to him." That was a reason *not* to vote for him.

DECEMBER 17: Well, I'm pretty depressed, and I ought to be giving up on Garth. I don't care if he's a dreamboat. What's the point? Hearing from him, sleeping with him, twice a month?

DECEMBER 18: Elisabeth Biondi's Christmas party. A very Teutonic spread of breads & sausages. Billy, the Irish painter whose chief theme is now onanism, was there; and Cora and Carl and Vance, who brought us all copies of the year-in-pictures issue of *Life*, complete with a shot of Al Sharpton in rollers . . . Fran & Howard were on their way to a second party, a reunion of *New Yorker* outlaws like Fran who tried to start another magazine after Gottlieb took over. They never got anywhere: they couldn't find anyone interested in the business side of things; they only wanted to work with people they liked; and they spent most of their time trying to decide what restaurants they should hold their meetings in.

DECEMBER 20: Early afternoon: corner of 3rd & 42nd. Guy in car swipes some bicyclists. I didn't actually see it; I arrived when one of the cyclists, a blond girl, was cursing the driver—10 fuckins per ½ minute—through his closed door. Crowd begins to gather. She lets loose her last "fuckin' asshole" and you think that'll be it. But no. A couple of fast kicks and she's broken his window. Before he can get out of his car with his bloodied lip, two guys jump out from the car behind—plainclothesmen. They grab the blond, handcuff her and proceed with the business of the arrest. Throughout this she is calm, smiling. All the anger & frenzy went out of her when she broke the window and drew blood.

DECEMBER 22: Had my haircut with Nancy, who was in a grumpy mood toward her husband, even though he's bought her a new house & Krugerrands.

. . .

. . . Heard the Bess [Myerson] verdict come in on the 11:00 news. Not guilty. Loony Sukhreet Gabel hugs her mother (against whom she testified) for the cameras and her nearly blind, doddering mom tells her "I'm proud of you, honey."

DECEMBER 25: Loree was in very good form—no sudden rages or calamities . . . Seán liked his microscope ("Mom! Do you want to look at the fruit fly's head?") . . . A big dinner, which we all ate with a remarkable lack of tension . . . I took the train back from Ronkonkoma. The conductor who punched my ticket was Billy McAleavey, with whom I played Little League ball 25, almost 30, years ago. They had about 10 kids in the family, I think; Daddy used to joke about the sight of the father carrying gallons of milk into the little Cape Cod house across from Stewart Manor School.

DECEMBER 26: I went to the Brooks Brothers sale today. It looked more like a Kmart clearance, though the women flinging ties up from the counter were all preppy and self-satisfied. Buying new epaulets for hubby's uniform.

DECEMBER 27: . . . Having a gloriously masturbatory time writing catalogue copy for *Stolen Words*.

DECEMBER 28: Strange weather. God in a bored, can't-make-up-His-mind mood. Mild and bright just before 4:00. Pane-rattling winds and rain at 5:00.

DECEMBER 30: Down with worst flu in at least 3 years. Surprisingly few AIDS-panic moments—time gets you used to the false alarms, even though I'm as likely to get it now as I ever was, if some of the statistics are right.

1989

JANUARY 1: Worst day yet. I should have called a doctor, but I didn't. For two reasons: one is that I don't have a doctor in NY, since I've never really needed one . . . Second is I'm scared. I'm afraid a visit will mean medical history, sexual history, talk of The Test, etc. I know they can't make you take The Test, but I don't want to get even that close to it. For some time I've thought I *ought* to have a doctor here, and today Greg gave me the # for his, but I want to see him for the first time when I'm healthy.

JANUARY 3: Watched an hour of public TV about Eudora Welty at 10:00 . . . She says you can't write about emotions without experiencing them. So who was he, Eudora?

JANUARY 7: [Greg and Ben and I] went to see *Torch Song Trilogy* after a dinner at Houlihan's at B'way & 64th . . . There aren't 2 realistic minutes in it—it represents Harvey Fierstein's fantasy life more than anything else (well, of *course* Matthew Broderick would fall on him declaring undying love) . . .

They're already stripping the walls of Scribner's. Went in there today for what may be the last time.

JANUARY 8: Garth, whom I never expected to hear from again, called tonight. He's been away for most of the last 3 weeks—back in Key West, where he's going to move . . . really, what difference does it make? . . . At one point while he was talking I was just bored & started working on a sentence in the ms. in front of me.

JANUARY 9: Ben spent the morning getting Cheryl Crane to a publicity appearance on a talk show. She's Lana Turner's daughter, the one who killed her mother's boyfriend. Last time it was Patty Hearst.

JANUARY 11: Jay Y. came over from the office tonight & we watched RR's uninspired farewell address together. What a lucky, improbable life.

JANUARY 13: Before Doug & I went to lunch at Squire's he gave me a tour of the Vanderbilt Y on 47th St.—it's his gym, only a couple of blocks from work. I've decided I'm going to join. It's only about $500 a year, and I'm enough into middle age to realize I need it. I'm still quite slim, but there's no pretending that gravity isn't a factor now.

JANUARY 14: Oh, my aching back. I don't know how it went out, but they say almost anything can do it. Patty says her sister threw hers out with a sneeze—had to hobble around with a mop, like a shepherd's crook, for 3 days.

I was miserable last night. Couldn't sleep until I took 2 shots of whiskey. (This after watching *The Lost Weekend* at 1 a.m. One of the liquor stores Ray Milland is staring into is, I think, right across from my old apartment next to St. Agnes'.)

JANUARY 16: Was running for the first time in weeks . . . It's Martin Luther King Day, and while I was warming up, I heard, through the Walkman, his sermon about what he told his little daughter when she asked why she couldn't go to Funtown, the segregated amusement park. Lord, how he worked that word: "Funtown"— he made it sound like both heaven and hell. It was chilling.

JANUARY 17: Georgia Jones-Davis calls from the *LA Times* to offer me a book. Jack Schwartz [*Newsday*'s books editor] calls to ask if I'd like to be a once-a-month Tuesday regular, so as to get $250 instead of $150 . . . I say OK—for 6 mos. Then we'll take another look. . . .

JANUARY 18: Patty's 40th birthday party in the evening . . . After everyone else had left, K & D & Patty & I sat in the living room & played with [Kathleen]. We also watched a tape of the Del Rubio triplets on the Pee-wee Herman Christmas special. The Del Rubios are the sisters of Lola Boyd, the ex- and annoying Chairman of the Spanish Dept. They are about 65 & perform in micro skirts & go-go boots. They have bouffant blond hair & strum guitars & sing in off-key Brooklynese. (No one knows where those vowels came from, since they grew up in Panama & Washington, D.C.) They sang "Winter Wonderland" & I gaped in amazement. Patty, who was tormented by Lola, is delighted by their embarrassing new success.

JANUARY 19: [Jack Schwartz] wants me to write a quick "appreciation" of Bruce Chatwin, who's just died. They say it's from some exotic disease he picked up on his travels, but everybody ("they" are the newspapers & "everybody" is everybody else) knows it's AIDS. I dug out the letters I had from him & a diary in which I located a description of his telephone call to me: April '84. In one of the letters, backing out of his Vassar visit, he says "Never count the chickens. . . ."

JANUARY 20: A kinder, gentler nation? George Bush gave a speech that was nothing much as rhetoric (standard-issue Peggy Noonan), but was modest and sensible in its message . . . RR looked very old all of a sudden in his white muffler. He's a strange, spooky man . . .
        . . .
    [Nick and Siri's] apartment is all right, but what a street (East 3rd, between 1st & 2nd Aves.). You can assume that there are a couple of drug dealers in your sight at any time. The Hell's Angels have their NY headquarters across the street & are considered a neighborhood asset.

JANUARY 22: Late word is that Scribner's may be saved after all, though today was supposed to be its last day. The Landmarks Commission is going to meet next month to see if they can keep a bookstore instead of a Benetton there.

JANUARY 23: The wait for Ted Bundy's execution dominates the news. He's finally confessing to it all. All these girls: it's as if they're rising from the grave. He's supposedly terror-stricken & is trying to buy time, like some diabolical Scheherazade—he thinks they'll let him live as long as he has new confessions to give, and thereby crimes to solve.

JANUARY 26: . . . The day of the NBCCs. Went down to 24 5th Ave. for the PPA luncheon. Sat with Ben; saw pretty Nina, smoking & looking nervous. Came back here in the afternoon & went down to NYU once more at 5:30 for the party . . . Couldn't stick the awards themselves. I came home via a couple of bars. Met someone very nice named Bill Bodenschotz [sic] . . .

JANUARY 27: Seán answers the phone like a grownup now. He won a poster contest at school—he made one against drunk driving. (God, whatever happened to Fire Prevention Week? They've got these poor kiddies conscious of booze, crack and AIDS by second grade.)

Dinner at Barocco with Elisabeth, Fran & Howard. Loud, new-wave Italian. Good risotto. Robert Altman dining across the room. I pick up the check: almost $200. I thought my Visa would melt, but it was clearly my turn . . . Talked about Susan Sontag & her AIDS book. Elisabeth says David Leavitt's agent has called *Vanity Fair* to complain because Leavitt is about to be James Wolcott's next Bum of the Month.

JANUARY 28: Went up to 57th St. to look at diaries in Dempsey + Carroll. I'm finally working on this *GQ* piece involving Chips Channon . . .

JANUARY 29: My Chatwin eulogy (pretty, but a little fussy, and with one egregious typo) is out.

JANUARY 30: . . . The account statement for *Arts & Sciences* . . . Lord, those returns.

FEBRUARY 2: I had lunch with George Doolittle today, a long, long lunch at Costello's with an ancient waiter who kept forgetting to bring our coffee. I hadn't seen George in 10 years. He looks very well, only gray-haired now. His speech is just as it was: he's consistently intelligent, even witty, as he goes about over-emphasizing everything. When we'd do imitations of him in high school the word we always used was "Absolutely!" What a model of sophistication he was for me then, and if, in his New Hampshire retirement, he seems a little provincial to me now, that doesn't take away from the real classiness he added to life at clunky Sewanhaka High School . . . He was a very important figure in my life, the man who got me to Brown & helped keep me there, bucking me up during that unhappy first semester . . .

. . .

. . . Up to George Plimpton's on E. 72nd St. for a publication party for Carol Houck Smith's author, Rick Bass. I spent part of the party trying to find a woman who, after her necklace of big fake Barbara Bush pearls broke, disappeared into the crowd. I walked around with the dozen or so I'd picked up, trying to find her. I held them in my open palm and probably looked as if I were distributing Quaaludes.

FEBRUARY 4: [At the Kiernans' in Sag Harbor] The usual orgy of eating, wine-drinking and dinner preparations. Vance worked so hard on this immense piece of pork & we all paid it so much attention that by the time it was ready it felt like another person in the house.

FEBRUARY 5: I drank too much Courvoisier too late last night & I didn't get out of bed until 11:20. I missed breakfast & Howard said they were talking about sending somebody up to put quarters over my eyes.

FEBRUARY 6: Feeling a little—more than a little—overwhelmed today. The junk I need for doing the [*Stolen Words*] footnotes is all over the apartment. I wake up with it, wade through it all day, go to sleep with it. I've come to the conclusion that you can write a novel in a studio apartment, but not a work of non-fiction.

FEBRUARY 7: The footnotes and [copyediting] are driving me crazy (Larry has a marginal note describing one page as "overcolonized"—it took me a long time to figure out he meant too many colons), but at least Marty Beiser [at GQ] says he loves the Chips piece & wants to see me next week to talk about doing more.

FEBRUARY 16: The *Wall St. Journal* messenger came for the *Billy Bathgate* review this morning. At 5:00 I was on the phone with David Brooks. He was telling me about the small changes he'd made. I suggested one more tinkering and he said he'd have to call downstairs to find out if they hadn't yet passed the point where each change costs $30,000.

FEBRUARY 17: Saw Nick at last in the library. He has been sick . . . We went out for tea on 41st St. He tells me that the tension over the Rushdie affair is getting to Siri at Viking. The rumor today is that the executives on 23rd St. are wearing bullet-proof vests. Another rumor: the ayatollah will call off the hit if he gets a sincere "apology." It hardly matters: Rushdie's life is ruined. He'll never live casually again.

FEBRUARY 19: Walked down to *Fiction Only* on 3rd Ave. . . . to get a copy of *Surprising Myself*, one of the gay novels blushing Jason Healy is using in his thesis. (Miracle of miracles, they still had *Arts & Sciences* on sale.)

FEBRUARY 22: Before dinner at the Pub we made a videotape of me playing with Kathleen in her red dress: Kathleen as Macy's Thanksgiving Parade balloon; Kathleen as infant alcoholic on *The Oprah Winfrey Show*; Kathleen as Queen Elizabeth opening Parliament; Kathleen doing pull-ups in the health club. We replayed it instantly, and it was awfully funny . . . I thought I looked good in it. Animated, handsome, a little more naturally butch than I would have expected. Much less awful than just hearing one's voice on a tape recorder. I wondered if I'll be dead a few years from now & it will bring a tear to the eyes of Karen, Patty & David. This is because I'm going through a bout of AIDS fear . . . I used to have these panic attacks almost weekly; now months usually separate them. But I realize there may still come the moment when you— I—realize that this is not a panic attack, this is not a false alarm; this is it.

FEBRUARY 25: Dinner at JG Melon on the West Side; *Working Girl* at the Regency; a couple of beers at The Works. David Morgan is adorable. He's about 30, went to Vanderbilt Law between college & Princeton, where he's now doing a Ph.D. in French. (He also practiced law for a couple of years in NY.) He has a thick South Carolina accent, looks very boyish, is obviously smart but endearingly slow on the uptake when it comes to jokes. The three of us had a good time—Ben made everything easy . . . I can say that this was the most enjoyable "fix-up" evening I've ever had.

FEBRUARY 27: At 6:00 I met Louise in front of the Paris Theatre up near the Plaza, and we went in to see *The Dressmaker*, a good little English movie made out of one of Beryl Bainbridge's gruesome books. Joan Plowright genuinely scary as the provincial-propriety mad aunt; she's wonderfully calmed by killing somebody.

FEBRUARY 28: When talking to Mom about Loree tonight, I asked her: "Who takes care of *me*? I don't have a life; I have a career."

MARCH 6: I am stretched as far as I can go. I spent all morning with Arthur Greene having my taxes done. He sat, as always, moving his pencil, silently, like the cartoon character Mr. Mum. Someone called up & he had to speak to him about a 79-year-old man who doesn't have enough money to live on because he gave it all away to his daughters to avoid estate taxes & they won't let him have any income from what he gave them.

Lunch at the Century Café with Eric Copage of *The NY Times Magazine*. I tried a couple of ideas out on him that met with varying degrees of enthusiasm. Some of them just shot down. I hate this part of writing—it makes me feel like a salesman with a suitcase full of ugly shoe samples.

MARCH 9: —San Juan—[Greg and I] had an easy flight down here . . . The toupeed City Council President, Andrew Stein, was on the plane, too—with 2 small children, what looked like a second wife, and an au pair.

. . . A few drinks before dinner. The man on the next seat at the bar gave us descriptions of all the local restaurants—*long* descriptions. I sometimes still can't get over the pedantry of gay men on the subject of food.

MARCH 10: I ran on the beach this morning—a good, exhausting run. The sand makes it a bit like running through tires on an obstacle course if you run far enough from the shoreline. I was beet-red & vein-beating by the time I got back to the wall near the hotel, where one of the ever-present prostitutes asked "Yes?" When it was clear the answer was no, he just encouraged me over my finish line: "You can do it" . . . A terrible dinner (at Oasis, where we were with each other 2 years ago) with Greg. He had absolutely nothing to say to me, and when I inquired if his silence meant something was bothering him, he snapped at me, said I was always criticizing him and so forth. It pretty much took my breath away, and dinner & the walk home became a duel of silences . . . The truth is that he wants his boyfriends and his friends to be just alike: totally controllable, utterly pliant ciphers . . . Walking home I thought: I don't particularly care if we cease to be friends, and I was calm.

MARCH 11: Walked through San Juan in the afternoon, in the direction away from the prosperous Condado. Lots of tacky stores advertising "Layaway Plans." A 50s feel to the neighborhood— the post office with Ike's name on the plaque still looking like the newest thing in the area . . . The truth is that I'm actually having a good time. No phones, no mail, lots of exercise, sun & stars.

MARCH 12: Everyone is at the bar with the rain pounding on the corrugated roof. Greg is sitting there with Joey & Darval, or Darvon, as I call him.

MARCH 13: Maria, a talkative lovelorn lesbian cab driver, took us to the Terrace restaurant. Lou, the 50-ish real-estate guy, told me about gay life in NYC in the early 60s: cruising techniques at the Rockefeller Center skating rink, bars called "316" and "The Annex" on 3rd Ave. in the lower 50s . . . Winding up on the terrace of the Atlantic Beach Hotel, watching the ocean and the cruise ships, like glittering silver corn cobs, sailing eastward.

MARCH 14: This was the day for Greg and me to go into Old San Juan . . . In the Ralph Lauren outlet he asked me which of 2 shirts I liked better & I said the second of the 2 because I don't really like wearing green & red together. He replied: "Can't you extrapolate (sic) anything beyond yourself? I want to know how it would look on *me*." . . . On the plane [home] he said to me: "I guess you're not very happy with my demeanor today." He explained that it was because he felt "jilted" last night. Never mind that he was asked twice to come along. Never mind that he has spent three years walking away from me & lots of his other friends whenever a vacant, passive face passed by.

MARCH 15: Saw Fran K. in the afternoon. She showed me the cover design for *Stolen Words*. It's wonderful: the sketch of a masked burglar stepping out of a big book while clutching a smaller one.

    She also says that she thinks she can get Cork to agree to a 2-book contract for me: *Aurora 7* plus a non-fiction work (they'd like a biography).

MARCH 18: Wrote my review of Patrick Gale—one of those pieces that I thought came out just right, like a snug bit of roofing.

    . . .

    David [Morgan] came by at about 8:15 and we had a couple of drinks so we would be fashionably late . . . The party was a pretty elaborate drunken affair—& as I write this on Sunday evening I've got as big a hangover as anybody. Greg, who called just before the party to make sure we'd be saying hello to each other, came with his ludicrous entourage . . . everything was giggles and gropings on Magno's bed downstairs . . . And to tell you some more unpleasant truth, David had a nice time joining in the little laughing petting party. So I seemed like an aging wallflower once more. Greg was, I'm sure, delighted that my drunken date had stopped paying attention to me by the end of the party. And David told me later that Greg & Joey et al. had suggested that he go home with them and "Forget about Tom."

On Tuesday night Greg [had] said, "I still consider you my best friend."

Well, David did go home with the one who brung him—me— and we drunkenly made it back in a cab. We slept together with our clothes on & when he left this morning I don't know which one of us was more embarrassed.

MARCH 22: At the library & began to gather things for the moon essay [for the *Times Book Review*]—*Mr. Sammler's Planet*; a pre-Apollo sci-fi anthology; James Michener. And in the reading room I'm reading a 1963 novel called *Apollo at Go*, in which the spunky bachelor astronaut who has to be left, dead, in lunar orbit, is named Mallon.

MARCH 23: A late dinner way down on Hudson St. (the block where Area used to be) at the Thai House Cafe, with Fran & Howard, Elisabeth, her friend Bettina (who looks like Barbara Hershey) and Fran's brother, a pleasant, campy decorator who lives in the Ansonia and has problems with the IRS . . . Talked about Janet Malcolm's articles on McGinniss & MacDonald[*] in *The New Yorker.* They have made a lot of writers nervous & angry.

MARCH 28: 82° today. What will the summer bring? Scores of hundred degree days when the reservoirs are empty? There's a feeling of nervousness, of impending environmental calamity. The oil is

---

[*] "The Journalist and the Murderer," *The New Yorker*, issues of March 5 and March 12, 1989, about the ethical questions arising from the writer Joe McGinniss's relationship with a subject, the killer Jeffrey MacDonald.

floating into the sea in Alaska; the mandatory recycling bill passed the City Council today: we'll all be sorting our trash come July. And ActUp protestors blocked City Hall this morning.

. . .

A few months ago a drunk or a car smashed the head off one of the huge black ceramic dogs outside the Physics institute near the corner. Today as I went to pick up my shirts I noticed a woman making a cast of the head of the undamaged dog so that the decapitated one can be fixed. The dogs are neighborhood conversation pieces & this little bit of restoration lifted my heart—maybe in defiance of the ecological & environmental disasters all around.

MARCH 31: . . . Went out for drinks. Ran into Michael Galligan & had a long chat, & then, to my delight, Bill Bodenschatz—an encounter which made me wonder why I had never called this man since January.

APRIL 1: Stayed in tonight & graded paper[s] & read tomorrow's *Times* & watched *Saturday Night Live*. Now what would it be like to spend a domestic evening like this *with* someone? I called Bill Bodenschatz late this afternoon & left a message on his machine.

APRIL 2: Bill called this morning, and this time we have a date . . . I'm happy, feeling I'm about to date someone really interested in me; someone who seems older and stronger; whose voice has a casual, very American kind of authority; who seems to have—as few of my real love objects ever did—a sense of humor.

APRIL 3: Wlady left a message on my machine. There's an execution scheduled at San Quentin for June 23 and he wants to know if I'd be interested in covering it.

APRIL 4: Bill called tonight. Not to set up details of dinner for Friday night—we'll do that Thursday—but "just to say how glad I was you called Saturday, how glad I was to run into you again, and how much I'm looking forward to Friday." Isn't it romantic? . . . Talked to Karen . . . She & Patty are going down to the huge women's march in Washington this weekend. And they're bringing Kathleen. I told her not to let Kathleen fall in with all the little lesbian babies wearing OshKosh overalls and eating granola zwieback toast.

APRIL 6: Feeling frustrated and hapless. I have the worst case of laryngitis I've ever had. I literally can't speak except for the occasional croak that emerges, almost accidentally, from a whisper. I have new empathy for the handicapped. When I'd go into a store today & need to talk to the clerk, I'd have to use gestures. And I had a slew of phone calls to return. I did editing, in hushed tones, with Becky Klock in Philadelphia & Georgia Jones-Davis in L.A. I sounded as if I were either being held hostage or attempting an obscene phone call.

APRIL 7: Worked at home all day just hoping my voice would come back. I gargled, poured tea and lemon juice & liquor down it, sprayed it, rattled lozenges in it—and I still had next to nothing . . . Well, we didn't cancel the date. Bill said, let's just order in & get a movie—that way you won't have to deal with restaurant noise & can just whisper if you have to without feeling self-conscious. So that's what we did. I arrived at E. 72nd St. (with flowers) a little after 8.

He is really wonderful. And only 43! What made me think older? Except for a receding hairline he's even a boyish 43, & in wonderful shape. From the time he left Washington Univ., from 1967 until 1984—for *seventeen years*—he lived monogamously with the same man . . . The relationship just eventually deteriorated, & the guy became abusive. They split up Fourth of July weekend in 1984 (the weekend, I creepily realized, when we knew Tommy had to go to the hospital).

He is funny, smart & immensely affectionate. Looking for all the right things. So potentially the right person for me that it made me nervous. So nervous that—honest to God—I threw up in the bathroom. But after that was fine. And we spent the evening listening to Sarah Vaughan and talking about ourselves and going to bed. We are *perfectly* comfortable there. We were safe & passionate. He accompanies every move with endearments and whispers & laughter. In some ways it seems too good to be true. And I don't know how to deal with being relaxed.

APRIL 8: When was the last time I laughed through breakfast with someone who just wanted to put jelly on my English muffin and smile at me and tell me I was special? Who wanted to go back into the bedroom, which we did, and say, "I can't hold you close enough." Someone I kept telling to slow down a little—even though I didn't want him to?

APRIL 9: On the phone . . . We set up tomorrow night. "I think you should stay over," he said when we were through making plans. What a relief to find someone who can just *say* that, without feeling he's taking some terrible risk or giving some piece of his power away. I said I'd bring a toothbrush.

APRIL 10: It's happening too fast. He's witty, perceptive ("There you go, Tommy, into the post-sex bunker. You're building up those walls, hammering as fast as you can"—& all the time he's saying it we're laughing & he's tickling me.) This man is on to me. If I could like myself as much as he does, I'd be fine.

APRIL 12: Patty tells me that she & Karen talked about me & Bill over lunch today & that Karen asked whether Tom had yet found a reason to let things make him miserable.

APRIL 13: Fran K. came here at 7:30 for a drink before we went up to the Equitable Center for a benefit for Yaddo . . . Calvin Trillin did a deadpan monologue at a lectern, and he was pretty funny. (Especially about the joke letter he sent to a coop board to which Joan Didion & John Gregory Dunne were applying.) At dinner Fran & I were seated next to Edward Said, Yasser Arafat's man in American academe & one of the authors of the declaration of independence for a Palestinian state. I *really* didn't want to discuss politics, so we stayed with such reliable professorial topics like what a pain it is to write letters of recommendation.

APRIL 14: Bill had a 7:30 dentist's appointment, so he kissed me good-bye early and I went back to sleep. When I got up at 9 I found he'd set out my clothes & left breakfast & coffee out and put a sweet note next to my chair. This is a whole new world. Can I deal with it?

APRIL 17: At 8 I was up at darling Billy's. It was "sandwich night"— adopted from *About Last Night*. We made plates with things he'd bought at Macy's & cracked open a bottle of wine. Watched *Murphy Brown* & *Designing Women*. He said he was goofy for me; I said I was crazy about him. These are safe ways of not (yet) having to use the "l" word.

And so to bed. Together.

APRIL 18: If [I'm] going to sleep happily with Bill a few nights each week, I'm going to have to get up before 10 the morning after. But the truth is that I'm not used to this much sex. And when he leaves for work he kisses me goodbye and straightens the covers & tells me to go back to sleep.

APRIL 20: Bill's bosses are Jewish, so he's got a few days off for Passover. We got up late and read the paper and played music & laughed. He's not much for politics, that's for sure, and I don't care: so what if he thinks Ortega is Noriega?

APRIL 21: Ran 5 miles up at the park this morning. And tonight the news is full of how a woman running up there was raped and nearly beaten to death the other night by a Harlem gang that had gone "wilding"—i.e., rampaging.

APRIL 23: Humor is of course fatal during sex, but nothing is better before and after. (It should also be noted here that Bill is no doubt the only person ever to have been driven to masturbation by *Arts & Sciences*. He says that yesterday he was reading a sex scene between Artie and Angela and was inspired to put the book aside and fantasize about me in Artie's place. I should notify the Houghton Mifflin sales department of this.)

APRIL 24: My schedule was too full before I had a boyfriend. Now that I do, I'm feeling frantic. I have got to do less & do it more efficiently.

. . .

Caught up on the rest of my phone messages—people now leave ones saying: "I know where *you* are. Well, call me tomorrow."

APRIL 26: Lucille Ball is dead, & I very nearly cried when I heard the news. But, instead, at dinner, I sang all the words to the *I Love Lucy* theme . . . She was everywhere on TV tonight—an hourlong special on CBS, even *Nightline*, which Bill & I watched on the phone with each other. I even called Mom; I'll bet a lot of people did similar things tonight—trying to touch base with the rest of the family after an aunt who'd been around forever died.

APRIL 27: I do think I may give up this diary, because I cannot any longer stand the idea of preserving disaster.

It had to happen—though not in the usual way. Not the sudden withdrawal, the admitted indifference. No, it has to be AIDS.

It was The Perfect Evening . . . We got to the Carlyle about 20 minutes before Dixie Carter comes on. We're sitting on a banquette in the corner . . . Pretty-boy couples throughout the room. Saks & Bloomie's spray-you-in-the-aisle boys having a big night before going back to apartments in Queens. A few straight couples. A tableful of Southern ladies who could have been straight out of *Designing Women*.

Dixie Carter[*] looks great, sings high. Alternates arty Jacques Brel numbers with funny ones like "Beans Taste Fine" and "I'm 27." Sings some of the Noël Coward lyrics to "Let's Do It" before doing the Cole Porter ones and slithering across the piano. We love her.

We walk out on air. Pass Sylvia Syms on the sidewalk. Walk home down 72nd St. happy as can be. Put on the record of Noël Coward singing his "Let's Do It". . . .

Then we do it. Safely, but with more gusto & feeling than

---

[*] Dixie Carter (1939–2010), actress and singer, performed many times at the Café Carlyle between the late 1980s and mid-2000s.

we've done it before. And then we lie back watching CNN at 1:00—in this age when you don't ever get to leave the news. And there's talk of a new AIDS drug. And I say again why I'd never have the test, and then, relaxed and half-asleep, I say, "You'd never get [the test] either, would you?"—something I'd never asked before because we've both been safe & I just assumed that like me, like most, he wouldn't want it.

And then he told me that, in fact, he had had it, two years ago. He tested positive.

APRIL 28: He's been agonizing, with his therapist, for weeks. If I were one of those people who insisted on knowing his test results—there are people who will ask you that 5 minutes after they've met you; and a negative result is the new status symbol, the way a Fire Island house used to be, in the gay world—I would have asked before. Would I have run if I'd known 3 weeks ago? Probably. Will I now? I don't know.

The irony? I'm probably + too. And he knows about Tommy. But the difference is *knowing the actual test result*. He had the test 2 years ago—the biggest mistake of his life, he now thinks—when someone he was becoming involved with insisted on it. His doctor & therapist advised against it. The person dumped him.

Should I get tested? No. I won't. I've lived with ambiguity for 5 years. I don't know if I could live with—with what? Isn't a + result ambiguous? Who's to say he'll ever get sick? Or, if he does, when? Who's to say I won't be sick in a year?

Within 5 minutes we'd explored every cul-de-sac and permutation. Who isn't an expert at this by now?

I'm not scared for myself. We've been safe. We could continue to be safe. What I mean is I'm not scared for myself *physically*. I'm scared emotionally, scared someone I've been falling in love with—someone who is completely in love with me—will get sick & die. Scared I'll be spooning peach ice cream into him at Columbia Presbyterian a year from now . . . I make it home. Talk to Doug, who immediately says DON'T LEAVE HIM. He's too good. He loves you. This could be your true chance for happiness in life. The love of your life. And if it lasts for 5 years or 2 years & ends in heartbreak you will at least have had what most people never get. Stay. As for sex—just keep not doing what you've been not doing.

. . .

. . . [Tonight] we sat in the living room & cried & told each other we loved each other—&, Christ, we meant it, too. . . .

APRIL 29: Talked to Jason Healy, after reading his "politically correct" radical thesis on gay men's fictions. Wanted just to say: oh, Jason, shut up. Why don't you live and suffer a little before you tell the world you've got it all figured out?

APRIL 30: Tonight I walked up to 72nd St., but Bill was out. So I kept walking around, calling him [from pay phones] every half-dozen blocks or so. Still no answer. I began to get alarmed . . . Took a cab home. Then he called. He'd been down at his friend Carol's in Stuy Town—crying his eyes out.

MAY 1: Joined [Fran] & Howard for dinner tonight down at Walker's on the corner of Varick & North Moore. Elisabeth was there with her painter friend Billy, along with the ponytailed editor of *Bomb*, who tells us that Mick Jagger has just had another facelift. Walker's like another era: a lot of sailors, one of them sitting next to an old man; a guy making out with his girlfriend; a tin ceiling. Howard & Fran rode me home . . . We dropped the *Bomb* editor off on his block near the Holland Tunnel—a street of transvestite prostitutes & crack dealers with one brownstone with a hall light burning.

MAY 2: Neither of us can get out of this conundrum. He imagines us both running into each other, 20 years from now, on a movie line, each of us healthy; afraid to have what we could have, we threw it away. I keep thinking of *The Beast in the Jungle* . . . We went into the bedroom and held each other & had sex in such a careful way that it was like an impassioned parody of lovemaking. I never relaxed for a second. I thought: could I go on like this? All the old questions: why don't *I* take the test? All the same dead ends.

MAY 3: Obika Gray, who now wears dreadlocks, was the Convocation speaker. The whole ceremony was an exercise in liberal First World breast-beating. Before he could talk to us about the evils of capitalism, [the president of Vassar] got on her anti–Allan Bloom broom again. It must be the only book she's read in the past 2 years.

MAY 4: Handed in the *Spectacle* proposal [for a book of essays that became *Rockets and Rodeos*] and the *A*7 précis to Fran, who says that Cork rather *likes* the idea of *Spectacle*, though he was quick to add to her that I shouldn't expect as much money for it as I would get for a biography. Fran says he's the cheapest man she knows— cheap in the way only WASPs can be. When she said they had to give me better advances than I'd been getting, Cork said: "Tom's not exactly on the street."

MAY 5: The proofs for *Stolen Words* arrived on Vanderbilt Ave. today . . . almost disbelieving that I will soon be free from this book.

. . .

. . . A letter from Yusupha Joof—my Save the Children kid in the Gambia. Either it was written by a field worker or the kid's a 10-year-old savant.

Worked until mid-evening when Chris Bull came by & we went down to Julius' for a drink. He'd already been to an ACT UP meeting. I don't tell him about Bill, but I listen to him talk about a new drug with keener interest than I might have.

MAY 8: Bill was amazed that what he thinks of as his pathetic, affectionate, puppy-dog neediness is one of the things I find *attractive* about him. My telling him that I found his sort of vulnerability to be generous came to him like an absolute revelation.

MAY 9: At 2:00 [my students] all came into the office bearing beer, wine, flowers & Cheetos & shouting surprise . . . I must have taught better than I knew this year. So we were chatting & I was asking everybody what their plans were after May 28. Exactly 2 out of 11 seniors have anything like definite ideas. So much for that 80s pre-professionalism.

MAY 10: The news from Mary E. is that Fran is going to make an offer, probably tomorrow, for both *Aurora 7* & *Spectacle*. Mary would like to get $25,000 but thinks $20,000 will be more like it. In any case, I'm excited, though with the *Stolen Words* proofs on my desk, it's a little bit like thinking about what you'll have for dinner when you're still eating breakfast.

. . .

. . . God, do I hate Rich the doorman. He never fails to point out how you'll never catch a cab in this weather, how your little umbrella will never stand up to the wind, etc.

MAY 11: The important thing is that I've sold my dream book, *Aurora 7*, & that I haven't chained myself to a literary biography. Instead I'm going to travel and write some good, quirky pieces. I'm already looking forward to the rodeo.

MAY 14: This was the evening that Greg was supposed to meet Bill, and he did, even though he'd reverted to a really bravura state of unpleasantness.

MAY 15: I tossed and turned, thinking that I have finally got to be done with Greg, for good and all. If the gesture weren't so petty and faggy, I'd take his name off the dedication on the galleys.

Bill & I read the *Times* together & played Dinah Washington records in the background. Not exactly Sunday-morning fare, but it was nice.

MAY 17: . . . To the ballet, where we saw three things (ABT). One was a recent thing called *The Informer*, set during the Irish Civil War. I thought: this looks like Agnes de Mille goes to Ireland, and told Bill when the lights went up. Then I found out it *is* Agnes de Mille. I wasn't sure she was still alive.

MAY 19: Sag Harbor . . . Fran went right to bed, and the rest of us had a decline-of-the-West conversation (Central Park rape, etc.) around the kitchen table over cold cuts from Balducci's.

MAY 20: Fran & I went shopping for food in Wainscott and Saga-ponack (at the store right across from the cemetery where James Jones is buried) . . . Late in the afternoon we planted the garden—snapdragons, marigolds, basil, arugula, lettuce, you name it. John, Fran, Elisabeth & I each had our own quadrants. We took pictures so we can see who wins the harvest competition this summer. We all rode to the beach & watched the trawlers and gulls . . . In the car coming home we listened to Aretha Franklin singing gospel music & I nearly choked up, thinking of how many things about my life I love, how worried I am about Bill, how happy I am about Bill, how worried I am about me & Bill, how afraid I am to die. (And I was also laughing, because Elisabeth told me this is the music they play in her aerobics class.)

MAY 23: Sweet Bill left early in the morning, telling groggy me that he was on his way to the dentist. I learned later that he'd gone to an acupuncturist for a no-smoking treatment. He's got two little staples in his ears and is a nervous wreck.

MAY 25: Ben said he had to take a # at the unemployment office today. He realized the wait would be long, so he killed the time by shopping at Barneys.

MAY 26: Bill & I went to *Forbidden Broadway* at a little theatre, or club, on E. 60th St. . . . A take-off on dirty-mouthed Mamet. The two actors of *Speed-the-Plow* sing, "We strain in vain to train Madonna's brain." And when she's able to say the words, one of them exclaims: "She's fuckin' got it!"

MAY 27: Uncle Joe died early this morning . . . I loved Joe—he was the funniest of all the uncles—but AIDS has changed me per-manently. I can't mourn for anyone over 60. I'll feel [grief] when I get out to Smithtown, but not as I might have 6 years ago.

MAY 29: Was at the funeral parlor a little after two . . . There was a couple—they looked like high-school kids—who were getting ready to bury a 3½-month-old baby who'd died of meningitis . . .

MAY 30: God, could Joe be funny. One time when Grandma was nearing 90, an old acquaintance ran into him & asked how she was—a discreet way of inquiring as to whether she was still alive. Joe said, "She's fine. She's gonna retire in another year or two." "Go on," the man said. "You don't mean to tell me she's still working." Joe quietly assured him that she continued to drive a beer truck for Rheingold.

JUNE 3: Down to Greg's . . . We ended the evening under the new, official city street sign making Christopher St. also "Stonewall Way." (The bar where it happened is now a plaqueless clothing store, after an interval as a Bagel Nosh.)

JUNE 5: [Billy] has a long work table in a room full of colored pencils and rulers and draftsman's lamps, and we've decided that this is where I'm going to do all the last work on the [plagiarism] book: checking each blessed quotation & making final, final, final adjustments to the page proofs . . . I love this man. There is no one easier to be with, no one who has ever loved me as much or who will again . . . I'm in a tumult of confusion. Fear and grimness—& I've never been happier either.

JUNE 6: . . . Down to 45th St.—passing Dag Hammarskjöld Plaza at 47th and rushing by the poor sodden Chinese democracy demonstrators.

JUNE 7: [Billy] tells me about one of his nicest memories of his mother. It was 1956 and Grace Kelly was getting married. The first films of it—just flown over from Monaco in those pre-satellite days—were about [to] be broadcast in St. Louis. She woke him up so they could watch together—& see the pretty dress. She was already sick and had less than a year to live.

JUNE 9: Bill & I wound up talking about IT in one of those sudden, unexpected ways. Actually it shouldn't be so sudden or unexpected: the huge [AIDS] conference has been going on in Montreal all this week. The news is very mixed. The numbers are appalling, but lots of new therapies are being discussed . . . Bill & I pulled all the philosophical stops out. At one point I mentioned that Keats [died] at 26. "Just like Jean Harlow," he said.

JUNE 10: [Chris Bull is] still young enough to hope for the moon. Still wants to convert his 94-year-old German-psychiatrist grandfather to acceptance of homosexuality. Can't understand why his mom is shocked when he tells her he's had sex with a PWA. ("You know, there is such a thing as safe sex, Mom.")

(It occurs to me that this is an 80s version of "Look, Ma, no cavities." So to speak.)

JUNE 11: Ran 5 miles this morning. Heavenly weather. About 80° with a strong, dry breeze. A big sign wishing the jogger a full recovery.

JUNE 12: The students on 47th St. have renamed Dag Hammarskjöld Park Tiananmen Square. There are hunger strikers lying in tents behind the funeral wreaths people have sent.

JUNE 13: I've reached the point of psychological takeover on the fact-checking. I spent 12 hours scurrying around the Reading & Catalogue rooms, as well as my apartment, today. As soon as I've tracked down one thing I convince myself another's gone amiss & I decide to look for that one too. And I fiddle with the text—with almost nothing gained in clarity & a good deal run up in expense. I was near tears by 10:30 tonight. . . .

. . .

Accuracy. An interesting study in it today. The *News* headlined the Hearns-Leonard fight of last night, which ended in a draw, as "A BEAUT OF A BOUT," saying it was a "mighty" contest. The *Post* said it was "A DREADFUL DRAW" between 2 geezers unable to show any stuff.

JUNE 14: . . . We went to Radio City to see Diana Ross . . . As Billy says, "she moves around like the great lady from Connecticut now," and it's true that D.R. doesn't break a sweat throughout the show. About the most strenuous thing she does is flick her hair like a Valley Girl. But the crowd was reverential. And interesting: a real mix: secretaries from Queens; dressed-up young black couples out on a big date; adoring gay men begging her to take their flowers (which she wouldn't).

JUNE 15: Spent part of the afternoon [researching *Aurora* 7] with the 1961–62 Manhattan telephone directory. All the pretty exchange names. I remember how Fownes [my father's office] was Murray Hill; realize that I'd be Oxford 7; and see that Louise's number, which I've dialed for years, is what it was in '62: Gramercy 5-7139.
      And Bill is Butterfield 8.

JUNE 16: I picked up the page proofs just before going down to the Morgan Library for my lunch with Charlie Pierce. Had I been told that his office was really Queen Elizabeth's, I would not have felt a bit of surprise. His hushed, baronial surroundings have finally given a suitable environment to that quiet maloccluded voice . . . We talked a lot about Vassar during and since his time. He tried to pretend less interest than he really felt, I thought . . . We were ideally suited to work with each other—we both had a taste for expeditiousness, a disinclination toward millenarianism. But each of us is not more than very slightly fond of the other. He respects my energies more than my intelligence . . .

JUNE 19: Handed the page proofs in to Fran & got a kiss. Cork came in to say he's been reading it & thinks it's very good: "I'm reading it very slowly, & with me that's a good sign." Tried to banish it completely from my mind; tried to tell myself I've sweat blood, done my best, and now it's over. But it was hard to fight down anxiety for much of the day, hard not to want just one last look.

JUNE 21: David Schorr, his ponytail in a braid, got here for drinks at about 7 . . . He talked about Wendy Gimbel, who's become the cultural editor at *Mirabella*, which has just run a piece of Phyllis's Josephine Baker book. The same week she was offered the *Mirabella* job she was offered the books editorship of *The Nation*. She sought Phyllis's advice, and it was "Wendy, you're not a 70-year-old Stalinist. Go to *Mirabella*."

JUNE 23: Billy was at a party in Greenwich so I rented *The Fountainhead* and watched Patricia Neal crash & claw her way through Ayn Rand's comic-book universe. (The comic book, specifically, is *Batman*—dark Gotham City, where the skyscrapers seem somehow always underground . . .)

JUNE 24: Worked happily in the science room of the NYPL late this morning, looking at NASA items. Came out and saw the bleachers set up and the banners hung for the Gay Pride parade tomorrow. Amazing to think that with this bunting the city officially celebrates what was a riot against its own police just twenty years ago. I remember the day, a week after graduation from [high school]. I was already working at Fownes & people were talking about Judy Garland, who was laid out up at Frank Campbell. I heard the news item about the riot sometime that weekend, I guess. I remember knowing dimly that this had something to do with me. . . .

JUNE 25: I ran a pretty easy 5 miles up at the park & came back to 72nd St. thinking: how great it is to be coming back to someone who's waiting for me, instead of to just a phone machine that only might be flashing . . . Bill cooked dinner for me & Doug & Bruce & the evening was a complete success. I was amazed at how relaxed I was; I could see that even hyper-critical Bruce was charmed by charming Billy. Doug took me aside in the work room & told me how lucky I was and not to worry about anything.

I took pictures. Am I already trying to save things up? Am I afraid this will be taken away from me?

JUNE 27: Manuela Hoelterhoff—she's David Brooks's successor at *The Wall Street Journal*—called to edit the *Apollo* review. Oh, *puh-lease*. She is terribly affected, and tries to sound disdainfully bril-

liant. With that name I suspect she's the child of a Nazi fugitive &
his sheltering South American mistress.

JUNE 28: Today I was straphanging [on the bus] by the seat of
one heavyset woman who must have been nearing 70. She was
in a short-sleeved summer dress, and I noticed her arm was tat-
tooed with a concentration-camp brand—blue numerals in a neat,
slightly archaic European style.

JUNE 29: Aux Trois Cavaliers is a little French restaurant right
around the block. I spotted it just when I moved to Turtle Bay
in '85 . . . a small, pretty, rustic-looking place with a garden . . .
somewhere in my mind I decided that I would never go there until
I had someone special to take. So tonight I took Billy. We sat in
the garden, under an umbrella, and had a bottle of wine with coq
au vin and steak au poivre. You could see the bricks of my building over the garden wall. And we had a lovely time, talking mostly
about growing up, and I thought: *at long last*. He's here.

JULY 2: The abandoned city is always depressing on holiday weekends, but this afternoon it seemed like one big Skid Row . . . the
little public plazas next to new office towers. The builders got tax
abatements to leave room for these "amenities," in which all you
see are desperate, shirtless, doped people sleeping at the feet of
skyscrapers.

JULY 3: Mary [Evans] called to say that *Arts & Sciences* has been
bought for French translation . . . Some hip line for the jeunesse,
I think . . . A 10,000-franc advance. I am of course delighted, but
it makes it seem all the more mysterious to me why it was never
sold for American paperback. . . .

     . . .

The abortion decision came down this morning. After all
these years and passions I'm still not sure what I believe deep in
my heart. But I do know that these male right-to-lifers give me
the creeps. One of them was crowing with hateful satisfaction
while beautiful, calm Faye Wattleton (Planned Parenthood) tried
to make a case against his.

JULY 4: I sat in the little chess players' park on E. 48th St. and wrote half of the new Mary Noonan scene; the story of Mom's mother suddenly came into it without my meaning [it] to . . . No interruptions except for one crazy lady who went by shouting "There's the man, officer!"—pointing at me for the benefit of a cop who didn't exist. A second later she'd shifted manias and was shouting toward another direction.

JULY 5: Talked on the phone to [L.B.], whom I can't stand. She's Houghton Mifflin's subrights person, and she's the one who botched the paperback sale of *Arts & Sciences*. Fran has told me that Katrina more or less pointed this out to her & there was very bad blood between them. As a result, [L.B.] doesn't seem terribly keen on me or on pushing my books.

JULY 7: [Sag Harbor] Fran & I read on the porch in the afternoon. David Leavitt came over . . . He has an article about himself & AIDS—"The Way I Live Now"—in this Sunday's *Times Magazine*, advance copies of which have been dispatched here. It seems to be required reading for tomorrow night's dinner party. I don't intend to do my homework. Really, what does this self-important person (Fran tells him she cried 3x reading the article & he asks her to tell him at precisely which points that happened) have to tell people who were burying friends and lovers five years ago? . . .

A dinner party a few blocks away at James Revson's. He's the *Newsday* gossip columnist and the man now in Giovanni Forti's life. Yes, *he* was there & Fran knew all about 2 years ago, or at least his version of it. We were very nice & smiling—but, God, he's so serious . . . We got bitten by mosquitoes in the yard (they're here in swarms this year because of all the June rain) & then went in to a nice dinner . . . An Italian journalist named Manuela Fontana referred to the "Bay of Porks" when the conversation turned to political history . . . While Fran & Sam Swope and I were walking to Revson's house, we heard, about 2 blocks from it, a huge dull crackle and then a long rumbling noise that lasted several seconds. It turned out that a huge old tree, near the Custom House and across from Revson's, had simply fallen down and died—on a night there was barely a breeze. I wondered if Chester A. Arthur, whose summer White House we passed on our walk, used to walk past it when it was young and in full leaf.

JULY 8: David Leavitt held forth endlessly on any number of topics, chief among them himself. Every time you think it's safe to open your ears again, you catch a phrase like "my Dutch publisher" coming at them like a mosquito. Elisabeth was bored by him, but she thinks he's just a little boy & doesn't get annoyed.

JULY 9: . . . Went out with Howard & Sam to step the mast on the *Sophie II*. After much difficulty with the stays we got it up nice & straight & then tethered the boat to a buoy in the harbor before rowing back to shore in a dinghy. I enjoyed the sun & the work, but sailing must be the most labor-intensive leisure in the world. . . .

Linda Asher, a very, very bright *New Yorker* editor, an amiably aggressive woman with gray hair and perhaps too much energy, came over for supper in the kitchen. She retains everything that has even so much as waded into her ken & she has little patience with a lot of young writers today, not because they don't have talent but because they're "dum-dums," just kids who don't know anything . . . She tired me out, but I liked her.

JULY 16: Read the paper up at Billy's. He thinks it's kismet that his copy was delivered with three *Book Review*s inside. [My essay "One Small Shelf for Literature," about how little important writing the moon landing spawned, was in it.]
. . .
Cooked a chicken dinner for Chris Bull, who arrived soaked from a sudden shower and who's a little discouraged with his job and apartment hunt. Sweet Chris, on the gay political cutting edge, admits that he fainted dead away at a film of Robert Mapplethorpe having his nipples pierced. He had to be carried out of the gallery where it was being shown and revived. When he told his hip father this story, his father's response was "You're repressed."

JULY 17: Bush's big space speech is scheduled for Thursday, the 20th anniversary . . . It will be a sad, strange thing if 20 years from now the only extraterrestrials left on earth are a few dying octogenarians.

JULY 19: So far it's been a relatively cool and peaceful summer in the city. There was this week the headline about the discovery of a "HUMAN CHOP SHOP," but since this Brooklyn enterprise was Mafia-run, no one really worries. They figure that people who died by the chop lived by the chop. The Mafia is much more careful about crossfire than non-connected drug dealers, and so people tend to think of them as the responsible criminal element. The only curious thing about the TV reporter's account was his saying that "all body parts except faces" were found.

JULY 23: To Billy's in the middle of the evening. Dennis [Cornelius, Bill's friend] has gone back to London—not without some worry. There's a work-to-rule slowdown at Gatwick, which means that customs officers will be asking even more than the usual number of questions of this sick-looking boy who's got no job & has medicine in his suitcase.

JULY 26: . . . Out to Mom's after a sweltering cab ride through midtown at lunch time. Read Proust on the way. She and I sat by the pool tonight for almost an hour, talking about everything. AIDS crept into the conversation, as it will . . . She said to me: "You know, if you ever got sick, I would take care of you. You could come out here. If these people didn't like it, we'd just move somewhere else."

JULY 29: At 1:00 up to Billy's. We took his friend Miriam to lunch at Stephanie's on 1st Ave.—the restaurant owned by Joan Bennett's daughter and decorated by Gene Moore [the Tiffany designer, and Bill's mentor]. Miriam is a 69-year-old redhead who worked for years in the dress business—a tough cookie who could reduce colleagues & competitors to tears, but to her friends a sweetie who would lie down in front of a bus for them. She can hardly keep from eating Billy up & blowing him kisses & calling him Bubby. I liked her right away.

JULY 31: [I was reporting an essay for the collection still called *Spectacle*.] . . . At noon to the U.N. Press Briefing. It'll be some time before I start going regularly, but I wanted to go today to hear what was being said after the execution of Col. Higgins (the U.S. marine attached to the U.N.) by the Hezbollah crazies who have been holding him hostage . . . Granted, it's off season, but there's an unbelievably low brain wattage apparent in the press & briefing rooms. (I knew more about the immediate situation with Higgins than did the questioners, because I'd watched TV while having my early lunch at home.)

AUGUST 1: Watched the mayoral debate on TV at 8:00. Koch, after 12 years and a little stroke, remains infinitely quicker than Goldin, Ravitch and Dinkins—who is just hopeless. He asked him: "Tell me, David, if they hadn't started to investigate, when would you have got around to paying your taxes? In the fifth year? The sixth? The tenth?" Goldin & Ravitch don't have a chance. I just hope that whoever does win—Koch or Dinkins—does so in the first round, because a runoff will be racial and ugly & bad for the city.

AUGUST 3: Poor Billy woke up with his morning anxieties. He just needs to be held like a puppy for a few minutes—and I'm happy to do it. He left me a love note to end all love notes in the kitchen.

AUGUST 4: Billy came by at 6:30 and after a drink we headed down 2nd Ave. in a taxi—a hot night—to meet Ben at the Orpheum & see Charles Busch in *The Lady in Question*, a campy send-up of 1940s anti-Nazi movies that has attracted a large "crossover" audience thanks to a rave from Frank Rich in the *Times*. (Four years ago I went to the opening night party, at Area, for one of his other plays—was taken there, improbably, by [W.]. The play is still running, having lasted about 16x longer than [W.] and I did.)

AUGUST 5: . . . Talked to Mom on the phone. She was in a very good mood over the good news about Parkinson's research, which made the front page of the *Times* the other day—just above good news about AZT. She excitedly read me some of the *Newsday* article, stumbling over the polysyllabic components of the new drug, marvelling at how smart these doctors "from your generation"— i.e., mine—are.

Went up to Billy's & we spent most of the evening in front of the TV and VCR. We watched a tape of Rosamond Bernier's lecture on Miró. She's sort of a cross between Margaret Thatcher & Julia Child—with the exact same overbite, Billy points out, as Gypsy Rose Lee.

AUGUST 8: *A Book of One's Own* will keep me in literary journalism for the rest of my life. The *Washington Post* today asked me to do Herbert Leibowitz's book about American autobiography; I had to say no because the *LA Times* has already asked me.

AUGUST 9: Should have gone to the gym, with its purgative powers, *after* I attended the meeting of the Special Committee Against Apartheid at the U.N. I got to the Trusteeship auditorium late & left early, after about 35 minutes of platitudes and agitprop. (No, I'm not for apartheid, jerk; but the language here was like Newspeak without the tang.) I'd say it was unspeakable, but they were speaking it. After a while I switched my earphone to Urdu or something so I wouldn't have to reflexively try to ascribe meanings to the words I was hearing.

. . .

. . . To Billy's for dinner. I stayed up late. While he was in bed, I went into the workroom to read spooky *Libra* almost to the end. Still, I don't believe any of it. I think Oswald was no more than Hinckley . . . I'll go to my grave believing he did it alone, haunted most by the thought of the night before, Thursday, Nov. 21, when he went to suburban Dallas (the house of Ruth Paine) to pick up the rifle. Playing with the babies & the neighbor children on the swings. Knowing he could still stop himself, but knowing he was going to wake up tomorrow & do it.

AUGUST 10: I like spending the day on 72nd St., going from room to room, missing Billy & thinking of him when I look at the stuffed cat, the cup of quarters for the laundry and bus, the way he's put everything out (including my breakfast) just so in the kitchen.

AUGUST 14: I've gotten myself into one of those reviewing over-loads, when my desk becomes an assembly line. Spent the day reading Louisa May Alcott's journals, outlining my Leibowitz piece, putting aside Chatwin and thinking about Berryman. But I will soon come to a patch of blue sky and get back to the novel.

AUGUST 15: Went to the "164th Meeting of the Committee on the Exercise of the Inalienable Rights of the Palestinian People." The entire meeting was devoted to discussion of other meetings. This body is so mentally numbing that Israel ought to give it a grant to keep it going.

AUGUST 16: The GMHC has begun urging people to have the AIDS test—if, that is, they can bear to. Can I bear to? I don't know. They say the medical advances make it worthwhile—it's no longer a case of "they can't do anything for you, so what's the point of knowing." A positive report now means an ominous diag-nosis rather than a quick death sentence.

I could take it; find out I'm negative; be released of the anxi-ety I've carried for 6 years. But would I start looking at Billy differently?

I could take it; find out I'm positive (as is likely); feel doomed and without any will; or begin getting treated for the virus and live years longer than if I hadn't had the test.

They say one should see a counselor before having the test. Can a counselor really change the above? Ladies and tigers.

AUGUST 18: We went to Café 57 . . Passed Billy's old apartment. Had a lovely meal at a table near a window. Billy asked me if I was as happy with this new life as he was, and I answered, with com-plete truth, yes.

AUGUST 19: We watched a video of *In Cold Blood* tonight. I've seen it at least 3x before, but I've never really been scared by it.

I realize I've just used the word "we" with no proper noun for it in this entry. And I realize whoever's reading this knows who it is. "We" = Billy + me. All of a sudden it comes naturally. Just as when Doug asks "What are you doing this weekend?" he means

"What are you two doing?"—as I've always meant through years of asking him.

AUGUST 21: I was on the 7:30 Pan Am Shuttle & got to the NASA Archives at about 9:30 . . . Went to the Vietnam Veterans Memorial just before 5:00. Sweating in my blue-&-white blazer . . . The wall itself did not especially move me. I walked up and down it respectfully. But I was appalled by the paper directory of names that makes you realize how many 55,000 are. A whole phone book full of people shot and exploded. The people coming to see the wall are more moving than the thing itself. You see pained looks, crinkling eyes. People leave flowers & poems. I found Johnny Olsen's name—the only one I could think of because of my blessed, draft-deferred youth—and stood quietly in front of the panel it was on. . . .

Had dinner with Damian Leader . . . Met him at the State Department, where he's on the French desk . . . Took me up to peer into James Baker's office, which has been tarted up with a lot of Federalist frou-frou that looks foolish in a post-war building. Damo's got a beautiful view of the Lincoln Memorial & a computer that's lead-lined so the Russian truck cruising the street out front can't pick anything up.

AUGUST 22: Back at the Archives in the afternoon. A great feeling of sadness comes over me. Not an unpleasant feeling, maybe a sense of tragic beauty; a feeling of the immense futility of our living and dying and saving what we can. I look at a portrait of FDR & think of his monumental life versus my little one & feel that I'm the one who matters because I'm *alive, now, this second*—& for however much longer. And yet there's no one more desperate to preserve himself in a neat little catalogued pile than I.

Took the Trump Shuttle home & was thrilled to see Billy light up when I brought him nothing more than a little china souvenir Washington, D.C., mug. "I'll have my coffee in it tomorrow morning," he said, before crushing me in a hug.

AUGUST 25: [Sag Harbor] Ran errands in town with Fran. Elisabeth arrived late in the afternoon and we conspired about the party. David Leavitt dropped in while Sam was making an interminable Indian dinner—to tell us all to be at a pro-choice rally in the Hamptons sometime tomorrow, because he was speaking . . . Elisabeth & I roll our eyes in opposite directions.

AUGUST 26: Guests arrived at about 8:00, smart Linda Asher among them . . . [G.G.] made the rounds with that dizzy moonbeaming face of his that he brings to within four inches of everyone else's. He says these terribly sincere things in a kitty-cat voice & seems bewildered and slightly hurt when anyone finds anything going on to be humorous.

AUGUST 28: . . . Letting out a whoop of joy at a letter from Alexandra Isles at the Museum of Broadcasting: they've agreed to buy the whole 10 hours of Aurora 7 coverage. Amazing good fortune. Also a letter today from Marjorie Ciarlante at the National Archives— she sends me a copy of a document she found: a speech drafted for LBJ to give if Carpenter didn't make it back. It is creepy, referring to his memory, his grieving family, etc. . . .

AUGUST 29: Fran & I talked late this afternoon. Cork is being pushed out of Houghton Mifflin—they're bringing in the guy who wrecked Weidenfeld. Fran has had it & will leave before the end of the year. I'm not going to worry about this: I've been through it before with James and Katrina. I do thank my stars the *Aurora* 7 & *Spectacle* contracts are signed, though.

        . . .

A call from Andy Pandolfo tonight. We're going to get together before the 20th Sewanhaka reunion. We were on the phone for nearly 2 hours—just like the gabby gay high schoolers we were 20 years ago. But tonight we were actually talking about our boyfriends, & who would believe that would ever come to pass?

AUGUST 31: I got Fran's message this morning that 2 copies of *Stolen Words* were waiting at the T&F receptionist's desk . . . Billy came over at 7:30 with a little bottle of Moët. When he saw his name had been added to the book in page proof he felt as if I'd handed him the moon. I LOVE HIM.

SEPTEMBER 1: Had lunch at the Glass Box with Ann & Doug. She's in town for a day or two. We had a lovely time. Doug asked, really eagerly: "Have you met Bill? He's adorable."

SEPTEMBER 2: Billy and I got the 9:50 to Vassar . . . We checked into Alumnae House Room #6 with all its chinoiserie. He loved the campus & I showed him everything . . . He liked and memorized it all. The whole place looks like a bucolic haven to him, so tired is he of the city, and he has to strain to realize how I longed to be free of it . . . I think Billy was shy about being among this bunch of Ph.D.s and was tickled by the silliness and ease of the conversation. I think he was especially taken with David [Littlefield]—part of a generation of straight men (for whom homosexuality is no big deal) that Billy's not been around much.

SEPTEMBER 3: We drove to Hyde Park and picnicked on the grounds of the Vanderbilt mansion on a bluff over the river. From there to FDR's house . . . The whole day was lived in golden light. I was so happy that I was inevitably melancholy. How long will this last?

SEPTEMBER 6: Richard Wilson was the Convocation speaker, and he gave a beautifully written & very funny speech, much of it about Aaron Copland. But he was preceded by Heather Fox, the student government president, who gave another guilt-wallowing speech about racism, homophobia, sexism, etc., that would make you think that Vassar is Selma, Alabama in 1950. She had the audience standing and sitting down, 6 different times, as a way of polling them about their various prejudices . . . The place is a little liberal police state, with any deviationists hunted down & scorned—as the place celebrates its diversity.

SEPTEMBER 7: Bob [Wilson at *USA Today*] is, in fact, the only book review editor with whom I ever actually talk books. Maybe it's just his leisurely style, but I don't think so. Most of the others are just shoving the meat into the sausage-maker without giving it a second look.

SEPTEMBER 8: Went to Ticknor & Fields to sign a boxful of complimentary copies of *SW*. The place is like a chaotic tomb: they're getting ready to move the office to Park Ave. So., and most of them are mourning the shabby treatment of Cork as they pack. . . .

SEPTEMBER 9: Walked home down First Avenue. A warm, pretty day that would later turn muggy. Bought Nick & Siri their wedding present: a hand-painted pitcher from Italy. Got it in a shop at 1st and 51st that Billy recommended.

Went out to the gym. Saw Martha Araya, my nice upstairs neighbor, coming in as I went out, and I held the door for her, rather grandly. "Are you joking?" I thought she said. I replied, with a big smile, "No." She looked confused. We waved goodbye. Then, dressed in my shorts with my Walkman in my ear, I realized she'd said, in her Spanish accent, "Are you jogging?" Oh, well.

SEPTEMBER 12: They're saying David Dinkins "paid his dues." I just wish he'd paid his taxes. He was surrounded in victory [in the Democratic primary] by every union leader who's going to milk the city dry during the next four years if he wins.

SEPTEMBER 14: Walked down to Louise's in the rain. We had supper & I gave her *Stolen Words* . . . We talked about the election (she voted for Dinkins) and walked down to the Astor Place Theatre to see a preview of *The Man Who Shot Lincoln*—a real barking turkey we decided to take a chance on . . . We laughed anticipating John Simon's review & had a drink at the Riviera. I walked her home to Peter Cooper and then took a taxi up to Billy's. God, how much nicer than a lonely walk home & 2 lonely beers at South Dakota on the way!

SEPTEMBER 15: I have really decided that the UN is a sinister place. No one can take that much unreality. After an hour in it I feel as if I'm suffering from radiation sickness, or oxygen deprivation.

SEPTEMBER 17: Why am I afraid of our living together? My workaholism? Fear that that will make things even harder if sickness comes? Fear of appearances? I don't know for sure, although I know it only makes sense. I now hate being alone in the evenings. I stayed down here to work tonight & couldn't stand it. Talked to him twice on the phone.

The subject of living together came up this morning, & when I gently brushed it aside I could see him holding back tears—not because I'd wounded him, but because he felt guilty—thought he'd upset me—upset the apple cart—thought, in fact, that he had no right to bring up something that was on his mind. *Blamed himself.* A legacy of his years with [his ex].

SEPTEMBER 19: Lunch on the 4th floor of the General Assembly Bldg. Huge portions of chicken, wine, dessert—while the UNICEF man was telling us about how Third World children needlessly die from diarrhea.

SEPTEMBER 20: A party at Jim Montoya's big new house . . . I did my imitation of Ed Koch looking for a boyfriend in retirement.

Sat next to Bob & at one point, when the conversation was subdividing, he mentioned to me that he "took a big step" this morning—he's had the AIDS test . . . I couldn't believe that even he could reduce this to cocktail party chit chat. He was always against getting the test, but now it's "standard practice," he says. Which is to say it's the Thing to Do—always the strongest appeal to Bob. Just as a negative result will be a status symbol, the way a big penis or a share on Fire Island was 10 years ago.

SEPTEMBER 23: Mary McCarthy is sick with pneumonia—& cancer on her pleurae. She's in New York Hospital & I went to visit her this morning. She was in very good spirits for all the tubes, and she took the usual intellectual pleasure she has in the *facts* of her illness: "They took *three* liters of fluid out of my lungs. I *saw* it." The familiar smile, and the familiar gesture with her first 2 fingers. She explained in lucid detail the procedure they'll use for treating the pleurae, & from there we went on to talking about *Stolen Words*. (She's already read 2/3 of it but didn't bring it down from Bard, "because I thought it would be dynamite in this room"—Barbara Epstein was planning to pay a visit that afternoon. "I'll make this quick," I said, and we both laughed.)

I talked to her about *Aurora* 7 and she was attentive & pleased. I got water for the flowers and was gone after 15 minutes. I managed to reach her at a good time—no meal or consultation or particular discomfort in progress. The visit was almost gay. I hope she pulls through this. Dear Mary—my mentor, my heroine, my friend.

SEPTEMBER 25: Our annual siege. George Bush came to the UN and we were all under house arrest as he arrived and departed. Most of the UN press corps couldn't get tickets—they were given out to the US mission & the reporters who travel with the President. So I sat here & got my first ¶ of the article out of the goings-on on the street.

SEPTEMBER 28: Poor Billy—my angel Billy—is not relaxed. He's having a crazy week at work & is pushing to get everything done before Italy. He was all hunched in on himself in bed tonight, & he made those funny little clicking noises that sound like Miriam Makeba.

SEPTEMBER 29: To the UN late in the morning. I caught the end of Mubarak's speech from the press gallery. There were lots of guns around—guards in the gallery, guards flanking him on the podium. But that was nothing compared to this afternoon when the Colombian president spoke. There were fears he'd be shot by the Medellín drug cartel . . .

SEPTEMBER 30: I wish I could make him SECURE. But he is at bottom worried that I'm somehow going to run away. But I'm not going anywhere. I am so fastidious & nervous about anything sexual that he's sometimes worried to start anything; and yet he feels the tepid sexual temperature may make me move somewhere else. I don't mind the tepid temperature or what's become the relative infrequency in the slightest. I am delighted to report that I think less about sex than I have in years. I'm too busy thinking about having someone to love—& the even greater novelty of being absolutely adored by somebody.

OCTOBER 2: Barbara Williams, the [Houghton Mifflin] lawyer, talked with me about subjects to avoid on the radio: don't discuss current aspects of the Sokolow case & don't speculate on his psychology & mental health.

OCTOBER 4: Billy & I met Fran & Howard & Elisabeth & Vance at the Thai House Café way down on Hudson, just after 9:00. It was Billy's debut dinner with the Sag Harbor crowd & he was clearly a hit. Fran is already talking about a November weekend with all of us. Billy liked her and *adored* Elisabeth, as I could have guessed.

OCTOBER 6: Sondra says the *Times* called up for another copy of *SW* & a picture; they say they'll be running a review next Thursday. My stomach will be contracted until then. Oh, God, if it isn't good I'm going to be in an awful mood on the plane Friday night. Please don't let this ruin my vacation and then let me ruin Billy's.

OCTOBER 7: Breakfast and the paper with dear Billy, who cried last night when I gave him a 6-mo. anniversary card. My sweet man.

OCTOBER 9: Faxed my piece to Wlady from the MCI desk in the UN press office this morning. A jolly Chinese man explained it all to me. Alas, this $57.50 job was coming out so faint as to be almost unusable on Wlady's end. I wound up having to Xerox & FedEx a copy anyway; I was glad to find a Xeroxer open on this shut-down day: it's both Columbus Day + Yom Kippur. And when [the piece] arrives a kid in the office still has to type it into their computer.* Editors are beginning to indulge me, and I don't know how much longer this can go on before I start losing work.

. . .

Billy and I went down to Carol's in Stuy Town, for dinner . . . We had a good Italian meal as the traffic from the FDR Dr. 9 floors down lapped like a calm tide. Easy, bluesy CDs playing in the background: Peggy Lee, Chet Baker, Harry Connick.

Carol has a friend at Met Life who can get Billy into Stuy Town when his sublet is over, and while we were walking out of

---

* I was still composing first drafts in longhand, then typing them on a typewriter.

the complex—past the pretty Oval, the bumless benches, the vast ivy patches, I was urging him, too strongly, to take her up on this. He doesn't want to think about it because he wants me to move in with him & he knows I'll never want to—because I wouldn't want to with anyone. I see its attractions—especially with Billy—and I sometimes think I could, but I always get back to my fear of that sort of melding. I ask him: aren't we happy as we are? "Yes," he says, but he wants to make a home for me.

OCTOBER 11: . . . I got a call from the *Times Book Review* to set up an interview (a "box"). This is good news, because they usually run those with sizable and reasonably favorable pieces. But it still added to my nervousness. . . .

OCTOBER 12: . . . Showing up at the Empire State Bldg.—the 55th floor—to do a Canadian Broadcasting interview with dear old Freda Garmaise, whom I got such a kick out of 4 or 5 years ago. I refused to go along with some gimmicky stuff (they wanted me to pretend I was in my Vassar office; the CBC now insists on "ambiance," even when it has to be faked) . . . Rushed back uptown to get my hair cut by Nancy. Delayed by joke-telling with Freda. ("What's tall, blonde, has a 38" bust-line and lives in Sweden? A: Salman Rushdie.")

OCTOBER 13: I'm up over the Atlantic & it's midnight. MY beloved Billy is sleeping next to me with a blanket around him . . . When he was going through his carry-on bag I noticed that he'd brought my anniversary card to him. I told him that was sweet & asked him why. He said, "if the plane goes down, I want that near my heart.". . . .

All hell broke loose with the Sokolow case today. Just after I got back from the gym & did the last editing of the UN piece with Wlady, I opened the mail. From Larry Cooper, the 10/5 edition of the *Concord Journal*. Front-page headline: SOKOLOW ADMITS TO PLAGIARISM—& inside: CENTER FOR AMERICAN STUDIES TO DISCUSS MALLON CHARGES . . .

Needless to say, I'm not relaxed about going away while everything's going on back home. But this is my honeymoon & 6-mo. anniversary trip all rolled into one & I wasn't about to defer it.

OCTOBER 14: Right as we were going through passport control in Milan I was hit by a huge crippling wave of Artie-Dunne-like panic, anxiety and pseudo-guilt. I was stunned and frightened by its force, though I shouldn't have been. It's been building up for months—all my little obsessive-compulsions taking more worry out of me—and this past week, with all the dread of reviews and the Sokolow situation, has pushed me over the edge. It, the panic, kept up almost all day, fueled as it was by exhaustion. We just kept going and going . . . The Milan train station is a huge Mussolinied affair from the early 30s. You can see the remains of "Fascisti" wiped out from underneath the Anno Domini carving . . . I imagined my grandfather, one of the two of them I never got to meet, going into the cathedral before he left for America at about 13.

OCTOBER 15: [Florence] We like our hotel. I sit in the lounge near the bar and do a little work while Billy takes a walk & runs errands. The he comes back and we write post cards together sitting not far from the gaudy, swirling green-glass chandelier. It's a beautiful monstrosity. One thing we've noticed all day is that the Italians have such an innate sense of design they even make their schlock stylish.

. . . From there to the Pitti Palace, built by a Medici rival (it was all Leona vs. Ivana back in those days) . . . We went out to Il Banchino, a very tiny restaurant, for a turistico menu . . . The cloth napkins all had the name "Elma" stitched into them—the name of Billy's dead, beloved aunt, whom he still imagines watching over him. He began to well up at this appearance of her spirit with us on this romantic night. I gave the waitress 10,000 extra lire at the end of the meal and told her we were pocketing the napkin & why. She loved the story.

OCTOBER 16: We went to the Duomo and climbed to the top of the Campanile and looked down on terra cotta Firenze. (Someone's initials from 1855 carved into one ledge—why is this more poignant than the rest of the trecento traces and monuments all about?) . . . Ended the evening back at Gilli. Billy adores its Belle Époque operettaness. He bought 2 plates from it for us to have our snacks on back home. The frilly, benign atmosphere was made only slightly sinister by the loud entrance of Claus von Bülow and his party. American mutters and whispers from other customers. Easy on the sweets, Claus—you know what you claim they did to Sunny!

OCTOBER 17: . . . Going into the Princes' Chapel, which seems to be made out of jade and emeralds instead of green marble. Our guidebook inexplicably calls it "grandiose but gloomy"; I could imagine someone booking it for a roller-skating birthday party. After looking at the gruesome reliquaries, we were on to the Academy to see David . . . Three times as large as I expected, and so thoroughly and immediately sexual that I was feeling not an aesthetic reaction but an almost purely erotic one. One just kept thinking not that the statue was beautiful but that *he* was so beautiful (even with dust on his shoulders, as Billy noticed).

OCTOBER 18: . . . I showed Billy around the Keats House just before it closed . . . A sadness came over me as we left. I just saw myself there 11 years ago and got the blues. I've done everything & more I could have wanted to. But the sadness rushed in anyway. It's only time and death and Daddy and everything else I can't control—it's only life.

OCTOBER 19: I knew as I looked up at the Temple of Antoninus & Faustina, a sharp, beautiful half-ruin against the lowering sun, that I was not feeling anything of ancient Rome—just the Rome of my 19th-century Englishmen, the home of twilight, crumblings & white melancholy.

OCTOBER 20: We spent most of the evening in the bar of the Hotel Bernini Bristol—partly to use its *gabinetto*, since there is no water at all in our first-class hotel, a fact that the management aren't even slightly apologetic about. They just tell you it's a problem up and down the street.

OCTOBER 22: We couldn't even sit together for the 8 ½-hour flight. There was so much bumping, overbooking and sheer confusion that we were six rows and two aisles apart. I tried to sleep, and I tried to work and I read A. N. Wilson's biography of Milton—the chapter containing Milton's time in Florence and his visit to the defeated Galileo in Fiesole . . . By the end of the flight *I missed Billy* and wrote him a love note that I put in his hand when I left the cab we got from the airport. I'll never forget our 9 days of complete togetherness. Not once did I feel so much as an irritated moment with him. I love him.

OCTOBER 23: No, the book is going to be a hit, because I have, at last, a great review from the *Book Review*. Walter Kendrick (a good choice at last!) says it's "lively, engrossing and provocative" and that I write "vivaciously." I have an immense sense of relief . . .

I did Lenny Lopate's radio show *New York Chronicle* on WNYC at 2:00.

OCTOBER 25: Mary McCarthy died today in New York Hospital. I was ready for it. Dixie told me this morning that she could go at any time. I got the message tonight when I got off the train from Vassar. There was also a message to call the Associated Press, which was compiling her obituary. I was giving facts and quotes to a woman 10 minutes after I'd gotten the news and I choked up, but she barrelled right along with her questions. The teletypes and word processors were chattering and the show was going on.

How glad I am to have had that last visit, when she was still herself. I sent her a postcard from Florence. . . .

I didn't get to Billy's until 11:00. His news? Miriam has lung cancer. His face was collapsed into a small boy's frightened one.

OCTOBER 30: down at the new Ticknor & Fields by 3:00. They're at Park Ave. So. & 17th now—right where Max's Kansas City used to be. Publishing has gone back to its pre-war self—leaving mid-town for downtown. . . .

OCTOBER 31: [The staff of The Center for American Studies at Concord] admit the "validity of the charges" that made them

accept JS's resignation, but they say I was remiss in not showing
JS a draft of the chapter before it was published. (Imagine 1973:
"Mr. President, my colleague Bob Woodward & I wonder if you'd
vet our article before it appears in the *Post*?")

NOVEMBER 2: Louise can't come to my publication party at Fran's
because she's going into NYU Hospital for colon-cancer surgery
on Monday. She's optimistic now, after a period of despair immediately after diagnosis. The irony is that, heavy smoker that she
is, she no doubt feared the lungs would get it. But her spirits are
strong and she's making jokes about how irritated she is to keep
hearing from the doctors that she's about to have "the same operation Reagan had."

NOVEMBER 6: . . . It's not easy for Billy now. He is going through a
terrible struggle with smoking—lapsing, feeling guilty—all much
worse than 6 mos. ago. He's stymied . . . doesn't know whether to
go back to the acupuncturist, to another doctor, or just give up . . .
He doesn't deserve this. And meanwhile all he does is worry about
me: he even sewed a rip in my suede jacket yesterday morning.
    Nicely dressed office girl crossing E. 57th St., saying to her
friend: "So I says, Herman, what the fuck is with you?"

NOVEMBER 7: It's 6 p.m. and Billy will be here by 9, at which time
we'll hear that that compassionate crook, that healing deadbeat,
the conciliating hack, David Dinkins, has been elected mayor. I
figure I'll get it over with by writing it down now. It has been a
preposterous campaign, with a tax cheat having daily bouquets
tossed him by the press. . . .

NOVEMBER 9: Watched the first few hours of the Aurora 7 tapes
at the museum today and was enchanted from beginning to end.
Everything held me, from the old Aerowax commercial (bullets
being fired at the "jet-age plastic") to Rene's taped interview, in
which, after saying Scott was suited to be an astronaut because of
his pioneer ancestors, she wondered: "What else corny can I say?"
Bad-girl astrowife!

NOVEMBER 10: Last night, while people were dancing on the Berlin Wall, Billy and I were being brave, trying to sound optimistic and sensible, feeling scared. He's gotten his once-every-four-months report and his count is way down. The doctor wants to see him Monday, and we're pretty sure he's going to be put on AZT. We knew this would come, and we know he may have years of excellent health ahead; he purposely started going to this doctor because he knows he'll get early, aggressive treatment for HIV. And it's not so silly to think that while AZT keeps it at bay for a few years, they may come up with something that will keep it at bay more or less permanently.

I may be the one living in a fool's paradise. My count could be lower than his. I know I should be tested—the GMHC has changed its mind on that score—but I am still too afraid. I keep telling myself I'll make a decision, but before I've finished this entry I'll have managed to put the question out of my mind.

NOVEMBER 12: I went down to see Louise at NYU. She looks tired but not unhealthy. She had a little pain today and the visit was a bit of a strain for her, so I left after a short while. Left wondering if I'd be visiting Billy there a year from now. Or if Louise would be visiting me. Sometimes I wonder if part of her doesn't resent me for not having gotten sick so far.

A beautiful day. A blue-and-gold sky, strong cold winds; I exulted in the day as I came back up First Ave. Life has that salted edge it had when Tommy first got sick; fear is making me percipient, appreciative.

NOVEMBER 14: Billy's doctor wants to do the test once more just to make sure that some little bug or anxiety over smoking didn't push his count way down last time . . . And I try to keep cheerful, reading things like a mailing from amfAR that says their goal—and not a utopian one—is to make AIDS something on the order of "diabetes or hypertension."

. . .

. . . Drinks & dinner ([at] Beach) with Billy, Carol & Miriam, who looks marvelous. She came out of a week of chemotherapy with her hair and spirits intact . . . tells about her encounter with Olivia de Havilland at some film seminar she went to—in Paris, I think. "She admired my dress, I admired hers. She admired my hair, I admired hers." Long pause. "She looked awful."

NOVEMBER 16: Billy and I got to Fran & Howard's on Park Ave. at just about 8:00. Fran had wanted to do this publication party weeks ago . . . Once Walter Kendrick weighed in I was relaxed and told her to go ahead . . . Carmella made the dinner and the apartment looked beautiful. There was a little stack of books, and some roses that were in a ginger jar instead of a tall vase because Dinah, one of the kittens, had chomped at the stalks the night before.

James and Anne Raimes came, and they were kept laughing by Freda Garmaise ("James Raimes?" she said when introduced to him. "That's not a real name") . . . I got up and made a person-by-person toast of thanks to everyone—heartfelt but unsyntactical. I realized how many people were there—James, Frank, Cork—[who] had left Ticknor & Fields unhappily. (Gwen goes soon, too.) But they had been so good to me . . . Billy was so proud, and nervous, uncomprehending as he is that nearly everyone who meets him feels cherishing and protective at once. He's very taken with Elisabeth, and was comfortable with Carol Smith (another ailurophile), but was scared to death, I think, of Linda Asher (who scares me, too, she's so bright) . . . We walked for several blocks before getting a cab, to let out the tension, and to let the feeling of exquisite pleasure take over. It was one of those evenings one so wanted to be perfect that one wanted it over with, as soon as possible, while it still was.

NOVEMBER 17: I was out to Andy's place in Glen Cove by 6:00 . . . We prepped ourselves for [our twentieth high-school] reunion by looking at the yearbook. (Jeff Gilbert, who is in jail for being one of the "stun-gun" torturers from that Queens police precinct, had "Machinist" as his ambition. Close.) . . . Cathy Hoffman was the prettiest, and the only woman I slow-danced with; she looks as if she's on *Knots Landing*, and, in fact, she does do TV commercials in Arizona. . . .

. . . Nick Mattia is a cop—he pulled Mr. Georgi [our tough sixth-grade teacher] over for speeding on Stewart Ave. a few years ago & was still too scared to give him a ticket . . . Most thrilling moment of the evening. Rhona Popeil comes up to me saying "Eddie Haugevik is looking for you!" Twenty years too late! He's still gorgeous and has become, of all things, a sculptor . . .

NOVEMBER 18: Went down to WNYC with Billy tonight. [He] sat in the studio while I did an hour, live, on the American Public Radio network. The show (*Modern Times*) was pre-empted in NY for a Brooklyn Academy of Music concert, but went out live to 21 other cities. The second half hour was for listeners' calls, and the loopy ones ("I think plagiarists ought to be stoned") came from California. One man seemed positively annoyed that I haven't been sued yet. Occasionally I would swivel my headphoned head and smile at darling Billy.

NOVEMBER 19: The paper at Billy's before going back to Turtle Bay to have brunch with Elmer & Sophie [Blistein], who were in town for the weekend and staying at the Beekman Towers . . . He says the [Brown English] department, which he still goes to a few times a week, is awful—"all the humanism is gone"—dominated no longer by the semioticians, who were coming on as I was leaving it, but the deconstructionists and political revisionists.

NOVEMBER 21: A very cold day. I worked out at the gym and spent the afternoon finishing up with the Aurora 7 tapes at the Museum of Broadcasting. I was so keyed up that when the moment came ("and alongside it a life raft, and sitting in it a gentleman named Carpenter") I started to cry . . . went downtown at 6:30 to meet Abby Tallmer for dinner at Delle Muse just south of Washington Square . . . God, I remember when Abby seemed, my first year [at Vassar], to be the scariest dyke on campus—all leather and hobnails. Now she's a coiffed, soft-spoken yuppie wondering if, at 29, she's too old to start graduate school.

NOVEMBER 23: Loree complained about her aches & pains, and Ollie has developed a curious, bitter sense of humor, but there was no fighting with Mom, and while anyone looking in on our Thanksgiving might have found it a little tense & even unpleasant, I'd give it, based on our own family standard, at least a B+.

NOVEMBER 25: It's Mom's 66th birthday (she's bothered by being as old as Dad was when he died).

And they're cheering Dubček in Prague.

NOVEMBER 26: . . . To Lincoln Center to see Suzanne Farrell's farewell performance . . . When all the group curtain calls were done the curtain rose once more and there she was, alone, in her white satin gown, and the hundreds of bouquets of thornless roses all took flight at the same second. And barrage after barrage after that until the stage was carpeted . . . Here at last you have someone honored, gone crazy over, for having created beauty, for thirty years, for having the discipline to do it that long—with a hip replacement along the way. If I were she I'd go home and eat chocolate cake every night and not care if I looked like Ethel Merman in a year's time.

. . . Talked about Billy's apartment hunting. He can be gotten into Stuy Town by Carol's cousin & he knows it makes financial sense. But he's afraid of doing it for that reason, for thinking he'd better save his money for AZT. "I always wanted a showplace of an apartment, to buy something beautiful and extravagant. If I move into Stuy Town I'll feel, somewhere inside me, that I'm settling, giving up, and just getting ready to die." To hear this from the least selfish, least self-pitying and least pretentious person I've ever known was heartbreaking.

NOVEMBER 27: The second test shows Billy's #s are up, so the doctor does not want him to start AZT now . . . This is a little gift—more time before the rain begins.

DECEMBER 2: Wrote my review of the Maugham biography, which isn't very good. I'm in reasonable shape with journalism just now: my review of Galbraith's novel is ready for the mail. (Will I soon be saying "ready for the modem"? Is that even how you spell it?)

DECEMBER 3: A bitter cold day. Read the paper at Billy's—all of it Yalta-to-Malta stories. The world is being remade and everybody is hoping that Gorbachev's cholesterol count and political skills are in good shape. All of this could fall apart in 10 minutes if he goes.

DECEMBER 5: Carol and I hugged each other in front of [my aunt] Belle's closed coffin this afternoon, and she said to me: "We're the old generation now." . . . I am taking this harder than I did Joe or Tom. Belle was my favorite—and the only one of all the relatives with whom Mom discussed my being gay. I just felt wretched in that room today—all these people I only see at funerals. She was laid out one "chapel" away from where Joe was in May.

DECEMBER 6: I went to sleep after finding myself famous—again, briefly, happily. Christopher Lehmann-Haupt has given *Stolen Words* a dream of a review in the daily *Times*. I'm almost as happy as I was over Naomi Bliven. [Billy and I] tried not to talk about it before going to the Korean deli at 11:00 [to get the *Times*]. We open the paper, see the picture—"Ooh, Tommy! You're in it!"—and then close it, waiting an eternity for the man to take my dollar and give me change. Reading it under the light outside & realizing it was good. And then choking up and actually crying a little as the tension unwound. The things I put Billy through.

DECEMBER 7: When I got up to Billy's tonight, he said "We're going out!" And we did: to Bemelmans Bar to drink champagne and listen to Barbara Carroll and celebrate the review . . . Wlady called, too. He says *The American Spectator* has assigned the book to Hugh Kenner, who's late sending in his piece. If it turns out negative, I probably won't be able to tell. I can never penetrate anything he writes.

DECEMBER 8: The computer arrived today . . . While grounding the plug I managed to hit the live wire with the screwdriver & extract a long flame and loud pop. And I was scared of the thing even before this. I walk up to the screen & keyboard + hard drive a little like a small kid approaching a German shepherd: nice doggie.

DECEMBER 9: We bought our Christmas tree at 3rd Ave. + 70th St. and the kid selling it turned out to be Nicholas Smithberg, an old student. "Mr. Mallon!" So we got $15 off and carried it home.

DECEMBER 10: Billy has made a tree so beautiful that you think you've wandered into Tiffany's or sat down for *The Nutcracker*. It's a miracle of plaid and gold bows, lights and baby's breath—as warm & elegant as any I've ever seen. We sat on the couch tonight and just kept bursting out with laughter over how gorgeous it was.

DECEMBER 11: I now have several pages of *Aurora* 7, an entire book review, and a portion of a Booth bibliography on the hard disk. I'm getting the hang of it . . . I can see why it's positively bad for the students, though. They hit hundreds of keys, fiddle and play and convince themselves they're writing.

DECEMBER 15: At 8:00 Billy and I set out for Elisabeth's in a cab. It was snowing hard when we left Turtle Bay, and by the time we got to Tribeca it was pouring . . . Billy was very quiet. He is intimidated by these people . . . Vance was chirping away about every last play he'd seen as well as his Garbo book; Fran was high about finishing her 7 *Days* piece; Elisabeth was talking about Helmut Newton; and I was being congratulated on Lehmann-Haupt. Billy was fighting his cold and almost scared to speak . . . We talked about it when we got home . . .

Elisabeth passed around a piece of the Berlin Wall tonight. It's not a 5th Ave. fake either, but something one of her old friends got firsthand. Everyone passed it around nervously, and with jokes, like a piece of political camp. She was flip about it too, but I know it meant something to her, and so when I handed it back to her, I said: "I think it's wonderful."

DECEMBER 16: We got Mom at Penn Station and steered her past the homeless . . . We took her up to Rockefeller Center to see the tree; it's never as big as one expects, and now the joke is that next year it will be a bonsai . . . Mom & Billy were immediately comfortable with each other ("He's *so* nice," she whispered to me later in the day), and she talked and talked and talked. He misses his aunts, & I think he felt at home. She was a little over-excited and her tremor seemed worse to me, but she's starting the new medication for Parkinson's soon . . . After lunch to the Ambassador for *The Circle*. My God, Rex Harrison. "He looks like a chimpanzee," said Billy, and it's true. He's aged in that simianizing way, and his skin is a mandarin orange. Glynis Johns, made up for the role like Tammy Faye Bakker, carried the play . . . Back to Billy's in a cab through the freezing cold. Mom couldn't get over the beautiful tree. We had coffee and cookies and I realized how lucky I was. Who could imagine such a scene, at least without a lot of lies and fictions, thirty years ago? Acceptance? *She* spent the whole week worrying if *he'd* like *her*.

DECEMBER 20: Billy + I went down to the East Village at 7:30 for dinner with Nick & Siri . . . [and] Anthony Jenkins . . . a handsome British reporter so full of himself and Cockburned-Hitchensy U-leftism that he might be a bit player in *Bonfire of the Vanities* . . . He left before we did (off to write 300 vicarious words about Panama), and the four of us were then quite jolly. Bill can't imagine how I once couldn't get on with Siri.

The evening had a considerable amount of charm lent to it by the presence of Baptiste, a huge glossy cat that I suspect is well moused. Whatever vermin may be lurking in it, though, East Third Street is much prettier in winter than summer. We were surprised at all the strings of Christmas lights in the windows; this is one taste apparently shared by the old Ukrainians and yuppie newcomers.

DECEMBER 22: Doug & I got into one of our discussions of the AIDS test & how we know we ought to do it but still can't . . . Dinner at Billy's with Carol & Miriam, who looked like a million bucks in her lynx coat & top-of-the-line wig. She goes in for her 3rd chemotherapy week just after New Year's. Bless her gallant heart. We all exchanged presents & ate the dinner Billy cooked. He was sad afterwards. He loves her very much & he knows she won't last much longer. There was nothing much I could say; all I can see is the larger shadow hanging over us.

DECEMBER 24: For the first time in my life I spent Christmas Eve with a man I love who loves me . . . Instead of watching Alastair Sim in [Mom's] living room I went into Billy's with a bagful of presents. The tree was lit, carols were playing, food was on the table and as he hugged me he burst into tears and had trouble stopping. He'd been waiting years to be happy on Christmas again.

DECEMBER 26: I reread a lot of Jim Bishop's Lincoln book, which I found thrilling over 25 years ago but which I now recognize as having been written in the floridly sentimental and "fateful" language known as Irish-American.

DECEMBER 28: The story is that there are no pictures of the Ceaușescus' execution—only ones of the bodies—because the firing squad couldn't wait for them to be stood against the wall & for the cameras to be turned on. They started shooting, gleefully, the moment they caught sight of them walking into the yard.

DECEMBER 29: Greg did something tonight that touched me. In fact, it made me feel closer to him than anything he's done all year—& we've had some miserable moments this year. A number of us were standing in Billy's bedroom, looking at the Firenze print (now hung), and just chattering. Greg saw the little night table with my picture & my books & the other pile of my stuff across from that and he gave me a hug. It meant: I'm happy for you, I know how much you wanted this.

DECEMBER 31: . . . A small, warm party at Jim Montoya's ski-chalet-like house near the [Vassar] golf course . . . The campus was almost thrillingly beautiful. To Billy it's a dream. He'd have us move to Poughkeepsie in a minute . . . Around midnight we called Mom—"HAPPY NEW YEAR, MRS. MALLON"—& Patty in Arizona . . . Iva called us—& I told her that I had *not* said they found her picture in Erich Honecker's hunting lodge* . . . We threw exorcising water, Cuban-style, over Jim's balcony at the stroke of midnight.

---

* Honecker was the newly deposed leader of East Germany.

1990

JANUARY 5: Mary E. says she was having trouble getting any glossy magazine to commission the rodeo piece . . . so this afternoon, after a little while at the library, I decided to follow through on the bright idea of calling Penny Laurans at *The Yale Review.*

JANUARY 6: Talked to Mom. The new Parkinson's medicine is working wonders. Her tremors are radically reduced, and she has no side effects. She feels wonderful. It's expensive—another $1200 a year—but I can do half of that & the (65+) reduction in her real estate taxes will give her the other half.

. . . Going with Billy to see *The Fabulous Baker Boys,* a sexy movie for grown-ups, with Michelle Pfeiffer & the Bridges Brothers. We met Greg (who was late of course) outside the Angelika Film Center at the corner of Houston and Mercer. It's new, and it tries to be hip, with a kind of café where popcorn might be—but mostly the exterior hipness disguises the interior truth: it's a suburban sixplex with teeny screens.

. . .

Do you remember Steve Smith? Look back in these books to late '85 & early '86 and you'll find him. He was at the movie tonight. I avoided his glance. I still have a bottle of vodka he brought over one night. Four years later and—bam!—you see the person. This must be one of the most common and moderately uncomfortable experiences gay men have in NY. At least his date tonight was good-looking!

JANUARY 8: Up to Billy's for the Rock Hudson movie, which I thought would be scary—i.e., watching it together. But it was too risibly enjoyable . . . They made Marc Christian seem like Tom Sawyer.

JANUARY 9: . . . Downtown, briefly, to the awful PEN holiday party at Garvin's on Waverly Place. A mob of people. Allen Ginsberg with a new Chinese boyfriend. People lunged at the trays with hors d'oeuvres. There was one canape for every ten people. You chased the trays and heard remarks like "She paperbacked the Mexico book . . ." as you whizzed by.

JANUARY 11: . . . To the Booth Theatre to see Robert Morse do *Tru*. It's terribly written (it's supposed to be set at Christmastime 1975 & yet there's a reference to Jonestown, which happened three years later), but fun . . . Morse can't really do the voice—he can't help butchly falling into a low register every now and then— but the gestures are superb.

JANUARY 12: I am, I realize, terribly afraid of missing him until it hurts. He gives me a little tin teddy from the bedroom to take with me. But I wonder why I'm going away at all. Yes, it's my work, and I'm always all business—but another truth is I'm *not* all business any more. I've blended into him nearly as much as he's blended into me. I LOVE HIM and can't imagine ten days without all our happy, childish rituals and sayings. If he's gone in 2 years, will I be angry at myself for not having spent every day with him?

JANUARY 14: [In Lubbock, staying with Jim and Pam Brink] We read the *Avalanche-Journal* and then went out for pancakes with Emily. (Imagine being back in a city where you time your departure for brunch in order to beat the after-church rush.) . . . God, what a lovely day! The party gave me a real sense of closure to the long Sokolow business . . . It's nearly 5 years since Briggs Twyman started the whole thing in Mary Hatfield's kitchen—"have we got a case for you."

. . .

An afternoon like any other with Mary + Lynn in the kitchen. A bird flying around; Wookie still alive; getting beer from the frig in the room with the ancient piano. Lynn telling his awful jokes; Mary laughing at all I say.

JANUARY 15: The [Texas Tech] University Center has gone somewhat upmarket, with franchised food concessions for the students so blond of hair, strong of limb, and moderate of brain power . . . The English building at 4 p.m. seemed quiet, haunted. The effect was increased by my coming upon Carolyn Rude in a roomful of desktop computers. The death of [her son] Ben has aged her fifteen years. Her words are slow and uninflected now. She talks the way dead people would if they could talk at all.

JANUARY 16: [Flying] over the West Texas landscape, the irrigation circles looking like cigarette burns, to Dallas & then up to Tulsa. Arrived in a sweet-smelling rain . . . Had dinner in an eerily deserted downtown. It's all malled over & restored—it took for a while, but it never came back after the oil slump.

The hotel is connected to the arena by a skywalk, so this couldn't be much easier. You can walk to the rodeo in the rain & never wet your feet—they've gone about as far as they can go.

JANUARY 17: Fell asleep reading Gail Sheehy's spooky hagiography of Gorbachev in *Vanity Fair.* It sounds like—has just the same diction as—the old paeans to Stalin.

JANUARY 18: Spent the morning at the very attractive Tulsa Library (*Arts & Sciences* has been checked out 13 times!) . . . then went to the first round of competition. Had a front-row seat for 3 hours & had lots of dirt kicked up on me.

JANUARY 20: Six hours of rodeo. Three in the afternoon and three in the evening. I don't know that I will ever get the announcers' voices out of my head. I learned from the shuttle launch that one should carry mosquito repellent; I learned from this that one ought to bring aspirin . . . I don't know what I would do without my phone calls from Billy. The pressure to *notice* everything, to be percipient, to figure things out—it takes a toll on the nerves. . . .

JANUARY 22: The flights went like clockwork—but what squalor one flies into. LaGuardia looks like a dump. Granted, there's construction going on, but they send you into this dirty mess with ten-year-old "New York Loves You" posters (Dick Cavett with 70s hair) to claim bags.

JANUARY 23: Jeffrey Simpson called from *AD* [*Architectural Digest*] today. It seems they are sponsoring a series of talks by great decorators to be delivered at the Smithsonian. If he gives me folders of bio material & pictures, would I interview 5 of them for about an hour and a half, and then write a thousand-word speech for each of them? The fee? Six thousand dollars. The project's appeal is purely financial—my God, what a sum for what I think would be a maximum of 2 weeks' work . . . But it *is* speechwriting, which somehow seems more honorable than ghostwriting, though there's no real shame in that (even Mary ghost-wrote H. V. Kaltenborn). It would pay my taxes this year.

JANUARY 25: [Mom] is very lonely. Mostly it's Belle's absence. They used to talk 3 or 4 times a week on the phone, and this gap in her routine makes her feel all the more isolated out there. But I also think, ironically, that her improved health is making her feel this way. Her Parkinson's symptoms have been so reduced by the new medicine that she's not thinking of herself, as she sometimes did over the last few years, as a semi-invalid. She wants to get out & there's nowhere to go.

JANUARY 27: Went to the gym, put the rest of *Aurora 7* into the computer, & then went down, with Billy, to sweet Chris Bull's new place on Avenue B, between 12th & 13th . . . At 8 p.m. there were dope smokers in doorways. When we came out at 11 people were making deals at pay phones and writing numbers on their sleeves.

JANUARY 30: Billy was here at dinnertime & we went to the Madison, across from Parnell's. There were 5 widows older than Mom eating by themselves, each in a little booth. A real First Avenue scene—outside the windows gay men & dogs, always. Inside the widows dining alone. There are few stretches of NY that can have changed less in the last 30 years.

FEBRUARY 1: Billy & I enter our first real crisis since April. I think we'll survive it, but I'm still in shock. It was sort of the last thing I expected.

He wasn't out with [B.] last night. He got a call from an old "date"—someone from last March, and the date came over & they wound up having a very modest sexual skirmish (sitting up on the edge of the bed). It goes back to what we talked of on Saturday. He didn't seek this out (I believe him), and it's the first time it's happened (I believe that too), but he says it happened last night because of the terrible way he's feeling about himself during this long sexual lull we're having . . . And then everything tumbled out: he confessed to terrible feelings of hurt & anger because I'm so addicted to my work. He loves me like he's never loved anyone in his life (I believe this, too), but he feels he will never come first . . .

FEBRUARY 2: . . . Elisabeth got sick, so it was just me & Fran & Howard & John up at The Gibbon on E. 80th . . . the *Seven Days* article terminates whatever relationship Fran had with Houghton Mifflin . . . [She] is not at all put out by this—greener pastures are beckoning since the article, including a possible "oral biography" of Mary McCarthy. She's already been calling around. She's spoken with Elizabeth Hardwick, who, when my name came up, gave a sort of exasperated sigh: "Oh, Tom Mallon. You know, I was thinking of buying that book." Just to see what it says. She claims the [*Stolen Words*] reviewers talk of nothing but the Epstein case—her poor little Jacob—and this couldn't be less true. Walter Kendrick never even mentioned it in *The NYTBR*. There's a rather nice review in *The Nation* this week, & that may be what she has in mind, but the reviewers in general have given much more attention to Sokolow.

FEBRUARY 3: I spent all day printing out a draft of *A7* on the ImageWriter. It hacked and chattered and gibbered for 3 hours & did a nice job. The noise was my delightful revenge on the woman next door . . .

FEBRUARY 6: Forget what I said about easy money. The *AD* job, I mean. At 5:00 today I went to Tom Britt's townhouse on E. 63rd St., near 5th. He wasn't there. I had to cool my heels on a bench near the wall of the park. After he showed up, he took me into his library—a weird little room full of busts of Caesar Augustus and bamboo shelves. Every "book" is wrapped in some sort of white paper with gold trim—but most of them are encyclopedia volumes & old copies of *Vogue*! . . . He immediately went into a tantrum over the topic, the format & having to share a platform with Michael DeSantis. He lunged for the phone & called Jeffrey Simpson and Beverly Perkins, a real editorial bitch in LA who pampered him on the speakerphone as if he were the genius of the age. (Speaking of geniuses: he's got Matisse and Picasso drawings, original pencil sketches, in the bathroom. I've never taken such an inspiring leak.) And she treated me like an indiscreet hired hand ("Can we not talk about Michael DeSantis in front of Tom Britt?"). I was there for 90 minutes—I got less than 40 of him on tape. The rest of the time he was being hysterical, taking phone calls, conducting his life. His assistant asked me who else I'd be seeing. I mentioned I had an appointment with Valerian Rybar next week. He responded: "You'd better hurry." AIDS, of course.[*]

FEBRUARY 8: Billy, bless his heart, has been doing a mock-up of the dust jacket, and it's a stunner: a sort of Roy Lichtenstein version of the Ralph Morse photo of Rene Carpenter watching the rocket go up. If we can get whatever permissions it may require, T & F would be crazy not to use it.

FEBRUARY 9: Not the butchest day I've ever spent, that's for sure. Spent the afternoon writing speeches for 2 interior decorators &

---

[*] Rybar died in June, of prostate cancer.

the evening at the Ballets Trockadero de Monte Carlo—the Trocks.

As for the speeches I've done for DeSantis and Britt: they may just be bad enough for *AD* to like them. I've never hit the italics key so many times . . . The Trocks were funny, and poignant. So many of these boys would like to be doing this stuff, and in the same outfits, not as travesty, but for real. You know they're slipping into their own honest-to-God childhood footlight fantasies in between muggings and winks. And they dance awfully well.

FEBRUARY 11: Lay in bed watching coverage of Nelson Mandela's release as Billy worked on his cover in the next room . . .

FEBRUARY 12: I was in Detroit by noon [to give a talk on plagiarism at Wayne State University].

. . . I would describe it as a contentious success, but hardly a pleasure . . . Later I learned that there were any number of faculty members in the audience who are hostile to this whole Center for Academic Ethics that had invited me. They see it as an organization put together by WSU's Silber-like president in an attempt to ride herd on faculty recalcitrance. Unaccomplished professors live in a world riddled with conspiracies, and I was clearly a guest of the Enemy.

FEBRUARY 14: I got out of the cab this morning in front of [Vassar's] Main Bldg. and learned that it was "occupied" by the students. They took it over at 5:45 a.m. to protest Moynihan's allegedly "racist" remark during his recent visit to campus on the Eleanor Roosevelt Chair. I tried to get in, was blocked, and had to listen to one of them—her face piggishly contorted, hateful, overprivileged—shout: "The campus belongs to the students!" I tried another door; it, too, was locked. Another one of our little Red Guards approached me—no doubt to re-educate me—and I told him to get lost . . .

Vassar has gone on one of its jags of moral imbecility . . . A resolution requesting that the students at least allow authorized personnel to enter Message Center—where fire alarms are received—did not pass because faculty members like Barbara Page thought it would send an unsympathetic "signal," if accompanied by nothing conciliatory to the noble children inside Main ... My one-day-a-week colleagues do not have the gumption or self-respect to pass a resolution that might keep the college from burning down.

FEBRUARY 15: In the afternoon I had my *AD* interview with Valerian Rybar, who looks like Dracula. Sounds like him, too, though very courteous & cooperative, even as his partner Jean-François Daigre, bullies and fends for him like a wife who's sick of her husband's invalidism. Their house on Sutton Place is, like all these places, over-decorated in such a luxurious way that you feel you've been trapped in a perfumed tomb. The butler and nurse came in and out as Rybar sat in his wheelchair, charming and trying hard, telling me stories about Christina Onassis and Herbert von Karajan. I was glad to get back out into the light of day.

FEBRUARY 20: Billy & I had our Tuesday dinner at the Madison— which is right near this place he points out called the GH Club. He says it's been there for years and years; and you think you knew everything about gay New York institutions. One look in the (dark) window shows that the clientele makes the Regent East look like a nursery school. These boys are *old*, and bless their hearts, they're still strutting it around. What does it stand for, the GH? Geriatric Homosexuals? Get Her?

FEBRUARY 21: The students were all in class today, including Dede & Ida, two pretty, blue-eyed occupiers wearing sheepish grins. They're nice kids, but I'll be damned if I write them letters of recommendation.

FEBRUARY 22: Mary E. called and we talked about *A7*, which I think she admires more than likes. She thinks it's ambitious, imaginative, interesting—if a little flat in its Godlike cadences of calm ... Dinner down at the Thai House Café on Hudson with Billy, Fran + Howard, Elisabeth, & Robert Nathan ... Elisabeth was carrying the issue of *Newsweek* about the imminent reunification of Germany. This led to a # of slightly nervous jokes.

FEBRUARY 23: . . . To the wacky Rubellian Royalton Hotel for coffee with Michael Wollaeger, the very handsome *AD* editor who's in town from LA. They like the work I've done so far & want to know if I'd do articles. I suppose so, but it's pretty thin frou-frou stuff they run. Still, a lot of writers—from Phyllis Rose to Gay Talese—are taking the money + running.

FEBRUARY 25: Back up to E. 72nd St. by 6:30. Nick & Siri were there an hour later for dinner and stayed until nearly midnight. A really lovely evening—Billy is fond of them both and curiously more at ease with them than he is with the flashy media crowd around Fran. Nick is a natural gentleman, doesn't parade his Oxonian learning or ways, laughs at himself and most everything else.

FEBRUARY 26: I threw myself into Booth today at the NYPL. Found the *Times* accounts of Major (by 1883 Colonel) Rathbone's killing of his wife. And get this: he was the son of the woman [Clara's] father took as his second wife.[*]

FEBRUARY 27: Billy was here before dinner & we went up to the Glass Box in our usual Tuesday alternation with the Madison. Before we left we went through my closet and weeded out clothes. (He's gently told me that I need to stop looking quite so much like a graduate student.). Most of what goes was Tommy's. By what miracle did I live long enough to wear it out?

MARCH 1: Doug called. He was watching Malcolm Forbes' funeral at St. Bart's from his office window.

MARCH 3: Tonight Billy and Miriam and I took a long cab ride down to Battery Park City to have dinner with his old St. Louis

---

[*] Henry Rathbone and Clara Harris, the doomed couple in the box at Ford's Theatre with the Lincolns, would become the subjects of my third novel, *Henry and Clara*.

friend Jennifer, who is as sweet and old-fashioned as one of those Mary Engelbreit cards he loves . . . You can see the Statue of Liberty from the bedroom window, and the huge Colgate clock is across the water. Jennifer says you wake up some mornings & see the QE2 gliding silently by . . . We listened to the *Tosca* music and ate a big meal (she called up her mother in Missouri when she got stuck on the chocolate sauce) and talked about everyone's feeling that as Eastern Europe liberates itself we sink further into race hatred and a swamp of drugs.

MARCH 4: Tonight Billy and I watched a tape of *The Boys in the Band*, which I'd never seen all the way through. In some ways it's irretrievably "dated"—pre-liberation, pre-AIDS. And yet there's one of most of those characters in my life; if not now, then in a past that's hardly remote. I was surprised at its "daring," too—after all, it was a mainstream-theater movie, and here they are talking about things like "rimming a snowman."

MARCH 6: John Herman called to say how much he likes *Aurora* 7. There's really very little he wants done . . . In fact, I'm eager to do some revisions & suspect they will be easy. I always thought of this as a book for which revision would be almost fun—because of the quick-take structure (I can tweezer scenes in and out without bringing down the whole house of cards, the way it usually happens if one tries to add or subtract a chapter) and because of the practically godlike vocal prerogatives I've given the narrator.

MARCH 7: . . . To the [Vassar] library to bring home Booth books for the vacation. Made nervous by seeing the name Gene Smith on all the charge cards—he's the guy who wrote *When the Cheering Stopped*, about Woodrow Wilson, and has taught a section or two of 207 for Demo.

MARCH 8: . . . Down again [to] NYU for the [NBCC] cocktail party and awards. All very repetitive. Had my annual in-person chats with Angeline [Goreau], Nina, Bob Wilson. The speeches at the ceremony tended to be in protest over what Random House is doing to Pantheon. E. L. Doctorow enjoyed the chance to be pious.

MARCH 9: . . . There won't be a Booth book . . . Gene Smith, whose number I got from Demo, is indeed doing one. It'll be out in '91. He says I ought to go ahead anyway. By the time I get one out in '94 or so, everyone will have forgotten about his. That's what he says and maybe he's right. He's an old warhorse whose respectable pop biographies have been in the book clubs, condensed by *Reader's Digest.* I know I'd do a better job, and for all I know there are a half dozen others at work on JWB right now, but *actually* knowing spoils it all . . . I'm just going on about this at length because I don't want to put down what happened late, when my various forms of panic got the best of me. My fear that I was losing control, losing Billy. I went out, down to South Dakota, and drank and felt sorry for myself, and ran into someone I'd met once before, a nice dull fellow, and we went back to his place and did something safely meaningless. At which point, in the middle of the night, I took a cab to Billy's, and arrived at his door, crying, run to earth, telling him the story, begging him not to make me feel I'd been expelled from what he's always told me is my home. And he took me in and put me to bed and held me.

MARCH 10: We've given ourselves a good scare. And the only reason we were able to do it is that we're scared all the time— meaning, we don't know how many years we've got even if things go as well as they can. And to be on the verge of pissing it all away, giving up our mainstays, each other, was the most frightening thing of all.

I got up late—wretched, shamed. Billy was in the other room reading the papers. And we didn't talk much at all about it. Just proceeded into a kind of silent certainty that we would go forward and try to make it.

. . .

Stumbled around the library looking for stuff on Rathbone— maybe this is the book I was meant to fall into, accidentally—in my best pick-yourself-up way. And tonight, battle-scarred Billy and I went up to Miriam's for dinner. She grilled us some steaks & she seemed in good form; she's already read the typescript of *Aurora 7* and is delighted to call herself my "East Side proofreader."

MARCH 11: Bill and I walked over to Symphony House at Broadway & 56th this afternoon to look at a huge studio apartment that he's going to take. "Our home," he kept saying—as if two days ago we'd faced down the point of no return & walked away from it & now we were safe. It was such a sunny day, and he loved the apartment so much—up on the 16th floor, right in his old neighborhood, the Hard Rock Café & the Biograph [Theater] visible through the window—that I could almost believe everything was all right.

MARCH 13: 85°. The old record beaten by 15°. More apocalyptic meteorological talk.

Sondra called from T&F to ask me to do an Australian radio show from Rockefeller Center. I said no. I told her that if they can't sell the book to England, it'll never be available in Australia, so why should I bother? . . .

Spent a lot of the day cleaning the apartment and getting ready for Elisabeth. I cooked chicken and Billy brought potatoes & carrots & sauteed mushrooms from the food shop at Macy's. She arrived tired, after some pitched battle at *Vanity Fair*, but the three of us had a good, cozy time.

MARCH 16: . . . A call today from David Garrow, who got a Pulitzer Prize a few years ago for his biography of Martin Luther King. It seems that the *PMLA* article that was put in front of me at Wayne State last month (about plagiarism in one of King's sermons) is just the tip of the tip of the iceberg. Garrow says that the story is soon going to break that King's doctoral dissertation on Tillich is massively plagiarized . . . Garrow expects fiasco & cover-up & wants to have lunch next week to talk about plagiarism. He's just read *Stolen Words*.

MARCH 17: David Brooks is moving to Brussels for 3 years to write on the New Europe for the *Journal*. So he and Jane gave themselves a farewell party up on W. 90th St. The usual right-wing suspects were there: Terry Teachout, whose belly extends a third of the way across the room; Donna Rifkind; Richard Brookhiser. No sign of Manuela Hoelterhoff, whom I was morbidly curious to lay eyes on.

MARCH 20: . . . Pounding rain, through which I walked to Café Un Deux Trois for my late lunch with David Garrow, who turns out to be baby-faced . . . He shows me the King dissertation & the borrowings. The extent? Let's put it this way: Garrow doesn't see how the Univ. of California could copyright the material in King's name. And I don't see how Boston University will be able to call King anything other than an honorary Doctor of Divinity after this comes out. King's greatness will finally absorb this blow, as it did the womanizing, but there will be a racially charged media orgy before that ever happens. Garrow says he's been depressed for about 6 months . . .

. . . [Billy] has the feeling that he's going to have to go on AZT just as he's moving into the real home he's always wanted; feels that his life might fall apart just when he's happiest. I held him & said all the right things, but I know I wasn't able to convey to him just how much I love his gentle, brave self.

MARCH 23: [John Herman and I] talked about Rathbone & he expressed real enthusiasm for—indeed, was the one who suggested—my doing it as a historical novel. I realize that he's enthusiastic enough about A_7 to think of me as a novelist now. This is a change in my relationship with T&F, which I think has always regarded me as an essayist with an understandable but somewhat regrettable tendency to want to write fiction too. If they think of me as a real novelist/essayist now, with each side of the slash having equal weight, so much the better. Could I ever think of myself that way?

MARCH 24: Went to the gym before Louise came by & we headed to MOMA for lunch in the dining room & a couple of hours through the regular painting galleries and the Tina Barney exhibit . . . Louise was in a good mood (she liked my telling her that Gene Moore wants to start a restaurant where smoking will be mandatory) . . .

MARCH 25: . . . Down to Stuyvesant Town for Miriam's 70th birthday party at Carol's . . . I like it there, but I know it isn't Billy. I'm glad he took his dream apartment at 56th + Broadway.

. . .

Miriam's sister Mildred is 72. She never married either, though she was always in Miriam's more glamorous shadow. She had a good job as an executive secretary and took care of their father in Bayonne. She only moved into Manhattan a few years ago—and she didn't move in with Miriam, who dreaded their becoming the old "Golombeck Girls." Mildred is obviously competitive, jealous, devoted—& terribly frightened of Miriam's illness. *She* was the one who choked up during "Happy Birthday."

But old Miriam may make it yet. She looked gorgeously alive in her wig & mink, & she has none of the wasted look that goes with cancer . . .

We came home very happy—& turned on the TV to see the bodies from the social club fire in the Bronx. Scores and scores of victims. And the wailing.

MARCH 26: Came down from Billy's to a phone message from Mark Miller at *The American Spectator.* "Good news. We're in." I get to spend next Monday night inside San Quentin, in the non-witness media room. I have to be inside the prison by 10 p.m. The execution takes place at 3 a.m. & after that we get to talk to the witnesses; after they emerge from seeing what they've seen. There are a number of rules and suggestions. Bluejeans not allowed (to lend dignity to the proceedings?).

MARCH 27: . . . The Magnificent Charles [Pierce], American male actress, down at the Ballroom doing Mae West, Bette Davis, Tallulah Bankhead and a couple of others. Billy & I had looked forward to this for months—& we were not disappointed. There's an ad for some new revue that says, "You'll laugh. You'll plotz. You'll pass a stone." They could have been talking about this.

Ancient jokes told with atomic-clock timing. And a couple of new ones. Tallulah went political when she started talking about her ancestor, "Cornhole" Bankhead, and asked the audience if they knew what Barbara Bush does with her old clothes . . . "She wears them." You had to be there. And we were, and we loved it. When Billy held up his lighter, offering to light one of Charles/Bette's cigarettes, he looked like a First Communicant, nervous in his jacket & tie. I loved him so much.

MARCH 28: Billy will start AZT next week. His count has gone down & the doctor says it's time . . . We say we are not scared, and I think we mean it. We were ready for this 6 months ago; we'd already crossed the bridge in our minds. But now we're going over it on foot, and at first it won't be easy. We tell ourselves all the useful things: thank God for the medicine; how different things are in 1990 from the way they were in '84; how we know people who've been on it & healthy for years; that it buys time until the breakthroughs, which are coming, get here; how it's no different from insulin or blood-pressure pills.

But it is, of course.

MARCH 29: A long flight to San Francisco . . . I read up on the [Robert Alton] Harris case & some more of Pat Brown 's book.[*]

MARCH 30: Word comes late in the afternoon that a judge on the 9th Circuit has stayed the execution. He feels Harris' lawyers' claims that RAH didn't get adequate psychiatric examination at the time of his trial (12 years ago!) should be the subject of a hearing . . . I call Wlady at his home in the evening & he says I might as well stay out here for a few days, since there's still a story and I can write a short piece for the magazine. That's okay, but it isn't going to get me any further ahead with *Spectacle* . . . I walked around earth-toned, sprouty Larkspur (no Cokes at The Good Earth restaurant). . . .

---

[*] *Public Justice, Private Mercy: A Governor's Education on Death Row* (1989). California governor Pat Brown's book arguing against capital punishment.

APRIL 1: Another routinely perfect day. I took the ferry across the bay and into San Francisco, practically scraping San Quentin along the way. The Port of San Francisco's piers now have more restaurants than ships, which seems in line with the death of Harry Bridges the other day. He & Harris fill the papers today. (Harris is shown holding a baby, like a politician, which in a sense he is; the returns come in tomorrow.)

APRIL 2: By a 6–3 [Supreme Court] vote Robert Alton Harris was allowed to live through the night. I spent the day outside the prison, covering the flute-playing Unitarians, the tract-passing fundamentalists, the aggrieved Main St. residents—and the enterprising ones who rented yard space to the TV affiliates' vans.

APRIL 4: I got to Kennedy at around midnight & took a $40 cab ride home, where Billy, bless him, was waiting. He started on the medicine yesterday & so far has had no reaction to it. He said that yesterday was hard, a frightening threshold to step across, and he tried to do that as matter-of-factly as he could. He took the first pill at a water-fountain near the NYU Medical Center pharmacy & got it over with.

APRIL 5: Left E. 72nd St. for the last time, and cried as I went out the door. It was looking at the corner where we had the Christmas tree that did it. I realized: this is where you've been happy. This is where you've been truly loved, for the first time since leaving home. Remember, whatever comes now: it's been worth it.

APRIL 6: [At a Vassar symposium held to celebrate the English department's move to new quarters] I found myself talking about how for me the English department is forever situated on its former premises—the odd little Gothic place that always seemed surrounded by its own self-generated atmosphere, like a poison gas. There was never an assistant professor who didn't feel a little like Jane Eyre the first time she entered it.

Jane Smiley is unaffected and gawky. At the luncheon we talked about being reviewed together on the same page of *Glamour* a few months ago—something that made a much bigger hit with her daughter than Mom's picture in *The NYTBR* . . . Andrew Towle was a bland, pretty Vassar boy. The lunch was upstairs in the lounge . . . [Bob] enjoying himself as Fran's footman. His life is one long glide across a ballroom floor. He never misses a step—& he'll never leave a footprint.

[Barbara Page] could have told about the time she dreamed she killed Susan Jane Turner & stuffed her body in the broom closet at the north end of Avery. As the dream went on she returned to the scene of the crime, thinking to dispose of the body more carefully. But when she opened the broom closet there was only a little pile of dust on the floor.

Was up at Billy's gorgeous, new, already carpeted place by mid-evening. I came with flowers and champagne. The move went well & he is very happy and proud. We went out to the Broadway Diner for supper. Our new home, high atop Broadway.

APRIL 7: I like this new nameless completely New York neighborhood. One of the things that makes it most like New York is that so many people here are guests: all the big hotels around. It gives you back a little of the exhilarating newness the city once had, when you first came here . . .

Billy's decided he's going to approach the medicine with style, insouciance. He bought himself a little silver pillbox at Tiffany for the five pills that make up his daily dose.

APRIL 10: . . . [Billy] shows me the catalogue for the auction of Bette Davis' effects that's going to [be] held at William Doyle tomorrow. He plans on going with Miriam. He'll bid for me on an autographed picture from Alan Shepard to B.D. Is there any artifact that could more happily symbolize our own odd union?

APRIL 12: Billy and I celebrated our anniversary tonight, a bit late. Dixie Carter is back at the Carlyle, looking and sounding great in a little black dress—and singing what are now our songs: "Come a Little Closer" and "Hold Out for the Real Thing." It was a lovely couple of hours and we didn't want it to end, so when it did we got in a cab and went down to the Ballroom, thinking we might catch [Charles Pierce's] late show at the bar. As it happens, there is no late show on Thursday nights, but Charles himself was grabbing [a] bite & stopped to chat on the way out. He was nice as could be (but *old*-looking? my *dears*) and we told him how much pleasure we'd gotten out of that video [of his act]. He did a little Barbara Stanwyck for us and then went out in the night, a gallant old figure who's been going on for years and years (and, we noticed, paying for his own food at the Ballroom).

APRIL 13: Spent the evening up at Billy's. We stayed in. Mom sent him a congratulations-on-your-new-home card with a refrigerator magnet inside that says: LOVE LIVES HERE.

APRIL 14: At 125 years to the minute after Booth was killing Lincoln and slashing Rathbone, I was sitting with Billy watching a John Waters movie called *Cry-Baby* that starred Johnny Depp and featured such superstars as Joey Heatherton & Patty Hearst.

APRIL 16: I realize that no matter how I've tried . . . I've lost confidence since the AZT came into the house.

APRIL 17: Went to the gym and had an early lunch at Aurora— what a gorgeous place that would be for the publication party— with [GQ's] Marty Beiser. We talked about essay topics & he told me he'd love for me to do something on [John] O'Hara. I left pleased.

    . . .

Everything seems so precarious. Miriam's cancer has spread into her arm & she will have to have more chemo.

When I got back from lunch today I was drawn, for some reason, to flip over the message tape on my answering machine & to play the side of it I used to use 5 or 6 years ago. The voices that came out of it! Katrina, Charles Edwards—& Tommy.

APRIL 18: Who needs this [Vassar job]? Do I? For the sake of 1/3 of my income + health insurance do I really want to be in a place where Milton is taught for the racism & sexism in his work?

APRIL 20: Back here late in the afternoon for Ann's arrival . . . Billy came by at 8:30 & the three of us went up to Stephanie's for dinner. Norman Mailer came in looking very old & paunchy, but I felt like standing up & giving him a bravo.

APRIL 21: We sang songs at the Duplex and even Doug, who turned 30 today, felt older than most of the crowd. Billy & I gave him a sweater from Bergdorf's. And Billy told me when we were home that he thinks that Doug is really dying to lead a sillier, campier, kick-up-his-heels life than he's able to with Bruce.

APRIL 22: Billy and I took the A train out to Brooklyn just before 6:00 for dinner at Wilma + Eddie [Atwell]'s* in Stuyvesant Heights, a pretty, quiet, middle-class black neighborhood. They've been restoring their 3-story house for 3 years now, & it's handsome . . . We had a huge meal topped off by a gut-busting chocolate cake. They are nice people & I love seeing Wilma's love for Billy, which is completely apparent . . . After a while I lost the awful self-consciousness one feels in these racially tense times . . . And yet, driving home, Eddie & Wilma in the front seat, Billy & I in the back, going through the nearly bombed-out neighborhoods before getting back to a middle-class land around the courts & before the bridge—it's then that the separateness, the unbridgeable gap, the insoluble dilemma of the whole tragic country reminds you about itself. Going through the bombed-out neighborhood, do Wilma & Eddie feel more akin to white, gay, middle-class me & Billy, or to the suffering angry black souls living an economic life completely unlike theirs? We never exchanged two political words tonight, a happy, warm evening wrapped in the national bafflement.

APRIL 23: Up to Billy's by 9. We clung to each other. More bad news about Miss Miriam. It's spread into the neck now. She is in great pain. . . .

---

* Wilma Atwell was a work colleague of Bill's. She and her husband, Eddie, were our friends.

APRIL 24: Billy—in whose endlessly loving arms I'll be in an hour—says he's worried about me: how little, he says, I enjoy life. How much aggravation I seem unable just to sweep aside.

Is it true? Does this book show someone who doesn't enjoy life?

APRIL 25: Billy's 45th birthday . . . We'd been planning on going to Café 57, which has sort of been our place—but it was all closed up, stripped of its sign, gone. Which kicked up, symbolically, all the scary feelings I've had since Billy went on the medicine.

APRIL 28: The party at Jim Montoya's house [at Vassar] was a big, big success. We could hear the sounds of Founder's Day coming from near Walker Field House . . . I got happily smashed and [had] my usual crowd-pleasing arguments with [Sid] Plotkin, who was laughing and laughing, though he's become deeply unhappy here. He's too much of a pedagogical conservative: he supports the kids' whole political agenda, but he can't stand their laziness, their anti-intellectualism . . .

APRIL 29: [Billy] cannot imagine a situation in which college professors aren't automatically figures of respect and authority; he doesn't know why students are listened to on any subject at all. This comes from having started college in the happier days of 1963.

MAY 1: Watched *Nightline*. What a way to spend the 1st post-Commie May Day—the guests included Angela Davis & Alexander Cockburn!

MAY 2: Went up to Billy's after getting my messages . . . & was settling in when [G.] called from work to say that [F.] had just called to say he'd taken 7 Valium. Would I stand by in case he needed me? I told him sure. Then he called from Chelsea. Now [F.] said it was 10. I got in a cab & we took him to St. Vincent's. He was woozy but awake. They pumped his stomach at the hospital. [G.] & I sat in the waiting room outside Emergency on what was, thank God, a calm night. An overdose; a minor car accident; somebody banged up in a fight.

Why did he do it? Who knows? He's not much smarter than a child & he has all sorts of fears—sometimes likes to sleep with the light on . . . There was [G.] in his business suit telling the triage nurse that he was the roommate . . . I guess they've seen stranger at St. Vincent's.

MAY 3: Slept late. Mary [Evans] called when I got back here. She makes the kind of option Radnitz* is planning to buy sound more like an option on an option, but I'm glad they're at least moving forward to some kind of deal. Marty Beiser called to say that Art Cooper will offer me $3000 for the O'Hara piece, so my coffers should remain brimful through the summer.

MAY 4: Went up to Billy's, where he and Carol & Jennifer & Miriam were already having drinks. This was Miriam's housewarming treat for Billy: she took us all down to dinner at the Symphony Café, a mere elevator ride away. The food was very good, but she had no appetite for it tonight—she's back on chemo. But we managed a lot of laughs, and some serious conversation about Dinkins. (One of his campaign foes, Jackie Mason, who has the worst dye job in the world, was at the next table.). Carol, who works on the city budget, says that the years coming up will make the mid-70s look flush.

MAY 5: Fran K. and I caught the 8:55 to Poughkeepsie for Vassar's memorial program for Mary [McCarthy] . . . We ran into Jim West—who was carrying a picture of the 4-year-old Mary for the Special Collections—as we went into the library. He is very banged up, missing Mary terribly. He sobbed, shoulders heaving, at a number of points in the day . . . Lunch was in the President's House. Fran & I sat with Carol Gelderman, who is hearty and smart, though, as Mary said, not at all literary. She told us, laugh-

---

* Robert B. Radnitz, the film producer of *Sounder* (1972) and *Cross Creek* (1983), took an option on *Aurora 7*.

ingly, about her struggles with Mary over the biography. Mary sent her one letter that said: "You don't know grammar, and you're too old to learn it." I was touched when Carol said, simply, "She liked you" & told me that Mary had once given her a copy of *A Book of One's Own*.

The program itself was in the Villard Room. Fran Fergusson gave a passable speech that exaggerated Mary's place in her life. Jane Kramer read a superb evocation of Mary. . . .

MAY 8: [In Washington, D.C.] This big conference celebrating the patent and copyright laws is supposed to stimulate American creativity, and it tells you something that about a third of the registrants at the opening cocktail party appeared to be Japanese.

MAY 9: I blew off the conference and went to the National Archives where I rather quickly located papers from the U.S. consulate in Brunswick and the legation in Berlin pertaining to the Rathbones. No bombshells, but enough to set me thinking about narrators. Maybe a Carraway-style one in the person of William C. Fox, the consul? Or an upright one in the person of Clara's sister, who took charge of the children & is described as sensible and devoted? . . . Met Geoff Stewart at his office in the building attached to the redone Willard Hotel, and we drove out to his beautiful house in NW Washington, not far from James Baker's . . . He drove me home after dinner, and we went out of our way to see Mrs. Surratt's boarding house—still standing, still tenanted, unplaqued! Part of D.C.'s little Chinatown. We rummaged around it in the rain & a Chinese fellow in an undershirt looked down on us suspiciously.

MAY 10: Walked in the sun to Dupont Circle & back before my speech. Over the bridge, browsing in the bookstores. And on my mind most of the time was The Test—which I'm still not facing up to. I *know* I ought to have it; if I'm + I could be adding years to my life with AZT. And yet I still can't face taking it. My thinking is trapped in 1984. And I keep deluding myself: I'm healthy, looking good as middle age comes. My hair is graying; I have a touch of arthritis in my right hand. I welcome these distant geriatric signals as promises of longevity, badges for the distance I've already made it over—nearly a decade of life more than Tommy had. . . .

Back at the hotel I snapped into my showtime mode. My speech went well and the panel was a hit . . . At the end of the table, Mary Higgins Clark, the zillion-selling author, whom I liked immensely. She's a nice old Irish gal (with a great facelift) who grew up in the Bronx, was widowed young with 5 kids and started writing radio scripts to support them. Then she found she had the talent, or let's say craft, to make millions with books. She's unpretentious and smart and she gave a nice little pitch for an American version of the library royalties system they've got in England and Canada.

James Michener was in the audience, and quite attentive too . . . He said some nice things to me afterwards as I kept quietly hoping he wouldn't remember something I once wrote about him, just last year, actually, in *The NYTBR* . . . The dinner was an immense affair. President Bush did not show up to present the awards; they got Teddy Kennedy instead. The Marine Corps Band played Sousa instead of "Hail to the Chief." Teddy was pretty awful as he passed out the awards—to Leonard Bernstein, Stevie Wonder, and S. Sondheim among others. TK seems barely able to read—he had trouble getting the word "tetracycline" out when he was honoring its inventor.

MAY 11: Went down to breakfast in the big hotel ballroom to hear Mark Craig of NASA talk about plans for the Mars mission. There is such a sense of non-urgency that comes through, a feeling that even they know they're kidding themselves, that they know the funds and national will will never be there. He even had trouble with the slide projector.

MAY 14: [At Vassar] Found Patty at Chicago Hall & we ran into Demo on our way to K+D's. (He tells us a Donald Trump joke—about the beautiful blonde who is so worshipful she asks if she can drop to her knees & give him a blow job. DT responds: "What's in it for me?")

MAY 17: Penny Laurans called this afternoon to say that *The Yale Review* not only likes my rodeo piece but is going to run all 9,000 words of it. She says [I] don't know what long is until I've seen a manuscript submitted by John Hollander.

. . .

Went to the gym and up to Billy's on the bus at about 9. He came in from dinner with Gene Moore at about 10 & we got into one of our periodic discussions about our fairly non-existent sex life—my fears (not of him but of everything more generally, including the test), my perplexities, and finally my sense—& even to a lesser extent his—that it hardly matters against all the rest we have, including a physical *affection* that seems more intimate to me than sex ever did. The truth is that I have never felt less sexy and less sexual—or more happy and more vital.

MAY 18: Met Louise in front of the Met—a clear, windy day—and we [saw] the show of French paintings from the Hermitage. How did Poussin even get thought of as great? The color is bland and the crowds are in poor perspective. Much more fun getting up to the Matisses. We went to the Right Bank on Madison after that— she's always glad when I suggest it, knowing that I ate there with Tommy years ago.

MAY 19: By 8:00 I was down at Greg's and he & Billy & John & Magno & I went down the street to the Cadillac Bar, which is loud and fun. We bought a round of tequilas from the girl who prowls the place wearing her shot-glass bandolier . . . From there to the Roxy at the end of W. 18th. This is the new place; it's even eclipsed Mars . . . Like all these clubs, I should think, the feeling is sexless. Everyone is self-contained and posing. (In fact, the dance of the moment is "Voguing," in which you strike a series of solitary poses.) The idea seems to be to show that you're too good, too beautiful & too exotic for sex. Dancers pose on platforms— one of them was a beautiful boy wearing an open silky bathrobe, dancing by himself and eating Chinese food out of a little carton. The decorations are somewhat elaborate—we sat on the swing— but it finally looks no better than the prom at a rich kids' high school. We were, at 11:30, almost the first people there, which is probably the only reason we were allowed in with our preppy clothes & lined faces.

MAY 20: Phyllis Rose and Laurent de Brunhoff were married last night at Wendy Gimbel's house, and this afternoon they had their reception at the top of the Beekman Tower. I went with Billy & he loved it—the Art Deco feel of the place and right in Auntie Mame's neighborhood. Phyllis looked beautiful—like an Ingres painting or a glass of champagne (Billy's choice). David was there, ponytail swinging, and I met Arthur, who is bald and quiet and not at all what I would have predicted. David has fallen in love against type, more than anyone I can think of . . . I'll bet Phyllis was seething because Annie Dillard was dressed in the same color . . . Billy thought Nan & Gay Talese were great looking . . . How *rational* New York looks from that high up! Such a thing of the mind, and such an achievement! Down on the ground the feeling these days is uglier.

MAY 22: Billy and I went to Freda's publication party up on West End Ave. in her disorderly apartment (the kitchen positively scared Billy). She was in boisterous form, but we didn't stay long, because people were packed together and shouting into one another's faces.

MAY 24: Bob Radnitz called to say that the option was announced on the front page of *The Hollywood Reporter*—& he's annoyed! He's mad at Mary for talking about it prematurely & without consulting him; he thinks he could have gotten better space in *Variety* or the *LA Times*.

MAY 25: Billy + I had dinner at the Broadway Diner and then went over to the new movie complex in my favorite new building, Worldwide Plaza, to see *Last Exit to Brooklyn*. Christ, what a brutal picture. It strives for a sort of stylized naturalism, if that's not a contradiction in terms.

MAY 26: The 7:45 Metroliner got me to Providence by 11:30 . . . The speech went well. I had 100 or so people, I'd say, and they seemed very appreciative. Lower Manning was a bit hot & noisy, but I made myself heard. Elmer introduced me . . . In the front row, back for his 50th reunion—none other than E. Howard Hunt & his new wife. I faltered when I got to the phrase "smoking gun" in my talk.

"Howard" knows Elmer & has for years—they were contemporaries here, & Elmer helped acquire EHH's spy-novel manuscripts for the Library. So EHH came back to Sophie & Elmer's for drinks afterwards, and was quiet and charming. He looks very fit for someone who's endured ridicule, a stroke and imprisonment, & he even talked a little about Watergate when conversation allowed—he says he was repelled by a recent Nixon appearance on *Larry King*. He said RN has learned nothing & is not the least bit sorry for anything. Sophie was surprised to hear EHH's own implied penitence here; he's never talked about Watergate in her presence before, & he is unreconstructedly right-wing . . . Rode back to the Biltmore [after dinner] with Elmer + Sophie + [librarian] Sam Streit . . . And then heard from the desk that Elmer had called while my line was busy. He left a message saying that I'd forgotten my camera at their house. But I looked across the room & saw that I hadn't: my camera was right there. I called him up & we realized it was Howard Hunt's. We wondered if he ever misplaced the microfilm in his CIA days. Actually, he didn't show perfect skills at the Watergate either.

MAY 27: I went to Mass in Sayles Hall, celebrated by Father O'Shea . . . He asked the parents, who are now all broke, to stand up. Everyone applauded them and I thought of Daddy, growing old and sick with worry and pride as he shelled out all 84 student-loan payments to the Dime Savings Bank. . . .

JUNE 1: Billy & I went out to Sag Harbor with Fran on the 4:00 jitney . . .

JUNE 2: We went shopping for food at Loaves & Fishes (where 3 hothouse tomatoes can cost $7.42) & Doug's Vegetable Patch (where Elisabeth ran into Annie Leibovitz) . . . Billy worries about being quiet and uninteresting amidst all the talk of books &

agents & articles, but he doesn't realize his own refreshing charm—in this setting as in any other.

JUNE 3: Billy + Elisabeth & I took a long, long walk on the beach. The weather was pleasantly rugged—windy, and just this side of raining. All the time I'm conscious of storing up memories, wondering what it would be like to live off them.

JUNE 5: I had my eyes examined by Dr. Dorothy Friedberg on Lexington Ave. across from the Shelburne. She's Billy's doctor & is very pleasant and competent. The form asks if one has AIDS. It also asks if one is at "high risk for AIDS." I checked yes. In her office she asked if I was HIV+. I said I didn't know my status, and feared a tsk-tsking about my own negligence. But she seemed to accept this as a reasonable response, & the subject was dropped. I realized in the waiting room that at least 3 gay men ("friends of Dorothy"?) were there.

JUNE 7: *Arts et Sciences* arrived this afternoon, looking wonderful. As nearly as my French will permit me to tell, I'd say the translation is fine, and the footnotes (to such American creations as Barbara Walters and Jell-O) are a hoot . . .

JUNE 8: I had coffee this morning with gorgeous Genny McSweeney, Vassar '80, the Cybill-Shepherd beauty who's about the only Republican I ever taught. She's married to Fred Ryan, Reagan's current chief of staff in LA. (She & Fred flew back from Washington to Calif. with Ron & Nancy.) She looked like a million & we went to the Peninsula Hotel . . . She's very protective of old Mr. Chips, wants me to be sure I have a good lawyer for this film deal—I should talk to Marty Ransohoff's son and so forth. It was a lot of fun. She has a kind of venture-capital company that at the moment is putting up money for some guy who wants to build a golf course in East Berlin. I remembered how 10 years ago she was talking to me about Reagan & I think I . . . said the country wouldn't elect him because he was too old.

Greg came over to Billy's for drinks & we went out to the Broadway Diner for a late supper. It's amazing how pleasant things are with him when he's around Bill . . . I realize, in fact, that if Bill hadn't come along, my friendship with Greg wouldn't have survived more than another couple of months.

JUNE 12: Police cars & sawhorses all around The Delegate at the corner. A window-washer's scaffolding fell. His belt saved him, but the crumbling masonry that wouldn't support the scaffold fell through the canopy right near the entrance. The awning was in tatters & what fell missed the doorman by about a foot, according to Rich.

JUNE 16: I picked Mom up at Penn Station and Billy & I took her to dinner at *Un Deux Trois* . . . From there to *Gypsy*, which Mom loved . . . Billy + I had a *lot* of reservations, but we didn't let Mom know it. (The truth is that Tyne Daly's the weakest thing in the show. She's smaller than life, much less Ethel Merman.) . . . We're becoming what we are: family.

JUNE 17: Mom is home. Billy & I went to brunch with her & I put her on the train at Penn Station. All this after she *sang* us a thank-you note she wrote this early morning that went to the tune of "I like New York in June." I of course nearly died of embarrassment, but Billy *adored* it.

JUNE 18: Went to the gym & talked to Patty before going up to Billy's. He was taping the *Ring* cycle, which is on PBS for four nights. Ghastly. They look like singing Teenage Mutant Ninja Turtles.

JUNE 20: The city went wild for Nelson Mandela today . . . [He] made a stop at a Bklyn high school asking students to raise money for black South African students, whose schools are so awful.

JUNE 23: . . . To Billy's for a big pasta dinner. Miriam & Carol were supposed to come over & watch *Amarcord* with us after we all ate. They did make it, but Miriam was having a very bad day (she's been spitting blood). It was heartbreaking to watch her, dressed & coiffed and gallant. But she could only stay a few minutes—just enough to ooh and aah at the latest things Billy has accomplished with the apartment, and to get very teary. "My eyes are happy," she said. Billy is her special chick, & she's so happy he's nested in a real home now, and with someone who loves him. I think she's doing what Daddy did ten years ago—waiting just long enough to see his progeny settled before letting go. Billy + Carol sense this too. Carol says that sometimes when she goes up to see Miriam she thinks about inventing a special new man she can say has come into her life.

JUNE 26: A response from Mrs. Kornfeld. A long letter—angry, friendly, emotional, hard to figure out in places. One thing is clear: she expected from the day she met me that [in *Stolen Words*] I would not take her side in the case. She never felt led on by me in the slightest, or by Fran, and this makes me feel good . . . Claims not to care either way about my opinions of the *Vintage* case, but this of course is nonsense. She displaces her anger, makes it high-minded, by attacking the book (mine) as "excruciatingly dull." (I would bet she never read a page besides the *Vintage* chapter.) The letter is condescending and voluble all at once—and slightly ridiculous only at the end, when she urges me—after talking about the *Vintage*-made scars on the bedrock of her heart and soul—not to take myself so seriously.

JUNE 27: Fran is back from her first interviewing trip to Maine. She thinks Lizzie Hardwick is making a kind of pathological play for Jim West. He squires her about a little up in Maine—and down here she's recently seen Bowden Broadwater. If Edmund Wilson weren't dead she'd probably be heading for Talcottville.

JUNE 28: Last night when [Billy] arrived home, happy and tipsy after dinner with Gene, he told me that Gene has asked him to do the Tiffany windows for Valentine's Day—5 women singers with their signature songs about love, sheet music spilling around the little mannequins and jewelry. He was so excited, and I was thrilled to think of his name in those little jewel-box windows. (I was already planning an "opening" party for him—a bunch of our friends at Top of the Sixes.). But by tonight he decided he wouldn't do it—too much like the old puppets he made with [his ex]. He'd talked himself into such a funk—& Billy is the least self-pitying person around—that I didn't think he would even come up with a new idea, as he said he would. I gave him a sort of Lady Macbeth motivational lecture, but I wasn't getting through. He was down, and all sorts of bad feelings were rushing down into the well.

JUNE 29: [A discussion in the Houghton Mifflin offices about cover designs for *Aurora* 7] . . . I said I hated them, that I did not want T&F to good-taste me to death; I wanted something fun & bold & laminated—not these weak matte productions that get smudged + torn a week after they're in the stores. The fact is no one has any idea why one cover works & another doesn't . . .

. . . The *Times* reports that Benno Schmidt is shutting down *The Yale Review* (after 79 yrs.) for lack of money and its failure adequately to reflect the writings of the Yale faculty. Just what we need—a house mouthpiece for Geoffrey Hartman . . . I called Penny Laurans and she says my rodeo piece is safe; it will be in the last issue, in fact.

. . .

We're so high up on the 16th floor that we can't hear the rain. We learn it's rained by watching the late news.

JULY 1: A lazy Sunday morning in the beautiful apartment. Billy went back to bed after breakfast & I lay on the couch reading "Andrea," one of O'Hara's coarse late ones.

JULY 2: At 5:30 I had my interview for the *AD* piece with Michael Christiano and Robert Metzger at their offices on East 58th . . . Metzger is hilariously over the top. As he talks to you he feeds his King Charles spaniel chopped meat out of his hand; he says things like, "When I saw those chairs I was hyperventilating!" It's been a while since anyone pawed me, bless his heart, but that's what he did when I came in. He said, "Can I offer you anything? Drink? Drugs?" We giggle. It was like being caught in a time warp, and I was smiling all the way home to Billy's . . . Walked west on 57th & could practically hear the opening-credits music

("Anything Goes") to *Boys in the Band* as I swung my briefcase in the afternoon sun.

JULY 3: Walking home from Bill's in the morning, my date-ridden brain recalled that it was 25 years ago today that I had my first sexual experience (if you could call it that)—with [K.N.], while Mom & Dad & Loree were in Glen Cove at the Macdonalds'. I reeked of guilt (and Palmolive soap) afterwards, though there wasn't even a need to wash. I spent much of the summer feeling guilty and trying to get into circumstances where it would happen again.

JULY 4: . . . In the sun, to the U.N. gates, where I used my expired press pass (with index finger over the date) to get us onto the back lawn for the fireworks . . . The crowd friendly and respectful. Probably most of them were foreigners, and they stood up for "The Star-Spangled Banner" during the finale.

JULY 6: He loves me, and I make him happy—I'm certain of these things—but as long as I work as hard as I do I'll never let us settle into the completely domestic life he'd like. "At least I know what my competition is," he says.

JULY 7: A great day. We had beautiful weather. K & D & Patty & Jimmy & Billy & I spent about 4 hours out on the boat tacking up the [Hudson] river in a very light breeze from Rondout to just below the bridge from Kingston. It was cool and calm and we sat there, sunblocked and well fed and completely serene. I proved a mean tillerman with dead-eye accuracy. Billy was laughing because I'm only happy, he knows, when I'm working or competing—if only against a wavering point of sail.

JULY 9: Over to Billy's carrying *My Turn* by Nancy Reagan. It arrived, inscribed by Nancy herself, as promised by Genny McSweeney . . . It attempts to settle a score on every page. The family chapters border on the unbelievable.

JULY 11: Lunch at Pete's Tavern with Diane Higgins . . . They're going to do two rounds of pre-pub quotes [for *Aurora* 7]—one with bound manuscripts and the other with galleys. We spent a lot of lunch deciding whom to put the touch on. She wants me to write notes myself where possible. It's an awful business—you don't know which feels more rude and embarrassing: importuning people you know or importuning people you don't.

JULY 13: We watched a tape of *From the Terrace*; long and trashy and absorbing. And with a real sudser of an ending. As the last credits ran, Billy said of O'Hara: "I don't know, John. You may have been a hard-drinkin', hard-fuckin' Irishman, but you've got a heart like a fairy."

JULY 14: Miriam is very bad. The cancer has spread to her brain & we're not sure she'll leave the hospital . . . I called her this afternoon and told her a joke and chatted about Robert Metzger (did my imitation for her), and she said she was "a little scared."

JULY 15: Maggie [Thatcher] had a hard 1/4-hour during *Question Time* tonight, we thought—all because Nicholas Ridley said about the Germans what everyone's thinking.

JULY 17: Fran is hearing all sorts of things with her tape recorder on and off. Alfred Kazin talks about how Bowden Broadwater picked up a boy at a party in the late 50s or 1960 when Mary was in Europe. He walked out with him and said to Kazin, as he passed with the boy, "You thought I was a little stick, didn't you?" Kazin liked him the better for it.

JULY 18: The option agreement is signed at last. I was on the phone with Radnitz tonight, and he told me what's required for the "treatment." I have to do numbered scene-by-scene summaries. I think it will be fun, and I think I'll learn from it. In fact, I've already put a page or two—complete with things like "OPEN-ING CREDITS"—into the computer.

JULY 19: By 6:30 Billy & Carol & I were up at Lenox Hill Hospital visiting Miriam, who was amazingly cheerful and energetic. She looked jaunty in her pink showercap, and she'd even put on some lipstick and eye shadow (actually, Miriam without eye shadow is inconceivable). We stayed almost two hours . . . She sat up, chatting, asking us about ourselves, deflecting conversation about all she's been through even as she's there in bed with big Xs on her arm marking the spots for radiation treatments.

JULY 21: Nancy Crampton came by at 4:30 and we went up to Peter Detmold Park to take the jacket photo for *Aurora 7*. "Oh, this is where I photographed Truman Capote three months before he died." Hmmm . . . Nancy is just back from England, where she photographed V. S. Pritchett, and Czechoslovakia, where she did some formerly dissident writers at Philip Roth's urging: "Nancy, they have *faces* over there. Not like us here."

JULY 23: I rattled around 60 Centre Street all day—watched the same Jane Alexander how-to-be-a-juror movie as three years ago . . . Before lunch I ran into a demonstration outside Central Criminal Court on behalf of the "Central Park Six"—i.e., the boys on trial for the rape and assault of the Jogger.

JULY 24: . . . It is not easy to get on a jury in a criminal case. More than half the people in the pool had to approach the bench when Judge Sudolnik asked if we'd ever been victims of a crime, convicted of a crime or witnesses in a criminal proceeding. Fun City! At lunch I saw Tim Minton of Eyewitness News pursuing one of the lawyers in the Jogger case. And in front of 111 Centre St. a white supremacist was screaming while a black man prepared to burn a flag.

JULY 25: By lunchtime I was seated on the jury of *The People of New York State vs. Larry Johnson*—a forcible sodomy + burglary case. On December 3, 1988, according to the indictment, Larry (as he's often called) pushed Rhonda Baker into her apartment and "ate her vagina" (the diction from the stand is a curious mix of the clinical and street) and put his finger in her rectum, and then said he would be back as soon as he could get a jar of honey, which he was going to smear all over her . . . Rhonda doesn't even have a phone. She made the call to 911 from the apartment of another friend upstairs—and he can't take the stand because he's on a respirator, dying of AIDS, at St. Luke's Hospital.

The defense attorney is George Haber, loud and grimacing and flamboyant, with an Eastern European accent. The assistant D.A. is Miss Bashford, who has a prosthetic leg and only two fingers on one of her hands and who has the sort of single-minded seriousness that is extremely impressive . . . The judge is Martin Rettinger, humorous, soothing, like a quiet version of Uncle Jimmy. When Haber reminds us of the Salem witch trials, he gently rebukes him: "Mr. Haber, we've got enough troubles here in New York."

JULY 26: Officer Ottley, the policeman who arrested Larry Johnson, takes the stand and testifies in a nervous, rehearsed way. Still, he seems credible, even if the police work was sloppy . . . He also helps redeem the case from its overwhelming racial and economic sadness. He's black; so is the chief court officer and one of the judge's courtroom clerks. You realize that if Harlem is a catastrophe compared to 30 years ago, it's partly because a lot of blacks have abandoned it for at least the lower reaches of the middle class in other neighborhoods. (Our black juror grew up in the projects but now lives on Staten Island.)

The demonstrations over the jogger case continue outside the courtroom. I rode in an elevator with Yusef Salaam's[*] mother today.

JULY 28: I started work on Larry Cooper's copyediting of *Aurora 7*. He's done his usual excellent job. I don't think he's right about all the common nouns he sticks in for pronouns, though. He's got a horror of grammatical ambiguity, but the effect of adding proper nouns is to distance the narration from the characters in places where I don't want that to happen.

JULY 30: The longest day of the trial . . . Larry Johnson took the stand in what I'm sure was the defense's dumbest move. Miss

---

[*] Yusef Salaam, b. 1974, one of the "Central Park Five," convicted and later exonerated.

Bashford managed on cross-examination to shred his story that this was a drugs-for-sex transaction that went wrong. She caught him in a huge lie, getting him to admit that he had return[ed] to the apartment, even though he denied that when Haber had him on direct. Rattled, Larry could only go back to the beginning of his well-rehearsed story, but whenever he tried to rewind the tape in his mind Miss Bashford would insist he answer her specific questions. She demolished him.

AUGUST 1: By early afternoon we had the case and were sequestered. Sandwiches were brought in. People were immensely eager to get talking and the result in the windowless room was near cacophony . . . By about 10:00 we were at a Days Inn near LaGuardia Airport, having been taken there in a small schoolbus. . . .

AUGUST 2: By 3:00 we had a verdict—after ten hours of deliberations, another readback (of Rhonda's testimony), a fair amount of argument, tedium, and mindchanging. And tension . . . We convicted him on all four counts. I was among the last to agree to the burglary charge . . . We went into the courtroom and took our seats. (William Kunstler, looking like a reptile with an extra set of eyes, his glasses perched on the bald dome above his gray fringe, was among the spectators; he was trying the next case to appear before "Shecky" Rettinger, as the court officers call him.) Roy, the foreman, said Guilty for [all] 4 counts, and then Larry came alive. Gone was the smoothly polite street hustler who apologized to the jury for having to use words like "pussy" during his testimony; here at last was the mean, crazy, real version, shouting that God and he would get us, that we'd never know peace.

. . .

What it came down to was this: we believed Rhonda Baker and the evidence we had. We believed that this unemployed drug abuser with a bunch of kids by a bunch of fathers was still deserving of the law's protection, deserving [of] a week of our lives and emotions. There was a certain majesty to this, amidst all of its squalor.

AUGUST 3: I heard about the Iraqis' invasion of Kuwait yesterday morning [in the hotel, while sequestered], but didn't really attend to it until today. I'm reentering the real world very slowly . . .

Billy + I met Carol + Jennifer at the Lincoln Center fountain . . . before we went over to the State Theatre for the City Opera's revival of *A Little Night Music* . . . Floating in a world of complete prettiness, I would be snatched back to W. 112th St. maybe once every half hour, thoughts of the past week sneaking up on me in the darkness of the theatre.

AUGUST 6: Fran came by at 11:30, and she interviewed me about Mary McCarthy for nearly 2 hours before we went out to lunch at Costello's. I found it very easy to talk about Mary—she was so vivid that it takes nothing at all to summon up one's memories of her. I also took out some old diaries from '82: the visits to her and Jim in Castine + in Paris . . .

AUGUST 12: Read more of Park Honan's pretentious book of essays. Well, it's better than John Gregory Dunne. I've been reading *Crooning* and I realize how far past I am any taste I ever had for him. Even the title, just like the last one [*Harp*], shows that phony, deracinated Irish tough-guy persona that I've found off-putting in O'Hara, for whom it was a generation less phony.

And then there's Madonna. Billy had a tape of her HBO concert "live from the Riviera." . . . The last half of it was interminable. Finally just another set of mannerisms; she might as well have been Jo Ann Castle [the piano player on *Lawrence Welk*] winking at the camera. One winks, the other grabs her crotch as she says "fuck." Signatures.

AUGUST 13: John H. is on vacation this week, so I talked with Caroline, who showed me the first sketch of the *Aurora 7* cover . . . *Absolutely not*, I told Caroline . . . It looks like the cover for a children's book, with this boy in a Buster Brown haircut looking up at a space capsule. At first glance it seems to be the picture of a little kid looking up because a safe, or a garbage can, is about to fall on his head . . .

AUGUST 14: Becky Sinkler has told me to go ahead and write a little essay on indexes that I proposed to her. She wants something by Oct. 1, and it will be easy. It will give me a bit of front-page publicity in the *Book Review* for *Aurora 7.* . . .

AUGUST 15: Down to Alison West's for dinner. An odd, charming evening . . . We talked very little about Mary, just a bit about how Jim's grief has taken the form of childishness and anger, which is what I hear from Fran, too. She says that Charles Edwards, who once adored her, dropped every thread of their relationship with hurtful, mysterious suddenness. A strange, strange boy, that one.

AUGUST 19: Miriam died early this morning. Mildred called while we were finishing the papers & muffins. She's said to have died peacefully (do they ever say anything else?) after an awful week.

She was fabulous. Bright, funny, self-educated, generous, glamorous, smoochy and vulnerable. She'll leave a tremendous impression with me, even though I knew her for only a little more than a year.

AUGUST 21: Billy and I took a cab up to Riverside . . . I don't think I've ever taken an elevator to a funeral parlor before. City living; or dying, I guess. Miriam was laid out in a chapel on the 4th floor. A rabbi who didn't know her spoke about her as if he did, even though he was always on the verge of forgetting her name. (One takes incompetent priests for granted; I never imagined an incompetent rabbi, though.)

Lenny's older brother, who worked with Miriam for years . . . recalled her coming for her job interview with him around 1960. She was trying to get out of [working at] Roaman's,[*] who were always behind paying their bills. "I'll never forget the way she looked—the red hair & the low-cut blouse. She said, 'I don't always dress this way. It's just that if you work for Roaman's this is the only way to get delivery.'"

. . . The graveside prayers were brief. The sky couldn't make up its mind really to rain . . . We went back to Mildred's on York

[*] Roaman's was a women's clothing store chain.

Ave. for food, and I walked home by myself in the drizzle—with that wonderful, guilty *alive* feeling one has after funerals. Feeling grateful and resolute, as on New Year's Eve.

AUGUST 23: At my Billy's by mid-evening. We watched [Saddam Hussein] dandle a terrified little Brit-kid hostage, and then listened to economists on *Nightline* talk about how much money we all stand to lose in the coming weeks.

AUGUST 24: Finished *Rabbit at Rest* at about 7:00 and began to cry. Harry is dead, unless you count the ever so slight ambiguity of the last page, which I don't. He was a wonderful creature—forever moving between transcendence and shame.

. . .

Dinner at Dick & Dennis' in our old place on E. 72nd . . . Dennis flounces through his days as a "professional AIDS victim"—his own description, self-hating, self-mocking, defiant and straightforward all at once. He watches TV, shops, goes to his support groups and writes Mayor Dinkins complaining about the quality of bus service for the handicapped. . . .

AUGUST 27: I got into Schenectady at dusk, during which it appeared like a slightly more northern Poughkeepsie. Went to my room at a Days Inn a couple of blocks from Union College [where I was researching what became *Henry and Clara*]. . . .

AUGUST 28: My mind is brimming with the bits and pieces learned today: Rathbone's being charged 13¢ for a broken glass; the orders he had direct from Lincoln in 1864; all the completely unreliable legends as to what happened to Clara's supposedly blood-spattered dress. I took lots of photos of the oldest campus buildings and touched the bell that used to call Rathbone to chapel—at least on those occasions when he bothered to show up.

I've got a book here, I know it: a great juicy novel.

AUGUST 29: Got a taxi to the Albany Institute of History & Art . . . There is one vivid glimpse of Clara . . in a diary kept in 1859 by [Henry's cousin] . . . After a party, he says, "Clara talked better than usual, she was less sarcastic" . . . That's how I imagine her—charming + repelling men with wit. Surely Mrs. Lincoln, with her own high-colored personality, wouldn't have befriended a milksop.

AUGUST 31: . . . As I found out talking to Larry Cooper, [I wasn't] even shown copy for the catalogue, which is already printed. I decided this afternoon that I am going to get out of there. If Carol Smith will buy both *Our Am[erican] Cousins* [an early, terrible title for *Henry and Clara*] & *Spectacle*, I am leaving . . . I am a well-regarded irrelevance at T&F, and I can't stand it anymore. And I can't stand working with John.

SEPTEMBER 6: My wallet was stolen this afternoon. Someone either scooped it up in the Food Emporium or noticed me drop it on E. 45th St., right when I came out of there . . . Two hours later—after I'd cancelled all the cards and counted myself lucky for only having about $40 in it, and for not getting slashed or punched—a man from E. 48th St., called to say he'd found it on 2nd Ave. in the usual condition: i.e., money gone, everything else there. He brought it by & I gave him a copy of *Stolen Words* with a jaunty inscription about thievery.

SEPTEMBER 7: The lady or the tiger?
After 6 years I have gone and done it. I have had the AIDS test . . . There is almost no one offering a serious argument against it any more. The years since Tommy's death have seen many changes. The fact is that now they can do something for you before you get sick; in '84 they couldn't do anything for you when you already were.

Gary Horbar was recommended to me by Doug, and I came right to the point with him. He gave me a strong, but appealingly unpushy, argument for taking the test. He knows the psychological torture of doing it, but every rational argument calls for it. He puts *everyone* who tests + on AZT, immediately. He doesn't believe in playing the T-cell stock market. He says he has 30 patients who have been on prophylactic AZT for 3 years; only one has gotten sick.

I still hesitated. We did the regular exam—including a chest X-ray and drawing blood for the regular tests. In his office he told me I look fine: clear X-ray, low blood pressure. I'm slender & I exercise. I have no apparent abnormalities in my lymph glands. I am not a candidate for cardiovascular disease or cancer . . . As I was putting my shirt on, waiting to go into his office, I knew that I had decided to take it. When we were sitting, and I was looking out at the treetops of Central Park across the street, I asked to have it. I went back in the examining room and the nurse drew more blood, which she instructed me to take to the City lab on First Avenue.

I walked down Fifth Avenue for a while before getting into a cab. I stopped in St. Patrick's & prayed, remembering how I went there in the fall if '83, right when I got here & asked God for a happy life here. In many ways—my God!—how I've had it! Billy; my books; so many undreamt-of or given-up-on things.

But always the terror of this disease . . . All day long I go back and forth—sure I'm positive, hopeful I'm negative, like a fast-motion version of the last 6 years. . . .

. . .

Billy is the only one I've told. I got through lunch with Doug w/o admitting it. [Billy] was shocked. But he thinks it's for the best, either way. But what else is in his mind? Does he worry, if I'm -, that I'll leave him? Or that, if I'm +, I won't be healthy enough to take care of him? Or he to take care of me?

My mind knows I've made the right decision, but my heart is sore afraid.

SEPTEMBER 10: Dr. Horbar called at 5:00 to say my routine blood work is "perfect" and that my cholesterol level is extremely low . . . I'm to call in Friday about the AIDS-test results, though they might take until Monday . . . At one point this morning my hand was trembling enough to make handwriting difficult.

SEPTEMBER 11: Mary E. called today to tell me John Herman has offered $15,000 for *Our American Cousins*. She wishes it were higher, and thinks she *may* be able to get twenty, but I can tell she's inclined to take it instead of trying Norton.

SEPTEMBER 12: On the train home [from Vassar]: thinking, thinking and praying, praying. Realizing that the next time I'm on it I'll know. Will have an idea of how long I might live.

If, that is, I don't die in the street violence with which everyone is obsessed. As the train pulled into the station, the conductor said: "Grand Central. Welcome to Dodge City. Stay alert, stay alive. Good luck."

Came back here and waited for Billy to arrive after his dinner with Mr. Gene . . . having just listened to Gene give one of his totally self-absorbed monologues, about his troubles with his 34-year-old boyfriend. (Maybe it's the 46-year age difference!)

SEPTEMBER 14: Gary Horbar called me back, at Billy's number, as I sat at the desk reading Brian Boyd's biography of Nabokov. The phone rang as I was reading a sentence, on p. 95 of the galley, with the word "immunize" in it. My solar plexus fired a gun.

"Tom, it's Gary. You're negative."

The lady.

I didn't know what to say. I was quickly overcome. He told me to go out and celebrate. "And now just don't get hit by a car."

I was racked with sobs after I put the receiver down. I fell to my knees and thanked God. To be given this news, this blessing after 5 years and more of dread. I am not worthy of it.

. . .

By the afternoon I was doing nothing out of the ordinary— just going about my miraculously happy routine of work. I went running, and fought back the tears as every song through the Walkman sounded impossibly beautiful.

I called Billy the minute after I thanked God, and I cried on the phone and hated myself for having this gift & not being able to give it to him . . . Never has sex seemed so inconsequential, and love and life so important . . . Billy and I drank champagne tonight. I didn't want to, but he insisted.

SEPTEMBER 15: Life is dazzlingly ordinary. I walk in disbelief.

SEPTEMBER 17: I threw my back out a couple of days ago and I've been hobbling around and taking Advil. A symbol of the increased possibility of my becoming a little old man?

SEPTEMBER 19: . . . Had a nice, almost fatherly chat with . . . a student in English 207 who was having a spell of What-Am-I-Going-to-Do-With-My-Life confusion. I think I was a more patient listener than I would have been a week ago. Knowing I'm negative has made me less negative. A kinder, gentler Tom Mallon. . . .

. . . Jennifer and I were bursting with pride for Billy: Gene Moore's book is out, with Billy's creations & name prominently displayed. "To Bill," it's inscribed, "a great artist whom I respect and love." Bless that old coot's heart. Billy delivered him some sketches this morning, and Gene asked for more windows.

SEPTEMBER 20: Had an early morning dream that Gary Horbar called to tell me he'd made a mistake about the test results.

SEPTEMBER 22: Scorsese's movie [*Goodfellas*] is brilliant, funny & incredibly brutal—lots of spraying heads & cloven chests. Billy hated it, which is not surprising—since his greatest movie experience this year was seeing the uncut version of *Star*, with Julie Andrews.

SEPTEMBER 25: Carol Smith called to say she wants to buy the Rathbone book, but that the package of it & *Spectacle* will be a tough sale to the Norton board. I wonder if I'm doing the right thing, why I'm even bothering to change. I could feel myself doing that self-salesmanship I hate when I was on the phone with her.

SEPTEMBER 27: Thrilled to get a nice jacket quotation for *Aurora* 7 from Michael Collins. Now who would have thought, when the rocket was flying to the moon 20 years ago, that the command-module pilot would one day be reading and recommending my nostalgic space book?

SEPTEMBER 29: The UN conference on children is here and the neighborhood is gridlocked with hundreds of representatives to it, many of them from corrupt dictatorships who've sent them to junket in New York and parade around with lots of colored folders and pamphlets as they go from pointless symposium to pricey restaurant. I don't see a lot of children getting fed and vaccinated from all this. It's good for all the local merchants, so I'm pleased on the Turtle-Bay level. On the global one I'm left cold.

OCTOBER 1: Spent the whole morning running around & avoiding the Bushlock around the U.N. I seemed to hit, with my feet, every button of my writing life. Made it to the post office, the Xeroxer, *Newsday*, the *Times*, GQ & the library, dropping off articles, talking with fact-checkers and returning books while I went.

OCTOBER 2: Germany was reunited several hours ago. "Happy Birthday, Dear Deutschland," sang the drunken young men waving flags in front of the Reichstag. How scary?

OCTOBER 3: This is the first time I've experienced the anniversary of Tommy's death without fear.

OCTOBER 5: Billy was off for the Jewish holiday, so we took the whole beautiful morning off and went to the Zoo. What an improvement it is over the thing I remember from 20 years ago! No more mangy tigers in rusting cages. Now all the creatures (except for the polar bears) are little ones who have been set out in large approximations of their natural environments amidst pretty brick columns and concrete eagles that I think are from the old Penn Station. It's lovely. We looked at the tufted puffins and the swimming penguins and the hairy ants and lots of tropical snakes, one of whom, all coiled up, looked like a big Day-Glo spinach knish.

OCTOBER 5: Billy & I, over the telephone, had what we almost never have—an argument. He wanted me to come down to Carol's tonight a little earlier than I said I'd be able to . . . (I do wonder about this argument, only because, when I think about it, I realize we've had several little ones—and that really isn't like us—in the past couple of weeks. Since the test results, in fact. Is Billy, pure-hearted as he is, the smallest, unconscious bit resentful that I got good news? It would be human, and I would love him all the more for it, but I hope that's not what's behind these little flare-ups. I hope nothing is behind them.)

OCTOBER 7: . . . The proofs of *Aurora 7*. I was at them for 12 hours. They've very clean (since it was originally set from the disk, you keep draining errors throughout the whole editing and production process; you don't have a typewriter introducing new ones).

OCTOBER 9: . . . Off to Norton for 2 hours talking to Carol Smith & her publicists—I still feel myself *selling* myself and I'm tired of it.

OCTOBER 10: Norton has made an offer that's a few thousand dollars more than the Ticknor one, but . . . I feel from my conversation with Carol that she might hover so closely over the books as I write them that I'd feel tyrannized. Maybe John Herman's inattentiveness is better.

OCTOBER 11: Billy is a good driver, and we had a lovely russet ride along Rts. 44 & 7 to Stockbridge. We went to the Norman Rockwell Museum . . . Say what you will about this Rotarian Hogarth, he created some extraordinary faces. The expressions are curiously subtle, even as they're performing their function of being emblematically broad. . . .

. . .

I love Billy, and we smiled at each other through dinner with that sweet solidarity that being on vacation brings—that feeling that you're a little vulnerable and are getting through something unfamiliar together.

OCTOBER 12: We spent the warm morning walking around Sturbridge Village and looking at the basket-maker, the lawyer, the printer and the rest of them. I even made a few notes about the

1830s lamps for [a] Rathbone chapter . . . We rode all the way up 95 to Portland . . . The Pomegranate Inn . . . a pretty, and rather extravagantly painted-up, place; it looks as though the Fauves & Matisse were competing against themselves to paint every wall in a bold south-of-France way.

OCTOBER 13: . . . I'm squeezing in bits of work, and am starting to want to go home. I am having a good time, but I am a terrible vacationer. And much as I love Billy, I am missing having my large daily blocks of time to work and think and worry.

OCTOBER 14: We were on the road by about 10:30. We stopped in Scarborough to walk along the beach and then headed toward Boston. We were in Cambridge by 2:30 . . . and went off on a long, long afternoon of sightseeing. We walked for hours, and I showed Billy great patches of Harvard . . . I get to bask in his adoring attention as I point out every sight—Warren House, Richards, Widener, the Yard, Adams House, the Coop, the Union, my old Harvard St. apartment . . . we walked around Radcliffe in the moonlight.

OCTOBER 15: I loved being at Harvard with Billy, loved having him trace my old paths with me. All those years ago, he was out there waiting for me.

OCTOBER 19: David [Schorr] said something perfectly simple & absolutely revealing tonight. It just came up when we were reminiscing about college and youthful awkwardness and stuff like that. "I've always been happy," he said—even when he was in a fraternity at Brown (sort of unimaginably). It was the kind of remark one never hears. First of all, the condition is rare, & people who don't have it would say, in a sour-grapes way, that it probably isn't worth having. But I was struck by the completely unaffected way in which David said this, and I realized that it was true for him & that he was twice blessed because he knew it.

OCTOBER 20: Waiting for the M104 this morning, just outside Billy's building, I saw all the cops and all the sawhorses getting ready for the antiwar demonstration in Columbus Circle. There were similar gatherings across the country today, and all the usuals, like Ramsey Clark, eagerly mounted the platforms. It is so obvious that these demonstrators are *delighted* by events in the Gulf, so happy that they can't even wait for the war to begin to start protesting. The posters, which look exactly like the ones for the moratoria 20 years ago, say "HELP BUILD THE MOVEMENT." They are hoping for a long, institutionalized struggle . . .

OCTOBER 21: . . . To the movies on E. 68th St.—*Reversal of Fortune*, Alan Dershowitz's self-loving account of the Claus von Bülow story. It has some ghoulishly funny stuff in it—Sunny eating a big sundae in the baronial dining room while smoking a cigarette and wearing dark glasses. We reminisced about seeing Claus in Gilli, & I insisted that Alexandra Isles is much prettier than the actress who plays her.

OCTOBER 23: Mary [Evans] called late in the afternoon to say that Carol Smith just pleaded with her to wait a day before accepting John's offer. Carol wants to go into the editors' meeting tomorrow & ask for a bit more money & a better payment schedule . . . This would have been complicated enough if I didn't have to head uptown, almost as soon as I got off the phone with Mary, and see Carol at Charlie Baxter's publication party. It was at his agent's Park Ave. apartment, a block or two north of Fran's. I took the bus up in the rain & hung around in the outer room when I got there, hesitant about facing Carol. I chatted with Cork Smith & Sheila & Gerry Howard and then Carol caught sight of me and called me over: "Tom, are we really going to lose you?" Oh, dear. I wished she wouldn't do this. I wished she'd just talk to Mary instead. I was evasive, told her I would sleep on it, that I was confused, that I was getting a lot of conflicting advice, that John had made a pitch to stay that I was finding hard to ignore. She said she understood, and we hugged each other, but I thought that deep down she was annoyed. . . .

OCTOBER 24: I called Mary's office at 9:00 and left word for her to accept John's offer. So that's that.

Loree and I had our long-planned lunch today. I met her at Penn Station and we went to Fiasco down on W. 23rd St. We didn't smoke the peace pipe so much as pretend there hadn't been a war. It was a white-knuckle afternoon for me nonetheless. She talked endlessly and loudly—but cheerfully. She asks a million questions and has no real interest in waiting for your answers, so after a while you realize you're not being rude by falling more or less silent. For *us* it wasn't such a bad day . . . once more I realized how *smart* Loree is, how many little things she knows, even as her temperament won't let her organize them into something really useful.

OCTOBER 25: [Mike Agnes] tells me he was talking to someone who used to work at *The NYRofBks*. He says he asked her what happened when *Stolen Words* came out. "We all hid it from her," she said about Barbara E.

OCTOBER 27: Billy and I took the jitney out to Manorville . . . [He] loved the house—it's just the sort of snug, knick-knack-filled place he'd love to have far from the city. And he & Mom get on terrifically. "I feel as if I have two sons," she says. He lets her chatter on; she goes for so long between real visits with people that she's desperate to talk and talk. And she likes him because he's a hugger. He thinks that Mom & I have a "nice, weird" relationship—it's obvious that I just tune her out for long stretches & it's just as obvious that she doesn't mind & doesn't take me all that seriously.

OCTOBER 28: Walked around the "Village" by myself before we left . . . It reminds me, as always, of some late-40s, early-50s development, full of the future, when America was still on the way up, and not, as it seems now, a collection of quarrelsome tribes . . . There is no sense of common purpose in the land—and that's a pretty dangerous thing for a country founded on abstractions.

OCTOBER 31: . . . A wonderful night. Mr. Gene's party was in full swing. Tiffany's was like a dream, full of pink light and red-&-white balloons. The jewelry was still in the cases, and you'd rest your drink on the glass counters whenever you wanted. Mr.

Gene—who's a delicate little thing, but still sharp as a tack & campy as a hatpin—received the adoring, including one beautiful boy in a Venetian Renaissance costume. Pauline Trigère laughed raucously. Paul Taylor (for whom the party was a benefit) stood nearby. Gene had designed costumes for some of his ballets. (Billy says Mr. Gene's principle here is simple: put as little as possible on the boys and as much as possible on the girls.). Gene, in his earlier Bonwit years, used to have an apartment across the street, above Wally Findlay; he'd go to it and trick on his lunch hour . . . I thought, peacefully: nothing can really kill New York. Not David Dinkins, not AIDS, not crack. It may have peaked decades ago, but some of the gorgeousness lives on, if only like the jewelry under the glass. Billy & I just looked at each other & smiled—& then the band played its last number, "Moon River" . . .

NOVEMBER 5: [In Rhode Island writing a political-campaign piece for what became *Rockets and Rodeos*] The Democrats had a loud but sparse rally in Kennedy Plaza at noon. Teddy Kennedy's face completely red from hairline to jowls, but he gives a good speech . . . I've already started to write portions of this diary-like piece & I'm feeling pleased with the material I have & my resourcefulness in getting it. *Spectacle* has really proved an adventure to someone with my bookish routine. I'm glad I'm doing it, and glad I'm doing it now. I'm not sure I'd have the needed energy + stamina even ten years from now.

NOVEMBER 6: Spent most of election night watching the parade of Republican losers at the Marriott. Then back here to the Biltmore, which was completely out of control with partying Democrats. I had to change rooms at 2:30 a.m. in the hopes of getting some sleep. But what a security guard told me gave me just the closing line I need for the whole piece.

NOVEMBER 9: Put the whole essay on to the computer— "keyboarded" it—& my little arthritic bump is jumping. . . .
    Ann's 40th birthday. Her parents told her to gather up a bunch of friends and take them all to dinner as their present to her . . . I

just hope she had a good time. Billy is very fond of her, but almost from the time he met her he's said, "Miss Ann is sad."

NOVEMBER 10: The Martin Luther King plagiarism scandal that David Garrow told me about months ago has finally broken. It was on the front page of yesterday's *Journal* & the front page of today's *Times*.

NOVEMBER 11: *People* magazine called today to interview me for their piece on the Martin Luther King story. They sent a car here to pick up a copy of *Stolen Words* to get to their writer in Brooklyn. The guy seems scrupulous, & I told him he couldn't use anything I said unless he also quoted something I said about King's greatness. This is not a subject I'm eager to wade into.

. . .

Down to Louise's for dinner. Mary + Missy were there with Annie & Oona [Louise's granddaughters] and we had a noisy, good-spirited Indian dinner. As usual, Louise and I drank beer afterwards, and at the very end, though I hadn't intended to, I told her about taking the test, and when I told her the result she threw her arms around me.

NOVEMBER 12: Billy has shingles. He thought the pain was a pinched nerve, but he started breaking out yesterday. He saw Dr. Jeff, as we call him, today. Dr. Jeff says it is *not* AIDS-related. They do see shingles in people with HIV, but not in people with AIDS.

NOVEMBER 15: I was on the 8:00 shuttle to Washington with Dave Garrow a number of rows ahead of me. He's all right, I guess, but there's something showoffy and unconsciously rude about him too. He always has to show you he knows a little more than you do about everything—whether it's *The Washington Post*, or television interviewers, or just the D.C. Metro . . . Anyway, he was all right once we got going. The interviewers were Betsy Aaron & Richard Threlkeld (married). I think he was the one who covered the Patty Hearst case years ago for CBS. Garrow & I worked well together, looking like good little boys in blue blazers, side by side on the couch. By 12:30 we were on a shuttle home, carrying our souvenir CBS *Nightwatch* coffee cups. And I was in the apartment by 2.

NOVEMBER 16: Billy and I got up at 2 a.m.—we'd set the alarm— to watch the CBS show. I thought I came out all right & it was a pleasant weird experience to be looking at this in the middle of the night. Curiously enough they cut the most controversial thing each of us said. When asked if we'd vote to revoke King's Ph.D. we both said yes—but that part never ran. Billy thought David Garrow had a "mean little mouth."

NOVEMBER 17: . . . To Monticello [with my grad-school buddies], which is less grand and much more fun than one expects. It's got all this kooky-wacky overlay of gadgetry (wine dumbwaiters, automatic doors, octagonal rooms, "polygraph" machines) that winds up being one's dominant impression. One knew of course that Jefferson dabbled in all these things, but you finally feel as if you're in Rube Goldberg's Little Pitti Palace . . .

NOVEMBER 19: Billy is better, thank God. The shingles are beginning to recede, and his sweet nature is coming back to the fore.

NOVEMBER 20: Marty Beiser called this morning and asked me if I had any suggestions for a new literary editor at *GQ*, and I said yeah, me. Why not? They want someone in the office 3 days a week for $50,000 a year. Somebody who'll buy fiction & essays and occasionally contribute & who'll give the magazine a higher literary profile in the city than Tom Jenks did. I told Marty I'd be perfect, & he said he thought so, too—he just didn't think I'd be interested.
    . . . Why pass up an opportunity to lunch with every important agent and publisher in NY? How can that hurt my own books?
    My mind raced all day, but my instinct stood its ground: take this. It's a large lovely plum that's fallen from the skies. That's what Billy says. I called him right away & we talked about it all through dinner at the Madison.

NOVEMBER 22: Billy & I had Thanksgiving together, just ourselves and sort of at home—downstairs in the Symphony Cafe.
(Phil Hartman, from *Saturday Night Live*, and his wife or girlfriend were at the table next to us, and their conversation sounded
like, well, a *Saturday Night Live* [sketch]—full of kissy-kissy therapist's talk about how they're so much happier now that they've
learned to communicate with each other.) . . . Saw the news on
a TV screen in the [restaurant]: THATCHER RESIGNS said a
paper that someone was holding up to the camera . . . Now that
both she & Ed Koch are gone, I can't think of a single politician
left who's got the least bit of guts & candor.

NOVEMBER 23: Got up late to a gray & rainy day. Billy went off
to Lord & Taylor to buy a coat & I went to the Mid-Manhattan
to look through the last three years of *GQ*, and put together my
letter to Art Cooper. The annual anti-fur demonstration charged
its way by as I was leaving.

NOVEMBER 27: I hand-delivered my letter to *GQ* this morning, &
Marty called this afternoon to say Art Cooper liked what was in it
and the "energy" it showed—and so, could I have lunch with them
both on Dec. 11 at the Four Seasons?

NOVEMBER 29: Irene Grabowski [the Vassar English department
secretary] died suddenly last night—from heart failure brought
on by an asthma attack. Her son wanted to take her to the hospital, but she wouldn't go and it was too late . . . Shock displaces all
other feelings. I said goodbye to her at 5:00 yesterday after we'd
had our usual bit of gossip and laughter. (Irene's taste in people
was wonderful. Her enthusiasms were reliable; her dislikes were
impeccable.) It's as if she's been kidnapped, snatched. Ann is dev-
astated; Barbara is puffy-eyed; Demo is weeping. It is horrible,
horrible.

I'll never lose the image of Irene behind her little wooden desk
in Avery, in a shirtwaist dress & cardigan sweater, a cigarette burning itself out in her ashtray . . . When she & I and Ann all arrived
at the department together in the fall of '79 we went around like

mice, wondering just what sort of Gothic horror-house we'd stumbled into. Irene was very shy & exceptionally discreet. But after about a year and a half she finally cocked an eyebrow or made a face about something, and our decade of dish began.

. . .

Billy & I went to the renovated Cafe 57 for dinner . . . On the way back up in the elevator a woman was wearing Norell & he breathed it in deep, trying to bring back Miriam, for just a moment.

NOVEMBER 30: Unravaged by a long illness, Irene looked very much like herself in her open coffin. Her lips were pursed in disapproval ready to give way to humor; her glasses were firmly on the little knob of a nose that her sister and all her children have too . . . Beverly and Ann and I went back to the DeMarias' for supper . . . We told stories about Irene's memory, stubbornness, shrewdness, kindness. She was too smart about people not to realize that we loved her: that's some comfort.

DECEMBER 1: When the Mass was over groups of people stood on the sidewalk outside Holy Trinity, on that little hill above Main Street, feebly laughing and angrily crying. Mostly the latter. The awful raw shock has not glazed over. Joanne Long cried and shook uncontrollably at one point, and Barbara and I sobbed in each other's arms. It was horrible.

DECEMBER 2: Billy was very blue on the phone this afternoon. "Sometimes I feel as if I'm just waiting to die." I've never heard him be so pessimistic about his situation before. It's not just HIV, he says, but everything is connected to that. Every time he starts a new freelance project these days, he quickly gets discouraged & puts the half-done thing down the incinerator. That happened this afternoon. He wonders how much his anger at the decline of New York is really a raging at the decline he fears in his health.

DECEMBER 3: Graded papers at home & found myself wishing that the *GQ* job would come through and take me away from this last bit of this, forever.

DECEMBER 4: Did I even mention my *PW* review? It's a rave, really: they think *A7* is "audacious" and "exhilarating" . . . Even *Bruce* called to tell me he's impressed.

DECEMBER 6: Had drinks with Jim Moser, a Brown classmate I barely knew back then . . . He's now a senior editor at Grove Weidenfeld . . . A very nice fellow, & courageous in his way: he was Tom Littler's boyfriend & a co-founder of the gay students' group at Brown back in '72, when the reaction of even the hippest antiwar people to such a thing was likely to be: *yuck.*

DECEMBER 8: . . . Down to LaGuardia Place for a birthday party for Nicholas Haylett. At 39 he's given up his job at the law firm to make one last full tilt at acting . . . We went to dinner at Rogers & Barbero in Chelsea . . . I enjoyed it, though Billy could probably have done without it. The plague hangs over all such occasions. There was one fellow across from me at the table who, I'm pretty sure, lost a lover. And John + Magno's old apartment (right across the hall from the new one) was bought by Keith Haring just before he died. One of his huge vodka-ad paintings hits you as you get off the elevator.

DECEMBER 11: Lunch with Art Cooper and Marty lasted for over two hours, and the Four Seasons was like a parody of itself. Joni Evans was eating with Erica Jong; Henry Kissinger (who looks as if he could use another bypass) was a few tables away; and at the table next to him, dining with Mort Janklow, was Jackie Onassis— who looks like a million bucks, which is probably what her extraordinarily subtle plastic surgery cost. I heard her utter one word, a breathy "hello," when Art Buchwald went over to her table. When she & Janklow were through and she stood up in her purple outfit, you could hear conversation in the restaurant—where a good table is defined not by its privacy but by its sight lines—hush its way to a near halt.

Art Cooper seemed to stop just short of offering me the job. He even talked money & days of the week & said he'd be calling me very soon. . . .

DECEMBER 13: I went up in the afternoon to the William Doyle Galleries for the Rex Harrison auction. I think I'll get a nice little thousand-word piece out of it; I also came away with a Christmas present. I bought his Victorian wine coaster for Loree.

DECEMBER 14: Had my teeth cleaned by Dr. Boris, who is about 30 years old. He told me I had very little tooth decay—"for a man of [my] age," that is. This is the first time I've heard this locution from a "health care professional"—but it's also the first time in the last six years that I haven't wondered if there was HIV in the blood I was spitting into the bowl and spattering onto his rubber gloves.

. . .

A dinner party at Fran Kiernan's . . . S.H. [Shirley Hazzard] actually drove me crazy—there's such a studied tweeness about her, and a kind of nonstop pedantry in her chatter about Italy. She's ferociously delicate, and one of those people one is supposed to think of as some cherishable treasure on the verge of extinction, but she's about as endangered as a truck.

Went back downtown with Alison [West] in a cab. She looks like a million but doesn't have a bean; I dropped her at 29th & Lex. & then had the guy swing back up to Billy's.

DECEMBER 19: The recession really must be in full slump. I was in Tiffany's & Bloomingdale's this morning & there were salespeople aplenty waiting to serve you, some of them chatting with each other, having no one to wait on.

DECEMBER 20: James Day [Vassar professor of classics] died suddenly last night . . . His heart gave out. Incredibly, he was only 63, the same age as Irene. James looked older than 63 when I first met him, more than 10 years ago. He was so ravaged by illness—mental and cardiac—that I can't remember a time when his face didn't have deep Audenesque canals.

He was a brilliant, outrageous man—irascible but not hateful. But what a handful in his manic, pre-lithium days . . . I think the first time I met James was in the Retreat. He approached the table and Bob [Pounder] said, "Fasten your seat belts." That may have been the day when poor old Miss Goudy—the rare-books librarian who looked like Little Lulu in kabuki makeup—passed by our table and James mused, loudly, "I'll bet she's the best fuck in Dutchess County."

DECEMBER 21: A message from Art Cooper on the machine. He tells me to sit tight for about another week. Things have just been stacked up there.

. . .

. . . Damian gave me the inside word on the State Department's guess as to whether there'll be war in the Persian Gulf: no one has the slightest idea.

DECEMBER 22: At about 5 Billy & Miss Carol got here in the rented car and we drove up to Ridgefield for Lenny + Diane's Christmas party. More Connecticut-country you couldn't get . . . It was a warm night & I spent part of it outside the house with the smokers, including someone named Arlene, who was complaining that her dog had been eating her painkillers. She also complained about how infrequently she has sex with her husband. "Tell me about it," said a pretty, younger woman, commenting. "But, honey," Arlene replied, "your husband is dead."

DECEMBER 23: At 7:30 I met Billy at Worldwide Plaza—the gorgeous building that's supposed to revive Eighth Avenue—and we saw *Home Alone* with adorable Macaulay Culkin, Radnitz' fondest hope to play Gregory Noonan. Never happen, but it was fun to think about.

DECEMBER 28: At 9:00 Billy & I met at the Carlyle & went in to hear our beloved Barbara Carroll . . . She stopped by our table to chat between long sets, and we told her we'd just about worn out the tape of *Old Friends*. About 8 loud boors made it hard to hear her for about a half hour—at one point she just stopped entirely, waiting for them to shut up. . . .

DECEMBER 31: New Year's Eve dinner [in Poughkeepsie] turned out to be candid-camera funny. We went to Antonio's, and they were obviously having some sort of kitchen-staff catastrophe. It took *3 hours* for them to get our dinners to us. We all sat there—Patty, Billy, me, Jimmy, Tom Matos, Sid & Marjorie Plotkin, Jimmy's friend Arthé—and got giddy with a sort of hostage humor. Some parties—the place was full—just upped and walked out, but we were having a good enough time to stay . . . a pleasant fiasco. . . .

1991

JANUARY 3: Well, I got the job. My appointment with Art Cooper turned into a drinking session with the boys. Marty & Paul Scanlon & Eliot Kaplan came into the office, too, and we knocked back a little single-malt scotch & vodka . . . I start Feb. 25, well after Alaska. It's $55,000 for 3 days a week. I felt a little giddy as all the numbers & handshakes proliferated, but I think this is a good thing for me—some money, some glamour, some change . . . Billy is thrilled . . . I stopped in Coliseum Books to buy some magazines. (I might as well get up to speed in my new world.). And I saw that *Aurora* 7 was already on the shelf—five copies, face out. We're almost 4 weeks away from pub. date, too.

JANUARY 4: Lunch at the Glass Box with Ann + Doug, who are very happy about it all. Afterwards Doug & I went shopping at Church's & Brooks Brothers for shoes and socks. He kept steering me toward fancier stuff, saying, "You work for *GQ* now."

JANUARY 7: Did paperwork with the Condé Nast personnel office this morning (all these well-dressed 23-year-old women sitting in front of framed old *Vogue* cover paintings out near the receptionist . . .). Went up to see Art & Marty afterwards. My first idea, fortunately, flies. They want me to get a reviewer for Norman

Mailer's CIA novel coming out in August—I suggest E. Howard Hunt (maybe I can get him through Elmer), and this is greeted with enthusiasm. I'm shown what will be my office ("Is that the one with the radon?" Kaplan jokes), and I meet my secretary, Jane O'Reilly. (Just writing this makes me think of Irene, of how everything is changing so suddenly.)

JANUARY 9: I walked through the sleet from Billy's to the New-York Historical Society to look at the things I knew they had pertaining to Jared Rathbone (Henry's father) . . . but I never expected the bonanza that was cross-referenced into the stuff: a letter that Clara Harris wrote on April 25, hours before Booth's capture. It's a stunner, complete with references to the blood that was on her face that night. . . .

JANUARY 11: Went back up to the Historical Society as a real snowstorm got underway. (It actual feels like winter.). Discovered two letters from Henry himself. Nice Jean Ashton, the head of the library, asks if I'd like to give a lecture in April, on historical fiction, and I said yes.

JANUARY 12: Talked to Loree and Mom, both of whom read *A7* in a single day & say they were moved by it. Mom started to cry over Jim Noonan. And Loree says she's been annotating her copy, so that years from now Seán and Christina will know that Jackson Heights was really Woodside, Mrs. Linley really Mrs. Leddy, etc.

JANUARY 15: It's 14 minutes to midnight, and as the deadline for [the Gulf] war arrives the neighborhood is eerie. The police have the street blocked off, making everyone state his business when he reaches the sawhorses. There was a huge demonstration this afternoon, mostly, it appeared, of perpetual dissidents, a lot of them wearing black-and-white checkerboard Yasser Arafat scarves. *Nightline* has just shown the U.N., calm and silent a hundred yards away.

JANUARY 16: I got the news that the war had started when the 7:13 pulled out of Poughkeepsie for New York. A woman, agitated and disbelieving, got on and said to me, with that compulsion to share the momentous, "They've started bombing Baghdad." For two hours, until the train got into Grand Central, I was in a news blackout. I walked home quickly. Passing John Barleycorn's, I looked through the window and saw President Bush on the bar TV.

JANUARY 17: Billy & I went down to a party at the Book Friends Cafe on W. 18th St.—it was given by St. Martin's Press (of course) for the staff of *The Advocate*. Chris Bull had asked us to come, and there he was, America's gay Jimmy Olsen, looking adorable. Ben was there, too, and in the back Quentin Crisp, all curled and scarved, was holding court.

Afterwards Billy & I went to Twigs for dinner . . . As soon as we entered the restaurant we heard that Iraq had fired missiles at Israel. Every overheard conversation in the restaurant—like every one overheard on the street—is about the war.

JANUARY 19: For the first time I can remember, the NYPL is now asking patrons to check their bookbags and briefcases before they go anywhere past the information and gift desks. There is a lot of talk about terrorist attacks upon landmark buildings and subway tunnels [and] so forth. Life gets a little grubbier every day. For a while going anywhere will be like going to an airport. The blocks around E. 45th remain an armed camp.

JANUARY 20: The *Newsday* review [of *Aurora* 7], done by Michael Gorra at Smith, is really good, very quotable. It's also well thought and well written; he was clearly willing to go against his own grain (he admits he was all set not to like the book), to stick with it and figure out what I was up to . . .

JANUARY 22: Finished the [film] treatment. Spent hours today mousing in the changes and printing it out.

Ran in the morning. (Coming out of the Y, past the Dag Hammarskjöld condo, I saw Imelda Marcos, best foot forward, getting into a limo with Jersey plates.)

JANUARY 23: Up betimes to begin what I'm determined to make my swan semester at Vassar: 7 years full-time; 3 years part-time; 2 years on leave—there we have it, 1979–91. Barbara and I spoke on the phone yesterday (she read *Aurora 7* in Key West over the weekend and, I could tell, had slightly contemptuous feelings for its religiosity, though she seemed to like it otherwise)—and I got the feeling that she thought I'd be back after this unpaid leave I'm taking next year. But that is not my intention. This is just one last safety valve, in case Condé Nast proves an immediate fiasco.

JANUARY 24: . . . A haircut from Nancy's husband, George. She was home with their sick daughter. In his thick Greek accent George tells me that there really isn't any Persian Gulf war going on—it's all lies. "Uh huh. A little shorter, George."

JANUARY 25: I have landed Howard Hunt for the *GQ* review of Mailer's book. In a note to me he says that he probably shouldn't do it, since Mailer has actually paid to quote chunks from two of EHH's books in *Harlot's Ghost*. But I called Art Cooper, and neither of us thinks this is terribly "disabling," to use Howard's word. So we sealed the deal when I called him in Texas. He rather improbably loves *Arts & Sciences*.

JANUARY 29: I went into Brentano's this morning + got next Sunday's *Times Book Review*. The review of *Aurora 7*, by someone named James Gordon Bennett, is just awful. It's malicious and supercilious and a half dozen other things, all of them bad. I read it with this horrible feeling . . . all over again. . . .

Is *Aurora 7* D.O.A.? Probably. This plus the recession will kill a paperback . . . This review is what's known as invincibly ignorant. The man complains of "coincidence" and arbitrary happy endings—without once mentioning the fact that God's arbitrariness is the explicit theme of the whole book. I could go on and on, but why bother? They win, you lose . . .

Maybe this will be the end of the line for me as a novelist. I feel absolutely no ambition to pick up the Rathbones. I am an essayist and that's it. . . .

JANUARY 30: I was OK. But then the strain of keeping up appearances took its toll, and when I was talking to Billy I lost it and cried my heart out for my poor maimed book & my poor ruined pride.

JANUARY 31: The only good news: *Entertainment Weekly*, a splashy Time Inc. magazine that is apparently doing quite well, is going to run a lead review, a good one, of the novel. They're sending a photographer here Saturday.

. . . Billy is trying everything, from bear hugs to tough love to telling me I'm a poor little thing to telling me I'm a spoiled brat. It is all done out of such obvious pain and love—a moment-by-moment improvisation, just looking for *something* that will work— that it only breaks my heart further. . . .

We went to see *Six Degrees of Separation* tonight, the John Guare play with Stockard Channing. It's better directed than it's written, but she was fun to watch. As Billy said—& he's not overly picky about these things—it's a little offputting how it manipulates homosexuality and AIDS for cheap melodramatic effect . . .

FEBRUARY 1: I took the LIRR to Port Washington and looked at nice Mrs. Gulotta's huge Japanese house for the *AD* article. It was so immensely bland and peaceful that I wanted to spend the rest of my life on one of its couches, just reading and sleeping and breathing the fresh air that came through the window.

But by 3:30 I was back home. Mary [Evans] called. She says that she and John have talked, that he's worried about the "distressed author" he has on his hands. I think he has a pep talk planned for Thursday morning. Mary says she can't understand why I'm not more excited about *Entertainment Weekly*; it's a big breakthrough for the book.

FEBRUARY 2: The photographers from *Entertainment Weekly* . . . arrived at 8:30 this morning and drove me out to Flushing Meadows, to the site of the old World's Fair. For two hours I was lying on my stomach, without my coat, as they set up and took pictures of me & the Unisphere—together again, for the first time since '64. After that it was an hour or two sitting on the roof of a Toyota parked in front of the old Titan and Atlas rockets by the Hall of

Science. It was all kind of creepy, like a J. G. Ballard story. I was cold and tired and really feeling the strain of smiling, but I kept going, knowing I was doing it for the book.

FEBRUARY 3: Radnitz just called. The *LA Times* has some criticisms of my "stoical" Catholicism, but they say I write wittily, that *A7* is put together with audacious cunning, and that it's "an original work by a promising novelist and literary critic." The book is "tender but chilly" and "more urbane than poetic." Well, I think he's right on the money—it's like the *Newsday* review, in fact. Both are intricate and professional, everything the *NYTBR* was not. . . .

FEBRUARY 4: Each day the book seems to grow a little stronger. The *Chicago Tribune* weighed in yesterday and said *A7* was "a real writer's novel, artfully contrived, firmly controlled and richly imagined." I now have some fight in me. . . .

. . .

[Preparing for my trip to rural Alaska, to write about the Poker Flat rocket range] I was at Billy's at 6:00 & we went shopping for my gear at Eastern Mountain Sports on W. 61st St., near Lincoln Center. I came away with heavy boots, "high-tech underwear," a face mask and some gloves and socks. The rest of what I need will be up there waiting for me.

FEBRUARY 5: I won't be completely cut off—I can even get Federal Express at the Chatanika Lodge; the sender just has to remember to include Milepost 28 in the address.

FEBRUARY 6: Fran K. was on the train with me to Vassar, going up and coming down . . . [She says] that in her letters to Jovanovich—which Fran went through today—Mary [McCarthy] discusses "one disappointment after another," aching over reviews, agonizing over sales. Maybe it just never gets better.

FEBRUARY 7: Met with John Herman & Evan [the publicist] down at T&F in the morning . . . John just smiles at you in this exasperating way, like a doctor trying to convince you that bad news is really good news. I suppose he just hopes for a miracle—a movie deal, a sudden surge of interest from the *Entertainment Weekly* piece. But the truth is he's probably forgotten about the book entirely. His head has turned its attention to other lists, other crapshoots. It's all so passive . . . I was off to the airport by 1:00. . . .

FEBRUARY 8: . . . How stunned I was as the plane travelled up the Alaska coast and on to Fairbanks . . . Vast quilts of mountains tufting their way into the sky; sometimes the clouds between them looked more like frozen rivers. It was, I think, -38° when I got to the airport, and I was nearly afraid to go out of the Terminal. But one quickly realizes that one's crisis attire is overdone and that survival is possible . . . A cab driver and his buddy (there are a lot of long-haired middle-aged hippies around, ones that have gone native) took me the thirty miles to Chatanika. On the way I saw about half a dozen moose and a stretch of the [oil] pipeline, which looks like easy pickings for terrorists.

. . .

I was out to the range at around 5:00. (Getting a ride is advisable; if you walk you're likely to run into a moose—they're in a mean mood this year, tired out from the deep snow.) . . . After 10 hours out there I had a good and happy sense of the place. You feel as if it's 30 years ago and you're helping to launch a Redstone.

FEBRUARY 9: I think that review is the most confidence-breaking thing that's happened to me as a writer. I feel as if I'm doomed as a novelist . . . I am busted, shaky. And of course I let it all show on the phone with Billy, who listens to me with the kind of unconditional love Daddy used to display, and which I exploit just as selfishly as I did twenty years ago.

FEBRUARY 10: Another long night, and neither rocket went up, but I had a good night on the Range—at Optics up on the hill and then back in the Blockhouse. (I prefer being down there; the engineers and mission grunts are more fun than the scientists.) . . . Everyone speaks candidly, and they see me with my pad all the time, and nobody tells me not to quote them—except for a few jokey don't-print-thats after they've sworn or something like that. This is going to be a friendly piece, but I'm still surprised by how naïve people can be around writers.

FEBRUARY 11: The Black Brant was launched with complete success a little after midnight . . . I stood out in the parking lot by the Blockhouse at around two in the morning, gazing up at these great emerald curtains of light [the aurora borealis].

. . . I think that one reason I am so disgustingly desirous of a good literary reputation is that in the last decade, since Tommy, I've carried around the feeling that I just might die young. And so leaving something fine and sterling behind became an obsession I can't shake. But I am probably just making excuses for myself. Even this entry has the usual loathsome little air of "performance" to it.

FEBRUARY 12: . . . Got a cab back down south to Fairbanks, which is so buried in snow—all the little houses seem to be gasping for air . . .

FEBRUARY 14: Talked to Mom. She says Loree has revived her store-window painting business. She does yellow ribbons (which now express longing for the return of troops instead of hostages) for $6 apiece.

FEBRUARY 15: A plane to Salt Lake, another to Dallas, another to New York, and then a taxi home, with that odd feeling that the city you're returning to *knows* so much that you don't.

FEBRUARY 16: Hovering in the background: an article in yesterday's *Times* about how AZT may not be as effective as they thought—at least for blacks and Hispanics. The news is poorly reported by Gina Kolata (which is not much of a surprise), and there's a lot of politics wrapped up in the science, and it's likely that it will turn out not to be a terribly important study. But Billy—for all his bravery and unwillingness to complain—is worried, and so am I. He should call Dr. Jeff about it, I think; but Billy says he doesn't want to be a nervous old queen bothering him over every snippet of news.

FEBRUARY 18: It wasn't the magazine piece, which was wonderful, but a review in *The Washington Post* that drenched me with hope and contentment. It is a rave such as I've never had, not even in the headiest days of *ABOOO*: "*Aurora 7*, as unpretentious in size as the space craft that bore its name, is vast with insight, charming and provocative—a brave mission of a book to put back the stars in any reader's eyes." I could go on . . . I feel as if the book is staggering to its feet reborn. Radnitz is doing handsprings. The combination of this piece & what's in the magazine may just be enough to let the book catch on. . . .

FEBRUARY 19: I continue to feel very, very good, and I just try to remind myself that the high is this high because the low was that low. Both are exaggerated and both come from the same basic problem—taking my validation from without instead of within. I know this sounds terribly 1970s, but there's a lot of truth to it.

FEBRUARY 20: No Vassar today. They're having a "teach-in" (i.e., a sentimental, defeatist, breast-beating orgy) on the war.

FEBRUARY 21: Up to school in the afternoon to give my make-up class . . . When I remarked that Mary McCarthy was remarkable for the lack of cynicism in all her worldliness, one student said he thought she was very cynical. When I asked him to elaborate, it became clear that he meant she was very judgmental. I point out that being judgmental is not the same as being cynical. His essential response was that this is *his* definition of cynicism, and that the word meant, really, whatever he wanted it to. There was no belligerence in this, just the sort of subjectivity that characterizes their approach to everything.

FEBRUARY 22: . . . The *USA Today* review is out and it's another super one. This whole experience is like a disjointed dream . . .
. . . I realize already, just by looking ahead at the week, that

doing both *GQ* and Vassar beyond this term is a complete impossibility. So Vassar goes. The long good-bye is at last complete.

FEBRUARY 23: . . . Went over to John Landau's[*] apartment in the Ansonia for dinner. He made chili for me [Billy was in St. Louis], Fran & Howard, and David Daniel, who writes about dance for *Vogue* . . . Says that if Suzanne Farrell hadn't met Balanchine she'd have been the lady who dives off the steel pier in Atlantic City on a horse . . . In the taxicab coming back to the East Side, I hear that the ground war had begun.

FEBRUARY 24: "Orientation" [to Condé Nast] in a conference room on the 19th floor. A video quotes Diana Vreeland. When someone told her about some amortization that was needed, she said, "I don't know what that means, but if it starts with 'amour,' I'm for it."

FEBRUARY 26: I read mss.; write rejection letters; talk to Jimmy Breslin's agent on the phone, struggle with the XyWrite computer program . . . Art ran a meeting in ten minutes this morning that would have taken 2 hours at Vassar. There's no rhetorical posturing and no compulsion to make every issue a moral issue.

FEBRUARY 27: The war ended tonight. It lasted only half a diary. President Bush announced that after midnight we would hold our fire. We have routed the enemy, and the Pax Americana people have been talking about seems suddenly real. We are the new good-guy Sparta, violent and oafish at home, a noble warrior-giant abroad.

FEBRUARY 28: Doug wants to know if there's any work to this *GQ* job, or if it's entirely perks. Today I went down—by limo—to Le Madri for a 2½-hr. lunch with Marty, Eliot Kaplan and Alan Richman. Very much a boys lunch—I suppose I feel a bit conspicuously gay at times, but I also think they like me well enough & that they're pleased with the fit. I am relaxed, too, because I don't,

_____
[*] Brother of Fran Kiernan.

as they seem to, worry about living and dying by Art's whim. If it doesn't work out, it doesn't work out.

MARCH 1: Spent most of the day whittling down the pile of mss. left behind by Tom Jenks . . . A little Zinfandel-tasting party in Art's office at 5:00 . . . Was at Billy's, after I ran, by 8:30. We had supper at our beloved Urban Grill II and then headed to Rainbow & Stars to catch Rosemary Clooney's late show. She was in wonderful voice, but the crowd was just awful. They profess their adoration of her, but all through her show they can't stop talking like jerks sitting around their VCRs back home in Jersey. I could have choked half a dozen of them.

MARCH 4: When I got back from lunch, Ruth, the nice receptionist, handed me a phone message from Mary [Evans]: "Have you seen this week's *New Yorker*?" I went back down to the lobby to buy one, and sure enough, there was a lovely review of *Aurora*. Not a huge Naomi Bliven, but a good-sized brief that likes the book a lot—a real selling review: And whoever did it is the only reviewer to recognize the model for Elizabeth Wheatley ("surely a very funny and knowing representation of Mary McCarthy").

MARCH 5: Tomorrow night [Billy] dines with Mr. Gene and tells him about the Tiffany windows he wants [him] to do for June. He's been making a mold at home and doing sketches, too, and he's excited about the idea he has for putting the jewels by little statues of famous women in wedding dresses cut from paper doilies. What he's described to me is simple & exquisite. . . .

Before dinner he had his once-every-six-weeks appointment with Dr. Jeff, who was quite untroubled by the Gina Kolata article from a little while back . . . In fact, he is more and more optimistic about combination therapies: that's where the breakthroughs will come, with treatment regimens that are highly individualized. What will really work in one patient won't work in another.

Every day people walk down Fifth Avenue past dozens and dozens of men who are HIV+, on AZT, fighting steadily for their lives. They are a city within a city, and they are invisible.

MARCH 6: On the train home I slept and then read a Frank Conroy memoir that we're going to run in the magazine. His sentences are so deadpan, so ordinary. But they always add up to something fine.

MARCH 8: This was the first day I edited rather than rejected a story. Jim Shepard's "Messiah" runs in the June issue and I wanted to make a few small revisions. So I called him up at Williams, where he teaches . . . I was nervous; I was used to conducting the diplomatic exercise that is phone-editing from the other end: the little negotiations, the trade-offs. Fortunately he was easy . . .

MARCH 10: Billy is going great guns on the ladies. I watched him work while I read the *Times*. My essay is out on the front page of the *Book Review*, but I'm too soured on them to take any real pleasure in it.

MARCH 12: Lunch with Kathy Rich . . . at Tropica in the Pan Am Bldg. She's spent her whole career on magazines & is endlessly on the prowl for new writers and new ideas. As soon as I started talking about Freda Garmaise I realized she might steal her from me before I had a chance to use her myself . . .

MARCH 13: What I suppose is a nice letter from Becky Sinkler arrived. It contains a lot of bull (how they were "all crushed by James Gordon Bennett's review") and how I'm a "prince" to have worked with them so soon after they ran it. . . .
. . .
Went to a cocktail party at Howard Kaminsky's apartment in the Apthorp. (I forgot my wallet, too, and a very nice Indian cab driver named Mr. Aziz, from Staten Island, agreed to let me send him a check.) The party was for a lot of Morrow authors, including pretty Michael Chabon, who tells me that Mary Evans described me as "a worthy person" for him to meet.

MARCH 16: We ran into the [St. Patrick's Day] parade on the way over [to Mildred's] (Dinkins got booed for marching with the gays who insisted on being in it—as if he wouldn't have gotten booed anyway) . . .

MARCH 17: I talked to Paul Sachner today, for the first time in 3 years, I think . . . He's switching to DDI from AZT, because his T-cells are dropping. In fact, Paul had never told me he's HIV+; it's been so long since we spoke that he forgot that. He's been on AZT for 2½ years. He coughed off and on during the conversation, but he says his health is pretty good. "I never feel great, but I'm not sick."

MARCH 18: . . . I came home to a letter from Andy Pandolfo. It started out as a warm, chatty thing, saying how much he'd just enjoyed *Aurora 7*. And then he mentioned that both he & Phil, just before Christmas, tested positive . . . Then I went over to Billy's and held him tight & never told him a word about Andy & Paul.

MARCH 20: . . . Over to Hotaling's out-of-town newsstand to get the *Rocky Mountain News* with the article about Scott Carpenter and me. (I find that these feature writers almost never seriously misquote you in terms of meaning—but what they do to your grammar!)

MARCH 23: The head of the research department, Tatiana [Strage], told me yesterday afternoon that she was having trouble locating the main source for James Salter's brothels piece. I told her I was going to the Fifth Ave. library over the weekend & would look through it for her. Well, I found it; and I found that there are a number of lines in it—I suspect there are more than I found— that Salter has lightfingeredly made his own . . . What a wonderful way to wind up on Page Six of the *Post*, or in the *New York* "Intelligencer" column; "GQ Lit Editor—Supposed Plagiarism Expert—Duped by Well-Known Author."

MARCH 24: . . . Headed to Elisabeth's farewell party. Vance + Fran + Howard + I gathered at Carl's loft on Walker St. (he lives below Red Grooms) and then we all went over to Puffy's on Hudson St. Elisabeth leaves Tuesday [for her native Germany], chasing the reunified Zeitgeist. She has a job on *Stern*. It is a good move, the right thing to do, to let oneself be swept along by one of history's cleaner tides.

MARCH 25: I brought Art the news that Salter's piece has a lot of plagiarism in it. "Thanks, I think," was his response. By the afternoon we'd decided to pull it from the June issue, and Art was feeling combative. He'd been depressed in the morning because we'd been shut out of the ASME [American Society of Magazine Editors] nominations. That Salter had gotten one for a piece he did for *Esquire* did not further endear him to Art, who now says he will leak the story to the press if Salter doesn't revise the piece or give us back our $5000. It was quite a day, and needless to say it's the big story on the 17th floor.

. . .

I went running and then up to Billy's for the Oscars. Billy has always loathed Kevin Costner, and I, who used to think he was fine, have begun to dislike him too. Married symbiosis.

MARCH 26: We called James Salter this afternoon. Art was on one line at his desk, and I was on another—over at the couch. We reached him in Boulder. Art told him there was a problem and that he was turning the conversation over to me but would stay on the line.

I really took no pleasure in it, but I had my ducks in a row and did pretty well. I never said plagiarism, but I said there were big problems with attribution and appropriated language. I could sense him sweating two time zones away, and he damn near died when I read him some of the original French. But he backed down; he ended up telling Art that he was "so embarrassed." At which point Art shot me a victory glance . . .

On top of everything else I managed to buy the excerpt from Breslin's Damon Runyon biography for $6000 instead of the $7500 we expected to pay.

MARCH 28: On the way home I saw David Dinkins in front of Grand Central addressing a crowd gathered to celebrate the night-time floodlight[ing] of the Terminal. Ordinary passersby betrayed not the slightest bit of curiosity in him.

Billy had dinner with Gene tonight. Gene's only comment when he saw the completed Elizabethan figure was, "Well, of course." What higher praise could there be? It's a beautiful work of art, and therefore it looks inevitable.

MARCH 31: Billy and I had Easter brunch at Nicole, in the Omni hotel. From there we walked in the sunshine to Fifth Ave. He went to the Presbyterian church (and was surprised at how happy and life-affirming everything in the service was compared to the Lutheran one); I walked home, through the Easter Parade. (I heard one tourist ask another, "What is it we're looking for, exactly?")

APRIL 4: At 4:00 we all had a champagne party in Art's office to welcome back pudgy little Michael Kelly from the Middle East. As the war was ending a couple of Iraqi soldiers, desperate to give up to anything that looked American, surrendered to him.

. . .

Met Louise for drinks at 5:30 at the InterContinental. We had a lively conversation over the loud piano. She's the first financial expert I've met who doesn't think paying off my mortgage is a bad idea.

APRIL 9: Art's moods were moving in a really rugged Alpine sine curve today. He cracked the whip at the 9:30 meeting—nobody was getting copy in fast enough, and so forth. Even I—still the fair-haired boy—caught a little of it. Hadn't I seen the pictures for the Conroy essay yet? Actually, I hadn't even edited it. But I took care of that in a trice . . . I called [Frank] in Iowa City, and there was no muss, no fuss. He didn't mind the jazzy title ("Jamming at Sugar Ray's") that we're putting on the piece, and he says he's eager to write more memoirs for us. We talked about New York, which he says he hates coming to nowadays: "It's like *Blade Runner*."

... Lunch with Liz Darhansoff at Saranac ... Alas, the writers I really want from L.D. are all struggling with novels and have no stories to ship out right now. This includes Charlie Baxter and William Kennedy.

APRIL 11: An odd, depressing lunch with LuAnn Walther of Vintage Books. We went to a new Lebanese restaurant near Random House. I *guess* she's not interested in paperbacking *A7*, but in fact the whole question never came up. When she insisted on having Random House pick up the check, saying, "It's the least I can do," I thought: "Is that a 'no'?" I guess it was. I suppose she had her own agenda, too: pitching Camille Paglia to *GQ* . . .

APRIL 15: Salter has responded to my latest request with enough friendliness for me to assume sarcasm . . . The piece is still unscheduled, but it's been turned over to the fact-checkers. God knows what they'll turn up.

APRIL 18: The guy who writes Page Six, the *Post*'s gossip sheet, called today to ask about a rumor that the piece of James Salter's nominated for a National Magazine Award, the one from *Esquire*, was in fact plagiarized from an old French magazine. Did I know anything about it? Well, no; and I played dumb about everything else, too. Art and I figure it's one of three things. Most likely the guy heard a garbled rumor, through the media grapevine that everybody here connects to, and in the course of the telling, as in a game of telephone, *GQ* became *Esquire*. Or, the guy from the *Post* knew the real story and was just fishing, trying to get me to say something. Or—least likely but most desired possibility—the *Esquire* piece is plagiarized, too . . .

APRIL 19: Norton has made an offer for the paperback rights to *Aurora*. The money is terrible, but I am feeling great. I reached John this morning and we decided that this is better than any other iron in the fire.

APRIL 20: Came back from Billy's—just as the doormen's strike was starting—to discover that they'd cut down all the bushes in front of my window and replaced them with little flowers, depriving me of what little privacy the apartment affords . . .

Read Raban's book for *USA Today* and then at about 7 Billy came here & we went off to Louise's dinner party. We came with flowers and books. There were 5 others, including her old artist friend, Roger Jorgensen, who did some of the paintings on the walls back in the 50s, and Judy Miller,* who's run a children's theatre company, The Paper Bag Players, for years . . . [Louise] & Billy seemed to take to each other nicely—his being a smoker gives him a great many extra points to start with.

APRIL 22: Almost since we met, Billy has been advising me to go into therapy—"just so you'll stop torturing yourself," he'll say. Today I decided to. I called up Dr. Bertram Slaff, whose name was given to Billy a long time ago by "Dr. Bob" (Brooks)—Billy's own therapist . . .

APRIL 25: This talk I gave at the Historical Society was probably the biggest deal in my speaking life since Convocation at Vassar six years ago . . . The library upstairs was a big, beautiful setting. Every part of my crazyquilt life was there [in the audience] . . . The speech went well, which is a good thing, since I'm going to give it in 3 other places. I could tell that I am really on to something with the Rathbone story—people actually gasped when I told them the kicker, and afterwards they could look at the original of Clara's letter, as well as the wanted poster for Booth & the conspirators, in the glass display cases . . . Billy & I and Miss Carol went out for dinner afterwards to celebrate his 46th birthday. My love. I gave him beautiful 1920s mother-of-pearl cufflinks from Paul Stuart. They were in the "estate items" section, and I wondered, with a sense of guilt and unluckiness as I bought them, if they'd come from the dresser drawer of a gay man who'd died of AIDS.

APRIL 26: On the telephone Frank Conroy's wife seems as nice as her husband. I called Iowa City today, trying to get a picture of FC when he was young, something we can run with the arti-

* Her stage name was Judith Martin (1918–2012).

cle . . . but she thinks he got rid of most of his youthful photos a long time ago—an interesting act, if true, for an autobiographer of childhood.

Billy and I celebrated his birthday as we do every year—by going to the Café Carlyle to hear Dixie Carter. She was really over the top this year—shaking a tambourine, slamming breath into a harmonica—and it was a wonderful show. Her husband, Hal Holbrook, was at the table just in front of us.

She did the songs we love, including "Warm," one of "our" songs. And I thanked God to be here with Billy, both of us still healthy, two years after that first traumatic night we heard her. I could see his eyes glistening with tears as he had the same thought.

APRIL 29: Talked to Frank Conroy about the pictures. He says there never really were very many—asks me to think about that no-'count family in *Stop-Time* in order to realize why. We're going to use the jacket photo from *Stop-Time* instead. He was thirty when it was taken, but he looks about ten years younger: he says he was hungover and the picture was taken by a kid in the Viking office.

APRIL 30: Went to a party at Mortimer's with Fran K. It was for her friend John Hart, who's formed a new film production company that's working with Paramount. Everyone there was vaguely recognizable and more or less famous: Ahmet Ertegun; Dominick Dunne; David Brown; Swifty Lazar. Billy Norwich was taking notes in a little pad for his *Daily News* column, and Fran and I thought about telling him lots of lies so tomorrow morning he'd have to put his head in the oven like Mr. Chatterbox [in *Vile Bodies*].

MAY 1: A very nice note from James Merrill, about how much he'd enjoyed *Aurora 7*. I suspect he saw the reference to Mary in the *New Yorker* review and went out to get the book.

. . .

Lynn Bartlett was the [Vassar] Convocation speaker, and the old boy did a fine job. He was moving, lucid & generous as he looked back on his life. (His emotions are always under his top layer of skin, and he nearly sobbed when he mentioned the boys from Lehigh who died in the Second World War.) What's funny is that Lynn had a perfect sense of occasion: he knew when to speed up, when to enunciate, how to pace. He had his big audience just where he wanted them. It's funny because in ordinary conversation, with one or two people, he has *no* sense of occasion: never knows when to stop, to move his face away from yours, to lower his voice. Anyway, I was happy for him; he is a kind soul and has been as nice as can be to me over the years.

MAY 2: I had my first appointment with Dr. Slaff today, up at Madison and 82nd, and shocked myself by bursting into hysterical sobs halfway through it. I said that if there were a cure for AIDS tomorrow morning, I would still never be able to disconnect sex and death. They are psycho-synonyms to me.

MAY 7: I left for Wilmington, on Amtrak, in the middle of the afternoon . . . My talk was to the friends of the Univ. of Delaware library, and it was at a country club deep in the pastures of DuPont country. I had some moments of peace before the cocktail chatter started, sitting, in a chair on an indoor patio, watching the golfers.

I spoke after dinner, and I cut some of what I gave at the Historical Society—the crowd was in large part old, tired and a little hard of hearing. Needless to say, they were also, for the most part, rich, and the librarians who invited me would have been delighted to see a couple of them drop dead over the soup, thereby turning into bequests before everyone else's eyes.

MAY 8: Well, after 11:00 I "went out." And had a couple of drinks. And "met somebody" for a few unsatisfying moments of what they call a "casual encounter."

I was so depressed by it, so upset that I could be doing anything to damage the happy home I've made with Billy, to put at the most infinitesimal risk the gift of my HIV- status (to risk "seroconversion"), so confused about why this was happening that I *did* wind up getting in a cab and going to Billy's at 2:30 a.m.— and telling him.

And he was as I knew I would find him—hurt, scared, soothing, understanding . . . We've built a world that is so tender and
warm and childlike that the erotic doesn't have a chance in it.

MAY 9: Getting through this. Together. Billy is wonderful, my
love, my life. We talked from the office, and he said this was
bound to happen, that it didn't have to sink us, that if it happened
again sometime it needn't be a catastrophe . . . we cannot assume
ourselves to be saints in the midst of coping with everything else.

MAY 12: Back home I put the changes to the Alaska piece onto the
diskette before heading down to Alison West's tea party on 29th
St. Dear Alison, who's off to Mongolia (yes) in a few weeks, had
finger sandwiches and strawberry tart spread out on the floor for
me and a few dancers and painters.

MAY 13: Had drinks with Lois Wallace at her agency on E. 70th St.
We liked each other a lot, I think. I'm trying to buy ½ of Elliott
Baker's essay on Robert Frost (and Mickey Cochrane) from her.
She thinks it's better for me to communicate with him directly,
since he's furious at her for telling him his new novel isn't publishable . . . She projects a deadpan, murmuring, humorous certainty
about everything—as if her greatest horror in life would be to register surprise over something. This should be terribly offputting,
but I found her charming. She's one of those people who's just too
smart to be annoying.

MAY 14: Had lunch with Doug for the first time in quite a while . . .
While he was waiting for me to come out of my office, he was
seated on a couch by the elevator with about a half-dozen drop-
dead handsome [male] models. "I couldn't work here," he told me.
He would crack under the pressure.

MAY 16: Had my second appointment with Dr. Slaff, which wasn't
as emotional as the first. I think he thinks what happened last
Wednesday was a good thing. I don't; and I don't think that we're
going to change each other's minds. Now he says we're ready to
talk about sexual fantasies. Oh, Lord, do we *have* to?

Art Cooper gave a cocktail party at his apartment on Sutton Place . . . Horn-rimmed Nick Lemann, this year's race-relations guru, was walking around. So was last year's, Tony Lukas. I met Esther Newberg, Chappaquiddick veteran and Jimmy Breslin's agent. She made an early getaway from the party, perhaps something she's learned to practice since July 1969.

MAY 20: Amy Cherry and I went to lunch at Café Un Deux Trois and she gave me the delightful news that Norton will be using Billy's pop-art painting of Rene Carpenter on the paperback cover of *Aurora*.

MAY 26: [My last Vassar commencement] Mathilde Krim gave the main address and Billy and I listened intently. It was short, specific and somber, but not despairing. My heart ached as I saw Billy, so attentive, listening for good news.

MAY 28: Billy got me up at 7:15 (no easy task) so that we could be at Tiffany by 8:00. We carried the four big cardboard boxes—light as can be—from Symphony House all along still-glamorous 57th St. Gene Moore came down to greet us and we took them up to his office on the freight elevator.

The old thing, still going strong at 81, is full of prunes. He was reading a new self-help book about obsessive love (at his ex-boyfriend's house) this weekend. The office is decorated from top to bottom with signed pictures of Audrey Hepburn, Dietrich, Colette, the works. He was scheduled to do an interview with a new magazine (*HOW*) this morning, and was pretending to be annoyed at the prospect.

MAY 30: . . . We headed up to Tiffany, in a taxi, to see the windows. The dolls, at night, lit by Gene's own direction, are, to put it mildly, spectacular. How the light gives contour, human shapeliness, to the faces! The cable TV kid came by with his video camera to tape the last 8 minutes of the show devoted to them. Poor Billy was nerve-wracked: this would be the night they were repaving the street *and* sandblasting one of the marble window borders. Well, I suppose it will all add up to New York ambiance, even if

Billy had to shout his answers to the questions. (Miss Carol and I appear at the end as strolling passersby.) . . . We went to the Plaza afterwards and ordered a bottle of champagne in the Oak Bar to celebrate . . . The United Nations Association dinner was breaking up . . . Some women in evening dresses, one of them spilling over a strapless one like an ice cream cone beginning to melt.

JUNE 1: . . . Off to Rockefeller Center for another [American Booksellers Association] party—Houghton Mifflin's—which took up the whole skating rink. Honestly, these publishers may be crying poor, but these are immense and lavish affairs . . . [Breslin] told me a little about the Runyon research. "You go down to the Hearst files at the University of Texas and you find a folder marked 'Mental Health—See Insanity.' That tells ya somethin'."

JUNE 7: Falling in love with the little town of Owosso [Michigan]. It'll all be in the piece,[*] and the real challenge will be how to keep the essay from being insipid. All day long in the beautiful warm weather: strolling along the river, going into Curwood's "castle," walking the street on which Tom Dewey grew up. This is the place the country used to fancy itself.

JUNE 8: I love it here. Couldn't Billy and I live here; couldn't he open a shop making stuffed kitties while upstairs I wrote on a mechanical typewriter whose clackings happily join the lawn mower noises?

But how much time do we have left together?

JUNE 9: I went up in an old open-sided Bell helicopter this morning, held in by only a seat belt, and looked at Owosso from the air. (It looks the same from above as it does on the ground, whereas New York from the air seems a much more wonderful and rational place than it does on the sidewalks.)

---

* "Why, O Why, O Why O, Do They Ever Leave Owosso?" appeared in *The American Spectator* and later in *Rockets and Rodeos*.

JUNE 10: The Breslin galleys came back with huge reform-school penmanship all over them, and then Sallie, the shy, Catholic girl from Research, presented me with a report that made me use the phrase "imaginative reconstruction" instead of the word "biography" in my editor's caption . . . One time when I was looking for her, Sallie was at church for Ascension Thursday, so I decided she wasn't up to enduring Breslin over the phone. I called up to do the research questions myself. When informed that Owney Madden didn't own the Parody Club in 1928, J.B.'s response was: "That's like sayin' you guys aren't owned by fuckin' Newhouse!"

JUNE 11: Jenny Egan, who's a client of Ginger's and who sold a couple of stories to Tom Jenks . . . She was my lunch guest, along with Amy Tardio, at Cafe Un Deux Trois today. She told a couple of funny stories about working for the Countess de Whatshername, the one who keeps writing books about having been a spy for the CIA.

JUNE 13: A long lunch at the Four Seasons with Art and Paul Scanlon and Mordecai Richler, who has a great big ruined eagle's face and a mop of limp hair. Paul and Art feed him the bonhomie and compliments he needs, even though he irritates them with his laziness and has probably reached a point where he needs the magazine more than it needs him. We got on fine—he talked about knowing Louis MacNeice many years ago—and Art was happy playing air-traffic controller with the celebrities at other tables. He kept giving us reports on what was going on with Si Newhouse & Tina Brown & Mike Ovitz, to all of whom Paul & I had our backs.

JUNE 16: [Billy] told me that he actually sees how I get all sorts of things from [Mom]: the way she tells a story, the sometimes comic abundance of detail and so forth. And I realized he's right.

JUNE 17: Billy is down, very down, and it's a lot of things at once—from post partum depression to the news coming out of the AIDS conference in Florence. The Americans are under fire because the administration, idiotically, won't be permitting HIV+ people into the country when the next big conference is held, next summer, in Boston. "It occurs to me," said Billy, never given to paranoia or political thoughts of any kind, "that the government wants me dead."

JUNE 21: Billy + I had a lovely Urban Grill dinner before going home to watch more *I, Claudius*. (Between the restaurant and home we went into Coliseum Books, where Carly Simon was browsing in a blond wig.)

JUNE 24: Jay Rockefeller's report on children is out, and the TV stations are showing all the thrown away, abused, malnourished millions. The country will never get off its drug-induced binge of trashiness, I think. No one is responsible for anything; we are all victims. And the "solutions" are as tiresome as ever. Rockefeller's tax credits would accomplish nothing, I'm sure . . . And I see the country getting more violent, crazy and disgusting. This is all being written by a patriot, but one who's very, very pessimistic these days.

JUNE 25: Read a lot of Richard Ford's *Wildlife* on the train—I can't understand why the reviews were often so sour. Maybe they were a useful corrective to past overpraising . . .

JUNE 26: [I was doing a profile of Vice President Dan Quayle for *The American Spectator*] David Broder from *The Washington Post*— a courteous, dull man—was on the plane. He and Bob Woodward are doing a lot of traveling with DQ and are planning some big splashy articles for August & September . . . Wlady and I originally thought of our piece on DQ for the September issue, but I'm going to ask him to push it up to August . . . I never thought I'd be trying to scoop Bob Woodward, but that's what it amounts to.

JUNE 27: . . . By 1:00 I was having a surprisingly relaxed lunch with John Herman at Metropolis off Union Square . . . He seems happy with the *Rockets and Rodeos* progress, and we talked about the long term, or beyond Rathbone.

... Up to Dr. Slaff at 5:50. I had absolutely nothing gloomy or fundamental on my mind, and it seemed like an awful waste of $150. But he says we assemble a picture of me from the good days as well as the bad.

JUNE 30: ... [Gay Pride Weekend] I feel no more pride in being gay than I do in being Irish, and I've never been drawn to the parade ... Went over to a rooftop party at [Doug Thornburg's friend] Walter's apartment house on Christopher Street ... Dougie's friends always remind me of a kind of gay high-school math club—they're very sweet and nerdy, and up there on the roof we were some contrast to the wild cutting-edge crowd in the streets below and out on the pier.

JULY 1: Poor Billy. He & Gene taped crazy Lynn Graham's cable show today, and when it became clear that he had no intention of giving her one of the dolls, as she seemed to expect he would, she turned bitchy. What an extorting cow. ...

JULY 2: Lunch with Marty at the Algonquin, during which we discuss the possibility of getting Art to start a real books column in the magazine. Mordecai's, after all, is called "Books and Things," and when he talks about the former at all, it's usually as a joke. Even Art is losing patience with him: he was supposed to turn in a column on Henry Miller's about-to-be-published first novel, but instead sent in a jokey piece about his Dutch translator.

JULY 3: Finished Richard Ford's novel and can now see the reason for the reviewers' irritation. That maddeningly passive, blank boy narrator can't sustain a whole novel.

JULY 4: Huntington, Indiana, was a good place to spend Fourth of July ... [Woodward] was nice to me, and beckoned me to join him when Dave Beckwith, the press sec'y, was giving him some extra bit of access. What a hustler, though! You'd think he was a 22-year-old kid ... He makes it his business to know the names of all the junior staffers, to chat up the Secret Service, to get to Quayle on the flight *out*, not just the one going back. (He accomplished this by telling Beckwith he had something he just had to give DQ. It turned out to be a Nixon in '92 button, but it did the trick.)

JULY 6: Billy and Chris Bull came by around 9 & we sat and drank and argued politics and mostly laughed . . . Sweet Chris, who is still so polite you expect him to say "sir" in the middle of a shouting match, was wearing some sort of love-bead necklace. Billy cannot get over the way this younger gay generation dresses.

JULY 10: Art loves the section of Talese I've recommended (it concerns GT's father's cousin, a tailor in Paris before WWI), and we've offered Lynn Nesbit $7500 for it. (Fortunately, she seems to have forgotten my connection to Jacob Epstein.) Si Newhouse himself has given us permission to go as high as $15,000. (And why not? *GQ* paying for a Knopf book? He might as well just shift money from one pants pocket to another.)

JULY 11: I'm nearly halfway through doing whatever work I'll manage to do in this life, but I still imagine myself as the new kid on the block. (Maura, in the copy department at the magazine, even calls me Sparky.) So I guess I feel wizened & peachfuzzy all at once.

JULY 12: Revised Quayle over the phone with Wlady. I don't think they're thrilled with it. I suspect they wanted more of a political piece, full of all the up-to-the-moment infighting, whereas what I turned in was, for want of better terms, atmospheric and psychological.

JULY 13: Howard Hunt's piece on Mailer showed up by Federal Express. He did it in record time, and it's good, too. The potential for fiasco was large, but what he's produced is shapely, witty, even generous. It will need some cutting, but I called him up in Florida to compliment him and relieve his anxiety, which seems to have been considerable. He pretty much sidestepped the issue of his own characterization in the novel . . .

JULY 15: I was spooked by a phone call from Fran K. this morning. We got to talking about James Revson, who died a few days ago. I hadn't even known he was sick. I just remembered his almost plump presence in Sag Harbor two summers ago . . . Fran tells me that Giovanni, who left James for someone else, is also + —and so is the fellow who's this summer's major domo at the house. There is so much death yet to come.

JULY 16: Marty and I took thin-lipped David Garrow to lunch at Sam's (Mariel Hemingway's place) in the Equitable Bldg. An "exploratory" discussion: it might lead to his doing a piece on abortion or on black conservatives, a hot topic since the Clarence Thomas nomination.

JULY 18: A certain crankiness at the magazine today. I felt a little of it myself as I wasted time modifying contracts for the remotest contingencies that agents dream up. And Eliot & Art seem to be down from their Tuesday high: the good news then was that circulation had reached 700,000. The bad news, that ad pages are down, came yesterday.

. . . I realize how much I'll miss [Billy] at Fran's this weekend, but I'm glad he made his excuses not to come. All that inane literary chatter and *au-courant* craziness leaves him feeling shy and awkward. Why should he bother with it? And yet he wants me to go and let my competitive nature swim in the summer literary waters, because it's good for me.

He is good for me, the best thing that ever happened.

JULY 20: A huge dinner party . . . Handsome, tortured Ben Taylor, who always makes me remember Tom Curley; and a nice, prematurely gray man named Louis, a Union Theological Seminary administrator. He's the boyfriend of Robert Jones, whose novel is out and being praised. . . .

JULY 21: One more appallingly hot day. I managed to do a little Rathbone outlining & read some manuscripts, but mostly I just wanted to sit on the porch, immobile, as if we were on the Mississippi Delta.

We drove over to the Strachans' late in the afternoon, to sit in the yard and see their new kittens. Fran, of course, brought champagne. Pat and Bill are lovely, and their cigarette company ought to sign them up for a promo. They fairly burst with good looks, brains, charm, and athletic bodies—and they both smoke like chimneys.

Back at the house we grilled hamburgers for dinner. (Life Today: the name of some long-ago acquaintance of Vance's came up, and Fran or Howard said, "He's dead," to which everyone just kind of nodded, as if whoever said it had said, "He's gotten divorced" or "He's left the city." AIDS is now just an ordinary life occurrence, a normal milestone, for gay men.)

JULY 22: The terrible heat kept up—the lights went out at Condé Nast just after lunch for about a half hour. People wandered the office in the semi-darkness, as their computer files died . . .

JULY 24: Jolted at the NYPL this afternoon when I found a poem about Tommy, by Katy Aisenberg, in the *Mississippi Review*. Louise had heard that one would be in there & had asked me to go looking for it. It is pretty harrowing in its specificity—how the bedroom in Baltimore looked; that blue coffeepot; the snapshots I took—and Katy has exaggerated & dramatized & self-pitied the bad-enough realities into something worse. Big Tom, called just that, making some drunken remarks at the wake, which he in fact never made. I hurried out of the library, agitated. . . .

JULY 26: Jimmy Breslin called yesterday, while I was out of the office. He told Art he loved the layout of the Runyon piece—to think I missed his first non-screaming communication!

JULY 29: All day long jokes about Jeffrey Dahmer (and the Milwaukee "slayfest") fly through the electronic inter-office mail. (JD's best pick-up line: "Hey, I know a great ribs place up the street.")

JULY 30: Ten years ago, when I regularly wrote for *National Review*, I prided myself on my ability to come up with my own titles, which they usually used. And I still like wrestling with puns and parody and then realizing the right one in a flash. But I spent half the day trying to come up with the right one for Howard Hunt's piece on Mailer and not really succeeding: "Artificial Intelligence"; "The Norman Context"; "Classified Mailer." Marty may actually have the best one—"The Prisoner of Text"—but even it's not right.

. . .

David Dinkins gave a speech about saving the city that absolutely no one paid the slightest attention to—as well they shouldn't have—and *The New York Times* suggests that there are reasons to be optimistic enough to stay in the city. For one thing, students' *math scores* are going up. Let's not all clap at once.

AUGUST 1: Robert Jones kept our lunch date at Sam's even though his lover, Louis, has gone to Roosevelt Hospital for a blood clot in his lung. Yes, he's HIV+. It goes on and on; no one expects anything else any more.

AUGUST 4: I realize that I enjoy my times with Mom more when Billy's there . . . the three of us play off one another naturally; we laugh and don't tire. This is a natural family, and Billy is more of a son-in-law than she's ever had. (He and I slept beneath the headboard of the bed on which I think I was conceived, the one that crowned the bed on which my parents spent their married life. And nothing could seem more right.)

AUGUST 6: I had dinner with Alison tonight at a little Chinese place on Third Avenue . . . On Thursday she goes in for surgery on her knee, after which she heads to Maine, where she'll be joined by Charles Edwards . . . He and Alison have reconciled after several years. He never blew up at her, as he did with me—just quietly cut her out of his life. Now they're friends again. With breathtaking matter-of-factness she tells me that she wants to make the most of time together with him, since he's HIV+.

He probably was the whole time we were together.

AUGUST 7: Art and I had our long-planned Four Seasons lunch with Gay Talese and Lynn Nesbit. She is a truly frightening woman, who at the end of the meal managed to harangue Art about our supposedly low fees. Talese himself was completely charming, leaning away from Lynn's little speech, telling me that he liked *Aurora 7*, recollecting how pretty Rene Carpenter was in '62. He gave us old family photos to use with the excerpt, and we all said hello to Si Newhouse, who gibbered his little simian way over to our table and told us that he has the pockets of his suits sewn shut so he can't stick things in them. Si's sewn pockets, it occurs to me, [were] a metaphorical opportunity for Lynn Nesbit, but she failed to see it or declined to use it.

AUGUST 8: Went up to Dr. Slaff's at 5:00. We discussed my ego—I use the term clinically—today. Frankly, I think the superego is much denigrated. The world would be a lot more dignified a place if we thought better of it.

AUGUST 10: Ran two miles before settling down to write 1500 words of the Rathbone novel. I'm getting to the point where I think I have Clara's voice.

Billy & I went down to Avenue B for Chris Bull's party . . . Sarah Schulman, the novelist, was there; a kid handing out cards advertising the anti-church documentary he's made . . . a boy who designed a Free Pee-wee Herman poster that was on Chris' wall. Also there was Fred, Chris' sweet, soon-to-be former boyfriend.

AUGUST 12: The city felt almost pleasant. I try to cheer myself with isolated bits (straws) of good news: that 1 in 7 black families are now making over $50,000 a year; that there are signs the crack epidemic is abating. The streets are as wretched as ever—there are 2 guys living in the doorway of the physics association building right on my block now—but one tries to hope.

. . .

And then, at 6, it was time for D. Keith Mano's publication party for *Topless*, which was held at the Star club on W. 33rd St. The first person I spotted was Jason Epstein, who looked quite a bit like a regular. Wilfrid Sheed was propped on two canes as he watched girls—pretty ones too—dance on the bar. Rick Brookhiser & Brad Miner from *National Review* were in danger of getting stiff necks. Mano got a huge amount of publicity out of it: the bright lights assisting various video interviewers were almost never off. DKM walked around with a fistful of bills, peeling them off and giving them to people in the cheapo publishing crowd, urging them to tip the girls since "they're human beings too." Jackie Deval tells me that he came to Lynn Goldberg's publicity outfit to see if they'd like to take on the job of promoting this novel. At one point during the interview he pointed to Jackie's breasts and told her she could make $2,000 a week with them.

AUGUST 15: Talked to Howard Hunt in the morning. He says again that *Silent Coup* is all nonsense. He dislikes John Dean but will give a deposition in support of Dean's lawsuit against the authors. Howard is pleased that the book at least gives Bob Woodward another black eye.

AUGUST 16: My long-planned visit to Loree's. That white-knuckle feeling on the train. In the end it wasn't so bad, but I took a while to relax. She is the only person whose presence makes me literally crave a drink. She says the children, or Oliver, I can't remember which, actually do imitations of me pacing.

AUGUST 18: At midnight, as I was brushing my teeth, Billy knocked on the bathroom door and told me to come out quickly and look at the TV: a bulletin had just come over CNN—Gorbachev was out. (Billy was smiling. Utterly uninterested in politics, he still knew that news this momentous would excite me, whether it was good or bad, and he offered it to me like a little present.)

Well, I hope Poland has her doors locked. This was bound to happen, of course, and one only wonders how ferociously the hard-liners (inevitably and inaccurately described as "right-wingers") will reassert themselves. Gorbachev was done in by the system he served for thirty years and reformed for six.

AUGUST 20: Spent some of the day fruitlessly trying to get Ward Just and Mario Cuomo to agree to do something on the upcoming

William Kennedy novel. "The Governor doesn't feel he could do it justice" with all he has to do in the next several months. Sounds as if he's planning a campaign.

Art is going crazy because *Esquire*, he's found out, is doing a JFK cover in December. We were planning one for January, since we've got some stuff on Oliver Stone's loony Jim Garrison film. Since *Esquire* will also have their piece of the Talese book a month before we have ours, Art feels beset & besieged: I did 5:00 bottle brigade in his office with Paul Scanlon.

AUGUST 21: Gorbachev is back—thanks to Yeltsin. The coup has failed, thrillingly. Billy & I watched MG get off his plane from the Crimea—Raisa looking frightened & the worse for wear . . .

AUGUST 22: *GQ* in Connecticut. Art had the editors and writers up to his house on Candlewood Lake. (What a house: an unweather-beaten, huge, genially showoffy place—if you were writing it up for *Architectural Digest* you'd want to call it "Art Nouveau.") . . . We had a big brainstorming bull session on the deck and came up with very little other than a decision to put George Foreman on one of the covers. After that it was all play . . . I went with Paul & Lucy & Johanna Schneller & Hilary on a motorboat tour of the lake, which is about 15 miles wide at one point. A local guy named Frank was our skipper & at some points he buzzed the boat up to 40 mph, making the wind and the wake absolutely blissful. Revolution in Russia? Race rioting in Crown Heights? No problem. We just sat back, in extasis, behind our sunglasses, and flew . . .

AUGUST 23: The Communist Party's activities have been outlawed in Russia and *Pravda* has been shut down.

(Less than a decade ago Ronald Reagan declared that Communism was a bizarre chapter in history that was approaching its end. Everyone laughed. Has one network or newspaper recalled that remark today?)

Gorbachev, who never granted one reform he knew he wouldn't have to, at least eventually, was toppled by people he appointed, and saved by those he opposed.

AUGUST 26: Lunch with Jackie Deval at Aquavit. She's now at Villard Books. When the meal was done we started to fight over the check & then stopped, realizing that Si Newhouse would be paying for it either way.

Talked to Wlady late in the afternoon and we agreed that I would go to Pearl Harbor for the 50th anniversary commemorations. He will pay for the hotel & as much of the plane fare as he can come up with. It's a good deal & a good idea, and if I can do my little trial beforehand and the film festival afterward, I'll have my book [*Rockets and Rodeos*].

AUGUST 28: [*Henry and Clara* research] Spent the afternoon at the NYPL and the Mechanics & Tradesmen's library. From the latter I got out a book on [wedding etiquette], which was last stamped as being due on May 19, 1909.

AUGUST 29: Billy's T-cell count has dropped to 280 over the last 4 months, and Dr. Jeff is going to switch him to DDI. This news hit us like a thunderclap, and we did some crying . . . All of our anxieties came tumbling out amidst declarations of love and of how we agreed the last 2½ years were the best of our lives. We do not feel victimized; we believe we've found and made a love, a home, a gentle world, that most people spend a lifetime looking for and never finding. We are not victims; we are part of the lucky few.

AUGUST 31: . . . At 8:30, Billy & I met outside the Ballroom . . . Tonight it was Lypsinka, a very clever guy named John Epperson whom even the newly hip *New Yorker* raves about. It was screamingly/silently funny—and it even included a brief mimed snatch from that ancient T. C. Jones record Billy has . . . We had a wonderful, happy time & were home with the paper & in our pajamas by 11:00.

SEPTEMBER 1: . . . Back over to Billy's for a pasta dinner with Doug & Bruce. We had a good time—Bruce is, in an odd way, a little afraid of Billy, and around him he remains on good behavior. Actually, it's not so odd: he knows Billy sees through him.

SEPTEMBER 3: Art wishes we had hot-racketed Jimmy Connors instead of defeated young Boris Becker on the cover we've got sitting on newsstands this week . . .

. . . [When we got home from a cocktail party in the Village hosted by some old friends of Bill's] Billy confessed that he was miserable. Why? Because almost the first thing Ed said to him when he got in the door, was: "Oh, we've got great news. Bob & I were just tested, and we're both negative." How can people be this stupid?

SEPTEMBER 4: Kathy Rich's 87-year-old great-aunt, who had a long career as a fashion editor in magazines and newspapers, has died. Kathy tells me that Kay Thomas once explained to her how she handled an abortion she required: "I didn't know which one was the father, so I made them all give me fifty dollars." Recently, when she needed something at Lenox Hill Hospital and felt the nurses weren't being quick enough about it, she'd dial 911.

SEPTEMBER 12: . . . Up to Billy's for drinks with Dick & Dennis . . . We went out for dinner to Aglio & Olio, & I felt less of that cloud of doom I've felt overhanging the table while eating at their house—this despite last week's bad news and Dennis' complaint of headaches: the fear that's even worse than brain tumor is encephalitis. He's going to be having a CAT scan. But he was cheerful, and he seems pleased to be working a day a week, on computers, for the PWA Coalition.

SEPTEMBER 15: Literary life in 1991: *Newsday* held a "literary tea" in the Grand Ballroom of the Waldorf in connection with the 5th Avenue book fair. The panelists were E. L. Doctorow (who said he is "haunted" by the thought that Communism might have collapsed sooner if the U.S. hadn't been so belligerent for 40 years); Joyce Carol Oates (who talked, mystifyingly, about how she seeks excuses to avoid her writing desk and throws a great many pages away); Marianne Wiggins (the ex-Mrs. Rushdie, who kept ungrammatically bashing England in an English accent she kept losing) . . . I listened to Breslin & Oates chat about boxing— a scene that cried out for a Max Beerbohm cartoon.

SEPTEMBER 17: Lunch at Vico, way up on Madison, with beautiful Alexandra Isles . . . We discussed what she might do with the love letters Oliver Gogarty [the real-life Buck Mulligan] wrote to her mother.

SEPTEMBER 18: Had lunch with Gerry Howard at the Algonquin . . . He is really a very smart guy, full of shrewd remarks about any author, past or present, that comes up. He breaks into these silly, breathy giggles every so often that are charming and just a little scary. He tells me what an operator Tom Jenks was, and I wonder if he thinks the same of me.

Fought my way up Madison (there are Con Ed projects everywhere) for a late afternoon appointment with Dr. Slaff, who does for me his imitation of Fulton J. Sheen, whom he mistakenly thought I was too young to remember. I know he blames all my anxieties, about everything, on Catholicism. I like him, but I am so absolutely, almost indecently, without curiosity about him that we'll probably never make much progress, whatever that may be. One is, after all, supposed to transfer certain emotions and hostilities to the analyst, no?

SEPTEMBER 26: Talked to Radnitz, who faxed me a letter from one of the screenwriters who's declined the offer to write a script for *Aurora 7*. It's somebody who worked on *Rebel Without a Cause* and *Rachel, Rachel* . . . he might have more success if he approached a few screenwriters under seventy.

SEPTEMBER 27: A haircut with Nancy. (She's going for her real-estate license and is thinking of sending in someone else to take the test, à la Teddy Kennedy.)

SEPTEMBER 29: . . . Up to Billy's to watch *Longtime Companion*, the AIDS movie [on] Channel 13 . . . There's a ludicrous fantasy scene of a Fire Island beach party, after a cure has been found, with all the dead characters [coming] back to life.

It's funny: we talked more about the movie as a movie—well made or badly made, etc.—than the real-life thing it's about. I guess we figured we'd been brave enough just watching it together.

OCTOBER 4: A little crisis I was hoping to avoid . . . Amy Cherry says that not only will Time-Life not give us permission to use Billy's pop-art rendition of the Ralph Morse photo, but they won't even entertain the request . . . It seems as if that painting of Rene Carpenter was never fated to be on the cover of any edition of *Aurora*. But Amy & the art director have agreed that Billy is to be given the commission for a new piece of art, if he's willing to take it—and, of course, bless him, he is.

OCTOBER 8: At the 9:30 staff meeting we got word that what Hugh Carey would call "the days of wine and roses" are over. Ad pages are down, the recession is hanging on, and we're all supposed to be more "sensible" about expense-account lunches and the rest of it.

. . .

Then, at 6:00, to Newark, in a car driven by two student interns. I was one of the guests on Allan Wolper's radio show, *Right to Know*, which comes out of the NPR affiliate on the Rutgers-Newark campus. Most of the program revolved around Fox Butterfield's plagiarized article on the plagiarizing Dean Maitre of B.U. . . . It was a dull, dumb, meandering show . . . A waste of time, but, hey, at least I got to see Newark.

Home to talk to Billy & watch Clarence Thomas' confirmation unravel . . . A matter that we all thought would reflect the great American race war will end up reflecting the great American sex war instead.

OCTOBER 13: Nobody can stop watching . . . One weird silver lining in all this. I don't think white people have ever watched blacks, hour after hour, this parade of articulate, professional witnesses, with so little consciousness of their color . . . It's about sex and careers and truth. . . .

OCTOBER 15: Art is out in Hollywood with his in-laws this week, so things are quiet at the magazine. I had one small near-crisis with a pull quote I did from T. C. Boyle's story: the p.q. shows the character injecting drugs, just the sort of thing to make a liquor advertiser on the facing page feel nervous. But it went through.

OCTOBER 17: [I was starting to cover a criminal trial for *Rockets and Rodeos*.] The city is crumbling faster than ever. There was an enormous water-main break near Grand Central this morning, and the East Side subways were put out of commission . . . On-duty taxi lights were as rare as stars of Bethlehem, but somehow found one on Fifth Ave. & made it downtown. (It poured, by the way, for much of the day.) Judge Rettinger is much as I remember him, a cross between Jimmy Breslin and [my uncle] Jimmy Moruzzi. The defendant, whose mother sat in the back on the same bench I did, is on trial for bank robbery and attempted murder. Rettinger tells me after the session (during which he granted another postponement, this time at the DA's request) that this will have lots of blood & pizzazz.

OCTOBER 18: Edited Gay Talese's piece in the office today. With a light hand, I might add. He has a tendency to use the perfect where the simple past would do . . .

How much nicer, I think, are my little ruts these days—to the Algonquin & Royalton & Cafe Un Deux Trois down 44th; the Mechanics library and the Mid-Manhattan and the NYPL on 44th and 5th; Brentano's a few blocks north; and back to Condé Nast on Madison—than the ruts I used to wear between Avery and the College Center and the College Center and the classroom.

OCTOBER 19: Billy has started DDI, which tastes awful, he says, and must be taken on a completely empty stomach. Alcohol is entirely forbidden; this, fortunately, is not much of a sacrifice for Billy, but I wonder if, while everyone is having cocktails, he'll have one more reminder that he is different, in danger.

OCTOBER 20: Dinner tonight down at Louise's . . . She sent me home with Tommy's old Paris guidebook (she may be over there the same week that Billy & I are) . . .

OCTOBER 21: Peter Richmond has started at *GQ*, trying a little too hard to please everyone, walking that fine line between charm and irritation.

OCTOBER 23: I bought Alice Adams' "Up the Coast" from Binky Urban's assistant this afternoon. I got it for $3000 without any haggling. It's a good story for us, and not the least of its virtues is brevity. We won't have to sacrifice someone's column to run it.

Just before I was leaving to go meet Billy tonight I got a call from Fran K. She'd already heard from Alice Adams in San Francisco, who already heard from Binky Urban in NY. You're surprised that someone who's been all over *The New Yorker* and in the O. Henry collections will still be excited about placing a story. Then you remember how few magazines pay them real money . . .

. . .

Miss Ann-Margret . . . looks very good. Billy & I saw her glitzy stage show at Radio City tonight. (Billy still beams like a little old lady from the Midwest when the Rockettes come out.) She hasn't got much of a voice, and the lasers and Dolby kabooming are way too much, but I'm glad we went . . . Billy's shrink turned out to be sitting in the same row we were.

OCTOBER 25: [At a writers' conference in Indianapolis] Charles Simic's plane was late, so I filled in for him at his public-library appearance downtown late in the afternoon. I read a few of his poems and chattered as sensibly as I could.

He'd shown up by the evening & together—along with Frances Sherwood, a nervous short-story writer, and David Wojahn, a professor-poet—we did a panel discussion to start the conference. A lot of fizzy, silly stuff about where writing comes from and why one does it (to think they made a video of all this!) . . .

OCTOBER 26: . . . Put in a little time in the library with Henry + Clara before going off to do my historical fiction speech yet again. A lot of enthusiasm and some very intelligent questions. Simic, big and hearty and warm—more Mediterranean than Slav—came with his wife & sat in the back row.

OCTOBER 29: Went over galleys with Gay Talese this morning. He's quietly touchy about any changes, and he has an almost pathological aversion to pronouns, but we got the job done happily enough.

OCTOBER 31: . . . To Mezzogiorno on Spring St. for Art's lunch welcoming Peter Richmond & David Granger (both from *The National [Sports Daily]*). Lots of red wine, about 9 of us around the table . . . We all went back to the Condé Nast Bldg. in 3 black limos: we looked like a mafia party leaving Umberto's or Sparks.

NOVEMBER 1: No trial today (defendant's religious day), so I went to the magazine and worked through my slush pile and negotiated with Irene Skolnick over Ed Allen. (Negotiations interrupted when Irene rushed out into Astor Place to observe Joe Papp's funeral, which had been passing below her window.)

There was a party for me at 4:00. (No wonder the Copy Dept. gets the occasional mouse; there's cake in there every couple of weeks.) There was champagne, and the icing said "Happy Birthday, Sparky"—Maura's nickname for me . . . How much harder this milestone birthday would be had I not gone to the magazine; I can hardly accuse myself of midlife stagnation.

NOVEMBER 2: This morning I woke up to a tableful of presents and a shower of love from the gentlest man in the world. I have had three times the career I ever expected; I'm rich in friends; I love my work; I'm alive and healthy. And grateful for every moment I've had & will have [with] Billy.

I'll take 40 over 30.

NOVEMBER 3: Took the #6 all the way up to 86th St. & met Billy at the National Academy of Design, for the farewell party for Laurent de Brunhoff's Babar exhibit. Phyllis looked like the ingenue empress of China in a gold robe; David had cut his hair & was desperately trying to please a date. Billy was amused as I did whatever little business the evening called for: chatting with Gay Talese and Jim Atlas, listening to Katha Pollitt complain about her poverty, making vague lunch plans with Wendy Gimbel . . . From the restaurant we came back here to 45th St. . . . and what should be in the mail but a letter from Scott Carpenter, a nice one, saying how much he'd enjoyed *Aurora* 7 and apologizing for his delay in writing. I'd long since given up on this. . . .

NOVEMBER 5: I was in Art's office this morning . . . and I mentioned Scott Carpenter's letter. Before I knew it we were deciding that I'd go out to Colorado soon, if MSC is willing, to do a "Class Act" feature on him. Does *GQ* make my life fun or what?

. . .

A small comfort: Dr. Jeff [Greene, Bill's physician] is on a very short list of the best AIDS doctors in the city in this week's *New York* magazine.

NOVEMBER 6: The Republicans are feeling shaky after yesterday's Senate election in Pennsylvania, but Mario continues to dither & play hard to get—to the point where people have become annoyed or bored.

NOVEMBER 7: Art's cocktail party for Gerri Hirshey, a new columnist, started at 6:30 [at] his apartment on Sutton Place . . . Everyone was talking about Magic Johnson's having tested HIV positive—a story that is dominating the news unbelievably. Art, who would like people to believe that he was a swinger in his pre-Amy days, asks Gay, "Heterosexual AIDS is very rare, isn't it?" Talese, who did a lot of sleazy primary research for *Thy Neighbor's Wife*, rushed to answer that it was *extremely* rare—no doubt trying to chase a couple of nervous-making memories from his mind. . . .

NOVEMBER 8: Dinner at the Century Club, around an enormous oval table, with the editorial board of *The American Scholar*. I came as Carol Smith's guest, and also because Joe Epstein had just bought my historical-fiction piece. What a neo-con crowd! Roger Kimball and Hilton Kramer (whom I rather liked) and Gertrude Himmelfarb.

NOVEMBER 10: . . . Off to Alison West's "birthday tea" down on 29th St. A crowd of people scrunched into her little apartment. Saw Margo Viscusi, Mary's executor, for the first time in quite a while, and she seemed unoffended by the sight of Alison's copy of *Aurora 7*, so I guess that's good.

NOVEMBER 15: Jerry Birenz, one of the Condé Nast lawyers, called to tell me that the James Brady story about [John] Fairchild has lots of potential problems. And the way we clear them up is to proceed from an absurd premise: since everyone will know the main character is Fairchild (it's even been in Liz Smith), he can complain about anything in the story that's *in*accurate. So we have to fact-check it as if it's a profile! Instead of worrying about the similarities between Bingo Marsh & John Fairchild, Jerry is troubled by the points of divergence. If Bingo is to say "wop," we've got to be able to show that Fairchild has been known to use ethnic slurs. Art was so disgusted by the nonsense of all this that he threw a shopping bag against the wall behind his desk.

NOVEMBER 17: . . . Christina [Frank] tells how she & Josh are going to be married in June by an Episcopal lesbian, but they have to pick a Sunday other than Gay Pride Day, because she doesn't work that day.

NOVEMBER 18: Steve Goldstein rested his case this morning and Mike Hardy rested his this afternoon. The only witness he called was Mrs. Batson—the bank robber's wife turns out to be an assistant vice-president at Shearson Lehman. When I comment on the strangeness of this, one of the ADAs sitting next to me tells me she's prosecuted bank tellers with perfect work records who were holding up Chinese restaurants at night.

NOVEMBER 19: [Billy] wants to buy an apartment and make me co-owner. He wants it to be a good-sized one, the kind I'll need "someday." And then we talked about "someday." He wants me to have the apartment when he's gone. It will have been our home together; he'll have decorated it; it will have all our things and memories; and it will be big enough for me to live the rest of my life in: I can sell the studio I'm in now. He would die knowing that I was set up, safe and secure, in our home.

NOVEMBER 20: Lunch in Art's office with Marty, Lisa, Paul & David Granger to pick the articles and issues we'll submit for this year's ASME awards. We had the twelve 1991 issues spread on the floor, and we walked around them, consideringly, winnowingly, as if we were picking shoes . . .

Met Billy outside the Met at 7:30 and we walked along Madison, down to the Carlyle & back, before going in to hear Rosamond Bernier (or Ros Russell, as she might now be called) lecture on Paris. It was a charming little run through her old neighborhood (she lived in Mme. de Staël's house), and you can't say she doesn't hold your attention. She stands to the side of the podium in a brightly colored evening dress and syntactically chatters on like a charming hostess in some old colonial outpost.

NOVEMBER 25: Billy called in the afternoon; *he* remembered Mom's birthday, though I didn't. We got flowers off just in time.

NOVEMBER 26: Oh, I didn't mention that James Brady came up to the magazine this morning to go over his Fairchild fiction with Art and me and Paul and the Condé Nast lawyer . . . Brady says it was he, not the Fairchild character in our excerpt, who experienced erection (or something close to it) in the still somehow arousing septuagenarian presence of Coco Chanel.

NOVEMBER 28: Our third Thanksgiving together . . . We went downstairs to glimpse the parade, staying out on Broadway long enough to spot Spider-Man and Kathleen Battle . . . Miss Carol came over around 4:00 and we went down to Symphony Cafe for dinner . . . There was a huge family right out of Martin Scorsese at the table next to us. Listening to them, Carol felt she might as well have stayed in Brooklyn—but then she remembered that Sue, her 78-year-old mother, wouldn't be there; she's in Atlantic City gambling.

We went to see *For the Boys*, the new Bette Midler movie. The Ziegfeld had only about a hundred people inside. It felt a little like a gay bar, too—lots of gay men with straight-women friends who looked as if they'd had too much of their own families today.

DECEMBER 1: Scott Carpenter called this afternoon & said he'd be delighted to get together for the *GQ* piece . . . There's a sweet, slow quality—hesitant, a little shy—to the way he talks. I told him I felt as if I should be hearing his voice through a crackle of static, the way I got used to hearing [it] on the flight tapes.

DECEMBER 2: A slightly frantic day of doing captions and pull quotes and galleys and still not quite getting either of my February pieces put to bed. Sid Blumenthal came by at 5 and we all had drinks and talked politics in Art's office . . . Art kept asking Sid if Mario Cuomo is going to run, and Sid's answer was "How should he know?"—he meaning Cuomo. A nice line. So there we were talking American political trivia and not saying a word about the dissolution of the USSR. The Ukraine left today . . .

DECEMBER 3: Had lunch with Eric Simonoff, Lynn Nesbit's very smart assistant. While waiting for him at the Algonquin I noticed that the . . . white-haired lady sitting all by herself was Eudora Welty. That sweet, homely face, the humped back, the quiet percipience that vibrates around her even now; it was all so inviting that I went right up to her and said, "Miss Welty, you'll never remember me, but years ago, during your visit to Vassar, we had lunch." She smiled and asked me about myself & said she did remember the visit. . . .

DECEMBER 4: [To Hawaii, to write about the fiftieth anniversary of Pearl Harbor] An interminable flight. It just went on and on, hour after hour, time zone after time zone, until it brought me to this airport hotel that is practically *under* the Nimitz Highway.

DECEMBER 7: At dawn we schlepped. Up at 1:15 so I could be at the media shed at Pearl before three. That's when the bus left to ride up the mountain (an extinct volcano, actually) to the Punchbowl cemetery to hear Bush give the first of three speeches. The next two were back down in the harbor—on the *Arizona* memorial and then on the Kilo 8 pier. They were poorly written but sincerely delivered.

DECEMBER 11: Radnitz called to tell me that James Bridges—who directed & wrote or co-wrote *Urban Cowboy, The China Syndrome,*

The Paper Chase and *Bright Lights, Big City*—has agreed to do a screenplay for *Aurora 7*. Now RR goes back to the studios.

. . .

Over to Billy's after watching [William Kennedy] Smith thank everyone who helped get him acquitted. He was lucky to meet up with the incredibly inept prosecutor he got. Everyone in New York seems to know a couple of women he's roughed up.

DECEMBER 12: . . . Up to Bert's [Dr. Slaff's] office. We are back, very far, into my childhood, and I am wondering (pointlessly?) about such things as why I cannot really remember how the room I slept in until I was nearly 7 looked or was laid out.

DECEMBER 13: Ed Allen was in town from Pahrump, Nevada— where he moved so that he could be near Las Vegas. He's a low roller, but he's a steady gambler, and he's doing a piece on the subject for us. I took him to lunch at the Algonquin and late in the afternoon we had a drink in Art's office. He's a very odd character—big, tall, and heavy, he looks a bit like a Southern sher- iff. You'd never take him for the author of a WASP-sophisticated story like "Celibacy-by-the-Atlantic," but there you are. He's also softspoken, quiet, not especially witty, as if reserving all his articu- lateness for paper.

DECEMBER 15: [Jeffrey Simpson's] party on W. 11th was amus- ing enough—there were some handsome architects he must moon over, and it was fun to watch his old bachelor nerves be rubbed raw by the sight of two little boys, the sons of one of his women friends, unplugging his TV and moving it under the bed that held the coats. I talked to [a] sparkly old British actress named Enid Rodgers, who's been in NY since 1948 and has done everything, I'm sure, from live TV to industrials.

. . .

. . . The window-shopping traffic on Fifth Avenue was still so thick at a quarter to nine that I got out of the blocked cab & walked the rest of the way home. On the way I checked out a building on E. 49th that's got an apartment we might be interested in.

DECEMBER 17: The *GQ* Christmas party was down at Tommy Tang's, and everybody except Art was very merry. There's really no figuring him. He came in with Bridget Fonda, and was feeling like Lord Bountiful, but when Michael Clinton, the publisher, gave a toast, you could see him going into deep gloom. He left early. The rest of us kept drinking and dancing . . . I talked to sweet Adam Smith from the Art department (Chris Bull, who knows his boyfriend, says that he's a big ACT UP supporter).

DECEMBER 18: Everyone very hungover this morning (some of them stayed over at the Royalton), but I tried to perk up for my lunch with Wendy Gimbel at the Century Club. Actually, looking lively is not hard to do there: all these wheezing old fellows for whom the Library Committee is now a big contentious deal. A lot of tired 60s lions down near the coat check: Tom Wicker, Arthur Schlesinger, John Chancellor. At the table next to us we had Rudy Giuliani, who at the Century passes for *le dernier cri*. (Across town Ed Koch, the man whose job he still wants, was collapsing at his health club.)

[Wendy] talked to me about her work at *Mirabella* & the book she's starting to write. When she was elected to the Century Club, she received a letter informing her of the fact. It began, "Sir."

DECEMBER 19: Art picked this day, beginning 36 hours after the Christmas party, for a 9–5 brainstorming session at the Omni Berkshire. Senior editors and writers going over everything from the fashion pages ("The models look like hoods," said Joe Nocera) to article ideas (Vietnam Veterans organizations with no vets leading them) to the state of the columnists. Art admits that Mordecai is his talisman, and that he'll never dump him, but I've at least got permission to give readers a supplementary bottle—200 words "GQ Recommends" reviews—with any literature pieces we run.

. . . Art always has to overdo it: from the hotel it was on to "21" for drinks and then Trattoria Dell'Arte for a gargantuan dinner. Only Lisa [Henricksson] had the guts to beg off. Fortunately, the restaurant is just a block from Billy's, but if I keep living the way I have been this week, I'll wind up with gout.

DECEMBER 20: David Granger and I had set up a lunch date for today, but we took one look at each other this morning & agreed we couldn't go through with it. Half-a-lettuce-leaf-for-the-rest-of-our-lives seemed like a reasonable diet after yesterday; we just couldn't face food.

DECEMBER 21: Bloomingdale's certainly proves the recession is hanging on. No pushing crowds, plenty of salespeople . . . I took care of Seán & Christina down at Alexander's, which was bustling with real people looking for real toys. Bloomingdale's, the clerk informed me, does not carry *Monopoly* . . . We got the train to Poughkeepsie and Patty met us at 2:40 . . . Jokes about all the huge coffee-table books (*Chapman Piloting, The PGA Manual of Golf*) that were obvious pass-alongs from my job at *GQ*.

DECEMBER 22: I edited [X's] piece until almost 1 in the morning. There's nothing terribly wrong with it, but he's got a tin ear; for all his Harvard education he doesn't know how to bring a sentence in for a smooth landing. Freda Garmaise, by contrast, left school at 16 and knows exactly what sounds right. You either got it or you ain't.

DECEMBER 25: I think this was the nicest Christmas I've had since Daddy died . . . There wasn't an unpleasant word or a raised voice. Loree & Oliver both liked Bill ("He's a nice guy," Ollie said to me in the driveway when we were leaving; this was said very deliberately, as an imprimatur, and it couldn't have been easy to deliver, given what it represents, for a farm boy from Ireland) . . . Mom & Billy went to bed & I stayed up to watch the news of Gorby's resignation and the lowering—no, the removal, forever—of the hammer + sickle from the Kremlin's flagpole.

DECEMBER 28: I haven't been to Paris for almost 10 years . . . The drive between Charles de Gaulle and the Étoile is a denser office-scape than ever, even when one subtracts from it all the buildings that appear at first to be offices but turn out to be apartment houses who've leased their rooftops to big corporate logos. (Does this practice exist anywhere in vulgar, "materialistic" America?)

The graffiti plague has also arrived here: it's everywhere now, even inside the Métro cars, something one no longer sees in even the New York subways. We walked down the Rue de Rennes and found the door to Mary's old building covered with it . . .

We're settled in at the nice little Hotel Récamier, right next to the Église Saint-Sulpice. We walked around all morning before we could check in: I took Billy to the Place Dauphine.

DECEMBER 29: The march of time: the late Yves Montand on the cover of *Paris Match*. And the *plus-ça-change* department: Johnny Hallyday, proclaiming from a magazine ad in the Métro: *"Je ne crois plus à l'amour."* . . . One last note of change and then I'll stop: the old hydraulic elevator that once took one up the Eiffel Tower is no more. A regular electric Otis now whizzes you up.

. . . At 7:00 to James Lord's beautiful apartment on the Rue des Beaux-Arts . . . Edmund White and I got on well, talking about Brown [University] & his Genet biography. One hears that he's been HIV+ for years, but he looks well, even chubby, and that made me feel good. (Billy + I immediately spotted him as a DDI taker when he declined champagne.)

DECEMBER 30: We went [to Beaubourg] to see the Gisèle Freund exhibit, which was satisfying and thorough, though it didn't include her picture of Mary. Perhaps it's just as well: Simone de Beauvoir was all over the walls.

DECEMBER 31: We went to the Givenchy exhibit at the Palais Galliera . . . The dress Jackie Kennedy wore to Versailles in 1961 was near another one that had been Babe Paley's. Sinatra records playing in the background. Everything simple, elegant, clean, no gimmicks. Billy was in heaven . . .

We had tea at the Plaza Athénée, sitting not far from the piano player and watching the women get into the elevator with their furs and little dogs and Esarac bags. We were on the Avenue Montaigne, and Marlene Dietrich was too—90 years old and behind one of the doors, though we didn't know which.

The Lyon Opera Ballet was performing *Romeo & Juliet* at the Théâtre de la Ville at Châtelet . . . (the Capulets were fascists and the Montagues were supposed to be "homeless") . . . Believe me, in this version love had nothing to do with it. The motivation was sex and more sex. Whenever they curled up together they didn't look tender so much as fucked out, and when Romeo was trying to revive her from what he misapprehends as her death, he throws her around in a way to indicate he's exasperated that his little sex machine is broken.

Afterwards we had a quick dinner at a brasserie named for Sarah Bernhardt, before squeezing into the Métro for a train to the Champs-Élysées. The crowd was loud, drunk and incredibly unthreatening by New York standards. We got out at George V and stood in the middle of the boulevard as horns blew, firecrackers exploded at our feet, champagne corks popped and everybody kissed. Us too.

1992

JANUARY 1: I read *Le Monde* in the station waiting room. Even now, the French are still the French: one of the lead items from the U.S. concerned a new rift between Angela Davis & Gus Hall. And over here they're still naming Métro stations for people like Jacques Duclos.

JANUARY 3: The Musée d'Orsay is new to me—that's how long it's been since I was last here—and we went to it this morning. It's a stroke of genius, really: gathering all that nineteenth-century art into the great fact and symbol of the nineteenth century—the railway station.

. . .

They say you should never go to the supermarket when you're hungry, and so I suppose you shouldn't shop for an overcoat when you're cold . . . I went looking at Daniel Hechter and all these little shops along the Boulevard Saint-Germain, and finally in Yves Saint-Laurent's Rive Gauche shop on the other side of the square from the hotel. I bought a thousand-dollar coat, on sale for about $700, a beautiful dark-green cashmere-and-wool thing that fit beautifully.

JANUARY 4: [Flying home] A clear demonstration of the effects Billy and I have had on each other over the last three years: for the first time in my life I had to pay customs duty and for the first time in his he didn't.

JANUARY 6: The New Year is off to a paranoid start at the magazine. Kathy Rich is gone, very unceremoniously, and is replaced by David Kamp, a tall, skinny kid from *Spy*. Art is really kind of crazy these days, and the place is becoming a boy's club. (So long as he gets along with Lisa Henricksson—The Pain Mistress—and Amy Tardio—The Daughter—he can convince himself he has no problem with women . . .)

. . .

Up to Bert's for my 5:50 appointment. Today he declared I "never was a child"—was full of high-seriousness and would-be maturity from about the age of two. Maybe.

JANUARY 10: Talked to Greg (he's still in LA) and to Chris Bull, who may be going to New Orleans to interview David Duke and ask him about his ex-boyfriends. Brave little Chris: there will be crosses burning on Avenue B when he gets back.

JANUARY 11: Louise was in very good spirits. I think she'd had one of the best Christmases she's had in a long time. I brought her some Fauchon spices from Paris and she gave me my annual fruitcake (which I actually look forward to—how many fruitcakes get that said about them?).

JANUARY 13: Lunch with Jim Atlas at Sam's. I'm beginning to like him. We talked about his Bellow biography, which we may get an early piece of. He's also going to send me an essay that made Shelley Wanger blush—it's on the dirtiest passages in High Literature. It was prompted I think by Nicholson Baker's high-brow phone sex novel, *Vox*. He tells me about a scolding letter that Mary [McCarthy] sent him about ten years ago. He recently dug it out at Fran's request and laughed over the extent to which Mary had his ambitious young number.

JANUARY 14: Lisa sat at Art's desk for this morning's Tuesday meeting looking as happy as Alexis Carrington Colby Dexter. When we got to my Carpenter piece on the May lineup, I said I'd be seeing Scott on the 27th. Since May copy is supposed to be in by Feb. 1, she said, "Well, I guess you'll have to write that chop-chop."

JANUARY 16: We got great news today. DDI has bounced Billy's T-Cell count up by over a hundred points. (Oh, God, please keep us a step ahead of the virus. Please keep it a step behind research.) We went out to Café 57 for a dinner that felt a little like a celebration.

　　. . .

　　. . . The end of the book seems suddenly in sight, and I am all excited, which I shouldn't be, since a book of essays (and that's still what it is) isn't going to make much of a splash.

JANUARY 20: The broker is showing Billy big alcove studios now—not the 1-bedroom we wanted but more or less equal to what he's renting now & much bigger than what I've got. There's one on E. 51st he saw late this afternoon. It's on the 8th floor, looks out over 2nd Ave., is roomy, has cedar-lined closets and a marble bathroom, and we could easily afford it. The monthly maintenance is only $479. Billy liked this one a lot, and I have a feeling it could be our home . . . We're also excited that the "spectacles" are coming to an end. I'm ready to stay put, out of the skies and at home, for a while.

JANUARY 24: [Out in Utah, writing about the Sundance Film Festival] *Poison Ivy*, with Drew Barrymore, who's grown into a sort of Satanic Brooke Shields, is a bad TV-movie-of-the-week, but its pompous director scolded an audience member during the Q-&-A as if the poor questioner had been paying insufficient attention to Proust.

JANUARY 25: The big party was out at the Park Meadows Racquet Club . . . "You know, a lot of these films *don't make sense,*" one realistic buyer told me. Deborah Harry, late of *Blondie*, was on the dance floor, a decade and a half out of her time, amiably hoping for attention and a role.

JANUARY 26: [Supper] with Nan and Tom . . . The Super Bowl finished during our dinner, and when we were through eating we shifted to the bar to watch Bill and Hillary Clinton on *60 Minutes* in a remake of *The Gary Hart Story.*

JANUARY 27: I was at [Scott Carpenter's in Vail] by 12:30 and we wound up spending more than four hours together. We broke into big grins when we first saw each other, and the initial encounter had that amused awkwardness of face-to-face meetings between people who've already been part of each other's awareness . . . I liked Barbara [his third wife] a lot. She's calm and humorous and enjoys the astronaut fame, which goes on and on. She was wearing a Mercury 7 pendant, and she told me about all the things that go along with Scott's "work," a word for which she mimed quotation marks: a trip to Paris for some event organized around the *Right Stuff* film; Mercury anniversaries. . . .

We taped about 20 or 30 minutes of "interview" for the *GQ* piece, some of it at the house and some of it at a Mexican restaurant Scott wanted to go to. (How will I explain a restaurant tab of only $13.10 to Art?) But the interview seemed silly, mostly because I knew it all already, but also because we were having a good time and just wanted to talk . . . He is gentle, very soft-and-slow-spoken. When he mentions something he really doesn't like, he sort of sighs, "But that's fine." He hardly takes his eyes off you, never says a swear word, and has beautiful, natural manners. (The photographer was crazy about him.)

JANUARY 28: . . . Stopped at a little truck stop in Downeyville and I got out and stretched and looked up at the mountains and felt wonderful. *Rockets and Rodeos* is a done deal, and I now know the man who's been staring down at my writing desk from that Ralph Morse photo for the last several years.

I could tell I was on my way back to New York when I heard a woman checking in at the Delta gate complain to her husband: "It's *hot* in here." She was wearing a fur coat.

FEBRUARY 1: Spent the day at the keyboard putting in the rest of the 54 pages of the trial essay. By 10:00 tonight I was writing my little piece on Scott, and Billy, on the phone, was gently characterizing me as "beyond obsessive." This is true, but before I met Billy work was the only absolutely reliable source of pleasure in my life.

FEBRUARY 4: Lunch with Hilton Kramer and Roger Kimball at Café Un Deux Trois . . . Hilton had just gotten the [last volume of Mary's memoirs] too. He says he remembers how 25 years ago, when he was still on good terms with Bob Silvers ("when I was still on good terms with" is a frequent opening phrase in his conversation), Silvers told him, excitedly, how Mary had just agreed to go to Vietnam for *The New York Review*. When Hilton asked if Mary knew anything much about Vietnam, Silvers said no, but that her going was still a good thing—otherwise she'd have nothing to do but keep writing that novel about how America was in decline because people no longer grew basil in little pots on their window sills.

FEBRUARY 5,: Did the last real editing on Ron Carlson's story and wondered if I really do care enough about others' writing besides my own to make a good editor (something Roger Kimball, who's also both, talked about yesterday).

FEBRUARY 6: Dinner at Joe Allen with Billy and Fran and Howard and Vance and John Landau. A very funny evening; no surprise there. Billy just loves to watch John call [his sister] Fran "Tiny" and tell her why her "road to hell is paved." It's like having dinner with the Glass children—their older brother is even named Seymour.

Norman Mailer came in with Norris Church toward the end of our meal. I'll have to remember to tell Howard Hunt.

FEBRUARY 8: Billy and I ordered a pizza and watched the opening ceremonies of the Winter Olympics (in his black coat Mitterrand looked like a cross between an undertaker and a corpse).

FEBRUARY 12: Art called me into his office this afternoon and closed the door and remarked that I'd now been here a year. "Do you want to stay?" he asked, in such a grave way that I assumed I was about to get a warning for some terrible fuck-up that had come to light. In fact, he wanted to tell me that I'm getting a $7,000 raise. . . .

FEBRUARY 13: This letter to [Clinton's] draft board that's surfaced—how familiar it sounds. 1969. There's nothing terrible in it; in fact, it's well written and rather touching. But it's a snow job—not on the draft board (there was no longer any need of that by 12/3/69) but on himself. You can hear him, a nice boy, trying to convince himself that he's been mostly making moral choices instead of career calculations.

FEBRUARY 14: Went down Broadway to *Harper's* for lunch with young (28) Robert Boynton, who's plump and blond and smart, a philosophy grad student turned journalist, a sort of liberal version of Roger Kimball. We went to the Time Café for lunch and talked about my finally doing that essay on Daddy's checks (which I've had in mind for ten years). . . .

The fiction boards were reconfigured, so I had to go over them once more in the afternoon. We all knocked off early, at around 4, and drank a case of fancy beer that a new advertiser had sent over.

FEBRUARY 18: [The New Hampshire primaries] Pat Buchanan has become the right-wing Gene McCarthy. On the Democratic side Clinton is probably the winner. He came in second but did better than he was expected to, and that's the only thing that matters.

FEBRUARY 19: Now, would I ever have gone to see Joan Collins in *Private Lives* if Billy hadn't gotten tickets? Well, no. But he thought it would be fun, and it was. We had dinner beforehand and then went off to the Broadhurst expecting high camp—but we found middle camp, by which I mean she really wasn't too bad . . . she was good at the shoving matches and phonograph-record-breaking in the middle of the play. Higher comedy eludes her, but it's not as if she didn't read the lines with a certain intelligence, and it's not as if she *forgot* any of them.

FEBRUARY 24: Had lunch at the Century Club with Mary's old friend Nicholas King. He talks in a continuous murmur, and one only catches a third of it, but he doesn't seem to expect any more than that from you, so it's relaxing enough. He'd just returned from New Hampshire, where he'd been shepherding a lot of foreign reporters around. . . .

No place makes one feel younger than the Century—all that WASP decrepitude (even Nicholas is related to Edith Wharton) . . . Even beautiful John Lindsay—how frail he looks! The face is still wonderful, but he's terribly thin and aged by sickness. Arthur Schlesinger went up to him down near the coat check and told him how good it was to have him back . . .

FEBRUARY 26: During the afternoon [I went over] Ed Allen's piece with Deidre [a copyeditor] and nearly screamed. She suggests twenty changes per page, nineteen of them pointless and none of her business. She means well, but she hasn't anything close to a realistic conception of her own job. It's not as if she's arrogant; I can tell, in fact, that she's nervous as can be while going over the stuff with me. And beyond telling her to use a lighter hand I find myself as incapable of scolding her as she does of staying her zealous little pencil. So I just sit there, trying to think of a hundredth new way to say, "I see what you mean, but maybe we'll just leave it."

FEBRUARY 28: One always knows whether Art is in or not. It doesn't matter whether or not you've seen him or heard of his whereabouts—you can always just sense his presence or absence, the way I can always feel what the weather must be like outside, even though my office doesn't have a window.

FEBRUARY 29: Walked from Billy's to Tiffany this morning to buy our 70th-birthday present for Louise: a painted bowl. Looked at the Venetian glass and felt peaceful while they wrapped it.

MARCH 1: Worked on the Sundance essay and went downtown at 9:00 to see Alison West's dance company perform at the Merce Cunningham Studio. Billy & I arrived late and had to sit on radiator covers—poor Billy's sciatica is giving him trouble, too. The performance was strange but engaging—sort of a combination of *Antigone* and *Beach Blanket Bingo*. The Viscusis were there, and so were Jim West and his new wife, Barbara, who is very pretty and who I'm sure was wearing Mary's old fur coat.

MARCH 5: Went up to Dr. Slaff late in the afternoon—I was considerably more calm than a couple of Saturdays ago. We talked more about anti-sexuality. I don't know if this [therapy] is getting me anywhere, but at least, now that I've been at Condé Nast for a year, some of it is covered.

MARCH 6: Holly Stevens [Wallace Stevens's daughter] is dead. I only met her a couple of times, once at Vassar and once at Beverly's party in New York. (Billy, who remembers everything we do together, remembers her from that night with perfect clarity.) She was supposedly brilliant, obviously excessive and very difficult; she embraced the worst possible fate a large person like herself could have—tending the memory of someone even larger.

MARCH 7: . . . Went up to Columbus Circle and finally saw . . . *JFK* with Chris Bull . . . There's barely a factual or honest moment in it. It's also cowardly. It's not afraid to smear anyone dead, from Earl Warren on down, but, no doubt fearing a lawsuit, it decides to call the still-living Ruth Paine (who was the poor Mrs. Surratt of the affair) "Janet Williams."

Billy wouldn't go. The thought of three hours of politics combined with Kevin Costner.

MARCH 10: Clinton, after today's primaries, is "inevitable."

MARCH 11: Took a cab early this morning to the office of the preposterous Carleton Varney at Dorothy Draper on E. 56th St. He was late for his appointment, having failed to walk the block from his Trump Tower apartment in time. Once settled, he responded

to my questions for the *Architectural Digest* article with the familiar self-aggrandizement the genre inspires. He's a blowhard on the
order of Tom Britt and he can't stop talking about bygone New
York glamour ("I saw the last of the best") and celebrity clients like
Joan Crawford. The thought of him waddling from room to room
in her antiseptic wake is a vivid one.

On top of this I had to have lunch with Jeffrey Simpson at
Oscar's. Each time I see him he's more unpleasant than the last.
The truth is that he's jealous of my books, and of my having Billy,
and he can't stop making little digs about the easy money Michael
Wollaeger is providing me with, and other stuff like that. He's very
intelligent in many ways, but self-deluded in a very standardized
one. Like many lonely and plain men his age (gay ones, anyway),
he is certain that all sorts of people, women and men, from Paige
Rense to Robert Metzger, are in love with him.

MARCH 12: Talked to Ward Just in Paris. He called to offer me
another essay besides the one he's going to try to do from Bucha-
rest. He leaves for eastern Europe tomorrow . . . He's entirely
pleasant to work with and has a great big laugh.

MARCH 13: It's poor, scared-eyed Seán's 11th birthday and God
only knows how [my nephew] survives all the shouting and tension in that house . . . I got him a test-pilot video and sent him
twenty bucks and a newspaper summary of the day he was born.
Poor little guy.

MARCH 16: Al Rubenstein, the production chief at the magazine,
is an odd duck. He dresses very conservatively but has a long gray
ponytail. His work life is one long Maalox moment, and he has
the disgusted expression to prove it . . . and is unafraid of pushing
anybody around.

Today he tried it with me, even though I have a reputation—
with him included—for being cooperative, turning materials
around quickly, meeting deadlines and coping with little crises . . .
Despite all this he barked at me over some simple computer mis-
understanding. That I would not have minded, except that he did
it in front of Alex and Adam in the art department. It left me angry

all day, but all I did was bitch about it to Maura, who's beleaguered herself and who tells me getting barked at by Al is part of the job.

But I let it gnaw at me all day and into the evening. . . .

MARCH 17: After the meeting I was still stewing, so I sat down and sent Al a firm but friendly piece of electronic mail. An hour later he came in and apologized and that—I think—is that.

I was left free to concentrate on the sounds of glockenspiels and pipes floating 17 floors up and through the window as the all-heterosexual (yeah, sure) St. Patrick's Day parade went on a block away. Paul and Lucy went out to Yamaguchi for lunch and said even it was trashed—you needed hip boots to negotiate the broken glass.

. . .

Tom McGuane has selected my rodeo piece for the next *Best American Sports Writing* collection from Houghton Mifflin. I feel like an idiot savant.

MARCH 18: [At the NBCC Awards] I found myself spending a lot of time listening to pitches by publicists and authors hoping to sell their wares to *GQ*: a new wrinkle in my literary life.

Philip Roth made a dignified acceptance speech, even though Carlin Romano, who once trashed him, was sitting on the dais a few feet away. Jane Smiley is an appealing person, but in many ways forever a Vassar undergraduate; she made an incoherent set of remarks about how Iowa was starting to resemble El Salvador. And Susan Faludi, in her tight groupie's dress, thanked the NBCC for "rocking the boat" by nominating a dangerous book like hers.

MARCH 22: Took a walk around Greenwood Village with Mom this morning . . . Sometimes the up-to-the-minute TV expressions she comes out with make me laugh. While complaining about one nosy neighbor, she told me: "I wanted to tell her, 'Get a life.'"

MARCH 23: A week ago today I was worrying about whether I'd have the gumption to call Al Rubenstein on the way he barked at me in the Art department; tonight I'm wondering how I'll rear-range my schedule on Wednesday so I can be at his funeral service.

He was killed last night by a hit-and-run driver at the corner of West End and 96th. The police have a license number but so far no driver. Al, whose whole life was devoted to the meticulous business of hyphenating and justifying margins and getting rid of widows, had to die in this ghastly, *sloppy* way . . . The weather last night was bad and snowy, and the streets were a mess. A plane crashed taking off at LaGuardia, and a lot of people died in the freezing water just past the runway.

He was an odd, skilled, eccentric man. I'm glad we made up our little quarrel as promptly as we did. (The last time I saw him was in the elevator on Friday, and we shared a laugh.)

MARCH 25: Everybody at the magazine went out to Al's funeral in Woodbury. We took two chartered buses at 11:30 . . . A very grim affair. The rabbi gave an angry speech about the murder, which is, after all, what it is. (Art has sent a letter to Dinkins and Lee Brown saying that he and Si Newhouse will be watching to see how aggressive the police investigation is and that CNP expects to publish something on it.) . . . Al had three beautiful sisters, younger ones, who described him as a wonderful protective older brother, a confidant—about the last role I can see him in but there you go . . .

There's something a bit unseemly about the way the higher-ups are mourning. (I'm glad I missed the boozy Monday lunch at P.J. Clarke's—there's nobody for whom it could have been less appropriate.) The people who actually knew Al best at the magazine—the women in the Copy Dept., all the people in the Art Dept.—are more or less left out . . .

Tonight Billy and I had supper in Times Square and went from that to *The Will Rogers Follies*   the chorus boys collecting for AIDS as you exited the theatre.

MARCH 26: The Japanese are coming to *GQ* in two weeks—a whole bunch of them who will be putting out their edition of the magazine. They're supposed to hover over us for two weeks and see what we do. The comic potential for all this is huge (they're bringing their own translators), and CNP ran an etiquette session for some of the brass today. Art told some of us about it over drinks this afternoon. (The first thing he should do is put away those *Victory at Sea* videotapes sitting near his office VCR.)

MARCH 30: Billy and I watched every bit of the Oscars, lying on top of the comforter. *Silence of the Lambs* won most of it, more or less shutting out *JFK*, thank goodness. Billy Crystal got big laughs when he sang about "Three Shots in the Plaza" to the tune of "Three Coins in the Fountain," proving that Stone has sped up the process of history to the extent that the assassination— far from being the open wound he claims it is—is now "only a movie"—i.e., unreal, a matter for jokey historical reference on the order of "Aside from that, Mrs. Lincoln, how did you like the play?" I wonder if Jackie Onassis was watching the awards in her apartment across town.

APRIL 1: At 6:15 we made our way to 251 E. 51st for our interview with the co-op board. We were dressed up like little diplomats and were ushered into the meeting room by a man who seemed obviously and reassuringly gay. In fact, far from having any apparent prejudice against a gay male couple, the board seemed anxious to confirm that we were indeed a couple, and that this didn't represent just an investment opportunity for the one who wouldn't be residing [full-time] in the apartment—that is, me.

APRIL 5: Brought the printed-out manuscript [of *Rockets and Rodeos*] to Billy . . . what counts is the dedication, and it could only be to [him]. For the first time in my life, as I made all these trips, I had someone to come home to.

APRIL 6: [Fran] told me that Giovanni Forti died last week. I can remember, five years ago, his extremely beautiful naked body lying under mine.

APRIL 7: The Japanese came to the Tuesday morning meeting, filling Art's office to capacity. The lineup sheets were translated with a sort of comic pointlessness. One encouraging thing: the Japanese seem no more organized than we do.

James Lord came over to Billy's for drinks and we went down to Dish of Salt for a very funny dinner. James will say anything that comes into his head, like a child. Tomorrow he goes over his memoirs with Roger Straus and Jonathan Galassi, and he told us about them as we ate. He says Peggy [Rosamond] Bernier's recollections of Picasso and everyone else are "absolute bullshit," and that when she and [her husband] divorced, she "carried on on two continents." But he thinks he's been a little nastier in the book than he should, so he may tone things down . . . James had his own affair with Stephen Spender, but more than the basic fact I did not learn . . . There are of course plenty of similarities between James and Mr. Gene, and Billy + I wondered what it would be like to get the two of them together over dinner. We decided they'd hate each other. . . .

APRIL 8: Went down to Ticknor to deliver my manuscript to John. A sunny morning, and Union Square was pleasantly alive with the Farmers' Market. John did a well-mannered job of feigning enthusiasm over *Rockets and Rodeos*.

APRIL 9: I could tell that Art disapproved of the loafers I had on, but I nonetheless accompanied him and Paul to the Four Seasons for lunch with Jim Brady . . . a peculiar combination of self-promotion and candor. He'll drop names faster than Art, but he'll also refer to things like "the time I was editing *Harper's Bazaar* and running it into the ground." Paul and I were really along to function as undersized Ed McMahons. . . .

APRIL 13: [Introducing two poets at the 92nd St. Y] Šalamun is rather nervous and donnish, not what I expected, and Charlie Simic was his hearty self: he was hobbling a bit with an old basketball injury that was kicking up. He was a crowd pleaser. Those funny, spare imagist poems—he seems as if he should be writing big overstuffed Rabelaisian pages instead, but what he does works wonderfully.

. . . Talked to Francine Prose . . . Her new novel has been

swatted down by Michiko Kakutani, and she has that awful defensive look, as if she's expecting everyone who approaches her to bring it up.

APRIL 14: Tonight was my night to help entertain the Japanese. Mims Walbridge and I sat on different sides of Mr. Shimanaka, the Si Newhouse of the operation, over dinner at La Reserve. His English is excellent, but conversation was still a strain. We talked about the depressed state of American publishing, and he told me it's really the fault of the American educational system—i.e., people who can't read don't want to buy books.

APRIL 17: Spent the morning in the office; Art showed me his letter to Jackie Onassis. It's a follow-up to a phone conversation they had—he's proposing lunch, but I think she's putting him off. Lorraine is much amused by what she overhears.

APRIL 18: Mom arrived at 2:00, and Billy and I took her to the Judy Garland exhibit at Lincoln Center . . . I can recall seeing Mom cry only twice while I was growing up—once when a lost wedding photograph of her parents turned up, and once when the TV broadcast a tribute to Judy Garland, shortly after her death.

. . . Realized again what a better, more attentive son Billy has made me.

APRIL 19: After an hour of reading the Archibald MacLeish biography (as awful as he probably was), I went off to the Parker Meridien to meet E. Howard Hunt for dinner. He is in town to tape a 20th-anniversary Watergate program for CBS, and he called a few days ago to let me know he'd be here. We went over to Cafe 57, and I can tell you that it was a really odd evening. In many ways he is charming and even touching—he wants to talk about Brown and books and something other than his notoriety. But he also likes to keep coming back to his notoriety—he will allude to episodes with women or adventure abroad that have a fantasist's feel to them. He seems to have been forever where anything was happening—aboard a nearby ship when Roosevelt and Churchill met on the Atlantic . . . in India at the time Galbraith ruled the embassy; with Averell Harriman in postwar Paris. Some of it is true, of course; bits, I suspect, are too good to be . . . For all his skill at survival, his intact emergence from prison, he remains, I think, essentially tragic—someone relegated to the raffish fringes of history, a man who wished to be consequential but couldn't stop himself from being bizarre.

APRIL 23: A phone call from Mary Evans informing me that John Herman is not going to publish *Rockets and Rodeos*.

The nakedness of what he's doing is beyond belief. He will not say a word against the book to either her or me. He admits it's a fine book. (He could hardly say otherwise, since he's seen most of the pieces one by one and has sent me enthusiastic notes about them—some of them ending "Onward!") He just says he always had doubts about the book, from the moment he learned Cork signed it up . . . He says he doesn't think he can make a commercial success of it, and so has "an obligation to the company" not to publish it. I asked him if he thought he might have an obligation to me, too.

The conversation was nauseating. I recognized those phony, emollient tones from my Harvard days, when those pompous creeps would say no to you about something and expect you to thank them for doing what, they assured you, was really in your best longterm interest. They would remain maddeningly calm, hoping you would lose your temper so they could accuse you of "immaturity," that worst of all sins.

I remained very calm. I told him that this was shabby on every level—professional and personal. I also told him that it raised real legal questions (I mentioned all those notes from him), and when I did I could sense him backing off.

He asked me if I hadn't done these pieces as a "working journalist"—in other words, wasn't their publication as a book incidental? I told him he ought to read his author's file. It's obvious that 11 of the 12 pieces were undertaken because of the book proposal: I sought the commissions so I could get the next chapter. I told him that if I'm a "working journalist" I must be a pretty bad one, since, to take one example, the rodeo piece must have cost me about $800 to write, for a return of $200 from *The Yale*

Review and—oh, yes—another $250 from John's parent company, Houghton Mifflin, for allowing the essay to be included in *The Best American Sports Writing 1992.*

John is swinging wildly. I think he's probably on the verge of losing his job and he's dropping inventory the way an airline pilot in trouble jettisons fuel . . .

APRIL 24: Down to Mary [Evans] this morning . . . While I was there, John called. Mary took the call in the back room, and when it was over she told me he'd reversed himself.

APRIL 25: . . . Billy's birthday celebration. He and Carol arrived at 7:30, and after drinks here we went up to Petaluma at 1st + 73rd . . . From there to the Carlyle for the late show (the last of her engagement) by our beloved Dixie Carter, who was wonderful and nervy, putting long comic monologues and trumpet playing into her already varied show. We held hands under the table when she sang "This Moment." . . . There was a festive, congratulatory air about closing night. Cybill Shepherd was out in the lobby; Hal Holbrook and Dixie's daddy were in the audience; Barbara Carroll came over from Bemelmans when Dixie was done, as did Sylvia Syms. John Wallowitch was at the back.

APRIL 30: Los Angeles is burning, just as in 1965. The jury in the Rodney King trial has, unbelievably enough, acquitted the white cops who beat a black motorist to a pulp—all of it visible on videotape to the whole country: 56 baton blows in 81 nauseating seconds.

MAY 1: Something close to panic swept across the city this afternoon. By 3:00 it felt, absurdly enough, the way the Cuban missile crisis did thirty years ago. I could feel the start of it a couple of hours earlier, when I went down to Chelsea. Mary [Evans] had the radio on and there were rumors of trouble in Brooklyn. And back out on W. 21st St., on my way back to the magazine, I could swear people were looking at one another in a funny way. (Paul and Lucy told me they felt the same thing while out for lunch in midtown.)

. . .

At 2:30 Condé Nast announced that it was closing, and most people cleared out fast. I hung around a little in Art's office with Marty and David Granger. Then Amy called Art from downstairs at *Mademoiselle* and told him they were smashing windows at Saks.

I left at around 3:30, and it was worse than the usual rush hour. There were long lines at the bus stop across Madison, and people were pouring into the Terminal. I got home and put the TV on, and then I learned that *absolutely nothing was going on*. The only thing running riot was rumor . . .

MAY 2: Out doing errands this afternoon Billy and I noticed the same thing: people were being unusually polite and friendly toward one another. Part of it was the sudden summer weather, but more of it was a feeling of relief—a sense that we'd all had a tremendous scare but somehow been spared the whirlwind, and maybe if we behaved better from now on the city would be a better place, liveable.

Mostly, though, I feel awful . . . this is all far more hopeless than what happened 25 years ago. Then it took place against the legislative revolution, and however frightened by the riots people were, many of them thought: well, the country is being remade into something more just, and perhaps it's going to be a more painful, convulsive process than we thought. There was a feeling that the country would eventually come out the other side. But nobody feels that now.

MAY 18: What a day to have to go to a publishing party co-sponsored by Houghton Mifflin. The other sponsor was *GQ*, since we'd run some of the book being celebrated (Dan Wakefield's *New York in the Fifties*). It was down at the Village Gate for nostalgia's sake, and all these old crocks like Bruce Jay Friedman & Ed Sorel were walking around. Wakefield, who seems genuinely grateful to Art, made an awkward, touching speech. Mort [Janklow] & Lynn [Nesbit] (Greed & Greed, as Swifty Lazar calls them) were there, the latter with Mia Farrow in a little *jeune-fille* sailor dress that I suppose she'd borrowed from one of her 35 children. Janet Malcolm was walking around, everyone wondering if she were Joan

Didion. I spent most of my time with Freda, getting very drunk on white wine and flirting crazily with her friend Keith Raffan, a wet Tory former MP. . . .

MAY 19: Alan Dershowitz is suing us for $100,000,000, which I know pleases Art, since it will keep us on Page Six of the *Post* for several days.

MAY 20: Norton will only make an offer for *Our American Cousins*, not for "the book of essays," as everyone now refers to it . . . Fran thinks I should just forget about the essays, flush them, because it's important to get out of T&F—at all costs . . .

When they (not Mary) look at *Rockets and Rodeos*, they see a complicating factor in a deal. I see myself in the bleachers at Cape Canaveral at 3 a.m. . . . falling asleep in the Poker Flat Block-house; waiting for Taps at sunrise at the Punchbowl cemetery. I wrapped a lot of the last 3 years around that book, and I have been jerked around like nobody's business for the last month. None of it's worth it. Writing is fine; publishing is awful.

MAY 22: We ended the evening watching Johnny Carson's last show . . . Carson is supposed to be aloof, cold, even cruel, and— what the media always mention with disgusted admiration— "private." All I know is I'm grateful to him for sending me off to sleep with a laugh ever since I was in the 6th grade.

MAY 24: . . . Finished McInerney's book. He tries to make the '87 crash a more resonant event than it was, and since he's got to put in AIDS without putting in gay people, he kills off the junkie nov-elist who's an isotope of himself.

MAY 26: Billy's count has dropped back to 260, about what it was before he switched to DDI last September. This is about what he was expecting. Dr. Jeff is not alarmed, but he will probably start testing every month or two instead of every 4. All other blood signs are good—"you could be drafted," he tells Billy.

MAY 27: You know, one definition of a bad-faith offer is an offer you know the intended recipient can't accept; and that's the kind of offer Norton made. So Mary and I turned them down this afternoon . . . How I'm going to manage my return to John is something I can't bring myself to think about right now.

. . . Fortunately things are slow at work; I even won a lot of points with Art by coming up with a title for one of Lisa's pieces ("Magna Cum Fraud") this afternoon. And Madison Bell has calmed down and already done his rewrites.

MAY 28: To Sutton Place to a party at Art Cooper's . . . I get my biggest ego boosts from Art these days. He brought me over to Si Newhouse himself tonight so he could say, "Si, this is one of the best hires I ever made." Art, you're all right.

MAY 29: Billy and I and Greg . . . went out for a drink at the ultra-chic Paramount Hotel bar tonight and had a surprisingly good time sitting and laughing and looking at these dozens of oddly dressed people from the fringes of the music business. The mirrored men's room is like one's idea of Mae West's bedroom. Billy + I got in a cab for home before midnight as Greg went off to hunt and gather.

MAY 30: Talked to Mom (she won't vote for Perot because he doesn't want gays in his cabinet) . . .

MAY 31: Went down to Alison's at 7:00: that peculiar neighborhood at Lexington & 29th—the mix of almost–Murray Hill townhouses; Indian restaurants; nearby prostitute hotels. We went out for Chinese food (I accommodatingly ate bean curd) on 3rd Avenue, and she told me about the manuscript of her sculpture book . . . She says that up in Castine Jim and Barbara are filling the house with things they buy from catalogues, things they have no use for and leave in their unopened boxes beneath the stairs. It's some symptom of old age, apparently—an elaborate, mail-order form of string-saving mania. Jim is only able to practice it now that he finally has credit cards, which Mary, in her Ludditism, used to forbid.

JUNE 3: Art is baching it for a few days, and I was left to drink with him alone from 7:30 until 9:00, when he could go off for his dinner. Not an appealing prospect, since Si is currently on his back about our low newsstand numbers. (The Seinfeld issue was, unaccountably, a disaster.)

JUNE 5: Feeling just awful. All the accumulated anger of the last weeks [about having to stay at Houghton Mifflin] has oozed toward the front of my head, the feelings of suspense having vacated the premises . . . I stopped up at the magazine, sopping wet, and found that Maura had put somebody in my office to take a copy-editing test. "Can I help you?" he asked. I went off to the bathroom and closed my eyes and gripped the sink and thought that, after six weeks, this is going to be the silly thing that makes me truly lose it, just dissolve in rage and tears.

JUNE 8: John Herman called this afternoon, after he'd talked to Mary. I think he was nicer to her than he was to me. He told her he'd be publishing *R+R* with vigor, though he had to remind me he thought it was still a mistake—for my career and his. It's pretty tacky for him to bring up the latter, but he did. He thinks it will hurt me because it will only sell a little and that will keep initial orders for the Rathbone novel down. He's probably right, but if every author has to base his career on marketing factors, then he won't write half his books.

JUNE 9: A publication party for Anna Shapiro at M. G. Lord's apartment near the Strand . . . Katha Pollitt was there, too, struggling between her roles as amiable person and feminist policewoman for *The Nation*. She asked if it was true that Art Cooper took "the entire senior editorial staff of *GQ*" to a topless bar. I told her it was not, so perhaps she'll sleep tonight.

JUNE 10: Lunch at the Algonquin with Jim Atlas. Talked about the piece he's doing for me (25th anniversary of *Couples, Portnoy* and *Myra Breckinridge*) and traded war stories. I told him about James Gordon Bennett's having the nerve to submit a story to me [after his review of *Aurora* 7], and he told me how not long ago Sven

Birkerts tried to chat him up at a party—6 years after his famous slaughter of *The Great Pretender* in *The New Republic*.

JUNE 11: John Herman called me today for advice about how Bob Stone should handle the plagiarism accusation that's been made against him, and Carol Smith called practically to demand a profile of Charlie Baxter ("our conscience") in *GQ*. Neither one of them seems to have considered that I might not be in a mood to do favors for Ticknor & Norton.

. . .

Billy and I ate in the little place a block down from the apartment. He told Irwin today that he's HIV+. Irwin was predictably wonderful, said his only concern was Billy's welfare, not the company's. He will make whatever arrangements Billy needs should his health get shaky . . . Billy seems relieved. We know that for all we face we have many blessings. Irwin Shama is not the least of them.

JUNE 12: On Thursday, at the library, a man approached the main desk in the catalog room and asked a librarian: "Do you have books on torture?" The librarian, hoping the man was doing political research, asked him: "Related to any particular place?" The man, expressing polite indifference, shrugged and said, "Europe?"

JUNE 15: I'm eager to get back to [my novel] and feel blessed to be able to read about Lincoln, Douglas, Breckinridge and Bell instead of Bush, Clinton and Perot.

JUNE 17: Lunch with Keith Raffan, Freda's ex-M.P. friend. Yes, that one. He had wanted to make a dinner date when I called him back last week, but I proposed lunch instead. "Safer," he joked. And it was. We went to Cafe Un Deux Trois and had a funny lunch (talked a lot about the royal-family crisis) that was only vaguely flirtatious.

. . .

Speaking of old crushes—I had a postcard today from my first great one-sided love, Eddie Haugevik, behind whom, in the ninth grade, I trotted like a desperate terrier. There's an exhibit

of his sculpture in Bridgehampton, and he sent me the announcement ... After 27 years my heart still pounded a little at the sight
of that left-leaning handwriting!

JUNE 18: The Paul Monette publishing party down at Wendy
Weil's was cancelled: he's sick.

JUNE 22: John Herman and I had our unbelievably uncomfortable
burying-the-hatchet lunch at La Galette on E. 22nd St. . . . When
we got out onto the street afterwards, we were reduced to talking
about the weather. He does seem genuinely enthusiastic about the
Rathbone book's potential—he said that T&F will be "pulling out
all the stops" for it, and that's a phrase I've never heard uttered on
my behalf in the dozen years I've been associated with them.

JUNE 23: ... Maura and I had a wonderful hour and a half
together in the afternoon; we banged into shape the tricky tenses
of Ward Just's Paris piece, and went about the business of burnish-
ing and plucking whatever needed to be burnished or plucked. I
don't know when I've had such a lovely time in front of the computer screen. Maura has a good, sensible ear and we worked well
together. Ward Just's prose is awfully good, plain stuff to begin
with, and we made the piece better . . . How fine not to walk away
from an afternoon's work with that empty feeling I used to have
after I'd finished grading a stack of student papers.

JUNE 30: Not since Pearl Harbor. Not again until the Second
Coming. The reaction at Condé Nast—the frenzy of gossip and
speculation, the paralysis of all else—to the firing of Bob Gottlieb from *The New Yorker* and his replacement with Tina Brown.
(Graydon Carter is taking over *Vanity Fair*.) The news broke just
after the 9:30 meeting ... The midtown phone lines must have
gotten tied up the way they did the afternoon of Kennedy's assassination. I talked to Fran (who told a *Newsday* reporter that it was
"appalling and unspeakable"); to Eric Simonoff (who thought it
was a joke); to Ward Just—who, while priding himself on being
out of the loop, could speak of nothing else. Art was exhilarated
to the point of dizziness by it all, and he came back from The

Four Seasons with a fresh batch of rumors: [Steve] Florio would be replaced by Ron Galotti; Elizabeth Drew would make way for Gail Sheehy.

. . . Maybe it's better to have glitz than simply to have [*The New Yorker*] die—that's what will probably happen without big changes . . . The rumor is that it loses Si $10 million a year. The people who make a fetish out of the magazine—and would sooner kill their firstborn than see a photograph in it—are growing older. In any event, one can bet that Tina Brown didn't ask for the job just to tinker. She'll be racing off to 43rd St. in her hot pink raincoat (I'll miss the sight of her dashing for her car on Madison), and she will be determined to do Great Things.

Billy and I went up to our first home on 72nd St. for dinner with Dick and Dennis [from whom Bill sublet] tonight. Dennis looks very good, Dick not so hot. Before we sat down to eat, an old lawyer friend of Dick's came over (they used to hang out at Julius' in the summer of 1965) so that Billy and I could be witnesses to Dick's will. We performed the task with civilized smiles and nonchalance.

JULY 2: The company closed for the holiday at 1:00 and I went home to get ready for [author photographer] Jerry Bauer. He's heavy and sweaty and *very* nervous: he made me a little crazy, in fact. But he travels light—no umbrellas and cables and dollies. Just a couple of Leicas. We did the whole shoot in two or three office-building colonnades along Second Avenue. He's got a bit of the 60s fashion photographer in him ("Now turn around. Take one step forward. Yes! That's great!"), and a bit of the mortician, too. He keeps telling you how he can airbrush out your wrinkles and your unruly hair. We had tea afterwards and he showed me a portfolio of his work—everybody from Henry Miller to Muriel Spark. "Would you believe she was 70 years old when I took that?"

JULY 8: I've got most of my boards for the September issue ready to ship, so I will be able to take the next week off.

JULY 9: Finished up at the magazine. (Just before I went, Art told me he wants "three knockout literary-essay ideas" from me at the

August "retreat" in Connecticut. Was there a hint of what-have-you-done-for-me-lately in this? Or just his endless quest for the bigger, better, flashier?)

. . .

Clinton has picked Gore for Vice-President. It would be a better ticket if it were reversed.

JULY 14: [In Albany for research on *Henry and Clara*] Norman Rice is a sweet, skinny old fellow . . . We had lunch in a dining room under the great brutal plaza that Rockefeller dropped onto the city, complete with flying-saucer theatre, a quarter century ago. And then we were off to Loudonville, over what used to be a plank road, to look at the old Harris country house and survey the Rathbone + Harris plots in the Albany Rural Cemetery . . . standing under the oaks and pines at the spot where J. Howard Rathbone was buried just two weeks before Lincoln was shot. I realized that the bones of almost everyone in my story were right here—even the skeletons of Thurlow Weed and Chester Arthur. Everybody was here, that is, except Henry and Clara: their bodies stayed in Germany & were pulverized by allied bombers 100 years after my book opens. Somehow their absence from these pretty grounds on this hot summer day made me aware of their tragedy, made me actually feel it, as I hadn't done before. It was a jolt I needed.

JULY 15: Billy came over after dinner and we watched Mario nominate Clinton. Norman Rice says that Matilda [Cuomo] is a nice woman. He's worked with her on the mansion. Says the Carey kids were awful—always coming to the Institute to borrow paintings they knew nothing about. He remembers the fire at the mansion in the early 60s. The first Mrs. Rockefeller was still around. She + Nelson had separate quarters in the house, and the governor didn't smoke; but when it was all over somebody noticed cigarette butts in the ashtray in his bedroom.

JULY 16: [Clinton] gave a very long acceptance speech tonight (he just never learns) after a video and speech by Al Gore that were both incredibly mawkish and effective. (If Reagan had used them the media would only have said mawkish, but since these are Democrats they're only saying effective.)

JULY 17: John [Herman], by the way, asked if I wouldn't mind changing the title. The marketers (always mentioned in the awe-struck tone one might reserve for the college of cardinals) prefer *American Spectacles*. That sounds more like a subtitle to me, and I've gotten quite fond of *R+R*, so I politely said no, and he politely said okay. "It's your book," he said. And it almost wasn't, thanks to him.

JULY 22: Liz Darhansoff's assistant, Leigh Feldman, sent over a story—a terrifically written story—by a guy named Dan Lyons. Alas, it contains a graphic rape scene that made me uncomfort-able, afraid some readers might take it the "wrong way." I asked Lucy [Kaylin] to read the piece and she had the same reaction—great writing, but some questionable angles to the presentation. We talked about this in her office until 6:30, and I finally decided I wouldn't buy it. But only after worrying that I was a p.c. victim.

And yet that's why I went to Lucy, who's smart, hip, right-thinking without being p.c. Our discussion was the most interest-ing I've had since I got to the magazine (and God knows more stimulating than what passed for serious literary discussion at Vas-sar). Not the least useful thing we realized was that this Lyons story would probably not be objectionable in *Paris Review* (George Plimpton & Jamie Linville have been sitting on it for 6 mos.). But in *GQ* it would be 5 pages from one of our beach-romp fashion spreads and some wiseassed article about sex in cars. These stories are not hermetically sealed; context counts. So I'm going to let Jamie have it.

JULY 23: Art had a 5:00 wine party in his office for Graydon Carter, who's just taken over *Vanity Fair*. G.C. is plump, leonine, Anglo-philic. Likes to say "fuck" in a clubby way. Art in his usual awe at the sight of a Player. Lots of jokes about all the enemies [Gray-don] made at *Spy*. Hey, it's not his fault if one of his employees saw Abe Rosenthal checking out of the video store with *Kinky Couples*.

JULY 24: Spent an unproductive afternoon at the NYPL (the dumbwaiters bringing books up to the Reading Room weren't working) . . .

JULY 27: Fran K. called this morning to say that while she thinks there is some beautiful writing in the first part of [*Henry and Clara*], she thinks there is one big problem. The story starts too slowly, and Pauline and Ira are not sufficiently interesting to get it going. Ask yourself, she told me: why is a reader supposed to be interested in Henry + Clara? And in a flash I knew what she knew, too, and what I should have known long ago: the book has to *begin* with Lincoln's assassination & the mystery of how Henry behaved in the box . . . She also told me that Alice Adams was out in Sag Harbor over the weekend. She read the Falcon Crest chapter of *Stolen Words* and liked it, though she says I was much too nice to Anita Clay Kornfeld, whom she knows and considers a witch. Well!

JULY 28: Put [my essay on Sinclair Lewis] into the magazine's computer before Michael Barone stopped by . . . the big scoop I got over lunch outdoors at Trattoria is that the Gore girls don't like Chelsea Clinton. The Gore girls are babe material and poor Chelsea has a mouthful of braces and looks terribly serious, but it turns out that during the convention the Gore girls kept asking very nobly what they could do to be of use whereas Chelsea, bless her heart, just wanted to shop.

JULY 29: Lunch with Linda Healey over at Billy's (the steakhouse, not my darling's) on First Avenue. She touted her upcoming wares from Pantheon and we gossiped about what Bob Gottlieb's payoff from Si is rumored to be . . . She says she would like to be editing more fiction than she is (when she was at FS&G, she says, Jonathan Galassi sort of hogged it), so maybe some day I could finally leave John and write for her. Pantheon seems a bit implausibly left-wing to be my publisher, but who knows? Linda is funny and smart (everyone always talks about what a fizzy lift she is from her dour husband, Tony Lukas) . . .

AUGUST 6: My inventory of fiction at the magazine is running very low, and the stuff that's been coming in is just awful. So I'm trying to shake some trees; called Neil Olson and Binky Urban, and it sounds as if she may have some stuff around Labor Day. This is a business like any other: slow seasons and supply problems.

AUGUST 11: . . . I do love my *GQ* perks. I came away from the office with a great new pair of Nike cross-training shoes today.

AUGUST 12: [The magazine's annual editorial retreat in Connecticut] Dinner was about 45 minutes away at the Hopkins Inn in, I think, New Preston. We ate outdoors, and I had a big tasty trout. Bottle after bottle of wine. Then it was time for our cover-subject discussion, which, to my amazement, revolved almost completely, for two hours, around my longshot I-thought-almost-not-worth-mentioning idea: scrap Christian Laettner for November and put Clinton and Gore on the cover instead. I was amazed at the enthusiasm for this: almost the whole discussion was about *how* to do it. After a nightcap discussion with Marty, Granger, Lucy and a few others, I went up to bed a hero!

AUGUST 13: Art's first choice for the Clinton cover story is Gore Vidal. It's highly unlikely that we'll get him (I've tried him for something else before) . . .

AUGUST 14: So far Gore has not said no. His agent, Owen Laster, called him in Italy and called me back and says there's a 50-50 chance he'll do it. Laster says he's "amazed" it got this far, since G.V. likes to write about politics only for non-general-interest magazines. The money ($10,000 for 3,000 wds.), the deadline (Sept. 11) and the approach (anything other than riding his Jerry Brown–like hobbyhorses) are all fine. He's apparently just doubtful about being able to write a piece that doesn't depend on their winning or losing. (We'll be on the stands two weeks before the election, and still on for two weeks after it.)

AUGUST 15: Chris Bull was burned out of his apartment on Avenue B by drug dealers the other night (Wednesday). He was awakened by the smell of smoke and had to rouse his sleeping roommate. They got out by the fire escape. The smoke ruined his computer. His books and clothes were drenched with it. He's moved to his uncle's old place in the West Village for the time being . . . Tonight Billy and I took him over to the Ballroom to see Lypsinka and have a few laughs. After that we went to Rumbul's, the little coffee-and-dessert place . . . where Fred works. Fred buried his head in Chris' shirt, sniffing for smoke, supposedly, but he really just wanted to nuzzle him.

AUGUST 17: We watched Buchanan deliver an over-the-top speech to the Republican convention, which is looking like a real hatefest. It's typical of Bush's weakness and his pathetic desire to be loved by the extreme right: he beats Buchanan in 33 out of 33 primaries, but then he lets Buchanan's people write the platform . . . I thought the election was supposed to be about foreign policy and economics, and it's turning out that the Republicans want to run on all this nauseating family-values stuff.

AUGUST 18: Very depressed over the convention, but elated over Gore Vidal's agreeing to do a piece on the election . . . Art is over the moon, and Marty took me to 44 to celebrate (Bianca Jagger, looking frowsy and slack-bodied, was at the bar.)

Everyone in New York is talking about Woody Allen (at least it's pushing Houston off the front pages). Things were no different at the dinner party I went to at Phyllis Rose's and Laurent de Brunhoff's on E. 82nd St. . . . Vivian Gornick, who wrote that book about her Communist parents, was at the end of the table.

AUGUST 19: It turns out that one of the "details" Owen wanted to work out was the difference between the $10,000 we were offering Vidal and the $25,000 they were asking. We split the difference at $17,500—exactly what [Dad] paid for the house in Stewart Manor in 1958 . . . Si Newhouse himself is delighted, according to Art . . .

. . .

. . . We watched Mary Fisher give a very well written and moving speech on AIDS to those hyenas in the Astrodome . . .

This woman, who looked Republican from head to toe (her red AIDS ribbon was really a piece of jewelry) and who worked for Gerry Ford (a braver President than George Bush in many ways) did a lot of good tonight.

AUGUST 20: I called Vidal in Italy this morning. I felt as if I were playing Dick Cavett or David Susskind, feeding him straight lines so he could keep shooting calm, funny, slightly canned replies. He's already written a draft of the piece, having been "inspired" by the Republican convention . . . He says Clinton may be a successful President because, like FDR, he's "completely without principle."

Having discussed all this, we turned to the subject of Woody Allen; GV has known him for years and feels sympathy. There's even, by the way, a Scott Carpenter connection to the scandal now. Mia Farrow has taken to speaking through her lifelong friend Maria Roach (Scott's second wife).

AUGUST 21: Good news from *Harper's*. Rob Boynton says Lewis Lapham loves the checks essay, will run it soon, and wants me to propose another piece right away.

AUGUST 27: . . . To the Martin Beck to see *Guys and Dolls*. Everything they say is true, and more . . . Not a dud tune or lyric in the whole thing. To think we saw wonderful Faith Prince struggling through *Nick and Nora* less than a year ago. . . .

AUGUST 29: [A trip to Dallas] I was in Dealey Plaza by 5:00, taking pictures, walking up and down the grassy knoll and generally feeling as if I were wandering around in a familiar dream, some little toy diorama that's been preserved like a secret basement room in the huge glass and concrete city that's been built over it . . . I spent about an hour and a half in the exhibit on "The Sixth Floor" (which is what they call [the museum]). It's done with great effectiveness and tasteful restraint—if Kennedy had been shot in northern California the museum devoted to the killing would look like this.

AUGUST 31: Worked for much of the day in the Dallas Public Library . . . Amused by one reader's annotations in their *Arts & Sciences* copy. Near the line about Angela's staring at someone "as if he were some particularly revolting peasant who'd leapt over the window sill of the Winter Palace," the reader has objected: "surely not a peasant, unless a mutinous soldier of peasant background."

. . .

More and more I find George Will saying the things I'm thinking: "Today honorable conservatives feel the sort of fury felt by honorable conservatives 40 years ago when Joe McCarthy was giving anti-Communism a bad name."

SEPTEMBER 1: Billy came by after a dinner with Mr. Gene. It turns out that Charles Pierce won't be performing at the Pauline Trigère benefit after all—as Charles told one of the organizers, he's up to a size 16 and couldn't possibly get down to a 12 in time.

SEPTEMBER 3: Took a taxi to the Plaza in the pouring rain at 3:00. Gore Vidal met me in his room on the twelfth floor. He is a huge, pleasant ruin—vastly overweight in the middle, but still vain about himself. (Whenever he shifted he would hold closed his unbuttoned sport coat.) . . . He is always, entirely, on. He looks away from you when he delivers most of his lines (which is what his conversation consists of), as if afraid he might establish too much of a human connection and crack his own persona. We talked about Harvard (Alan Heimert was an Exeter classmate of his) after I confessed to being an ex-hack of academe (he loved my quoting him). We got on to historical fiction and the Rathbones, and he confirmed Fran's good advice about the assassination prologue. "Oh, I'd open with the bang-bang," he said. "It's the hack's solution, but sometimes that's what works." Further talk of Henry and Clara led to my mentioning Chester Arthur, whose daughter-in-law, Vidal informed me, used to operate "the biggest dyke salon in Paris."

. . .

I read his Clinton piece while he lay on the bed and watched me. When I laughed at something, he asked me what line I was at, and nothing gave him greater pleasure in our whole discussion, or provoked a bigger smile, than my telling him that Clinton and Gore had refused to pose for the *GQ* cover when they found out he was our writer.

SEPTEMBER 4: Lorraine Mead was wondering if Condé Nast couldn't have some sort of relief drive for the [Hurricane Andrew] victims. (She was struck by the sight of everyone carrying Evian bottles in the elevator, while some people in Florida have no water at all.) Later I heard Art talking to someone about this on the phone: "What are we gonna send them?" he wondered. "Three hundred little black dresses?"

SEPTEMBER 8: Suddenly Si has cooled toward Gore—after enthusing over lunch with Art and cheering through the print order meeting. This morning he told Art that Gore (Random House's—i.e., Si's—leading novelist) is a "silly man." Poor Art was crestfallen. My theory is that either Tina Brown or Graydon said something snide to the suggestible Si at Alexander Liberman's 412th birthday party out in Quogue over the weekend. They don't want *GQ* playing in their ballpark . . . Watch: if the issue sells well, Si will tell him what a fine idea it was.

SEPTEMBER 11: Faxed Gore his proofs and then went over them with him on the phone. Very easy and agreeable. The research dep't. wanted to know his sources for the FDR anecdotes; he said they could be found in pretty much any Roosevelt biography but that, if the fact-checkers couldn't locate them, we could claim that FDR just told the stories to Gore's father. When we were finished with the proofs, we chatted about H. L. Mencken and political correctness. He said he'd just had a letter objecting to his use of the word "man" for humankind. "It was as if," he said of the sender, "this word 'man' were a giant cock coming straight at her."

SEPTEMBER 14: Art gave a party for Graydon Carter down at Peter Bart's townhouse, which looks like the inside of a rectory, on E. 19th Street . . . Jeffrey Katzenberg, who *looks* like a Disney character, was standing still, and Bob Evans, former actor and movie mogul looking like a drug dealer down on his luck, was also present . . . Joan Rivers has a face that's been redesigned for television but not life: it is beyond surgery, beyond reconstruction. One can only call it a head transplant.

SEPTEMBER 15: Escaped the office at four, leaving the Gore boards in the hands of Lauren, my ambitious new Harvard-graduate assistant. To Bert's for my 5:50. We discussed workaholism (he believes I am afraid of leisure, truly doing nothing, because I am afraid of my own thoughts) . . .

SEPTEMBER 16: Flew to New Orleans with a lot of other writers on the 9:35 a.m. flight: Nick Lemann working at his laptop; Pete Hamill came butchly bounding up the aisle . . . (One reason Lemann is back home here in New Orleans is [to] give a deposition. Perry Russo, Jim Garrison's star witness, who still drives a cab here, is suing *GQ* over Lemann's description of him as a "grifter" in an article about Garrison and Oliver Stone's movie.) . . .

I'm in the Hilton, right by the river, a scape of barges, bridges and cargo containers. The conference itself, at the Sonesta on Bourbon Street, is very plush. At the cocktail party, one of the writers whose story I critiqued in connection with the Walker Percy award, went into a sputtering rage at me, the representative of Success and Mammon. I knew nothing about Art and her absolute need to write. Actually, I have a copy of my comments on her story: they are entirely friendly and constructive. Most of the people who come to these things are *excessively* humble, but there's often the angry lunatic fringe, too.

Dinner was at the Windsor Court Hotel . . . I got stuck at the hairy-chested table of Lucian Truscott (Ralph Kramden as writer) . . .

SEPTEMBER 19: Two panels in the afternoon, one on essays, the other on short fiction, both involving Richard Ford doing his the-bigger-they-are-the-nicer-they-are routine. Robert Ward showed up feeling no pain, and after the fiction panel, Binky Urban . . . came up to ask us (she'd come in late) if it was as dumb as it sounded.

SEPTEMBER 20: A panel called Writers' Writers in the after-noon . . . Pete Hamill claims to be a reader of Henry James's note-books, and Bob Ward babbled bibulously. . . .

The evening party—(black tie: I was in Bill's tux wearing his Tiffany studs from Mr. Gene)—was held at Anne Rice's slightly (deliberately) creepy house in the Garden District. A lifesize statue of St. Joseph (or St. Francis, I couldn't tell), holding an infant, inside the dining room. I'll say this for her: you can tell that most of the books in her huge library have been read. The spines are cracked, the jackets are torn, and little slips of paper are stuck in them . . . David Brinkley wandered around pouting. Molly Ivins did her act and looked for adoration. The whole thing seemed to be over as quickly as it began; everyone boarded the bus back to the Sonesta as in a fast-forwarded movie.

Wandered Bourbon Street, which is totally unraffish in any real way. It's about as real in feeling as Tom Sawyer's Island at Disneyland.

SEPTEMBER 21: The big closing luncheon in the main ballroom of the Sonesta. I presented the Walker Percy Prize . . . Rita Mae Brown gave a shameless take-the-money-and-run speech after we'd eaten, but I enjoyed myself nonetheless. I sat near [former congresswoman] Lindy Boggs and told her how I'd fallen asleep last night watching her daughter Cokie Roberts try repeatedly to get an answer out of the maddening Ross Perot. He's on the ballot in 50 states now, and she wanted to know if he's coming back into the race. He treated the question as an impertinence. I told Mrs. Boggs how frustrating I thought her daughter must have found it. [She replied:] "Has that girl forgotten her Southern training? She should have just cried!"

SEPTEMBER 24: At 6:00 Billy and I went to the National Arts Club off Gramercy Park. Gene was being given a sort of Life Achieve-ment award, and there was a grand cocktail party followed by the presentation and a slide show, which was accompanied by Gene's own commentary, delivered from a chair. He showed four differ-ent things that Billy had done, and the audience oohed and aahed and I was very proud and happy. Gene was at his most endearingly cranky during the question-and-answer session, screwing his face into an expression of baffled annoyance at every query.

SEPTEMBER 28: Art was in a grumpy mood today, and everyone was giving him a wide berth. (The grumpiness was due, it seems, to his having had to spend the weekend with his sister-in-law's crying baby. The scene is almost literally unimaginable; the closest I can come to picturing it is seeing Art trying to calm the kid down with a martini.)

OCTOBER 1: Amy Cooper is out at *Mademoiselle* . . . So far Art seems to be taking it well, concocting schemes of petty revenge and realizing there's not much else he can do by way of gallantry. Everyone's biggest fear on the 17th floor was that he might quit in a huff. But that was never very likely . . . Lucy was going off to a 2:00 interview with Marla Maples (the Donald's cookie) when she got the news. This was actually for a freelanced piece for *Mademoiselle*, so she had a double what-happens-now feeling.

OCTOBER 2: Up to the Carlyle for lunch with Claire Blunden . . . when we went off to the Frick she was amazingly avid and knowledgeable, making me look at some things closer than I ever had before. (How silly and cartoonish those little faces in the Turner—the one of Dieppe—look!)

OCTOBER 3: Billy and I rented *Walk on the Wild Side*. Between this and *Dead Ringer* we seem to be in a camp-noir period. . . .

Overheard on 2nd Avenue, angry mother to small child: "Well, *I* asked Santa for a Porsche, and I didn't get what *I* wanted!"

OCTOBER 7: The city slowed down because of Yom Kippur. I took Scott Omelianuk out to lunch, and we talked about writing ideas for him. A couple of guys at the magazine, Marty especially, have more or less given up on him; he no doubt seems too smartassed and complaining to them. But I found out long ago that you just have to knock the chip off his shoulder and he turns very sweet. You don't even have to knock it off: you can just brush it away, like dandruff.

OCTOBER 8: Graydon Carter gave a party in one of the Royalton penthouses for David Kamp and Aimée Bell, who will be married in about ten days. They are both his protégés and are clearly Rising Stars at CNP and in the magazine world beyond. It was a creepy party—not just because the room seemed denuded of furniture, and not just because the lights came up from the floor, as if you were on a subway platform or being lit for a horror movie. It was creepy because Art and Amy showed up and had to endure a couple of hours with Graydon . . . after he'd gone out of his way to tell *The Observer* what a wonderful thing Gabé Doppelt's appointment to *Mademoiselle* is. Amy is still hurting, and Art was boozy and teary. Out on the terrace, all of the upper neon of Times Square visible in the near distance, he let his thoughts run in all directions: maybe Si will fire him, too; maybe he'll go to *Esquire* and take everyone with him ("Will Blythe is history!"), and so forth. I told him he would get over this, that he was blessed by being a creature of enthusiasms: in a week or two he'll be excited by some new writer or cover idea or piece of gossip, and all of the unpleasantness will fade. He knew what I was talking about, but he insisted, "It's no fun anymore."

OCTOBER 9: I was at home this afternoon when Marty called. He'd had lunch with Lisa, and they're concerned that Art is drinking too much when he ought to be on his guard. No one knows what knives are out at the moment. In fact, there's a rumor going around that Charles Gandee is going to be picked to replace Art. This is so preposterous—Mahatma Gandhi would make more sense—that, in CNP logic, there just may be something to it. He has been taken from *HG* to *Vogue* by Anna Wintour, who hates Art and hopes to be the next Liberman. And Si Newhouse is nearly as enamoured of her as he is of Tina. On the other hand, why make *GQ* into something hip and downtown and gay (as Charles would surely make it) when *Details* is already taking care of that territory?

OCTOBER 10: Ran and worked on *Henry & Clara* until it was time to go down to La Bohème for dinner with Billy and [his second cousin] Lynn and Miss Carol . . . I even took pictures in the restaurant: I never for one day forget that Billy is a temporary gift to me, that I must hoard whatever life we live together, preserve it, keep it available for lonely times ahead.

OCTOBER 11: Billy + Lynn went to a matinee of *The Will Rogers Follies* and came back to report that Marla Maples' chorus-line kicks are not exactly stratospheric . . .

OCTOBER 13: . . . Lynn and I kissed each other goodbye, and as she hugged me, she said, very quietly, with Billy out of earshot: "Take care of Bill." Was I imagining that she said it with some urgency, that she'd *planned* to say it? . . .

Quayle and Gore debated tonight . . . Gore was robotic and condescending. Vidal is wrong: he's not Tom Sawyer, he's Sid. It was the best night the Republicans have had in ages.

OCTOBER 15: Art was called down to see Si this morning, and when he came back up he called all of us into his office. This is it, we thought. Well, it wasn't. It turns out that Si wanted to tell him we'll be going to a new, heavier paper stock in January, two months before *Esquire* does. Everyone exhaled a great burst of relief.

OCTOBER 18: Dinner with Billy and Dick and Dennis at Stephanie's. They're just back from England and Italy, and Dennis looks better than ever. Dick looks even thinner than last time. Dennis does a comic riff on his gruff-workingman father's recent visit to NY—sitting in the living room without his shirt on and so forth. Underneath the story, which he couldn't bring himself to reveal overtly, were fear and tenderness. His father had never been able to accept Dennis' homosexuality, had barely been able to remember him amidst his seven brothers and sisters—now, suddenly, for the first time, he shows up in New York. Doubtlessly because Dennis' mother told him there might not be another time.

OCTOBER 20: Gore Vidal called this afternoon, from a Miami fat farm, to ask how the issue was selling. Since it's just come on to the stands, I didn't have much to tell him. He wants to be kept abreast of all reaction to the piece; he is, of course, hoping to be abused, or at least to find a little fray into which he can jump. . . .

... [Art] is still terribly low about Amy; he's lapping up the vodka and trying to pick fights with everyone from Pam van Zandt to Billy Norwich. (He's mad at the latter for implying that *Mademoiselle* under Amy was boring. So he glowers at him in the elevator . . .) He's abusing Graydon & Tina and all the British editors at every opportunity. Lucy and I and Paul sat with him, trying to be cheerful and calming, until it was past 7.

... Vidal told me he liked my Sinclair Lewis piece, though he doesn't think Lewis was as down about everything as I make him out to be. Some of it, GV insists, was just the bilious tone that Mencken had made fashionable.

OCTOBER 23: Billy arrived here late, saying that Pat [Kennedy] Lawford called [Donald] Brooks while they were having drinks and reminded him to watch Maria Shriver's interview with Fidel Castro. And there you have the Cuban Missile Crisis + 30 years.

OCTOBER 26: John Herman called this morning, and I called him back when I got in from running. He's at last read the first part of the Rathbones, and his verdict is mixed. He likes Clara a lot—finds her witty and delightful; otherwise he thinks the narrative voice is too distant and that we don't have a strong enough sense of Henry. He wants me to keep going and then go back and address these things.

. . .

Learned that the rodeo essay, aside from being in the sports-writing anthology, has made the list of "notable" pieces in this year's *Best American Essays*, edited by Susan Sontag. (I guess being her kid helps you to get in the actual text: she had the gall to put in one of David Rieff's pieces.)

OCTOBER 27: Art took me to The Four Seasons today to celebrate the Vidal cover. We had a lot of laughs, but he is still obviously raw over Amy. Si's being on the other side of the room—and Grace Mirabella, another of his spectacular victims, being at the next table—didn't help.

NOVEMBER 1: Kept revising Part 2 until it was time for us to head out to Brooklyn for dinner at Wilma and Eddie's . . . They've got two new dogs, Duke and Ella, and the boy is hilariously frisky. Wilma made me a big chocolate birthday cake ringed with strawberries, and we finished the evening by watching part of a TV comedy special about the election. . . .

NOVEMBER 2: This was an altogether easier birthday to contemplate than last year's. (For one thing, 41 somehow sounds younger than 40.)

NOVEMBER 3: Bill Clinton is the 42nd President of the United States . . . Turnout seemed enormous: this morning at the school across the street people were lined up out the door and down the sidewalk, holding their umbrellas over their heads. I voted for Bush, again, albeit reluctantly. He made a gracious concession speech, and Clinton was even more generous in victory. (The first problem he mentioned, in a list of those he'd go to work on, was AIDS.) I expect inflation and foreign-policy confusion, many failures though no Carter-like debacle. There will be successes, too, though not the kind people are hoping for—the country's social problems are simply too huge and intractable and fundamental. But how can one not wish him well?

NOVEMBER 4: Lucy greeted me by saying "It's morning in America." She meant it too.
    . . . Had lunch at Jean Lafitte on W. 58th with Owen Laster, Gore's agent. He presented me with an autographed copy of the Clinton-Gore cover—Gore V. put his inscription to me right on his kinsman's forehead . . . Owen says G.V. is impatient with his biographer, Walter Clemons. He wants the book to come out soon, so that it will cause lots of fights he can jump into.

NOVEMBER 5: At 7:00 I got a cab and made the difficult, rain-soaked, traffic-clogged journey up and across town to Equinox, the health club at Amsterdam and 76th, where GQ was having a party to celebrate the new Personal Best section of the magazine.

Weird health-food *hors d'oeuvres*: you'd be drinking a light beer and someone would come by with a tray of citrus-fruit slices.

NOVEMBER 6: To Alexandra Isles' for a birthday dinner for Elisa Shokoff... The life of the party was Richard Osterweil, who reminded me of Ben, and who is increasingly famous as a bad painter and gate crasher. His exploits in the latter field are being celebrated in a new documentary movie that the Arts and Leisure section will be puffing this Sunday.

NOVEMBER 9: Had Bert at 5:50. Not so stimulating a session as the last one, but still useful. We're working on workaholism.

NOVEMBER 10: Ann came by at 6:00 to celebrate our birthdays and we killed the $250 bottle of wine Art gave to "console" me over the election. I tried to come up with adjectives to report to Art and Alan: she thought it was spicy, I thought it smelled of the forest....

NOVEMBER 11: Lucy is being driven crazy by complaints from Charlie Rose and his publicist over her saying he's more like a lapdog than a pit bull on his show... They've made *three* phone calls so far, two of them to Art (yesterday). It's past the point where they should be told to fuck off, but Lucy is depressed.

NOVEMBER 12: Scott Carpenter called tonight from Vail. He'll be in New York next week and we'll have dinner or lunch. He also has a proposition for me. He's getting ready to start a book about his grandfather Victor Noxon, the editor, and he wants to know if I'll help him out... I'd find helping him fun, but I don't have big chunks of time & won't take his or even his agent's money. If he wants to pay me back, he can teach me to ski in Vail some week....

NOVEMBER 16: I had lunch at Le Max with Hilary [Sterne], who always seems on the verge of exploding (actually, she does explode some afternoons in the office—a door-slamming meltdown). She is very bright but does not have enough—or a clear indication of what—to do. So she spends a lot of time in office arguments and intrigue and eating her guts out about David Kamp's meteoric rise. . . .

NOVEMBER 20: A trying morning. First a letter from a genealogist distantly descended from the Harris family. He makes a strong objection to the phrase "whiff of incest" in my *American Scholar* article and provides evidence that Clara may be 6 years older than I now think. I don't state any age in the *Scholar* article, so there's nothing incorrect there, but suddenly my [novel's] first 50 pages seem shaky. They'll have to be rethought. As Fran said when I called her about it, better to learn this now than when the book is out. I put in calls for help to Norman Rice and Melinda Yates in Albany.

Then my strange call to Vail. Having had no word from Scott all week I thought I'd call to find out if I'd misheard him when he said he'd be here this week; if he was here and couldn't get hold of me, I thought, maybe he'll access the message machine in Vail. So I called and got Barbara who said she knew nothing about a trip to New York, that Scott was in Orlando. I had the feeling I'd put a lump of ice into her stomach.

NOVEMBER 23: Richard Ford called from Montana, where he was probably in the process of killing something with Tom McGuane. He doesn't want to do the essay on Clint Eastwood that Lisa suggested to him but says he'd like to do something for me soon. He also asks why I didn't send him *Rockets and Rodeos* for a blurb.

NOVEMBER 24: Another daylong editorial conference. It's too soon after Connecticut, but there's no stopping Art. He rented a penthouse at the Royalton . . . [and] had to make wretched excess out of the day: drinks at the Wyndham, dinner at Trattoria Dell'Arte; nightcaps on the top floor of the Peninsula. And I sloshed and soldiered on to the end.

NOVEMBER 26: [Thanksgiving] We went to Symphony Cafe this year, with Miss Carol, and had a wonderful time . . . It was a rainy day (the doorman in Billy's building said the two Rockettes who live there were crying as they left to go dance in the Macy's parade) . . .

NOVEMBER 27: The first sound I hear in the morning, at 7:00, is that of Billy in the kitchen, grinding up his medicine with the mortar and pestle. This should be depressing, a grim reminder with which to start the day, but it really isn't. I'm happy we at least have the medicine. It's a familiar, comforting sound—like coffee brewing.

NOVEMBER 28: Scott Carpenter called this afternoon, apologetic and evasive, except to say that he did try to reach me—and that he and Barbara are "splitting." He says this has been coming for a long time; other than that he was no more inclined to talk about the matter than he might be to discuss Rene or Maria. I don't know what situation I stumbled into, or what complication I caused, but that's that. Three wives, children by each, and still, at 67, he's, as they say, "searching for something."

DECEMBER 1: A crazy day at the office. Richard Johnson's column reported on the continuing rumors about Art and wondered who's fueling them. (It's Anna Wintour, everyone feels pretty certain . . . David Kamp now refers to the Anglicization of the Newhouse empire as the "ethnic cleansing" of the company.) By late afternoon Art was hitting the vodka bottle and having a long, edgy telephone conversation with Graydon.

DECEMBER 2: I was in Washington by 9:30 and went straight to the Archives. Found the letters written on Henry's behalf in 1877. The family mounted quite a campaign to get him a diplomatic post—everyone from Ambrose Burnside to the Bishop of Albany wrote . . . Walked around Capitol Hill—the inaugural platform is going up and Clinton tee-shirts are already everywhere. . . .

    . . .

The *American Spectator* 25th-anniversary banquet at the Capital Hilton . . . I knew almost no one except for Wlady, but I smiled merrily in my tuxedo, sitting at the left wing of Richard Perle during dinner. P. J. O'Rourke was the emcee . . . longing for the 1980s, "when saying you'd slept with the President only meant that you'd been to a Cabinet meeting." A major theme of the evening was the relief it will be for the magazine to be in opposition rather than trying to be for an administration it could only half believe in. The references to Bush were tepid, whereas mentions of Reagan raised the roof.

DECEMBER 4: More rumors about Art. Now Adam Moss (*Seven Days*) is being touted as his successor. Another rumor probably generated by Anna Wintour (or perhaps John Fairchild?). Art is obsessive about it all, immobilized. He spins his theories and recaps them endlessly and every visit to his office to do business turns into a therapy session.

What a place. Tina Brown fired six writers yesterday (among them Ved Mehta and Bernstein), and she's badmouthing Graydon all around town. Wants him to fail so *VF* will be remembered only for its golden era under her, and wants to get revenge for all the fun he made of her at *Spy*.

DECEMBER 7: Fran was dreading having to appear at this party for Carol Brightman [and her biography of Mary McCarthy]— the competition—and I wasn't looking forward to the [Bob] show. Actually, it wasn't so bad: he was enormously busy, what with the likes of Joan Didion and Arthur Schlesinger to suck up to, and we never even looked at each other. I talked to Jim West, who is beginning to fail and be forgetful, and to Kate McCarthy, Kevin's still-young second wife, who never especially liked Mary. Lizzie Hardwick shook my hand for the first time in years.

Went out to dinner afterwards, across town at Etats-Unis, with Fran and Alison, who tells me that Charles Edwards is not expected to live past Christmas . . . We told funny, sad stories about [him] . . . Fran saw him as a sort of Holly Golightly figure, and by the end of the meal he might as well have been dead for some time.

DECEMBER 9: I worked the Wilson galleys and read the fiction boards, changing a "bow" tie to a "bad" tie when I noticed the illustrator had ignored the text and given the character the latter kind. Lucy and I had a drink with Art, who'd been to Si's annual holiday luncheon for the editors-in-chief. He (Si) said that Condé Nast was "like a family." The Corleones, I suggested; no, the Mansons, Lucy insisted.

DECEMBER 10: Si has cold feet about John Sack's piece on the death camps run by Jews in Poland in 1945. He wants Elie Wiesel to read it and offer comment in the same issue—not very fair to Sack, I think. Or to Wiesel, for that matter: it's unclear whether he's being asked to comment on the morality of the situation or to affirm or deny [the story] from the point of view of a Holocaust scholar. The best thing, of course, would be to publish the piece and let anyone comment on it in due course, but Si is insistent— he even made a phone call from the pay phone at his gym to see how Art was proceeding with the matter.

. . .

I had Bert at 5:50, and I talked about Charles Edwards and my inability to cry for him. There are so many deaths, they come so early and so close together and so frequently, that you quickly process them—like slapping on a toe tag in the morgue—and get ready for the next one.

DECEMBER 13: . . . Gazed at the first bound copy of *Rockets and Rodeos*, which arrived yesterday with a nauseating note of "congratulations" from John Herman.

At 7:30 Billy and I headed down to West 11th St. to a dinner party (a delicious pork roast) at Jeffrey Simpson's. We had a surprisingly good time. Billy liked all the old furniture and talk of Chautauqua. He thought Jeffrey himself was all right: "He's sort of like Aunt Pittypat," he said as we started for home.

DECEMBER 15: It appears that John Mortimer will do an essay on Prince Charles (for $12,500), and Art likes the Russell Banks story, so both sides of my cupboard at the magazine are full, and I am pleased. (The dark note today: the John Sack piece on the death camps has been killed—for public-relations reasons masquerading as legal ones.)

DECEMBER 16: Paul Sachner is dead. He was 42. His obituary was in the *Times* this morning: he died in a hospital in Connecticut . . . Paul was a handsome, smart, serious man—fundamentally self-loathing, I would say. We didn't especially like each other. I remember his nervous laugh, his intellectual snobbery, his occasional burst of feeling and tenderness (I do think he loved Tommy).

DECEMBER 17: From Billy's I went down to Nell's on 14th Street, where *GQ*, in keeping with our tradition of wretched excess, was having a second party in two nights—this one with the Ford Modeling Agency to celebrate the January swimsuit spread . . . Nell's is not what it used to be. It's less the venue for brat-pack writers and more a club for rough music groups. The bouncers were really a huge goon squad, and late in the evening they beat up David Handelman, who works at *Vogue* and is married to Susan Morrison, the *New York Observer*'s editor. A great scene on the sidewalk: bored cops; bleeding 80s husband, take-charge 90s wife; Art peeling off a $10 bill to give to a guy in a wheelchair who says he saw the whole thing; Lucy and I trying to get Art away from the whole business, since we both felt pretty sure there was at least one gun amidst this group of "security" guys who were as scary as anything this side of Attica. Finally, Art drove me home in his stretch limo—after, that is, we both walked Lucy home to her little apartment near a palm reader around the block.

DECEMBER 22: I had Bert at 5:50, and we talked about Paul Sachner and death, and I felt absolutely dry—no emotions at all. After all I've already seen, and all that's yet to come, I refuse, somewhere inside myself, to admit that AIDS is the chief catastrophe—perhaps even the central event—of my life history . . . Bert and I went over and over this, but it seemed much more like philosophy and politics than therapy. It was abstract, dispassionate.

DECEMBER 23: WELCOME BACK, CARTER. That would have been my morning headline if I wrote them for the tabloids. Clinton has appointed his key foreign-policy people, a collection of Jimmyite retreads and mediocrities: Anthony Lake; Warren

Christopher; Les Aspin (less bad than the rest); even Madeleine Albright. . . .

Lunch at the Royalton with Joe Queenan, an odd duck but an interesting one. He had a rough childhood in a South Philadelphia housing project; a drunken father; years of writing unpublishable novels and working for ex-pornographer Ralph Ginzburg; and, since 1986, huge, prolific success as a magazine humorist . . . You have to let him monologue and quote himself for about a half hour, and then he settles into being good company, listens to your questions, tells you interesting things about himself, not just *shtick*.

DECEMBER 25: Thanks to Billy, two non-catastrophic Christmases in a row—practically a Mallon record. Not only did nobody explode at anyone else—in fact, we all got on festively and famously. Loree really *likes* Bill, understands his sweet nature and wants his approval.

DECEMBER 27: We went to see (hear, I suppose) the *Messiah* at Carnegie Hall—the last one to be conducted by David Randolph. Billy, who fell in love with it in the 9th grade, still finds it enchanting. I must say I thought it was . . . long. But I did have a little brainstorm about Henry and Clara as I listened.

DECEMBER 31: I buckled down in the reading room, writing Henry's walk around Lafayette Square; I stayed until they turned off the chandeliers and only the little lamps on the tables, half of which don't work, were left on.

It was a wonderful New Year's. Patty and I went to Billy's at 7, and Karen and David arrived from Staten Island an hour later. We had dinner at the Zephyr Grill in the Beekman Hotel (whose lit rooftop is visible every night from Billy's window), and came back to 51st St. a little before midnight . . . Billy and I hugged and thought about the four wonderful New Year's Eves we've had, from Poughkeepsie to Paris. I pray for at least a few more—though the last month (Charlie, Paul) has left me shaken, brought me back to my pessimistic senses.

1993

JANUARY 3: Tonight we all watch multiple Amy Fisher stories on television; it's as meaninglessly meaningful a view of American culture in the 1990s as you can find. "I loved him. And we had great sex. And he fixed my car."

JANUARY 4: David Kamp came to me complaining about an idea that Marty shot down—one he knows Art would have approved if he'd only gone to him directly. He's learning the essential difference between the two: Marty enjoys power by saying no, whereas Art enjoys it by saying yes, dispensing a favor, doling out the goodies.

[Art] and I took a car to the Wyndham Hotel at 5:00 to meet John Mortimer, who came shuffling down to the lobby looking alarmingly feeble. We went across the street to The Oyster Bar for a drink, which proved great fun. He's very limber up top, and it's clear he's going to do a first-rate, fun piece on Prince Charles. He was full of fresh gossip and anecdotes about the times he's been at a lunch or dinner with either of them. He sat next to Diana once and found her charming: she laughed at his jokes and seemed aware of who he was. Art asked him if he thought she'd read his books. "I shouldn't think so," he replied.

JANUARY 11: I began jury duty on this gray slushy day. I'm in a civil court down on Thomas St. I never even had a *voir dire*—just hours of waiting—sometimes without a seat—in the main room, presided over by a fat long-haired bureaucrat who thinks he's a comedian. He does loud shtick all day, tormenting those trying to read and bringing guffaws from the rest. Every other person hacks and coughs and sneezes—or mumbles—or snores. God help me. I'll scream if I have two weeks of this.

JANUARY 12: *Newsday* ran a long review of *Rockets & Rodeos* today, and for the most part I'm pleased. It picks and chooses among the essays, as all the rest of them will, but it's full of quotable things—says I'm "always elegant," that the book is "low-key but eloquent"; especially likes the Alaska piece and says Owosso rates with the best of Garrison Keillor. The complaints are that I'm too detached and unemotional—he wants me to whoop over the rodeo and bawl at Pearl Harbor.

JANUARY 14: . . . Corrected the transcript of an interview I did with Kristin van Ogtrop for one of those *Dictionary of Literary Biography* volumes, and was amazed at how verbose and ungrammatical I sounded.

JANUARY 15: I left the courthouse clutching my proof-of-service slip like an immigrant's citizenship papers.

JANUARY 17: [Old Harvard friends] . . . Early in the evening I called Micheluccio in San Francisco. I'd had a letter from him. I've been scared to call—these days you expect the worst. And if you don't get it, you get something nearly as bad: Michele is fine, but Jim Janke is sick—nearly died last fall.

JANUARY 18: Andy [Pandolfo] told me tonight that Phil has been very sick for a month. Andy—the most warm-hearted fellow alive—spent the holidays crying himself to sleep.

And at some point his own turn to be sick will come.

JANUARY 20: . . . William Jefferson Clinton (not "Bill") took the oath of office as 42nd President of the United States. He delivered a short, unmemorable speech, which was followed by a bad but well-read poem by Maya Angelou. . . .

A busy day at work. Art thinks the Chris Isaak cover won't sell, so he wants to push John Mortimer's piece up into April and, going for broke, put Prince Charles on the cover. We'll see. I talked to Mortimer today—he's faxing the piece on Monday—and he says the whole story is heating up. There are rumors MI5 is bugging the royals' phones and that it's a Thatcherite plot: she wants the monarchy to crumble so that it will be replaced by a new constitution that will allow her to run for President!

JANUARY 21: Gary Krist came by to go over his story this morning. I had complimented him on its smooth logistics, the way he keeps members of a large cast of characters moving from room to room without ever confusing the reader. It turns out that he has a part-time job designing logic puzzles—two days a week at Stanley Kaplan . . . My darling, beloved Audrey Hepburn, gone too soon at 63 . . . Oh, the happiness you gave me! And, as long as there's a VCR anywhere, always will. My darling Holly, Jo, Sabrina, Regina, Joanna.

JANUARY 23: On our way to the Manhattan Theatre Club we went into Coliseum Books and found a nice stack of *Rockets and Rodeos* in the "Travelog" section, near those Peter Mayle books on Provence. It's under a different rubric in every store.

JANUARY 25: Went down to Hotaling's at lunchtime and then sat in Bryant Park with yesterday's *Chicago Tribune*. The review it has of *R+R* is very good: a big spread shared with Diane Johnson's latest book, and a reviewer who urges readers not to let political disagreements put them off the book's literary merits . . .

The Mortimer piece is good, so Art is pleased. He's asked me if I'm willing to edit Mordecai Richler; his thought is that I (perhaps because I'm a writer myself) will get more out of him than Paul, get him to do the big books he now avoids. Well, I'm *not* sure I can get any more out of him than Paul does now, and I've decided to tell Art (he told me to sleep on it) that I want to do the column myself. Mordecai belongs in the well, writing humor, travel and memoirs. He's wasted on books, and books are wasted on him.

JANUARY 26: This morning I told Art I wanted the column. He seemed surprised and intrigued, said he had to think about it . . . The two of us had a good time this afternoon looking at pick-up photos of Prince Charles. Art and I and Robert Priest tried to find one where he didn't look too fish-faced, and which could accommodate the GQ logo.

JANUARY 28: Talked to Jeffrey Simpson (depressed about love and work) and Greg—who now believes he will not make partner and that he doomed his chances when he told them he was gay.

JANUARY 29: One form [Art's] excitement over a piece takes is an inability to approve a title for it, the fear we won't have the *perfect* one. He's doing this with Mortimer. Nothing I offer ("Good Luck, Sweet Prince," "Thy Kingdom Come") is quite good enough . . . I've been busier than a one-armed paperhanger this week, but I had to take time out for a long expensive lunch at San Giusto on 2nd Ave. with Keith Raffan, who, fortunately, no longer makes me feel any attraction . . . We talked about the Mortimer piece, and he told me about some encounters he had with Charles when he was still an M.P. He's very much of the Prince's party (Charles was willing to say all sorts of bold, thoughtful things—even, say, in favor of proportional representation), and he loathes Diana, a shrewish airhead, he insists.

Greg came by in the evening, and we went across the street to Chapter XI (the late Billy Munk) for dinner . . . What Greg says about himself is true: he's lost confidence during the last two years because of the way things have been for him at the firm. What one can't say to him—because they *have* been unjust to him—is that defeat has made him a much nicer person.

JANUARY 30: "Reign, Man"? "Noblesse Besieged"?

JANUARY 31: Billy is down, ready to give up on the cows [figures for Tiffany's windows]. I see him do this with so many projects: he works and works, solves the crucial problems, and then finds a reason to turn the whole thing against himself. I gave him something between a pep talk and a stern lecture tonight.

FEBRUARY 1: At five it was time to go to Bert's. I talked more about my recent phone conversations with Andy than anything else. When the time comes, will I have the strength to care for Billy the way he's caring for Phil? I may lack HIV, but I also lack Andy's natural generosity.

Billy and I ordered Chinese food. (The elevator is always full of people bringing take-out food and videos up to their particular cubes in the vertical ice-cube tray; the same thing goes on all over the city, which for the most part lives just like any other suburb in America.) After we'd watched some television, he went to sleep, and I went to read on the couch, as I do most nights, until or past midnight, when the lights atop the Beekman Hotel flash off.

FEBRUARY 3: Did the fact-checking of the Jim Atlas piece (a second session) with the amazingly labor-intensive Tatiana Strage, who, I think, finds herself excited by saying some of the naughty bits aloud. Last week she asked me if I had a page reference in *Myra Breckinridge* for the "anal rape with a dildo."

FEBRUARY 4: Billy and I arrived, with Lucy, for my reading at Brentano's at seven on the dot. I had a good crowd. (We papered the house with invitations to everyone at *GQ*, and Art kicked in for a catered reception afterwards.). The podium and microphone were all the way at the top of the staircase, and I felt a bit like Mussolini as I read to the crowd far below. In fact, they were so far removed that I felt I was doing a radio broadcast. I had hardly any sense of whether it was going over well or not.

FEBRUARY 5: Billy and I stayed in our own places tonight, he working on the cows, and I on Clara's Hanover diary. I was very blue by the end of the evening, without really knowing why, until Billy, on the phone, gave me the obvious, and actual, explanation: it's the *material* that's depressing me—writing about poor Clara, trapped in that boarding house, giving up the love of her life to madness, and unaware that her own violent death is fast approaching.

FEBRUARY 9: We were supposed to take Jeffrey Simpson out to dinner, but Gene Moore—thinking his dinner with Billy tomorrow night was actually for tonight—showed up five minutes before Jeffrey. It was a fairly felicitous mixup: each of these characters wouldn't work easily with a lot of others, but the two of them have a lot of common interests (Gene is something of a legend to Jeffrey) and they got on fine. For one thing, they had John Loring in common (he's been at both Tiffany and *AD*), available for running down. We went out to the Zephyr Grill and Gene (who would not admit his scheduling mistake) gradually warmed up by talking about himself, himself, himself . . . He is, I think, genuinely distressed over Audrey Hepburn's death, having loved her since he did some fashion photographs of her more than forty years ago, when she came to New York to do *Gigi*.

FEBRUARY 10: Art is back from Japan, even fatter somehow, but glad to be once more in the saddle.

I had lunch with Colin Harrison, my new "rabbi" (as Marty would say) at *Harper's*, now that Rob Boynton, who couldn't get most of the stuff he bought onto the schedule, has left. That failure includes my checks piece, which Colin thinks he can get through . . . Colin is a slightly plump, easygoing, smart, all-American fellow, a novelist who's married to Kathryn Harrison, whose second novel is about to get a huge Binky build-up: the full ICM-Newhouse treatment, complete with a party to which Madonna's invited.

FEBRUARY 11: The American correspondent of *Yomiuri Shimbun*, the huge Japanese newspaper, came to interview me this afternoon. (His wife, who acts as his photographer, accompanied him and took my picture.). He'd seen *Rockets & Rodeos* in Brentano's window and wanted to write it up, even though I have no Japanese publisher. He's been over here since October, after being their Middle East man (Arafat made a pass at his wife). I asked him what stories he's been filing home lately: Katie Beers [the kidnapped Long Island girl] and Amy Fisher.

FEBRUARY 13: Clara died at 4:30 this afternoon in the main reading room of the NYPL. I wrote for hours, and by the time I was through I had a catch in my throat—not because I did it all that affectingly; only because I'll miss her. I got up to pace the hall as soon as I finished. It's a grisly Gothic scene, but while I wrote it I was less preoccupied by gore than logistics. I'd never really written a murder before . . . and the business of her getting [Henry] out of the children's room, his having a gun in one hand and a knife in the other—it was all tricky.

FEBRUARY 17: I must have faith in this book. I must not allow John Herman to publish it in his usual surreptitious manner.

FEBRUARY 18: David Gates . . . has written a wonderful story called "Wonders of the Invisible World." Sloan Harris sent it over, and I am hugely keen on buying it. The only problem is that it's very long—probably 7000 words. Art grimaced when I gave it to him—he's been hoping the fiction would start to get shorter, and now I hand him this. To top things off, he was in a bad mood. After I came out of the office, Lorraine asked what possessed me to bring something like this to him today.

FEBRUARY 19: Nina King called from Washington to ask if I'd like to review Jonathan Yardley's new book [for the *Post*], something about the mid-Atlantic. He has let it be known that my review of his Mencken book was the most sensible one he saw. Oh, really? Well, too bad he was sent into such a half-snit by the style of *Stolen Words*. I told Nina I felt I should decline. She says they're having trouble thinking of anyone he hasn't had a whack at.

FEBRUARY 22: Art is going to let me buy the David Gates story. He admits it's terrific, even though it kills him to commit the space. I promised to show him haikus and sonnets for the next six months.

FEBRUARY 25: An editorial lunch at Trattoria Dell'Arte, in the chilly room where they keep the wine. Art at his worst—full of himself and full of the magazine after being lionized at "focus groups" in Dallas and Atlanta. No idea seemed good enough today. These brainstorming sessions are always peculiar . . . they're not so much about sharing ideas as killing them. Someone puts forth a modest notion, and it's immediately set upon and shredded, like meat before wolves.

FEBRUARY 26: Took the Metroliner down through a snowy eastern corridor to Washington. Read Shacochis and scribbled changes onto *Henry and Clara*. Lunch in Union Station with Michael Barone, who says he's going to suggest me to the Quayle people to be DQ's ghostwriter on his memoirs. Seriously. DQ himself asked Michael, who said no . . . Did an AP radio interview at the Gannett Building in Arlington late in the afternoon. The interviewer was Bill Thompson, who'd worked at a station in Providence and liked the Pell piece. Just before taping the program I heard the news of the World Trade Center bombing.

I stayed with Geoff and Marybeth [Stewart] at their huge new house in northwest Washington. The neighborhood is called Spring Valley, and since it's the only Republican-voting one in the District, they don't get their streets plowed.

MARCH 1: . . . [Billy] says Jennifer was at home on Friday when the Trade Center bomb went off; she looked out her windows near the Battery, thinking a boat had blown up.

MARCH 3: Bert actually got on to something very interesting tonight . . . We were talking about my need to slow down, to take a sort of sabbatical . . . and in the course of his saying that a period without intense work would recharge my artistic batteries, nourish my imagination, I rather casually objected to his characterization of me as an artist. I have never considered myself one. A good writer, a good craftsman, yes, but hardly an artist. Why not claim the word? he wanted to know. I'm, after all, entitled to it: three serious novels, and so forth. No, I said: I just think of myself as a good working writer, closer to a small businessman than anything else. Is this, perhaps, one reason that I don't slow down? I mean, would I consider that a slothful sin against my bourgeois calling, rather than—as I *could* consider it—a necessary part of my "artistic" vocation?

MARCH 4: . . . The day's real low point came when Art called in all the senior editors and up for a collective dressing down, Captain-Queeg style. It seems *Esquire* has Richard Ben Cramer writing about the Sicilian mafia, just as we have John Lombardi doing such a piece. And there were people who knew about Cramer's assignment but didn't tell Art . . . He was impossible (and more than a little wasted from his lunch). There was no screaming, but the whole thing was pointless and insulting. Marty got his head bitten off when he suggested that it wouldn't be so terrible if both Lombardi and Cramer did their pieces; he was no doubt recalling Art's frequent dictum that we pay no attention to *Esquire*. No matter: Art needed some *hysteria du jour*. The end result? A half dozen disgusted editors. It really isn't like this very often; but lately . . .

. . . A clutch of absolutely glowing reviews [for *Rockets and Rodeos*]. I wish they were from bigger places than Cleveland, Orlando and Flint, but I was happy to get them.

MARCH 6: I delivered [*Henry and Clara*] to Mary this afternoon. I brought it down to E. 5th St. and left it behind her iron gate, underneath the brownstone's steps. She had an earthenware jug with a manufacturer's mark—So. Pearl St., Albany, N.Y.—that I took to be a good omen. I enclosed a note with the typescript, saying my chief hope for the book is that it get me out of the miserable, humiliating editorial relationship I'm in.

. . . I picked up a phone message from Ruth's desk. Rick Horgan from HarperCollins called me yesterday afternoon. The message: "calling at the suggestion of Dan Quayle". . . .

I can't say yes. Or can I? the money would be tempting . . . but would one want it known? (I wouldn't want an "as told to" credit, but if I could do it anonymously?) Mary doesn't think it would be a bad thing for my resume (and she's a Quayle-hating Hoosier), and she thinks I'm overdue for a big paycheck. I don't know: here I am having just finished this serious novel (I must admit that

DQ's timing is good), and being encouraged by Bert to think of myself as an artist. And yet . . . we're only talking about a matter of months, aren't we?

MARCH 8: [Out in northern California to write a *GQ* piece on the Search for Extraterrestrial Intelligence (SETI) Institute] Mountain View is a pretty, less aggressively pure version of the towns one finds in Marin County, and I had a good day. Frank Drake, the SETI guru, is a rather weary fellow for someone so sure he'll see his dream—of finding "ETI"—come true by 2000. (Note the way one begins to write just the number, and not the whole phrase "the year 2000.")

MARCH 9: Spent the whole day at Ames Research Center, a weird landscape of wind tunnels and test facilities. I had a wonderful time, of course, imagining myself as a low-level toiler there, a life in a low-bid office, putting my scrawny shoulder to the space wheel . . . I probably had my best interview with Barney Oliver, one of the real SETI pioneers, a sputtering volcano now, nearly 80. When I muttered that I might have trouble handling some of the math in a paper he offered me to read, he barked: "That's not math, that's arithmetic!"

Bob and Joanne DeMaria are living in Palo Alto this year, and tonight we went out to dinner . . . I entertained them with the Quayle story and was surprised by their enthusiasm for my doing it. They clearly think it's a *prestige* project—and Karen & Patty (according to reports from Billy) feel the same way. Academic awe at the real world?

MARCH 10: . . . interview with Kent Cullers, the blind-from-birth chief of signal detection. I asked him if being blind ever caused him to think along different lines from other people in the project, ever enabled [him] to make intuitive leaps that they couldn't. He suggested, with a smile, that I close my eyes and see if I felt any smarter.

MARCH 13: I called Billy in the morning, and he said he could barely see across 2nd Ave. My flight was cancelled, along with everything else going to the east coast . . . The whole country is essentially "down," though here in Pasadena it was the prettiest June day you ever saw. By evening I was a despairing caged bear, determined to get myself out of here no matter how much of Si Newhouse's money it takes . . . No one knows when the east-coast airports are going to reopen, but I shall try to claw my way across the country, time zone by time zone. Anything will be better than another day in this plush hotel.

MARCH 14: I nearly made it home, but when I got to Chicago I discovered that I'd overplayed my hand: the 4:30 flight to New York had just been cancelled. And so I joined the lost world inside O'Hare: thousands and thousands of people trying to get east, putting themselves on standby lists (futile), and realizing that they may not get out until Tuesday . . . There aren't even enough hotel rooms in Chicago to accommodate the stranded. It's all lines, improvisation and shouting matches.

MARCH 16: Mary [Evans] has read the Rathbone novel . . . Now what happens? I know she is uncomfortable about showing it to other publishers while it's still under contract to John. This bothers me not at all, not after what he did to me last year. I could just break the contract right now, of course. That would mean I'd have to pay back the advance (something that doesn't trouble me as much as it does Mary), and that I'd be without my bird in the hand (something that *does* trouble me). . . .

. . .

Marty took me along to the Jewel of India for lunch with Walter Russell Mead (a big burly [Jim] Brink of a man), who's going to travel to Russia for *GQ* and write about trying to sell his idea, to the Russians, that the U.S. should solve everyone's problems by buying Siberia. (He has already floated this on an Op-Ed page.)

Billy and I had a quiet evening at home. He is very down: he's overworked, terribly, at the office . . . I think Billy is tired out from the cows, too. (The four he's done are hilariously ingenious.)

The good news: his T-cell count is 210. That's a drop, but a statistically insignificant one, according to Dr. Jeff's office.

MARCH 17: Came down to Washington on the shuttle through a driving rain. Checked into the Hay-Adams (the *GQ* contingent arrives tomorrow), and stood out on my room's balcony listening to the noontime bells of St. John's Church, trying to imagine my Clara hearing them 120 years ago as she took her babies into the park.

By 2:30 I was down at the end of K Street, where Dan Quayle has some temporary office space. We spent over 2½ hours talking together, and by the time I left it seemed pretty clear to me that this is going to happen. We were both talking about exactly how we *would* work together, and leaving off the ifs . . . I told him that I was not a social-issue conservative, that I blame Buchanan for a lot of what went wrong in '92, and that I thought we could make areas of disagreement work to the project's advantage. He seemed to feel the same. (I did not tell him that I love *Murphy Brown*: disclosure has its limits.) . . .

MARCH 18: Began the day with [John] McConnell, DQ's nice, square-jawed, true-believing, incredibly polite kid speechwriter. He took me over to the [American Enterprise Institute] to meet Bill Kristol . . . perhaps the most open Bush-basher of the lot . . . Horgan says I am DQ's preference, though Quayle has also told Horgan that he could work with the other remaining candidate— the less "bold" choice—as well. So it all depends on how much Bill Shinker, the head guy at HarperCollins, likes bold. I'm supposed to meet with him at 3:30 on Monday. So this will drag on through the weekend. Will I be relieved if it all falls through?

. . .

The Michael Kelly book party, which began with cocktails in Art's suite and then a huge gathering at Sequoia (about 5 blocks down from DQ on K Street, right on the river), was a big success. Art bagged most of the celebrities he wanted: Sally Quinn, James Carville, Mary Matalin . . . Dinner was at I Ricci, another wretched-excess repast . . . My partner was Andrew Sullivan, the gay, Catholic, relatively conservative editor of *The New Republic*, who is so hot now that he even appears in Gap ads. He talked about his boyfriend and bashed the Clinton people (soulless nerds) with even more gusto than I could have summoned.

MARCH 21: . . . Andy called to tell me that Phil died last week. He was calm and strong and obviously exhausted on the phone.

MARCH 22: I went back to the office by 5 and found a message from Mary. She'd just had a call from Jonathan Galassi at Farrar, Straus: Helene Atwan says Tom Mallon might like to leave Ticknor. Could they talk about it?

MARCH 25: Mary really must have played hardball, because she's gotten me the $100,000 I wanted [to do the Quayle book]: a $90,000 fee plus $10,000 in expenses. She's not through yet, either: she figures she can go back for more at least one more time before they get sick of us. I think we were lucky to have Bob Barnett in all this: he's so used to dealing in big sums for the high and mighty that he probably thought [another] $25,000 was a trivial matter . . . So I'm going to do it. It seemed preposterous a month ago when Michael Barone first mentioned it. But I think now that it will be easy, and that it won't make any impact on my career one way or the other. Yes, some people will know, but my name won't be on the book and HarperCollins has agreed not to do a press release. It will be my little brush with history, and it will leave me richer.

MARCH 26: Did some frantic phone-dealing for a very short Ann Beattie story that we need right away. (Art bit [a production editor's] head off yesterday, when Craig revealed he'd miscalculated the runover by 12 columns; the long Tom Rayfiel story had to be bumped to August.)

MARCH 29: Arthur Greene did my taxes in the morning. My return has become so complicated that I have no idea whether I owe a large sum or am entitled to one back.

APRIL 1: Marilyn Quayle opened the door—none too friendly, I thought. We chatted in the living room (it's DQ's aunt's house) while DQ was on the phone. I told her I thought he and I could do a good book, that he had an interesting story to tell, and she responded that "it was fascinating—if you didn't have to live it." I think she's shattered and angry.

He and I get on just fine . . . he tells a pretty good story; has a sense of useful detail; doesn't need much prompting; and doesn't mind interruption. The tapes already have some very choice bits, though I suspect he's going to choke when it comes to actually using some of the stuff.

APRIL 2: DQ picked me up at Congressional [Country Club], and on the way to Potomac he told me that Marilyn had agreed— reluctantly—to talk about 1988 with me. She was sitting in the living room, sullen, when we arrived, and she warned me that she didn't like "touchy-feely questions." But once I turned the tape recorder on, I couldn't get her to stop—tears, anger, score-settling, and lots of vivid detail.

APRIL 3: Took Ann Beattie's editorial changes over the phone (she was surprisingly easy, agreeing to just about all I'd suggested), before Billy and I went down to Jay Yost's housewarming party. He and his boyfriend Wade (who's like a skinnier version of Jay) have bought a huge loft-turned-apartment on E. 19th St. They had about 50 people over, a big affair with two handsome gay waiters pushing complicated hors d'oeuvres . . . As always, I found myself wondering how many of the guests were sick.

APRIL 8: Another day with DQ . . . [His son Tucker,] home from Lehigh for Easter vacation, joined us for about a half hour so I could tape his memories of '88 and of life in the VP mansion. (You could play lacrosse indoors, because the bulletproof windows wouldn't break.)

APRIL 9: Marty called from the office to tell me that the Prince Charles issue—to everyone's surprise—is selling very well. . . .

Billy and I rented *My Favorite Year*, the Peter O'Toole comedy about the early days of television. It's a mess that ends nowhere, but it has its touching moments. I always like movies about guys just starting out (the Mark Linn-Baker character). In fact, I'd like to be starting out forever: it's my preferred, enduring image of myself.

APRIL 12: It's past midnight and I am in a little Amtrak room-ette underneath Penn Station. I'm about to go to sleep on the train they call "the smallest hotel in NY." One car of cunningly designed sleepers—really, what I'm in is as cleverly put together as the Mercury space capsule, and a thousand times as comfortable.

. . .

[Earlier in the evening] At Billy's by 8:30. In the cold wind we went out of the building to catch a cab and head for Tiffany's. And there they were—the cows—in all their charming, whimsical glory, beautifully lit. I was so proud of him. I told him so, told him how much I loved him. And then I headed off in another cab to come here.

APRIL 13: It should have been a relaxing ride [home from Wash-ington], but I was actually frantic. I'd played back some of the last 2 tapes and realized that failing batteries had rendered DQ and [me] to sounding like Donald Duck or the Chipmunks. By the end the volume was extremely low and the words so fast as to be unin-telligible. Back home, Billy and I tested and retested and could in no way improve them. Most of the day's material is usable, come what may, and I still have my notes. For the rest, Billy and I were looking at tape doctors in the Yellow Pages.

APRIL 14: "I do all the Gotti tapes," said the Russian-born dubber, proudly. I found his studio a block south of Condé Nast; he was used to reviving tapes made by no-tech lawyers, and in a matter of hours, for $186, he succeeded in bringing the Quayle recordings back to life. I don't think he ever recognized who was on them, not even when DQ was talking about his former boss' lack of ideas and initiatives. "You use these in litigation?" the Russian asked.

APRIL 15: Spent the morning at home, reading and rejecting man-uscripts. I have so many good things right now—Lorrie Moore, Francine Prose and Rick DeMarinis—that I can't possibly buy: no room.

APRIL 17: By 4:30, having flown the last miles over those huge brown and green circular farms (laid out for irrigation purposes), I was back in Lubbock, being greeted by Mary and Lynn, who look very little older than they did fifteen years ago. They're in a new International Style house now, very peculiar for Lubbock, and closer in to the university. It was built in 1938, ancient for these parts; you can see dust-storm scratchings on the dining-room windows.

They threw a nice party for me tonight, full of familiar folk from Tech . . . In many ways like the old days, except . . . All the woe and travail that's swept through these past few years. The ugly Marshall divorce; the accidental death of the Rudes' son; the suicide of Wendell Aycock's boy (the same little one, I think, who used to be in the English building on Saturday morning, drinking Dr Pepper); the nasty lawsuit by Pat Shaw against Leon Higdon. Chris Hatfield's wife Dot has already left him—the 2-year-old son William now shuffles between them. Liz Smitten getting more lonely and eccentric as the years without Jeff go by. One old constant: Wookie, the black cat I used to play the piano with (doing glissandos with her paws) is *still alive*. A little black bag of bones.

APRIL 18: From there to the Book Gallery, in the upscale Kingsgate Center at 82nd & Quaker, for my reading . . . There's so little going on in Lubbock that a TV reporter showed up to do an interview . . .

APRIL 19: I took off from Dallas at about 1:30, and I wonder now if I might have spotted the burning Waco cult compound if I'd looked out the window. Some of the few survivors, fire victims, were already on their way, I think, to the burn center at Parkland Hospital. I had no idea any of this was happening until I saw the news tonight, though this morning, when Mary had on *Good Morning America*, I did notice them showing shots of Koresh's stronghold with hints that something might be up.

APRIL 20: It seems that Paul did an end run around Marty with my SETI piece—never showed it to him before putting it into production. Now Art and Marty both say it needs some rewriting, which would be normal and fine if I hadn't been sitting here for two weeks thinking there was no problem.

APRIL 23: We began our celebration of Bill's birthday at Café Greco, where we used to go with Miss Miriam, and then it was on to the Carlyle for our beloved Dixie, who looked especially sleek and beautiful this year. She sang our songs, and we sat on the same banquette as last year. She's added a funny number about Woody and Mia, probably written by John Wallowitch. . . .

APRIL 25: Spent the afternoon doing a dry run of Quayle writing. Carol Shookhoff's transcripts are marvelous, and in two hours, with them and some press clips and the speech file, I'd put together 2500 words on the Tower nomination fight. I hope it all goes this smoothly. Enough of his phrasing survives in the text so that it sounds like him. I'm putting it directly into the computer: it feels just the way doing those old *Architectural Digest* speeches used to feel—much more like editing than writing.

APRIL 26: Paul came back from vacation today, and Art chewed him out within an inch of his job . . . It fell to me to have lunch with him at Yamaguchi, his usual place with Lucy, as he tried to calm his nerves. So, instead of *my* getting stroked today—after a week of demoralizing nonsense—I was in the role of therapist. Tomorrow we'll get to work on the piece itself . . . Art wants a more personal essay, more explicit point of view, less reportage. Well, fine. If that had been the original assignment, I'd have been even happier to do the piece.

APRIL 27: Art handled the SETI piece's disappearance from the lineup with a nice finesse at the 9:30 meeting. He said it was being moved to September "because Tom Mallon promises us a major discovery by then." . . . Fretted about how thin I'm stretched when I was at Bert's. He came out to the waiting room to get me; I had my eyes closed, my head back; the sun was on my face and I was nearly asleep; that was how, if I had to be there at all, I wanted to spend the hour.

APRIL 29: To Billy's by nine. The cows have come home, fresh from their Tiffany triumph. Mr. Gene already wants him to do a sequel: kitties. Cat on a Hot Tin Roof, Cat in the Hat, Cat o' Nine Tails—the feline possibilities are even bigger than the bovine ones.

MAY 1: The trees in the Quayles' front yard were in full flower. But DQ and I spent the whole morning and most of the afternoon in the basement, taping his recollections of the Gulf War. He handed me his diary, which contains some vivid and touching things—it would be nice to reproduce a page or two of it with the photographs, but we'd have to find an orthographically perfect one.

. . .

I got a 5:00 shuttle back from Washington, and was in my apartment just before Andy Pandolfo arrived. He looks well, if quite a bit older. (His hair is entirely gone but for a gray fringe; I would almost have sworn I was seeing his father, Paul.) He talked cheerfully about Phil and how much he misses him, how a friend is even trying to put him in touch with a "channeler." I nodded encouragingly, no matter how sad I thought this was.

MAY 4: [In Arizona, working on the Quayle book at DQ's parents' house] John McConnell picked me up in a Lincoln (a loan from one of the dealers DQ is addressing down here) and we drove an hour or so into the desert to Wickenburg, past tumbleweeds and cacti and squatly looming ridges.

MAY 5: . . . Got up in the sun-filled guest house. Birds chattering everywhere. Rabbits and tiny quail (yes) running around outside . . . Corinne Quayle is very pretty . . . She calls her son "Danny" and shakes her head in a bewildered way over the memory of every shot that was fired at him.

DQ and I sat out by the pool, in shorts and sunglasses, taping hour after hour on the '92 campaign. (He thinks the Bush people let him run his own operation this time, "because they could only screw up one campaign at a time.") . . . In the afternoon, Dan went off to golf 36 holes, while McConnell and I went out with a guide from the nearby ranch. We were on some quiet old horses (mine was Adam, a great muncher of wildflowers), and we rode a few miles into the hills . . . wonderfully peaceful, listening to the clopping sounds one has only heard in movie westerns . . . patches of red soil; flaming shoots of ocotillo; century trees that grow so fast you can hear them.

. . .

Jim and Corinne seemed very happy to have us; it was as if Danny were still a college boy and he'd brought two classmates home for spring break. After dinner, Jim stayed inside and the rest of us went out to look at the Little Dipper and a moon so bright it appeared to be a disk of radium.

MAY 6: More hours of taping. And we're pretty much through with it . . . Even gay rights: no, DQ would not mind if all the sodomy laws were quietly repealed. And he notes how Bush-Quayle put through lots of non-discriminatory rules for government workers, except in the military—where he thinks gays will quietly continue to serve without being asked about their orientation. I have plenty of disagreements with him here, but it's important to remember that with these positions he would have been considered a wild-eyed radical on the subject of gay rights as little as 15 years ago . . . I thought these 3 days would be pleasant enough, but I never figured they'd be as much fun as they have. The landscape has been a constant thrill to my eyes, and the fact is I've become fond of DQ and his parents, too.

MAY 7: . . . Breakfast with Jim and Corinne. He rode me to the airport. (Bless his heart: he stiffens up easily, and the long ride could not have been a picnic.) We passed the slow-motion explosion of outer Phoenix's growth, and he left me at one of the *slightly* older terminals—not the one recently named for Barry Goldwater, who was still giving cantankerous quotes to the newspaper this week.

MAY 11: I'd had a productive day at the office, banging a new version of the SETI piece into the computer, when Mary [Evans] called at 5:10 to say that Jonathan Galassi and FSG have passed on the novel . . .

I don't know what to do. My life feels so *incoherent*. I don't

mind being busy, but I cannot keep all these plates in the air, especially when the one to which I seem to give the least attention—my
own writing—is the one that's supposed to be the most important
to me. I don't mind working hard; in fact, I can't imagine life any
other way. But my life doesn't make *sense*. I'm trying to conduct
three careers at once . . . What I want is to be just a writer. At long
last. Not a writer who's also a teacher, editor, ghostwriter and so
on and so on.

MAY 12: I'm losing faith in that novel, and I have to stop this at
all costs.

MAY 13: Helped Art polish his commencement address to the
Penn State journalism graduates. It's more like a series of after-
dinner jokes, but still better than what I spent years listening to on
Sunday mornings in Poughkeepsie.

MAY 14: David Brooks . . . is in town, and we went out to lunch with
Adam Bellow—Saul's son—an editor at Macmillan's Free Press.
David is probably looking to shop a book proposal, but there was
no particular business at hand, just a friendly lunch among still-
youngish neocons. Adam has, unmistakably, his father's eyes . . .
David has been covering Europe for three years now. He says he
went to Brussels admiring bourgeois values, but he's become sick
of the orderliness, the "café stare" and lack of animation. He's
longing now for the antisocial mayhem of New York, even if it
means bringing his children back into it.

MAY 16: Slept until noon—like some sort of drugged water buffalo. Billy says he's sure I do it to escape the world—the constant
fretting about the half dozen pots I'm stirring at once, not to mention all the bigger fears and anxieties.
   I'm a little anxious about him just now. A new medicine he's
on is having some uncomfortable side effects: nothing major, but
some digestive upset and facial blotches. Otherwise he seems fine.
Better, certainly, than Dennis, who's in Lenox Hill with TB . . .
   . . . Went down to Louise's for a nightcap. It was months since
we'd seen each other . . . Her old New Dealer's heart was surpris-

ingly tickled by the Quayle news, and she wanted lots of detail. She inquired very attentively about Billy's health, and we talked about the gays-in-the-military controversy, which seems to be coming to a rest at the "don't ask, don't tell" compromise.

MAY 17: Billy saw Dr. Jeff tonight. JG spent much of yesterday showing a surgical amphitheatre to Barbra Streisand, who is about to make a film of Larry Kramer's *The Normal Heart*. (Kramer is also a patient of Dr. Jeff's. His nurse, Lillian, says he's "the sweetest person" and that his screaming shtick is simply a strategic persona.) Dr. Jeff says Streisand—the ultimate Clintonista—asked him how he felt about HMOs. He responded that he felt about the way she would if she had to let someone else direct her movie.

MAY 19: Mary [Evans] called to read me a letter she got from Jonathan Galassi. It expresses continuing interest in me—he wants to talk more at their lunch next month. He says he has by no means given the novel a final turndown. Well, this is nice, but it doesn't help much . . .

Dennis is not doing well. Billy talked to him this afternoon, and his pancreas is now giving him problems. This could be the point, the endgame, where everything begins to give out and shut down . . . When he goes, there will be one less railing between us and the cliff; that's how it will feel.

MAY 20: If I ever write my Condé Nast novel, I've got my fact-checking story. [P.K.], a very handsome young man whose vacant, lovely face makes Dan Quayle's look craggy with complexities, was doing research on a profile of William Weld. It contained a sentence about how Weld must decide whether he wants to "go for the brass ring" and run for President in '96. Well, [P.K.] called the White House to ask if it was true *that new Presidents received brass rings*. I am not making this up. Marty had to call him into his office the morning, to ask the poor gorgeous lummox what planet he was from.

MAY 22: Wrote about 3000 words on the Bentsen debate . . . I'm amazed by how quickly this goes. Someday I should try to write a first-person novel; I bet it feels easier than what I've been doing all these years.

. . .

Bill and I went out to the Broadway Diner (East Side branch) for supper. And then we made a cabaret evening of it. Up to hear Barbara Carroll at the Carlyle and then down in a cab to the Ballroom.

MAY 24: SETI is fine. Art got back from Connecticut around lunchtime and came into my office to tell me he thought it was excellent, much stronger, easier to follow, and quite beautifully written in places. I am absolutely delighted. Now *GQ* can go back to being the happy, low-maintenance part of my life it's been for 3 years . . . [But then there's] Mordecai: his review of Halberstam's Fifties book, in the June issue, hits rock bottom. He is stealing Art's money, and we will never mean anything in the book world, no matter what efforts I make with fiction and essays and small reviews, until he's glossily banished to the well, where he can do travel pieces, leaving the book column to someone else—e.g., me.

MAY 26: Caught the 8:30 shuttle to D.C. . . . Walked around in the spring air before getting a cab to Potomac. I was out at Dan Quayle's by 11:00. We went over the outline and 2 of the sections (Bentsen and the convention) . . . Bill Kristol—brilliant, pudgy, putting out a sort of aggressive intellectual calm—came by for lunch. He, too, liked what's been written, and he had some useful suggestions . . .

MAY 27: [Getting ready to give a talk at my twentieth college reunion at Brown] I see from the brochure, by the way, that one of my competitors for an audience Saturday morning will be Jane Fonda, that buoyant feather of the Zeitgeist. She'll be with her husband, Ted Turner, as he picks up an honorary degree; she herself will be speaking in Sayles Hall. She's gone from clapping her hands atop an anti-aircraft gun to having a boob job to please her billionaire hubby . . .

Had a letter from Gore Vidal . . . "Huck's [Clinton's] absence of principle has, so far, not been as fruitful, in every sense, as I had hoped—I've finished yet another film—I am the villain—so relaxing to be in a film with no responsibility at all except to be there. My life unfolds before me on the page like some vast inside joke. Can't wait for the punchline."

MAY 28: [In Providence] John F. Kennedy Jr., back for his tenth, was milling through the crowd toward George St.

We all went back to Harkness and faded fast. The people across the way in Chapin—Class of '63—seemed to have more stamina, but I suppose their children are grown, whereas people like Deborah and Jay are used to going to bed at 9:30.

MAY 29: My talk was scheduled for 10:30 . . . Once inside my nervousness increased: they had put me into a big lecture hall behind a large podium. Oh, dear. What I had—some offhand remarks and the "Held in Check" essay—seemed so *slight*, especially now that the room was filling with twice as many people as I'd expected.

I was truly surprised to see how many of my classmates showed up. And there was Sophie [Blistein] about ten rows back. Anne Diffily introduced me, and I got going—looking every so often at Jay and Nan in the front row—and when I got into the checks essay, I knew something very good was happening. Everyone was here to think about the past; every person was in search of his old self; and I realized that this essay, about looking for traces of a parent who went broke sending his kid to Brown, was the perfect thing for the occasion.

. . .

Rob and Sam Streit and I walked all the way to Alumni Ave. to drop in on Elmer, and although he was on his oxygen tube he was jaunty (in a track suit) and humorous and complaining about "Saint Sophia," who won't stop hovering over him.

MAY 30: . . . How much *nicer* people are after 35. The suspicion and one-upsmanship fade. Having been cut up and exalted by life, everyone has a healthy respect for its brevity and power, is glad simply to see old faces that are alive and well. . . .

JUNE 1: Went to Bert at 5:50—told him that I never felt more like a writer than I did this weekend. We talk about why I seem to have such a hard time, after so many years and books, really believing I am one—why it still seems so presumptuous. What self-loathing is at work *there*?

JUNE 3: All the competing agenda [with the Quayle memoir] . . . Horgan [the editor] wants emotion; Kristol wants issues; Zondervan [a division of HarperCollins] wants religion; and DQ wants '96. . . .

Billy and I went up to Lenox Hill Hospital tonight to visit Dennis, who looks terrible, and was groggy with medication, but who seems, amazingly, to be bounding back. They were ready to give up on him a week ago, but his pancreas is now fighting off the infection. He is blessed with what Tommy lacked completely: the will to live.

JUNE 4: John Herman has responded to the Rathbones . . . For the first time he expresses some real enthusiasm for the book and coherently talks about the single thing holding it back: Henry's character . . . As things stand Henry is too much like Iago, too little like Othello—he is so dark from the start that the assassination hardly has much chance to change him.

JUNE 5: Mom arrived on the jitney from Manorville. We took her to Sardi's for dinner, the three of us sitting beneath Jessica Tandy's caricature. From there we went next door to the Helen Hayes to see Lynn Redgrave's *Shakespeare for My Father* . . . She does some funny imitations of Maggie Smith and Edith Evans and Noël Coward. But the bits about her family and her father are mostly mawkish and embarrassing—completely Oprah-ratic. (Exorcism of Daddy dearest before inevitable "reconciliation" with one's memories.) How completely Americanized L.R. is. Her loony Marxist sister could never have perpetrated this.

But Mom loved it and, bless her heart, got up in her little pink suit to join in the standing ovation . . .

JUNE 6: Breakfast with Mom and Billy at the Lexington Ave. Grill. He gets impatient with me when I get impatient with her chatter. (I forgive myself by thinking that my spurts of impatience are so familiar to her they make her feel secure.)

JUNE 11: Mary [Evans] called after her lunch with Jonathan Galassi. "He'd really like you to write a book on the Irish in America." She was all excited about this, but an hour after we got off the phone I could see myself backing into another *Stolen Words*.

JUNE 12: Up to Doug and Bruce's around 7:30. Ben and Peter came too, and after drinks we went out to a Mexican restaurant. Puerto Rican flags all around the neighborhood in anticipation of tomorrow's parade. Bruce . . . more tedious than ever, unable to believe Ben pronounces *chaise longue* the way 95% of all Americans do . . . We ended the evening down at the new Barnes & Noble—a huge city block of a store on Broadway in the lower 80s. It felt like Saturday night at a suburban mall. The store has a coffee bar & lots of tables and chairs. It's beautifully stocked (no problem finding any of my own in-print titles, which of course I looked for), but you wonder how many people have actually come to buy.

JUNE 13: [Bill was in California.] Some friend of Michael's in San Francisco steered Billy to a special hotel deal that has him staying for $180 a night in the St. Francis Hotel suite where Queen Elizabeth and Prince Philip lodged in 1983. It's got a dining room with twelve chairs, and Billy says it's especially hard not to think of the royals whenever one ventures into the bathroom.

   . . .

    In our apartment, by myself, reading in bed, doing dishes, looking at the lights atop the Beekman Tower Hotel: a vision of myself, rather frightening, in the days when Billy will be gone.

JUNE 15: John Mortimer called this morning, agreeing to do a little piece on the Inns of Court. While he had me on the line he asked about the location and procedures of the New York City morgue. (He's writing a story in which a character has a heart attack while bidding at Christie's and then dies, still unidentified, at Lenox Hill.) I told him I'd have to get back to him.

JUNE 19: Billy and I went to see *Much Ado About Nothing* tonight . . . There's this terrible air of self-congratulation about the whole enterprise, an inability to have any witty line delivered without a thigh being slapped appreciatively. It's not so much a movie as a long reaction shot. (The truth is the play itself has too much of this, too many lines reminding the audience how witty Beatrice is.)

JUNE 21: Finally dug back into *Henry and Clara* tonight. I'm beginning to figure out how to move Henry in the direction he needs to go. One thing that needs changing: his taste for apocalypse.

JUNE 22: Back home in bed Billy and I watched the obituaries for Pat Nixon, and I cried.

JUNE 29: I met Fran and Gerry Howard for lunch at Tropica, and we picked the winner of the *GQ* fiction contest. It's a witty story by someone completely unknown named Talton Weber. Art will be pleased because it involves pretty Amish girls riding around in a Corvette. They may or may not be witches, according to Fran, who apparently read with greater closeness than I did. It wasn't Gerry's favorite in the stack he had to read, but as he said with some accuracy: "It has a good beat and you can dance to it."

JUNE 30: I was with [Art] almost all day—we had another big editorial lunch at Trattoria Dell'Arte, the antipasto drowned in garlic and olive oil; and then he called me in when he was talking to Kamp about Philip Roth. Most of the time I was just schmoozing or nodding, but he leaves one exhausted. He is as comical and silly and predictable as can be, but he is also smart, and full of this crazy touching gusto that just sucks the life out of everyone around him.

JULY 1: . . . Billy's count has dropped to 176. Dr. Jeff took blood on Monday. No change in regimen is anticipated, but he has dropped below the old magic # of 200.

JULY 5: While I folded laundry I watched a bit of the *Twilight Zone* marathon on Channel 11. How I still love Rod Serling's overwritten intros and codas. You were supposed to detect a trace of their style in the first little section of *Aurora 7*.

JULY 6: I called our fiction-contest winner this afternoon. Talton Weber is 37 years old, and he makes his living publishing high-school and college yearbooks. He has published only a couple of stories in local magazines, and his biggest break has been a grant from the Ohio Arts Council. I felt like the Publishers Clearing House Prize Patrol, or Ed McMahon, telling him he'd won $5000, publication in the November issue, and a trip to New York, where we'll give him a party stocked with editors and agents. He told me he was going back to his computer "reborn," and apologized for being eager to end the conversation, but he just had to get off the phone and scream.

JULY 7: Horgan is used to "crashing" celebrity books through the publishing pipeline, and he thinks, I fear, that I'm proceeding with Flaubertian slowness . . . Sick of it all. Longing to get back to *Henry & Clara*. . . .

JULY 10: Andy picked us up at the Glen Cove station. A squall had blown through his bit of the north shore a few hours before, felling trees and strewing branches everywhere. Some of the traffic lights were out, and the power coming to Andy's house brought light bulbs to only the dimmest life. He showed us pictures of Phil and the panel he's made, with friends, for the AIDS quilt . . . On the train home, Billy said, out of the blue, "I think I'm a lot farther along than Andy"—i.e., he surmises his T-cell count is lower.

JULY 15: Saturday night [Doug and Bruce are] off to the White Party on Fire Island, wearing shorts and pearls and bare chests and stuff like that. This is quite a change for Bruce, who used to hate anything that appeared overtly homosexual, and who is now making the same sorts of judgments about the discreet that he once reserved for the flamboyant.

JULY 16: Tonight Billy and I went to Radio City to see beautiful Chris Isaak and then—the hardest-working woman in show business—Miss Tina Turner, who shook her thing, and belted, and got atop a hydraulic lift, and never stopped for almost two hours. She had the audience limp by the time she was through.

JULY 17: I think I'm doing it well enough, but I have made a firm One Time Only vow as far as ghosting goes—otherwise, before long, I'll be writing sentences like "John Sununu could be stubborn as all get out" in my *own* voice. It's like what mothers tell their kids when they cross their eyes: if you keep doing that, they'll *stay* crossed.

JULY 18: Billy and I had an early dinner at Nations cafe. Through the plate-glass windows I spotted Si Newhouse exit his UN Plaza apartment and hail a cab. Si generally shuns limos and on weekdays walks so fast to his lunches, and so inattentively to traffic, that at *GQ* we've imagined headlines like: MIDGET MAG MOGUL MOWED DOWN ON MADISON.

JULY 20: When I went up to Dr. Slaff's this afternoon, I told him that I felt as if I were carrying a mile-high stack of plates that was swaying and swaying, and that if a single sprig of parsley were dropped on to it, the whole thing would come crashing down.

. . .

Billy and I ate at the new Italian place on 2nd & 50th tonight. A woman at the table next to us had the single loudest conversational voice I've ever heard in New York. Across the aisle sat a very handsome young man, who was reading, believe it or not, *How to Win Friends and Influence People*. He was more than 3/4 of the way through it, and he was dining alone.

JULY 24: . . . At intervals I've been reading the galley of Gerald Posner's *Case Closed* . . . In its exhaustive, plodding, day-by-day account of Oswald's life, it has, curiously enough, the force of revelation. For twenty years all the real evidence has been pushed aside so that the fantastical stuff could be piled up on the table. Now the old facts look fresh and convincing.

JULY 28: In green, flat clean Indianapolis by 6:00. I'm in a Radisson in a suburban office park, not far from Carmel, where Dan and Marilyn and the gentry live.

Talked to Billy, had room service bring up dinner, and sat down to write about Mikhail Gorbachev.

JULY 30: [DQ] told me that he last saw Nixon early this year, up in New Jersey. RN advised him "not to suck up to your critics" in the book . . . I went out to the house in Carmel around 7:30. The cab driver couldn't quite find the street I'd asked for, but while he was looking for it, he pointed out a big house, in the manner of a tour guide, and said, "That's where Quayle's living now." "Good," I replied, telling him to pull over.

AUGUST 1: . . . Billy called around 10 p.m. He had a wonderful time, but he left St. Louis in an emotional state, thinking about how he loves this little remnant of his family, and of how, when Nathan and Andrew and Nikki make their first trips to New York—probably in high school, the boys and their parents guessed—he's not likely to be alive.

AUGUST 2: Billy is very down. Dr. Jeff points out that he's lost 10 pounds. While he's lost weight in previous summers, it's still not good news.

AUGUST 5: Marty came into my office this morning with a galley of my James Merrill review and asked if the books I was doing in the Critiques column weren't sometimes a little elitist. I told him that this was a book Joe Nocera and Art were urging me to look at for excerpting and that I'd said no to that. So maybe he should talk to them. And if we overcompensate a little for Mordecai Richler (his November books column is on two self-help sex tomes), maybe the solution is to hold Art's feet to the fire and make sure Mordecai loses the column. . . .

Lunch with David Gates at Inagiku in the Waldorf. We couldn't linger too long, since he had to get back to *Newsweek* to finish a piece on Philip Larkin (that elitist author I'll soon be writing about). He's a twitchy, furtive sort, and we had a restrained discussion of Jane Austen and John O'Hara. He really came alive, though, on the subject of the Kennedy assassination (how did it even come up?). He is a major conspiracy freak, *Newsweek*'s resident expert on the subject. He knows a number of "researchers," who call him up from places like British Columbia and whisper sinister theories about "the Priscilla Johnson connection."

. . .

The day's good news: Billy's count is back to 200. Dr. Jeff did one on Monday night.

AUGUST 6: [Vermont] The Littlefields live down the road [from Middlebury] in Cornwall, on about 90 acres with only another house or two in sight. They've added a whole series of upstairs rooms, like a string of railroad cars with treacherous head-banging ceilings, onto the old farmhouse below . . . Dave Sr. is exactly Billy's idea of an elegant college professor . . . At dinner Jeannie told the story of how her Alabama father took the 16-year-old Tallulah Bankhead to her very first New York play. At the restaurant the prim young thing sniffed at her drink, checking very carefully to make sure it contained no alcohol.

AUGUST 7: It rained all afternoon, so we had our Bread Loaf picnic on the porch of one of the houses there and then went for coffee in the big converted barn . . . Dinner, presided over by DL Sr., who has the gentle, huggy ways of a Unitarian minister, turned very funny, as we brought out all the old stories of Vassar eccentrics like Lola Boyd. God, even Billy's heard them five times by now!

AUGUST 12: Peter Richmond is back from Guadalcanal, where he went to look around the old battle site, since his father was there during WW2. He's doing an essay for us . . . This afternoon he told me that he now "really knew" what it felt like to be on that island during WW2. This revelation comes, apparently, from finding a couple of old belt buckles and shell casings. That he went and came home from the island on a Condé Nast expense account, rather than on a troopship and in a body bag, seems to have eluded him . . .

. . . My dreary dinner with Jeffrey Simpson (Aunt Pitty, as

Billy calls him). We went to Chin-chin, where he jaw-jawed about problems with his parents in the nursing home; small treacheries at *AD*; his unpublished manuscript; his envy of his friend David McCullough. He ate and ate and talked and talked, and I was so tired I thought I would scream. What a relief to get over to 51st St. and rest my head on my favorite spot between Billy's shoulder and neck.

AUGUST 13: Encountered . . . on my way to Penn Station this morning, after I'd told the cabdriver, stuck in traffic, to let me out: Father Mike. Who looks as merry as ever . . . We had an embarrassed chat, our first in four years. He told me that he'd been reading *Rockets and Rodeos* . . . It's a good thing I had a train to catch. I just wanted to strip the clothes from his slim little body and go to bed with him, without any of the scrupulosity of 6 years ago. I mean: look at all the grubby things we've learned about priests since then. Father Mike looks quite disciplined and upstanding compared to all of that.

AUGUST 14: Went for a run before dinner with Mom, during which she teared up about how lonely she is, and how worried about Loree's marriage. She can do little about the latter, though her worries for Loree are compounded by her *embarrassment* over how the world perceives marital disarray. To Mom, the world = the neighbors. And she has no real idea that half of all marriages end badly these days.

AUGUST 16: I was at the office until 6:30, arguing with Maura that the phrase "young womanhood" should not be n-dashed to read "young woman–hood." She made her elaborate grammatical arguments to me (she had everything but common sense on her side), and I overruled her, and her lower lip came out.

AUGUST 17: At the Tuesday lineup meeting this morning, Art announced that I would be taking over the Books column from Mordecai beginning in December. Surprised expressions throughout the room. This is a good thing, but I'm already feeling pressure from him & Marty to throw some hot popular books into my literary mix: I assured Art that I would do Mikal Gilmore's book after the Larkin letters, and that seemed to please him.

. . .

Continued talk of workaholism with Bert. Throughout my 20s, I said, it kept me from having to face sex in any realistic way. But I was a compulsive worker long before I was trying to run away from anything . . . So what made me embrace the compulsion before I was ten? He says it's nothing so simple as a mere avoidance mechanism, though on occasion it may function as such. He said I have to remember all the healthy gratification it brings, too. It's not a *useless* compulsion (say, handwashing). . . .

AUGUST 18: *GQ* in Connecticut . . . We made the long, twisty drive to New Preston for dinner at the Hopkins Inn. We were then stuffed as much as the goose who became the foie gras . . . Afterwards, back indoors for the cheese course, we had a discussion of covers (the usual one that never leads to any lasting changes), and Art proceeded to bite off everyone's heads in a rather stunning display of know-it-all inebriation. It was so unpleasant that Marty held off presenting him the Tiffany clock that is our present to mark his 10 years as editor.

AUGUST 19: Interesting to watch meeting styles. Lucy bravely pipes up with ideas of her own and in support of others; Lisa sneers or cocks an equivocating eyebrow, but *never ever* offers a proposal of her own; Alan Richman avoids being swatted by donning his cap and bells and offering comic relief.

I was sort of sick of the whole thing (in fact, I got up at a quarter to seven at the inn to take a hot bath, call Billy, and feel pure by working on my novel for an hour). There comes a point where, if you hear the word "piece" once more, you think you're going to shriek.

AUGUST 24: Months ago, a Japanese journalist named Takagi interviewed and photographed me for a piece on *Rockets and Rodeos*. The story has finally run, and he's faxed it to me. Strange Kafkaesque feeling to see your picture surrounded by a language of which you can decipher not a character. Makes you feel you've done something terrible. I finally called him up at his office in Rockefeller Center for a précis.

AUGUST 25: This morning I passed Scott + Lamar's office, and Scooter called me in (to the boys I am an avuncular figure): "Hey, Tom," he said excitedly, "Lamar found a dead guy last night." Some downtown junkie looked peculiar to him, as he stepped over the limp form . . . There was no sign of respiration, and a filmy gunk had begun to form over the lifeless eyes. Lamar reported the sighting to some cops, who radio'd a unit about a "possible corpse."

AUGUST 26: Billy and I took Fran and Howard and John Landau out to Vivolo, on 74th St., for Fran's birthday. Virginia Graham, Grand Old Broad, was two tables away. On the way over to the restaurant John's taxi had hit a very handsome young skateboarder. The cab was coming out of the park and the boy was skateboarding against the light. He flipped up into the air, flew, came down with a thud—and is okay.

AUGUST 28: [Sag Harbor] Trent Duffy, a free-lance editor, is Fran's major domo this summer. I sat next to him at dinner. Karen Marta from *Allure* across from me. Gwyneth Cravens arrived with Henry Beard, who got quite manic and boisterous for no apparent reason, not even drink. Ben Taylor, who's always reminded me of Tommy, was there, too: I see his face only once every year or two, and it's disconcerting—it's as if I'm watching Tommy, in some afterlife, as he goes about aging with the rest of us.

AUGUST 29: . . . We went over to Linda and Aaron Asher's in Sagaponack . . . Everyone stood drinking cocktails while the orange setting sun looked as if it were about to bowl a strike, straight down the green yard and into the house. William Gaddis was there, going on through his drinker's nose about how awful Robert Moses was, and how dumb each Rockefeller brother managed to be. Aaron at one point took me into an old shed with the promise of showing me something I could give to the Quayle museum. It turned out to be Bill Kristol's rusty old tricycle, a hand-me-down from Gertrude Himmelfarb and Irving K. more than 30 years ago, when Linda and Aaron were their neighbors and Linda first became pregnant.

SEPTEMBER 2: Breakfast with Dan Quayle at the New York Athletic Club. I think the median age in the dining room dropped by 20 years when we walked in . . . We talked a little about New York City politics. The new schools chancellor is obviously gay, and that's fine with DQ, since his social agenda is very moderate. (In fact, it's the more conservative voters on the school board who brought him in from San Francisco. It's the gay radicals who are tormenting him right now.)

SEPTEMBER 3: Betty Froelich called tonight and told me that Elmer died this morning. The last ten days were very rough, but he was allowed to remain at home: Sophie arranged round-the-clock care from a hospice. I knew that things were much worse than they'd been in May: late in July he sent me a letter that he had to dictate to one of his sons. It's still on my desk, unanswered . . .

A merry man, generous, harmlessly vain, uxorious (and with reason to be), a wonderful teacher and encourager. He helped me to find my voice, and thus my life. Tonight I felt a little as if Mary were dying all over again.

And Tommy would have been 40 years old today.

SEPTEMBER 4: "A proper man, as one shall see in a summer's day, a most lovely gentlemanlike man." The Oriental-sounding [florist] listened very carefully as I gave him this, from *A Midsummer Night's Dream*, to put on the card I was sending to Sophie.

SEPTEMBER 6: . . . Wigstock. A big issue in the East Village city-council-seat race . . . Antonio Pagán, the openly gay incumbent, has reasonable positions (i.e., he doesn't think everyone should be permitted to run wild) on the so-called "quality-of-life" issues. Miriam Friedlander, this old Stalinist type he ousted 2 years ago, wants her seat back, so she is arguing that Wigstock should be allowed to go on for 8 hours, whereas Pagán says it should be, like other loud, outdoor events, limited to four.

SEPTEMBER 7: Sophie called from Providence tonight (24 years to the day after I arrived on campus), and she told me how hard it's been . . . Five hundred people came to the synagogue yesterday. One of them told her of overhearing a man on some street in Providence saying to his companion, "You know, Elmer Blistein's life shows that money doesn't mean a damned thing."

SEPTEMBER 8: The headline on Elmer's obituary in the *Times* refers to him as "Humorist and Professor." The order would amuse him . . . I called Howard Hunt in the afternoon. Sophie was eager that he not read the news in the papers before someone could tell it to him personally. Fortunately, someone else did get to him with it, just an hour or two before I did. We reminisced about Elmer, and at the end of the brief conversation he was choked up and had to excuse himself and hang up.

SEPTEMBER 10: Worked for most of the day on Clara's dinner party—the new chapter set in 1873. If anyone ever wants to do a mini-series of the book, this will be his chance for a big Gilded Age scene.

SEPTEMBER 11: Revised DQ before it was time to go up to Billy's and await the arrival of Lucy and Mr. Chris [Bull]. He's in town . . . for a convention of gay journalists, and Lucy is covering the same convention for a piece she's doing for *GQ*. So we all decided to go out to dinner at the Metropolitan Café. The two of them brought me a tee-shirt from the convention: WE'RE HERE. WE'RE QUEER. WE'RE ON DEADLINE. Mr. Chris was cute as could be in his white shirt and tie (he'd just finished doing a panel); he's like some sort of nephew to Billy and me: we're just so damned proud of him, you know.

SEPTEMBER 13: John Butler, the choreographer, is dead. I always used to see him on First Avenue walking his dog, his great eyebrows preceding him, like whisk brooms.

SEPTEMBER 14: David Leavitt is in the middle of a little plagiarism scandal. Not really plagiarism so much as bad manners. He's taken a chapter of Spender's *World Within World* and made it the basis of his new novel (*While England Sleeps*). And Spender is screaming his octogenarian head off.

Billy and I went to Bette Midler's opening at Radio City tonight with Wilma and Eddie. We had a wonderful time. Is there another entertainer who so effortlessly alters the mood of what she does from moment to moment? The audience was full of sub-urban folk; the dreary kind of celebrity mogul (Barry Diller); and older gay men, who remember her from her first time around and now, fifteen years later, look burdened by loss and illness as they walk through the lobby at intermission.

SEPTEMBER 15: Have had moments of depression over the last few days, and Billy pinpointed the cause: "You're caught up with your work," he says. "You can't handle the lack of pressure."

SEPTEMBER 16: Art likes the Larkin piece—a lot, I think—though I know he's worried I won't be able to lower the high brow every once in a while.

SEPTEMBER 21: Terry McDonnell is out at *Esquire*, and Ed Kosner (from *New York*) is replacing him. Art is sky high. This couldn't have happened at a better time—the week of his 10th-anniversary celebrations. The news will be reported as evidence of *GQ*'s supremacy, and it's made sweeter by Ed Kosner's having fired Art from *Newsweek* years ago. Now Art has the chance to go head to head with him. "It's Patton versus Rommel," he was saying, "and I can smell the cordite."

SEPTEMBER 22: The whole staff assembled at 7:30 a.m. in a big fashion-photography studio down on Broadway near Houston . . . Timothy Greenfield-Sanders, an adorable little photographer (sort of a bald Lord Alfred Douglas), had us standing on boxes, sitting on ladders, lowering our chins and sticking our heads for-ward, just a little bit, in that way that takes off five years. The pic-ture is an anniversary present for Art, who remains highly elated. The press is playing the *Esquire* story just as he wants it to.

SEPTEMBER 23: Art's 10th-anniversary party began at 6:00 at "21." It was almost as much of a crush as he wanted. Ed Kosner showed up, and the press had a good time getting pictures of the new rivals. Si Newhouse made an awkward, incoherent toast, which everyone nevertheless raved about because it was so *long*. To most people, Si is like the early Garbo: they have never heard (and can't imagine) him speaking at all. Peter Gallagher, all eyebrows and handsomeness, was there with his wife; Carl Bernstein, alone, was walking back and forth as purposefully as someone in a pick-up bar at 3 a.m . . .

At dinner upstairs . . . Si sat next to Kathie Lee Gifford, and one can only imagine what he made of her cascading talk-show patter. Frank Gifford's toast to Art managed to make one realize how little there really is to their friendship. Alan Richman and Eliot Kaplan, up from Philadelphia, both did much better, and eventually the evening developed a little life and warmth.

SEPTEMBER 24: Art doesn't want the week to end, and I can't blame him. But most of us could have done without the spur-of-the-moment lunch at the Royalton. He wanted to be seen in his new role as Undisputed Master in front of people like Anna Wintour, so he took me and Lucy and Friedman and Hilary and Marty and Kamp and Granger over for a big lunch and much more wine than our hungover heads required. I went home at about four, exhausted . . .

SEPTEMBER 26: Wrote the potato chapter [of the Quayle book], and realized that my hard drive, weighted down with about 800 pages of Danny and *Henry and Clara* and everything else, is just about out of room . . . I've begun to move old files to floppies, bailing my high-tech boat.

SEPTEMBER 27: Clinton was in town (making a fool of himself by more or less saying that the only reason anybody could be voting against Dinkins is racism; his four-year record is that fabulous, I guess) . . .

SEPTEMBER 29: Never a dull moment at CNP. Gabé Doppelt, Anna's little protégée at *Mademoiselle*, has resigned after Si and Liberman more or less had Lucy Sissman editing that disastrously repositioned magazine behind her back. Art, on Amy's behalf, now feels vindicated. The last ten days have been glorious for him.

. . . At 6:00 Art and Lucy and I took a car over to Carnegie Hall for Frank Conroy's book party . . . To my surprise, Joe Kanon himself came over to say hello to me, and Irene Williams, the head Houghton Mifflin publicist, also marched up. I didn't recognize either one of them until they said their names, but each seemed aware of *Henry and Clara* as something from me with brighter than usual prospects . . . Maybe they will finally stop publishing me as if I'm part of the federal Witness Protection Program.

Rode home past the fat Botero sculptures that have taken up temporary residence on the Park Avenue malls. They're like those huge monstrosities at the opera house, or Macy's parade balloons that have fallen to earth. They'll be fun to have around for a while.

SEPTEMBER 30: PETA, the anti-fur people, invaded the building and sat in on the *Vogue* floor until they were dragged away by the cops. They failed to get to Anna, who slipped down the stairs and out to lunch with Calvin Klein, but soon we will all have to get picture IDs. (They will probably pay for the new security program with a couple more Blackglama ads.)

. . .

. . . Watch[ed] pieces of a couple of Susan Hayward movies on TNT. God, what a march through 50s "biopics": from the wheel-chair to the bottle to the gas chamber.

Looked at Avedon's pictures of all the old Camelot personali-ties in this week's *New Yorker*. I fail to see his talent in his so-called serious work. He should be a passport photographer, or a coro-ner's. He doesn't bring out a subject's personality; he just *drains* the subject of it . . . Billy thinks all the hideous "serious" stuff is done as a sort of weird artistic penance for his glitzy, high-fashion work—all of which (though Avedon will never believe it) is actu-ally much more artful.

OCTOBER 2: Over to Billy's with the *Times*. He was cleaning out his closets, as he does each year at this time. He fills up a big bag for the *GQ* clothing drive, and before I take it to the CNP building I take out about a third of the stuff, which is always in mint condition, for myself. "Billy, you can't give *this* away." Unless it's to me, of course.

OCTOBER 4: Had trouble sleeping, and so, at 3 a.m. I turned on the television. Live pictures of Yeltsin's assault on the Russian parliament building. CNN must have had a half dozen cameras set up, and all day long they showed tracer bullets, flaming windows, surrendering "rebels" (old-style Communists, actually), prone bodies that had been hit by snipers. It was the most ridiculously intimate spectacle, like watching something going on a few miles away at City Hall.

. . .

John Herman called . . . they need to settle on a title. I think *Henry & Clara* will be it . . . Just their names—two good, solid, 19th-century-American ones—will do it. And never mind if Fred Busch had *Harry & Catherine* and there was a biography of the Luces called *Henry & Clare*.

OCTOBER 7: Elmer's farewell.

I took a 9:30 train to Providence . . . The ceremony began at 4:30 in gloomy Sayles Hall, where only a few months before I'd been making merry with Jay and Nan and Geoff and Rob and Deborah. The speeches were well done, and I was moved by the way Dick Nurse ('61) told about Elmer's giving him confidence back when Dick was one of only two black men on campus. Andy Sabol played the organ, and even threw in a funereal rendition of the Brown fight song.

OCTOBER 12: . . . To Barocco for dinner with Art & Amy + Lucy. Don't ask me what made him think of us as a foursome. Lucy and I were sort of dreading it, particularly when we saw Amy in her leather poor-boy hat & fashion crucifix, this Mary-Quant-meets-the-Mineshaft outfit she's been wearing all the time lately. But it turned out to be fine. We (Lucy & I) expected to have to endure an *Esquire*-vs.-us-and-why-we're-winning monologue from Art, but the conversation turned out to be lively and general, a lot of it about the Clintons' health plan, in fact. This may have to do with the fact that Art has been having some ominous neurological problems lately—he has numbness in one of his legs. It's time for him to drop 50 pounds, to throw away the cigarettes, and to cap the vodka bottle.

OCTOBER 13: Scott Talton Weber, our Frederick Exley fiction contest winner, came to town today. He's a big overgrown, 37-year-old kid, straight off the turnip truck; he spent a lot of the day marvelling at skyscrapers and taxi drivers' habits.

I took him to lunch at the Royalton with Sarah, Ellen Ryder and Paula Bernstein, before sending him off to an appointment I'd set up for him with Sloan Harris at ICM.

At 6:00 he was the man of the hour down at the Lion's Head. We threw a big party to celebrate the award . . . The bar (which is headed into Chapter 11 with a leaky roof) was jammed with writers, editors and agents and every kid from the magazine. People stayed late and drank. Art and I spoke, and Exley's old subject Frank Gifford (the element I was most worried about) then got up to present Scott with his award. But he turned out to be immensely charming—infinitely better than he'd been at Art's anniversary party. He told some touching stories about Exley (who drank himself toward death at the Lion's Head) and generally sprinkled an odd glamor on the occasion. (Fran Kiernan, not exactly the football-hero type, was absolutely melting.)

That we really are beating *Esquire* was evident in all sorts of ways tonight, not the least of which involved Morgan Entrekin and Jay McInerney doing some deliberate schmoozing with me . . . I guess they realize Ed Kosner may no longer have so plush a welcome mat out in front of the Hearst Building.

Art was mad for Freda's daughter, who at one point looked around the room and told her mum: "I should have worn something more sluttish."

OCTOBER 19: Marty Xeroxes the big *USA Today* article on DQ's Huntington appearance and circles the paragraph that says, "If successful, Quayle's book could signal the launch of a 1996 presidential bid." Annotation: "Thanks a lot, Tom."

OCTOBER 22: The Mary McCarthy conference at Bard. A fiasco.

I drove up with Fran and Dan Max, who'll be writing a piece on it, no doubt comical, for *The Observer*. It's hard to say who did worse: the verbose, empty, overprepared academics, whose ugly-sounding speeches betrayed a complete cluelessness as to what Mary was like and about, or the "celebrity" writers like . . . Nancy Milford and Frankie FitzGerald, who did 15 minutes of ad libs at the mike . . or the conference organizers, who so over-scheduled the thing that there was never any discussion among the "panelists," let alone questions from the audience. It was hour after hour of forced marches up to the microphone, one unevocative speech after another. Once in a while you'd smile at something or prick up your ears and then realize it was just a quotation from Mary you were hearing, sandwiched between great soggy slabs of cardboard rhetoric . . . Tom Flanagan and Maureen Howard and a couple of others had their moments, but more typical of the day was Carol Brightman, standing up at the podium, voluminous in her dropcloth of a dress, paging through *The New Yorker*, hunting for passages in Janet Malcolm that she wanted to "discuss," and occasionally looking at a wadded-up piece of notepaper, only to confess that she couldn't read her own writing.

OCTOBER 26: *GQ* is certainly hot right now. I've finally gotten a William Trevor story (if I can seal the money deal) and Lois Wallace says Wm. Buckley would like to do a piece on his nephew's ordination (at a French monastery) for us. Well, the last won't fly (Art once said he thought *GQ* was "a substitute for God") . . .

OCTOBER 27: The mayoral campaign . . . do the opponents of Giuliani really think they can make a case against him by arguing, in effect, that he's too zealous against criminals? Do they really expect people in New York in 1993 to find that such a bad thing? . . . When Giuliani's men handcuffed the Wall Street traders 6 years ago, the act was hailed as a blow against Reaganism and greed; now it's seen as the tactic of a fascist.

OCTOBER 29: I hit rock bottom in my feelings toward New York today. The mail brought a tax bill from the city's Department of Finance. It claims I owe them $6400 in back taxes, interest and penalties—the "unincorporated business tax" it claims I should have been paying between 1988 and 1991. They picked the figures out of thin air, $1000 for each year. . . .

Arthur Greene's assistant explained to me that this is not taxation; it's a shakedown. The city, desperate for revenue, has madly been billing anyone who files a Schedule C. The computers don't look beyond that—they just decide that since Schedule C filers *might* be the kind of people who owe "UBT," they'll send a bill. Without even looking at the W-2s and business-expense deductions also filed by those people. You can write the check and let yourself be the victim of extortion, or you can protest, file lots of paperwork and hear from them a year later, or never. They're hoping you're the kind of person who doesn't like things hanging over his head, or has a guilty conscience about some other part of his taxes; if a lot of these people, even 10% of them, write checks, the shakedown has had a good yield.

. . .

. . . I was a real mess by the end of the day, when it was time for us to go up to the Carlyle. Hearing Barbara Cook was one of my birthday presents, and it was lovely (even if that vibrato in her soprano sometimes sounds like the whinnying of a pony). Yes, we love the Carlyle, and what could be more New York? But I'll bet Barbara Cook sometimes plays Indianapolis, maybe even Owosso, and is it worth all the degradation and hassle of New York just to sit two tables away from Matthew Broderick and Sarah Jessica Parker?

OCTOBER 30: . . . I am feeling so beleaguered in this city I worked so hard to get to ten years ago.

NOVEMBER 2: We got up and voted early, Billy at the synagogue on 51st and I at the preschool across from The Sands. The place was packed . . . I went off to Condé Nast, wearing a "RUDY" button I'd dusted off from four years ago . . . I was about to lose hope when suddenly all three networks, within minutes of one another, declared Rudy the winner. They'd all realized that Queens and Staten Island were running behind the other boroughs in reporting results . . . I wanted to sing the old *Follies* song—"I got through David Dinkins, and I'm here." Some of his gangster supporters, like Sharpton, were already crying racism, but the Mayor himself—I'll give him this—went more than the extra mile of graciousness when he conceded.

NOVEMBER 5: Ran into Nonnie Moore [GQ's fashion editor] in the cafeteria. She was just back from the Calvin Klein show in Bryant Park. She says the whole week has been a big success, and that the tents are more fabulous than some of the clothes.

NOVEMBER 6: Was in the air, on my way to Indianapolis, by 3:00. Started Anna Shapiro's new novel as we flew. Landed amidst snowflakes and freezing air, and my suitcase came off the plane with a ripped handle. Someone's single shoe preceded it on the carousel.

NOVEMBER 8: DQ and I were at the book for 14 hours today, out at the house in Carmel.

NOVEMBER 11: Art wants me to name my book column. Speaking Volumes? By the Book? Shelf Life? Bound and Determined? Lucy favors the simple Mallon on Books.

NOVEMBER 17: Marty has decided that I should have his original Sorel sketch of Dan Quayle, which touched me. (Dare I put it on one of the new [office's] walls right away? DQ might, after all, come up to my office to work on the ms. a couple of weeks from now.)

NOVEMBER 18: Kamp tells me that Art recently told him about our first meeting: "He'd just written that O'Hara piece, and the prose was so muscular. I expected this big guy to walk into The Four Seasons, and in comes—Tom!"

NOVEMBER 22: [Art's] courtship by *New York* continues. It's clear he's at least on the short list, and I think he may get an offer. He claims that's all he wants, something he can show Si, prompting a raise and additional perks—but I'm not so sure. The tone of his voice makes me think he'd like to give it a try. He'd be giving up a national magazine for a local one, but he'd be a player in the city and state—a guy who could get a lunch with Cuomo and Giuliani whenever he wanted. And there would be the proud pleasure of walking away from Condé Nast (something no editor ever does) instead of waiting to be fired (something every editor experiences).

NOVEMBER 23: [Art] chewed out Harry Schwartz for not getting our December issues to us in time, telling him that he should watch out when he sees Mallon in the elevators. Why? wondered Harry. "He's Bugsy Siegel's grandson." And Harry now believes this.

. . .

A letter from Gore Vidal: he says Clinton and Gore, with their generous figures, now look like "comforting matrons after jitterbug warrior Bush."

NOVEMBER 24: At 8:00 I was off to Jim Atlas' party. Impossible traffic all the way up Madison and across the park. Why? I wondered until we got across. Of course: the balloons. They were blowing them up right under Jim and Anna's apartment on 77th St.—the whole reason for having a party on this night. One almost couldn't get down the block—it was like 45th St. on the day of a presidential visit: one had to give the cops at the sawhorses a convincing story.

The party was crowded, with Philip Roth's head bobbing above nearly everyone else's. I chatted with Katha Pollitt-buro . . . I liked [her] back in my days at the Y, but I only feel nervous around her now. Jonathan Galassi and I exchanged a few words about being together at Harvard years ago, and I was desperate not to do business, not to pick up where his lunch with Mary left off, not to work my ticket. I just wanted a night off from the lit biz—and what a place to think I might have one! . . . By 10:30 the balloons were beginning to grow, to rise from the pavement like huge, sweet, dumb, human-dependent dogs . . . The nicest person I met at the party tonight was a young man named Vladimir, a

Bosnian who has been here for a year. I asked him what he wanted America to do over there. He said he had hoped for military intervention a year ago, after they declared independence. Now there's nothing like a nation left to save.

NOVEMBER 25: [Thanksgiving dinner at] a restaurant in the 7th Regiment Armory on Park Avenue. It was dark and echoing as we walked into the building, like a museum after hours. We walked under old oil portraits and tattered flags to the elevator, which was also being used by residents of the shelter on the 3rd floor. But at the top was this big restaurant that looked like a banquet hall with an old Irish wedding in progress. The crowd was on the old side, with a sprinkling of East Side kids in blazers. The guy who used to do caricatures for the *Daily News* had an easel set up, and there was a bad singer at a piano. "Kooky wacky," as Billy would say, but we had a good time. Back at Susan's we heard about her great-aunt Rose, who in 1912 murdered the man who made her pregnant.

NOVEMBER 27: Mom came in on the jitney . . . the revival of *She Loves Me* at the Brooks Atkinson. The girl singer was no Barbara Cook, but the show was charming and well put together. Too bad the theatre was like an oven. The entire audience was fanning itself with the *Playbill*—the house looked like a field of lilies in the wind.

NOVEMBER 30: At lunchtime I took Sallie Motsch up to the new Four Seasons Hotel to meet DQ. (The hotel, designed by I. M. Pei, is very cold and very elegant. You feel as if you're in the world's most beautiful new office building.) Dan and Sallie charmed each other, and she explained her fact-checking m.o. (Mustn't misspell "George Shultz," as Mrs. Thatcher does throughout her Harper-Collins memoir.)

DECEMBER 9: Something like a genuine pall has settled over people in the wake of what happened on the LIRR [a mass shooting]. Even the *Post's* Sean Delonas hasn't attempted a cartoon; the sick *Challenger*-style jokes one would have expected to hear making their way uptown have never arrived.

DECEMBER 11: Below the Kamps' window was a lot with Christmas trees for sale. Beside it was a tiny motor home. Each year the same family comes down from Vermont and lives in the trailer on Jane St. for a few weeks, selling their trees.

DECEMBER 13: Patty called from Poughkeepsie and said that Earl, the huge and scary Vassar security man (the one who would frighten the life out of you, if you were working late in Avery and you spotted him making his rounds), has committed suicide. A big, lonely, alcoholic man, he once sent Patty flowers and tried to date her.

DECEMBER 14: Back to the office, where Molly Ivins arrived at 5, for drinks, and stayed until past 7 . . . Art was in love by the time she left. She told Texas stories and newspaper tales in that studied, soft voice, and he was ready to sign her up for anything. She left agreeing to do a profile of Charlie Wilson, some gonzo congressman she's fond of. (About Capitol Hill secretaries, he says: "You can teach 'em to type, but you can't make 'em grow tits.") In the course of talking about her unhappy stint at the *Times*, she told the story of rumpled reporter Mo Waldron's job interview there. He already had a Pulitzer Prize, but Clifton Daniel (reputed to wear silk underpants) looked across his desk at him and asked, "Mr. Waldron, what makes you think you're qualified to work at *The New York Times*?" After a long, thoughtful pause, Waldron answered: "Well, I once fucked a woman who belonged to the Junior League."

DECEMBER 15: The *GQ* Christmas party down at Kin Khao on Spring St. Art's good mood (he's had a wonderful year) fairly infectious. Not an especially rowdy night, but a happy one . . . Afterwards a lot of the party transferred itself to Ahnell around the block on Prince. There things revved up. Craig wanted to fight some young investment bankers (straight out of an 80s movie) after they seemed to insult Maura. He sent Tyler in for him, and Tyler ended up being like the dog who licks the burglar: he started trading yuks with them and came back to us holding one of their business cards.

DECEMBER 21: A rubric at last. Art insisted on some sort of adjective, and I told him that the critical traits I would most want emphasized were skepticism and exactingness, so *GQ*'s Books column, by Thomas Mallon, is now called Doubting Thomas. It's growing on me.

DECEMBER 23: Shopped for Mom in the afternoon, and on the way home I picked up a cat toy for Billy. He has wanted another kitty for years—he still mourns the one he had all those years on Jane St.—and the other night he told me that he has pretty much decided to get one when we're back from England. He could tell I wasn't crazy about the idea, and I got the toy today to let him know that it's fine, and that I'll love the kitty, too.

You know what I'm thinking. Me and the cat—when he's gone. I can't keep a plant alive. But I'll take care of this animal and love it as long as it lives, because it made Billy happy. "Don't deny him this," Lucy told me when we discussed it on our shopping trip. "That man has so much love he needs one more outlet for it."

DECEMBER 25: This is my fifth Christmas with Billy, and the third that he's spent with Mom, Loree, Oliver and the kids. He truly feels like part of the family now, and yet he still retains some sort of novel magic that keeps Loree on an even keel and prevents the old family explosions from doing their holiday eruptions.

DECEMBER 27: Billy and I left for Kennedy in a limo at four o'clock. The bitter cold was beginning to ease off . . . [He] thinks of everything, right down to bringing all the audio cassettes that mean the most to the two of us. We've got Dixie and Barbara Carroll and even Charles along. He sleeps as I read, and from time to time I watch over him; I spring to life when he needs water for taking his pill, and I feel a fierce protectiveness that is probably the truest love I will ever know.

DECEMBER 28: . . . We stopped in the National Portrait Gallery. Wait until I tell Art that the faces of Harry Evans and Tina Brown are among the latest additions . . . On [to] the Wyndham to see Diana Rigg's wonderful *Medea* . . . What fun for the 2 little boys playing the children: no lines to memorize and the chance to cover themselves in red stage blood and scream.

DECEMBER 29: We set out for Cambridge after breakfast. Liverpool Street Station, redone and rededicated in 1991, proved a shock. They've put a cheesy everymall under the old lattice-work. Instead of the old grime and grunge, one smells a great wave of freshly warmed croissants from all the boutique bakeries. The whole thing is so little like the old depressing place that it feels completely depressing.

DECEMBER 30: . . . To the Adelphi for *Sunset Boulevard*.

Mr. DeMille, I'm ready for my Maalox. God, what a bomb. A hundred missed opportunities; a vamping score; a title song that sounds like something from the lounge-act send-up Bill Murray used to do on *Saturday Night Live* . . .

DECEMBER 31: We went to an exhibition of coronation robes at Kensington Palace (Diana's wedding dress has been "temporarily" removed) . . .

1994

JANUARY I: The Profumo case is back in the news. The 30-year-rule on releasing certain Cabinet files has gone into effect for 1993, so the papers are once more running pictures of Christine Keeler and Dr. Ward. Fame lasts longer than 15 minutes over here. Turn on the TV and you'll find some woman talking about the one of the Kray brothers that she's just married. And Cliff Richard is still grinning up from the tabloid party pictures. They all go on and on, just like the Queen Mum.

JANUARY 3: We got back to New York just ahead of some very nasty weather . . . I began to go through the mail: early Christmas bills and late Christmas cards for the most part, but in the middle of it all a letter from the Ingram Merrill Foundation saying I'd been awarded $20,000 . . . I suppose it's all James Merrill's doing—I remember the letter from him, out of the blue, expressing admiration for *Aurora 7*, and Fran says the foundation once lavished one of these awards on Mary (she used it to buy a fur coat).

JANUARY 4: I brought my letter of acceptance (all the award requires) to the office of the law firm, on E. 40th, where the foundation does its business. "Have you come for your money?" asked one old man in this WASPy place. And an old secretary named Miss Wilcox said they could give me the check then and there. "Oh, no!" I protested. "There's no rush. I just thought I would bring this letter around by hand since your letter to me had been sitting in my apartment for a week before I caught up with it." The whole thing seems so strange, like the old TV series *The Millionaire*.

JANUARY 6: Could it be that this is my year? Mary called today to say that someone in Scott Rudin's office at Paramount wants an immediate look at *Henry and Clara*.

JANUARY 7: Sick as can be. Dropped everything and stayed in bed . . . Drinking Robitussin from plastic individual-serving bottles that look like crack vials.

JANUARY 8: . . . I managed to get to the office for my stuff on Donleavy. I brought it back to Billy's and wrote my April column lying in bed, while he, on the other side of the breakfront, worked on the kitties [for Tiffany].

JANUARY 9: Went to the CNP building to work with Sallie Motsch on fact-checking the Quayle manuscript. She remains all golden laughter and cheerfulness as she goes about her meticulous work, getting the right spelling for George Bush's Velamints or the exact age for his granddaughter Noelle. She'll call the American embassy in Paraguay if that's what it takes to confirm a name or a date. She'll earn her $6000 three times over.

JANUARY 10: John Herman is gone, as I always hoped and knew he would be, in a puff of smoke. Ticknor & Fields is being folded into Houghton Mifflin and all of the Ticknor authors are being reassigned to editors in Boston. I couldn't be more delighted, whoever the new editor turns out to be. All the misery this man put me through is over. . . .

. . .

You would think New York was a Republican town the way the waiters and patrons of [Remi] come up to Dan and tell him how good it is to see him, how right he was about Murphy [Brown], how much they hope to see him in '96. But it's just the usual worship of celebrity. If David Dinkins had walked in instead, the same people would have been kissing his ring.

We went off to the theatre in a big stretch limo to see *Crazy for You*. The theatre was his idea. The flack who escorted us down the aisle to our seats had given [his assistant] a note saying how many shots would be fired in each act, so that we all wouldn't duck.

JANUARY 13: DQ is so aware that it's long since past time to be making changes on a manuscript everyone is happy with, and so aware that he can't stop himself from doing so, despite my exasperation, that when he called me in the office, he began by saying "Don't hang up on me."

JANUARY 14: Late in the day Mary E. called to say that the trade division at Harcourt Brace had just been decimated: Cork and Pat Strachan and a bunch of others are out. What an industry!

JANUARY 16: Andy drove in from Long Island. After drinks at Billy's we went down to Pescatore for dinner. He talked a little about Phil, and Eddie Haugevik (I think he has a crush on him all over again, thirty years later), and converting to Episcopalianism—because of the Catholic church's hostility toward gays. He explained this to his mother, and she said, "Oh, I see," the same hurt, baffled expression I can remember Josie Pandolfo using three decades ago. Sweet Andy; with all he's been through and all he faces, he goes on, warm and uncomplaining.

JANUARY 18: I finally got down to Bleecker St. for a late dinner with Fran & Howard & Carl & Elisabeth Biondi—Dollface!—who's back here for a visit. First time I've seen her since she went to Germany. She seemed much older, but quite happy. We all got sort of uproarious over nothing except the sick stories in the paper—the assault on Nancy Kerrigan, the Menendez brothers.

JANUARY 20: Had Bert in the afternoon. We talked about my longtime back-of-the-mind idea of going to Bosnia to write about relief work. I said I didn't think my motives were pure: maybe it was some bit of vestigial machismo, or some desire for attention, or just because Mary had gone to Vietnam. But I do feel I should be writing *something* about this central, terrible event that is almost wholly ignored. He asked me why my motives *had* to be pure, and why I thought motives could *ever* be pure.

JANUARY 24: Ran at the Y and then went to Billy's. He'd been to Dr. Jeff, who gave him the results of a new test—not the T-cell count, but a count of how much HIV they actually find in the blood. The quantity in Billy is *amazingly low*, enough to cause conversations between Dr. Jeff . . . and the test's inventor. Exactly what it means is unclear. But any significance it has can only be good.

JANUARY 26: Si Newhouse is in one of his creative moods, and he's thrown the company into a tizzy by replacing ancient Alexander Liberman with trendy young James Truman.

JANUARY 27: Paige Rense, the dowager empress of *Architectural Digest*, is quoted in the papers, saying "If James Truman tries to tell me how to run my magazine, I'm going to spank him and put him to bed without his dinner." Art will probably send her roses for that. He is predictably obsessed with all the fuss—another development: Ron Galotti is going to be *Esquire*'s publisher—and at 5:00 was knocking back the vodka, bouncing war cries off Paul and working the phones. When he's in this state, it doesn't matter whether the news is good or bad, so long as there's *news*, and so long as it keeps coming.

JANUARY 28: Billy and I went up to Dick and Dennis' for dinner. Dick opened the door, and we were cheered by the sight of him—heavier, altogether more hearty than he was the last time. But then Denny came out of the bedroom, and we were horrified. He looks 60 years old; his hair is wild and patchy; his face white and dry, as if he'd been hit with a sack of flour. It's unclear whether it's the progression of the disease or the side effects of the medicine that's making him look so much worse than he did in the hospital . . .

God bless and keep the two of them, taking care of each other, hooking up their drips every night before bedtime.

JANUARY 31: [Fran] asked me what I thought of Stephen Spender's [courtroom] victory over David Leavitt in England. "Well," I told her, "I've been remaindered, but I've never been pulped."

. . .

Over to Billy's early, greeted by a new blond, ponytailed doorman. Gentlemanly, Teutonic Erich retired from the building on Friday after 35 years. Billy and I gave him some champagne on our way out to Dick and Dennis'. He was dutiful to the end, handing me Billy's Macy's bill, which had been misdirected to another box . . . "Good evening, Mr. Mallon," he would say every night when I arrived. He made you feel the height of bourgeois respectability . . .

FEBRUARY 3: . . . Sallie soldiers on, tying up every loose factual end of the book, even as she goes about her day job, which at the moment entails checking my column on Donleavy. The two tasks recently blended into a nightmare for the poor girl: she dreamed that Marilyn Quayle had moved all of us working on DQ's memoir to a farmhouse in Ireland, where we lacked all the equipment—computers, faxes and so forth—necessary to produce the book and where she enforced a variety of bizarre rules, including one that insisted we wear shoes to bed.

FEBRUARY 7: . . . Was at [Dr. Horbar's] for an overdue physical, and the news was good. He says I'm lean and fit and that everything—even an EKG and chest X-ray—seem perfect. He did, however, note "a wisp of a heart murmur," but even that may be good news: it's possible I have a ventricle so peppy and eager to work that it slams shut a little louder than it needs to.

FEBRUARY 8: The New School program on Irish-American writers went on, despite the snow. A few dozen hardy souls turned out, including some recent arrivals from Ireland. They made the discussion a lot better than it would have been otherwise. Rosemary Mahoney (*Whoredom in Kimmage*) is smart and sharp-featured, with no nonsense or pretension about her. Bill O'Sullivan (*Precious Blood*), rumpled and hairy, bewildered and hurt by the publishing world . . . I liked Maureen Howard no better than I liked her book. After it was over and Bob Polito took us to Café Loup, she sat at the head of the table, pronouncing ideas and carving people up.

FEBRUARY 9: The snow is piled up, and the weather is awful, but Alida Becker and I both managed to get to our lunch at the Algonquin. And we had fun. She really has too much personality to work at the *Times Book Review*.

FEBRUARY 11: Jackie Kennedy has non-Hodgkin's lymphoma, and though her prognosis is not too bad, I found myself surprisingly depressed by the news. I admire her, and I don't want us to lose the queen. There's no one to replace her.

FEBRUARY 14: At 3:30 I went over to the Algonquin to meet Larry Cooper and Janet Silver, who had just come from Seymour Lawrence's memorial at the Harvard Club. The hotel lobby was full of Houghton Mifflin writers . . . [Janet] stressed that I was part of the "family," that they could provide "continuity" and help to build my career. She drew me out about my problems with John and assured me I wasn't the only author to have them.

FEBRUARY 15: The kitties are in! Billy and I went up to Tiffany's at 7:30 to see them spotlit in their windows. They look wonderful. Gene has supplied all the right touches, even little fans to sway the bad cat's birdcage, the sleeping kitty's pajamas, and The Cat's Out of the Bag's boa. What a warm, witty quintet—hundreds of thousands of people are going to stop and smile at them during the next few weeks . . . I am so proud of Billy. He was so happy tonight, almost as pleased as he was when the brides went in.

From there . . . to Anna Shapiro's for a dinner party . . . down Bank St. to Westbeth, the old Bell Telephone lab that's now an artists' residence. Anna's apartment has pipes running all around its high ceiling (and she still has a rotary phone) . . . [She] made a big hearty winter meal, a roast and potatoes and a pie, and M.G. [Lord] told funny stories about the history of the Barbie doll, her current book subject. (The real-life Ken—gay, as one always knew he had to be—is a man in his 50s who lives in the Village and does architectural restoration.)

FEBRUARY 17: [P.R.] lunges on story after story, frankly says he has to "pull rank" on [L.] when there's something they both really want, and then turns in the usual underresearched sentimental dreck (as he will do in soggy spades with Rosemary Clooney). He's just amazing. He comes into my office today, asking for a synonym for something, and instead of just saying "I'm stuck for a word," he walks in carrying a galley and saying, "I'm working on the April cover . . ."

FEBRUARY 18: Lucy and I were supposed to go to Delmonico's for lunch, to check it out for my post-book-party dinner (Art thought it would be fun to go to a restaurant actually mentioned in *Henry and Clara*), but it's closed for renovations.

FEBRUARY 20: Summer! The piles of black snow are going down the drains, and people are walking around in shirtsleeves.

FEBRUARY 22: Art and Marty were in Washington this morning for a press conference about Walter Russell Mead's half-comic, half-serious article about how the U.S. should buy Siberia. When Art got back this afternoon, he said that a lot of people from the Russian embassy next door had dropped in for the free food.

FEBRUARY 23: Read the ms. of Heller's sequel to *Catch-22* past midnight. It's awful. I hope Art says no to our doing a piece of it.

MARCH 3: I handed in the first half of the [Quayle] galleys to Rick Horgan this afternoon (DQ actually does a good imitation of him with his pouting lower lip), but not until after one more meeting with Dan, who wanted me to look at the captions with him and Sallie. So we had a room-service lunch at the Four Seasons . . . He was all excited—nervous about being finished . . . in a super, playful mood . . . He kissed Sallie goodbye and brushed my cheek with his hand, showing a tenderness that surprised me.

MARCH 4: This afternoon, on the phone from work, Billy told me what has really been making him so depressed and irritable all week . . . that he's found a small spot on his side that he thinks may be KS. I looked at it tonight and I feel almost certain it's not (he's got Dr. Jeff on Monday), but once he told me, I realized how hellish his last few days have been. When I said, in response to his worries about disfigurement, that I would love him no matter how he looked, he burst into tears.

MARCH 5: . . . Turned to Larry Cooper's copyediting queries on the Rathbones . . . he seems, at times now, to be morbidly sensitive to repetitions, and allergic to the slightest adverb. Still, he's done a wonderful job toning down my packaging of the dialogue, which I do, as always, with far too many pokes in the rib to the reader (all those loaded speaking verbs and so forth). It will be a much better book for Larry's work, and the narrative pace will be 5 mph faster.

MARCH 7: Late this afternoon I was on the phone with Dan Quayle as both Chris Bull and Trey Graham were trying to reach me. Chris was calling to warn me that Graham, an editor at Washington's gay newspaper, the *Blade*, was trying to write an item about me and Quayle . . . (Hasn't the story of gay conservatives—the media's shocked discovery that there are loads of them—gotten to be a boring story in any case?) . . . I told Billy about this tonight, and he burst into tears. He hates politicians on all sides (liberal + conservative, in office or in the media) and he hates the thought that this may be painful for me. We should have been joyful: the spot on Billy's side is nothing.

MARCH 8: By the end of the day I called back Trey Graham, because it was clear that he wouldn't leave me alone until I did. Messages were piling up at home and at the office, and I couldn't leave my ringer off forever at CNP. So tonight I called him and said that I was sorry, but I never discuss the Quayle book with anyone. I said goodbye before he could pepper me with questions . . . Chris Bull has been absolutely wonderful these last two days. A true friend.

MARCH 9: . . . I had to join the whole *GQ* crew up at the Post House for an enormous dinner (I had buffalo for the first time), during which we had plenty of red wine, and after which we were awash in port. It was then that I told Art what I've been going through these last few days, and he was, as I knew he would be, completely tender and, as they say, "supportive." Is there anything he can do? he asked. Is there, for instance, anyone I'd like killed?

MARCH 11: Chris called to tell me there was nothing in the *Blade*. He also let me know that he called Eric Marcus [the source of the story] and complained to him about being used. Eric apologized and asked for my number, but I'm not really expecting him to call: there's nothing in it for him.

Talked to Dan Quayle about what's been going on. Same reaction as Horgan: no surprise, just sincere distress that I've had to put up with it. A relief to talk to him . . . He does think I should reconsider the question of the Acknowledgments, and he makes a decent political argument: if there's not at least some oblique reference to me, some reporter, gay or mainstream, who's heard about my participation, will smell a story. Does Dan Quayle have a problem with Mallon's being gay? Is that why he was "dropped" from the Acknowledgments? Is Mallon ashamed of helping Quayle? Is that why he didn't go in? . . .

. . . I have to remember that I owe the ease with which I was able to bring this problem to Art and to Dan to a lot of brave people, braver than I, who years ago brought gay rights into the realm of the reasonable. My own conservatism—stronger as the years go by—will never to me feel incompatible with the fight they fought and what they achieved. It's just sad that in the process they swallowed so much of the left-wing hog and forgot that privacy was one of the things they were striving to protect in the first place.

MARCH 14: I agreed to go into the Acknowledgments, vaguely and amidst dozens of other names: "Tom Mallon, who wrote an even-handed essay about me while I was in office, provided a great deal of help for which I'm grateful." Having made this concession, I can now tell the HarperCollins publicity department that they absolutely have to stiff any reporter making an inquiry about me.

MARCH 16: Howard Hunt is back in my life. Because of the [Aldrich] Ames* case, Art would like him to do an "Enthusiasms" piece on "Why We Need Spies." So I called him in Florida, and he accepted right away. The only other solicitations he gets involve Watergate . . .

John Corry, the conservative *Times* reporter who's now written his memoirs, was the guest of honor at a party thrown tonight by *The American Spectator* at the National Women's Republican Club on W. 51st St. (You pass a huge painting of Nancy Reagan as you mount the staircase to the ballroom.) Corry is now writing the *Spectator*'s media column, but when Abe Rosenthal, looking like a hairy walnut in a bowtie, went up to the microphone to offer a toast, he couldn't keep the magazine's name straight, referring to it as the *Statesman*, while Bob Tyrrell stood a few steps away. . . .

Over to Billy's. Mom called to tell us both about her Florida trip, which turned out to be a fabulous time for her. She couldn't get over the surprise of this. When Billy and I told her we were tired, she said, "Well, you've got each other, and that's what counts. That's what I still miss."

MARCH 17: The most awful day of the year in New York, when my people evolve backwards and drag their knuckles along the ground in that colorless parade. Billy [was] kept up tonight by all the noise coming from The Green Derby and the other Irish bars along 2nd Avenue.

MARCH 18: Art opened up the expensive wine from Si this afternoon: we've gotten an ASME nomination for General Excellence. Of course we're up against Tina, so we'll probably lose.

MARCH 19: Lied to Jeffrey Simpson and told him Billy was in St. Louis, thereby sparing Billy the dinner party Jeffrey threw to welcome Larry Carroll (a former *AD* colleague who's the new managing editor of *Allure*) to New York . . . One older businessman, a couple of sweet young things, a handsome sees-everything, knows-everybody architect named Ted Porter who makes Vance

---

* Ames, a CIA officer, had been exposed as a double agent who spied for the Soviets.

Muse look like a shut-in . . . The food, a good hearty pot roast and winter vegetables, was more satisfying than anything else. Jeffrey—always on the prowl for imagined slights—a nervous host.

Coming back uptown, I got into conversation with my cab driver, a Pakistani who's been here for seven years. Back home he has a wife and children—the children are doing very well in school—who have never been permitted over here for so much as a visit, because of immigration restrictions. He's soon going home with all the money he's saved driving a cab and living in two rooms in Brooklyn. I ask him if he's had a chance to see any part of the country other than New York; only Jersey and DC, he says. When we pass Limelight, the old church turned disco, he says that you could never do such a thing with a mosque.

MARCH 20: Just before bed I took out a pen and pad and started giving names to the *Dewey Defeats Truman* characters [for my next novel] who have been taking (still very insubstantial) life inside my head. And as soon as they had these names I could see them taking on color and bulk, little Frankensteins getting up off their tables and starting to introduce themselves to one another.

MARCH 21: Molly Ivins' piece on Charlie Wilson finally came in— or at least half of it did—and it's pretty funny. Lazy, but pretty funny.

MARCH 24: Greg called from India. His amorous adventures are made so ambiguous and complicated by language and cultural differences that he can't tell if he's being flirted with or blackmailed.

MARCH 25: The Hunt piece is surprisingly restrained. It reads like an ordinary Op-Ed piece from a neocon think tank. I actually had to call Howard in Miami—I woke him up from his nap—to tell him to jazz it up a bit.

MARCH 29: Sallie came in to pour out the troubles of the Research Dept. [P.K.]—an amiable boy so stupid that the other day he had to ask his fellow fact-checkers if "Hebe" was a derogatory word— e-mailed everyone he works with the news, and exact amount, of his raise. And now Sallie knows that this dolt is making more than she is.

MARCH 31: At last there's an offer for *Henry & Clara*. The [David L.] Wolper protégés have come through and gotten ABC Films to take an option . . . I'd like to see the money come up, but the important thing is to have an offer *now*, while there's still time for it to do the book some good: jazz up the sales reps and give the subrights people a better shot.

APRIL 2: [Off to Pasadena to write a space article] The plane took off on time and I managed to read for most of the five hours. I'm either a man of broad interests or a mess: my reading was made up of Edith Sitwell's letters; a James Ellroy noir-fest; and a book about comets.

APRIL 3: [Easter Mass in Pasadena] A beautiful, huge near-cathedral, each of its pillars a different color of marble. Packed: about half "Anglos," the other half Hispanic, all the kids from all the big families looking scrubbed and sweet in their white straw hats and new shoes. The priest gave a simple, sensible sermon, and I felt peaceful. (There was even a gay couple a couple of rows in front of me.) I thanked God for Billy and prayed for his health. Tears came to my eyes a few times, good tears, not sad ones, just ones that came from feeling fully alive, big and open instead of frantic.

Spent some of the afternoon at the Norton Simon Museum, whose brick exterior looks like the tiled bottom of the space shuttle . . . Two paintings of St. Jerome (one by Goya and another by Bouts) in his penitential phase. What a contrast the haggard, self-tormenting figure makes to the stately El Greco version one is used to seeing in the Frick.

APRIL 4: I got to the [Jet Propulsion Laboratory] by 10:45, and it felt pleasantly familiar—the billboard tracking Galileo and Ulysses still going strong, even if the dining room of the cafeteria was closed for earthquake repairs . . . Back here in the afternoon I tried to pretend I was on vacation: reading Ellroy by the pool, working the Stairmaster, waiting for Billy to call. But there's just so much leisure I can take.

APRIL 5: In the afternoon I went down to the Planetary Society to interview the director, Louis Friedman, a big, loud retro guy (you can picture him in the Playboy Mansion), who is a manned-space-exploration booster (unlike the JPL guys), but who shares the JPL view of the real villain of the space program: the shuttle.

APRIL 8: Made a decision to write my August column about the David Leavitt–Stephen Spender ruckus, which goes on and on, and which David has made much worse by a revolting piece he did for last Sunday's *Times Magazine*. In counterattacking Spender, he manages to be beside every single point, and to raise this great billowing smokescreen of homophobia.

APRIL 11: Art (to keep up with Tina) bought a table at this year's PEN gala, so I was down there by a quarter to eight, as soon as Billy tied my black tie. The event was held in the newly, superbly refurbished waiting room of Grand Central, and there still wasn't enough space. (In a common touch, there was no special bathroom for the revelers. All those Armani tuxes and Geoffrey Beene gowns made their way past the homeless toward the urinals and stalls.) At the *GQ* table we had me, Art, Amy, Joe and Francesca Queenan, Marty and Kathy, Mr. and Mrs. Morley Safer (he was our "literary host"), and his friend Schuyler Chapin and his much-younger date. S.C. is now Rudy Giuliani's culture czar, but he still keeps up with the opera and told us how difficult Kathleen Battle really was. Maureen Dowd was also with us, but she kept leaning over to the table full of her *Times* colleagues. . . .

Peter Jennings was the smooth master of ceremonies; he got caught up in the left-wing spirit of the evening, at one point referring to "Reaganism" as if it were one of those definitive historical evils. In this crowd it comes off the tongue as easily as Stalinism. The 6 speeches by writers were mostly nonsense. Toni Morrison's had some eloquence, but the five others drove me crazy—among them Tony Kushner inveighing against capitalism (all those nasty ticket sales for *Angels in America*) and Edna O'Brien going on about how good the gulag was for Solzhenitsyn's writing. At the end of the evening I ran into Bob Tyrrell, who told me, "This is all such bullshit. *We're* the counterculture!"

Absolutely everyone was there—the literary predictables (McInerney, Conroy, Kennedy) and the pure celebrities. Chief among the latter were Donald and Marla Trump. She has the two most perfect breasts I've ever seen, and finding them was, she made sure, no problem at all.

APRIL 15: Out of the blue, a letter from Scott Carpenter. He broke his clavicle on the ski slopes the other day and finds himself with time on his hands. He says he's coming to NY in June with "Patty" (a 4th wife? a new girlfriend?) and hopes we can get together.

APRIL 18: Just got the news that Nixon has had a stroke and can't speak. And just yesterday, on the phone, Mom and I were wondering how much longer poor Jackie Onassis has left. "I keep picturing her in that yellow suit," said Mom. "The one she had on with de Gaulle."

Colin [Harrison] called me late in the afternoon to say he "loved" the Jupiter piece. "Now let's see if they buy it on Thursday." *Harper's* is some drill.

APRIL 21: "Lift the arms embargo!" they've been yelling outside my window for much of the last hour. And they're right. Why won't Clinton let the Bosnians "fight for their lives," as Jeane Kirkpatrick would put it (with, for all we know, as much success as the armed Afghans eventually had)? He prefers to hope it will all go away, or that they will quietly die to the soothing, burbling sounds of Warren Christopher and Boutros Boutros-Ghali.

APRIL 22: Colin Harrison called at 5:00 to tell me that the editorial meeting had "not come out in [my] favor." Some people liked the first half of the essay but not the second; for others it was the opposite . . . Every piece, contracted or not, is really a spec piece, and Lapham uses kill fees as a cheap way of getting a lot of finished, polished pieces from which to choose.

. . .

Tried not to let this get me too down as Billy and I made our annual pilgrimage to see Dixie Carter at the Carlyle. The show was familiar and elegant—a trifle more subdued than usual—and she sang some of our songs. We walked home, down Madison Avenue, happy; still in love with each other; grateful.

And came home to the news that Richard Nixon, a man who let me down again and again, and to whom I felt deeply connected—whether I was wearing a Nixon-Lodge button at the age of 9, or having a shouting match with my father over the Cambodia invasion ten years after that—had died, at 9:08 p.m., at the age of 81. There was never a time in my life when he wasn't on the scene; he was already a Senator when I was born. And now he's gone, and I sat before the television sobbing.

APRIL 25: Billy's birthday; and when I came in the door with flowers tonight he burst into tears. He had just been reading some pamphlets on health insurance and disability and suddenly the idea of leaving Catton Bros.* seemed overwhelming, impossible. It was the first time I have ever seen him sob over what HIV is doing to his life. We held on to each other and talked things out, and I told him that we would find a way.

APRIL 26: Billy is better; he's pulled himself together, and we're going on. The rarity of last night makes me realize how brave he is every day of the week; how little he leans on me or lets me see his fears; how much, instead, he attends to my petty complaints and worries.

The TV option is settled. It's going to Scripps-Howard's production company, not ABC, although David Stevens is still involved. I don't understand it all, but the money is up and there's a consultant's fee on top of it.

APRIL 29: The Jupiter piece will go to Wlady. Nancy Franklin says she likes it but that it's too much of an "essay" for *The New Yorker* (tells you something about the Tina years) . . .

---

* Children's wear company where Bill was the art director.

MAY 2: A long day, but a useful one. I finally have a story for August: something witty and summery and charming by Amy Hempel . . . And the noontime brought manna: Frank Conroy's memoir of his freshman-writing teacher at Haverford. Lovely stuff. . . .

Lunch at the Paramount Hotel with amiable David Gernert, the Doubleday editor-in-chief who never has to do anything in life after publishing John Grisham. . . .

After 5:00 , Sallie and I spent more than two hours putting her fact-checking work onto the *Henry and Clara* galleys. (Whew! I had Clara talking with Sumner months after he was dead.)

MAY 3: Talked to a somewhat nervous DQ this afternoon . . . He feels all right about the press coverage so far. Says he still hasn't heard anything about the book from Bush. He ran into him at the Nixon funeral and asked what he thought. Bush replied: "Haven't read it yet. Bar got hold of it." So DQ asked her. She said she'd read the first four parts and liked them, but was holding off on '92, as that would be painful.

. . .

Sallie and I did most of the rest of the Rathbone fact-checking after five . . . and then [at home] I noticed the back cover of the just-arrived bound galley had the most outrageous misprint imaginable. When they transcribed a line of the catalog copy—"[Mallon's] powers as a novelist are fully in evidence in this astonishing and moving story"—"fully" became "finally"!

MAY 4: A ferocious day. I had to run the *Henry and Clara* page proofs down to Houghton Mifflin (16th & 17th Sts. were cordoned off because a gunman was holding a hostage) and straighten out the back cover with Barbara Henricks. Fortunately, none of the galleys went out and there's time to do a patch.

. . .

I had a call from Rebecca Johnson at *The New Yorker*. They were thinking of doing a "Talk of the Town" piece on me—as DQ's collaborator. I told them I wouldn't talk to them, and she got all snide and aggressive and media-megalomaniacal, as if I had some nerve turning down the free publicity.

MAY 7: Talked to John McConnell in the morning. He told me he really likes the [Quayle] book, and we had a post mortem of the first week's coverage. Next Thursday there'll be a big party for it, with a dinner to follow, down in Washington. I'm not going, since I don't want to get any questions from all the press who will be around. . . .

MAY 8: [DQ] flew from Washington to NY early in the evening (he has the *Today* show tomorrow), and took me and Sallie and [his assistant] out to dinner at Jean Lafitte (I made the reservation) to celebrate. He was at his absolute best, sweet as can be, grateful for all our work, philosophical about [Sam] Donaldson, curious about us and what we'd be doing next, excited about his next two months on the road. He signed books for me and Sallie and Mom. This thoroughly nice and decent man . . . *why* does he want to return to the scummy world of politics and the media? Why can't he find someplace to, I don't know, start a small business and coach the local Little League team? He's going to jump back in in '96—he's already jumped back in—and he's going to be shredded to bits.

MAY 11: [*The Observer's*] piece—"Media Whispers Name of Quayle's 'Ghost'"—ran on the front page, which tells you what important things the *Observer* covers . . . Took some comfort and amusement in Jonathan Yardley's review . . . He says that it's not a bad book, & that he only fell asleep twice in a whole day spent reading it—which, in comparison to his experience with the Carter, Ford and Kissinger memoirs is "like being wired for life."

MAY 12: I called [Jim] Windolf to complain about all the snideness and inaccuracy in his [*Observer*] piece, and, above all, to protest the way (I've learned) [Joe] Conason [his editor] called Marty—one of my bosses!—to inquire about my sexuality. This is apparently his idea of how one checks an "outing" item. It never occurs to him that the subject's boss might be one of the very people he might not want to "know"? Why not call his wife? Jim Windolf's exact response to my complaint: "Yeah, I guess that was a little gauche."

Amused by Frank Rich's column . . . delivers a tirade against the Quayle book but says it's "surprisingly readable."

MAY 15: John [McConnell] went to the big party Thursday night in Washington, and he told me stories, as did Sallie, who got her behind brushed by the ninety-year-old hand of Strom Thurmond.

MAY 17: Had lunch with Valerie Lester, up from Annapolis and as wonderfully sexy and fizzy as ever. We went to the Algonquin, and on the way she reminisced about her flight-attendant days in the early 60s, when she lived in the Hotel Iroquois and would get phone calls from "summer widowers" who wanted her to come down to the Algonquin bar for a drink.

MAY 19: . . . The news came that Jackie Onassis was dead . . . Jackie's passing leaves me sadder about the *present*, whereas Nixon's passing made me mourn the past. Her death should do that too, make me feel that my childhood is *really* over, but I feel her loss as that of something current and vital. Whenever I've been down on NY, I've thought: it's still good enough for Jackie. She still thrives here and finds ways of being a good citizen. My mind should be thinking of Dealey Plaza and Camelot and rest of it, but I'm mostly aware of the loss to New York.

Fran called me this afternoon, hours before the death, but already near tears; she'd just seen all the sound trucks and the crowd in front of the apartment at 86th St.

MAY 25: Lunch with Phyllis Rose at the Royalton. (Si & Anna and Michael Kinsley and James Truman on the banquettes. Anna, rumored to be in trouble, looking very eager to please.) Phyllis was full of laughter and apparent contentment . . . She says her friendship with [David Schorr] has deepened from their appreciation of the fact that they'll actually be there for each other in their old age—whereas most of David's friends are dying or dead of AIDS and Phyllis doesn't expect Laurent, a good deal older than she is, to go on forever.

MAY 26: Granger, Paul and I took Adrienne Miller, our new assistant who somewhat eerily reminds me of Sharon Tate, to lunch at Sushiden, near Saks. After assistants from Radcliffe and Princeton, it's nice to have one from Miami University of Ohio: she is thrilled to be in New York, beside herself to be typing up our contracts and reading my slush pile.

MAY 28: [The American Booksellers Association convention in Los Angeles] The big party tonight was actually Houghton Mifflin's, out in Hollywood on the New York street-scene set of the Paramount lot. (They've got a book coming out about the first twenty years of *Saturday Night Live*.) The buildings, at least the facades, are amazingly substantial, real brick and stone, not great Styrofoam block as I'd always sort of imagined. There are brownstones, lofts, a chunk of the Citicorp Building, and a corner marked 7th Avenue and E. 57th . . . Reruns of *Saturday Night Live* were playing on TVs in the windows of the brownstones.

MAY 29: The big party this evening was Grove Press' at the Chateau Marmont, the seedy Sunset Blvd. hotel (with its sinister neon sign) where John Belushi speedballed himself into the hereafter a dozen years ago. The faces of Jack Nicholson and Michelle Pfeiffer stared down from a billboard onto the poolside patio. . . .

Stars by the pool: Peter Weller, Michael York, Sydney Pollack. David Kamp, who was staying at the hotel, told me he was upstairs with Keanu Reeves. Other than that, it was like a New York publishing party that had been pointlessly flown 3000 miles west . . .

. . . . Talked to strange Michael Silverblatt, who once wrote an interesting review of *Aurora* 7 and who has a radio show about books. He seemed to have an almost eerie knowledge of my books; he's read them all, even *Arts & Sciences*, which Lionel Abel had sent him. He says the plagiarism one was of special interest to him since long ago he spent three years pretending he was someone else . . . As James Ellroy might say: weird juju.

MAY 30: I called Billy and got the news that Dennis died last night. He went peacefully, in his sleep; he'd managed to get up in the morning and shower and get dressed. He was miraculous, pure steel under the screaming campy exterior.

JUNE 1: Janet Silver called this afternoon with the *Kirkus* review of *Henry and Clara*: "enjoyable, but depressing." (Well, no kidding.) I have no real problem with this, but when she called and told me, I realized it was all starting and that I'm too depleted to go through it . . .

JUNE 2: Trying for once to focus on others' troubles. Linda Asher was badly injured in a car accident—the same one that killed E. J. Kahn—over the weekend.

JUNE 5: Clinton in Europe for D-Day: I feel sorry for him, actually. He looks about as comfortable as George Bush would having to put up a 25th-anniversary plaque at Woodstock.

JUNE 10: Billy and I had our dinner with Dick Snyder* tonight. After drinks at the apartment, we took him over to Zephyr Grill. Dick is butching it out in his straight-laced way. He's already gotten everything in order, has already had a little reminiscence-service in the apartment (a week to the day after Dennis died, while we were still in Atlanta). He's going to California and then France . . . Not much talk about Dennis, because I don't think he could really bear it.

JUNE 14: Called Scott Carpenter about tomorrow's lunch arrangements. Got a wrong number. When I asked for Scott by name, a raspy old New York voice said: "What? Is he still up in space?"

JUNE 15: Scott and I had a long lunch at Arizona 206 near Bloomingdale's. It was a hot, hot day and we were both near to dripping when we arrived. But it was a lovely time. He's one of the few famous people I've met (and there was a time when he was *very* famous) who would prefer to listen than talk about himself.

JUNE 17: O.J. Simpson managed to escape from the Los Angeles police today. We were all in Art's office late in the afternoon

* Partner of Dennis Cornelius, who had died of AIDS.

to watch a press conference during which, we thought, O.J.'s arraignment would be announced; instead, a very angry cop told the reporters, who went berserk with excitement, that the department had no idea where Mr. Simpson was. It's the most public screw-up of a police force since Dallas in November '63.

Everything became much more bizarre tonight, when they found O.J. and tailed his car as it made its way back to his home in Brentwood. He was inside, with a gun to his own head, being driven by an old friend. Helicopters with cameras broadcast live pictures to the whole country. It was like watching the burning Symbionese Liberation Army house all over again . . . Billy and I, mildly disgusted with ourselves, watched the whole thing until it was over. Barbara Walters said that the screaming people along the route, the ones shouting "Go, Juice, go!" were evidence of the love there still was for this man, despite whatever he had done. Actually, they were the same people who shout "Jump!" when somebody is out on a ledge.

JUNE 18: [At the Writers at Work conference in Utah] This time they've put most of the writers into condos out in Deer Valley . . . I'm sharing one with William Kittredge and his partner, Annick Smith.

JUNE 19: Awakened in the middle of the night by the sharp odor of a skunk (memories of how they would always be outside my screened window in Poughkeepsie), and a few hours after that by the singing of hundreds of birds.

. . .

[Kittredge and Smith], my condo-mates, were tonight's readers. He boomed out a Whitmanic tract about saving the environment; her piece of fiction was much better. They clearly think of themselves as The Best of the West, which is, I think, the name of an anthology they did—everything about them is meant to shout Montana and Anti-Development, from his plaid shirts to her turquoise ring and Indian-beaded hair clip. (Their environmentalism doesn't stop them from leaving the lights on and throwing Coke cans into the unrecycled garbage can back at the condo.) All in all, a bit affected, but good company on our ride back up the mountain.

JUNE 20: After dinner François Camoin and Agha Shahid Ali were up: he's a Kashmir aristocrat, a Shiite Muslim who looks like a chubby little Ganesha, frankly craves applause and does a stand-up comic's patter between poems. He's one of Carol Houck Smith's pets, and Carol does her usual, quite unbelievable, routine at readings. If she's sitting near you, she monitors your reactions: are you laughing often enough, applauding loudly enough, exhibiting sufficient adoration toward her discovery?

JUNE 21: Just as I was about to leave for my walk down the mountainside, I got a call from Sallie. The *PW* review is out, and it's grand: a star, a juicy description . . . The reading went well (the first three chapters of Part 3), although I had to rush a bit. James Thomas followed; we were the Grim Brothers. I ended with Clara throwing away her bloody dress, and he finished with a Greek graduate student who hangs himself in a barn.

JUNE 22: . . . The 2:00 panel I was on with Phyllis Barber, Janet Burroway, Shahid and François. It was about "Writing Out of Culture," and I guess I was the half-dead white male perspective, lacking as I do the hint of Mediterranean spice provided by François' cedilla. Actually, the whole thing was fun, and I got my chance to speak a little piece about the new Balkanization of bookstores.
    . . .
    The readings tonight were down at the Kimball Art Center. Mark Strand was quite wonderful. He looks and sounds like Clint Eastwood and is funny and unreconstructed about sex. Pam Houston has gotten a bit grand with success: talked about how she's leaving Park City because of all the development. . . .

JUNE 23: Nan came by the condo mid-morning and the two of us rode up to Silver Lake and took the chair lift to the top of the mountain . . . The view coming down on the chair was so beautiful, and the air so quiet, that I wanted to cry. Tonight, while he was at the Streisand concert in New York, I left a message on Billy's answering machine, just four words that I asked him to put in his head and think about, like a whisper: "Christmas in the Rockies."

. . .

. . . The dance. My happiest moment: dancing with willowy Phyllis Barber to "Hey, Good Lookin'."

JUNE 25: Went to the office to catch up and, of course, found that Art was there, too. (On Monday he goes to Milan.) He told me what I'd missed this week, including Tommy Hilfiger's sending over three thousand dollars' worth of red wine in response to Scooter's article. And then we got to talking obsessively about O.J.

JUNE 26: Woke up with a head cold; let Billy and Patty go off to breakfast by themselves. I went back to 45th St., and had to show my ID to get to my apartment: 25 years ago the cops were busting gay heads at Stonewall; today they were making sure that nobody bothers the gay marchers starting out from the United Nations.

JUNE 30: The *Advocate* item is out, exactly as Chris predicted it. I'm "credited with keeping the antigay Quayle rhetoric that marred the campaign out of the book" . . . if it gets the gay press off my back, wonderful. I have no idea what "mainstream" publications may decide to pick up the item, but I think I've gotten off lucky.

JULY 1: Went up to a dinner party hosted by Scott Carpenter and Patty Snyder, at her apartment on 5th and 89th, across the street from the Guggenheim . . . There was a Russian filmmaker, plump, voluble and funny, named, I swear, Ninotchka. (She knew Brodsky and Akhmatova when she was a girl in Leningrad.) Finally, there was Scott's youngest daughter, Candace, and her boyfriend; they both play guitars and sing at clubs in the Village . . . At one point during the dinner conversation, "Nina" malapropped the words "ozone" and "testosterone." When her error was pointed out, she asked for a definition of testosterone. Candy pointed to her father and said, "Ask the expert."

JULY 5: *Vanity Fair*'s "Hot Type" lists *Henry and Clara* for August.

JULY 8: Tonight Sallie threw Paul Scanlon a surprise 50th-birthday [party] down at her little place on Hudson St. "I haven't been in an apartment like this in 30 years!" exclaimed Richard Merkin (who looked like a cross-eyed Casey at the Bat in his cap). He meant the tininess, the layers of paint, the shower in the kitchen. But it's new to Sallie, and she's thrilled to be on her own down on Hudson and W. 10th, away from the room she used to rent from Nellie, away from all of Nellie's ancient Russian friends. The party she threw wound up being a sort of Holly Golightly affair, a big roaring success, mostly because it was stocked with so many of Paul's friends from the Lion's Head.

It was sweltering and loud and boozy. Ellroy showed up. I talked to him and his wife about Mikal Gilmore. (She used to date him, and Ellroy talked about the apparent commercial failure of *Shot in the Heart*, despite the good reviews, with a barely suppressed flood of crocodile tears.) Sinatra was on the tape player just as Jonathan Schwartz came in and kissed Paul with Hollywood sincerity, lavishing upon him a lot of birthday CDs that were no doubt review copies. The Baroness Sheri de Borchgrave told everyone about her next book, a series of erotic adventures in Tahiti. A Staten Island friend of Paul's brought along his cousin, an Irish priest, who blessed Sallie's new apartment, sprinkling the place with holy water while Pete Hamill's little brother held the prayer book and the smell of pot drifted out of the nearby kitchen.

JULY 13: Lunch with Jack Schwartz at Campagna on E. 21st . . . He got to reminiscing about his early days as a copy boy on the *Mirror* . . . Told me about the has-been barking Walter Winchell used to do, and about the night Sputnik went up. He went racing in to the managing editor with the teletype copy, but the M.F. just said "Sit down, kid" and wouldn't listen to a word Jack had to say until the John Garfield picture that was on the Late Show finished up.

JULY 14: . . . Billy dropped by with the video camera (our early Christmas present to ourselves), which we tried out with great success. We talk about all the special events we'll be wanting it for—my book party, the Christmas windows, our vacation. But I want us to tape reels and reels of the ordinary, silly, precious things of simple days together at home. The things I'll need to live off when he's gone.

JULY 16: The revival of *Damn Yankees* . . . Bebe Neuwirth was too wrongly perfect as Lola. She danced and sang and moved with such intelligence and precision that there was no sexiness to her performance. You couldn't believe this woman would ever have *needed* to sell her soul to the devil.

JULY 19: *Henry and Clara* is already on the shelves of Brentano's and Barnes & Noble on Fifth Avenue. I'm not sure I like this. The book will be eating up some of its shelf life weeks before reviews appear. Well, I suppose the opposite situation would be worse.

JULY 21: A glam day. Billy got me ready this morning and I left from 51st in a cab down to Industria, a big photo studio in the meat-packing district. *GQ* does some shoots there; the individual rooms of the old warehouse are so big that the photographers can drive their cars right up the ramps and park them inside. The photographer for *Entertainment Weekly* was Fran Collin; there was also a very sexy stylist, who made me up and combed my hair. I complicated the photographer's life by refusing to be shot without my shadow-producing glasses, but otherwise it was smooth sailing. The only hard part: I couldn't smile. They want, I think, to do a triptych of me and Henry and Clara, so a somber expression was in order. Whenever we cracked up over something, I had to get back into character.

JULY 24: My summer trip to Loree's . . . We ate out on the deck, and then we went back inside to watch years of slides that she's finally gotten organized since Bill and I gave her the projector last Christmas. So many dead people; and while it was startling, and even thrilling, to see them almost large as life on the screen, after just a week with the video camera I felt frustrated: I wanted Daddy and Grandma and Tom and Belle and Joe to begin *moving*, and, above all, speaking.

JULY 25: Billy and I had dinner at Zephyr with Mr. Gene, between drinks at his apartment in U.N. Plaza (suffocatingly beautiful, exquisitely overdecorated) and a bit of videotaping there later on . . . We teased him about always claiming to be the oldest person around, pointing out that, at 104, Rose Kennedy could be his mother. Gene said that would have been awful, and Billy agreed, reminding us all that if Rose *had* been his mother, then Gene couldn't have been such good friends with Gloria Swanson.

JULY 27: Some good news about the book, I think. Fresh Air, the NPR show, will be reviewing it on air (the reviews run nationally and several times). And we now have dates for Albany (Sept. 21) and Washington (Sept. 10, at Chapters). The Archives may do something later, in the fall, or at Ford's Theatre in February.

JULY 28: Talked to Brady Udall, an Iowa workshop writer who placed second in the fiction contest and whose story, "Midnight Raid," I'm buying nonetheless. He's delighted, even though (I learned on a second call) a *Story* editor who's also made an offer for it chewed him out. They "discovered" him, says Lois [Rosenthal]. So now they want to keep his light under a bushel.

JULY 30: [Sag Harbor] Dinner was taken over by another literary comedy. M.G. [Lord] was sitting with three people who have had to turn down excerpts from her book on the cultural history of Barbie: me at *GQ*, Stanley at *Newsday*, and Karen at *Vogue*. ("I hate Barbie," said Anna. End of discussion.). The rejection at the latter is the one that really bothers M.G., and if the flowers hadn't been between them, [she and Karen] might have come to blows. They flared over something else, of course, but we knew what they were really talking about. . . .

All the predictable talk about how Tina has hired Michael Kelly away from the *Times*, and how so-and-so left *Mirabella* for thus-and-such: this is "getting away for the weekend"?

JULY 31: Linda Healey and Tony Lukas came over for drinks at four. Linda always lovely; he less dour than usual (he talked a lot about the Watergate anniversary and of how he's sympathetic to the "silent coup" theory), but he's always on the verge of scolding her.

AUGUST 2: I almost forgot: before coming home this afternoon, I had to stop at Billy's. I zigzagged my way there from CNP, and at about a quarter to two I found myself on 49th St. between 2nd and 3rd; and there she was. Poor old Katharine Hepburn, heading for home with her companion. At 86, she looks much older than Gene. She was leaning on a heavy black cane, and her face was terribly mottled, a sort of red-and-white checkerboard. It was a pitiable sight; what a brute life is.

AUGUST 3: Nonnie's retirement party was held early this evening in the MOMA sculpture garden. (What? No Libermans?). The men's designers flocked to the occasion. Little Tommy Hilfiger, and Abboud, and Calvin Klein (who came in with Donna Karan) looking a lot older and more badly complected than his photographs. [Condé Nast's Lisa] Hintelmann, [Lisa] Henricksson & [Lucy] Kaylin, all in little black dresses and looking like the girls in the old Robert Palmer video, attracted the attention of the *Times'* Bill Cunningham, who took picture after picture of them. . . .

AUGUST 4: *Entertainment Weekly's* photo editor calls, wanting to know if there was a make-up and hair stylist present at my photo shoot. "Are the pictures that bad?" I ask. They're fine, she says, but they've lost the stylist's name and they're wondering who it is they're to credit.

AUGUST 5: *Dateline*, one of NBC's magazine shows, came by to tape a segment on . . . political diaries . . . We made the video in Art's office after he'd gone to Connecticut for the weekend. (Wait until he sees the "establishing shots" of me, in a Valentino jacket borrowed from the Fashion Dept., typing at his typewriter and signing a letter at his desk.)

AUGUST 8: Lunch, at Oscar's, with Jeffrey Simpson, and once again I get up from the table thinking *never again*. An hour and a half spent mostly listening to his intricate recitation of the ways he's been wronged and slighted and snubbed by Condé Nast or Chautauqua or some person I've never heard of. At one point he'd made himself so red-faced over the tale of a check that was lost in the mail that he had to feel his own pulse.

AUGUST 9: As I expected, Janet Silver wants the letters book but not *Dewey Defeats Truman*. She tells Mary it seems more like a short story than a novel.

Well, it's time for me to go. They are never going to think of me as a novelist . . . For years now I've been passed down to editor after editor, like a piece of the office furniture.

AUGUST 11: Went up to Dr. Horbar at 4:00. I cannot shake this cold without some help. He says he's been seeing dozens of people with what I've got: all the humidity this summer has turned their membranes into tropical breeding grounds for viruses. "Your uvula is twice its normal size," he tells me, "and it's laying there like a lox."

AUGUST 12: Art will give a dinner for me (18 people) after my Players Club party on September 12. All I can think of is: how will I be able to face all those people if the *Times* review is bad? How will I get through my reading on the 30th, and the rest of it?

AUGUST 15: Nightmare avoided . . . The only time I could say the *Times* has treated my fiction fairly. Not the rave I was secretly hoping for through all my anxiousness, but something I can live with. Janet thinks it's strong, and Barbara and Mary are pleased. Fran, after she read it, could tell how strung out I was: "You should be much more pleased than you are. You're too exhausted to enjoy it."

It's true, because I was also too exhausted to enjoy the rave that *did* show up—a piece by George Garrett in *The Washington Post*. An unbelievably generous appraisal . . .

AUGUST 16: Curiously depressed, even as everyone comes by to congratulate me on the reviews, which Art insisted be circulated. My desperate need for praise; my inability to accept or believe it. Maybe I'm still just sick. And tired.

AUGUST 17: [Connecticut editorial retreat] We were all sitting on Art's deck talking story ideas when the portable phone rang. It was Connie, his assistant, calling from the office: *The New Yorker* had just called her, trying to arrange a photo shoot. They need a picture of me to accompany the review of *Henry and Clara* that John Updike is doing for the Sept. 5 issue . . . For the first time since *A Book of One's Own*, ten years ago, a book I've written is going to exceed my expectations and my hopes. I'm just stunned—as Mary was when I called her. This will quite possibly change everything. This book is going to take off . . . Yes, I'm assuming J.U. will like it; how often does he whack the relatively obscure?

AUGUST 18: I called Mary, who says that Janet Silver is now saying that I am *not* yet free to go elsewhere (a direct contradiction of what she told me on Monday)—this is all per Joe Kanon, who told Janet that they have not yet had a chance to exercise their option. What this means is that Janet has been told by higher-ups that she blew it, passing on my new novel proposal just as my fiction was finally breaking through.

AUGUST 19: Pretty little Eileen Travell, the *New Yorker* photographer, showed up at the office with her Brady-like box camera around 9:30. She took dozens of photos and thought she had nailed it, but late in the afternoon, *The New Yorker*'s photo editor (a job title that still sounds odd) called to ask if I'd do a reshoot. The pictures are beautiful, she says, but too staid and solemn. They look like a minister's author photos. So tomorrow morning Eileen and I will try again. (Best news of the day: Eileen says, "I can't wait to read your book. Updike's review is great! Oh, I'm not supposed to tell you that—please don't tell anyone, I could get in trouble.")

. . . Barbara Henricks says they had a marketing meeting this

morning and the only question was how big the *NY Times* ad for *Henry and Clara* will be, not whether they'll take one.

AUGUST 20: Got up early and ran a couple of miles before it was time to meet Eileen Travell for the reshoot. We did it in Peter Detmold Park, where Nancy Crampton photographed me, in the rain, four years ago . . . I tried to look less solemn than I did yesterday; I put on a corduroy shirt and bluejeans and appeared like a less butch John Irving.

AUGUST 22: Came back from lunch with Doug at Grand Central Cafe to find that Terry Sullivan had faxed me yesterday's full-page *Chicago Tribune* review of *Henry and Clara*. "A big wet kiss in the ear," he wrote on his cover sheet. . . .

AUGUST 24: Rabbit is Rhapsodic! Mary called this afternoon, upon receiving a fax of the mechanicals of Updike's review. (The ads aren't even on the pages; she called in a favor over at *The New Yorker*, and the person who sent them to her could lose her job.) It's five pages long, and not only does it call *Henry and Clara* "amazing," "ingenious," "deeply felt," moving, poignant, and quite a number of other things—I could go on—but he describes it as my breakout book. He went back to everything: *ABOOO*, *Stolen Words* and both other novels, which he says "for all their wit and compass were rather bloodless." (He does say *Aurora* was "shimmering" and "gleaming.") Of course, I know what he means. But the idea of him writing a fat ¶ on *Arts and Sciences*! If I'd known he was up in Beverly Farms this past month reading (re-reading?) all my books, I'd have died of fright. But that's what he was doing, and that's what led him to the last two sentences, which made Mary and me cry: "He has shown himself to be, at the age of forty-three, one of the most interesting American novelists at work. Some times the long way round is the only way home."

. . . After this review no one will ever think of me as "primarily a non-fiction writer" again. "Breakout"? I feel as if I've been shot from a cannon.

AUGUST 26: Houghton Mifflin have gone back for a second printing . . .

AUGUST 29: Ran at the Y (a horde of 20 high-school boys sprinting around the track as I tried to jog) and picked up my shirts before I went into a little magazine store on 49th to buy *The New Yorker*: not wanting the anticipation to be quite over. It looks wonderful. My picture makes me appear about 25 and as if I'm a bit afraid of all the good news that surrounds it . . .

. . . Art wants to tell Si that Sonny should take me on at Knopf, and Mary says, great, go ahead, let's get some action going. The Luce, just home, called to ask me if it had all sunk in yet.

It hasn't.

AUGUST 30: Art calls Sonny, and Sonny calls Mary, and Mary sends him the proposals, and he promises an answer within 24 hours. All from that one review . . .

AUGUST 31: Sonny Mehta has offered $100,000 for *Dewey Defeats Truman* and *Yours Ever*. The negotiation with Mary took minutes. One of his only conditions: he wants the novel *first*. (The opposite of what it would have been at Houghton Mifflin if they'd wanted the novel at all.) He'll publish me at Pantheon since he thinks I might get "lost" at Knopf. He'll handle all the marketing, and Dan Frank will actually edit me.

SEPTEMBER 8: Tried to get a start on my Peter Høeg piece, but these are not normal days. Art seems to spend about half his time preparing for Monday night's party. Alan Richman called in from Lyon so they could talk about the wine list.

SEPTEMBER 10: [At Chapters, in Washington, D.C.] The shop owner introduced me by saying that their brochure, which was printed pre-Updike and described me as a "woefully undersung man of letters," was now of course obsolete. The crowd laughed and applauded, and I think it was at that moment that this great event in my life, this great change, really sank in.

SEPTEMBER 12: [At the Players Club] I barely moved from one spot all evening . . . standing beneath Edwin Booth's portrait, ready to shake [everyone's hand] . . . Dozens and dozens of people in my life from Christopher Field to Joe Queenan, Alison West to Freda Garmaise, James Raimes to Linda Healey. There were over a hundred of them, and I don't think there were more than five who didn't mention the Updike review. I've been knighted. I stood there in my new suit and red silk power tie and had the authentic clichéd feeling that this couldn't possibly be all for me.

SEPTEMBER 16: After a long day in the office—I stayed there until 7:30—I walked up to Carnegie Hall, where Billy was waiting for me outside. It was our night to see Lena [Horne]. We'd worried a little about this. Her new album is terrific, but was it a miracle of engineering? . . .

She walked out with no fanfare, and she was moving stiffly. You feared that she would fall, worried as she stood there singing—singing soft and slowly—but awfully well—for the first twenty minutes or so. But steadily, imperceptibly, it was building, building and before the first hour was over she was sashaying and belting and hitting and holding notes that made you gasp. People were roaring, screaming, on their feet again and again for what wasn't just a musical triumph, or a "legendary night in the theatre." It was a human miracle, a beautiful, beautiful thing, which ended with "Stormy Weather." That was her encore, and that's what she left you with. No denouement, no easy back-down-to-earth goodbye song, just "Stormy Weather" better than she sang it 40 years ago. Lights up. And straight down off a cliff. Billy and I were shaking.

Acknowledgments

I am grateful to David Remnick, Dorothy Wickenden, and Valerie Steiker at *The New Yorker,* the home for much of my writing over the past three decades, where portions of this book first appeared.

I am fortunate to be represented by the Wylie Agency, whose Katie Cacouris handles my work with matchless efficiency and warmth.

At Knopf, I want to express real appreciation to Edward Kastenmeier, Brian Etling, Margot Lee, Patrick Dillon, Claire Leonard, Nicholas Latimer, and Kathy Zuckerman. Thanks, too, to Reagan Arthur.

For the continuing preservation of these diaries, along with the rest of my literary and personal papers, I am indebted to Robert Rulon-Miller and to the Library of Congress' Ryan Reft, Janice Ruth, Marie Arana, Mark Sweeney, and Roswell Encina.

ILLUSTRATION CREDITS

All photographs are courtesy of the author unless otherwise noted.

A NOTE ABOUT THE AUTHOR

Thomas Mallon is the author of eleven novels, including *Henry and Clara*, *Dewey Defeats Truman*, *Fellow Travelers*, *Watergate*, *Landfall*, and *Up With the Sun*. He is a frequent contributor to *The New Yorker*, *The New York Times Book Review*, and other publications. In 2011 he received the American Academy of Arts and Letters' Harold D. Vursell Memorial Award for prose style. He has been the literary editor of *GQ* and the deputy chairman of the National Endowment for the Humanities. He lives in Washington, D.C.

A NOTE ON THE TYPE

This book was set in Janson, a typeface long thought to have
been made by the Dutchman Anton Janson, who was a practicing typefounder in Leipzig during the years 1668–1687.
However, it has been conclusively demonstrated that these
types are actually the work of Nicholas Kis (1650–1702), a
Hungarian, who most probably learned his trade from the
master Dutch typefounder Dirk Voskens. The type is an
excellent example of the influential and sturdy Dutch types
that prevailed in England up to the time William Caslon
(1692–1766) developed his own incomparable designs from
them.

Composed by North Market Street Graphics,
Lancaster, Pennsylvania